MASTER THE GMAT CAT 2004

MASTER THE GMAT CAT 2004

Thomas H. Martinson

THOMSON ARCO™

Australia • Canada • Mexico • Singapore • Spain • United Kingdom • United States

An ARCO Book

ARCO is a registered trademark of Thomson Learning, Inc., and is used herein under license by Peterson's.

About The Thomson Corporation and Peterson's

With revenues of US$7.8 billion, The Thomson Corporation (www.thomson.com) is a leading global provider of integrated information solutions for business, education, and professional customers. Its Learning businesses and brands (www.thomsonlearning.com) serve the needs of individuals, learning institutions, and corporations with products and services for both traditional and distributed learning.

Peterson's, part of The Thomson Corporation, is one of the nation's most respected providers of lifelong learning online resources, software, reference guides, and books. The Education Supersite℠ at www.petersons.com—the Internet's most heavily traveled education resources—has searchable databases and interactive tools for contacting U.S.-accredited institutions and programs. In addition, Peterson's serves more than 105 million education consumers annually.

For more information, contact Peterson's, 2000 Lenox Drive, Lawrenceville, NJ 08648; 800-338-3282; or find us on the World Wide Web at: www.petersons.com/about

COPYRIGHT © 2003 Petersons, a division of Thomson Learning, Inc.
Thomson Learning™ is a trademark used herein under license.

Previous editions © 1980, 1986, 1990, 1992, 1993, 1994, 1997, 2001, 2002

ALL RIGHTS RESERVED. No part of this work covered by the copyright herein may be reproduced or used in any form or by any means—graphic, electronic, or mechanical, including photocopying, recording, taping, Web distribution, or information storage and retrieval systems—without the prior written permission of the publisher.

For permission to use material from this text or product, contact us by
Phone: 800-730-2214
Fax: 800-730-2215
Web: www.thomsonrights.com

ISSN: International Standard Serial Number information available upon request.
ISBN (book only): 0-7689-1203-2
ISBN (book with CD-ROM): 0-7689-1202-4

Printed in the United States of America

10 9 8 7 6 5 4 3 2 1 05 04 03

Contents

PART VI: FIVE PRACTICE TESTS

PART VII: GMAT MATH REVIEW

Before You Begin

HOW WILL THIS BOOK HELP YOU?

Taking the GMAT is a skill, so it shares some things in common with other skills such as playing basketball or singing opera. These are skills that can be improved by coaching, but ultimately improvement also requires practice. This book gives you both.

- On the next page, you'll find a list of the top ten ways to raise your score, followed by a chart to help you track your progress.
- Part I provides essential information about the GMAT CAT. Part II is a full-length diagnostic test that is your first chance to work with samples of every GMAT question type. It can show you where your skills are strong—and where they need some shoring up.
- Parts III through V are the coaching program. They analyze each question type for you and give you powerful test-taking strategies. These strategies are based on 20-plus years of careful study of the GMAT, both in its paper-based form and in its newer CAT version.
- Part VI contains five practice tests followed by a detailed analysis of each question. The detailed analysis is very important because it is there that you can learn from your mistakes.
- Part VII is a full-scale review of GMAT mathematics. If your math skills are rusty and need refreshing, this section is for you.

Top 10 Ways to Raise Your Score

When it comes to taking the GMAT CAT, some test-taking skills will do you more good than others. There are concepts you can learn, techniques you can follow, and tricks you can use that will help you to do your very best. Here's our pick for the top 10 ways to raise your score:

1. **Create a study plan and follow it.** The right GMAT study plan will help you get the most out of this book in whatever time you have. *See chapter 1.*
2. **Don't get stuck on any one question.** Since you have to answer questions in order to keep moving, you can't afford to spend too much time on any one problem. *See chapter 2.*
3. **Learn the directions in advance.** If you already know the directions, you won't have to waste your precious test time reading them. You'll be able to jump right in and start answering questions as soon as the test clock starts. *See chapter 3.*
4. **Read passages for structure, not details.** When you read GMAT passages, don't stop for details. Most of the questions will ask about the structure of the passage rather than specific facts. *See chapter 5.*
5. **In sentence corrections, save time by skipping the first choice.** It always repeats the original sentence so there's no point in reading it. *See chapter 6.*
6. **In critical reasoning questions, start by finding the conclusion.** Since the conclusion is the main point of the argument, it's the key to answering every question of this type. *See chapter 7.*
7. **If a problem-solving math question stumps you, work backward from the answers.** The right answer has to be one of the five choices. Since the choices are arranged in size order, starting with choice (C) results in the fewest calculations. *See chapter 8.*
8. **Do only as much work as you have to for data sufficiency questions.** Your task is only to decide if you have enough information to answer the question. You don't have to solve it. *See chapter 9.*
9. **Use the "three main points" approach in the analytical writing assessment.** This plan will give your essay structure and strength. *See chapter 10.*
10. **Polish up rusty math skills with the GMAT Math Review.** If your math skills need some shoring up, the Math Review covers all the basic concepts of arithmetic, elementary algebra, and geometry that you're likely to encounter on the GMAT. *See chapters 11, 12, and 13.*

TRACK YOUR PROGRESS

For each exam:

1. Enter the number of questions that you answered *correctly* in each part (Verbal and Math) in the appropriate rows. (Ignore incorrect responses.)
2. Enter the total number of questions that you answered correctly for both the Verbal and Math parts for that exam in the "TOTAL" row.
3. Enter your Verbal and Math subscores using the table provided on page 9.
4. To keep track of your progress in each of the content areas, enter the number of items of each type that you answered correctly into the appropriate row.
5. Enter your overall (3-digit) score using the table provided on page 10.
6. Note: Exercise caution in interpreting the data. Because a book-based exam cannot simulate in every respect a computer-based exam, results tend to be volatile. Do not place too much emphasis on small differences in performance.

GMAT Score Tracker

	Diagnostic Test	Practice Test 1	Practice Test 2	Practice Test 3	Practice Test 4	Final Practice Test
Verbal						
Math						
TOTAL						
Verbal Subscore						
Sentence Correction Subtotal						
Critical Reasoning Subtotal						
Reading Comp. Subtotal						
Math Subscore						
Problem Solving						
Data Sufficiency						
Overall Score						

PART I

GMAT BASICS

Getting Started

chapter 1

OVERVIEW

- **Can you prepare for the GMAT?**
- **What is a GMAT study plan?**
- **How can you tell if your work is paying off?**

CAN YOU PREPARE FOR THE GMAT?

This is the question of the day. Can you indeed prepare for a test that purports to test your aptitude for success in business school rather than your mastery of any particular subject? Of course you can. The GMAT is long, and some of its questions are tough, but it's not unconquerable.

There are many ways to prepare and many tricks and tips to learn. One of the most important things to learn is to think like the test makers so you can find the answers they have designated as best. Once you learn "GMAT thinking," you'll be more likely to pick the best answer—and up will go your scores.

WHAT IS A GMAT STUDY PLAN?

As you can tell, this book contains a lot of information about the GMAT, and you'll need a plan for getting through it. The right study plan will help you manage your time so that you get the most out of this book whether you have three months, three weeks, or only three days to prepare. It will help you work efficiently and keep you from getting stressed out.

Choose the Plan That's Right for You

To decide on your study plan, answer these two questions: (1) How long do you have until the test? (2) How much time can you devote to GMAT study?

Here are some suggestions to make your job easier. If you are starting early and the GMAT is two or three months away, you can do it all. You can study from beginning to end, you can use the CAT test on the CD-ROM, you can take advantage of the valuable Private Tutor classes on the CD-ROM, and you can visit the Author's Edge at www.petersons.com/authorsedge/gmat to get even more study materials and help. If the GMAT is a month or less away and you need a more concentrated course, take the diagnostic test and tailor your study plan to your areas of weakness, and cover those parts of the book that will be of most value to you.

NOTE

Is there a secret to preparing for the GMAT? There's no secret, but you have to have a plan. You can follow one of the plans here or create your own. Either way, a plan will keep you on track.

HOW CAN YOU TELL IF YOUR WORK IS PAYING OFF?

Again, no matter how much time you have to prepare, you should start by taking the diagnostic test. After you score it, you'll be able to see where you need to concentrate your efforts.

The next step is to see how you do with the exercises at the end of each chapter. Compare your scores to your results on the diagnostic test. Have you improved? Where do you still need work?

After you score a practice test, make another comparison to the chapter exercises and to the diagnostic test. This will show you how your work is paying off.

TIP

Start with the tough stuff. To make the most of your study time, study the difficult sections first. If you run out of time later, you can just skim the sections that are easy for you.

All about the GMAT

OVERVIEW

- **What is the GMAT?**
- **What is the CAT?**
- **How do you register for the GMAT?**
- **What kinds of questions are on the test?**
- **How is the test structured?**
- **How is the test scored?**
- **How can I predict my GMAT score?**
- **What smart test-takers know**

chapter 2

WHAT IS THE GMAT?

The letters GMAT stand for Graduate Management Admission Test, which is a standardized exam given at various locations in the United States and Canada and around the world. Throughout North America and in many international locations, the GMAT is administered only via computer. In those international locations where an extensive network of computers has not yet been established, the GMAT is offered either at temporary computer-based testing centers on a limited schedule or as a paper-based test (given once or twice a year) at local testing centers.

WHAT IS THE CAT?

The computer-based version of the GMAT is called a Computer-Adaptive Test (CAT). The CAT differs from the old paper-based GMAT in that a computer program chooses problems based on a candidate's responses to previous questions. Thus, the CAT is "adaptive" or "interactive." Whereas candidates taking the old paper-based test were presented with a range of questions (including easy, moderately difficult, and difficult items), the CAT selects questions according to each candidate's ability. During a CAT, the computer controls the order in which test items appear, basing its selection on the candidate's responses to earlier items.

At the risk of oversimplifying, the testing procedure can be described as follows. The computer has access to a large number of test items classified according to question type (sentence correction, reading comprehension, critical thinking, problem solving, and data sufficiency—the question types that you will study below) and arranged in order of difficulty. At the outset, the computer presents you with one or two "seed" questions, items of average level of difficulty. If you answer those successfully, the program selects for the next question an item of greater difficulty; if you do not answer the "seed" questions correctly, the program lowers the level of difficulty. This process is repeated, with the program continuing to adjust the level of difficulty of questions, until you have provided all the answers that the computer needs to calculate your score.

HOW DO YOU REGISTER FOR THE GMAT?

TIP

Get the latest GMAT information on the Web. You can get up-to-the-minute GMAT information on the World Wide Web. The address is www.mba.com.

GMAT information and registration forms can be found in the *GMAT Bulletin*, which is available from your Career Placement Office or by contacting:

Graduate Management Admission Test
Educational Testing Service
P.O. Box 6108
Princeton, NJ 08541-6108
Telephone: (609) 771-7330
E-mail: gmat@ets.org
On-line: www.mba.com

You can also register in either of the following two ways:

- On-line using the URL above if you have a Visa card, MasterCard, or American Express card.
- By phone by calling one of the hundreds of test centers listed in the *Bulletin*.

To schedule your test, you must call one of the designated test centers and make an appointment. While it is possible to make the appointment even just a few days before you would like to take the test, it is better to schedule a few weeks in advance to ensure that you get an appointment that is convenient for you.

WHAT KINDS OF QUESTIONS ARE ON THE TEST?

Verbal Questions

There are three types of verbal questions:

- **Sentence Correction.** This type tests grammar and expression. Sentence correction items consist of a sentence, all or part of which has been underlined, with five associated answer choices. You must choose the best way of rendering the underlined part. This question type tests your ability to recognize standard English.

- **Critical Thinking.** This type tests logical thinking. Critical thinking items present an argument that you are asked to analyze. Questions may require you to draw a conclusion, to identify assumptions, or to recognize strengths or weaknesses in the argument.
- **Reading Comprehension.** This type tests your ability to read critically. Reading comprehension questions relate to a passage that is provided for you to read. The passage can be about almost anything, and the questions about it test how well you understand the passage and the information in it.

Quantitative Questions

There are two types of quantitative questions:

- **Problem Solving.** This type tests your quantitative reasoning ability. Problem-solving questions present multiple-choice problems in arithmetic, basic algebra, and elementary geometry. The task is to solve the problems and choose the correct answer from among five answer choices.
- **Data Sufficiency.** This type tests your quantitative reasoning ability using an unusual set of directions. You are given a question with two associated statements that provide information that might be useful in answering the question. You then have to determine whether either statement alone is sufficient to answer the question; whether both are needed to answer the question; or whether there isn't enough information given to answer the question.

There is also an essay component. The essay component is called the Analytical Writing Assessment or AWA. The AWA consists of two 30-minute writing exercises:

- One "prompt" or topic asks you to *analyze an issue.*
- A second "prompt" or topic asks you to *analyze an argument.*

HOW IS THE TEST STRUCTURED?

The following chart shows the structure of a typical GMAT Computer-Adaptive Test.

ANATOMY OF A TYPICAL GMAT

Section	Number of Questions	Time
Warm-up Period		—
Analytical Writing Assessment		
Issue Topic		30 min.
Argument Topic		30 min.
(optional break)		5 min.
Quantitative Section	37	75 min.
(optional break)		5 min.
Verbal Section	41	75 min.

The Warm-up period is untimed and contains no questions that count toward a score. Instead, the Warm-up period allows you to become familiar with the computer (the mouse and scroll bar functions in particular) and with the peculiarities of the program itself.

HOW IS THE TEST SCORED?

NOTE

Why does the GMAT use scaled scores? Quite frankly, because they are convenient. They are the "bar codes" of business school admissions.

The multiple-choice parts of the test are not scored in the traditional way; that is, a grader does not compare a completed answer document to a key in order to calculate a final score based upon total performance. Rather, the computer "builds" your score as you work your way through the questions.

Initially, the computer knows nothing about your quantitative or verbal skills, so it "assumes" that you are average and gives you a question of average level of difficulty. Based upon your response, the computer adjusts the initial assumption either in the direction of "above average" or "below average" and fires off another question. Then, based upon your first two responses, the computer readjusts the assumption and gives you a third question. The process continues until the computer has "built" a score for you.

A word of caution. Your final score is not based solely on the last question that you answer. The algorithm used to build a score is more complicated than that. This means that you can make a silly mistake and answer incorrectly and that the computer will recognize that item as an anomaly. In other words, don't worry that if you miss the first question that your score will fall somewhere in the bottom half of the range. However, the first 5 questions are important as a whole, because they go a long way to determining your score potential.

Each of the two essays in the Analytical Writing part of the test is graded on a scale of 0 (the minimum) to 6 (the maximum):

0 An essay that is totally illegible or obviously not written on the assigned topic.
1 An essay that is fundamentally deficient.
2 An essay that is seriously flawed.
3 An essay that is seriously limited.
4 An essay that is merely adequate.
5 An essay that is strong.
6 An essay that is outstanding.

Each essay will be given two grades, one of which may be generated by an E-rater®. The E-rater is an electronic system that evaluates more than 50 linguistic and structural features.

HOW CAN I PREDICT MY GMAT SCORE?

The use of computer adaptive testing technology makes it difficult to predict your *actual* GMAT score based on your performance on a paper-and-pencil practice test. We have tried, however, to develop a scoring table that provides a general idea of your performance at this point in your preparation. To predict your score on the practice tests in this book, count the correct answers in each section and find that number in the left column of the charts below. The corresponding number in the right column represents an approximation of your GMAT test score.

VERBAL SUBSCORE (C = CORRECT; S = SCORE)

C	S	C	S	C	S	C	S	C	S	C	S
41	60	34	48	27	34	20	20	13	6	6	0
40	60	33	46	26	32	19	18	12	4	5	0
39	58	32	44	25	30	18	16	11	2	4	0
38	56	31	42	24	28	17	14	10	0	3	0
37	54	30	40	23	26	16	12	9	0	2	0
36	52	29	38	22	24	15	10	8	0	1	0
35	50	28	36	21	22	14	8	7	0	0	0

MATH SUBSCORE (C = CORRECT; S = SCORE)

C	S	C	S	C	S	C	S	C	S
37	60	29	46	21	30	13	14	5	0
36	60	28	44	20	28	12	12	4	0
35	58	27	42	19	26	11	10	3	0
34	56	26	40	18	24	10	8	2	0
33	54	25	38	17	22	9	6	1	0
32	52	24	36	16	20	8	4	0	0
31	50	23	34	15	18	7	2		
30	48	22	32	14	16	6	0		

GMAT SCORE (C = CORRECT; S = SCORE)

C	S	C	S	C	S	C	S	C	S
78	800	62	660	46	500	30	340	14	200
77	800	61	650	45	490	29	330	13	200
76	800	60	640	44	480	28	320	12	200
75	790	59	630	43	470	27	310	11	200
74	780	58	620	42	460	26	300	10	200
73	770	57	610	41	450	25	290	9	200
72	760	56	600	40	440	24	280	8	200
71	750	55	590	39	430	23	270	7	200
70	740	54	580	38	420	22	260	6	200
69	730	53	570	37	410	21	250	5	200
68	720	52	560	36	400	20	240	4	200
67	710	51	550	35	390	19	230	3	200
66	700	50	540	34	380	18	220	2	200
65	690	49	530	33	370	17	200	1	200
64	680	48	520	32	360	16	200	0	200
63	670	47	510	31	350	15	200		

WHAT SMART TEST-TAKERS KNOW

Each essay will be graded by two readers, one of which may be an E-rater, and in most cases, the final score will be the average of the two scores awarded. Thus, if an essay receives a 3 from one reader and a 4 from the other, the final score for that essay is 3.5. In the event that the individual graders assign scores that are more than one point apart, e.g., 2 and 4, then the essay is graded by a third reader.

YOU CAN ENJOY THE "BUTTERFLIES."

Taking the GMAT is an anxiety-generating experience. Fortunately, "butterflies" are just a symptom of performance anxiety—a kind of adrenaline rush. This was true even of the paper-based version of the GMAT. The "butterflies" are nature's way of saying that you are raring to go.

YOUR JOB IS TO FOCUS ON THE TASK.

When placed in a strange and stressful situation, it is natural to worry—sometimes about the wrong things because their significance is not clear. In order to make the CAT experience as non-stressful as possible, the testing authority has gone to great pains to create a detailed list of "specs" to which each computerized testing center must conform—right down to the number and size of the storage lockers that are available for personal items not permitted in the testing room. You should be concerned only about things that will make a difference in your score.

YOU SHOULD CONCENTRATE ON FLYING THE PLANE; THE COMPUTER IS YOUR NAVIGATOR.

Don't worry about where you are going. The computer will take care of the navigation, moving you up or down the algorithmic ladder of difficulty until you arrive at the appropriate score—which is your final destination. If you try second-guessing the computer (am I moving up or down?), then you are wasting mental energy that is needed to answer questions.

IF YOU ARE A "COMPUTER DUMMY," YOU SHOULD BUY, BEG, BORROW, OR RENT ONE.
Now, first of all, you are not a "complete dummy" even if you have never used a computer. You've certainly seen them in a bank, or a grocery store, or at a friend's home, so you have some idea of what one looks like and what it is supposed to do. But there is a big difference between knowing what a car looks like and knowing how to drive one. If you have to, go down to your local office service store or local library and buy an hour or two of time on a computer. Play with the machine. If you purchased the book/disk version of this guide, take your disk with you. A technical support rep will help you load it onto the computer so that you can practice taking a CAT.

Then, during the Warm-up period at the testing center, do the tutorial three or four times, so that you are confident that you feel comfortable with the particular machine that you are using.

IF YOU ARE A "COMPUTER WHIZ," YOU CAN USE THE "PLUS 10" SYSTEM DURING THE WARM UP.
Take time to learn how to manipulate the devices—even if you use a mouse every day. In fact, if you use a computer frequently, you probably have grown used to your particular piece of hardware and find it comfortable. A different physical shape may take some getting used to. In addition, although you may be familiar with each of the individual functions of the testing program, e.g., the need to confirm a choice, the function may not work in exactly the way that you expect. Plus, the unusual combination of functions may cause some confusion. When you finally say to yourself "I can handle this," spend 10 more minutes playing around.

IF YOU KNOW THE DIRECTIONS IN ADVANCE, YOU WON'T HAVE TO WASTE TIME READING THEM.
Your allotted time is all the time you get for a section. No additional time is given for reading instructions. If you spend a minute or two reading directions, you are losing points because you could be spending more time analyzing the questions. The solution to this problem is to be thoroughly familiar with the directions for each question type before you go for your appointment to take the exam.

THE ANSWERS ARE ON THE SCREEN.
Because of the multiple-choice format, you have a real advantage over the GMAT. The correct answer is always right there on the screen. To be sure, it's surrounded by wrong choices, but it may be possible to eliminate one or more of those other choices as non-answers. Look at the following reading comprehension question:

The author argues that the evidence supporting the new theory is

(A) hypothetical

(B) biased

(C) empirical

(D) speculative

(E) fragmentary

You might think that it is impossible to make any progress on a reading comprehension question without the reading selection, but you can eliminate three of the five answers in this question as non-answers. How? Read on.

Study the question stem. We can infer that the author of the selection has at least implicitly passed judgment on the evidence supporting the new theory. What kind of judgment might someone make about the evidence adduced to support a theory? (A), (C), and (D) all seem extremely unlikely. As for (A), while the theory is itself a hypothesis, the evidence supporting the theory would not be hypothetical. As for (C), evidence is empirical by definition. So it is unlikely that anyone would argue "This evidence is empirical." And (D) can be eliminated for the same reason as (A). Admittedly, this leaves you with a choice of (B) or (E), a choice that depends on the content of the reading selection; but at least you have a 50–50 chance of getting the question correct—even without reading the selection.

YOU MUST ANSWER QUESTIONS IN THE ORDER PRESENTED.

On a CAT exam, you must answer every question in the order presented. Since the exam adapts itself in response to your answers, you cannot skip and later return to any questions. And, you cannot rethink and change your answer at a later time. You cannot seek out and answer the easier question styles first. In other words, you must do the best you can to answer each question. Choose the answer that you have determined is best, confirm your choice, and move on to the next question.

TIP

When you're guessing, play the odds. If you can eliminate one answer choice, your guess has a 25% chance of being right. Eliminate two choices, and you have a $33\frac{1}{3}\%$ chance. Eliminate three choices and you have a 50% chance of guessing correctly.

"TO GUESS OR NOT TO GUESS" IS NOT AN ISSUE.

With a paper-based test, there is always the issue of whether it is a good idea to guess or not. With the GMAT CAT, the question is simply irrelevant. You have to answer one item before the computer will let you move onto the next. So even if you don't have any idea of how to solve the problem, you still have to "click" on an oval and confirm it as your response. Is that guessing, or is that answering in a state of ignorance out of necessity? Who cares? Just do it.

YOU MUST ANSWER EVERY QUESTION.

"Algorithm" is the fancy name that the test designers use to describe the way that the computer moves you up or down the ladder of difficulty. The algorithm is apparently enormously complex and is proprietary, that is, it belongs to the GMAT people and they are not sharing it with anybody else. You don't need to worry about how it works, but you do need to know one thing: You must answer every question. (If you want more on this, consult the *GMAT Bulletin.*)

YOU CAN'T AFFORD TO GET BOGGED DOWN ON ANY ONE QUESTION.

Your average time per question on the CAT is between one and three-quarters and two minutes. Because you have to answer each question in order to move on, you can't afford to get bogged down on any one item. If after a minute and a half, you see that you're going nowhere, take your best guess and click on an answer. Your time will probably be better spent on other questions later in the section.

THE OPTIONAL BREAKS ARE MANDATORY.

You will be given the option of taking five-minute breaks between sections. These breaks are mandatory. After you finish one part of the test, you may feel that you are really on a roll and have the energy to push right on through the next part. But remember, the next part is 75-minutes long. What if you have overestimated your "fuel reserve"? You cannot stop in the middle of the next section to take a five-minute break without losing points. So, make the scheduled pit stop.

BIORHYTHMS COUNT.

We all have biorhythms. Some of us are morning people, some afternoon. Schedule your appointment for the GMAT for a time when you are likely to be at your peak.

GMAT Questions: A First Look

chapter 3

OVERVIEW

- **What can you expect on the test?**
- **How does the GMAT test verbal reasoning ability?**
- **How does the GMAT test quantitative reasoning ability?**

WHAT CAN YOU EXPECT ON THE TEST?

The GMAT uses five different types of multiple-choice questions to test your verbal and quantitative abilities plus the AWA. This chapter will describe each question type in turn and show you samples. Learning the question types in advance is the best way to prepare for the GMAT. This way, you'll know what to expect, and you won't have any unpleasant surprises on test day.

NOTE: On the computer-based GMAT, the answer choices appear as blank ovals, and you click on an oval to register your choice. The questions look like this:

> What is the sum of the areas of two squares with sides of 2 and 3, respectively?
>
> ○ 1
>
> ○ 5
>
> ○ 13
>
> ○ 25
>
> ○ 36

In this book, however, you will see letters in parentheses, so questions will look like this:

What is the sum of the areas of two squares with sides of 2 and 3, respectively?

(A) 1

(B) 5

(C) 13

(D) 25

(E) 36

The letters are provided for you as a convenient tool for locating the appropriate answer explanation as you study.

HOW DOES THE GMAT TEST VERBAL REASONING ABILITY?

The GMAT tests your verbal reasoning ability with these three question types:

- Reading comprehension
- Sentence correction
- Critical reasoning

Reading Comprehension

Reading comprehension questions, as the name implies, test your ability to understand the substance and logical structure of a written selection. The GMAT uses reading passages of approximately 200 to 350 words. Each passage has three or more questions based on its content. The questions ask about the main point of the passage, about what the author specifically states, about what can be logically inferred from the passage, and about the author's attitude or tone.

Here are the directions for reading comprehension questions and an example of a short reading passage. (Real passages are longer and are followed by three or more questions.)

Directions for reading comprehension questions: Each passage is followed by questions or incomplete statements about the passage. Each statement or question is followed by lettered words or expressions. Select the word or expression that most satisfactorily completes each statement or answers each question in accordance with the meaning of the passage.

The international software market represents a significant business opportunity for U.S. microcomputer software companies, but illegal copying of programs is limiting the growth of sales abroad. If not dealt with quickly, international piracy of software could become one of the most serious trade problems faced by the United States.

Software piracy is already the biggest barrier to U.S. software companies entering foreign markets. One reason is that software is extremely easy and inexpensive to duplicate compared to the cost of developing and marketing the software. The actual cost of duplicating a software program, which may have a retail value of $400 or more, can be as little as a dollar or two—the main component being the cost of the CD. The cost of counterfeiting software is substantially less than the cost of duplicating watches, books, or blue jeans. Given that the difference between the true value of the original and the cost of the counterfeit is so great for software, international piracy has become big business. Unfortunately, many foreign governments view software piracy as an industry in and of itself and look the other way.

U.S. firms stand to lose millions of dollars in new business, and diminished U.S. sales not only harm individual firms but also adversely affect the entire U.S. economy.

1. In this passage, the author's primary purpose is to
   - **(A)** criticize foreign governments for stealing U.S. computer secrets
   - **(B)** describe the economic hazards software piracy poses to the United States
   - **(C)** demand that software pirates immediately cease their illegal operations
   - **(D)** present a comprehensive proposal to counteract the effects of international software piracy
   - **(E)** disparage the attempts of the U.S. government to control software piracy

The correct answer is (B). This question, typical of the GMAT, asks about the main point of the selection. (A) is incorrect. Though the author implies criticism of foreign governments, their mistake, so far as we are told, is not stealing secrets but tacitly allowing the operation of a software black market. (C) is incorrect since this is not the main point of the selection. You can infer that the author would approve of such a demand, but issuing the demand is not the main point of the

TIP

It's an "open-book" test. In GMAT reading comprehension questions, the answers will always be directly stated or implied in the passage.

selection you just read. (D) can be eliminated for a similar reason. Though the author might elsewhere offer a specific proposal, there is no such proposal in the selection you just read. (E) also is wrong since no such attempts are ever discussed. Finally, notice how well (B) does describe the main issue. The author's concern is to identify a problem and to discuss its causes.

2. The author's attitude toward international software piracy can best be described as

(A) concern

(B) rage

(C) disinterest

(D) pride

(E) condescension

The correct answer is (A). This question asks about the tone of the passage, and concern very neatly captures that tone. You can eliminate (B) as an overstatement. Though the author condemns the piracy, the tone is not so violent as to qualify as rage. (C) must surely be incorrect since the author does express concern and, therefore, cannot be disinterested.

Sentence Correction

Sentence correction questions test your mastery of standard written English. Your task is to evaluate the grammar, logic, and effectiveness of a given sentence and to choose the best of several suggested revisions.

Here are the directions for sentence correction questions, followed by two sample items.

> **Directions for sentence correction questions:** In questions of this type, either part or all of a sentence is underlined. The sentence is followed by five ways of writing the underlined part. Choice (A) repeats the original; the other answer choices vary. If you think that the original phrasing is the best, choose (A). If you think one of the other answer choices is the best, select that choice.

Sentence correction questions test your ability to recognize correct and effective expression. Follow the requirements of standard written English: grammar, choice of words, and sentence construction. Choose the answer that results in the clearest, most exact sentence, but do not change the meaning of the original sentence.

3. The possibility of massive earthquakes <u>are regarded by most area residents with</u> a mixture of skepticism and caution.

(A) are regarded by most area residents with

(B) is regarded by most area residents with

(C) is regarded by most area residents as

(D) is mostly regarded by area residents with

(E) by most area residents is regarded with

The correct answer is (B). In the original, the verb "are" does not agree with the subject "possibility." (B), (C), and (D) make the needed correction. (C) is wrong, however, because "as" is not idiomatic, and (D) is wrong because the placement of "mostly" makes it modify "regarded" rather than "area residents," thereby changing the meaning of the sentence.

4. Despite the repeated warnings against drug abuse and the numerous fatalities, drug use is <u>equally as prevalent, if not more so than, a decade ago.</u>

(A) equally as prevalent, if not more so than, a decade ago.

(B) equally as prevalent, if not more so than, it was a decade ago.

(C) as prevalent, if not more than a decade ago.

(D) as prevalent as, if not more prevalent than, it was a decade ago.

(E) as prevalent, if not more so than a decade ago.

The correct answer is (D). The original is incorrect because the problem idiom is "as prevalent as," but the second "as" does not appear in the sentence. Only (D) makes the needed correction.

Critical Reasoning

Critical reasoning questions present brief statements or arguments and ask you to evaluate the form or content of the statement or argument.

Here are the directions for critical reasoning questions, along with two sample items.

Directions for critical reasoning questions: The following questions ask you to analyze and evaluate the reasoning in short paragraphs or passages. For some questions, all of the answer choices may conceivably be answers to the question asked. You should select the best answer to the question, that is, an answer that does not require you to make assumptions that violate common-sense standards by being implausible, redundant, irrelevant, or inconsistent.

ALERT!

Make the best of it. Note that these directions ask you to choose the *best* answer. That's why you should always read all the answer choices before you make your final selection.

5. In an extensive study of the reading habits of magazine subscribers, it was found that an average of between four and five people actually read each copy of the most popular weekly news magazine. On this basis, we estimate that the 12,000 copies of *Poets and Poetry* that are sold each month are actually read by 48,000 to 60,000 people.

   The estimate above assumes that

   (A) individual magazine readers generally enjoy more than one type of magazine

   (B) most of the readers of *Poets and Poetry* subscribe to the magazine

   (C) the ratio of readers to copies is the same for *Poets and Poetry* as for the weekly news magazine

   (D) the number of readers of the weekly news magazine is similar to the number of readers of *Poets and Poetry*

   (E) most readers enjoy sharing copies of their favorite magazines with friends and family members

The correct answer is (C). The argument draws an analogy between the popular weekly news magazine and *Poets and Poetry.* Based on the analogy, the speaker reaches a conclusion about the readership of *Poets and Poetry.* That argument assumes, however, that the ratio between copies and readers is similar for both magazines.

NOTE

What other kinds of questions will there be on the GMAT?
What you see is what you get. The questions on these pages show you what you'll find.

6. If military aid to Latin American countries is to be stopped because it creates instability in the region, then all foreign aid must be stopped.

   Which of the following is most like the argument above in its logical structure?

   (A) If a war in Central America is to be condemned because all killing is immoral, then all war must be condemned.

   (B) If charitable donations are obligatory for those who are rich, then it is certain that the poor will be provided for.

   (C) If the fascist government in Chile is to be overthrown because it violates the rights of the people, then all government must be overthrown.

   (D) If a proposed weapons system is to be rejected because there are insufficient funds to pay for it, then the system must be purchased when the funds are available.

   (E) If a sociological theory is widely accepted but later proven wrong by facts, then a new theory should be proposed that takes account of the additional data.

The correct answer is (C). The argument in the question stem commits the fallacy of hasty generalization in two respects. It reasons from military aid to Latin America (a particular type of aid to a certain region) to the general conclusion that all aid must be stopped, regardless of type or of recipient. (C) parallels this. From a particular conclusion about one form of government in one country, it moves to a general conclusion about all government—regardless of form or of society. Although (A), (B), and (D) have superficial similarities of content (war, donation, military), the logical structures of these arguments differ from that of the stem paragraph. (A) is a valid argument: Given anything that is a war, if any war is to be condemned, then all wars are to be condemned. (B) is not a valid argument but a nonsequitur. It does not follow that an obligation on one party guarantees a benefit to any other. For example, there may not be enough rich to provide for all the poor. (D) is also a nonsequitur. That we reject a system now because we lack the money to buy it does not imply we should buy it when we have funds. Finally, (E) is not really an argument but only a statement. Not all "If . . . , then . . . ." statements mean "P, therefore Q." For example, "If you do not do the assignment, you will fail the course" is not an argument with a premise and a conclusion but a single statement that describes a causal relation.

HOW DOES THE GMAT TEST QUANTITATIVE REASONING ABILITY?

The GMAT tests quantitative reasoning ability with these two question types:

- Problem solving
- Data sufficiency

Problem Solving

Problem-solving questions are ordinary multiple-choice math questions. They test your mastery of basic mathematical skills and your ability to solve problems using arithmetic, basic algebra, and geometry. Some problems will be plain mathematical calculations; the rest will be presented as real-life word problems which will require mathematical solutions.

Here are the directions for problem solving questions, along with two sample items:

Directions for problem solving questions: For each of the following questions, select the best of the answer choices.
Numbers: All numbers used are real numbers.
Figures: The diagrams and figures that accompany these questions are for the purpose of providing information useful in answering the questions. Unless it is stated that a specific figure is not drawn to scale, the diagrams and figures are drawn as accurately as possible. All figures are in a plane unless otherwise indicated.

7. Betty left home with $60 in her wallet. She spent $\frac{1}{3}$ of that amount at the supermarket, and she spent $\frac{1}{2}$ of what remained at the drugstore. If Betty made no other expenditures, how much money did she have when she returned home?

(A) $10
(B) $15
(C) $20
(D) $40
(E) $50

A quick calculation will show that the correct answer is (C). Betty spent $\frac{1}{3}$ of $60, or $20, at the supermarket, leaving her with $40. Of the $40, she spent $\frac{1}{2}$, or $20, at the drugstore, leaving her with $20 when she returned home.

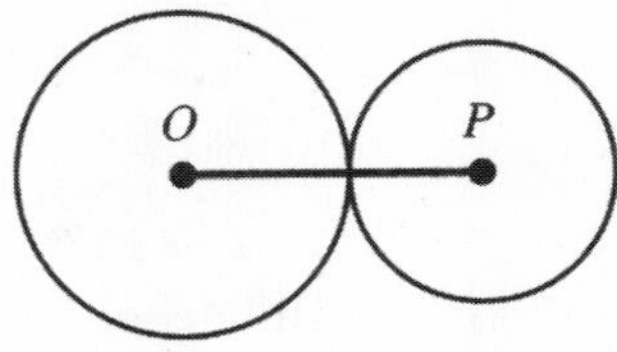

8. In the figure above, circle *O* and circle *P* are tangent to each other. If the circle with center *O* has a diameter of 8 and the circle with center *P* has a diameter of 6, what is the length of *OP*?

(A) 7
(B) 10
(C) 14
(D) 20
(E) 28

The correct answer is (A). *OP* is made up of the radius of circle *O* and the radius of circle *P*. To find the length of *OP*, you need to know the lengths of the two radii. Since the length of the radius is one half that of the diameter, the radius of circle *O* is $\frac{1}{2}(8)$ or 4, and the radius of circle *P* is $\frac{1}{2}(6)$ or 3. So the length of *OP* is $3 + 4 = 7$.

Data Sufficiency

Data sufficiency is a unique type of math question created especially for the GMAT. Each item consists of the question itself followed by two numbered statements. You must decide whether the statements—either singly or in combination—provide enough information to answer the question.

Here are the directions for data sufficiency questions, followed by two sample items:

Directions for data sufficiency questions: Each question below is followed by two numbered facts. You are to determine whether the data given in the statements is sufficient for answering the question. Use the data given, plus your knowledge of math and everyday facts, to choose between the five possible answers. Choose:

(A) if statement 1 alone is sufficient to answer the question, but statement 2 alone is not sufficient

(B) if statement 2 alone is sufficient to answer the question, but statement 1 alone is not sufficient

(C) if both statements together are needed to answer the question, but neither statement alone is sufficient

(D) if either statement by itself is sufficient to answer the question

(E) if not enough facts are given to answer the question

9. Which copy machine, X or Y, makes copies at the faster rate?

(1) Machine X makes 90 copies per minute.

(2) In 3 minutes, X makes 1.5 more copies than Y.

The correct answer is (B). Statement (1) is not sufficient because it provides no information about machine Y. Statement (2), however, is sufficient because it tells you that X is faster than Y.

NOTE

Do you need to know college-level math to do well on the GMAT?

No, you do not need to know college-level math. The GMAT quantitative sections test only the basic math concepts you learned in high school.

SUMMING IT UP:

What You Need to Know About the GMAT

Review this page the night before you take the GMAT. It will help you to recall important basic information about the test.

- The GMAT is a test of verbal and quantitative reasoning ability.
- There are three verbal reasoning question types: reading comprehension, sentence correction, and critical reasoning.
- There are two quantitative reasoning question types: problem solving and data sufficiency.
- There is also an essay component called the Analytical Writing Assessment. It consists of two 30-minute writing exercises.
- On the computer-adaptive test (CAT) version of the GMAT, the computer chooses problems based on a candidate's answers to previous questions.
- The GMAT is a multiple-choice test, so the answers will always be right on the screen in front of you.
- By learning the directions for each question type in advance, you won't have to waste time reading them.
- On the CAT, you have to answer the question on the screen in front of you before you can proceed to the next question; and it is to your advantage to answer every question before time runs out.
- On the CAT, you have to answer the questions in the order in which they are presented.

PART II

DIAGNOSING STRENGTHS AND WEAKNESSES

Diagnostic Test

chapter 4

ANALYTICAL WRITING ASSESSMENT

I. Analysis of an Issue

Time—30 Minutes

Directions: In this section you will have 30 minutes to analyze and explain your views on the topic presented below. Read the statement and directions carefully. Make notes to organize your thoughts in your test booklet. Then write your answer in the separate answer document for this essay question. Write only on the topic given. An essay on a topic other than the one assigned will automatically be assigned a grade of 0.

Note: On the CAT version you will keyboard your essay. For this exercise, allow yourself three sides of regular $8\frac{1}{2} \times 11$- inch paper for each essay response.

> Some people complain that professional athletes are overpaid. They note that many athletes make more than lawyers, doctors, and business executives, people who often have many more years of formal education. Other people point out that there are relatively few professional athletes compared to the number of members that other professions have and that professional athletes have relatively short careers. Thus, it is concluded that professional athletes are not overpaid.

Which position do you find more compelling? Explain your position using reasons and/or examples drawn from your personal experience, observations, or readings.

II. Analysis of an Argument

Time—30 Minutes

Directions: In this section you will have 30 minutes to write a critique of the argument presented below. Read the argument and directions carefully. Make notes to organize your response in your test booklet. Then write your answer in the separate answer document for this essay question. Write only on the topic given. An essay on a topic other than the one assigned will automatically be assigned a grade of 0.

Note: On the CAT version you will keyboard your essay. For this exercise, allow yourself three sides of regular $8\frac{1}{2} \times 11$- inch paper for each essay response.

> Washington County, a rural area that has experienced considerable population growth in the past few years, still has many intersections that are either unmarked or marked only with a "YIELD" sign. All of these intersections should be re-marked either with "STOP" signs or with traffic lights. A rush program to install the new marking within 18 months will ensure that the number of traffic accidents in the county will not increase significantly as the population continues to grow.

How persuasive do you find this argument? Explain your point of view by analyzing the line of reasoning and the use of evidence in the argument. Discuss also what, if anything, would make the argument more persuasive or would help you better to evaluate its conclusion.

Quantitative Section

37 Questions • 75 Minutes

Directions: For each of the following questions, choose the correct answer. To simulate the experience of taking the CAT, answer each question in order. Do not skip any questions, and do not go back to any questions you have already answered.

Numbers: All numbers used are real numbers.

Figures: The diagrams and figures that accompany these questions are for the purpose of providing information useful in answering the questions. Unless it is stated that a specific figure is not drawn to scale, the diagrams and figures are drawn as accurately as possible. All figures are in a plane unless otherwise indicated.

For Data Sufficiency questions: Each question is followed by two numbered facts. You are to determine whether the data given in the statements are sufficient for answering the question. Use the data given, plus your knowledge of math and everyday facts, to choose between the five possible answers.

Example:

Q Which copy machine, X or Y, makes copies at the faster rate?

(1) Machine X makes 90 copies per minute.

(2) In 3 minutes, X makes 1.5 more copies than Y.

(A) statement 1 alone is sufficient to answer the question, but statement 2 alone is not sufficient

(B) statement 2 alone is sufficient to answer the question, but statement 1 alone is not sufficient

(C) both statements together are needed to answer the question, but neither statement alone is sufficient

(D) either statement by itself is sufficient to answer the question

(E) not enough facts are given to answer the question

A **The correct answer is (B).**

1. If $x + 5 = 4x - 10$, then $x =$
   (A) –15
   (B) –5
   (C) –3
   (D) 3
   (E) 5

2. $\frac{2^6 - 8^2}{4^3} =$
   (A) 0
   (B) 1
   (C) 2
   (D) 4
   (E) 8

3. Attendance at a certain play was 8% higher on Saturday night than it was on Friday night. What was the attendance on Saturday night?
   (1) Friday night's attendance was 200.
   (2) Attendance increased from Friday night to Saturday night by 16 people.
   (A) statement 1 alone is sufficient to answer the question, but statement 2 alone is not sufficient
   (B) statement 2 alone is sufficient to answer the question, but statement 1 alone is not sufficient
   (C) both statements together are needed to answer the question, but neither statement alone is sufficient
   (D) either statement by itself is sufficient to answer the question
   (E) not enough facts are given to answer the question

4. At a street fair, a concessionaire sold both bracelets and necklaces. How much money did she take in on the sale of the bracelets?
   (1) She took in a total of $540 on the sale of bracelets and necklaces.
   (2) She took in $12 for each of the 25 necklaces she sold.
   (A) statement 1 alone is sufficient to answer the question, but statement 2 alone is not sufficient
   (B) statement 2 alone is sufficient to answer the question, but statement 1 alone is not sufficient
   (C) both statements together are needed to answer the question, but neither statement alone is sufficient
   (D) either statement by itself is sufficient to answer the question
   (E) not enough facts are given to answer the question

5. How many people visited a certain museum in 1985?
   (1) In 1985, four times as many people visited the museum as in 1984.
   (2) In its first year of operation, 3000 people visited the museum.
   (A) statement 1 alone is sufficient to answer the question, but statement 2 alone is not sufficient
   (B) statement 2 alone is sufficient to answer the question, but statement 1 alone is not sufficient
   (C) both statements together are needed to answer the question, but neither statement alone is sufficient
   (D) either statement by itself is sufficient to answer the question
   (E) not enough facts are given to answer the question

6. A box is filled with cookies ranging in weight from 3.2 grams to 3.8 grams. How many cookies are in the box?

(1) The gross weight of the box and the cookies is 130 grams.

(2) The net weight of the cookies is 112 grams.

(A) statement 1 alone is sufficient to answer the question, but statement 2 alone is not sufficient

(B) statement 2 alone is sufficient to answer the question, but statement 1 alone is not sufficient

(C) both statements together are needed to answer the question, but neither statement alone is sufficient

(D) either statement by itself is sufficient to answer the question

(E) not enough facts are given to answer the question

7. Is $x + 3 > 0$?

(1) $x + 5 > 0$

(2) $x < 0$

(A) statement 1 alone is sufficient to answer the question, but statement 2 alone is not sufficient

(B) statement 2 alone is sufficient to answer the question, but statement 1 alone is not sufficient

(C) both statements together are needed to answer the question, but neither statement alone is sufficient

(D) either statement by itself is sufficient to answer the question

(E) not enough facts are given to answer the question

8. What is the area of Circle O?

(1) The diameter of Circle O is 4.

(2) The circumference of Circle O is 4π.

(A) statement 1 alone is sufficient to answer the question, but statement 2 alone is not sufficient

(B) statement 2 alone is sufficient to answer the question, but statement 1 alone is not sufficient

(C) both statements together are needed to answer the question, but neither statement alone is sufficient

(D) either statement by itself is sufficient to answer the question

(E) not enough facts are given to answer the question

9. A square floor with a side of 3 meters is to be covered with square tiles. If each tile has a perimeter of 1 meter, what is the minimum number of tiles needed to cover the floor?

(A) 3

(B) 9

(C) 12

(D) 36

(E) 144

10. In a certain city, the average income for a family of four rose from \$12,200 in 1980 to \$16,300 in 1986. This represents an increase of *approximately*

(A) 4%

(B) 25%

(C) $33\frac{1}{3}\%$

(D) 40%

(E) 60%

diagnostic test

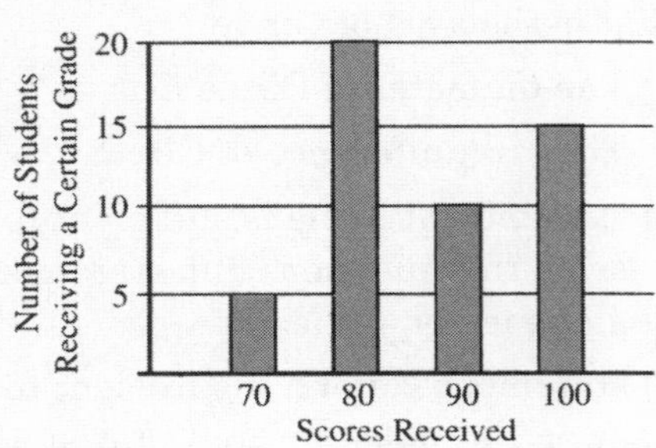

11. The graph above shows the distribution of test scores for a certain class. What was the average (arithmetic mean) score?

(A) 87

(B) 81

(C) 80

(D) 78

(E) 75

SHIPPING RATES

	Regular Service	Express Service
First pound	\$5.10	\$17.50
Each additional pound or fraction of a pound up to 10 pounds	\$1.80	\$2.60
Each additional pound or fraction of a pound over 10 pounds	\$1.50	\$1.20

12. According to the table of shipping rates above, how much does it cost to send a package weighing 23.5 pounds by Express Service?

(A) \$22.50

(B) \$42.50

(C) \$57.70

(D) \$64.30

(E) \$66.20

13. Which of the following is the greatest?

(A) 8×0.012

(B) 3×0.122

(C) 0.7^5

(D) 0.3% of 7

(E) 0.98×3

C B E F D A

14. Rearrange the six blocks shown above so that the letters are in alphabetical order, reading from left to right. What is the minimum number of blocks that must be moved to arrive at the desired arrangement?

(A) 2

(B) 3

(C) 4

(D) 5

(E) 6

15. Is it cheaper to buy bagels by the dozen rather than singly?

(1) A single bagel costs 30 cents.

(2) A dozen bagels cost ten times as much as a single bagel.

(A) statement 1 alone is sufficient to answer the question, but statement 2 alone is not sufficient

(B) statement 2 alone is sufficient to answer the question, but statement 1 alone is not sufficient

(C) both statements together are needed to answer the question, but neither statement alone is sufficient

(D) either statement by itself is sufficient to answer the question

(E) not enough facts are given to answer the question

16. In a certain company, 55% of the workers are men. If 30% of the workers are full-time employees and 60% of these are women, what percentage of the full-time workers in the company are men?

(A) 12%

(B) 40%

(C) 60%

(D) $66\frac{2}{3}\%$

(E) $77\frac{7}{9}\%$

17. What was the greatest difference between the high and low test scores of any particular student in the third grade at PS 11?

(1) The highest test score earned by any student in the third grade at PS 11 was 98.

(2) The lowest test score earned by any student in the third grade at PS 11 was 44.

(A) statement 1 alone is sufficient to answer the question, but statement 2 alone is not sufficient

(B) statement 2 alone is sufficient to answer the question, but statement 1 alone is not sufficient

(C) both statements together are needed to answer the question, but neither statement alone is sufficient

(D) either statement by itself is sufficient to answer the question

(E) not enough facts are given to answer the question

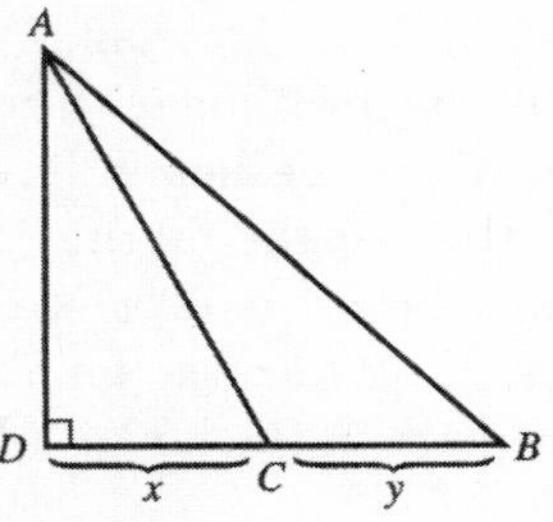

18. In the figure above, $x = y$. What is the ratio area $\frac{\Delta ABC}{\text{area } \Delta ADC}$?

(A) $\frac{1}{2}(x + y)$

(B) $x + y$

(C) xy

(D) $\frac{1}{2}$

(E) 1

19. If in a certain shipment of new cars, the cost of car X is twice the average of the other 11 cars in the shipment, what fraction of the total cost of 12 cars is the cost of car X?

(A) $\frac{1}{12}$

(B) $\frac{1}{11}$

(C) $\frac{2}{13}$

(D) $\frac{2}{11}$

(E) $\frac{1}{6}$

diagnostic test

20. The weight of a glass jar is 20% of the weight of the jar filled with coffee beans. After some of the beans have been removed, the weight of the jar and the remaining beans is 60% of the original total weight. What fractional part of the beans remain in the jar?

(A) $\frac{1}{5}$

(B) $\frac{1}{3}$

(C) $\frac{2}{5}$

(D) $\frac{1}{2}$

(E) $\frac{2}{3}$

21. If x is an integer such that $2 < x < 12$, $4 < x < 21$, $9 > x > -1$, $8 > x > 0$, and $x + 1 < 7$, then x is

(A) 3

(B) 5

(C) 6

(D) 8

(E) It cannot be determined.

$$\begin{array}{r} 729 \\ 5X3 \\ +\ 9X1 \\ \hline 2,2X3 \end{array}$$

22. In the addition calculation above, the number X must be

(A) 0

(B) 2

(C) 3

(D) 7

(E) 9

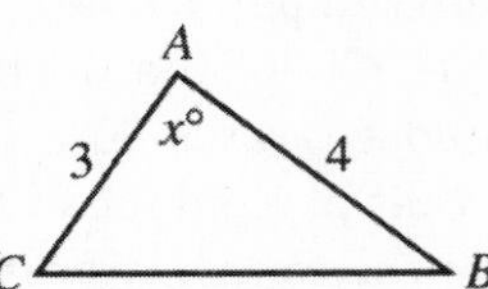

23. What is the area of the triangle shown above?

(1) $AB^2 = BC^2 - AC^2$

(2) $x = 90$

(A) statement 1 alone is sufficient to answer the question, but statement 2 alone is not sufficient

(B) statement 2 alone is sufficient to answer the question, but statement 1 alone is not sufficient

(C) both statements together are needed to answer the question, but neither statement alone is sufficient

(D) either statement by itself is sufficient to answer the question

(E) not enough facts are given to answer the question

24. An airplane took off from airport P and later landed at airport R at the same time that another airplane landed at airport R, completing its flight from airport Q. If both flights were nonstop flights, which airplane flew at the faster average speed?

(1) The first plane took off a half hour before the second plane.

(2) The distance from P to R is greater than the distance from Q to R.

(A) statement 1 alone is sufficient to answer the question, but statement 2 alone is not sufficient

(B) statement 2 alone is sufficient to answer the question, but statement 1 alone is not sufficient

(C) both statements together are needed to answer the question, but neither statement alone is sufficient

(D) either statement by itself is sufficient to answer the question

(E) not enough facts are given to answer the question

25. Is x a positive number?

(1) $2x - 5 > 0$

(2) $2x + 1 > 2$

(A) statement 1 alone is sufficient to answer the question, but statement 2 alone is not sufficient

(B) statement 2 alone is sufficient to answer the question, but statement 1 alone is not sufficient

(C) both statements together are needed to answer the question, but neither statement alone is sufficient

(D) either statement by itself is sufficient to answer the question

(E) not enough facts are given to answer the question

26. A container manufactured for the transport of liquids is a right circular cylinder. If it has a diameter of 40 inches, what is its volume?

(1) The surface area of the container, excluding the top and the bottom, is 1200π square inches.

(2) The entire surface area of the container is 2000π square inches.

(A) statement 1 alone is sufficient to answer the question, but statement 2 alone is not sufficient

(B) statement 2 alone is sufficient to answer the question, but statement 1 alone is not sufficient

(C) both statements together are needed to answer the question, but neither statement alone is sufficient

(D) either statement by itself is sufficient to answer the question

(E) not enough facts are given to answer the question

27. Edna has exactly 73 cents in her pocket, in dimes and nickels and pennies. How many nickels does she have in her pocket?

(1) She has twice as many dimes as she has pennies.

(2) She has three pennies.

(A) statement 1 alone is sufficient to answer the question, but statement 2 alone is not sufficient

(B) statement 2 alone is sufficient to answer the question, but statement 1 alone is not sufficient

(C) both statements together are needed to answer the question, but neither statement alone is sufficient

(D) either statement by itself is sufficient to answer the question

(E) not enough facts are given to answer the question

28. In 1985, the Party Time Catering Hall spent a total of $1,200 for metered water. How much did it spend for metered water in 1986?

(1) In 1986, Party Time Catering Hall purchased 10% more metered water than it did in 1985.

(2) The average price per gallon of metered water purchased by Party Time Catering Hall in 1986 was 5% more than that for 1985.

(A) statement 1 alone is sufficient to answer the question, but statement 2 alone is not sufficient

(B) statement 2 alone is sufficient to answer the question, but statement 1 alone is not sufficient

(C) both statements together are needed to answer the question, but neither statement alone is sufficient

(D) either statement by itself is sufficient to answer the question

(E) not enough facts are given to answer the question

29. The value of a share of stock P and the value of a share of stock Q each increased by 16%. If the value of a share of stock P increased by 16 cents and the value of a share of stock Q increased by $1.68, what is the difference between the value of stock Q and the value of stock P *before* the increases?

(A) $8.00
(B) $9.50
(C) $10.00
(D) $10.50
(E) $11.02

30. An express train traveled at an average speed of 100 kilometers per hour, stopping for 3 minutes after every 75 kilometers. A local train traveled at an average speed of 50 kilometers, stopping for 1 minute after every 25 kilometers. If the trains began traveling at the same time, how many kilometers did the local train travel in the time it took the express train to travel 600 kilometers?

(A) 300
(B) 305
(C) 307.5
(D) 1200
(E) 1236

31. The number 45 is what percentage of 9000?

(A) 0.05%
(B) 0.405%
(C) 0.5%
(D) 4.05%
(E) 5%

32. If $3x = 6$ and $x - y = 0$, then $y =$

(A) –2
(B) 0
(C) 2
(D) 6
(E) 12

33. A demographic survey of 100 families in which two parents were present revealed that the average age, A, of the oldest child is 20 years less than $\frac{1}{2}$ the sum of the ages of the two parents. If F represents the age of one parent and M the age of the other parent, then which of the following is equivalent to A?

(A) $\frac{F+M-20}{2}$

(B) $\frac{F+M}{2}+20$

(C) $\frac{F+M}{2}-20$

(D) $F+M-10$

(E) $F+M+10$

34. A professional athlete was offered a three-year contract to play with Team K that provided for an annual salary of $100,000 in the first year, an increase in annual salary of 20% over the previous year for the next two years, and a bonus of $50,000 on signing. Team L offered a three-year contract providing for an annual salary of $150,000 in the first year, an increase in annual salary of 10% over the previous year for the next two years, and no signing bonus. If he accepts the offer of Team L and fulfills the three-year contract terms, the athlete will receive how much more money by choosing Team L over Team K?

(A) $32,500
(B) $50,000
(C) $82,500
(D) $92,000
(E) $100,000

35. What is the value of $x + y$?

(1) $x + y + z = x + y - z + 1$

(2) $x - y + z = 0$

(A) statement 1 alone is sufficient to answer the question, but statement 2 alone is not sufficient

(B) statement 2 alone is sufficient to answer the question, but statement 1 alone is not sufficient

(C) both statements together are needed to answer the question, but neither statement alone is sufficient

(D) either statement by itself is sufficient to answer the question

(E) not enough facts are given to answer the question

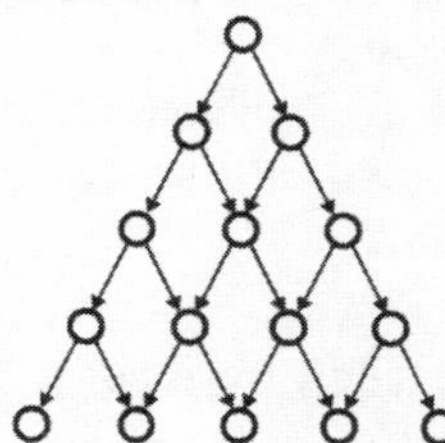

36. The figure above illustrates a managerial table of organization in which each person, except those on the lowest level, supervises exactly two persons on the next lower level. If each lower level contains exactly one person more than the next higher level, which of the following could be the total number of persons in an organization built on such a pattern?

(A) 7

(B) 16

(C) 20

(D) 28

(E) 35

37. How many rectangular cereal boxes can be shipped in a certain cardboard carton?

(1) Each cereal box has a volume of 120 cubic centimeters.

(2) The cardboard carton has a volume of 2400 cubic centimeters.

(A) statement 1 alone is sufficient to answer the question, but statement 2 alone is not sufficient

(B) statement 2 alone is sufficient to answer the question, but statement 1 alone is not sufficient

(C) both statements together are needed to answer the question, but neither statement alone is sufficient

(D) either statement by itself is sufficient to answer the question

(E) not enough facts are given to answer the question

Verbal Section

41 Questions • 75 Minutes

Directions: For each of the following questions, choose the correct answer. To simulate the experience of taking the CAT, answer each question in order. Do not skip any questions, and do not go back to any questions you have already answered.

For Sentence Correction questions: In questions of this type, either part or all of a sentence is underlined. The sentence is followed by five ways of writing the underlined part. Choice (A) repeats the original; the other answer choices vary. If you think that the original phrasing is the best, choose (A). If you think one of the other answer choices is the best, select that choice.

Sentence Correction questions test your ability to recognize correct and effective expression. Follow the requirements of Standard Written English: grammar, choice of words, and sentence construction. Choose the answer that results in the clearest, most exact sentence, but do not change the meaning of the original sentence.

Example:

Q The possibility of massive earthquakes <u>are regarded by most area residents with</u> a mixture of skepticism and caution.

(A) are regarded by most area residents with
(B) is regarded by most area residents with
(C) is regarded by most area residents as
(D) is mostly regarded by area residents with
(E) by most area residents is regarded with

A **The correct answer is (B).**

For Critical Reasoning questions: Questions of this type ask you to analyze and evaluate the reasoning in short paragraphs or passages. For some questions, all of the answer choices may conceivably be answers to the question asked. You should select the *best* answer to the question, that is, an answer that does not require you to make assumptions that violate common-sense standards by being implausible, redundant, irrelevant, or inconsistent.

Example:

 In an extensive study of the reading habits of magazine subscribers, it was found that an average of between four and five people actually read each copy of the most popular weekly news magazine. On this basis, we estimate that the 12,000 copies of *Poets and Poetry* that are sold each month are actually read by 48,000 to 60,000 people.

The estimate above assumes that

(A) individual magazine readers generally enjoy more than one type of magazine

(B) most of the readers of *Poets and Poetry* subscribe to the magazine

(C) the ratio of readers to copies is the same for *Poets and Poetry* as for the weekly news magazine

(D) the number of readers of the weekly news magazine is similar to the number of readers of *Poets and Poetry*

(E) most readers enjoy sharing copies of their favorite magazines with friends and family members

A **The correct answer is (C).**

For Reading Comprehension questions: Each passage is followed by questions or incomplete statements about the passage. Each statement or question is followed by lettered words or expressions. Select the word or expression that most satisfactorily completes each statement or answers each question in accordance with the meaning of the passage.

1. Because of the accident, toxic fumes were released into the atmosphere and the inhabitants of several communities had to be relocated to an army base from their homes 20 miles away.

   (A) had to be relocated to an army base from their homes 20 miles away.

   (B) have to be relocated to an army base from their homes 20 miles away.

   (C) had to be relocated 20 miles away from their homes to an army base.

   (D) had to be relocated to an army base, 20 miles away from their homes.

   (E) has to be relocated to an army base, 20 miles away from their house.

2. The numerous constraints placed on the members of the First Family has made it difficult for them to engage in normal social activities such as going to the movies.

   (A) has made it difficult for them to engage in normal social activities such as going to the movies.

   (B) have made it difficult engaging in normal social activities such as going to the movies.

   (C) has made the engagement in normal social activities such as going to the movies difficult.

   (D) have made it difficult to engage in normal social activities such as going to the movies.

   (E) has made their engagement in normal social activities such as going to the movies difficult.

3. Like their counterparts in other countries, the student movement in the United States in the 1960s was a powerful one and probably helped to bring the war in Vietnam to an end.

   (A) Like their counterparts in other countries, the student movement in the United States in the 1960s

   (B) As in other countries, the student movement in the United States in the 1960s,

   (C) Just as the student movements in other countries, the student movement in the United States in the 1960s,

   (D) Like its counterparts in other countries, the student movement in the United States in the 1960s

   (E) The student movement in the United States in the 1960s, like in other countries,

4. MME. CHARPENTIER: Research has demonstrated that the United States, which has the most extensive health care industry in the world, has only the 17th lowest infant mortality rate in the world. This forces me to conclude that medical technology causes babies to die.

   M. ADAMANTE: That is ludicrous. We know that medical care is not equally available to all. Infant mortality is more likely a function of low income than of medical technology.

   M. Adamante attacks Mme. Charpentier's reasoning in which of the following ways?

   (A) By questioning the validity of her supporting data

   (B) By offering an alternative explanation of the data

   (C) By suggesting that her argument is circular

   (D) By defining an intermediate cause

   (E) By implying that her data leads to the opposite conclusion

5. When this proposal to reduce welfare benefits is brought up for debate, we are sure to hear claims by the liberal Congressmen that the bill will be detrimental to poor people. These politicians fail to understand, however, that budget reductions are accompanied by tax cuts—so everyone will have more money to spend, not less.

Which of the following, if true, would undermine the author's position?

(A) Poor people tend to vote for liberal politicians who promise to raise welfare benefits.

(B) Politicians often make campaign promises that they do not fulfill.

(C) Poor people pay little or no taxes, so a tax cut would be of little advantage to them.

(D) Any tax advantage enjoyed by the poor will not be offset by cuts in services.

(E) Budget reductions, when accompanied by tax cuts, often stimulate economic growth.

6. The Metropolitan Museum of Art will soon add a wing devoted entirely to modern art, whereas before other museums exhibited modern art while the Met ignored it.

(A) art, whereas before other museums exhibited modern art while the Met ignored it.

(B) art, while before other museums exhibited modern art while the Met ignored it.

(C) art, meanwhile before the other museums had exhibited the art while the Met ignored it.

(D) art, other museums exhibited the art before with the Met ignoring it.

(E) art; until now, other museums exhibited modern art, but the Met ignored it.

QUESTIONS 7 AND 8

An artist must suffer for his art say these successful entrepreneurs who attempt to pass themselves off as artists. They auction off to the highest bidder, usually a fool in his own right, the most mediocre of drawings; and then, from their well-laid tables, they have the unmitigated gall to imply that they themselves ______(7)______.

7. Choose the answer that best completes the paragraph.

(A) are connoisseurs of art

(B) suffer deprivation for the sake of their work

(C) are artists

(D) know art better than the art critics do

(E) do not enjoy a good meal

8. Which of the following must underlie the author's position?

(A) One must actually suffer to do great art.

(B) Financial deprivation is the only suffering an artist undergoes.

(C) Art critics have little real expertise and are consequently easily deceived.

(D) Most mediocre artists are fools.

(E) All successful entrepreneurs are fools.

9. Deregulated in 1984, the researchers at AT&T continue to produce new and important ideas and products such as undersea fiberoptic cable.

(A) Deregulated in 1984, the researchers at AT&T continue to produce

(B) Having been deregulated in 1984, the researchers at AT&T are continuing to produce

(C) The researchers at AT&T, even though it was deregulated in 1984, continues to produce

(D) Although AT&T was deregulated in 1984, its researchers continue to produce

(E) Despite its being deregulated in 1984, the researchers for AT&T continue to produce

10. The success scientists have had developing treatments for once incurable types of cancer have led to a host of patent lawsuits which will effect the prices individuals will pay for the cure.

(A) The success scientists have had developing treatments for once incurable types of cancer have led to a host of patent lawsuits which will effect the prices individuals will pay for the cure.

(B) The success scientists have had in developing treatments for once incurable types of cancer has led to a host of patent lawsuits which will affect the prices individuals will pay for the cure.

(C) The success scientists has had in the development of treatments for once incurable types of cancer have led to a host of patent lawsuits which affect the prices individuals will pay for the cure.

(D) The success scientists had had in the development of treatments for once incurable types of cancer have led to a host of patent lawsuits which would affect the prices individuals would pay for a cure.

(E) Scientists have had success in the development of treatments for once incurable types of cancer which have led to a host of patent lawsuits which will effect the prices individuals will pay for the cure.

11. The senator was so popular that she was reelected with as wide of a margin as any candidate in the state's history.

(A) she was reelected with as wide of a margin as any candidate in the state's history.

(B) she had been reelected with as wide of a margin as any candidate in the state's history.

(C) having been reelected with as wide a margin as any candidate in the state's history.

(D) she was reelected with as wide a margin as any candidate in the state's history.

(E) she was reelected with as wide a margin than any candidate in the state's history.

QUESTIONS 12–18

At the present time, 98% of the world energy consumption comes from stored sources, such as fossil fuels or nuclear fuel. Only hydroelectric and wood energy represent completely renewable sources on ordinary time scales. Discovery of large additional fossil fuel reserves, solution of the nuclear safety and waste disposal problems, or the development of controlled thermonuclear fusion will provide only a short-term solution to the world's energy crisis. Within about 100 years, the thermal pollution resulting from our increased energy consumption will make solar energy a necessity at any cost.

Man's energy consumption is currently about one part in ten thousand that of the energy we receive from the sun. However, it is growing at a 5% rate, of which about 2% represents a population growth and 3% a per capita energy increase. If this growth continues, within 100 years our energy consumption will be about 1 percent of the absorbed solar energy, enough to increase the average temperature of the earth by about one degree centigrade if stored energy continues to be our predominant source. This will be the point at which there will be significant effects in our climate, including the melting of the polar ice caps, a phenomenon that will raise the level of the oceans and flood parts of our major cities. There is positive feedback associated with this process, since the polar ice cap contributes to the partial reflectivity of the energy arriving from the sun: As the ice caps begin to melt, the reflectivity will decrease, thus heating the earth still further.

It is often stated that the growth rate will decline or that energy conservation measures will preclude any long-range problem. Instead, this only postpones the problem by a few years. Conservation by a factor of 2, together with a maintenance of the 5% growth rate, delays the problem by only 14 years. Reduction of the growth rate to 4% postpones the problem by only 25 years; in addition, the inequities in standards of living throughout the world will provide pressure toward an increase in growth rate, particularly if cheap energy is available. The problem of a changing climate will not be evident until perhaps 10 years before it becomes critical due to the nature of an exponential growth rate together with the normal annual weather variations. This may be too short a period to circumvent the problem by converting to other energy sources, so advance planning is a necessity.

The only practical means of avoiding the problem of thermal pollution appears to be the use of solar energy. (Schemes to "air-condition" the earth do not appear to be feasible before the twenty-second century.) Using the solar energy before it is dissipated to heat does not increase the earth's energy balance. The cost of solar energy is extremely favorable now, particularly when compared to the cost of relocating many of our major cities.

12. The author is primarily concerned with

(A) describing a phenomenon and explaining its causes

(B) outlining a position and supporting it with statistics

(C) isolating an ambiguity and clarifying it by definition

(D) presenting a problem and advocating a solution for it

(E) citing a counterargument and refuting it

13. According to the passage, all of the following are factors which will tend to increase thermal pollution EXCEPT

(A) the earth's increasing population

(B) melting of the polar ice caps

(C) increase in per capita energy consumption

(D) pressure to redress standard of living inequities by increasing energy consumption

(E) expected anomalies in weather patterns

14. The positive feedback mentioned in lines 35–39 means that the melting of the polar ice caps will

(A) reduce per capita energy consumption

(B) accelerate the transition to solar energy

(C) intensify the effects of thermal pollution

(D) necessitate a shift to alternative energy sources

(E) result in the inundations of major cities

15. The author mentions the possibility of energy conservation (lines 42–45) in order to

(A) preempt and refute a possible objection to his position

(B) support directly the central thesis of the passage

(C) minimize the significance of a contradiction in the passage

(D) prove that such measures are ineffective and counterproductive

(E) supply the reader with additional background information

16. It can be inferred that the "air-conditioning" of the earth (lines 68–70) refers to proposals to

(A) distribute frigid air from the polar ice caps to coastal cities as the temperature increases due to thermal pollution

(B) dissipate the surplus of the release of stored solar energy over absorbed solar energy into space

(C) conserve completely renewable energy sources by requiring that industry replace these resources

(D) avoid further thermal pollution by converting to solar energy as opposed to conventional and nuclear sources

(E) utilize hydroelectric and wood energy to replace nonconventional energy sources such as nuclear energy

17. The tone of the passage is best described as one of

(A) unmitigated outrage

(B) cautious optimism

(C) reckless abandon

(D) smug self-assurance

(E) pronounced alarm

18. Which of the following would be the most logical topic for the author to address in a succeeding paragraph?

(A) The problems of nuclear safety and waste disposal

(B) A history of the development of solar energy

(C) The availability and cost of solar energy technology

(D) The practical effects of flooding of coastal cities

(E) The feasibility of geothermal energy

19. Many people ask, "How effective is Painaway?" So to find out we have been checking the medicine cabinets of the apartments in this typical building. As it turns out, eight out of ten contain a bottle of Painaway. Doesn't it stand to reason that you too should have the most effective pain-reliever on the market?

The appeal of this advertisement would be most weakened by which of the following pieces of evidence?

(A) Painaway distributed complimentary bottles of medicine to most apartments in the building two days before the advertisement was made.

(B) The actor who made the advertisement takes a pain-reliever manufactured by a competitor of Painaway.

(C) Most people want a fast, effective pain-reliever.

(D) Many people take the advice of their neighborhood druggists about pain-relievers.

(E) A government survey shows that many people take a pain-reliever before it is really needed.

QUESTIONS 20 AND 21

Stock market analysts always attribute a sudden drop in the market to some domestic or international political crisis. I maintain, however, that these declines are attributable to the phases of the moon, which also cause periodic political upheavals and increases in tension in world affairs.

20. Which of the following best describes the author's method of questioning the claim of market analysts?

(A) He presents a counterexample.

(B) He presents statistical evidence.

(C) He suggests an alternative causal linkage.

(D) He appeals to generally accepted beliefs.

(E) He demonstrates that market analysts' reports are unreliable.

21. It can be inferred that the author is critical of the stock analysts because he

(A) believes that they have oversimplified the connection between political crisis and fluctuations of the market

(B) knows that the stock market generally shows more gains than losses

(C) suspects that stock analysts have a vested interest in the stock market, and are therefore likely to distort their explanations

(D) anticipates making large profits in the market himself

(E) is worried that if the connection between political events and stock market prices becomes well-known, unscrupulous investors will take advantage of the information

22. Like Andy Warhol, the "pop art" of Roy Lichtenstein is full of familiar images such as cartoon characters.

(A) Like Andy Warhol, the "pop art" of Roy Lichtenstein

(B) As with that of Andy Warhol, the "pop art" of Roy Lichtenstein

(C) Like the work of Andy Warhol, the "pop art" of Roy Lichtenstein

(D) The "pop art" of Roy Lichtenstein similar to Andy Warhol

(E) It being similar to Andy Warhol's, the "pop art" of Roy Lichtenstein

23. The smoking of cigarettes being injurious to nonsmokers is rapidly becoming a major concern of public health officials.

(A) The smoking of cigarettes being injurious to nonsmokers is

(B) Cigarette smoking being injurious to nonsmokers is

(C) The fact that cigarette smoking is injurious to nonsmokers are

(D) It being injurious to nonsmokers, cigarette smoking is

(E) The fact that cigarette smoking is injurious to nonsmokers is

24. A substance from the licorice plant, 50 times sweeter than sucrose, was recently discovered, is not only a natural sweetener but also prevents tooth decay.

(A) A substance from the licorice plant, 50 times sweeter than sucrose, was recently discovered,

(B) A substance, which was recently discovered, from the licorice plant, 50 times sweeter than sucrose,

(C) A substance from the licorice plant, which was recently discovered to be 50 times sweeter than sucrose,

(D) A substance from the licorice plant, 50 times sweeter than sucrose, which was recently discovered,

(E) A recently discovered substance, 50 times sweeter than sucrose from the licorice plant,

25. This piece of pottery must surely date from the late Minoan period. The dress of the female figures, particularly the bare and emphasized breasts, and the activities of the people depicted—note especially the importance of the bull—are both highly suggestive of this period. These factors, when coupled with the black, semigloss glaze that results from firing the pot in a sealed kiln at a low temperature, makes the conclusion a virtual certainty.

Which of the following is a basic assumption made by the author of this explanation?

(A) Black, semigloss glazed pottery was made only during the late Minoan period.

(B) The bull is an animal that was important to most ancient cultures.

(C) Throughout the long history of the Minoan people, their artisans decorated pottery with seminude women and bulls.

(D) By analyzing the style and materials of any work of art, an expert can pinpoint the date of its creation.

(E) There are key characteristics of works of art that can be shown to be typical of a particular period.

26. Most radicals who argue for violent revolution and complete overthrow of our existing society have no clear idea of what will emerge from the destruction. They just assert that things are so bad now that any change would have to be a change for the better. But surely this is mistaken, for things might actually turn out to be worse.

The most effective point that can be raised against this argument is that the author says nothing about

(A) the manner in which the radicals might foment their revolution

(B) the specific results of the revolution, which would be changes for the worse

(C) the economic arguments the radicals use to persuade people to join in their cause

(D) the fact that most people are really satisfied with the present system so that the chance of total revolution is very small

(E) the loss of life and property that is likely to accompany total destruction of a society

27. Doctors, in seeking a cure for *aphroditis melancholias,* are guided by their research into the causes of *metaeritocas polymanias* because the symptoms of the two diseases occur in populations of similar ages, manifesting symptoms in both cases of high fever, swollen glands, and lack of appetite. Moreover, the incubation period for both diseases is virtually identical. So these medical researchers are convinced that the virus responsible for *aphroditis melancholias* is very similar to that responsible for *metaeritocas polymanias.*

The conclusion of the author rests on the presupposition that

(A) *metaeritocas polymanias* is a more serious public health hazard than *aphroditis melancholias*

(B) for every disease, modern medical science will eventually find a cure

(C) saving human life is the single most important goal of modern technology

(D) *aphroditis melancholias* is a disease that occurs only in human beings

(E) diseases with similar symptoms will have similar causes

QUESTIONS 28–34

It would be enormously convenient to have a single, generally accepted index of the economic and social welfare of the people of the United States. A glance at it would tell us how much better or worse off we had become each year, and we would judge the desirability of any proposed action by asking whether it would raise or lower this index. Some recent discussion implies that such an index could be constructed. Articles in the popular press even criticize the Gross National Product (GNP) because it is not such a complete index of welfare, ignoring, on the one hand, that it was never intended to be, and suggesting, on the other, that with appropriate changes it could be converted into one.

The output available to satisfy our wants and needs is one important determinant of welfare. Whatever want, need, or social problem engages our attention, we ordinarily can more easily find resources to deal with it when output is large and growing than when it is not. GNP measures output fairly well, but to evaluate welfare we would need additional measures which would be far more difficult to construct. We would need an index of real costs incurred in production, because we are better off if we get the same output at less cost. Use of just man-hours for welfare evaluation would unreasonably imply that to increase total hours by raising the hours of eight women from 60 to 65 a week imposes no more burden than raising the hours of eight men from 40 to 45 a week, or even than hiring one involuntarily unemployed person for 40 hours a week. A measure of real costs of labor would also have to consider working conditions. Most of us spend almost half of our waking hours on the job and our welfare is vitally affected by the circumstances in which we spend those hours.

To measure welfare we would need a measure of changes in the need our output must satisfy. One aspect, population change, is now handled by converting output to a per capita basis on the assumption that, other things equal, twice as many people need twice as many goods and services to be equally well off. But an index of needs would also account for differences in the requirements for living as the population becomes more urbanized and suburbanized; for the changes in national defense requirements; and for changes in the effect of weather on our needs. The index would have to tell us the cost of meeting our needs in a base year compared with the cost of meeting them equally well under the circumstances prevailing in every other year.

Measures of "needs" shade into measures of the human and physical environment in which we live. We all are enormously affected by the people around us. Can we go where we like without fear of attack? We are also affected by the physical environment—purity of water and air, accessibility of parkland and other conditions. To measure this requires accurate data, but such data are generally deficient. Moreover, weighting is required: to combine robberies and murders in a crime index; to combine pollution of the Potomac and pollution of Lake Erie into a water pollution index; and then to combine crime and water pollution into some general index. But there is no basis for weighting these beyond individual preference.

There are further problems. To measure welfare we would need an index of the "goodness" of the distribution of income. There is surely consensus that given the same total income and output, a distribution with fewer families in poverty would be better, but what is the ideal distribution? Even if we could construct indexes of output, real costs, needs, state of the environment, we could not compute a welfare index because we have no system of weights to combine them.

28. The author's primary concern is to

(A) refute arguments for a position

(B) make a proposal and defend it

(C) attack the sincerity of an opponent

(D) show defects in a proposal

(E) review literature relevant to a problem

29. The author implies that use of man-hours is not an appropriate measure of real cost because it

(A) ignores the conditions under which the output is generated

(B) fails to take into consideration the environmental costs of production

(C) overemphasizes the output of real goods as opposed to services

(D) is not an effective method for reducing unemployment

(E) was never intended to be a general measure of welfare

30. It can be inferred from the passage that the most important reason a single index of welfare cannot be designed is

(A) the cost associated with producing the index would be prohibitive

(B) considerable empirical research would have to be done regarding output and needs

(C) any weighting of various measures into a general index would be inherently subjective and arbitrary

(D) production of the relevant data would require time, thus the index would be only a reflection of past welfare

(E) accurate statistics on crime and pollution are not yet available

31. The author regards the idea of a general index of welfare as

(A) an unrealistic dream

(B) a scientific reality

(C) an important contribution

(D) a future necessity

(E) a desirable change

32. According to the passage, the GNP is

(A) a fairly accurate measure of output

(B) a reliable estimate of needs

(C) an accurate forecaster of welfare

(D) a precise measure of welfare

(E) a potential measure of general welfare

33. According to the passage, an adequate measure of need must take into account all of the following EXCEPT

(A) changing size of the population

(B) changing effects on people of the weather

(C) differences in needs of urban and suburban populations

(D) changing requirements for governmental programs such as defense

(E) accessibility of parkland and other amenities

34. The passage is most likely

(A) an address to a symposium on public policy decisions

(B) a chapter in a general introduction to statistics

(C) a pamphlet on government programs to aid the poor

(D) the introduction to a treatise on the foundations of government

(E) a speech by a university president to a graduating class

QUESTIONS 35 AND 36

Having just completed Introductory Logic 9, I feel competent to instruct others in the intricacies of this wonderful discipline. Logic is concerned with correct reasoning in the form of syllogisms. A syllogism consists of three statements, two of which are premises, the third of which is the conclusion. Here is an example:

MAJOR PREMISE: The American buffalo is disappearing.

MINOR PREMISE: This animal is an American buffalo.

CONCLUSION: Therefore, this animal is disappearing.

Once one has been indoctrinated into the mysteries of this arcane science, there is no statement one may not assert with complete confidence.

35. The reasoning of the author's example is most similar to that contained in which of the following arguments?

(A) Any endangered species must be protected; this species is endangered; therefore, it should be protected.

(B) All whales are mammals; this animal is a whale; therefore, this animal is a mammal.

(C) Engaging in sexual intercourse with a person to whom one is not married is a sin; and since premarital intercourse is, by definition, without the institution of marriage, it is, therefore, a sin.

(D) There are 60 seconds in a minute; there are 60 minutes in an hour; therefore, there are 3600 seconds in an hour.

(E) Wealthy people pay most of the taxes; this man is wealthy; therefore, this man pays most of the taxes.

36. The main purpose of the author's argument is to

(A) provide instruction in logic

(B) supply a definition

(C) cast doubt on the value of formal logic

(D) present an argument for the protection of the American buffalo

(E) show the precise relationship between the premises and the conclusion of his example

37. It is widely accepted by scientists that chlorofluorocarbons released into the atmosphere as a result of industrial refrigeration and insulation is the main cause of the huge gaps in the earth's ozone layer.

(A) released into the atmosphere as a result of industrial refrigeration and insulation is

(B) released into the atmosphere as a result of industrial refrigeration and insulation are

(C) resulting from industrial refrigeration and insulation released into the atmosphere are

(D) being released into the atmosphere as a result of industrial refrigeration and insulation is

(E) having been released into the atmosphere and resulting from industrial refrigeration and insulation are

38. There are over 110 million dogs and cats in the United States, which is more than the population of any Western European country.

(A) which is more than the population of any Western European country.

(B) which are more than the population of any Western European country.

(C) being more than the population of any Western European country.

(D) more than any Western European country in population.

(E) more than in any Western European country by population.

diagnostic test

QUESTIONS 39 AND 40

On a recent trip to the Mediterranean, I made the acquaintance of a young man who warned me against trusting Cretans. "Everything they say is a lie," he told me, "and I should know because I come from Crete myself." I thanked the fellow for his advice but told him in light of what he had said I had no intention of believing it.

39. Which of the following best describes the author's behavior?

(A) It was unwarranted because the young man was merely trying to be helpful to a stranger.

(B) It was paradoxical, for in discounting the advice he implicitly relied on it.

(C) It was understandable inasmuch as the young man, by his own admission, could not possibly be telling the truth.

(D) It was high-handed and just the sort of thing that gives American tourists a bad name.

(E) It was overly cautious, for not everyone in a foreign country will try to take advantage of a tourist.

40. Which of the following is most nearly analogous to the warning issued by the young man?

(A) An admission by a witness under cross-examination that he has lied.

(B) A sign put up by the Chamber of Commerce of a large city alerting visitors to the dangers of pickpockets.

(C) The command of a military leader to his marching troops to do an about-face.

(D) A sentence written in chalk on a blackboard that says, "This sentence is false."

(E) The advice of a veteran worker to a newly hired person: "You don't actually have to work hard so long as you look like you're working hard."

41. <u>Autism, where a child may be severely retarded, have problems speaking, and exhibit bizarre behavior, occur</u> in 5 of every 10,000 children.

(A) Autism, where a child may be severely retarded, have problems speaking, and exhibit bizarre behavior, occur

(B) Autism, which manifests itself in children in severe retardation, speech problems and bizarre behavior, occurs

(C) Autism is a disease in which a child may be severely retarded, have problems speaking and also bizarre behavior and it occurs

(D) A disease causing severe retardation, speech problems, and behavior may be bizarre, is autism which occurs

(E) Autism, causing severe retardation, speech problems and bizarre behavior, and occurring

answers

ANSWER KEY

Quantitative Section

1. E	8. D	15. B	22. D	29. B	36. D
2. A	9. E	16. B	23. D	30. C	37. E
3. D	10. C	17. E	24. E	31. C	
4. C	11. A	18. E	25. D	32. C	
5. E	12. C	19. C	26. D	33. C	
6. E	13. E	20. D	27. A	34. C	
7. E	14. B	21. B	28. C	35. E	

Verbal Section

1. D	9. D	17. B	25. E	33. E	41. B
2. D	10. B	18. C	26. B	34. A	
3. D	11. D	19. A	27. E	35. E	
4. B	12. D	20. C	28. D	36. C	
5. C	13. E	21. A	29. A	37. B	
6. E	14. C	22. C	30. C	38. A	
7. B	15. A	23. E	31. A	39. B	
8. B	16. B	24. C	32. A	40. D	

EXPLANATORY ANSWERS

Quantitative Section

1. **The correct answer is (E).** This question is easily solved by manipulating the equation to find the value of x:

   Subtract x from both sides:

   $$x + 5 = 4x - 10$$
   $$-x \quad -x$$
   $$5 = 3x - 10$$

   Add 10 to each side:

   $$+10 \quad +10$$
   $$15 = 3x$$

   Rearrange if you wish:

   $$3x = 15$$

   Divide both sides by 3:

   $$\frac{3x}{3} = \frac{15}{3}$$
   $$x = 5$$

2. **The correct answer is (A).** This question is most easily solved by manipulating exponents rather than by a complicated and lengthy series of multiplications. Since 8 is equal to 2 to the third power, we can substitute 2^3 for 8:

   $$\frac{2^6 - (2^3)^2}{4^3}$$

   The second term of the numerator indicates that 2 to the third power is being raised to the second power. The rules of exponents require that we multiply in this situation:

   $$(2^3)^2 = 2^6$$

Now it becomes clear that the value of the numerator is 0, so the value of the entire expression is 0.

3. **The correct answer is (D).** Statement (1) coupled with the information supplied in the question stem is sufficient to answer the question asked. An increase of 8% over Friday night's attendance would be an increase of 16 people (8% of 200 = 16), so 216 people attended Saturday night.

   Statement (2), when coupled with the information supplied in the stem, is also sufficient to answer the question asked. The increase of 16 people is equal to an increase of 8%:

   8% of Friday night's attendance = 16 people

   So Friday night's attendance = $\frac{16}{0.8}$

   Friday night's attendance = 200 people
   Given that, plus the information about the increase, we establish that Saturday night's attendance was 216.

4. **The correct answer is (C).** Statement (1) is clearly not sufficient to answer the question, for it does not break down the receipts between the two categories.

   Statement (2) is alone not sufficient to answer the question, for it gives you only the receipts derived from the sale of necklaces—not bracelets.

   The two statements taken together, however, do answer the question. You can use statement (2) to find the money taken in from the sale of necklaces and subtract that total from $540, the amount specified in statement (1), to find the money taken in from the sale of bracelets.

5. **The correct answer is (E).** Statement (1) does nothing to establish the *number* of people who visited the museum in 1985, and statement (2) does nothing to establish the number of people who visited the museum in 1985. So we eliminate choices (A), (B), and (D), and check for a possible interaction between (1) and (2). As it turns out, there is no way of relating the information given in one to that given in another, so the correct choice is (E).

6. **The correct answer is (E).** Statement (1) is insufficient since it does not even allow us to determine the weight of the cookies in the container. Statement (2) has the merit of overcoming this by establishing directly the weight of the cookies, but even that is not sufficient to establish the *number* of cookies in the box because of the variation in weight. Using extreme cases to illustrate the possibilities, if only one cookie weighs 3.8 grams and all others weigh 3.2 (or as close to 3.2 as possible), then the box would contain 1 cookie weighing 3.8 grams plus $(112 - 3.8) \div 3.2 = 1 + 33 = 34$ cookies. But if the opposite were true, then the box would contain 1 cookie weighing 3.2 grams plus $(112 - 3.2) \div 3.8 = 1 + 28 = 29$ cookies. So the box could contain anywhere from 29 to 34 cookies.

7. **The correct answer is (E).** Statement (1) is not sufficient to answer the question, for it establishes only that $x > -5$. If x is -4, then $x + 3$ is not more than 0, but if x is -1, then $x + 3$ is greater than 0.
   Statement (2) is also insufficient for the same reason. Are they sufficient when taken together? No. Taken together they establish only that x is greater than -5 and less than 0: $-5 < x < 0$

   But given that range, it is impossible to determine whether $x + 3$ is greater than 0.

8. **The correct answer is (D).** Statement (1) is sufficient to establish the area of the circle. The radius of a circle is one-half its diameter, and the formula for computing the area of a circle is $A = \pi r^2$.

   Statement (2) is also sufficient. The formula for finding the circumference of a circle is $C = 2\pi r$. Given the circumference, it is possible to find the radius, and with that the area.

9. **The correct answer is (E).** Obviously, to answer the question you must know the length of the side of a piece of tile. Since each tile is square and has a perimeter of 1 meter, each side is 1 divided by 4, or $\frac{1}{4}$ meters in length. Then, the length of the side of the square to be tiled is 3 meters, and 3 divided by $\frac{1}{4}$ is 12. So you would need 12 such tiles laid side by side to cover one edge of the area. Finally, since the area to be covered is 3 meters by 3 meters, you would need at least 12 times 12, or 144 tiles.

10. **The correct answer is (C).** This question involves the computation of a percentage increase. The formula for finding a percentage change is Increase/Original Total.

Notice also that the question specifically allows you to use an approximation:

$$\frac{16,300-12,200}{12,200}=\frac{4,100}{12,200}\cong\frac{1}{3}=33\frac{1}{3}\%$$

So the closest approximation is (C).

11. **The correct answer is (A).** The information for this question is presented in graphic form. The solution requires the computation of a weighted average; that is, to find the overall class average, we must make sure we give proper weight to each score according to the number of students who achieved that score:

	5 × 70	=	350
	20 × 80	=	1,600
	10 × 90	=	900
	15 × 100	=	1,500
Totals:	50 students		4,350 points

To find the average, we divide the total number of points by the total number of students:

$$\frac{4,350}{50} = 87$$

12. **The correct answer is (C).** This question tests nothing more than your ability to do some simple, if tedious, bookkeeping. To find the cost of sending a 23.5-pound package by Express Service, we must use all three express rates:

First lb.	\$17.50
Next 9 lbs.	9 × \$2.60 = \$23.40
Additional 13.5 lbs.	14 × \$1.20 = \$16.80
Total:	\$57.70

13. **The correct answer is (E).** This question is more easily solved by using common sense than by doing the operations indicated. Without making a final decision about (A) and (B), you can see that they are similar, so don't try to compare them at first. Then, (C) involves raising a fraction to the fifth power, and as you do that, the numbers get smaller and smaller. So (C) is going to be much smaller than either (A) or (B). (D), however, when rewritten as 0.003 × 7, looks very much like (A) and (B). So go on to (E). (E) is somewhat like (A), (B) and (D), except that the decimal number in (E) is much larger than those of the other choices. Consequently, (E) will be correspondingly larger than any of the others. And you can reach this conclusion without actually doing any multiplication.

14. **The correct answer is (B).** To a certain extent, answering this question is a matter of trial and error. One way of arriving at the desired arrangement is:

	C	**B**	**E**	**F**	**D**	**A**
STEP 1:	A	C	B	E	F	D
STEP 2:	A	B	C	E	F	D
STEP 3:	A	B	C	D	E	F

While this is not the only way of doing it, a little experimentation will show you that it cannot be done in fewer steps.

Further, we can offer a sort of informal proof that it is not possible to do the job in fewer steps.

answers

Given the arrangement:

C B E F D A

We know that we must move A to the left of B, C to the right of B and D to the left of E. That will require a minimum of three steps.

15. The correct answer is (B). Statement (1) is not sufficient because it does not supply the comparison between the cost of a single bagel and the cost of a dozen bagels.

Statement (2), however, is by itself sufficient. If 12 bagels cost only 10 times as much as one bagel, then bagels are cheaper by the dozen. If the cost were the same, then a dozen bagels would cost 12 times as much as a single bagel.

Be careful, however, not to assume that you need statement (1) as well. Once you know that a dozen bagels cost only 10 times what one bagel purchased singly costs, you can answer the question. Yes, they are cheaper by the dozen. You do not need the actual unit cost to reach that conclusion.

16. The correct answer is (B). This question can be solved using a table:

	Full-Time	Part-Time	Total
Men			
Women			
Total			

The table or matrix shows the possibilities. We begin to fill in the individual squares, or cells, by using the information provided:

	Full-Time	Part-Time	Total
Men			55%
Women			
Total	30%		

But we know that the total labor force is 100%, and this means that the percentages for full-time and part-time must equal 100 and that the percentages for Men and Women must equal 100. So we can fill in some further information:

	Full-Time	Part-Time	Total
Men			55%
Women			45%
Total	30%	70%	100%

Next we reason that 60% of the 30% who are full-time employees are women. In other words, full-time women workers account for 60% of 30% of the work force:

	Full-Time	Part-Time	Total
Men			55%
Women	18%		45%
Total	30%	70%	100%

Now, since we have totals indicated, we can use arithmetic to find the missing information:

	Full-Time	Part-Time	Total
Men	12%	43%	55%
Women	18%	27%	45%
Total	30%	70%	100%

Notice that all totals check out.

The final step is to use the information to answer the question:

$$\frac{\text{Men Full-Time}}{\text{Total Full-Time}} = \frac{.12}{.30} = \frac{2}{5} = 40\%$$

17. The correct answer is (E). Here you must read the question carefully. The question asks for the greatest difference for any *student*—not the greatest difference between the lowest score recorded (of all students) and the highest score recorded (of all students). It is true that the statements, taken together, establish that the range among all students was 44 to 98, or 54 points. But nothing establishes that this was the range of a particular student. And the question asks for the greatest range of scores for a single student.

18. The correct answer is (E). The trick here is to recognize that both triangles, *ADC* and *ABC*, have the same altitude, *AD*:

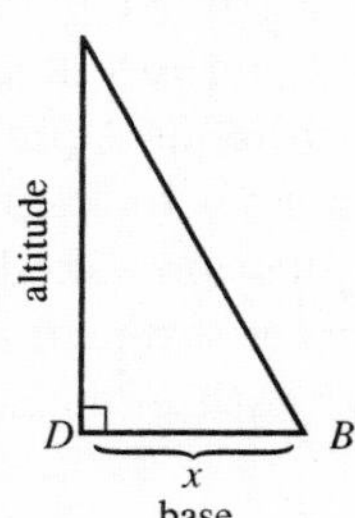

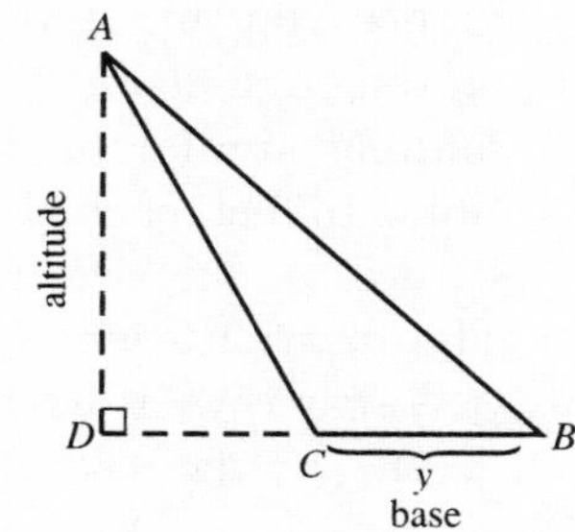

Now you use the standard formula ($\frac{1}{2}$ × altitude × base) to find the area of each triangle. For ΔADC it is $\frac{1}{2}(x)(AD)$ and for ΔABC it is $\frac{1}{2}(y)(AD)$. Then you set up your ratio:

$$\frac{\frac{1}{2}(x)(AD)}{\frac{1}{2}(y)(AD)}=\frac{x}{y}$$

But since x and y are equal, the ratio is just 1.

19. The correct answer is (C). A good approach to this question is to try to express the information given in English in algebraic terms. We are told that the cost of car X is twice the average of the other 11 cars. To express the average cost of the other 11 cars we can use the letter T to represent their total cost (all 11 combined), and so the average will be $\frac{T}{11}$. Then we are told that the cost of X is twice this, or $\frac{2T}{11}$. We now have all costs represented in terms of T, and we can address ourselves to the question asked: "what fraction of total is car X?" Expressed with symbols:

$$\frac{\text{Cost of Car } X}{\text{Total of All}}$$

The total cost of the cars in the shipment will be the cost of the 11 cars plus the cost of car X: Total Cost = $T + \frac{2T}{11} = \frac{13T}{11}$. Now we substitute this into the fraction above:

$$\frac{\frac{2T}{11}}{\frac{13T}{11}}=\frac{2T}{11}\times\frac{11}{13T}=\frac{2}{13}$$

20. The correct answer is (D). Above, we solved the problem using "official" algebraic unknowns, but in other situations we have used actual numbers. Question 19 could also have been handled in such a way. For this question, let us use the alternative method rather than the "official" algebraic approach.

We are not told the weight of the jar or its contents, so we can arbitrarily supply our own numbers. Let us pick a convenient number to work with, say 10 pounds. If the total weight of the jar and its contents is 10 pounds, then the jar alone weighs 20% of 10 pounds, or 2 pounds, and the coffee therefore weighs 8 pounds. Now if we remove beans so that the combined weight of the jar and the remaining beans is 60% of the original total, the new combined weight is only 6 pounds, of which 2 pounds is glass jar and 4 pounds is coffee. So we have only 4 pounds of coffee remaining out of an original total of 8 pounds. Therefore, we have removed 4 out of 8 pounds or exactly $\frac{1}{2}$ of the coffee.

21. The correct answer is (B). A simple approach to this question is to combine the information given in an informal way, rather than trying to perform precise manipulations by the rules. First, on the lower end, we know that x must be larger than 2, larger than 4, larger than –1, and larger than 0, which means simply that x is bigger than 4. On the other side, x is less than 12, less than 21, less than 9, less than 8, and less than 6 (if $x + 1 < 7$ then $x < 6$). Therefore, x (which is said to be an integer) is bigger than 4 and less than 6, so x must be 5.

22. The correct answer is (D). Perhaps the very best way to solve this question is just to test each answer choice to find out which one works. If you test each choice by substitution into the calculation for X, you will find that only 7 works:

$$\begin{array}{r} 729 \\ 573 \\ +\,971 \\ \hline 2{,}273 \end{array}$$

23. The correct answer is (D). Statement (1) is enough to establish that this is a right triangle. We usually think of the Pythagorean Theorem as saying that in a right triangle the square of the longest side (the hypotenuse) is equal to the sum of the squares of the other two sides. But the converse is also true. Any triangle in which the square of the longest side is equal to the sum of the squares of the other two sides *is necessarily* a right triangle. Statement (1), when rewritten as $AB^2 + AC^2 = BC^2$, says that this triangle fits the Pythagorean Theorem.

Once we know that angle A is a right angle, then we can calculate the area of the triangle. We can use CA as an altitude and BA as a base, and the area is $\frac{1}{2} \times$ altitude $\times$ base, or 6.

Statement (2) is also sufficient and operates in an even more direct fashion. If $x = 90$ degrees, then, as described above, we can use CA as an altitude and BA as the base for purposes of computing the area.

24. The correct answer is (E). Statement (1) does not establish the relative speeds, for it makes a statement about time only, saying nothing about distance.

Statement (2) suffers from the opposite deficiency, making a statement about distance but not about time.

So neither statement alone can be sufficient. But even together they fail to answer the question. They establish that the first plane flew farther and flew for a longer period of time, but that does not determine whether it flew faster than the second plane.

25. The correct answer is (D). At first glance you might think we need both statements, using them together in a manner similar to simultaneous equations. In fact, each statement is by itself sufficient to answer the question asked. The question is whether x is greater than 0. We can rewrite each of the statements.

(1) $2x - 5 > 0$

$2x > 5$

$x > 2.5$

So x is more than 2.5 and therefore greater than 0.

(2) $2x + 1 > 2$

$2x > 1$

$x > \frac{1}{2}$

So x is greater than $\frac{1}{2}$ and therefore greater than 0.

26. The correct answer is (D). The key to this question is the technique for finding the surface area of a cylinder. Notice we say "technique" and not "formula." There really is no point in trying to memorize such a rule, for the surface area of a cylinder can be analyzed into three components:

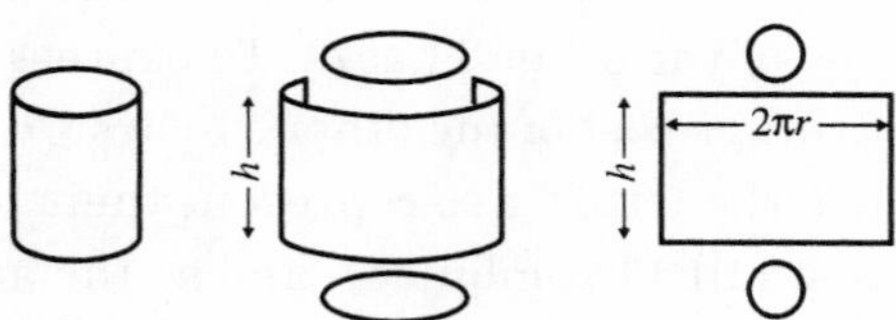

As the exploded view shows, the surface area consists of the top and the bottom and the wrap-around side. As the diagram shows, the top and the bottom are both circles, whereas the wrap-around area is really a rectangle wrapped into a cylindrical shape. The width of the wrap-around rectangle is the same as the circumference of the circle.

To find the entire surface area you need only two dimensions: the radius of the top or bottom and the height. The radius of the top and bottom is given in the question stem, so any information that provides the height is all that is required to answer the question.

Statement (1) gives the information. If the rectangular wraparound has an area of 1200π square inches, and if one side (as we know) is equal to the circumference of a circle of known radius, then we can find the other side of the rectangular wraparound. And that is the height of the cylinder.

Statement (2) also provides the needed information. We know from the question stem the areas of the top and bottom. Then given the total surface area of the cylinder, we simply subtract the top and the bottom and are left with the area of the rectangular wraparound. After that, we find the height in the method just described.

27. The correct answer is (A). Statement (2) is not sufficient to answer the question because it does not fix the number of nickels or dimes. For example, she might have 6 dimes, 2 nickels, and 3 pennies. Or she might have 1 dime, 12 nickels, and 3 pennies.

Statement (1), however, is sufficient to answer the question. Try the various possibilities. The minimum number of pennies Edna might have is 3. If she has 3 pennies, then she would have 6 dimes, for a total of 63 cents, and therefore 2 nickels. Then try the next possibility. Could Edna have exactly 8 pennies? No, for if she has twice as many dimes as pennies, 8 pennies would mean 16 dimes, for a total of 168 cents. But that is more than stipulated by the question. So if Edna has twice as many dimes as pennies, then she must have exactly 3 pennies and 6 dimes and 2 nickels. And that is sufficient to answer the question asked.

28. The correct answer is (C). This question requires only that you see that to find a total cost you need the per unit price and the number of items purchased. In this case, the information is supplied in a somewhat indirect fashion, for the question stem does not give us the unit price of the earlier year.

Since no unit price is given, it is unknown and we can call it x. In other words, the per-gallon price for metered water in 1985 was $\$x$ per gallon. Also we do not know the number of gallons purchased in 1985, so we can call that y. We do know, however, that the price multiplied by the number of gallons gives the total amount spent: $\$x$/gallons times y gallons = \$1,200. Or put in official algebra:

$$xy = 1{,}200$$

Notice that both numbered statements give some information related to this equation. Statement (1) gives information that relates 1986 to x, and statement (2) gives information that relates 1986 to y. But neither alone is sufficient.

Taken together, however, they are sufficient. Statement (1) establishes the 1986 price as 10% more than x, or $1.1x$. And statement (2) establishes that 1986 consumption was 5% more than y, or $1.05y$. Combining the two, 1986 consumption was $1.1x\,(1.05y) = 1.115xy$. This means that 1986 charges were 11.5% more than the \$1,200 spent in 1985, and that is enough to answer the question.

Of course, there is no reason to work out the final numbers. We are concerned only to determine when information is sufficient, not to arrive at final numerical solutions.

29. The correct answer is (B). Here we have a percentage question that involves several manipulations. Only one basic insight, however, is needed to handle the problem. Knowing the amount and percent of an increase is sufficient to allow you to calculate the starting and ending amounts. In this case, we need the starting amounts.

For stock P we know that an increase of 16 cents is equal to 16% of the original value of the stock:

$$\$0.16 = 16\% \text{ of Original Value}$$
$$\$0.16 = .16 \times OV$$
$$\frac{\$0.16}{.16} = OV$$
$$\text{Original Value} = \$1.00$$

For stock Q we know that an increase of \$1.68 is equal to 16% of the original value of the stock:

$$\$1.68 = 16\% \text{ of Original Value}$$
$$\$1.68 = .16 \times OV$$
$$\frac{\$1.68}{.16} = OV$$
$$\text{Original Value} = \$10.50$$

Now we find the difference between the original values:

$$\$10.50 - \$1.00 = \$9.50$$

30. The correct answer is (C). This problem is rather tedious because it requires calculating the times for these two trains that stop and start. How long does it take the express train to travel 600 kilometers? Since it travels at the rate of 100 kilometers per hour, the total time while actually moving will be:

$$\frac{600 \text{ kilometers}}{100 \text{ kilometers}} \text{ per hour} = 6 \text{ hours}$$

Now we calculate the non-moving time:

75 kilometers, total traveled of 75, then first stop
75 kilometers, total traveled of 150, then second stop
75 kilometers, total traveled of 225, then third stop
75 kilometers, total traveled of 300, then fourth stop
75 kilometers, total traveled of 375, then fifth stop
75 kilometers, total traveled of 450, then sixth stop
75 kilometers, total traveled of 525, then seventh stop
75 kilometers, total traveled of 600

Note that when the train reaches 600 kilometers, you do not add in another stop. The question requires that you calculate the time needed to *travel* 600 kilometers. So the total time is 6 hours plus 7×3 minutes, or 6 hours and 21 minutes.

Now how far can the local train travel in that length of time? Since the local train travels at 50 kilometers per hour, it will cover 25 kilometers in 30 minutes:

$$\frac{25 \text{ kilometers}}{50 \text{ kilometers}} \text{ per hour} = .5 \text{ hours, or } 30 \text{ minutes}$$

This means that the train will travel $12 \times 25 = 300$ kilometers in exactly 6 hours, but that includes 12 1-minute stops. So in 6 hours and 12 minutes the local train travels 300 kilometers and completes its final stop. Now the train starts up again and runs for another 9 minutes, to give our total of 6 hours and 21 minutes. How far does it travel in 9 minutes?

$$50 \text{ kilometers per hour} \times \frac{9}{60} \text{ hours} = 7.5 \text{ km.}$$

The local train travels a total of 307.5 kilometers in the same time it takes the express train to travel 600 kilometers.

31. The correct answer is (C). This is a fairly straightforward calculation problem. To answer a question of the sort "x is what percent of y," you create a fraction using the y term (the object of the preposition "of") as the denominator and using the x term as the numerator: $\frac{45}{9000} = 0.005$. (Be sure to keep track of your decimal point!) Then rename that decimal as a percentage by moving the decimal two places to the right: $0.005 = 0.5\%$

32. The correct answer is (C). You can solve for y by treating the information as simultaneous equations. First solve for x in the equation $3x = 6$: $x = \frac{6}{3} = 2$. Then substitute that value for x in the other equation: $2 - y = 0$, so $2 = y$.

33. The correct answer is (C). Here is a question that asks you to translate English into "algebra." We are told that A is equal to 20 years less than $\frac{1}{2}$ the sum of the ages of the two parents. Since F and M designate the ages of the two parents, the sum of the ages of the two parents is just $F+M$. And the $\frac{1}{2}$ of that is just $F+M$ divided by 2. So we render that as

$$\frac{F+M}{2}$$

Next, A is 20 years less than that, so the formula is:

$$\frac{F+M}{2} - 20$$

34. The correct answer is (C). This question is pretty much just a matter of bookkeeping, even though it does get a little complicated because of the mass of information. In the end, we want to know how much more the athlete will receive in the package offered by Team L than in the package offered by Team K. What does each offer?

First, K offers \$100,000 for the first year, \$100,000 + 20% of 100,000 = \$120,000 in the second year, and \$120,000 + 20% of \$120,000 = \$144,000 in the third year, plus the signing bonus of \$50,000:

\$100,000 + \$120,000 + \$144,000 + \$50,000 = \$414,000

L offers a salary of \$150,000 in the first year, \$150,000 + 10% of \$150,000 = \$165,000 in the second year, and \$165,000 + 10% of \$165,000 = \$181,500 in the third year:

\$150,000 + \$165,000 + \$181,500 = \$496,500

So L pays more than K: \$496,500 – \$414,000 = \$82,500

35. The correct answer is (E). The numbered statements here are two equations. To determine the sufficiency of the data provided we need to simplify each equation.

As for statement (1):

$$\begin{aligned} x+y+z &= x+y-z+1 \\ x+z &= x-z+1 \\ z &= -z+1 \\ 2z &= 1 \\ \text{so } z &= \tfrac{1}{2} \end{aligned}$$

As for statement (2), although the equation can be rewritten, it cannot be further simplified. That is, we cannot eliminate any of the three variables. Thus, neither statement alone is sufficient.

But can they work together to provide a solution? Substituting our result from the manipulation of statement (1) into the equation in statement (2), we have:

$$\begin{aligned} x-y+\frac{1}{2} &= 0 \\ x-y &= -\frac{1}{2} \end{aligned}$$

Even that, however, is not enough. For knowing only the value of x *minus* y is not sufficient to determine the value of x *plus* y.

36. The correct answer is (D). To answer this question you do not need any advanced mathematics, just some good common sense. The pyramid structure shown in the drawing looks like the pin setup in bowling (ten pins). And the principle is the same. Each subsequent row contains one more member than the earlier row. So the progression is 1, 2, 3, 4, 5, etc. And the total number of members goes 1, 3, 6, 10, 15, 21, 28, etc. So to answer the question you just need to count until you find one of the "magic" numbers in the choices.

37. The correct answer is (E). To answer the question we need to know the volume of the overall container and the volume of the individual packages to be placed in the larger container. But that is not enough. We must also know the dimensions of each, that is the shape of each. Even using both numbered statements, we have no information about the shape of either the larger carton or the individual boxes.

Verbal Section

1. **The correct answer is (D).** The original is incorrect because the order of the phrases "to an army base," "from their homes," and "20 miles away" does not correctly reflect the logic of the underlying thought of the sentence. (D) represents the best ordering of those phrases. Although (E) also uses the correct order, (E) introduces an error in its use of "has." "Has" fails to agree with the subject, and is the wrong verb tense.

2. **The correct answer is (D).** The original sentence is wrong because the subject "constraints" is plural and the verb "has made" is singular. (C) and (E) fail to correct the error. (B) corrects that error but introduces a new problem by using the *-ing* verb form instead of the infinitive.

3. **The correct answer is (D).** The "their" is intended to refer to "movement." But "movement" is singular. (D) corrects this error by using "its." (B) does correct the original error but introduces a new error, a faulty comparison. (B) implies a comparison between "countries" and "student movement." (E) commits a similar error. Finally, (C) is wrong because "Just as the student movements in other countries" doesn't express a complete thought. Ordinarily, that kind of phrasing would be used in the following situation: "Just as their parents did, many adults today are. . . ."

4. **The correct answer is (B).** The basic move by M. Adamante is to offer a competing explanation for the phenomenon. That is, he seems to agree that the United States has the 17th lowest infant mortality rate, but he attributes this to distributional factors rather than to medical technology itself. (D) is the second most attractive answer. But Adamante does not introduce any intervening variables, e.g., technology allows more pregnancies that would otherwise abort to go to term, which in turn means that weaker infants are born, and so more die. (A) is incorrect since Adamante seems to accept the validity of the data and to contest the explanation. (E) is incorrect for the same reason. Finally, (C) is incorrect since Adamante does not suggest that the first speaker has made a logical error—only a factual one.

5. **The correct answer is (C).** The speaker is arguing that the budget cuts will not ultimately be detrimental to the poor. (C) attacks this conclusion directly by pointing out that they will receive little or no advantage. (A) and (B) are wrong because they are irrelevant: how or why politicians are elected is not a concern of the speaker. And (D) and (E) both seem to strengthen the speaker's position by suggesting ways in which the poor would benefit.

6. **The correct answer is (E).** The original sentence suffers from two defects. First, the phrasing is very awkward. Additionally, the "before" does not pinpoint the time frame intended. Does it mean before the moment at which the speaker is speaking or the time when the museum will open its new wing? Only (E), with its change in phrasing and punctuation, corrects these errors.

7. **The correct answer is (B).** The author is accusing the artists of being inconsistent, claiming that they give lip service to the idea that an artist must suffer, but that they then live in material comfort—so they do not themselves suffer. Only (B) completes the paragraph in a way so that this inconsistency comes out. (A) and (D) can be dismissed because the author is attacking *artists,* not connoisseurs or purchasers of art, nor critics of art. (C) is inadequate for it does not reveal the inconsistency. The author apparently allows that these people are, after a fashion, artists, but objects to their claiming that it is necessary to

suffer while they do not themselves suffer. (E) is the second best answer, but it fails, too. The difficulty with (E) is that the author's point is that there is a contradiction between the actions and the words of artists: They claim to suffer but they do not. But the claimed suffering goes beyond matters of eating and has to do with deprivation generally.

8. **The correct answer is (B).** Choice (B) is an assumption of the author because the inconsistency of which the author accuses others would disappear if, though they were not poor, they nonetheless endured great suffering, e.g., emotional pain or poor health. (A) is not an assumption of the author. The author is trying to prove the existence of a contradiction in another's words and actions: It is the others who insist suffering is necessary. The author never says one way or the other whether suffering is necessary to produce art—only that these others claim it is, and then eat well. (C) incorrectly construes the author's reference to purchasers of art. There is no mention of the role of the critic. (D) and (E) both make the mistake of applying the term "fools" to a category other than "bidders."

9. **The correct answer is (D).** Choice (A) is incorrect because of a misplaced modifier. The sentence actually says that the researchers were deregulated. (B) repeats this error. (C) is grammatically incorrect (the verb does not agree with the subject), and it is needlessly wordy and awkward. (E) is incorrect because "its" does not have a clear referent.

10. **The correct answer is (B).** The original sentence fails on two counts. First, "success" is singular and requires a singular verb form. The original sentence says that "success . . . have led." There is also a mistake in diction. The correct word is the verb "affect" not "effect." (B) corrects these two errors without introducing new ones. (C) repeats one of the errors; (D) introduces an incorrect verb tense; and (E) repeats the second error.

11. **The correct answer is (D).** The original sentence makes a mistake of diction. "As wide of a" is not standard English. Both (B) and (C) introduce incorrect verb tenses. (E) introduces a new error: "as wide than" is not idiomatic.

12. **The correct answer is (D).** This is a main idea question. The two things the author does in this passage describe the problem of increasing thermal pollution and suggest that solar energy will solve the problem. (D) neatly describes this double development. (A) is incorrect, for in addition to describing the phenomenon of thermal pollution and its causes, the author also proposes a solution. (B) is incorrect since it fails to make reference to the fact that an important part of the passage is the description of a problem. It can be argued that (B) does make an attempt to describe the development of the passage, but it does not do as nicely as (D) does. (C) is easily eliminated since no ambiguity is mentioned. Finally, (E) is incorrect because the author never cites and then refuses a counterargument.

13. **The correct answer is (E).** This is an explicit-idea question. (A), (B), and (C) are mentioned in the second paragraph as factors contributing to thermal pollution. (D) is mentioned in the third paragraph as a pressure increasing thermal pollution. (E) is mentioned in the third paragraph—but not as a factor contributing to thermal pollution. Unpredictable weather patterns make it difficult to predict when the thermal pollution problem will reach the critical stage, but the patterns do not contribute to thermal pollution.

14. **The correct answer is (C).** This is an inference question. In discussing the melting of the polar ice caps, the author notes that there is a positive feedback mecha-

answers

nism: Since the ice caps reflect sunlight and therefore dissipate solar energy which would otherwise be absorbed by the earth, the melting of the ice caps increases the amount of energy captured by the earth, which in turn contributes to the melting of the ice caps, and so on. (C) correctly describes this as intensifying the effects of thermal pollution. (A) is easily eliminated since this feedback mechanism has nothing to do with a possible reduction in per capita energy consumption. (B) is incorrect, for though this feedback loop increases the problem, and thereby the urgency for the changeover to solar energy, the loop itself will not cause a change in policy. (D) is incorrect for the same reason. Finally, though the melting of the polar ice caps will result in flooding, this flooding is not an explanation of the feedback loop. Rather it is the result of the general phenomenon of the melting of the ice caps.

15. **The correct answer is (A).** This is a logical detail question. Why does the author discuss energy conservation? Conservation may appear as a possible alternative to solar energy. The author argues, however, that a closer examination shows that conservation cannot avert but only postpone the crisis. In terms of tactics, the author's move is to raise a possible objection and give an answer to it—as stated in (A). (B) is incorrect, for the refutation of a possible objection does not support the central thesis directly, only indirectly by eliminating a possible counterargument. (C) is incorrect since the author never acknowledges having fallen into any contradiction. (D) is incorrect since it overstates the case. The author admits that conservation has a beneficial effect, but denies that conservation obviates the need for solar energy. Finally, (E) is incorrect since the point is argumentative and not merely informational.

16. **The correct answer is (B).** This is an inference question. In the final paragraph the author makes references to the possibility of "air-conditioning" the earth. A word placed in quotation marks indicates that it is being used in a nonstandard way. Ordinarily, we use the word "air-condition" to mean to cool, say, a room or an entire building. Obviously, the author is not referring to some gigantic air-conditioning unit mounted, say, on top of the earth. But the general idea of removing heat seems to be what the term means in this context. This is consonant with the passage as well. Thermal pollution is the buildup of energy, and we are showing a positive buildup because fossil fuel and other sources of energy release energy which was only stored. So this, coupled with the sun's energy which comes in each moment, gives us a positive (though not desirable) balance of energy retention over energy loss. The idea of air-conditioning the earth, though not feasible to the passage, must refer to schemes to get rid of this energy, say, into outer space. This is the idea presented in (B). As for (A), redistribution of thermal energy within the earth's energy system will not solve the problem of accumulated energy, so that cannot be what proponents of "air conditioning" have in mind. (C) is a good definition of conservation, but not "air conditioning." (D) is the recommendation given by the author, but that is not a response to this question. Finally, (E) is incorrect for the reason that burning wood is not going to cool the earth.

17. **The correct answer is (B).** This is a tone question. The author describes a very dangerous situation, but also shows the way to solve the problem. The author does not necessarily believe that the battle for solar energy has been won; otherwise, why advocate a shift to solar energy? On balance, the tone of the passage is hope

or optimism, qualified by the realization that solar energy is not yet a high priority. This qualified hope is best described by (B). (A) is incorrect since this is not the tone of the passage. Though the author may be distressed at the perceived shortsightedness of policy makers, this distress does not color the writing in the passage. (C) is totally inappropriate since the author is analytical. (D) is inconsistent with the author's concern. Finally, (E) overstates the case. The author is concerned, but not panicked.

18. **The correct answer is (C).** This is an application question. We are looking for the *most* logical continuation. Since the author has urged us to adopt solar energy, an appropriate continuation would be a discussion of how to implement solar energy. And (C) would be a part of this discussion. (B) can be eliminated since the proposal depends upon the cost and feasibility of solar energy, not on its history. (A) and (E) can be eliminated since the author has explicitly asserted that *only* solar energy will solve the problem of thermal pollution. Finally, (D) is incorrect since the author need not regale us with the gory details of this situation. The point has already been made. As readers, we will want to see the practical details of his plan to avoid disaster.

19. **The correct answer is (A).** The author reasons from the premise "there are bottles of this product in the apartments" to the conclusion "therefore, these people believe the product is effective." The ad obviously wants the hearer to infer that the residents of the apartments decided themselves to purchase the product because they believed it to be effective. (A) directly attacks this linkage. If it were true that the company gave away bottles of the product, this would sever that link. (B) does weaken the ad, but only marginally. To be sure, we might say to ourselves, "Well, a person who touts a product and does not use it is not fully to be trusted." But it does not aim at the very structure of the argument as (A) does. (C) can hardly weaken the argument, since it appears to be a premise on which the argument itself is built. (C), therefore, actually strengthens the appeal of the advertisement. It also does not link to Painaway's effectiveness. (D) seems to be irrelevant to the *appeal* of the ad. The ad is designed to *change* the hearer's mind, so the fact that the hearer does not now accept the conclusion of the ad is not an argument against the ability of the ad to accomplish its stated objective. Finally, (E) is irrelevant to the purpose of the ad for reasons very similar to those cited for (D).

20. **The correct answer is (C).** Take careful note of the exact position the author ascribes to the analysis: They *always* attribute a sudden drop to a crisis. The author then attacks this simple causal explanation by explaining that, though a crisis is followed by a market drop, the reason is not that the crisis causes the drop but that both are the effects of some common cause, the changing of the moon. Of course, the argument seems implausible, but our task is not to grade the argument, only to describe its structure. (A) is not a proper characterization of that structure since the author never provides a specific example. (B), too, is inapplicable since no statistics are produced. (D) can be rejected since the author is attacking generally accepted beliefs rather than appealing to them to support his position. Finally, though the author concedes the reliability of the reports in question, he wants to draw a different conclusion from the data, (E).

21. **The correct answer is (A).** Given the implausibility of the author's alternative explanation, he is probably speaking tongue-in-cheek, that is, he is ridiculing the analysts for *always* attributing a

drop in the market to a political crisis. But whether you took the argument in this way or as a serious attempt to explain the fluctuations of the stock market, (A) will be the correct answer. (E) surely goes beyond the mere factual description at which the author is aiming, as does (D) as well. The author is concerned with the *causes* of fluctuations; nothing suggests that he or anyone else is in a position to exploit those fluctuations. (C) finds no support in the paragraph for nothing suggests that he wishes to attack the credibility of the source rather than the argument itself. Finally, (B) is inappropriate to the main point of the passage. Whether the market ultimately evens itself out has nothing to do with the causes of the fluctuations.

22. **The correct answer is (C).** The original sentence makes an incorrect comparison between Andy Warhol and the work of Roy Lichtenstein. (B) makes a correct comparison of the art of Lichtenstein and that of Warhol but uses "as with" to make the comparison, which is incorrect. (D) repeats the incorrect comparison. (E) is incorrect because the "it being similar" is not acceptable in standard written English.

23. **The correct answer is (E).** The original sentence commits a grammatical mistake. The phrase modifying the gerund "being" should be in the possessive case. But the resulting phrase "smoking of cigarettes being injurious" is very awkward. The best course of action is to eliminate that phrase altogether, as (C) and (E) both do. (C), however, is wrong because the verb "are" does not agree with the new subject, "fact."

24. **The correct answer is (C).** The original sentence runs several ideas together. (C) correctly separates them, and places them in a logical order.

25. **The correct answer is (E).** The assumption necessary to the author's reasoning is the fairly abstract or minimal one that there is a connection between the characteristics of a work of art and the period during which it was produced. If there were no such connection, that is, if there were no styles of art that lasted for some time but only randomly produced works unrelated to one another by medium, content, or detail, the argument would fail. Every other answer, however, attributes too much to the author. (D), for example, states that the expert can *pinpoint* the date of the work, but this goes far beyond the author's attempt to date generally a particular piece of pottery. (C) says more than the author does. The author mentions that the details of seminude women and bulls are characteristic of the *late* Minoan period, not that they generally characterize the entire history of that people. (B) also goes far beyond the details offered. The author connects the bull with a period of *Minoan* civilization—not ancient civilizations in general. Finally, (A) fails because, while the author apparently believes that Minoan pottery of this period was made in a certain way, there is no claim that all such pottery came from this period. The author uses a group of characteristics in combination to date the pottery: It is the combination that is unique to the period, not each individual characteristic taken in isolation.

26. **The correct answer is (B).** The weakness in the argument is that it makes an assertion without any supporting argumentation. The author states that things might turn out to be worse, but never mentions any specific way in which the result might be considered less desirable than what presently exists. As for (A), the author might have chosen to attack the radicals in this way, but not having adopted a particular line of attack is not

nearly so severe a criticism as that expressed by (B)—that the line of attack that was adopted is defective, or at least incomplete. The same reasoning applies to both (C) and (E). It is true the author might have taken the attack proposed by (C), but choosing not to is not nearly so serious a weakness as that pointed out by (B). (E) comes perhaps the closest to expressing what (B) says more explicitly. (E) hints at the specific consequences that might occur, but it is restricted to the *transition* period. It is not really detailing the bad results which might finally come out of a revolution, only the disadvantages of undertaking the change. Finally, (D) describes existing conditions, but it does not treat the question whether there *should* be a revolution; and, in any event, to defend against the question whether there *should* be a revolution by arguing there *will not be* one would itself be weak, had the author used the argument.

27. **The correct answer is (E).** The author cites a series of similarities between the two diseases, and then in his last sentence writes, "So . . . ," indicating that the conclusion that the causes of the two diseases are similar rests upon the other similarities the author has listed. Answer (E) correctly describes the basis of the argument. (A) is incorrect, for nothing in the passage indicates that either disease is a public health hazard, much less that one disease is a greater hazard than the other. (B) is unwarranted, for the author states only that the scientists are looking for a cure for *aphroditis melancholias,* not that they will be successful; and even if there is a hint of that in the argument, we surely would not want to conclude on that basis that scientists will eventually find a cure for *every* disease. (C), like (A), is unrelated to the conclusion the author seeks to establish that similarities in the symptoms suggest that scientists should look for similarities in the causes of these diseases. The author offers no opinion of the ultimate goal of modern technology. The argument is complete without any such addition. (D) is probably the second best answer, but it is still completely wrong. The author's argument, based on the assumption that similarity of effect depends upon similarity of cause, would neither gain nor lose persuasive force if (D) were true. After all, many diseases occur in both man and other animals, but at least (D) has the merit—which (A), (B), and (C) all lack—of trying to say something about the connection between the causes and effects of disease.

28. **The correct answer is (D).** This is a main idea question. The author begins by stating that it would be useful to have a general index to measure welfare and notes that some have even suggested the GNP might be adapted for that purpose. Then the author proceeds to demonstrate why such an index cannot be constructed. Generally, then, the author shows the defects in a proposal for a general index of welfare, and (D) nicely describes this development. (A) is incorrect for the author never produces any arguments for the position being attacked. Even when raising points such as the suggestion that hours worked might be a measure of cost of production, the author is only mentioning the position to attack it. (B) is incorrect since the author is attacking and not defending the proposal discussed. (C) is easily eliminated because the author never attacks the sincerity of an opponent. Finally, (E) is wrong, for the author never reviews any literature on the subject under discussion.

29. **The correct answer is (A).** This is an inference question. In the second paragraph the author mentions that a general index of welfare would have to include some measure of the cost of produc-

answers

ing the output. The author first suggests that someone might think hours worked would do the trick, but then rejects that position by noting that hours worked, as a statistic, does not take account of the quality of the work time, e.g., long hours versus short hours, working conditions, satisfaction of workers. Answer (A) best describes this argument. (B) is incorrect, for the author discusses environmental costs in connection with another aspect of a general index. (C) is incorrect since this distinction is never used by the author. (D) is incorrect since this is not mentioned as a goal of such a measure. Finally, (E) confuses the GNP, mentioned in the first part of the paragraph, with the index to measure real costs.

30. **The correct answer is (C).** This is an inference question that asks about the main point of the passage. The author adduces several objections to the idea of a general index of welfare. Then the final blow is delivered in the last paragraph: Even if you could devise measures for these various components of a general index, any combination or weighting of the individual measures would reflect only the judgment (personal preference) of the weighter. For this reason alone, argues the author, the entire idea is unworkable. (C) makes this point. (A) and (D) can be eliminated since the author never uses cost or time as arguments against the index. (B) can be eliminated on similar ground. The author recognizes that considerable research would be needed to attempt such measures, yet does not bother to use that as an objection. (E) can be eliminated for a similar reason. The author may have some arguments against the way such statistics are gathered now, but does not bother to make them. The author's argument has the structure: Even assuming there are such data, we cannot combine these statistics to get a general measure of the quality of the environment.

31. **The correct answer is (A).** This is a tone question, and the justification for (A) is already implicit in the discussion thus far. The author sees fatal theoretical weaknesses inherent in the idea of an index of welfare, regarding such a notion as an unrealistic, that is, unachievable, dream. (B) is incorrect because the author does not believe the idea can ever be implemented. (C), (D), and (E) can be eliminated on substantially the same ground.

32. **The correct answer is (A).** This is an explicit idea question. In the second paragraph, the author acknowledges that the GNP is a fairly accurate measure of output. There is no suggestion made that the GNP can estimate needs, predict welfare, or measure welfare generally. So we can eliminate the remaining choices.

33. **The correct answer is (E).** This is an explicit idea question, with a thought reverser. (A), (B), (C), and (D) are all mentioned in the third paragraph as aspects of a needs index. The fourth paragraph does not treat the idea of a needs index but the idea of a physical environment index. That is where the author discusses the items mentioned in (E). So the author does mention the items covered by (E), but not as part of a needs index.

34. **The correct answer is (A).** This is an application question. We are looking for the most likely place for the passage. To be sure, it is possible that the passage might appear in any of the five suggested locations, but the most likely place is that suggested by (A). This could easily be one of a series of papers addressed to a group meeting to discuss public policy decisions. As for (B), it is not likely that the passage would be an introduction to a general text on statistics. It is too firmly dedicated to a particular idea, and the use of statistics is in a way subordinate to

the theoretical discussion. (C) is inappropriate since the discussion bears only remotely on programs to aid the poor. (D) is even less likely since the passage does not discuss the foundations of government. Finally, (E) is to a certain extent plausible, but (A) is more closely connected to the content of the passage.

35. **The correct answer is (E).** The sample syllogism uses its terms in an ambiguous way. In the first premise the category "American buffalo" is used to refer to the group as a whole, but in the second premise it is used to denote a particular member of that group. In the first premise, "disappearing" refers to extinction of a group, but in the second premise "disappearing" apparently means fading from view. (E) is fraught with similar ambiguities. The argument there moves from wealthy people as a group to a particular wealthy person, an illegitimate shifting of terminology. (A) is a distraction. It mentions subject matter similar to that of the question stem, but our task is to parallel the *form* of the argument, not to find an argument on a similar topic. (A), incidentally, is an unambiguous and valid argument. So too is (B), and a moment's reflection will reveal that it is very similar to (A). (C) is not similar to (A) and (B), but then again it is not parallel to the question stem. (C) contains circular reasoning—the very thing to be proved had to be assumed in the first place—but while circular reasoning is incorrect reasoning, it does not parallel the error committed by the question stem: ambiguity. (D) is clearly a correct argument, so it cannot be parallel to the question stem, which contains a fallacious argument.

36. **The correct answer is (C).** The tone of the paragraph is tongue-in-cheek. The author uses phrases such as "mysteries of this arcane science" and "wonderful discipline," but then gives a silly example of the utility of logic. Obviously, the intention is to be ironic. The real point the author wants to make is that formal logic has little utility and that it may even lead one to make foolish errors. (A) cannot be correct because the example is clearly not an illustration of correct reasoning. (B) can be rejected since the author does not attempt to define the term "logic," but only to give an example of its use. (D) is a distraction. The particular illustration does mention the American buffalo, but could as easily have another species of animal or any other group term that would lend itself to the ambiguous treatment of this syllogism. (E) is incorrect since the author never examines the relationship between the premises and the conclusion. The author gives the example and lets it speak for itself.

37. **The correct answer is (B).** The original sentence is wrong because the subject "chlorofluorocarbons," which is plural, cannot have the singular verb "is." (B) corrects this error without introducing new ones. (C) is not logical because it says that insulation and refrigeration are released into the atmosphere. (D) uses an incorrect verb form "being released" and repeats the error of subject/verb agreement. (E) is awkward and wordy.

38. **The correct answer is (A).** (B) is incorrect because of the plural verb form "are." (C) is incorrect because a clause, not an adjective phrase, is needed to express the complete thought underlined in the original sentence. (D) changes the meaning of the original by making an illogical comparison. And (E) is not idiomatic.

39. **The correct answer is (B).** The author's behavior is paradoxical because he is going along with the young man's paradoxical statement. He concludes the young man is lying because the young man told him so, but that depends on believing

what the young man told him is true. So he accepts the content of the young man's statement in order to reject the statement. Once it is seen that there is a logical twist to this problem, the other answer choices can easily be rejected. (A), of course, overlooks the paradoxical nature of the tourist's behavior. The stranger may have been trying to be helpful, but what is curious about the tourist's behavior is not that he rejected the stranger's offer of advice, *but* that he relied on that very advice at the moment he rejected it! (C) also overlooks the paradox. It is true the tourist rejects the advice, but his rejection is not *understandable;* if anything it is self-contradictory, and therefore completely incomprehensible. (D) is the poorest possible choice since it makes a value judgment totally unrelated to the point of the passage. Finally, (E) would have been correct only if the tourist were possibly being victimized.

40. **The correct answer is (D).** As explained in the previous question, the tourist's behavior is self-contradictory. So, too, the sentence mentioned in (D) is self-contradictory. For if the sentence is taken to be true, what it asserts must be the case, so the sentence turns out to be false. On the other hand, if the sentence is taken to be false, then what it says is correct, so the sentence must be true. In other words, the sentence is true only if it is false, and false only if it is true: a paradox. (A) is not paradoxical. The witness *later* admits that he lied in the first instance. Thus, though his later testimony contradicts his earlier testimony, the statements taken as a group are not paradoxical, since he is not claiming that the first and the second are true *at the same time.* (B) and (C) do not have even the flavor of paradox. They are just straightforward statements. Do not be deceived by the fact that (C) refers to an about-face. To change directions, or even one's testimony, is not self-contradictory—see (A). Finally, (E) is a straightforward, self-consistent statement. Although the worker is advised to dissemble, he does not claim that he is both telling the truth and presenting a false image at the same time.

41. **The correct answer is (B).** The original sentence is incorrect on two counts. The "where" cannot refer to autism ("where" cannot introduce an adjective clause). The original also fails because the subject, "autism," needs a singular verb—"occurs," not "occur." (B) corrects both of the problems. (C) and (D) both fail because their elements are not in parallel form. (E) is incorrect since the resulting sentences lack a main verb.

PART III

GMAT VERBAL QUESTIONS

Reading Comprehension

chapter 5

OVERVIEW

- **What is reading comprehension?**
- **How do you answer reading comprehension questions?**
- **What smart test-takers know**

WHAT IS READING COMPREHENSION?

GMAT reading comprehension is a test of your ability to read and understand unfamiliar materials and to answer questions about them. You will be presented with passages drawn from a variety of subject areas, including both the humanities and the sciences. The questions will ask you to analyze what is stated in the passage and to identify underlying assumptions and implications.

GMAT Reading Comprehension Questions

On the GMAT, reading comprehension passages and questions appear in the 75-minute verbal section. Within the section, the sets of passages and questions are not grouped together. Instead, they are interspersed with the sentence correction and critical reasoning questions.

The reading comprehension passages are approximately 200 to 350 words long. Each one is followed by three or more questions about its content.

Question Format

Reading comprehension questions follow the standard multiple-choice format with five answer choices each. All of the questions fall into one of the following six categories:

- The main idea of the passage
- Specific details mentioned in the passage
- The author's attitude or tone
- The logical structure of the passage
- Further inferences that might be drawn from the text
- Application of the ideas in the text to new situations

Here is how to spot each question type:

1. **Main idea questions.** Main idea questions are usually worded as follows:

    Which of the following best summarizes the main point of the passage?

    The author is primarily concerned with . . .

    Which of the following is the best title for the passage?

    Regardless of form, this question asks about the overall theme or main point of the selection. Answering it will help you to solidify your understanding of the passage.

2. **Specific detail questions.** This kind of question is easy to recognize:

    According to the passage, . . .

    According to the author, . . .

    The author mentions all of the following EXCEPT

    In line ##, the author says that . . .

    Questions with this form are just asking about concrete details. You do not have to have a theory to answer them.

3. **Author's attitude or tone questions.** Question of this type look like this:

    The author's attitude can best be described as . . .

    Which of the following best describes the tone of the passage?

    Attitude/tone questions are usually fairly easy.

4. **Logical structure questions.** These questions ask about the overall development of the passage or about why the author introduces a specific point:

    The author develops the passage primarily by which of the following means?

    The author introduces the point at line ## in order to . . .

    These questions focus on the logical development of the passage. If you understand the main organizing theme, then you should be able to answer them.

5. **Inference questions.** These questions ask you to go beyond what is explicitly stated in the passage. They often are phrased like this:

    The author implies that . . .

    It can be inferred that . . .

    Questions in this category are often among the most difficult reading comprehension questions.

6. **Application questions.** These questions are often worded as follows:

    The author would most likely agree with which of the following statements?

    These questions are also often very difficult.

Now let's look at the directions for GMAT reading comprehension, along with a passage, some sample questions, and their explanations.

Anatomy of a Reading Comprehension Passage

Directions: The passage below is followed by questions based upon its content. After reading the passage, choose the best answer to each question. Answer all of the questions on the basis of what is stated or implied in the passage.

(This is a much abbreviated reading comprehension passage, but it exhibits all of the important features that you can expect to find on the passages in your GMAT.)

Instead of casting aside traditional values, the Meiji Restoration of 1868 dismantled feudalism and modernized the country while preserving certain traditions as the foundations for a modern Japan. The oldest tradition and basis of the entire Japanese value system was respect for and even worship of the Emperor. During the early centuries of Japanese history, the Shinto cult in which the imperial family traced its ancestry to the Sun Goddess became the people's sustaining faith. Although later subordinated to imported Buddhism and Confucianism, Shintoism was perpetuated in Ise and Izumo until the Meiji modernizers established it as a quasi state religion.

Another enduring tradition was the hierarchical system of social relations based on feudalism and reinforced by Neo-Confucianism which had been the official ideology of the pre-modern world. Confucianism prescribed a pattern of ethical conduct between groups of people within a fixed hierarchy. Four of the five Confucian relationships were vertical, requiring loyalty and obedience from the inferior toward the superior. Only the relationship between friend and friend was horizontal, and even there the emphasis was on reciprocal duties.

(**Summary:** *The passage has a main theme that is developed with supporting arguments:*

The Meiji Restoration modernized Japan without repudiating traditional values. It did dismantle feudalism. But it preserved important traditions. This kind of organization is typical of GMAT reading passages.

Note the point of the second paragraph: An important feature of Japanese society that was preserved was a hierarchical system of social relations.)

1. The author is primarily concerned with

(A) providing a history of the rise of feudalism in Japan

(B) identifying the influences of Confucianism on Japanese society

(C) speculating on the probable development of Japanese society

(D) developing a history of religion in Japan

(E) describing some important features of the Meiji Restoration

This question asks about the main idea or theme of the passage. The correct answer is (E).

2. The passage mentions all of the following as being elements of Japanese society EXCEPT:
   - **(A)** obedience to authority
   - **(B)** sense of duty
   - **(C)** respect for the Emperor
   - **(D)** concern for education
   - **(E)** loyalty to one's superior

This question asks about details mentioned in the passage. The correct answer is (D) because the author does not mention education.

3. It can be inferred from the passage that those who led Japan into the modern age were concerned primarily with
   - **(A)** maintaining a stable society
   - **(B)** building a new industrial base
   - **(C)** expanding the nation's territory
   - **(D)** gaining new adherents of Confucianism
   - **(E)** creating a new middle class

This question asks about an idea that can be inferred from the passage. The correct answer is (A).

ALERT!

Don't let unfamiliar topics throw you. There's no need to worry about what you know or don't know about the topic in a reading passage. The answers are all based on information in the passage, and you won't be required to draw on outside knowledge.

HOW DO YOU ANSWER READING COMPREHENSION QUESTIONS?

To answer reading comprehension questions, follow these steps:

Reading Comprehension: Getting It Right

❶ Preview key sentences.

❷ Read for structure; ignore details.

❸ Do a mental wrap-up.

Let's look at this process in more detail.

❶ **Preview key sentences.** The first sentence of a paragraph is often the topic sentence. It will give you an overview of the paragraph. Previewing the first sentence of each paragraph will give you a general sense of the logical structure of the passage. You should also preview the very last sentence of the passage because it often contains the main conclusion of the passage. On the computer, you can view key sentences by scrolling through the passage as it appears on screen.

❷ **Read for structure; ignore details.** Most of the questions ask about the structure of the passage rather than specific facts. As you read, consciously ask yourself "What is the main point of the passage?" and "Why is the author introducing this idea?"

Your academic training has taught you to read for details because you know that you will be tested on them. Do not dwell on the particulars. In the first place, there are only a few questions per passage, so there are not likely to be many questions about details. And in the second place, this is an open-book test, so you can refer to the passage. You do not have to memorize anything.

❸ **Do a mental wrap-up.** Before moving on to the questions, pause for just a few seconds and review in your mind what you have just read. Try to summarize in your own words the main point of the selection (think up a title for the passage) and to see in your mind's eye an outline of the passage.

Now let's look at another sample reading comprehension passage and questions about it. As you read the explanations, think about how the solution process applies.

Directions: Each reading passage is followed by questions or incomplete statements about the passage. Each statement or question is followed by five lettered words or expressions. Select the word or expression that most satisfactorily completes each statement or answers each question in accordance with the meaning of the passage based upon its content.

A fundamental principle of pharmacology is that all drugs have multiple actions. Actions that are desirable in the treatment of disease are considered therapeutic, while those that are undesirable or pose risks to the patient are called "effects." Adverse drug effects range from the trivial, e.g., nausea or dry mouth, to the serious, e.g., massive gastrointestinal bleeding or thromboembolism; and some drugs can be lethal. Therefore, an effective system for the detection of adverse drug effects is an important component of the health care system of any advanced nation. Much of the research conducted on new drugs aims at identifying the conditions of use that maximize beneficial effects and minimize the risk of adverse effects. The intent of drug labeling is to reflect this body of knowledge accurately so that physicians can properly prescribe the drug; or, if it is to be sold without prescription, so that consumers can properly use the drug.

(In this passage the author announces a "fundamental principle" of pharmacology. The paragraph then goes on to contrast "desirable" and "adverse" drug effects. The author emphasizes the need for an effective system of making this information available to doctors.)

The current system of drug investigation in the United States has proved very useful and accurate in identifying the common side effects associated with new prescription drugs. By the time a new drug is approved by the Food and Drug Administration, its side effects are usually well described in the package insert for physicians. The investigational process, however, cannot be counted on to detect all adverse effects because of the relatively small number of patients involved in premarketing studies and the relatively short duration of the studies. Animal toxicology studies are, of course, done prior to marketing in an attempt to identify any potential for toxicity, but negative results do not guarantee the safety of a drug in humans, as evidenced by such well known examples as the birth deformities due to thalidomide.

(In this next paragraph, the author says that the current system of drug investigation is useful and accurate. But then the author goes on to identify some weaknesses in the system.)

This recognition prompted the establishment in many countries of programs to which physicians report adverse drug effects. The United States and other countries also send reports to an international program operated by the World Health Organization. These programs, however, are voluntary reporting programs and are intended to serve a limited goal: alerting a government or private agency to adverse drug effects detected by physicians in the course of practice. Other approaches must be used to confirm suspected drug reactions and to estimate incidence rates. These other approaches include conducting retrospective control studies; for example, the studies associating endometrial cancer with estrogen use, and systematic monitoring of hospitalized patients to determine the incidence of acute common side effects, as typified by the Boston Collaborative Drug Surveillance Program.

(In the next paragraph, the author claims that the system has been improved by establishing programs that keep records of reports by doctors of adverse drug consequences. But, the author notes, these reporting programs are not perfect.)

Thus, the overall drug surveillance system of the United States is composed of a set of information bases, special studies, and monitoring programs, each contributing in its own way to our knowledge about marketed drugs. The system is decentralized among a number of governmental units and is not administered as a coordinated function. Still, it would be inappropriate at this time to attempt to unite all of the disparate elements into a comprehensive surveillance program. Instead, the challenge is to improve each segment of the system and to take advantage of new computer strategies to improve coordination and communication.

(In the final paragraph, the author summarizes by saying that the system is a composite one with many different aspects. And the last sentence summarizes the conclusion of the passage.)

1. The author is primarily concerned with discussing

(A) methods for testing the effects of new drugs on humans

(B) the importance of having accurate information about the effects of drugs

(C) procedures for determining the long-term effects of new drugs

(D) attempts to curb the abuse of prescription drugs

(E) the difference between the therapeutic and nontherapeutic actions of drugs

This is a main idea question. (B) correctly describes the overall point of the passage. The author starts by stating that all drugs have both good and bad effects, and that correct use of a drug requires balancing the effects. For such a balancing to take place, it is essential to have good information about how the drugs work. Some of this can be obtained prior to approval of the drug, but some information will not become available until after years of use.

(A) is incorrect, for the different methods for testing drugs are mentioned only as a part of the development just described. The author is not concerned with talking about how drugs are tested but about why it is important that they be tested. (C) is incorrect for the same reason. As for (E), this is the starting point for the discussion—not the main point of the discussion. Finally, as for (D), the idea of drug abuse is not part of the passage at all.

2. The author implies that a drug with adverse side effects

(A) will not be approved for use by consumers without a doctor's prescription

(B) must wait for approval until lengthy studies prove the effects are not permanent

(C) should be used only if its therapeutic value outweighs its adverse effects

(D) should be withdrawn from the marketplace pending a government investigation

(E) could be used in foreign countries even though it is not approved for use in the United States

TIP

The main idea of the passage is critical. Every GMAT reading comprehension passage is organized around a main idea. All else is supporting argument and detail. If you can say in your own words what that idea is, you are half-way home to answering most of the questions.

This is an inference question, and the correct answer is (C). In the first paragraph, the author states that all drugs have effects and that these effects range from the unimportant to the very important. One purpose of drug labeling is to ensure that physicians (and ultimately consumers) are aware of these effects. We can infer, therefore, that drugs with side effects are used—provided the gain is worth the risk. And this is what (C) says.

(A) seems to be contradicted by the passage. One purpose of labeling, according to the author, is to let consumers of nonprescription drugs know of possible side effects of those drugs. As for (B) and (D), the analysis in the preceding paragraph clearly shows that drugs are approved for use and used even though they have unwanted side effects. Finally, there is nothing in the passage to support the conclusion expressed in (E).

3. Which of the following can be inferred from the passage?

(A) Drugs with serious side effects are never approved for distribution.

(B) A centralized drug oversight function would improve public health.

(C) Most physicians are not aware that prescription drugs have side effects.

(D) Some rare adverse drug effects are not discovered during the limited testing.

(E) Consumers are seldom unable to understand directions for proper use of a drug.

This is an inference question, and the correct answer is (D). Although this conclusion is not stated in so many words, the author does say that some effects are not uncovered because of the short duration of the studies. We may therefore infer that some effects do not manifest themselves for a long period.

4. The author introduces the example of thalidomide (line 39) to show that some

(A) drugs do not have the same actions in humans that they do in animals

(B) drug testing procedures are ignored by careless laboratory workers

(C) drugs have no therapeutic value for humans

(D) drugs have adverse side effects as well as beneficial actions

(E) drugs are prescribed by physicians who have not read the manufacturer's recommendations

This is a logical structure question, and the correct answer is (A). The example is introduced in lines 34–39 where the author is discussing animal studies. The author says that the fact that a drug shows no dangerous effects in animals does not necessarily mean that it will not adversely affect humans and then gives the example. Thus, the example proves that a drug does not necessarily work in humans the same way it does in animals.

5. The author of the passage regards current drug investigation procedures as

(A) important but generally ineffectual

(B) lackadaisical and generally in need of improvement

(C) necessary and generally effective

(D) comprehensive but generally unnecessary

(E) superfluous but generally harmless

This is an author's attitude question, and the correct answer is (C). We have already determined that the author regards drug investigation procedures as necessary, so we can eliminate (D) and (E). And at various points in the passage the author speaks of the current mechanism for gathering information as effective. For example, the author states that unwanted side effects are usually described in detail in the pamphlets distributed to physicians and also mentions that there is an entire discipline devoted to this area, so you can eliminate (A) and (B).

TIP

Most details are irrelevant. A passage can include a lot of details. However, with all the different types of questions that are asked, there can't be many devoted solely to details. Therefore, most of the details are not important.

6. It can be inferred that the estrogen study mentioned in lines 54–55

(A) uncovered long term side effects of a drug that had already been approved for sale by the Food and Drug Administration

(B) discovered potential side effects of a drug that was still awaiting approval for sale by the Food and Drug Administration

(C) revealed possible new applications of a drug that had previously been approved for a different treatment

(D) is an example of a study that could be more efficiently conducted by a centralized authority than by volunteer reporting

(E) proved that the use of the drug estrogen was not associated with side effects such as thromboembolism

ALERT!

"So what" answers are traps. Test writers love to include something actually mentioned in the passage as a wrong answer. People look at the answer and think "Yes, that is in the passage, so it must be right." But it can be in the passage and still not be an answer to the question asked.

This is an inference question, and the correct answer is (A). The key to this question is the word "retrospective." This tells you that the control study mentioned was done after the drug was already in use. (B) is incorrect because although the study uncovered harmful side effects, according to the passage, the drug was already in use. (C) is incorrect because the paragraph in which this study is mentioned deals with methods of reporting adverse drug effects, not new applications for drugs. (D) is incorrect first because the author does not mention the efficiency of the study and second because the author is not in favor of a centralized authority. In fact, in the last paragraph the author says that it would be inappropriate at this time to attempt to unite all of the disparate elements into a comprehensive surveillance program. Finally, (E) is incorrect because although thromboembolism is mentioned in the passage as one of the possible harmful side effects of drugs, it is not mentioned in connection with estrogen. The use of estrogen is mentioned in connection with endometrial cancer.

7. The author is most probably leading up to a discussion of some suggestions about how to

(A) centralize authority for drug surveillance in the United States

(B) centralize authority for drug surveillance among international agencies

(C) coordinate better the sharing of information among the drug surveillance agencies

(D) eliminate the availability and sale of certain drugs now on the market

(E) improve drug testing procedures to detect dangerous effects before drugs are approved

This is an application question, and the correct answer is (C). In the last paragraph the author suggests that uniting disparate elements into a comprehensive surveillance program is inappropriate at this time. This eliminates choices (A) and (B). The author suggests, however, that improvements are possible in each segment of the system and urges reliance on computers to improve coordination and communication, so (C) is the correct answer. (D) is wrong because although the author might advocate the elimination of the availability of certain drugs, that is not what the passage is leading up to. As for (E), although the author acknowledges that preapproval studies are not infallible, this notion is too narrow in scope to be the next logical topic for discussion.

8. The author relies on which of the following in developing the passage?

(A) statistics

(B) analogy

(C) examples

(D) authority

(E) rhetorical questions

This is a logical structure question, and the correct answer is (C). The author frequently illustrates the argument's points with examples. In the first paragraph there are examples of side effects, in the second an example of side effects not detected by animal studies, in the third the Boston Collaborative Drug Surveillance Program. The author does not, however, use statistics (no numbers in this passage), an analogy (no "this is like that"), or authority (citing an example is not the same as appealing to an authority), and doesn't use rhetorical questions.

WHAT SMART TEST-TAKERS KNOW

READING COMPREHENSION QUESTIONS CALL FOR DIFFERENT LEVELS OF UNDERSTANDING.

According to the test-writers, good reading involves three levels of understanding and evaluation. First, you must be able to grasp the overall idea or main point of the selection along with its general organization. Second, you must be able to subject the specific details to greater scrutiny and explain what something means and why it was introduced. Finally, you should be able to evaluate what the author has written, determining what further conclusions might be drawn and judging whether the argument is good or bad. This sequence dictates the strategy you should follow in reading the selection.

DETAILS CAN BOG YOU DOWN.

If a part of a passage gets too detailed, just skip it. Bracket it in your mind. You do not need to have a full understanding of every single detail to appreciate the organization of the passage and to answer most of the questions.

THE GMAT USES SIX—AND ONLY SIX—READING COMPREHENSION QUESTIONS.

Identify the type of question asked, and you are halfway home to finding the correct answer.

1. Main idea questions ask about the central theme or main point of the passage.
2. Specific detail questions ask about details included by the author to support or to develop the main theme.
3. Inference questions ask about ideas that are not explicitly stated in the selection but are strongly implied.
4. Logical structure questions ask about the organization or the overall development of the passage.
5. Application questions ask you to take what you have learned from the passage and apply it to a new situation.
6. Attitude or tone questions ask you to identify the overall tone of the passage or the author's attitude toward something discussed in the passage.

For each of the six question types, there are special clues in the answer choices that help you tell right ones from wrong ones.

IN MAIN IDEA QUESTIONS, THE "GOLDILOCKS PRINCIPLE" APPLIES.

On a main idea question, choose an answer that refers to all of the important elements of the passage without going beyond the scope of the passage. The correct answer to a main idea question will summarize the main point of the passage. The wrong answers are too broad or too narrow. Some will attribute too much to the passage. Others will be too narrow and focus on one small element of the selection, thereby ignoring the overall point. The correct answer will be "just right."

IN SOME MAIN IDEA QUESTIONS, THE ANSWER LIES IN THE FIRST WORD OF EACH CHOICE.

Some main idea questions are phrased as sentence completions. With a main idea question in sentence completion form, the first word of each choice may be all you need to pick the answer. Here's an example:

The author's primary purpose is to

(A) argue for . . .

(B) criticize . . .

(C) describe . . .

(D) persuade . . .

(E) denounce . . .

Note that the first word in each choice describes the passage differently. If the selection were neutral in tone, providing nothing more than a description of some phenomenon, you could safely eliminate (A), (B), (D), and (E).

IN SPECIFIC DETAIL QUESTIONS, LOCATOR WORDS POINT THE WAY.

A detail question basically asks "What did the author say?" So, the correct answer to a detail question will be found right there in the passage. There often will be a word or phrase in the question stem to direct you to the appropriate part of the passage. Just find the relevant information and answer the question.

IN SPECIFIC DETAIL QUESTIONS, "SO WHAT" ANSWERS ARE WRONG.

Often, wrong answer choices look like right ones because they refer to specific points in the passage. The point is right there in the passage, but it is not an answer to the question asked. So your reaction to such answer choices should be "Yes, this is mentioned, but so what?"

IN SPECIFIC DETAIL QUESTIONS, "WAY OUT" ANSWERS ARE WRONG.

Wrong answers can also refer to things never mentioned in the selection. On a detail question, eliminate answer choices referring to something not mentioned in the passage or anything going beyond the scope of the passage. Test-writers prepare wrong answers by mentioning things related to the general topic of the selection but not specifically discussed there. An answer to an explicit question will appear in the selection.

IN SOME SPECIFIC DETAIL QUESTIONS, THOUGHT-REVERSERS TURN A QUESTION INSIDE-OUT.

Sometimes the test-writer will use a thought-reverser. For example:

The author mentions all of the following EXCEPT

Sometimes a detail question uses a thought-reverser. In that case, it is asking for what is not mentioned in the selection. Out of the five choices, four will actually appear in the selection. The fifth, and wrong, choice will not.

ALERT!

"Categorical" answers are traps. Common sense says that categorical statements that use "all," "always," and "never" are more likely to be proved wrong than statements that use "some," "sometimes," and "seldom." The test-writers know this and use categorical statements as wrong answers.

INFERENCE QUESTIONS CALL FOR AN UNSTATED CONCLUSION.

An inference question should not require a long chain of deductive reasoning. It is usually a one-step inference. For example, the selection might make a statement to the effect that "X only occurs in the presence of Y." The question might ask, "In the absence of Y, what result should be expected?" The correct answer would be: "X does not occur."

LOGICAL STRUCTURE QUESTIONS ARE ALL ABOUT ORGANIZATION.

Some logical structure questions ask about the overall structure of the passage. The correct answer to this kind of question should describe in general terms the overall development of the selection.

Another kind of logical structure question asks about the logical function of specific details. For this kind of question, find the appropriate reference and determine why the author introduced the detail at just that point.

ALERT!

Your academic training is hazardous to your test-taking health. In college, you are rewarded for memorizing details. The GMAT penalizes for this. This is an open-book test. Do not waste time trying to understand insignificant points.

APPLICATION QUESTIONS ARE THE TOUGHEST, AND YOU MAY HAVE TO GUESS, SO THAT YOU CAN MOVE ON.

Application questions are the most abstract and therefore the most difficult kind of question. There is no "silver bullet" for this type of question, and you may find that it is better to make a guess and just move on.

FOR ATTITUDE/TONE QUESTIONS, THE ANSWER CHOICES RUN A GAMUT.

Attitude or tone questions often have answer choices that run a gamut of judgments or emotions, from negative to positive. On this kind of question, try to create a continuum of the answer choices and locate the author's attitude or tone on that continuum. Here's an example:

The tone of the passage is best described as one of

(A) outrage

(B) approval

(C) objectivity

(D) alarm

(E) enthusiasm

Arrange these attitudes in a line, from the most negative to the most positive:

(–) . . outrage . . alarm . . objectivity . . approval . . enthusiasm . . (+)

EXERCISE 1: READING COMPREHENSION

35 Questions • 50 Minutes

Directions: Below each of the following passages, you will find questions or incomplete statements about the passage. Each statement or question is followed by lettered words or expressions. Select the word or expression that most satisfactorily completes each statement or answers each question in accordance with the meaning of the passage.

QUESTIONS 1–6

Our current system of unemployment compensation has increased nearly all sources of adult unemployment: seasonal and cyclical variations in the demand for labor, weak labor force attachment and unnecessarily long durations of unemployment. First, for those who are already unemployed, the system greatly reduces the cost of extending the period of unemployment. Second, for all types of unsteady work—seasonal, cyclical, and casual—it raises the net wage to the employee, relative to the cost of the employer.

As for the first, consider a worker who earns $500 per month or $6,000 per year if she experiences no unemployment. If she is unemployed for one month, she loses $500 in gross earnings but only $116 in net income. How does this occur? A reduction of $500 in annual earnings reduces her federal, payroll and state tax liability by $134. Unemployment compensation consists of 50% of her wage or $250. Her net income therefore falls from $366 if she is employed, to $250 paid as unemployment compensation. Moreover, part of the higher income from employment is offset by the cost of transportation to work and other expenses associated with employment; and in some industries, the cost of unemployment is reduced further or even made negative by the supplementary unemployment benefits paid by employers under collective bargaining agreements. The overall effect is to increase the duration of a typical spell of unemployment and to increase the frequency with which individuals lose jobs and become unemployed.

The more general effect of unemployment compensation is to increase the seasonal and cyclical fluctuations in the demand for labor and the relative number of short-lived casual jobs. A worker who accepts such work knows she will be laid off when the season ends. If there were no unemployment compensation, workers could be induced to accept such unstable jobs only if the wage rate were sufficiently higher in those jobs than in the more stable alternative. The higher cost of labor, then, would induce employers to reduce the instability of employment by smoothing production through increased variation in inventories and delivery lags, by additional development of off-season work, and by the introduction of new production techniques, e.g., new methods of outdoor work in bad weather.

Employers contribute to the state unemployment compensation fund on the basis of the unemployment experience of their own previous employees. Within limits, the more benefits that those former employees draw, the higher is the employer's tax rate. The theory of experience rating is clear. If an employer paid the full cost of the unemployment benefits that his former employees received, unemployment compensation would provide no incentive to an excess use of unstable employment. In practice, however, experience rating is limited by a maximum rate of employer contribution. For any firm that pays the maximum rate, there is no cost for additional unemployment and no gain from a small reduction in unemployment.

The challenge at this time is to restructure the unemployment system in a way that strengthens its good features while reducing the harmful disincentive effects. Some gains can be achieved by removing the ceiling on the employer's rate of contribution and by lowering the minimum rate to zero. Employers would then pay the full price of unemployment insurance benefits and this would encourage employers to stabilize employment and production. Further improvement could be achieved if unemployment insurance benefits were taxed in the same way as other earnings. This would eliminate the anomalous situations in which a worker's net income is actually reduced when he returns to work.

1. The author's primary concern is to
   (A) defend the system of unemployment compensation against criticism
   (B) advocate expanding the benefits and scope of coverage of unemployment compensation
   (C) point to weaknesses inherent in government programs that subsidize individuals
   (D) suggest reforms to eliminate inefficiencies in unemployment compensation
   (E) propose methods of increasing the effectiveness of government programs to reduce unemployment

2. The author cites the example of a worker earning $500 per month (lines 15–27) in order to
   (A) show the disincentive created by unemployment compensation for that worker to return to work
   (B) demonstrate that employers do not bear the full cost of worker compensation
   (C) prove that unemployed workers would not be able to survive without unemployment compensation
   (D) explain why employers prefer to hire seasonal workers instead of permanent workers for short-term jobs
   (E) condemn workers who prefer to live on unemployment compensation to taking a job

3. The author recommends which of the following changes be made to the unemployment compensation system?
   (A) Eliminating taxes on benefits paid to workers
   (B) Shortening the time during which a worker can draw benefits
   (C) Removing any cap on the maximum rate of employer contribution
   (D) Providing workers with job retraining as a condition of benefits
   (E) Requiring unemployed workers to accept public works positions

4. The author mentions all of the following as ways by which employers might reduce seasonal and cyclical unemployment EXCEPT
   (A) developing new techniques of production not affected by weather
   (B) slowing delivery schedules to provide work during slow seasons
   (C) adopting a system of supplementary benefits for workers laid off in slow periods
   (D) manipulating inventory supplies to require year-round rather than short-term employment
   (E) finding new jobs to be done by workers during the off-season

5. With which of the following statements about experience rating (lines 63–70) would the author most likely agree?
   (A) Experience rating is theoretically sound, but its effectiveness in practice is undermined by maximum contribution ceilings.
   (B) Experience rating is an inefficient method of computing employer contribution because an employer has no control over the length of an employee's unemployment.
   (C) Experience rating is theoretically invalid and should be replaced by a system in which the employee contributes the full amount of benefits he will later receive.
   (D) Experience rating is basically fair, but its performance could be improved by requiring large firms to pay more than small firms.
   (E) Experience rating requires an employer to pay a contribution that is completely unrelated to the amount his employees draw in unemployment compensation benefits.

6. The author makes which of the following criticisms of the unemployment compensation system?
   (A) It places an unfair burden on firms whose production is cyclical or seasonal.
   (B) It encourages out-of-work employees to extend the length of time they are unemployed.
   (C) It constitutes a drain on state treasuries, which must subsidize unemployment compensation funds.
   (D) It provides a source of income for employees who have no income or have only reduced income from employment.
   (E) The experience rating system means that employers responsible for higher-than-average turnover in staff pay higher-than-average premiums.

QUESTIONS 7–12

There is extraordinary exposure in the United States to the risks of injury and death from motor vehicle accidents. More than 80 percent of all households own passenger cars or light trucks and each of these is driven an average of more than 11,000 miles each year. Almost one-half of fatally injured drivers have a blood alcohol concentration (BAC) of 0.1 percent or higher. For the average adult, over five ounces of 80 proof spirits would have to be consumed over a short period of time to attain these levels. A third of drivers who have been drinking, but fewer than 4 percent of all drivers, demonstrate these levels. Although less than 1 percent of drivers with BAC's of 0.1 percent or more are involved in fatal crashes, the probability of their involvement is 27 times higher than for those without alcohol in their blood.

There are a number of different approaches to reducing injuries in which intoxication plays a role. Based on the observation that excessive consumption correlates with the total alcohol consumption of a country's population, it has been suggested that higher taxes on alcohol would reduce both. While the heaviest drinkers would be taxed the most, anyone who drinks at all would be penalized by this approach.

To make drinking and driving a criminal offense is an approach directed only at intoxicated drivers. In some states, the law empowers police to request breath tests of drivers cited for any traffic offense and elevated BAC can be the basis for arrest. The National Highway Traffic Safety Administration estimates, however, that even with increased arrests, there are about 700 violations for every arrest. At this level there is little evidence that laws serve as deterrents to driving while intoxicated. In Britain, motor vehicle fatalities fell 25 percent immediately following implementation of the Road Safety Act in 1967. As Britishers increasingly recognized that they could drink and not be stopped, the effectiveness declined, although in the ensuing three years the fatality rate seldom reached that observed in the seven years prior to the Act.

Whether penalties for driving with a high BAC or excessive taxation on consumption of alcoholic beverages will deter the excessive drinker responsible for most fatalities is unclear. In part, the answer depends on the extent to which those with high BAC's involved in crashes are capable of controlling their intake in response to economic or penal threat. Therapeutic programs which range from individual and group counseling and psychotherapy to chemotherapy constitute another approach, but they have not diminished the proportion of accidents in which alcohol was a factor. In the few controlled trials that have been reported there is little evidence that rehabilitation programs for those repeatedly arrested for drunken behavior have reduced either the recidivism or crash rates. Thus far, there is no firm evidence that Alcohol Safety Action Project-supported programs, in which rehabilitation measures are requested by the court, have decreased recidivism or crash involvement for clients exposed to them, although knowledge and attitudes have improved. One thing is clear, however; unless we deal with automobile and highway safety and reduce accidents in which alcoholic intoxication plays a role, many will continue to die.

7. The author is primarily concerned with

(A) interpreting the results of surveys on traffic fatalities

(B) reviewing the effectiveness of attempts to curb drunk driving

(C) suggesting reasons for the prevalence of drunk driving in the United States

(D) analyzing the causes of the large number of annual traffic fatalities

(E) making an international comparison of experience with drunk driving

8. It can be inferred that the 1967 Road Safety Act in Britain

(A) changed an existing law to lower the BAC level that defined driving while intoxicated

(B) made it illegal to drive while intoxicated

(C) increased the number of drunk driving arrests

(D) placed a tax on the sale of alcoholic drinks

(E) required drivers convicted under the law to undergo rehabilitation therapy

9. The author implies that a BAC of 0.1 percent
   (A) is unreasonably high as a definition of intoxication for purposes of driving
   (B) penalizes the moderate drinker while allowing the heavy drinker to consume without limit
   (C) will operate as an effective deterrent to over 90 percent of the people who might drink and drive
   (D) is well below the BAC of most drivers who are involved in fatal collisions
   (E) proves that a driver has consumed five ounces of 80 proof spirits over a short time

10. With which of the following statements about making driving while intoxicated a criminal offense versus increasing taxes on alcohol consumption would the author most likely agree?
    (A) Making driving while intoxicated a criminal offense is preferable to increased taxes on alcohol because the former is aimed only at those who abuse alcohol by driving while intoxicated.
    (B) Increased taxation on alcohol consumption is likely to be more effective in reducing traffic fatalities because taxation covers all consumers and not just those who drive.
    (C) Increased taxation on alcohol will constitute less of an interference with personal liberty because of the necessity of blood alcohol tests to determine BAC's in drivers suspected of intoxication.
    (D) Since neither increased taxation nor enforcement of criminal laws against drunk drivers is likely to have any significant impact, neither measure is warranted.
    (E) Because arrests of intoxicated drivers have proved to be expensive and administratively cumbersome, increased taxation on alcohol is the most promising means of reducing traffic fatalities.

11. The author cites the British example in order to
    (A) show that the problem of drunk driving is worse in Britain than in the U.S.
    (B) prove that stricter enforcement of laws against intoxicated drivers would reduce traffic deaths
    (C) prove that a slight increase in the number of arrests of intoxicated drivers will not deter drunk driving
    (D) suggest that taxation of alcohol consumption may be more effective than criminal laws
    (E) demonstrate the need to lower BAC levels in states that have laws against drunk driving

12. Which of the following, if true, most weakens the author's statement that the effectiveness of proposals to stop the intoxicated driver depends, in part, on the extent to which the high-BAC driver can control his intake?
    (A) Even if the heavy drinker cannot control his intake, criminal laws against driving while intoxicated can deter him from driving while intoxicated.
    (B) Rehabilitation programs aimed at drivers convicted of driving while intoxicated have not significantly reduced traffic fatalities.
    (C) Many traffic fatalities are caused by factors unrelated to excessive alcohol consumption on the part of the driver.
    (D) Even though severe penalties may not deter intoxicated drivers, these laws will punish them for the harm they cause if they drive while intoxicated.
    (E) Some sort of therapy may be effective in helping problem drinkers to control their intake of alcohol, thereby keeping them off the road.

QUESTIONS 13–18

Helplessness and passivity are central themes in describing human depression. Laboratory experiments with animals have uncovered a phenomenon designated "learned helplessness." Dogs given inescapable shock initially show intense emotionality, but later become passive in the same situation. When the situation is changed from inescapable to escapable shock, the dogs fail to escape even though escape is possible. Neurochemical changes resulting from learned helplessness produce an avoidance-escape deficit in laboratory animals.

Is the avoidance deficit caused by prior exposure to inescapable shock learned helplessness or is it simply stress-induced noradrenergic deficiency leading to a deficit in motor activation? Avoidance-escape deficit can be produced in rats by stress alone, i.e., by a brief swim in cold water. But a deficit produced by exposure to extremely traumatic events must be produced by a very different mechanism than the deficit produced by exposure to the less traumatic uncontrollable aversive events in the learned-helplessness experiments. A nonaversive parallel to the learned helplessness induced by uncontrollable shock, e.g., induced by uncontrollable food delivery, produces similar results. Moreover, studies have shown the importance of prior experience in learned helplessness. Dogs can be "immunized" against learned helplessness by prior experience with controllable shock. Rats also show a "mastery effect" after extended experience with escapable shock. They work far longer trying to escape from inescapable shock than do rats lacking this prior mastery experience. Conversely, weanling rats given inescapable shock fail to escape shock as adults. These adult rats are also poor to nonaversive discrimination learning.

Certain similarities have been noted between conditions produced in animals by the learned-helplessness procedure and by the experimental neurosis paradigm. In the latter, animals are first trained on a discrimination task and are then tested with discriminative stimuli of increasing similarity. Eventually, as the discrimination becomes very difficult, animals fail to respond and begin displaying abnormal behaviors: first agitation, then lethargy.

It has been suggested that both learned helplessness and experimental neurosis involve inhibition of motivation centers and pathways by limbic forebrain inhibitory centers, especially in the septal area. The main function of this inhibition is compensatory, providing relief from anxiety or distress. In rats subjected to the learned-helplessness and experimental-neurosis paradigms, stimulation of the septum produces behavioral arrest, lack of behavioral initiation and lethargy, while rats with septal lesions do not show learned helplessness.

How analogous the model of learned helplessness and the paradigm of stress-induced neurosis are to human depression is not entirely clear. Inescapable noise or unsolvable problems have been shown to result in conditions in humans similar to those induced in laboratory animals, but an adequate model of human depression must also be able to account for the cognitive complexity of human depression.

13. The primary purpose of the passage is to

(A) propose a cure for depression in human beings

(B) discuss research possibly relevant to depression in human beings

(C) criticize the result of experiments which induce depression in laboratory animals

(D) raise some questions about the propriety of using laboratory animals for research

(E) suggest some ways in which depression in animals differs from depression in humans

14. The author raises the question at the beginning of the second paragraph in order to
   (A) prove that learned helplessness is caused by neurochemical changes
   (B) demonstrate that learned helplessness is also caused by nonaversive discrimination learning
   (C) suggest that further research is needed to determine the exact causes of learned helplessness
   (D) refute a possible objection based on an alternative explanation of the cause of learned helplessness
   (E) express doubts about the structure of the experiments which created learned helplessness in dogs

15. It can be inferred from the passage that rats with septal lesions (lines 72–74) do not show learned helplessness because
   (A) such rats were immunized against learned helplessness by prior training
   (B) the lesions blocked communication between the limbic forebrain inhibitory centers and motivation centers
   (C) the lesions prevented the rats from understanding the inescapability of the helplessness situation
   (D) a lack of stimulation of the septal area does not necessarily result in excited behavior
   (E) lethargy and other behavior associated with learned helplessness can be induced by the neurosis paradigm

16. It can be inferred that the most important difference between experiments inducing learned helplessness by inescapable shock and the nonaversive parallel mentioned in lines 29–30 is that the nonaversive parallel
   (A) did not use pain as a stimuli to be avoided
   (B) failed to induce learned helplessness in subject animals
   (C) reduced the extent of learned helplessness
   (D) caused a more traumatic reaction in the animals
   (E) used only rats rather than dogs as subjects

17. The author cites the "mastery effect" primarily in order to
   (A) prove the avoidance deficit caused by exposure to inescapable shock is not caused by shock per se but by the inescapability
   (B) cast doubts on the validity of models of animal depression when applied to depression in human beings
   (C) explain the neurochemical changes in the brain which cause learned helplessness
   (D) suggest that the experimental-neurosis paradigm and the learned-helplessness procedure produce similar behavior in animals
   (E) argue that learned helplessness is simply a stress-induced noradrenergic deficiency

18. Which of the following would be the most logical continuation of the passage?
   (A) An explanation of the connection between the septum and the motivation centers of the brains of rats
   (B) An examination of techniques used to cure animals of learned helplessness
   (C) A review of experiments designed to create stress-induced noradrenergic deficiencies in humans
   (D) A proposal for an experiment to produce learned helplessness and experimental neurosis in humans
   (E) An elaboration of the differences between human depression and similar animal behavior

exercises

QUESTIONS 19–24

Reverse discrimination, minority recruitment, racial quotas, and, more generally, affirmative action are phrases that carry powerful emotional charges. But why should affirmative action, of all government policies, be so controversial? In a sense, affirmative action is like other government programs, e.g., defense, conservation, and public schools. Affirmative action programs are designed to achieve legitimate government objectives such as improved economic efficiency, reduced social tension, and general betterment of the public welfare. While it cannot be denied that there is no guarantee that affirmative action will achieve these results, neither can it be denied that there are plausible, even powerful, sociological and economic arguments pointing to its likely success.

Government programs, however, entail a cost; i.e., the expenditure of social or economic resources. Setting aside cases in which the specific user is charged a fee for service (toll roads and tuition at state institutions), the burdens and benefits of publicly funded or mandated programs are widely shared. When an individual benefits personally from a government program, it is only because she or he is one member of a larger beneficiary class, e.g., a farmer; and most government revenue is obtained through a scheme of general taxation to which all are subject.

Affirmative action programs are exceptions to this general rule, though not, as it might at first seem, because the beneficiaries of the programs are specific individuals. It is still the case that those who ultimately benefit from affirmative action do so only by virtue of their status as a member of a larger group, a particular minority. Rather the difference is the location of the burden. In affirmative action, the burden of "funding" the program is not shared universally, and that is inherent in the nature of the case, as can be seen clearly in the case of affirmative action in employment. Often job promotions are allocated along a single dimension—seniority. When an employer promotes a less senior worker from a minority group, the person disadvantaged by the move is easily identified: the worker with greatest seniority on a combined minority-nonminority list passed over for promotion.

Now we are confronted with two competing moral sentiments. On the one hand, there is the idea that those who have been unfairly disadvantaged by past discriminatory practices are entitled to some kind of assistance. On the other, there is the feeling that no person ought to be deprived of what is rightfully his, even for the worthwhile service of his fellow humans. In this respect, disability due to past racial discrimination, at least in so far as there is no connection to the passed-over worker, is like a natural evil. When a villainous man willfully and without provocation strikes and injures another, there is not only the feeling that the injured person ought to be compensated but there is also consensus that the appropriate party to bear the cost is the one who inflicted the injury. Yet, if the same innocent man stumbled and injured himself, it would be surprising to hear someone argue that the villainous man ought to be taxed for the injury simply because he might have tripped the victim had he been given the opportunity. There may very well be agreement that the victim should be aided in his recovery with money and personal assistance, and many will give willingly, but there is also agreement that no one individual ought to be singled out and forced to do what must ultimately be considered an act of charity.

exercises

19. The passage is primarily concerned with
   (A) comparing affirmative action programs to other government programs
   (B) arguing that affirmative action programs are morally justified
   (C) analyzing the basis for moral judgments about affirmative action programs
   (D) introducing the reader to the importance of affirmative action as a social issue
   (E) describing the benefits which can be obtained through affirmative action programs

20. The author mentions toll roads and tuition at state institutions (lines 25–26) in order to
   (A) anticipate a possible objection based on counterexamples
   (B) avoid a contradiction between moral sentiments
   (C) provide illustrations of common government programs
   (D) voice doubts about the social and economic value of affirmative action
   (E) offer examples of government programs that are too costly

21. With which of the following statements would the author most likely agree?
   (A) Affirmative action programs should be discontinued because they place an unfair burden on nonminority persons who bear the cost of the programs.
   (B) Affirmative action programs may be able to achieve legitimate social and economic goals such as improved efficiency.
   (C) Affirmative action programs are justified because they are the only way of correcting injustices created by past discrimination.
   (D) Affirmative action programs must be redesigned so that society as a whole, rather than particular individuals, bears the cost of the programs.
   (E) Affirmative action programs should be abandoned because they serve no useful social function and place unfair burdens on particular individuals.

22. The author most likely places the word "funding" in quotation marks (lines 46–47) in order to remind the reader that
   (A) affirmative action programs are costly in terms of government revenues
   (B) particular individuals may bear a disproportionate share of the burden of affirmative action
   (C) the cost of most government programs is shared by society at large
   (D) the beneficiaries of affirmative action are members of larger groups
   (E) the cost of affirmative action is not only a monetary expenditure

23. The "villainous man" introduced at line 73 functions primarily as a(n)
   (A) illustration
   (B) counterexample
   (C) authority
   (D) analogy
   (E) disclaimer

24. According to the passage, affirmative action programs are different from most other government programs in the
   (A) legitimacy of the goals the programs are designed to achieve
   (B) ways in which costs of the programs are distributed
   (C) methods for allocating the benefits of the programs
   (D) legal structures that are enacted to achieve the objectives
   (E) discretion granted to the executive for implementing the programs

QUESTIONS 25–30

Nitroglycerin has long been famous for its relief of angina pectoris attacks but ruled out for heart attacks on the theory that it harmfully lowers blood pressure and increases heart rate. A heart attack, unlike an angina attack, always involves some localized, fairly rapid heart muscle death, or myocardial infarction. This acute emergency happens when the arteriosclerotic occlusive process in one of the coronary arterial branches culminates so suddenly and completely that the local myocardium—the muscle area that was fed by the occluded coronary—stops contracting and dies over a period of hours, to be replaced over a period of weeks by a scar, or "healed infarct."

In 1974, in experiments with dogs, it was discovered that administration of nitroglycerin during the acute stage of myocardial infarction consistently reduced the extent of myocardial injury, provided that the dogs' heart rate and blood pressure were maintained in the normal range. Soon after, scientists made a preliminary confirmation of the clinical applicability of nitroglycerin in acute heart attack in human patients. Five of twelve human subjects developed some degree of congestive heart failure. Curiously, the nitroglycerin alone was enough to reduce the magnitude of injury in these five patients, but the other seven patients, whose heart attacks were not complicated by any congestive heart failure, were not consistently helped by the nitroglycerin until another drug, phenylephrine, was added to abolish the nitroglycerin-induced drop in blood pressure. One explanation for this is that the reflex responses in heart rate, mediated through the autonomic nervous system, are so blunted in congestive heart failure that a fall in blood pressure prompts less of the cardiac acceleration which otherwise worsens the damage of acute myocardial infarction.

It appears that the size of the infarct that would otherwise result from a coronary occlusion might be greatly reduced, and vitally needed heart muscle thus saved, by the actions of certain drugs and other measures taken during the acute phase of the heart attack. This is because the size of the myocardial infarct is not really determined at the moment of the coronary occlusion as previously thought. The fate of the stricken myocardial segment remains largely undetermined, hanging on the balance of myocardial oxygen supply and demand which can be favorably influenced for many hours after the coronary occlusion. So it is possible to reduce the myocardial ischemic injury during acute human heart attacks by means of nitroglycerin, either alone or in combination with phenylephrine.

Other drugs are also being tested to reduce myocardial infarct size, particularly drugs presumed to affect myocardial oxygen supply and demand, including not only vessel dilators such as nitroglycerin but also antihypertensives, which block the sympathetic nerve reflexes that increase heart rate and work in response to exertion and stress. Such measures are still experimental, and there is no proof of benefit with regard to the great complications of heart attack such as cardiogenic shock, angina, or mortality. But the drugs for reducing infarct size now hold center stage in experimental frameworks.

25. According to the passage, the primary difference between a heart attack and an angina attack is that a heart attack

(A) involves an acceleration of the heartbeat

(B) cannot be treated with nitroglycerin

(C) generally results in congestive heart failure

(D) takes place within a relatively short period of time

(E) always results in damage to muscle tissue of the heart

26. In the study referred to in lines 28–30, the patients who developed congestive heart failure did not experience cardiac acceleration because

(A) the nitroglycerin was not administered soon enough after the onset of the heart attack

(B) the severity of the heart attack blocked the autonomic response to the nitroglycerin-induced drop in blood pressure

(C) administering phenylephrine mitigated the severity of the drop in blood pressure caused by nitroglycerin

(D) doctors were able to maintain blood pressure, and thus indirectly pulse rate, in those patients

(E) those patients did not experience a drop in blood pressure as a result of the heart attack

27. The passage provides information to answer all of the following questions EXCEPT:

(A) What are some of the physiological manifestations of a heart attack?

(B) What determines the size of a myocardial infarct following a heart attack?

(C) What effect does nitroglycerin have when administered to a patient experiencing a heart attack?

(D) What are the most important causes of heart attacks?

(E) What is the physiological effect of phenylephrine?

28. It can be inferred from the passage that nitroglycerin is of value in treating heart attacks because it

(A) lowers the blood pressure

(B) stimulates healing of an infarct

(C) causes cardiac acceleration

(D) dilates blood vessels

(E) counteracts hypertension

29. The author's attitude toward the use of nitroglycerin and other drugs to treat heart attack can best be described as one of

(A) concern

(B) resignation

(C) anxiety

(D) disinterest

(E) optimism

30. It can be inferred that the phenylephrine is administered in conjunction with nitroglycerin during a heart attack in order to

(A) prevent the cardiac acceleration caused by a drop in blood pressure

(B) block sympathetic nerve reflexes that increase the pulse rate

(C) blunt the autonomic nervous system which accelerates the pulse rate

(D) reduce the size of a myocardial infarct by increasing oxygen supply

(E) prevent arteriosclerotic occlusion in the coronary arterial branches

QUESTIONS 31–35

From the time they were first proposed, the 1962 Amendments to the Food, Drug, and Cosmetic Act have been the subject of controversy among some elements of the health community and the pharmaceutical industry. The Amendments added a new requirement for Food and Drug Administration approval of any new drug: The drug must be demonstrated to be effective by substantial evidence consisting of adequate and well-controlled investigations. To meet this effectiveness requirement, a pharmaceutical company must spend considerable time and effort in clinical research before it can market a new product in the United States. Only then can it begin to recoup its investment. Critics of the requirement argue that the added expense of the research to establish effectiveness is reflected in higher drug costs, decreased profits, or both, and that this has resulted in a "drug lag."

The term drug lag has been used in several different ways. It has been argued that the research required to prove effectiveness creates a lag between the time when a drug could theoretically be marketed without proving effectiveness and the time when it is actually marketed. Drug lag has also been used to refer to the difference between the number of new drugs introduced annually before 1962 and the number of new drugs introduced each year after that date. It is also argued that the Amendments resulted in a lag between the time when new drugs are available in other countries and the time when the same drugs are available in the United States. And drug lag has also been used to refer to a difference in the number of new drugs introduced per year in other advanced nations and the number introduced in the same year in the United States.

Some critics have used drug lag arguments in an attempt to prove that the 1962 Amendments have actually reduced the quality of health care in the United States and that, on balance, they have done more harm than good. These critics recommend that the effectiveness requirements be drastically modified or even scrapped. Most of the specific claims of the drug lag theoreticians, however, have been refuted. The drop in new drugs approved annually, for example, began at least as early as 1959, perhaps five years before the new law was fully effective. In most instances, when a new drug was available in a foreign country but not in the United States, other effective drugs for the condition were available in this country and sometimes not available in the foreign country used for comparison. Further, although the number of new chemical entities introduced annually dropped from more than 50 in 1959 to about 12 to 18 in the 1960s and 1970s, the number of these that can be termed important—some of them of "breakthrough" caliber—has remained reasonably close to 5 or 6 per year. Few, if any, specific examples have actually been offered to show how the effectiveness requirements have done significant harm to the health of Americans. The requirement does ensure that a patient exposed to a drug has the likelihood of benefiting from it, an assessment that is most important, considering the possibility, always present, that adverse effects will be discovered later.

31. The author is primarily concerned with

(A) outlining a proposal

(B) evaluating studies

(C) posing a question

(D) countering arguments

(E) discussing a law

32. The passage states that the phrase "drug lag" has been used to refer to all of the following situations EXCEPT

(A) a lag between the time when a new drug becomes available in a foreign country and its availability in the United States

(B) the time period between which a new drug would be marketed if no effectiveness research were required and the time it is actually marketed

(C) the increased cost of drugs to the consumer and the decreased profit margins of the pharmaceutical industry

(D) the difference between the number of drugs introduced annually before 1962 and the number introduced after 1962

(E) the difference between the number of new drugs introduced in a foreign country and the number introduced in the United States

33. The author would most likely agree with which of the following statements?

(A) Whatever "drug lag" may exist because of the 1962 Amendments is justified by the benefit of effectiveness studies.

(B) The 1962 Amendments have been beneficial in detecting adverse effects of new drugs before they are released on the market.

(C) Because of the requirement of effectiveness studies, drug consumers in the United States pay higher prices than consumers in foreign countries.

(D) The United States should limit the number of new drugs which can be introduced into this country from foreign countries.

(E) Effectiveness studies do not require a significant investment of time or money on the part of the pharmaceutical industry.

34. The author points out the drop in new drugs approved annually before 1959 in order to

(A) draw an analogy between two situations

(B) suggest an alternative causal explanation

(C) attack the credibility of an opponent

(D) justify the introduction of statistics

(E) show an opponent misquoted statistics

35. The author implies that the nonavailability of a drug in the United States and its availability in a foreign country is not necessarily proof of a drug lag because this comparison fails to take into account

(A) the number of new drugs introduced annually before 1959

(B) the amount of research done on the effectiveness of drugs in the United States

(C) the possible availability of another drug to treat the same condition

(D) the seriousness of possible unwanted side effects from untested drugs

(E) the length of time needed to accumulate effectiveness research

EXERCISE 2: READING COMPREHENSION

20 Questions • 25 Minutes

Directions: Below each of the following passages, you will find questions or incomplete statements about the passage. Each statement or question is followed by lettered words or expressions. Select the word or expression that most satisfactorily completes each statement or answers each question in accordance with the meaning of the passage.

QUESTIONS 1–7

Like our political society, the university is under severe attack today and perhaps for the same reason; namely, that we have accomplished much of what we have set out to do in this generation, that we have done so imperfectly, and while we have been doing so, we have said a lot of things that simply are not true. For example, we have earnestly declared that full equality of opportunity in universities exists for everyone, regardless of economic circumstance, race, or religion.

This has never been true. When it was least true, the assertion was not attacked. Now that it is nearly true, not only the assertion but the university itself is locked in mortal combat with the seekers of perfection. In another sense the university has failed. It has stored great quantities of knowledge; it teaches more people; and despite its failures, it teaches them better. It is in the application of this knowledge that the failure has come. Of the great branches of knowledge—the sciences, the social sciences, and the humanities—the sciences are applied, sometimes almost as soon as they are learned. Strenuous and occasionally successful efforts are made to apply the social sciences, but almost never are the humanities well applied. We do not use philosophy in defining our conduct. We do not use literature as a source of real and vicarious experience to save us the trouble of living every life again on our own.

The great tasks of the university in the next generation are to search the past to form the future, to begin an earnest search for a new and relevant set of values, and to learn to use the knowledge we have for the questions that come before us. The university should use one-fourth of a student's time in his undergraduate years and organize it into courses which might be called history, and literature and philosophy, and anything else appropriate and organize these around primary problems. The difference between a primary problem and a secondary or even tertiary problem is that primary problems tend to be around for a long time, whereas the less important ones get solved.

One primary problem is that of interfering with what some call human destiny and others call biological development, which is partly the result of genetic circumstance and partly the result of accidental environmental conditions. It is anticipated that the next generation, and perhaps this one, will be able to interfere chemically with the actual development of an individual and perhaps biologically by interfering with his genes. Obviously, there are benefits both to individuals and to society from eliminating, or at least improving, mentally and physically deformed persons. On the other hand, there could be very serious consequences if this knowledge were used with premeditation to produce superior and subordinate classes, each genetically prepared to carry out a predetermined mission. This can be done, but what happens to free will and the rights of the individual? Here we have a primary problem that will still exist when we are all dead. Of course, the traditional faculty members would say, "But the students won't learn enough to go to graduate school." And certainly they would not learn everything we are in the habit of making them learn, but they would learn some other things. Surely, in the other three-quarters of their time, they would learn what they usually do, and they might even learn to think about it by carrying new habits into their more conventional courses. The advantages would be overwhelmingly greater than the disadvantages. After all, the purpose of education is not only to impart knowledge but to teach students to use the knowledge that they either have or will find, to teach them to ask and seek answers for important questions.

1. The author suggests that the university's greatest shortcoming is its failure to
   (A) attempt to provide equal opportunity for all
   (B) offer courses in philosophy and the humanities
   (C) prepare students adequately for professional studies
   (D) help students see the relevance of the humanities to real problems
   (E) require students to include in their curricula liberal arts courses

2. It can be inferred that the author presupposes that the reader will regard a course in literature as a course
   (A) with little or no practical value
   (B) of interest only to academic scholars
   (C) required by most universities for graduation
   (D) uniquely relevant to today's primary problems
   (E) used to teach students good writing skills

3. Which of the following questions does the author answer in the passage?
   (A) What are some of the secondary problems faced by the past generation?
   (B) How can we improve the performance of our political society?
   (C) Has any particular educational institution tried the proposal introduced by the author?
   (D) What is a possible objection to the proposal offered in the passage?
   (E) Why is the university of today a better imparter of knowledge than the university of the past?

4. Which of the following questions would the author most likely consider a primary question?
   (A) Should Congress increase the level of Social Security benefits?
   (B) Is it appropriate for the state to use capital punishment?
   (C) Who is the best candidate for president in the next presidential election?
   (D) At what month can the fetus be considered medically viable outside the mother's womb?
   (E) What measures should be taken to solve the problem of world hunger?

5. With which of the following statements about the use of scientific techniques to change an individual's genetic makeup would the author LEAST likely agree?

(A) Society has no right to use such techniques without the informed consent of the individual.

(B) Such techniques can have a positive benefit for the individual in some cases.

(C) Use of such techniques may be appropriate even though society, but not the individual, benefits.

(D) The question of the use of such techniques must be placed in a philosophical as well as a scientific context.

(E) The answers to questions about the use of such techniques will have important implications for the structure of our society.

6. The primary purpose of the passage is to

(A) discuss a problem and propose a solution

(B) analyze a system and defend it

(C) present both sides of an issue and allow the reader to draw a conclusion

(D) outline a new idea and criticize it

(E) raise several questions and provide answers to them

7. The development discussed in the passage is primarily a problem of

(A) political philosophy

(B) educational philosophy

(C) scientific philosophy

(D) practical science

(E) practical politics

QUESTIONS 8–14

The high unemployment rates of the early 1960s occasioned a spirited debate within the economics profession. One group found the primary cause of unemployment in slow growth and the solution in economic expansion. The other found the major explanation in changes that had occurred in the supply and demand for labor and stressed measures for matching demand with supply.

The expansionist school of thought, with the Council of Economic Advisers as its leading advocates, attributed the persistently high unemployment level to a slow rate of economic growth resulting from a deficiency of aggregate demand for goods and services. The majority of this school endorsed the position of the Council that tax reduction would eventually reduce the unemployment level to 4% of the labor force with no other assistance. At 4%, bottlenecks in skilled labor, middle-level manpower, and professional personnel were expected to retard growth and generate wage-price pressures. To go beyond 4%, the interim goal of the Council, it was recognized that improved education, training and retraining, and other structural measures would be required. Some expansionists insisted that the demand for goods and services was nearly satiated and that it was impossible for the private sector to absorb a significant increase in output. In their estimate, only the lower-income fifth of the population and the public sector offered sufficient outlets for the productive efforts of the potential labor force. The fact that the needs of the poor and the many unmet demands for public services held higher priority than the demands of the marketplace in the value structure of this group no doubt influenced their economic judgments.

Those who found the major cause of unemployment in structural features were primarily labor economists, concerned professionally with efficient functioning of labor markets through programs to develop skills and place individual workers. They maintained that increased aggregate demand was a necessary but not sufficient condition for reaching either the CEA's 4% target or their own preferred 3%. This pessimism was based, in part, on the conclusion that unemployment among the young, the unskilled, minority groups, and depressed geographical areas is not easily attacked by increasing general demand. Further, their estimate of the numbers of potential members of the labor force who had withdrawn or not entered because of lack of employment opportunity was substantially higher than that of the CEA. They also projected that increased demand would put added pressure on skills already in short supply rather than employ the unemployed, and that because of technological change, which was replacing manpower, much higher levels of demand would be necessary to create the same number of jobs.

The structural school, too, had its hyperenthusiasts: Fiscal conservatives who, as an alternative to expansionary policies, argued the not very plausible position that a job was available for every person, provided only that he or she had the requisite skills or would relocate. Such extremist positions aside, there was actually considerable agreement between two main groups, though this was not recognized at the time. Both realized the advisability of a tax cut to increase demand, and both needed to reduce unemployment below a point around 4%. In either case, the policy implications differed in emphasis and not in content.

8. The primary purpose of the passage is to

(A) suggest some ways in which tools to manipulate aggregate demand and eliminate structural deficiencies can be used to reduce the level of unemployment

(B) demonstrate that there was a good deal of agreement between the expansionist and structuralist theories on how to reduce unemployment in the 1960s

(C) explain the way in which structural inefficiencies prevent the achievement of a low rate of unemployment without wage-price pressures

(D) discuss the disunity within the expansionist and structuralist schools to show its relationship to the inability of the government to reduce unemployment to 4%

(E) describe the role of the Council of Economic Advisers in advocating expansionist policies to reduce unemployment to 4%

9. Which of the following is not mentioned in the passage as a possible barrier to achieving a 4% unemployment rate through increased aggregate demand?

(A) Technological innovation reduces the need for workers, so larger increases in demand are needed to employ the same number of workers.

(B) The increase in output necessary to meet an increase in aggregate demand requires skilled labor, which is already in short supply, rather than unskilled labor, which is available.

(C) An increase in aggregate demand will not create jobs for certain subgroups of unemployed persons such as minority groups and young and unskilled workers.

(D) Even if the tax reduction increases aggregate demand, many unemployed workers will be unwilling to relocate to jobs located in areas where there is a shortage of labor.

(E) An increase in the number of available jobs will encourage people not in the labor market to enter it, which in turn will keep the unemployment rate high.

exercises

10. The author's treatment of the "hyperenthusiasts" (lines 75–81) can best be described as one of

(A) strong approval

(B) lighthearted appreciation

(C) summary dismissal

(D) contemptuous sarcasm

(E) malicious rebuke

11. Which of the following best describes the difference between the position taken by the Council of Economic Advisers and that taken by dissenting expansionists (lines 30–35)?

(A) Whereas the Council of Economic Advisers emphasized the need for a tax cut to stimulate general demand, the dissenters stressed the importance of structural measures such as education and training.

(B) Although the dissenters agreed that an increase in demand was necessary to reduce unemployment, they argued government spending to increase demand should fund programs for lower income groups and public services.

(C) The Council of Economic Advisers set a 4% unemployment rate as its goal, and dissenting expansionists advocated a goal of 3%.

(D) The Council of Economic Advisers rejected the contention, advanced by the dissenting expansionists, that a tax cut would help to create increased demand.

(E) The dissenting expansionists were critical of the Council of Economic Advisers because members of the Council advocated politically conservative policies.

12. The passage contains information that helps to explain which of the following?

(A) The fact that the economy did not expand rapidly in the early 1960s.

(B) The start of wage-price pressures as the unemployment rate approaches 4%.

(C) The harmful effects of unemployment on an individual worker.

(D) The domination of the Council of Economics by expansionists.

(E) The lack of education and training among workers in some sectors.

13. Which of the following best describes the author's attitude toward the expansionists mentioned in line 11?

(A) The author doubts the validity of their conclusions because they were not trained economists.

(B) The author discounts the value of their judgment because it was colored by their political viewpoint.

(C) The author refuses to evaluate the value of their contention because he lacks sufficient information.

(D) The author accepts their viewpoint until it can be demonstrated that it is incorrect.

(E) The author endorses the principles on which their conclusions are based but believes their proposal to be impractical.

14. It can be inferred from the passage that the hyperenthusiasts (lines 75–81) contended that

(A) the problem of unemployment could be solved without government retraining and education programs

(B) the number of persons unemployed was greatly overestimated by the Council of Economic Advisers

(C) a goal of 3% unemployment could not be reached unless the government enacted retraining and education programs

(D) the poor had a greater need for expanded government services than the more affluent portion of the population

(E) fiscal policies alone were powerful enough to reduce the unemployment rate to 4% of the work force

QUESTIONS 15–20

An assumption that underlies most discussions of electric facility siting is that the initial selection of a site is the responsibility of the utility concerned—subject to governmental review and approval only after the site has been chosen. This assumption must be changed so that site selection becomes a joint responsibility of the utilities and the appropriate governmental authorities from the outset. Siting decisions would be made in accordance with either of two strategies. The metropolitan strategy takes the existing distribution of population and supporting facilities as given. An attempt is then made to choose between dispersed or concentrated siting and to locate generating facilities in accordance with some economic principle. For example, the economic objectives of least-cost construction and rapid start-up may be achieved, in part, by a metropolitan strategy that takes advantage of existing elements of social and physical infrastructure in the big cities.

Under the frontier strategy, the energy park may be taken as an independent variable, subject to manipulation by policymakers as a means of achieving desired demographic or social goals, e.g., rural-town-city mix. Thus, population distribution is taken as a goal of national social policy, not as a given of a national energy policy. In the frontier strategy, the option of dispersed siting is irrelevant from the standpoint of community impact because there is no preexisting community of any size.

Traditionally, the resource endowment of a location—and especially its situation relative to the primary industry of the hinterland—has had a special importance in American history. In the early agricultural period, the most valued natural endowment was arable land with good climate and available water. America's oldest cities were mercantile outposts of such agricultural areas. Deepwater ports developed to serve the agricultural hinterlands, which produced staple commodities in demand on the world market. From the 1840s onward, the juxtaposition of coal, iron ore, and markets afforded the impetus for manufacturing growth in the northeastern United States. The American manufacturing heartland developed westward to encompass Lake Superior iron ores, the Pennsylvania coalfields, and the Northeast's financial, entrepreneurial, and manufacturing roles. Subsequent metropolitan growth has been organized around this national core.

Against the theory of urban development, it is essential to bear in mind the unprecedented dimensions of an energy park. The existing electric power plant at Four Corners in the southwest United States—the only human artifact visible to orbiting astronauts—generates only 4,000 megawatts of electricity. The smallest energy parks will concentrate five times the thermal energy represented by the Four Corners plant. An energy park, then, would seem every bit as formidable as the natural harbor conditions or coal deposits that underwrote the growth of the great cities of the past—with a crucial difference. The founders of past settlements could not choose the geographic locations of their natural advantages.

The frontier strategy implements the principle of man-made opportunity; and this helps explain why some environmentalists perceive the energy park idea as a threat to nature. But the problems of modern society, with or without energy parks, require ever more comprehensive planning. And energy parks are a means of advancing American social history rather than merely responding to power needs in an unplanned, *ad hoc* manner.

15. Which of the following statements best describes the main point of the passage?

(A) Government regulatory authorities should participate in electric facility site selection to further social goals.

(B) Energy parks will have a significant influence on the demographic features of the American population.

(C) Urban growth in the United States was largely the result of economic forces rather than conscientious planning.

(D) Under the frontier siting strategy for energy parks, siting decisions are influenced by the natural features of the land.

(E) America needs larger power-producing facilities in urban and rural areas to meet the increased demand for energy.

16. All of the following are mentioned in the passage as characteristics of energy parks EXCEPT

(A) energy parks will be built on previously undeveloped sites

(B) energy parks will be built in areas remote from major population centers

(C) energy parks will produce considerably more thermal energy than existing facilities

(D) energy parks will be built at sites that are near fuel sources such as coal

(E) energy parks may have considerable effects on population distribution

17. According to the passage, which of the following is the most important feature of the traditional process of siting decisions for electric facilities?

(A) Sites were selected for the ability to advance social history.

(B) Siting was viewed as a tool for achieving economic goals.

(C) The primary responsibility for siting resided with the utility.

(D) Decisions were made jointly by utilities and government.

(E) Groups of affected citizens participated on advisory panels.

18. Which of the following, if true, would most seriously weaken the author's position?
    - **(A)** The first settlements in America were established in order to provide trading posts with Native Americans.
    - **(B)** The cost of constructing an electric power plant in an urban area is not significantly greater than that for a rural area.
    - **(C)** An energy park will be so large that it will be impossible to predict the demographic consequences of its construction.
    - **(D)** Cities in European countries grew up in response to political pressures during the feudal period rather than economic pressures.
    - **(E)** The United States is presently in a period of population migration that will change the rural-town-city mix.

19. With which one of the following statements would the author most likely agree?
    - **(A)** Decisions about the locations for power plant construction should be left in the hands of the utilities.
    - **(B)** Government leaders in the nineteenth century were irresponsible in not supervising urban growth more closely.
    - **(C)** Natural features of a region such as cultivatable land and water supply are no longer important to urban growth.
    - **(D)** Modern society is so complex that governments must take greater responsibility for decisions such as power plant siting.
    - **(E)** The electric power plant at Four Corners should not have been built because of its mammoth size.

20. According to the passage, the most important difference between the natural advantages of early cities and the features of an energy park is
    - **(A)** the features of an energy park will be located where the builders choose
    - **(B)** natural advantages are no longer as important as they once were
    - **(C)** natural features cannot be observed from outer space but energy parks can
    - **(D)** early cities grew up close to agricultural areas, but energy parks will be located in mountains
    - **(E)** policy planners have learned to minimize the effects of energy parks on nature

Exercise 1: ANSWER KEY AND EXPLANATIONS

1. D	8. B	15. B	22. E	29. E
2. A	9. A	16. A	23. D	30. A
3. C	10. A	17. A	24. B	31. D
4. C	11. C	18. E	25. E	32. C
5. A	12. A	19. C	26. B	33. A
6. B	13. B	20. A	27. D	34. B
7. B	14. D	21. B	28. D	35. C

1. **The correct answer is (D).** This is a main idea question. The main idea of the passage is fairly clear: Suggest reforms to correct the problems discussed. Choice (D) is a very good description of this development. (A) is incorrect since the author criticizes the system. (B) is incorrect since no recommendation for expanding benefits and scope is made by the author. (C) overstates the case. The author indicts only unemployment compensation and believes that the shortcomings of the system can be remedied. (E) is incorrect because the author is discussing unemployment compensation, not government programs designed to achieve full employment generally. We may infer from the passage that unemployment compensation is not a program designed to achieve full employment, but a program designed to alleviate the hardship of unemployment. On balance, (D) is the most precise description given of the development of the passage.

2. **The correct answer is (A).** This is a logical detail question. In the second paragraph the author introduces the example of a worker who loses surprisingly little by being unemployed. The author does this to show that unemployment encourages people to remain unemployed by reducing the net cost of unemployment. (A) makes this point. (B) is incorrect, for the author does not discuss the problem of employer contribution until the fourth paragraph. (C) is incorrect, for this is not the reason that the author introduces the point. (D) is incorrect because the topic is not taken up until the third paragraph. Finally, (E) is incorrect since the author analyzes the situation in a neutral fashion; there is no hint of condemnation.

3. **The correct answer is (C).** This is an explicit idea, or specific detail, question. (C) is a recommendation made by the author in the final paragraph. (A) is actually inconsistent with statements made in that paragraph, for the author proposes taxing benefits in the same way as wages. (B), (D), and (E) are interesting ideas, but they are nowhere mentioned in the passage—so they cannot possibly be answers to an explicit idea question.

4. **The correct answer is (C).** Here, too, we have an explicit idea question. (A), (B), (D), and (E) are all mentioned in the third paragraph as ways by which an employer might reduce seasonal and cyclical fluctuations in labor needs. (C), however, was not mentioned as a way to minimize unemployment. Indeed, we may

infer from other information supplied by the passage that supplementary benefits actually increase unemployment.

5. **The correct answer is (A).** This is an application question. We are asked to apply the author's analysis of the rating system to conclusions given in the answer choices. The author is critical of the rating system because it does not place the full burden of unemployment on the employer. This is because there is a maximum contribution limit, and in the final paragraph the author recommends the ceiling be eliminated. From these remarks, we may infer that the author believes the rating system is, in theory, sound, but that practically it needs to be adjusted. Choice (A) neatly describes this judgment. (B) can be eliminated since the author implies that the system is, in principle, sound. Moreover, the author implies that the employer does have some control over the time his former employees remain out of work. The maximum limit on employer contribution allows the employer to exploit this control. As for (C), this is contradicted by our analysis thus far and for the further reason that the passage never suggests employee contribution should replace employer contribution. Indeed, the author implies that the system serves a useful and necessary social function. (D) can be eliminated because the author never draws a distinction between contributions by large firms and contributions by small firms. Finally, (E) is incorrect since the experience rating system is theoretically tied to the amount drawn by employees. The difficulty is not with the theory of the system, but with its implementation.

6. **The correct answer is (B).** This is an explicit detail question. We are looking for criticisms that are made in the passage. (B) is such a criticism, and it can be found in the very opening sentence. As for (A), the author actually states the opposite: The system allows firms of this sort to use the unemployment compensation system as a subsidy for their employees, reducing their own costs of production. As for (C), the author only states that employers contribute to the fund from which benefits are paid. No mention is ever made of a state contribution. (D) is certainly a goal of the system, but it is not mentioned as a weakness of the system by the author. Finally, (E) is true, as mentioned in the final paragraph. But this is not a criticism of the system. In fact, the author views it in a positive light and as a basis for a recommendation for reform.

7. **The correct answer is (B).** This is a main idea question. The author begins by stating that a large number of auto traffic fatalities can be attributed to drivers who are intoxicated, and then reviews two approaches to controlling this problem: taxation and drunk driving laws. Neither is very successful. The author finally notes that therapy may be useful, though the extent of its value has not yet been proved. (B) fairly well describes this development. (A) can be eliminated since any conclusions drawn by the author from studies on drunk driving are used for the larger objective described in (B). (C) is incorrect since, aside from suggesting possible ways to reduce the extent of the problem, the author never treats the causes of drunk driving. (D) is incorrect for the same reason. Finally, (E) is incorrect, because the comparison between the U.S. and Britain is only a small part of the passage.

8. **The correct answer is (B).** This is an inference question. In the third paragraph, the author discusses the effect of drunk driving laws, stating that after the implementation of the Road Safety Act in Britain, motor vehicle fatalities fell considerably. On this basis, we infer that the RSA was a law aimed at drunk

answers

driving. We can eliminate (D) and (E) on this ground. (C) can be eliminated as not warranted on the basis of this information. It is not clear whether the number of arrests increased. Equally consistent with the passage is the conclusion that the number of arrests dropped because people were no longer driving while intoxicated. (C) is incorrect for a further reason, the justification for (B). (B) and (A) are fairly close since both describe the RSA as a law aimed at drunk driving. But the last sentence of the third paragraph calls for (B) over (A). As people learned that they would not get caught for drunk driving, the law became less effective. This suggests that the RSA made drunk driving illegal, not that it lowered the BAC required for conviction. This makes sense of the sentence " . . . they could drink and not be stopped." If (A) were correct, this sentence would have to read " . . . they could drink the same amount and not be convicted."

9. **The correct answer is (A).** This is an inference question. In the first paragraph, the author states that to attain a BAC of 0.1 percent, a person would need to drink over five ounces of 80 proof spirits over a short period of time. The author is trying to impress on us that that is a considerable quantity of alcohol for most people to drink. (A) explains why the author makes this comment. (B) is incorrect and confuses the first paragraph with the second paragraph. (C) is incorrect since the point of the example is that the BAC is so high most people will not exceed it. This is not to say, however, that people will not drink and drive because of laws establishing maximum BAC levels. Rather, they can continue to drink and drive because the law allows them a considerable margin in the level of BAC. (D) is a misreading of that first paragraph. Of all the very drunk drivers (BAC in excess of 0.1), only 1 percent are involved in accidents. But this does not say that most drivers involved in fatal collisions have BAC levels in excess of 0.1 percent, and that is what (D) says. As for (E), the author never states that the only way to attain a BAC of 0.1 percent is to drink five ounces of 80 proof spirits in a short time—there may be other ways of becoming intoxicated.

10. **The correct answer is (A).** This is an application question. In the second paragraph, the author states that increased taxation on alcohol would tax the heaviest drinkers most, but notes that this would also penalize the moderate and light drinker. In other words, the remedy is not sufficiently focused on the problem. Then, in the third paragraph, the author notes that drunk driving laws are aimed at the specific problem drivers. We can infer from this discussion that the author would likely advocate drunk driving laws over taxation for the reasons just given. This reasoning is presented in answer (A). (B) is incorrect for the reasons just given and for the further reason that the passage never suggests that taxation is likely to be more effective in solving the problem. The author never really evaluates the effectiveness of taxation in reducing drunk driving. (C) is incorrect for the reason given in support of (A) and for the further reason that the author never raises the issue of personal liberty in conjunction with the BAC test. (D) can be eliminated because the author does not discount the effectiveness of anti-drunk driving measures entirely. Even the British example gives some support to the conclusion that such laws have an effect. (E) is incorrect for the author never mentions the expense or administrative feasibility of BAC tests.

11. **The correct answer is (C).** This is a question about the logical structure of the passage. In paragraph 3, the author notes that stricter enforcement of laws

against drunk driving may result in a few more arrests; but a few more arrests are not likely to have much impact on the problem because the number of arrests is small compared to those who do not get caught. As a consequence, people will continue to drink and drive. The author supports this with the British experience. Once people realize that the chances of being caught are relatively small, they will drink and drive. This is the conclusion of answer (C). (A) is incorrect since the passage does not support the conclusion that the problem is any worse or any better in one country or the other. (B) is incorrect since this is the conclusion the author is arguing against. (D) is wrong because the author is not discussing the effectiveness of taxation in paragraph 3. (E) is a statement the author would likely accept, but that is not the reason for introducing the British example. So choice (E) is true but nonresponsive.

12. **The correct answer is (A).** This is an application question which asks us to examine the logical structure of the argument. In the fourth paragraph, the author argues that the effectiveness of deterrents to drunk driving will depend upon the drinker's ability to control consumption. But drunk driving has two aspects: drunk and driving. The author assumes that drunk driving is a function of drinking only as indicated by the suggestion that control of consumption is necessary as opposed to helpful. (A) attacks this assumption by pointing out that it is possible to drink to excess without driving. It is possible that stiff penalties could be effective deterrents to drunk driving if not to drinking to excess. (B) is incorrect because the author actually makes this point, so this choice does not weaken the argument. (C) is incorrect since the author is concerned only with the problem of fatalities caused by drunk driving. Then (D) can be eliminated since the author is concerned to eliminate fatalities caused by drunk driving. No position is taken on whether the drunk driver ought to be punished, only that the drunk driver ought to be deterred from driving while intoxicated. (E) is not a strong attack on the argument since the author does leave open the question of the value of therapy in combating drunk driving.

13. **The correct answer is (B).** This is obviously a main idea question. The main purpose of the passage is to review the findings of some research on animal behavior and suggest that this may have implications for the study of depression in humans. (B) neatly restates this. (A) can be overruled since the author proposes no such cure, and even notes that there are complex issues remaining to be solved. (C) is incorrect since the author does not criticize any experiments. It is important to recognize that in the second paragraph the author is not being critical of any study in which rats were immersed in cold water, but rather anticipating a possible interpretation of those results and moving to block it. So, the author's criticism is of a possible interpretation of the experiment, not the experiment itself or the results. In any event, that can in no way be interpreted as the main theme of the passage. (D) is wide of the mark. Though one might object to the use of animals for experimentation, that is not the author's point. Finally, (E) is incorrect because the author mentions this only in closing, almost as a qualification on the main theme of the passage.

14. **The correct answer is (D).** This is a logical detail question. As we have just noted, the author introduces the question in the second paragraph to anticipate a possible objection: Perhaps the animal's inability to act was caused by the trauma of the shock rather than the

fact that it could not escape the shock. The author then lists some experiments whose conclusions refute this alternative explanation. (A) is incorrect since the question represents an interruption of the flow of argument, not a continuation of the first paragraph. (B) is incorrect and might be just a confusion of answer and question. (C) can be eliminated since that is not the reason for raising the question, though it may be the overall theme of the passage. Here we cannot answer a question about a specific logical detail by referring to the main point of the text. Finally, (E) is incorrect since the author does not criticize the experiments but rather defends them.

15. **The correct answer is (B).** This is an inference question. We are referred by the question stem to lines 71–73. There we find that stimulation of the septal region inhibits behavior "while rats with septal lesions do not show learned helplessness." We infer that the septum somehow sends "messages" that tell the action centers not to act. If ordinary rats learn helplessness and rats with septal lesions do not, this suggests that the communication between the two areas of the brain has been interrupted. This idea is captured by (B). (A) is incorrect and confuses the indicated reference with the discussion of "immunized" dogs in line 35. (C) seems to offer an explanation, but the text never suggests that rats have "understanding." (D) is incorrect since it does not offer an explanation: Why don't rats with septal lesions learn helplessness? Finally, (E) is irrelevant to the question asked.

16. **The correct answer is (A).** This is an inferred idea question. The author contrasts the inescapable shock experiment with a "nonaversive parallel" in order to demonstrate that inescapability rather than trauma caused inaction in the animals. So the critical difference must be the trauma—it is present in the shock experiments and not in the nonaversive parallels. This is further supported by the example of a nonaversive parallel, the uncontrollable delivery of food. So the relevant difference is articulated by (A). (B) is incorrect since the author specifically states that the nonaversive parallels did succeed in inducing learned helplessness. (C) is incorrect for the same reason. (D) is incorrect since the value of the nonaversive parallel to the logical structure of the argument is that it was not traumatic at all. Finally, (E) is incorrect because even if one experiment used rats and the other dogs, that is not the defining difference between the shock experiments and the nonaversive-parallel experiments.

17. **The correct answer is (A).** This is a logical detail question, and it is related to the matters discussed above. The author raises the question in paragraph two in order to anticipate a possible objection; namely, that the shock, not the unavoidability, caused inaction. The author then offers a refutation of this position by arguing that we get the same results using similar experiments with nonaversive stimuli. Moreover, if trauma of shock caused the inaction, then we would expect to find learned helplessness induced in rats by the shock, regardless of prior experience with shock. The "mastery effect," however, contradicts this expectation. This is essentially the explanation provided in (A). (B) is incorrect since the author does not mention this until the end of the passage. (C) can be eliminated since the "mastery effect" reference is not included to support the conclusion that neurochemical changes cause the learned helplessness. (D) is incorrect, for though the author makes such an assertion, the "mastery effect" data is not adduced to

support that particular assertion. Finally, (E) is the point against which the author is arguing when mentioning the "mastery effect" experiments.

18. **The correct answer is (E).** This is a further application question. The author closes with a disclaimer that the human cognitive makeup is more complex than that of laboratory animals and that for this reason the findings regarding learned helplessness and induced neurosis may or may not be applicable to humans. The author does not, however, explain what the differences are between the experimental subjects and humans. A logical continuation would be to supply the reader with this elaboration. By comparison, the other answer choices are less likely. (B) is unlikely since the author begins and ends with references to human depression, and that is evidently the motivation for writing the article. (C) is not supported by the text since it is nowhere indicated that any such experiments have been undertaken. (D) fails for a similar reason. We cannot conclude that the author would want to test humans by similar experimentation. Finally, (A) is perhaps the second best answer. Its value is that it suggests the mechanism should be studied further. But the most important question is not how the mechanism works in rats but whether that mechanism also works in humans.

19. **The correct answer is (C).** This is a main idea question. The author begins by posing the following question: Why are affirmative action programs so controversial? He then argues that affirmative action is unlike ordinary government programs in the way it allocates the burden of the program. Because of this, he concludes, we are torn between supporting the programs (because they have legitimate goals) and condemning the programs (because of the way the cost is allocated). (C) neatly describes this development. The author analyzes the structure of the moral dilemma. (A) is incorrect since the comparison is but a subpart of the overall development and is used in the service of the larger analysis. (B) is incorrect since the author reaches no such clear-cut decision. Rather, we are left with the question posed by the dilemma. (D) is incorrect since the author presupposes in his presentation that the reader already understands the importance of the issue. Finally, (E) is incorrect since the advantages of the programs are mentioned only in passing.

20. **The correct answer is (A).** This is a logical structure question. In the second paragraph the author will describe the general structure of government programs in order to set up the contrast with affirmative action. The discussion begins with "Setting aside . . . ," indicating that the author recognizes such cases and does not wish to discuss them in detail. Tolls and tuition are exceptions to the general rule, so the author explicitly sets them aside in order to preempt a possible objection to his analysis based on claimed counterexamples. (B) is incorrect since the overall point of the passage is to discuss this dilemma, but the main point of the passage will not answer the question about the logical substructure of the argument. (C) is incorrect since tolls and tuition are not ordinary government programs. (D) is incorrect since the author never raises such doubts. Finally, (E) misses the point of the examples. The point is not that they are costly but that the cost is born by the specific user.

21. **The correct answer is (B).** This is an application question. In the first paragraph the author states that affirmative action is designed to achieve social and economic objectives. Although he quali-

answers

fies his claim, he seems to believe that the arguments are in favor of affirmative action. So (B) is clearly supported by the text. (A) is not supported by the text since the author leaves us with a question; he does not resolve the issue. (C) can be eliminated on the same ground. The author neither embraces nor rejects affirmative action. (D) goes beyond the scope of the argument. While the author might wish this were possible, nothing in the passage indicates such restructuring is possible. Indeed, in paragraph three the author remarks that the "funding" problem seems to be inherent. Finally, (E) can be eliminated on the same ground as (A). Though the author recognizes the unfairness of affirmative action, he also believes that the programs are valuable.

22. **The correct answer is (E).** In paragraph two the author mentions that government programs entail both social and economic costs. Then, the cost of a specific example, the passed-over worker, is not a government expenditure in the sense that money is laid out to purchase something. So the author is using the term "funding" in a nonstandard way, and he wishes to call his readers' attention to this. (E) parallels this explanation. (A) is incorrect since it is inconsistent with the reasoning just provided. (B) is incorrect, for though the author may believe that individuals bear a disproportionate share of the burden, this is not a response to the question asked. (C) is incorrect for the same reason: It is a true but nonresponsive statement. Finally, (D) fails for the same reason. Though the author notes that affirmative action programs are similar to other government programs in this respect, this is not an explanation for the author's placing "funding" in quotation marks.

23. **The correct answer is (D).** This is a logical structure question. In the final paragraph, the author analyzes another similar situation. This technique is called "arguing from analogy." The strength of the argument depends on our seeing the similarity and accepting the conclusion of the one argument (the villainous man) as applicable to the other argument (affirmative action). (A) is perhaps the second-best response, but the author is not offering an illustration, e.g., an example of affirmative action. To be sure, the author is attempting to prove a point, but attempting to prove a conclusion is not equivalent to illustrating a contention. (B) is incorrect since the author adduces the situation to support his contention. (C) is incorrect, for the author cites no authority. Finally, (E) can be eliminated since the author uses the case of the villanious man to support, not to weaken, the case.

24. **The correct answer is (B).** This is an explicit idea question. In paragraph one, the author mentions that affirmative action is like other government programs in that it is designed to achieve certain social and economic goals. So, (A) cites a similarity rather than a difference. (C) can also be eliminated. In paragraph three the author states that the relevant difference is not the method of allocating benefits. The salient difference is set forth in the same paragraph, and it is the difference described by (B). (D) and (E) are simply not mentioned anywhere in the selection.

25. **The correct answer is (E).** This is an explicit idea question. The answer can be found in the first paragraph, where the author notes that a heart attack is unlike an angina attack because the heart attack always involves the death of heart muscle. As for (A), although a heart attack may involve acceleration of the heartbeat, this is not what distinguishes it from angina. (B) is incorrect since the author describes the way in which nitroglycerin may be used to treat heart at-

tack. (C) is incorrect both because this is not a statement that can be justified by the text and because it is not the defining characteristic of a heart attack. Finally, (D) is incorrect, for though the heart attack involves rapid muscle death, it is the death of tissue and not the length of time of the attack that is the distinguishing feature.

26. **The correct answer is (B).** This, too, is an explicit idea question, but it is more difficult than the preceding one. The author cites the "curious" result that the nitroglycerin helped the most seriously stricken patients but did not help the less seriously stricken patients. The author explains that in the more seriously stricken patients the ordinary automatic response to a drop in blood pressure, which would be a faster heart rate, did not occur. Apparently, the congestive heart failure effectively blocked this reaction. Consequently, the drop in blood pressure caused by the nitroglycerin did not invite the normal increase in heart rate. This explanation is presented by choice (B). (A) is incorrect since no mention is made of any delay in administering drugs. (C) is incorrect since phenylephrine was not available to the twelve patients at the time of the study. Phenylephrine was later used to counter the drop in blood pressure caused by nitroglycerin. (D) is incorrect since the passage states that blood pressure did drop in those patients with congestive heart failure. The difference between those patients and the less seriously stricken ones was that the drop in blood pressure did not cause an increase in heart rate. For the same reason, (E) must also be eliminated.

27. **The correct answer is (D).** This is an explicit idea question. As for (A), several results of heart attack are mentioned at various points in the text. The answer to (B) is explicitly provided in the third paragraph. As for (C), the author mentions the effect of nitroglycerin at various points, e.g., dilates blood vessels, reduces blood pressure. Finally, (E) is answered in the second paragraph. (D), however, is not answered in the passage. The author discusses the effects of heart attack, but not the causes of heart attack.

28. **The correct answer is (D).** The answer to this inference question can be found in the final paragraph. There the author states that research is being done on drugs that affect myocardial oxygen supply and demand "including . . . vessel dilators such as nitroglycerin." From this we can infer that nitroglycerin dilates blood vessels and this somehow affects the oxygen balance in the heart muscle. This is the value of the drug. (A) is incorrect because the lowering of blood pressure is an unwanted side effect of nitroglycerin, not its medical value. (B) is incorrect since the value of nitroglycerin is to prevent damage, not to aid in healing. (C) is incorrect for the same reason that (A) is incorrect. Finally, (E) is incorrect because nitroglycerin is mentioned as a vessel dilator in the final paragraph, not as a drug that counters hypertension.

29. **The correct answer is (E).** This is a tone question. The author's attitude is best studied in the final paragraph. Having described the possibility of treating heart attacks with nitroglycerin, the author adds the disclaimer that there is no proof yet of the value of the treatment in very serious cases. From this we may infer, however, that the author believes it has some value in less serious cases and possibly in other cases as well. This attitude is best described as one of optimism. Since the passage has, on balance, a positive tone, we can eliminate (B), (C), and (D). As for (A), though the author may be concerned about the treatment of heart attacks, the overall tone of the

discussion is not concern or worry, but rather hope or optimism.

30. **The correct answer is (A).** This is an inference question, the answer to which is found in the second paragraph. There it is stated that phenylephrine is used to maintain blood pressure, but that simple statement is not enough to answer the question. We must dig deeper. Why is it important to maintain blood pressure? The final sentence of the paragraph states that a drop in blood pressure causes the heart to speed up. It is this increase in heart rate that "worsens the damage." So the value of phenylephrine is that it prevents cardiac acceleration by maintaining blood pressure. This is the explanation given in choice (A). (B) and (C) make essentially the same statement using language drawn from different parts of the passage, but they describe something other than the effect of phenylephrine. (D) is incorrect since the phenylephrine has a particular use that complements nitroglycerin. Although the effect of both drugs taken together may be something like that described in (D), this is not an answer to the question asked. Finally, (E) is just language taken from the first paragraph and is not an answer to the question asked.

31. **The correct answer is (D).** This is a main idea question. The author cites several arguments in favor of the "drug lag" theory, then offers refutations of at least some of them. The conclusion drawn is that the arguments for "drug lag" are not conclusive and that, contrary to the view of the "drug lag" theoreticians, the 1962 Amendments are not, on balance, harmful. The main technique of development is refutation of arguments cited. (D) is therefore the best answer to this question. (A) can be eliminated since the author does not outline a proposal. Discussing the effectiveness of some past action is not outlining a proposal. (B) has some merit because the author does analyze the evidence presented by the "drug lag" theoreticians. This analysis, however, is not the final objective of the passage. It is presented in order to further the goal of refuting the general position of that group. (C) is incorrect since the author poses no question, and indeed seems to answer any question that might be implicit in the passage regarding the value of the Amendments. (E) has some merit since the focus of the passage is a law. But the intent of the author is not to discuss the law per se. Rather, the intent of the passage is to refute objections to the law. On balance, (D) more precisely describes the main idea than the other choices.

32. **The correct answer is (C).** (A), (B), (D), and (E) are all mentioned as "drug lag" arguments in the second paragraph. As for (C), the argument that effectiveness studies cost money is mentioned in the first paragraph. But "drug lag" results from the time and cost of effectiveness studies. "Drug lag" is not the increased cost itself.

33. **The correct answer is (A).** This is an application question. Support for (A) is found in the closing sentences of the passage. In the final paragraph, the author insists that there are few, if any, examples of harm done by the requirements of effectiveness studies. Then the author says that we are at least assured that the drug, which might actually prove harmful, does have some benefit. The qualified nature of the claim suggests that the author would acknowledge that some "drug lag" does exist but that, on balance, it is justified. This thought is captured by choice (A). (B) is incorrect because the author never states the effectiveness studies are designed to determine whether the drug has unwanted effects. Apparently, effectiveness studies, as the name implies, are designed to

test the value of the drug. This is not to say that such studies may not, in fact, uncover unwanted side effects, but given the information in the passage, (B) is a more tenuous inference than (A). (C) is incorrect for two reasons. First, the passage never states that the cost of drugs is higher in the United States than in other countries. The passage states only that the proponents of the "drug lag" theory argue that the effectiveness study requirement increases the cost of drugs here. That makes no comparison with a foreign country. Second, the author seems to discount the significance of the increased cost. (D) is incorrect because there is no basis for such a recommendation in the passage. Finally, (E) is incorrect because the passage never states that the studies do not cost money or time. The author only doubts whether the cost or time create profit pressures serious enough to cause "drug lag."

34. **The correct answer is (B).** This is a logical structure question. In the final paragraph the author states that the drop in new drugs introduced annually began before the Amendments took effect. The author does not deny that the drop occurred but rather, points out that it predated the supposed cause. In other words, the author is suggesting that there must be some other reason for the drop. Answer (B) correctly describes the author's logical move. (E) is directly contradicted by this analysis. The author does not deny that there was a drop in the number of new drugs introduced every year. As for (A), the author does not point to any similarity between two situations, saying only that the situation being studied existed even before the Amendments took effect. (C) is incorrect because the author never questions the credibility of an opponent, only the value of the opponent's arguments. Finally, (D) is incorrect because the author uses statistics to prove some further conclusion, not to justify the use of statistics.

35. **The correct answer is (C).** This is a logical structure question. In the second paragraph, the author cites, as one argument for the existence of "drug lag," the nonavailability in the United States of a drug that is available in a foreign country. The third paragraph offers a refutation of this argument. The simple availability/nonavailability comparison is not valid because consumers may not suffer from the nonavailability of that particular drug if another drug is available to treat the same condition. Choice (C) correctly describes the structure of this argument. The remaining answer choices are in various ways related to the overall argument of the passage, but they are not answers to this particular question.

answers

Exercise 2: ANSWER KEY AND EXPLANATIONS

1. D	5. A	9. D	13. B	17. C
2. A	6. A	10. C	14. A	18. C
3. D	7. B	11. B	15. A	19. D
4. B	8. B	12. B	16. D	20. A

1. **The correct answer is (D).** This is a fairly easy inference question. We are asked to determine which of the problems mentioned by the author is the most important. (B) can be eliminated because the author's criticism is not that such courses are not offered, nor even that such courses are not required. So we eliminate (E) as well. The most important shortcoming, according to the author, is that students have not been encouraged to apply the principles learned in the humanities. The support for this conclusion is to be found at the end of the second paragraph. As for (C), this is not mentioned by the author as a weakness in the present curriculum structure. Rather, the author anticipates that this is a possible objection to the proposal to require students to devote part of their time to the study of primary problems. (A) is indeed a weakness of the university, and the author does admit that the university has not yet achieved equal opportunity for all. But this is discussed in the first paragraph, where the university's successes are outlined. Only in the second paragraph does the discussion of the university's failure begin. This indicates that the author does not regard the university's failure to achieve complete equality of opportunity as a serious problem.

2. **The correct answer is (A).** This is an inference question as well, though of a greater degree of difficulty. It seems possible to eliminate (C) and (E) as fairly implausible. The author's remarks about literature (at the end of the second paragraph), addressed to us as readers, do not suggest that we believe literature is required, nor that it is used to teach writing. As for (D), the author apparently presupposes that we, the readers, do not see the relevance of literature to real problems, for that it is relevant is at least part of the burden of his argument. (B) is perhaps the second best answer. It may very well be that most people regard literature as something scholarly, but that does not prove that (B) is a presupposition of the argument. The author states that literature is a source of real and vicarious experience. What is the value of that? According to the author, it relieves us of the necessity of living everyone else's life. The author is trying to show that literature has a real, practical value. The crucial question, then, is why the author is attempting to prove that literature has real value. The answer is because the author presupposes that we disagree with this conclusion. There is a subtle but important difference between a presupposition that literature is scholarly and a presupposition that literature has no practical value. After all, there are many nonscholarly undertakings that may lack practical value.

3. **The correct answer is (D).** This is an explicit idea question. It is important to keep in mind that an explicit idea question is almost always answerable on the basis of information actually stated in the text. With a format of this sort, this means that the question should be readily answerable without speculation, and that

answers

this answer should be fairly complete. (D) is correct because the author raises a possible objection in the final paragraph. (A) is incorrect because the author never gives any such examples. (B) is incorrect because the author never addresses the issue of political society. That is mentioned only as a point of reference in the introductory remarks. (C) is not answered since no university is ever named. And (E) is incorrect since the author makes the assertion, without elaborating, that the university is a better teacher today than in the past. There is a further point to be made. It is possible to argue that (B) is partially answered. After all, if we improve our students' ability to pose and answer questions, is this not also a way to improve the performance of our political society? But that is clearly more attenuated than the answer we find to question (D). The same reasoning may be applied to other incorrect answers as well. It may be possible to construct arguments in their favor, but this is a standardized exam. And there is a clear, easy answer to (D) in the text, indicating that this is the answer the test-writer intends that you choose.

4. **The correct answer is (B).** This is an application question. The author uses the term "primary problems" to refer to questions of grave importance that are not susceptible to an easy answer. Each of the incorrect answers poses a question that can be answered with a short answer. (A) can be answered with a yes or no. (C) can be answered with a name. (D) can be answered with a date. (E) can be answered with a series of proposals. And even if the answers are not absolutely indisputable, the questions will soon become dead issues. The only problem that is likely to still be around after "we are all dead" is the one of capital punishment.

5. **The correct answer is (A).** This is an application question—with a thought reverser. The question asks us to identify the statement with which the author would be least likely to agree. In the fourth paragraph, the author introduces an example of a primary problem. What makes this a primary problem is that there are competing arguments on both sides of the issue: There are benefits to the individual and to society, but there are dangers as well. (A) is not likely to get the author's agreement since the author acknowledges that the question is an open one. The author implies that society may have such a right, but points out also that the use of such measures must be studied very carefully. That same paragraph strongly suggests that the author would accept choices (B) and (C). As for (D) and (E), these are strands that are woven into the text at several points.

6. **The correct answer is (A).** This is a main idea question. The author describes a problem and proposes a solution. (B) is incorrect since the analysis of the system leads the author to propose a reform. (C) is incorrect since the author makes a definite recommendation. (D) is incorrect since the new idea the author outlines is defended in the text, not criticized. (E) is incorrect since the author does not develop the passage by raising questions.

7. **The correct answer is (B).** This too is a main idea question in that the question asks, What is the general topic? (B) is the best answer since the author is speaking about the university and he is addressing fundamental questions of educational philosophy. (A) and (C) are incorrect since politics and science are only tangentially related to the argument. (D) and (E) can be eliminated on the same ground and on the additional ground that though the author wants to make education practical, the decision to do that will be a decision based on philosophical concerns.

8. **The correct answer is (B).** This is a main idea question presented in the format of a sentence completion. We are looking for the answer choice that, when added to the question stem, produces a sentence that summarizes the main thesis of the passage. Insofar as the verbs are concerned, that is, the first words of each choice, each choice seems acceptable. One could say that the author is concerned to "suggest," "demonstrate," "explain," "discuss," or "describe." So we must look at the fuller content of each choice. The author begins the passage by noting that there were two schools of thought on how to reduce unemployment, and then proceeds to describe the main ideas of both schools of thought. Finally, the author concludes by noting that, for all of their avowed differences, both schools share considerable common ground. This development is captured very well by (B). (A) is perhaps the second best choice. It is true that the author does mention some economic tools that can be used to control unemployment, but the main thesis is not that such ways exist. Rather, the main thesis, as pointed out by (B), is that the two groups, during the 1960s, had seemingly different yet ultimately similar views on how the tools could best be used. (C) is incorrect since the discussion of structural inefficiencies is only a minor part of the development. (D) is incorrect because the discussion of disunity is included simply to give a more complete picture of the debate and not to show that this prevented the achievement of full employment. Finally, the CEA is mentioned as a matter of historical interest, but its role is not the central focus of the passage.

9. **The correct answer is (D).** This is an explicit idea question. Each of the incorrect answers is mentioned as a possible barrier to achieving 4% unemployment in the discussion of structural inefficiencies of the third paragraph. There reference is made to the effect of technological innovation, the shortage of skilled labor, the problem of minority and unskilled labor, and the reserve of workers not yet counted as being in the labor force. There is no mention, however, of the need to relocate workers to areas of labor shortage. The only reference to relocation is in the final paragraph. Since (D) is never mentioned as a possible barrier to achieving the 4% goal, it is the correct answer.

10. **The correct answer is (C).** This is an attitude or tone question. The author refers to the position of the hyperenthusiasts as "not very plausible," which indicates the author does not endorse the position. On this ground we can eliminate (A). (B) can be eliminated on the same ground, and on the further ground that "lighthearted" is not a good description of the tone of the passage. (D) and (E), however, are overstatements. Though the author obviously rejects the position of the hyperenthusiasts, there is no evidence of so negative an attitude as those suggested by (D) and (E). (C) describes well what the author means by mentioning the position and then not even bothering to discuss it.

11. **The correct answer is (B).** This is an explicit idea question. The needed reference is found in the second paragraph. The difference between the CEA and the dissenting expansionists grew out of the question of where to spend the money that would be used to stimulate the economy. The dissenting faction wanted to target the expansionary spending for public services and low-income groups. (B) presents this difference very well. (A) is incorrect and conflates the dissenting expansionists (paragraph two) and the structuralists (paragraph three). (C) commits the same error. (D) represents a misreading of the second paragraph: The CEA were expansionists. (E) is incorrect

since the passage does not state that the CEA were conservatives.

12. **The correct answer is (B).** This is an explicit idea question. Information that would bear on the issue raised by (B) is included in the third paragraph. As for (A), there is no such information in the passage. In the first paragraph, the author mentions that the economy failed to expand rapidly in the early 1960s, but offers no explanation for that phenomenon. And (C) is never mentioned at any point in the text. (D) is a political question that is not addressed by the passage, and (E) is an historical one that is not answered.

13. **The correct answer is (B).** The author mentions a dissenting group of expansionists in the closing lines of paragraph two. The author remarks of their arguments that their commitment to certain political ideals likely interfered with their economic judgments. For this reason the author places very little faith in their arguments. (B) nicely brings out this point. (A) is incorrect. The author does discount the value of their conclusions, but not because they were not trained as economists. As for (C), there is nothing that suggests that the author lacks information. Rather, it seems from the passage that the author has sufficient information to discount the position. (D) is clearly in contradiction to this analysis and must be incorrect, and (E) can be eliminated on the same ground.

14. **The correct answer is (A).** Here we have a relatively easy inference question. The hyperenthusiasts used structuralist-type arguments to contend that jobs were already available. That being the case, the hyperenthusiasts dissented from both the positions of the expansionists and the structuralists who believed unemployment to be a problem. We may infer, then, that the essence of the hyperenthusiasts' position was that no government action was needed at all—at least no government action of the sort being discussed by the main camps described by the author. As for (B), nowhere in the passage does the author state or even hint that anyone overestimated the number of people out of work. As for (C), this represents a reading that confuses the hyperenthusiasts (paragraph four) with the main-line structuralists (paragraph three). (D) is incorrect and conflates the hyperenthusiasts of the expansionary school of thought with those of the structuralist school. Finally, (E) is incorrect since it describes the position of the main group of expansionists.

15. **The correct answer is (A).** Here we have a main idea question. The structure of the passage is first to explain that previous siting decisions have been made by regulatory agencies with only a review function exercised by government. The author then explains that in the past the most important features affecting the demographic characteristics of the population were natural ones. Then the author argues that, given the effect siting decisions will have in the future, the government ought to take an active role in making those decisions, and that the government ought to take social considerations into account in making such decisions. Given this brief synopsis of the argument, we can see that (A) neatly restates this thesis. Further, we can see that (B) constitutes only a part, not the entirety, of the argument. (C), too, forms only one subpart of the whole analysis. (D) can be eliminated since the author believes that future siting decisions need not be governed by only natural features. Finally, (E) may very well be true, but it surely is not the main point of the argument presented.

16. **The correct answer is (D).** This is an explicit idea question. (A) is mentioned in the final sentence of the first para-

answers

graph along with (B). (E) is a theme which runs generally through that paragraph, and (C) is specifically mentioned in the third paragraph. Nowhere does the author suggest that proximity to fuel sources needs to be taken into the siting decision.

17. **The correct answer is (C).** This is a specific detail question, so the answer will be explicitly provided in the text. Your main task is to find the right part of the passage. The answer is given in the first paragraph, where the author explains that, traditionally, siting decisions were made by the utilities with government relegated to a review function. (A) and (B) are mentioned in the passage, but as advantages of a different process, or, if you prefer, they're mentioned, but in the wrong place to answer this question. (D), of course, contradicts the selection, and (E) is just not mentioned by the author.

18. **The correct answer is (C).** This is a logical structure question. The author's analysis and recommendation depend on the assumption that it will be possible to predict the demographic consequences of an energy park. Without this assumption, the recommendation that the government use electric facility siting decisions to effect social goals loses much of its persuasiveness. As for (A) and (D), the historical explanation is in large part expository only, that is, background information which is not, strictly speaking, essential to the argument supporting the recommendation. To the extent, then, that either (A) or (D) does weaken the historical analysis, and that is doubtful, the damage to the overall argument would not be great. As for (B) and (E), these are both irrelevant, and the proof is that whether (B) and (E) are true or false does not affect the argument.

19. **The correct answer is (D).** The correct answer to this application question is clearly supported by the concluding remarks of the passage. (A) is contradicted by these remarks and must be incorrect. (B) goes beyond the scope of the passage. We cannot attribute such a critical judgment ("were irresponsible") to the author. In fact, the passage at least implies that decisions during the nineteenth century were made in a natural (no pun intended) way. (C) overstates the case. Though the author believes that siting decisions for power plants need not depend on natural features, there is no support in the text for such a broad conclusion as that given in (C). Finally, as for (E), there is no evidence that the author would make such a judgment.

20. **The correct answer is (A).** This is an explicit idea question, the answer to which is found at the end of the third paragraph. The most important feature of an energy park is that the place in which the massive effects will be manifested can be chosen. So, unlike the harbor, a natural feature located without regard to human desires, the energy park can be located where it will serve goals other than the production of energy. As for (B), even to the extent that (B) makes an accurate statement, the statement is not responsive to the question. This is not an important difference between the natural advantages of an early city and the man-made features of the energy park. A similar argument invalidates (D). As for (C), this is obviously irrelevant to the question asked. Finally, (E) is incorrect for two reasons. First, such a conclusion is not supported by the passage. Second, it is not a response to the question asked.

Sentence Correction

chapter 6

OVERVIEW

- **What is sentence correction?**
- **How do you answer sentence correction questions?**
- **What smart test-takers know**

WHAT IS SENTENCE CORRECTION?

Sentence correction questions test your mastery of standard written English. You must demonstrate your ability to recognize correct (grammatical and logical) and effective (clear, concise, and idiomatic) expression and choose the best of several suggested revisions. Each question begins with a sentence, all or part of which has been underlined. The answer choices represent different ways of rendering the underlined part. Choice (A) always repeats the original wording; the other choices offer various alternatives. About a fifth of the time, the original sentence is correct. In the other cases, the underlined part contains one or more errors. The correct choice will correct all of the errors without introducing any new mistakes.

GMAT Sentence Correction Questions

On the GMAT, the sentence correction questions appear in the 75-minute verbal section. Within the section, they are not grouped all together. Instead, they are interspersed among the reading comprehension and critical reasoning questions.

Here are the directions for sentence correction questions, along with some sample questions and explanations.

Anatomy of Sentence Correction Questions

Directions: In the following sentence correction problems, either part or all of the sentence is underlined. The sentence is followed by five ways of writing the underlined part. Choice (A) repeats the original; the other answer choices vary. If you think that the original phrasing is the best, choose (A). If you think that one of the other answer choices is the best, select that choice.

These problems test the ability to recognize correct and effective expression. Follow the requirements of Standard Written English: grammar, choice of words, and sentence construction. Choose the answer that results in the clearest, most exact sentence, but do not change the meaning of the original sentence.

1. <u>Beautifully sanded and revarnished, Bill proudly displayed the antique desk in his den.</u>

- **(A)** Beautifully sanded and revarnished, Bill proudly displayed the antique desk in his den.
- **(B)** Beautiful, sanded, and revarnished, Bill proudly displayed the antique desk in his den.
- **(C)** An antique, and beautifully sanded and revarnished, in his den Bill proudly displayed the desk.
- **(D)** Bill, beautifully sanded and revarnished in the den, proudly displayed the antique desk.
- **(E)** Bill proudly displayed the antique desk, beautifully sanded and revarnished, in his den.

In this item, the entire sentence is underlined. Notice that choice (A) repeats the original. You would choose (A) if the original rendering is correct. In this case, however, the original is wrong. The correct answer is (E). The sentence as originally written suggests that it was Bill who was sanded and revarnished. Only (E) makes it clear that it was the desk, not Bill, that was refurbished.

2. <u>With</u> only two percent of the votes counted, the network announced that the incumbent would be reelected by a substantial majority.

- **(A)** With
- **(B)** Being
- **(C)** On account of
- **(D)** Due to
- **(E)** Because of

Here only a part of the original is underlined, and the correct answer is (A). The sentence is correct as written. The logical structure of the thought is best expressed by *with*.

HOW DO YOU ANSWER SENTENCE CORRECTION QUESTIONS?

Here is a simple, four-step plan for answering GMAT sentence correction questions.

Sentence Correction: Getting It Right

1. Read the sentence carefully, trying to identify an error.
2. If no error is apparent, ask yourself:
   - Is the sentence grammatically correct?
   - Is the sentence properly structured?
   - Does the sentence use correct diction?

   If you find one or more errors, look for an answer that makes the corrections.
3. If you cannot find an error, read the answer choices. Focus on the *differences* between each choice and the original. Often this will turn up an error that you overlooked.
4. Eliminate choices that contain errors and choose from among those that remain.

NOTE

Does sentence correction test technical grammar terms?

No, but it does test technical points of grammar. You have to be able to recognize the points—even if you do not know the technical name. The technical terms used in this book will probably be familiar from high school and college, but you do not have to memorize them.

Now let's examine some sample GMAT sentence correction questions. As you read each question and its answer, think how the four-step solution process applies.

The most important food-energy source of three-fourths of the world's population are grains.

(A) of three-fourths of the world's population are grains

(B) for three-fourths of the world's population are grains

(C) for three-fourths of the world's population is grains

(D) for three-fourths of the worlds' population is grains

(E) for three-fourths of the world's population is grain

The original sentence contains an error of grammar. The verb *are* fails to agree in number with its subject, *source.* The correct verb is *is.* Additionally, the *of* is not idiomatic, for *of* here creates the impression of ownership, e.g., that the population is in possession of the source. Finally, the use of *grains* is not idiomatic; *grain* would be preferable. (B) corrects the second error but not the first and third. (C) and (D) correct the first and second errors but not the third. Additionally, (D) changes the meaning of the original by implying that the sentence is describing several different worlds. Only (E) corrects all three errors.

The possibility of massive earthquakes are regarded by most area residents with a mixture of skepticism and caution.

(A) are regarded by most area residents with

(B) is regarded by most area residents with

(C) is regarded by most area residents as

(D) is mostly regarded by area residents with

(E) by most area residents is regarded with

The original sentence contains an error of grammar. The verb *are* fails to agree with its subject, *possibility*. The correct verb is *is*. Each of the other choices makes the needed correction, but three of them introduce new problems. (C) changes the meaning of the original. The use of *as* implies that the residents think earthquakes are like a mixture of skepticism and caution. (D) changes the meaning of the original by qualifying the belief with *mostly* (a low-level usage in itself) and failing to quantify the number of residents who hold the belief. Finally, in (E) the use of *by* implies that the residents will themselves cause the earthquakes. Thus, choice (B) is the correct answer.

WHAT SMART TEST-TAKERS KNOW

Agreement is key. Always make sure that the verb of the sentence agrees with the subject. This error is used very often by the test-writers.

Getting a Grip on Grammar

SUBJECTS AND VERBS MUST ALWAYS AGREE.

The phenomena of public education is another example of the workings of democracy.

(A) The phenomena of public education is another example of the workings of democracy.

(B) The phenomena of public education is yet another example of democracy at work.

(C) The phenomenon of public education is another example of how the workings of democracy work.

(D) The phenomenon of public education is another example of democracy at work.

(E) Public education, a phenomena, is another working example of democracy.

In this example there is a lack of agreement in number between the subject (*phenomena*) and the verb (*is*) because *phenomena* is plural (*phenomenon* is singular). The same error eliminates choices (B) and (E) ("a phenomena" is incorrect). Choice (C) is redundant ("the workings of democracy work"). Choice (D) is correct. The general rule is that a singular subject requires a singular verb, and a plural subject requires a plural verb.

Everyone on both sides except the pitcher and me was injured in that game.

(A) except the pitcher and me was

(B) except the pitcher and me were

(C) except the pitcher and I was

(D) accept the pitcher and I were

(E) accept the pitcher and me was

The underlined portion contains no errors, choice (A) is correct. The *was* is correctly used since *Everyone* is always considered to be singular. *Everyone* is an indefinite pronoun, of which there are three types. The pronouns of the first type are always singular: *everyone, each, either, neither, someone, somebody, nobody, anyone, anybody, everybody, one*, and *no one*. Those of the second type are always plural: *both, few, many,* and *several.* Those of the third type may be singular or plural, depending on whether the noun to which they refer is singular or plural: *some, more, most,* and *all* ("some of the cake [singular] is . . ."; "some of the boys [plural] are . . ."). In choice (C), *I* should be *me* because it is the object of *except.* Choices (D) and (E) are both incorrect because *accept* is a verb, not a preposition (an error of diction).

His dog, <u>along with his cat and goldfish, prevent</u> him from taking long trips.

(A) along with his cat and goldfish, prevent

(B) as well as his cat and goldfish, prevents

(C) in addition to his cat and goldfish, are preventing

(D) together with his cat and goldfish, were preventing

(E) accompanied by his cat and goldfish, prevent

The subject of the sentence is *dog*, which is singular; therefore, a singular verb is required. Only choice (B) has a singular verb (*prevents*). The general rule is that the joining of a singular subject with another noun or pronoun, or with several nouns or pronouns, by prepositions such as *along with, together with, with, as well as, in addition to,* or *accompanied by* does not make the singular subject into a plural one. (Only *and* can join two singular subjects and make them act as a plural one.) Choice (D) also changes the meaning of the original by making the tense of the verb past instead of present.

<u>Neither the council members nor the mayor take</u> responsibility for the passage of the controversial bill.

(A) Neither the council members nor the mayor take

(B) Neither the council members or the mayor takes

(C) Neither the council members take nor the mayor takes

(D) Neither the mayor nor the council members takes

(E) Neither the council members nor the mayor takes

Choice (E) is correct. The general rule is that when two distinct words or phrases are joined by the correlatives *either . . . or, neither . . . nor*, or *not only . . . but also*, the number (singular or plural) of the word or phrase nearer to the verb determines the number of the verb. Choices (A) and (D) are wrong for that reason ("mayor take" and "council members takes"). Choice (B) is wrong because *Neither* is incorrectly correlated with *or* (rather than *nor*). Choice (C) is wrong because of the insertion of *take*; in this construction, both *neither* and *nor* must be followed by the same part of speech.

PRONOUNS MUST AGREE WITH THE WORDS TO WHICH THEY REFER.

The preacher said <u>that everyone will burn in eternal damnation for their sins</u>.

(A) that everyone will burn in eternal damnation for their sins

(B) that everyone for his sins in eternal damnation will burn

(C) that everyone will burn in eternal damnation for his sins

(D) about everyone that they will burn in eternal damnation for their sins

(E) that all of us should burn in eternal damnation for their sins

Everyone is always singular. Therefore, any pronoun that refers to *everyone* must also be singular. Choices (A) and (D) use *their* (plural) instead of *his* (singular) to refer to *everyone* and are therefore wrong. Choice (B) uses *his* correctly but places its prepositional phrase modifiers awkwardly. Choice (E) uses *their* correctly to refer to "all of us" (plural *all* because of *us*, which is plural), but changes the meaning of the sentence to "should burn" instead of "will burn." Choice (C) is correct.

TIP

Check for multiple errors. Many sentences contain multiple errors. The right answer is the one that corrects all of them.

Of the two leaders, neither Trotsky nor Lenin <u>was most brilliant, but each worked in their sphere</u> for the party.

(A) was most brilliant, but each worked in their sphere

(B) was most brilliant, but each worked in their own sphere

(C) was most brilliant, but each worked in his sphere

(D) was more brilliant, but each worked in their own sphere worked

(E) was more brilliant, but each worked in his sphere

Each is always singular. Therefore, any pronoun that refers back to *each* must also be singular. Choices (A), (B), and (D) use *their* (plural) instead of "his" (singular) to refer to "each" and are therefore wrong. After the commas in choices (C) and (E), the wording is the same and is correct. In choice (C) *most* is incorrect because only two people are mentioned in the sentence: a comparison between two people or things uses the comparative degree (more + adjective or adjective ending in -*er*), not the superlative degree (most + adjective or adjective ending in -*est*). Both (D) and (E) use the proper comparative form, but (A), (B), and (C) do not. Choice (E) is the correct answer.

PRONOUNS MUST BE IN THE CORRECT CASE.

Every conservative candidate <u>except Smith and she</u> was defeated in the primary election.

(A) except Smith and she

(B) except Smith and her

(C) excepting Smith and she

(D) but not she and Smith

(E) outside of her and Smith

Since *except* is a preposition, it must take an object (*her*), not a subject (*she*). Therefore, choices (A) and (C) are wrong. Choice (C) is also wrong because *excepting* is poor diction as used in this context, as a substitute for *except*. In choice (E), *outside of* is also poor diction; either *except* or *other than* should be used instead. In choice (D), "but not she and Smith" is wrong for the same reason as (A); when used as a preposition, *but* takes the object *her*. (B) is correct.

> If I were he, I would lay that manuscript on the sofa and keep it away from the kitchen table.
>
> **(A)** If I were he, I would lay
>
> **(B)** If I were him, I would lay
>
> **(C)** If I were he, I would lie
>
> **(D)** If I was he, I would lay
>
> **(E)** If I was he, I would lie

The various answer choices in this example contain three places where an error may occur: *was* or *were*; *he* or *him*; and *lay* or *lie*. The correct choices from the three pairs of alternatives are *were* because the first clause is contrary to fact (the *I* is not *he*) and therefore requires the subjunctive mood of the verb (*I were* rather than the normal, or indicative, mood, *I was*); *he* because whenever a form of the verb *to be* is used (in this case, *were*), the pronouns on both sides of the verb must be subjects (the *I* is a subject, and the *he* is a predicate nominative); and *lay*, which means "to put or place," not *lie*, which means "to recline" (an error of diction). Therefore, the correct answer is (A).

> The contest judges were told to give the prize to whomever drew the best picture.
>
> **(A)** to give the prize to whomever drew the best picture.
>
> **(B)** to give the prize to whoever drew the best picture.
>
> **(C)** to give whomever drew the best picture the prize.
>
> **(D)** to give to whomever drew the best picture the prize.
>
> **(E)** to give the prize to whomever it was who drew the best picture.

In this sentence the preposition *to* (the second *to* of the sentence) has as its object the rest of the sentence, not merely the word *whomever*. The part of the sentence after the second *to* is a clause (a group of words containing a subject and a verb) which has *whomever* as its subject (*drew* is its verb, and *picture* is the object of *drew*). But *whomever* is an object; the correct word is *whoever*. That eliminates choices (A), (C), and (E). Choice (D) is awkwardly phrased because *the prize* does not immediately follow *give*. Therefore, choice (B) is correct. As a comparison, a sentence that uses *whomever* correctly (as the object of the verb *liked*) would be the following: ". . . to give the prize to whomever the audience liked best."

EVERY PRONOUN MUST REFER TO A NOUN OR TO ANOTHER PRONOUN.

The coal strike reduced Indiana's energy reserves, which caused unemployment among the workers.

- **(A)** which caused unemployment among the workers
- **(B)** which caused the workers to unemployed
- **(C)** a circumstance that resulted in unemployment
- **(D)** a fact that created unemployed workers
- **(E)** which led many workers to be unemployed

In this sentence, *which* has no other word in the sentence to which it can logically refer: neither the *reserves* nor the *strike* "caused unemployment," but rather the fact that the energy reserves were reduced caused unemployment. Therefore, choices (A), (B), and (E) are incorrect. Either *a circumstance* or *a fact* is correct. Since the reduction of energy reserves did not create workers (unemployed or otherwise), choice (C) is correct. The *circumstance* resulted in unemployment (and unemployment of workers is understood; the context implies that it is workers, and not some other group, who are unemployed). The general rule is that a pronoun in a sentence must unambiguously refer to some other noun or pronoun in the sentence. Otherwise, as here, another word (*circumstance*) must be supplied.

ALERT!

To correct the error, you usually need to read more than the underlined part. Many errors involve not just one word but different words or parts of the sentence. For example: Three members of the company's upper-level management was justifiably fired for incompetence. The verb was does not agree with the subject members.

In this article they imply that everybody who dislike this philosophy must still accept its principal tenet.

- **(A)** In this article they imply that everybody who dislike this philosophy must still accept its principal tenet.
- **(B)** The author of this article implies that everybody who dislikes this philosophy must still except its principal tenet.
- **(C)** The author of this article implies that everybody who dislikes this philosophy must still accept its principal tenet.
- **(D)** The author in this article implies that everybody who dislike this philosophy must still except its principle tenet.
- **(E)** The author implies that everybody who dislike this philosophy must still accept its principle tenet.

In this sentence, *they* has no reference, unambiguous or otherwise. Therefore, an appropriate change must be made, as in choices (B), (C), (D), or (E) ("The author"). Choices (A), (D), and (E) contain a second error, namely, *dislike* instead of *dislikes*, because *who* refers to *everybody*, and *everybody* is singular. Choices (B) and (D) contain diction errors (the use of *except* instead of *accept*), so those choices are incorrect. Choices (D) and (E) contain a second diction error, the use of *principle* instead of *principal*. Choice (C) is correct.

VERB TENSES MUST REFLECT THE SEQUENCE OF EVENTS.

When I opened the hood and saw smoke pouring from the engine, I realized that I forgot to add oil.

(A) realized that I forgot to add oil.

(B) had realized that I forgot to add oil.

(C) had realized that I forgotten to add oil.

(D) realized that I would forget to add oil.

(E) realized that I had forgotten to add oil.

Verb tenses must be in proper sequence. When two or more events have taken place, are taking place, or will take place at the same time, their tenses must be the same. If two events have taken place in the past but one event occurred prior to the other, the later of the two events must be in the past tense, and the earlier of the two must be in the past perfect tense (*had* plus the past tense of the verb). In this sentence, the "opening," the "seeing," and the "realizing" all took place in the past at the same time and therefore should all be in the (simple) past tense. So choices (B) and (C) (with *had realized*, which is the past perfect tense) are wrong. The "forgetting" also took place in the past but prior to the other three events and therefore should be in the past perfect tense (*had forgotten*). So choices (A), (B), and (D) are wrong. Only choice (E) contains the proper sequence of tenses.

If they would have paid attention, they would not have had to be told again.

(A) would have paid

(B) would pay

(C) had paid

(D) paid

(E) were to pay

This sentence provides another example of the proper sequence of tenses in a slightly different format. If the two events had actually occurred (neither event did occur), the "paying attention" would have occurred prior to the "having to be told again." Therefore, the earlier event must be in the past perfect tense (*had paid*). Only choice (C) has the correct form of the verb. The *if* clause is known as a condition contrary to fact (in fact, they did not pay attention).

ELLIPTICAL VERB PHRASES MUST BE CONSTRUCTED PROPERLY.

She is not and does not intend to run for political office.

(A) is not and does not intend to run

(B) is not running and does not intend to

(C) is not and will not run

(D) is not running and does not intend to run

(E) has not and does not run

NOTE

Should you read every answer choice?
No. Do not read choice (A) because it simply repeats the original underlined part. But do read (B), (C), (D), and (E) carefully before making a final choice.

This sentence contains an example of an ellipsis (the omission of a word or words from a sentence) in the omission of some form of *run* after the first *not.* In a construction like this one, the verb may properly be omitted only if it is in the same form as another appearance of the same verb. Since *running* is the omitted form and *run* is the form that appears later in the sentence, *running* must appear after the first *not.* Choice (B) corrects that error but omits *run* at the end of the underlined portion; therefore, choice (B) is wrong. Choices (C) and (E) do not correct the error of the original; furthermore, the meaning of the original is changed by the changing of tenses. Only choice (D) is correct.

A PRONOUN MODIFYING A GERUND MUST BE IN THE POSSESSIVE CASE.

He disapproves of you insisting that the rope of pearls were misplaced on purpose.

(A) He disapproves of you insisting that the rope of pearls were misplaced on purpose.

(B) He disapproves of you insisting that the rope of pearls were purposely misplaced.

(C) He disapproves of your insisting that the rope of pearls was purposely misplaced.

(D) He disapproves of you insisting that she misplaced the rope of pearls purposely.

(E) How could you insist she misplaced the rope of pearls on purpose?

In this sentence the object of the preposition *of* is *insisting*, not *you*. Therefore, *your*, not *you*, must be used since that word is acting as a modifier of *insisting* (which is a gerund or a verb form ending in *-ing* that acts as a noun). Choices (B) and (D) contain the same error. Additionally, choices (A) and (B) contain an error of agreement between the subject of a clause (*rope*) and its verb (*were misplaced*). The fact that the *rope* is *of pearls* (plural) does not make the subject grammatically plural. Choices (D) and (E) also change the meaning of the original (the reader does not know who misplaced the pearls). Either *on purpose*, choices (A) and (E), or *purposely*, choices (B), (C), and (D), may be used without affecting the grammar or meaning of the sentence. Only choice (C) contains no errors.

ADVERBS, NOT ADJECTIVES, MODIFY VERBS.

The car runs quieter when I add a more heavy transmission fluid.

(A) The car runs quieter when I add a more heavy transmission fluid.

(B) The car runs more quietly when I add a heavier transmission fluid.

(C) The car runs quieter when I add a more heavier transmission fluid.

(D) The car runs more quietly when I add a more heavy transmission fluid.

(E) The car runs quieter when I add a heavier transmission fluid.

The glaring grammatical error in this sentence is the use of *quieter* (the adjective form of *quiet*) instead of *more quietly*. *Quieter* (or *more quietly*) modifies *run* (a verb) and therefore should be in its adverb form (adverbs modify verbs, adjectives, or other adverbs) rather than its adjective form (adjectives modify nouns and pronouns). The other error in the original is the use of *more heavy* instead of *heavier*. In general the shorter adjectives form the comparative by adding *-er* and the superlative by adding *-est*. The longer adjectives and most adverbs form the comparative by the use of *more* (or *less*) and the superlative by the use of *most* (or *least*). Choices (C) and (E) do not correct the *quieter* error; additionally, in choice (C), *more heavier* is incorrect because it joins two comparative forms in one construction. Choice (D) does not correct the *more heavy* error. Therefore, choice (B) is correct.

Sizing Up Sentence Structure

COMPARISONS MUST BE PHRASED CORRECTLY.

John maintained that his scholastic record was better or at least as good as hers.

(A) was better or at least as good as hers

(B) at its least was as good as hers

(C) was as good or better than hers

(D) was better or at least as good as her scholastic record

(E) was better than or at least as good as hers

When two items are being compared and one is stated to be better than the others, the *than* in the comparison is essential. Likewise, when one item is stated to be as good as another, the second *as* is essential. Therefore, the correct construction in the sentence above should be "... better than or at least as good as hers" or "... at least as good as or better than hers" (either order is acceptable). Choices (A) and (D) omit *than*, and choice (C) omits the second *as*. Choice (B) changes the meaning of the sentence slightly and therefore is incorrect. In choice (D), it is unnecessary to replace *hers* (at the end of the sentence) with *her scholastic record*. Only choice (E) contains no errors.

TIP

Pay attention to elements of sentence structure. Do not think only in terms of grammar mistakes. Elements such as parallelism and logical structure are also very important.

COMPARISONS MUST BE LOGICAL.

A speaker's physical impact including gestures, facial expression and body carriage is as important as listening to the message.

(A) A speaker's physical impact including gestures, facial expression, and body carriage is

(B) A speaker's physical impact gestures, facial expression, and body carriage are

(C) The examination of a speaker's physical impact including gestures, facial expression, and body carriage is

(D) Examining a speaker's physical impact gestures, facial expression, and body carriage are

(E) Examining a speaker's physical impact including gestures, facial expression, and body carriage is

This question is relatively difficult. The sentence as it stands makes a comparison between *impact* and *listening*, which are neither grammatically nor conceptually parallel. Since *listening* is not underlined, the subject of the sentence, *impact,* must be changed so as to be parallel with *listening. Examination* comes close, but *Examining* is even closer to being parallel with *listening.* Thus the correct answer is either (D) or (E). Since the subject of the sentence is singular *impact* in (A) and (B), *examination* in (C), and *Examining* in choices (D) and (E), the verb must be singular (*is* instead of *are*) even though the subject seems to be plural ("gestures, facial expression, and body carriage" does not make the subject plural). Thus, choices (B) and (D) are incorrect. Furthermore, (B) and (D) are wrong because they eliminate *including* before *gestures* and therefore imply that "gestures, facial expression, and body carriage" are the only characteristics of a "speaker's physical impact," whereas *including* implies that there may be other characteristics. Therefore, choices (B) and (D) slightly change the meaning of the original underlined portion. Thus, only choice (E) is correct.

Your courage is as great as any other man in defending your country.

(A) as great as any other

(B) so great as any other

(C) great like any other

(D) as great as that of any other

(E) as that of any

A comparison is being made in this sentence between *Your courage* and *any other man.* But *courage* and *man* are not like classes of things. Since *courage* is not underlined, *any other man* must be altered to make the comparison logical. Only (D) corrects the error, by comparing *courage* to *that of any other man,* that is, to the courage of any other man. The correct construction could be either choice (D) or "as great as the courage of any other man" or "as great as any other man's courage" or "as great as any other man's" (where "courage" after "man's" would be understood).

SENTENCE PARTS MUST BE PARALLEL.

The stranger was affable, with good manners and has a keen wit.

(A) with good manners and has a keen wit
(B) with good manners and a keen wit
(C) well mannered and keen witted
(D) good manners as well as keen witted
(E) and has good manners as well as a keen wit

This sentence contains two illustrations of a lack of parallelism among grammatically equivalent elements of the sentence. *Affable,* an adjective, is used to describe the *stranger*. Therefore, the other two descriptions of the stranger must agree in form (that is, must be parallel) with *affable*. "With good manners" is a prepositional phrase and "has a keen wit" is the predicate portion of a clause; both must be changed into their adjective forms. Only choice (C) makes that correction.

To run for an important political office, to manage a large organization, and practicing law effectively all require organizational and problem solving skills.

(A) To run for an important political office, to manage a large organization, and practicing
(B) To run for an important political office and to manage a large organization, practicing
(C) Running for an important political office, managing a large organization and to practice
(D) To run and manage political offices and large organizations and practicing
(E) Running for an important office, managing a large organization, and practicing

This sentence, like the previous example, is a very straightforward example of lack of parallelism: Two infinitives (*to run* and *to manage*) are used along with a gerund (*practicing;* a gerund is a verb form that ends in *-ing* and functions as a noun). All three terms must be either infinitives or gerunds. Only choice (E) uniformly uses one construction or the other.

Edward not only resists learning to correlate new facts but also remembering old lessons.

(A) not only resists learning to correlate new facts but also remembering
(B) not only resists learning to correlate new facts but also to remember
(C) resists not only learning to correlate new facts but also remembering
(D) resists not only learning to correlate new facts but also to remember
(E) resists learning to correlate new facts and remembering

NOTE

Does every item contain a mistake?

No. For about one-fifth of the items, the original is correct.

The terms *not only* and *but also* (just like *neither* and *nor* and *either* and *or*) must introduce grammatically equivalent, and therefore parallel, sentence elements. In this sentence, *not only* introduces *resists* and *but also* introduces *remembering. Resists* is the verb of the sentence, and *remembering,* along with *learning,* is an object of *resists.* One way to correct this error would be "Edward not only resists learning . . . but also resists remembering. . . ." But the use of *resists* twice is unnecessarily wordy. A better way to correct the error is choice (C), the correct answer. Choice (B) compounds the error of the original underlined portion by using *to remember* instead of *remembering,* so that the new term is not parallel with *learning.* Choice (D) corrects the original error, but makes the same mistake as choice (B). Choice (E) slightly changes the meaning of the original sentence by eliminating the comparative emphasis between *learning* and *remembering.*

MODIFIERS MUST STAY CLOSE TO HOME.

By leading trump, the contract was defeated resoundingly by the defenders.

(A) By leading trump, the contract was defeated resoundingly by the defenders.

(B) By leading trump, the defenders defeated the contract resoundingly.

(C) The defenders resounded the defeat of the contract by leading trump.

(D) The contract, by leading trump, was defeated resoundingly by the defenders.

(E) Resoundingly, the contract was defeated by the defenders by leading trump.

An introductory modifier of a noun or pronoun, in this case the prepositional phrase "By leading trump," must modify the subject of the main clause, in this case "the contract." But clearly the *contract* did not lead trump; rather, the *defenders* led trump and "defeated the contract resoundingly." Therefore, the subject of the main clause must be *defenders,* if "By leading trump" is to remain the introductory modifier. The error here is known as a dangling, or misplaced, modifier. Choice (B) corrects the error and is the correct answer. Choice (C) changes the meaning of the original by stating that "The defenders resounded the defeat . . ." (D) and (E) still imply, grammatically, that the contract led trump. An additional point concerning the construction of these answer choices is that, as a matter of writing style (but not as a matter of grammar or usage), the active voice ("the defenders defeated the contract") is preferable to the passive voice ("the contract was defeated by the defenders").

In addition to those specified for professions, the corporations maintained endowments in purely academic fields, especially in the physical sciences.

- **(A)** the corporations maintained endowments in purely academic fields, especially in the physical sciences.
- **(B)** the corporations had maintained purely academic endowments like those of the physical sciences.
- **(C)** in purely academic fields, endowments, especially in the physical sciences, were maintained by the corporations.
- **(D)** the endowments were maintained in purely academic fields, especially in the physical sciences, by the corporations.
- **(E)** purely academic endowments, especially for those fields like the physical sciences, were maintained by the corporations.

Grammatically, this sentence states that *the corporations* are "In addition to those specified for professions," whereas it is the *endowments* that are "In addition to those specified for professions." One way to classify this error is to say that the nonunderlined portion of the sentence is a dangling, or misplaced, modifier because it grammatically modifies *the corporations* but logically should modify the *endowments.* Another way to classify the error is to say that the reference of the pronoun *those* is ambiguous because *those* grammatically refers to *corporations* (the general rule is that a pronoun should refer, whenever possible, to the noun or other pronoun closest to it in the sentence) but logically should refer to *endowments.* In either case, the subject of the main clause must be *endowments* rather than *corporations.* (C), (D), and (E) all use *endowments* as the subject of the main clause. In choice (C) the prepositional phrase modifiers "in purely academic fields" and "especially in the physical sciences" are misplaced so that the sentence is awkward and confusing. Choice (D) corrects the awkwardness of choice (C) and is therefore the correct answer. Choice (E) is more concise in its use of "purely academic endowments" rather than "endowments in purely academic fields," but changes the meaning of the original sentence; the endowments were maintained "especially in the physical sciences," not "especially for those fields like the physical sciences."

ALERT!

Know a sentence fragment when you see one. No matter how long or wordy a phrase may be, if it doesn't contain a subject and a verb, it's not a complete sentence.

SENTENCE FRAGMENTS DON'T CUT IT.

The lovestruck boy was sad because the girl who he loved and who had left him for another.

- **(A)** the girl who he loved and who had left him for another
- **(B)** the girl whom he loved and whom had left him for another
- **(C)** the girl whom he loved and who had left him for
- **(D)** the girl whom he loved had left him for another
- **(E)** the girl who he loved had left him for another

The underlined portion of this sentence is a fragment because it contains a subject (*girl*) but no verb to act as a predicate for the subject (the two clauses that begin with *who* act as modifiers of *girl*). Removing *and who* after *loved* will correct this error, as in choices (D) and (E); *had left* then becomes the verb that acts as the predicate for *girl*. Another error in the original underlined portion is the first *who*, which is in the form of a subject but which should be in the form of an object (*whom*) since it acts as the object of *loved* (*he* is the subject of *loved*). The second *who* is correct since it is the subject of *had left* (*him* is the object). Therefore, choice (D) is correct.

RUN-ON SENTENCES DON'T MAKE IT.

Initially Bob was the group's spokesperson, <u>afterwards it occurred to them that</u> Jane was more articulate and more diplomatic.

(A) afterwards it occurred to them that

(B) that wasn't the best thing to do since

(C) but they came to realize that

(D) they concluded, however, that

(E) then they decided that

This sentence is an example of a run-on sentence, that is, a sentence containing two independent clauses that are not properly joined. The portion of this sentence before the comma is an independent clause (which means a clause that can act as a sentence all by itself), and the portion of the sentence after the comma is also an independent clause. A comma by itself is not sufficient to separate two independent clauses; rather, a coordinating conjunction like *and, but, yet, for, or,* or *nor* must be used between the comma and the second independent clause. Only choice (C) provides such a conjunction at the beginning of the second clause. Since "they came to realize" has virtually the same meaning as "it occurred to them," choice (C) is the correct answer. The main consideration here is that choices (A), (B), (D), and (E) are run-on sentences.

SUBORDINATE CLAUSES MUST HAVE A LOGICAL CONNECTION.

The Beatles were to be honored <u>on account they bolstered</u> the sagging British economy.

(A) on account they bolstered

(B) being that they bolstered

(C) when they bolstered

(D) the reason being on account of their bolstering

(E) since they bolstered

The underlined portion of this sentence is a subordinate (or dependent) clause, that is, one that cannot stand by itself as a complete sentence but which must be joined to an independent or other dependent clause by a subordinate conjunction. Both (C) and (E) introduce the clause by a subordinate conjunction (*when* and *since*). Since the relationship between the two clauses of the sentence is one of cause and effect, *since* is a better word than *when. On account,* if used at all, should be in the form *on account of;* furthermore, since *of* is a preposition, it must take an object, for example, "their bolstering of the sagging British economy." *Being that* is not acceptable in Standard Written English as a substitute for *since* or *because.* Choice (D) is redundant (*the reason being* and *on account of* say the same thing). Therefore, choice (E) is correct.

BECAUSE IS NO WAY TO START A NOUN CLAUSE.

Because he agrees with you does not signify that his reasons are the same as yours.

(A) Because he agrees with you

(B) If he agrees with you

(C) When he agrees with you

(D) Because you and he agree

(E) That he agrees with you

The underlined portion of the sentence acts as the subject of the sentence, that is, the underlined portion "does not signify . . .." The correct answer is choice (E) because *That* is short for *The fact that,* and *fact* is the true subject of the sentence. The omission of *The fact* from choice (E) is another example of an ellipsis (the omission of a word or words from a sentence). None of the other choices can act as the subject of the sentence.

ALERT!

Do not trap yourself by making a needless change. Do not make a change unless you have a good reason for it. Remember that about one-fifth of the originals are correct.

Choosing the Right Word

FAULTY DICTION IS OFTEN THE PROBLEM.

The prisoner was expedited from California to Florida.

(A) The prisoner was expedited from California to Florida.

(B) From California to Florida, the prisoner was expedited.

(C) The prisoner from California was extradited to Florida.

(D) The prisoner was extradited from California to Florida.

(E) From California, the prisoner was expedited to Florida.

In this example, *expedited* (meaning "speeded up, hastened, or accomplished promptly") is used incorrectly; therefore, answer choices (A), (B), and (E) should be eliminated. The proper word to use in this context is *extradited* (meaning "surrendered by one state or authority to another"), which appears in choices (C) and (D). The meaning of the original is changed in (C): "The prisoner from California" seems to mean that the prisoner is a person from the state of California, not necessarily that the state of California is extraditing the prisoner. The error in choice (C) is an example of a misplaced modifier (in this instance, the prepositional phrase "from California"). Therefore, choice (D) is correct.

WORDY ANSWER CHOICES ARE NO SOLUTION.

If one begins to smoke at an early age, it is likely that he will go on smoking further.

(A) it is likely that he will go on smoking further

(B) he will probably keep smoking more and more

(C) it is hard to stop him from smoking more

(D) he is likely to continue smoking

(E) he will have a tendency to continue smoking

This example illustrates an unnecessarily wordy original sentence. In shortening a wordy expression, you need to make sure that the meaning of the original is preserved. Choice (C) changes the meaning of the original and therefore should be eliminated. Choice (E) changes the meaning slightly but is a possibility. Choices (A) and (B) are quite wordy in comparison with the correct answer, choice (D). Choice (D) expresses the meaning of the original clearly and concisely. None of the answer choices in this question contains any grammatical mistakes, which is rare. Also, you should not blindly choose the shortest answer choice.

ALERT!

Pompous prose poses pitfalls. Do not select an answer choice just because it sounds "important." A complex rendering may be incorrect for the very reason that it is not the most direct way of expressing the idea.

After being in school for sixteen years, Jack couldn't wait to get out to get a job.

(A) Jack couldn't wait to get out to get a job

(B) there was great desire in Jack to get out and get a job

(C) Jack was eager to get a job

(D) Jack wanted out and a job badly

(E) Jack arranged to look for a job

This example illustrates a lack of brevity of expression. Choice (C) expresses the idea of the underlined portion clearly and concisely. In choice (D) *out* used without *to get* is poor diction. Choice (E) changes the meaning of the original by using "arranged to look" (the reader of the sentence does not know what steps, if any, Jack has taken in pursuit of a job). Both choices (A) and (B) are wordy.

The scholar's reluctance over committing himself as to judging the authenticity of the manuscript may be caused as a result of his uncertainty of its recent history.

(A) over committing himself as to judging the authenticity of the manuscript may be caused as a result of

(B) to judge the authenticity of the manuscript may be caused as a result of

(C) to judge the authenticity of the manuscript may be a result of

(D) over committing himself as to judgment of the authenticity of the manuscript may be caused by

(E) over committing himself as to judging of the authenticity of the manuscript may be a result of

The underlined portion of this sentence uses too many words to express two ideas and also uses poor diction. "Over committing himself as to judging" should be either "to commit himself to judge" ("reluctance over committing" uses poor diction; *reluctance* in this context should be followed by an infinitive) or merely *to judge*, which is even better. "Caused as a result of" is redundant: his reluctance either "is caused by his uncertainty" or "is a result of his uncertainty," not both. Therefore, the correct answer is (C).

Focusing Your Attention

READING CHOICE (A) IS A TIME-WASTER.

Choice (A) always repeats the original sentence, so there is no point in reading it.

SOME SENTENCES CONTAIN MULTIPLE ERRORS.

The underlined portion of some sentences contains more than one error. The correct answer choice must correct all of the errors in the underlined part of the original sentence.

YOU WON'T FIND ERRORS IN SPELLING OR CAPITALIZATION.

Sentence correction items test correct (grammatical and logical) and effective (clear, concise, and idiomatic) expression. They do not test spelling or capitalization.

EXERCISE 1: SENTENCE CORRECTION

30 Questions • 38 Minutes

Directions: In each problem below, either part or all of the sentence is underlined. The sentence is followed by five ways of writing the underlined part. Choice (A) repeats the original; the other answer choices vary. If you think that the original phrasing is the best, choose (A). If you think one of the other answer choices is the best, select that choice.

This section tests the ability to recognize correct and effective expression. Follow the requirements of Standard Written English: grammar, choice of words, and sentence construction. Choose the answer that results in the clearest, most exact sentence, but do not change the meaning of the original sentence.

Example:

Q The possibility of massive earthquakes <u>are regarded by most area residents with</u> a mixture of skepticism and caution.

(A) are regarded by most area residents with

(B) is regarded by most area residents with

(C) is regarded by most area residents as

(D) is mostly regarded by area residents with

(E) by most area residents is regarded with

A **The correct answer is (B).**

1. A career in the medical profession, <u>which requires an enormous investment of time and money, do not guarantee success as there is so much competition.</u>

(A) which requires an enormous investment of time and money, do not guarantee success as there is so much competition.

(B) which requires an enormous investment of time and money, does not guarantee success since there is so much competition.

(C) requiring an enormous investment of time and money, without guarantee because there is so much competition.

(D) requires an enormous investment of time and money, and it cannot guarantee success because there is so much competition.

(E) requires that an enormous investment of time and money be made and success cannot be guaranteed due to the competition.

2. It was believed that a thorough knowledge of Latin would not only enable students to read the classics, also enabling them to think clearly and precisely.

(A) It was believed that a thorough knowledge of Latin would not only enable students to read the classics, also enabling them to think clearly and precisely.

(B) It had been believed that a thorough knowledge of Latin would not only enable students to read the classics but rather enable them to think clearly and precisely.

(C) It was believed that a thorough knowledge of Latin would not only enable students to read the classics but also enabling them to think clearly and precisely.

(D) It used to be believed that a thorough knowledge of Latin would enable a student to be able to read the classics but also enable them to think clearly and precisely.

(E) It was believed that a thorough knowledge of Latin would enable students not only to read the classics, but also to think clearly and precisely.

3. Most adolescents struggle to be free both of parental domination but also from peer pressure.

(A) both of parental domination but also from peer pressure.

(B) both of parental domination and also from peer pressure.

(C) both of parental domination and also of peer pressure.

(D) both of parental domination and of peer pressure as well.

(E) of parental domination and their peer pressure as well.

4. The president of the block association tried to convince her neighbors they should join forces to prevent crime in the neighborhood rather than continuing to be victimized.

(A) they should join forces to prevent crime in the neighborhood rather than continuing to be victimized.

(B) that they should join forces to prevent crime in the neighborhood rather than continue to be victimized.

(C) about joining forces to prevent crime in the neighborhood instead of continuing to be victimized.

(D) for the joining of forces to prevent crime in the neighborhood rather than continue to be victimized.

(E) to join forces to prevent crime in the neighborhood rather than continuing to be victimized.

5. Although he is as gifted as, if not more gifted than many of his colleagues, he is extremely modest and his poetry is unpublished.

(A) Although he is as gifted as, if not more gifted than many of his colleagues, he is extremely modest and his poetry is unpublished.

(B) Although he is as gifted, if not more gifted, than many of his colleagues, he is extremely modest with his poetry remaining unpublished.

(C) Although he is as gifted as, if not more gifted than, many of his colleagues, he is extremely modest and will not publish his poetry.

(D) Despite his being gifted, if not more gifted than his colleagues, he is extremely modest and will not publish his poetry.

(E) Being as gifted as, or more gifted than, many of his colleagues, he is extremely modest and his poetry is unpublished.

exercises

6. Although the manager agreed to a more flexible work schedule, he said that it must be posted on the bulletin board so that both management and labor will know what everyone is assigned to do.

   (A) he said that it must be posted on the bulletin board so that both management and labor will know what everyone is

   (B) he said it had to be posted on the bulletin board so that both management and labor knows what everyone is

   (C) he said that they would have to post the assignments on the bulletin board so that management and labor knew what everyone was

   (D) he said that the schedule would have to be posted on the bulletin board so that both management and labor would know what everyone was

   (E) saying that the schedule had to be posted on the bulletin board so that both management and labor would know what everyone had been

7. With just several quick strokes of the pen, the monkeys were drawn by the artist, capturing their antics.

   (A) the monkeys were drawn by the artist, capturing their antics.

   (B) the artist sketched the monkeys, capturing their antics.

   (C) the artist captured the antics of the monkeys, sketching them.

   (D) the artist sketched the monkeys and also capturing their antics.

   (E) the monkeys and their antics were sketched by the artist.

8. Primarily accomplished through the use of the electron microscope, researchers have recently vastly increased their knowledge of the process of cell division.

   (A) Primarily accomplished through the use of the electron microscope,

   (B) Through the competent use of advanced electron microscopy,

   (C) Primarily through the use of electron microscopy,

   (D) In a large sense through the use of the electron microscope,

   (E) In the main, particularly through the use of electron microscopes,

9. Though garlic is often associated with Italian cuisine, it is actually the use of oregano which most distinguishes the Italians from the French.

   (A) which most distinguishes the Italians from the French

   (B) which primarily distinguishes Italians from Frenchmen

   (C) which generally serves to distinguish an Italian sauce from a French one

   (D) which is the major distinction between the two great cuisines

   (E) which most distinguishes Italian cookery from French

10. While controversy rages over whether the sign language taught to some great apes is truly human-like speech, there is no similar dispute that our powers of communication are greater by far than that of any other animal.

   (A) are greater by far than that of any other animal

   (B) are far greater than that of any other animal

   (C) are greater by far than any other animal

   (D) are far greater than those of any other animal

   (E) have been far greater than those of other animals

11. Despite the money that has been invested by industry in the attempt to persuade Americans that highly processed foods are the best foods, the populace stubbornly clings to the belief that such foods <u>are neither particularly healthy or tasty.</u>

(A) are neither particularly healthy or tasty

(B) are neither particularly healthful nor tasty

(C) are not particularly health or tasty

(D) are not particularly healthful or tasteful

(E) are not very healthy nor tasty

12. <u>While it is certainly true that almost all literate citizens could be taught to improve their ability to read and reason, it must first be demonstrated that such an undertaking would increase the general welfare.</u>

(A) While it is certainly true that almost all literate citizens could be taught to improve their ability to read and reason, it must first be demonstrated that such an undertaking would increase the general welfare.

(B) While it is certainly true that almost all literate citizens could improve their reading and reasoning skills, such a vast undertaking requires a clear demonstration of benefit before being undertaken.

(C) Before undertaking to improve the reading and reasoning of almost all citizens, it is necessary to show that the project will work.

(D) Before the project of improving almost all citizens' reading and reasoning skills is undertaken, that the outcome will be increased happiness must be demonstrated.

(E) Prior to the improvement of citizens' reading and reasoning skills, it must be shown that they will be happier with the improved skills than they are now.

13. The closing of small, inexpensive hospitals while large expensive hospitals remain open <u>seems a luxury that we can no longer afford in order to maintain them</u>.

(A) seems a luxury that we can no longer afford in order to maintain them

(B) seems to emphasize luxury over economy, which we can no longer afford

(C) seems to be a waste of valuable resources

(D) seems a luxury we can no longer afford

(E) seems too luxurious to be any longer affordable

14. The ancient question of the exact difference between plants and animals, which was so complicated with the discovery of microscopic members of both groups, was somewhat side-stepped with the establishment of a third phylum, the Protista, <u>reserved just for them</u>.

(A) reserved just for them

(B) consisting only of them

(C) inhabited only by them

(D) which includes all microscopic life

(E) which would have included all microscopic plants and animals

exercises

15. The Lake Manyara Park in Tanzania affords the visitor with unequaled opportunities to photograph lions playing in trees without the aid of telephoto lenses.

(A) The Lake Manyara Park in Tanzania affords the visitor with unequaled opportunities to photograph lions playing in trees without the aid of telephoto lenses.

(B) The Lake Manyara Park in Tanzania permits the visitor unequaled opportunities to photograph lions playing in trees without the aid of telephoto lenses.

(C) The Lake Manyara Park in Tanzania gives the visitor the unequaled opportunity to photograph lions playing in trees without telephoto lenses.

(D) The visitor to the Lake Manyara Park in Tanzania has the unequaled opportunity to photograph lions playing in trees without the aid of telephoto lenses.

(E) Even without the aid of telephoto lenses, the visitor to Tanzania's Lake Manyara Park has an unequaled opportunity to photograph lions playing in trees.

16. In the Renaissance, painters were so impressed with da Vinci that they ignored their own training and designate as a masterpiece anything he painted.

(A) were so impressed with da Vinci that they ignored

(B) were impressed with da Vinci to such an extent that they were to ignore

(C) were so impressed with da Vinci as to ignore

(D) were so impressed with da Vinci that they had to ignore

(E) were as impressed with da Vinci as to ignore

17. Most members of the trade union rejected the mayor's demand that they return to work.

(A) that they return to work.

(B) that the members return to work.

(C) for them to return to work.

(D) that they would return to work.

(E) that they ought to return to work.

18. The players were often punished by the referee's lack of alertness who penalized all those who were involved in fighting, regardless of who had instigated it.

(A) The players were often punished by the referee's lack of alertness who penalized

(B) The referee's lack of alertness often caused him to penalize

(C) The players were punished by the lack of alertness of the referee who penalized often

(D) Lacking alertness, the referee's choice was to penalize often

(E) His lack of alertness to brutality often caused the referee to penalize

19. The New York City Police Department was not only responsible for the maintenance of order in the metropolitan area but also for rebuilding the bonds among the various ethnic groups.

(A) not only responsible for the maintenance of order in the metropolitan area but also for rebuilding the bonds

(B) responsible not only for maintaining order in the metropolitan area but also for rebuilding the bonds

(C) responsible not only for the maintenance of order in the metropolitan area and also for rebuilding

(D) responsible not only for the maintenance of order in the metropolitan area and also for the rebuilding of bonds

(E) not only responsible for maintaining order in the metropolitan area but also for rebuilding the bonds

20. In comparison with the literature created by the ancient Greeks, today's Greeks have written nothing worth describing.
    - **(A)** In comparison with the literature created by the ancient Greeks, today's Greeks have written nothing worth describing.
    - **(B)** In comparison with the literature created by the ancient Greeks, the literature of today's Greeks are containing nothing worth describing.
    - **(C)** Compared to that of the ancient Greeks, today's Greeks have written nothing worth describing.
    - **(D)** Compared to that of the ancient Greeks, the literature of today's Greeks is not worth describing.
    - **(E)** Compared to the ancient Greek's literature, today's Greeks have written nothing worth describing.

21. Steve, along with his oldest brothers, are going to make a large real estate investment.
    - **(A)** Steve, along with his oldest brothers, are
    - **(B)** Steve, along with his oldest brothers, is
    - **(C)** Steve, in addition to his oldest brothers, are
    - **(D)** Steve, as well as his oldest brothers, are
    - **(E)** Steve and his oldest brothers is

22. During the war, when it looked as if the German army was going to cross into France, English mercenaries joined the French to resist the assault.
    - **(A)** it looked as if the German army was going to cross
    - **(B)** it looked like the German army was going to cross
    - **(C)** it looked like the German army would have crossed
    - **(D)** appearances were that the German army would be crossing
    - **(E)** it appeared that the German army would cross

23. In stating the argument that the President does not care about the plight of the poor, a prominent Democrat inferred that Republicans have never been concerned about them.
    - **(A)** a prominent Democrat inferred that Republicans have never been concerned about them.
    - **(B)** a prominent Democrat inferred that Republicans have never been concerned about the poor.
    - **(C)** a prominent Democrat implied that Republicans have never been concerned about them.
    - **(D)** a prominent Democrat inferred that Republicans have never been concerned about it.
    - **(E)** a prominent Democrat implied that Republicans have never been concerned about it.

24. Many travelers state unequivocally that the streets in Paris are more beautiful than any other city.
    - **(A)** that the streets in Paris are more beautiful than any other city.
    - **(B)** that the streets in Paris are more beautiful than those in any other city.
    - **(C)** that Parisian streets are more beautiful than in any other city.
    - **(D)** that, unlike any other city, Parisian streets are more beautiful.
    - **(E)** that the streets of Paris are more beautiful than the streets in any other city.

25. The mayor's media advisor, together with his three top aides, are traveling with him on a tour of European capital cities.

(A) media advisor, together with his three top aides, are

(B) media advisor, also his three top aides, are

(C) media advisor, as well as his three top aides, is

(D) media advisor, along with his three top aides, are

(E) media advisor, all in the company of his three top aides, is

26. Lawyers and doctors alike both agree that something should be done about the rise in medical malpractice suits which are on the increase.

(A) alike both agree that something should be done about the rise in medical malpractice suits which are on the increase.

(B) alike agree that something should be done about the rise in medical malpractice suits.

(C) both agree that something should be done about the increasing rise in medical malpractice suits.

(D) agree that something should be done about the rise in medical malpractice suits, which are increasing.

(E) agree that something should be done about the rise in the number of medical malpractice suits.

27. The obviously bitter actress stated that had the director known what he was doing, the play would have run for more than one night.

(A) had the director known what he was doing, the play would have run

(B) if the director would have known what he was doing, the play would have run

(C) if the director had known what he was doing, they would run

(D) had the director known what he was doing, they would run

(E) if the director knew what he was doing, they would have run

28. Dr. Smith's findings that emotions affect blood pressure are different from those published by his colleague, Dr. Loeb.

(A) affect blood pressure are different from those

(B) effect blood pressure are different from those

(C) effect blood pressure are different than those

(D) affect blood pressure are different than those

(E) affect blood pressure are different from that

29. Entering professional tennis as a talented but shy and awkward teenager, for the past eight years Steffi Graf was the dominant force on the woman's circuit, a powerful and consistent player.

(A) Entering professional tennis as a talented but shy and awkward teenager, for the past eight years Steffi Graf was

(B) A talented yet shy and awkward teenager when she entered professional tennis, for the last eight years Steffi Graf has been

(C) Steffi Graf entered professional tennis as a talented yet shy and awkward teenager, and was

(D) For the past eight years, having entered professional tennis as a talented yet shy and awkward teenager, Steffi Graf has been

(E) Having entered professional tennis as a teenager who was talented yet shy and awkward, for the past eight years Steffi Graf has been

30. The jurors agreed that of all the reasons the defense attorney gave for finding his client not guilty, the last two of them were the most absurd.

(A) the last two of them were the most absurd.

(B) the latter two were the most absurd.

(C) the last two of these were the most absurd.

(D) the last two of them were the absurdest.

(E) the last two were the most absurd.

exercises

EXERCISE 2: SENTENCE CORRECTION

15 Questions • 18 Minutes

Directions: In each problem below, either part or all of the sentence is underlined. The sentence is followed by five ways of writing the underlined part. Choice (A) repeats the original; the other answer choices vary. If you think that the original phrasing is the best, choose (A). If you think one of the other answer choices is the best, select that choice.

This section tests the ability to recognize correct and effective expression. Follow the requirements of Standard Written English: grammar, choice of words, and sentence construction. Choose the answer that results in the clearest, most exact sentence, but do not change the meaning of the original sentence.

Example:

Q The possibility of massive earthquakes are regarded by most area residents with a mixture of skepticism and caution.

(A) are regarded by most area residents with

(B) is regarded by most area residents with

(C) is regarded by most area residents as

(D) is mostly regarded by area residents with

(E) by most area residents is regarded with

A The correct answer is (B).

1. The court order's requirement that each transit worker return to work was generally ignored.

(A) that each transit worker return to work

(B) that each transit worker would return to work

(C) that each transit worker should return to work

(D) for each transit worker to return to work

(E) that each transit worker returns to work

2. Having been ordered by the judge to resume alimony payments, Ms. Jones was still not required by it to see her children on weekends.

(A) was still not required by it

(B) still had not been required by it

(C) still was not to be required

(D) was still not required

(E) was not sufficiently required

exercises

3. The police officers throughout the department were so distrustful of the new commissioner that they refused to carry out his orders.

(A) were so distrustful of the new commissioner that they refused

(B) was so distrustful of the new commissioner that they refused

(C) were distrustful of the new commissioner to such an extent that they were to refuse

(D) were so distrustful of the new commissioner that they had to refuse

(E) were as distrustful of the new commissioner that they refused

4. To consider a diagnosis on the basis of inadequate or misleading evidence is neglecting years of specialized medical training.

(A) To consider a diagnosis on the basis of inadequate or misleading evidence is neglecting

(B) To consider a diagnosis on the basis of inadequate or misleading evidence is to neglect

(C) In considering a diagnosis on the basis of inadequate or misleading evidence is neglecting

(D) Considering a diagnosis on the basis of inadequate or misleading evidence is to neglect

(E) Considering a diagnosis on the basis of inadequate or misleading evidence amounts to neglecting

5. Twenty years ago, on my graduation from law school, I would have liked to have had the chance to join the partnership, but the substantial investment required would have made such a move impossible.

(A) I would have liked to have had the chance

(B) I would like to have the chance

(C) I like to have the chance

(D) I will like to have had the chance

(E) I would like to have had the chance

6. The recent discovery of Tutankhamen's tomb by Egyptologists has provided information that suggests that the wealth accumulated by ancient Egyptian pharaohs was greater than believed.

(A) believed.

(B) is believed.

(C) was believed before.

(D) they have believed before.

(E) had been believed.

7. The accident victim was very grateful to the hospital that had saved his life, but viewed his insurance company with suspicion out of fear that it will refuse to pay his claim and very expensive medical bills.

(A) out of fear that it will refuse

(B) in fear that it will refuse

(C) out of fear that it would refuse

(D) out of fear that it is refusing

(E) out of fear that they will refuse

8. A panel from the World Health Organization concluded that malnutrition is the most serious health problem facing the third world countries, but it could or will be eradicated with the assistance of developed countries.

(A) but it could or will

(B) but they could or will

(C) but that it would be or could

(D) but that it can and will

(E) but it would and should

9. Having discovered the Roman aristocrats to be suffering from lead poisoning, it is now thought that this was a major cause of their inability to reproduce.

   (A) Having discovered the Roman aristocrats to be suffering from lead poisoning,

   (B) To have discovered the Roman aristocrats to be suffering from lead poisoning,

   (C) Since scientists have discovered that the Roman aristocrats suffered from lead poisoning,

   (D) Since the suffering of lead poisoning by Roman aristocrats was discovered by scientists,

   (E) Due to the fact Roman aristocrats were suffering from lead poisoning was discovered by scientists,

10. Henry Wadsworth Longfellow was a professor of Modern Languages at Harvard, at the same time also one of America's greatest poets.

    (A) Harvard, at the same time also one of America's greatest poets.

    (B) Harvard, and at the same time was also one of America's greatest poets.

    (C) Harvard, at the same time as he was one of America's greatest poets.

    (D) Harvard, at the same time that he had been one of America's greatest poets.

    (E) Harvard, being one of America's greatest poets at the same time.

11. Despite her harsh criticism of the competition, the actress was at the ceremony to accept her award.

    (A) Despite her harsh criticism of the competition,

    (B) Always harshly criticizing such competitions,

    (C) Any competition was criticized, yet

    (D) Saying that all competitions should be harshly criticized,

    (E) In spite of criticizing all such competitions,

12. While many citizens feel powerless to influence national policy, it is actually effective to write to a Congressperson with an opinion.

    (A) it is actually effective to write to a Congressperson with an opinion.

    (B) writing to your Congressperson with your opinion is actually effective.

    (C) to write to a Congressperson with an opinion is effective.

    (D) that writing your opinion to your Congressperson is effective.

    (E) the writing of an opinion to a Congressperson may be effective.

13. In light of the increasing evidence of the complexity of the body's immune system, they now realize that their approach to finding a cure for cancer has been too simplistic.

    (A) they now realize that their approach to finding a cure for cancer has been too simplistic.

    (B) scientists now realize that their approach to finding a cure for cancer has been too simplistic.

    (C) it is now realized that the approach at curing cancer was too simplistic in their approach.

    (D) approaches by them at curing cancer have been too simplistic.

    (E) they now realize that their approaches to curing cancer has been too simplistic.

14. It is characteristic of the Metropolitan Opera, as of every major international company, that the casting is based more on the availability of singers as it is on the tastes of the music director and the public.

(A) as of every major international company, that the casting is based more on the availability of singers as it is

(B) as it is of every major international company, that the casting is based more on the availability of singers than it is

(C) as it is of every major international company, that the casting had been based more on the availability of singers as

(D) as about every major international company, that casting is based more on the availability of singers than it was

(E) as it is of every major international company, where the casting is based more on the availability of singers than it is

15. Although all dogs are descended from the wolf and the jackal, the various breeds of dog are so different from one another that it hardly seems possible that they had a common ancestry.

(A) are so different from one another that it hardly seems possible that they had a common ancestry.

(B) are so different from each other that it hardly seems possible that they have a common ancestry.

(C) are so different, one from another, that their having a common ancestor hardly seems possible.

(D) being so different from one another makes it hard to believe that they had a common ancestry.

(E) that having a common ancestry hardly seem possible in that they are so different from one another.

exercises

Exercise 1: ANSWER KEY AND EXPLANATIONS

1. B	7. B	13. D	19. B	25. C
2. E	8. C	14. D	20. D	26. E
3. D	9. E	15. E	21. B	27. A
4. B	10. D	16. C	22. E	28. A
5. C	11. B	17. A	23. E	29. D
6. A	12. A	18. B	24. B	30. E

1. **The correct answer is (B).** The original sentence is incorrect because the subject and verb do not agree. Further, it is incorrect to use "as" to mean "because." (C) is incorrect because the resulting sentence lacks a main verb. (D) is incorrect because the "it" has no antecedent. (E) is not technically wrong, but it is too wordy.

2. **The correct answer is (E).** The correct construction for this sentence is "not only *x* but *y*." (B) introduces an incorrect verb tense, "it had been believed," and a construction, "not *x* but rather *y*," which is incorrect. (C) uses the proper construction but fails to make the verbs parallel. (D) is illogical because there is no reason for the "but" since there is no comparison made.

3. **The correct answer is (D).** The phrase "but also" implies a contrast between two ideas, but no such contrast is supported by the original. (D), by using the simple conjunction "and," makes it clear that the two ideas are parallel. The other choices include a superfluous "also."

4. **The correct answer is (B).** The original sentence commits the error of faulty parallelism. The "this rather than that" construction requires two elements of the same form: "join rather than continue." (D) and (E) fail on the grounds of parallelism. As for (C), the phrase "convince about" is not idiomatic English.

5. **The correct answer is (C).** The first part of the original sentence (from "although" to "colleagues") is correct. The comparison is logical and properly completed. So (B), (D), and (E), which make changes in that part of the original, are incorrect. The second part of the original, however, contains a logical error. The "and" fails to specify the nature of the connection between the person's modesty and the fact that the poetry is unpublished. (C) correctly supplies the connection.

6. **The correct answer is (A).** The original sentence contains no error. (B) makes two errors. First, in changing the present tense "must" to "had," it introduces an error of logic. The requirement of posting is ongoing, not contained in the past. Second, the verb "knows" does not agree with the plural subject "both management and labor." (C) is incorrect because the verb "knew" does not correctly reflect the fact that the requirement of posting is an ongoing one. (D) and (E) are both incorrect because the use of the verb "would" implies a condition that is not mentioned or suggested by the sentence.

7. **The correct answer is (B).** The original sentence contains a misplaced modifier. As a rule, a modifier should be placed as close to the element modified as possible. (B), therefore, is better than the original. (C), (D), and (E) all make un-

needed changes and result in awkward sentences.

8. **The correct answer is (C).** The element of the sentence following the introductory descriptor or modifier must apply to the first noun after the comma. The researchers were not "primarily accomplished" through the use of electron microscopes, so (A) is out. Though (B)'s idea of competence is not unacceptable, (B) drops the idea of the primacy of the electron microscope in the work, which is wrong. (D) and (E) use locutions that are either meaningless or wordy. (C) keeps everything in order.

9. **The correct answer is (E).** The first part of the sentence speaks of the cuisine, so we do not want to shift suddenly to the peoples themselves as the original does. (B) fails for the same reason. (C) limits itself to sauces, which is unfounded. (D) fails to mention the French cuisine, which is in error. Thus (E) is correct, because then the word "cookery" can be carried forward in the reader's mind to yield French cookery being compared to Italian cookery.

10. **The correct answer is (D).** The original errs in its use of "that," which is singular, while "powers," for which it stands, is plural. This eliminates (A) and (B). (C) fails because it is comparing our powers of communication with other animals, rather than with the powers of communication of the other animals. (E) is inferior to (D) because it changes the tense to "have been" without cause. (D)'s change to "far greater," while not strictly necessary, does leave the meaning intact and even improves the sentence.

11. **The correct answer is (B).** "Healthy" refers to the state of health of some organism. "Healthful" is the proper way to describe something that promotes health. "Tasty" refers to the quality of having a good taste when eaten. "Tasteful" refers to being in accord with good aesthetic taste, or having such taste. In addition, the original erred in having "neither . . . or," when "neither . . . nor" is required. Only (B) conveys the intended meaning of the original.

12. **The correct answer is (A).** The original, while not a wonderful sentence, is not wrong. (B) omits the standard of judging benefit (general welfare). (C) leaves aside all consideration of benefit and focuses only on the feasibility of the project. (D) is perhaps second best, though a little convoluted. However, it omits the certainty that the project could be accomplished. (E) incorrectly refers to the happiness of the individuals, while the original referred to the general welfare, which might not be the same thing at all.

13. **The correct answer is (D).** The part of the sentence after "in" is surplus. (D) correctly dispenses with that part and preserves the rest.

14. **The correct answer is (D).** The "them" is unclear, eliminating (A), (B), and (C). (D)'s use of the present tense is acceptable since the classification presumably still does what it was set up to do. (E)'s use of the "would" construction is not acceptable since there is no doubt about what is included.

15. **The correct answer is (E).** The original sentence has the lions playing with lenses while in the trees. This is clearly unacceptable. Only (E) corrects the situation to make it clear that the visitor is the one concerned with telephoto lenses, not the lions.

16. **The correct answer is (C).** (A) and (D) express simple result ("so impressed . . . that"), but (C) adds the sense of *to such an extent* ("so impressed . . . as to.") That this sense is the one intended is shown in the original by the second result "designate," which is in the infinitive form; the two results together then should be "so

impressed . . . as to ignore . . . and designate. . . . " (B) takes more wordage than (C) to stress "to such an extent that," and "were to ignore" changes the time sense. (E) is not idiomatic.

17. **The correct answer is (A).** (A) is correct because the way to specify a "demand" that someone do something is in a "that" clause using the present subjunctive (*do* "return"). (C) weakens the effect by confusing "demand that" with "demand for." (D) and (E) make incorrect use of the auxiliary verbs "would" and "ought." With "ought" (E) even changes the meaning. (B) needlessly repeats "the members" instead of using the pronoun "they."

18. **The correct answer is (B).** The original confuses two sources of punishment, the "referee's lack" and the referee himself, resulting in awkward use of "who" and needless use of both "punished" and "penalized." (C) better manages to link "referee" and "who," but it still requires both "punished" and "penalized." (D) and (E) change the meaning, (D) by implying that the referee is conscious of his "lack," (E) by adding "brutality."

19. **The correct answer is (B).** (A) and (E) suffer from faulty parallelism. When two or more phrases/clauses branch off from the same word, that word should come first and they should be in parallel structure ("responsible not only for . . . but also for . . . "). (C) and (D) have the right word order but a wrong word—the idiom is "not only . . . but also," and (C) changes the meaning. Furthermore, (A), (C), and (D) are wordy, using "the maintenance of order" when "maintaining order" will do.

20. **The correct answer is (D).** (A), (C), and (E) are marred by faulty parallelism: Ancient Greek literature is compared with today's Greek people. (C) even leaves "literature" to be inferred, and (E) compares the ancient *Greek* with modern *Greeks.* (B) does achieve parallelism, but errs in using the plural (and here unidiomatic) verb "are containing" with the singular noun "literature." Only (D) lines up the ideas correctly.

21. **The correct answer is (B).** In (A), (C), and (D), the phrases about the "oldest brothers" are parenthetical; they are not part of the subject. Steve, the true subject, is singular, requiring not "are" but "is," as in (B). In (E), "his oldest brothers" is linked with "Steve" by "and," thus creating a plural subject requiring not "is" but "are."

22. **The correct answer is (E).** In Standard Written English, "looked like" and "looked as if" are not synonyms for "appeared that," eliminating (A), (B), and (C). "Would have" in (C) changes the meaning. "Appearances were that" and "would be crossing" make (D) wordier than the succinct, and correct, (E).

23. **The correct answer is (E).** (A), (B), and (D) incorrectly use "inferred" to mean "implied." (A) and (C) use the pronoun "them" instead of "it" (the antecedent is "plight").

24. **The correct answer is (B).** (A) creates ambiguity through faulty parallelism: Are streets being compared with streets or with cities? (E) eliminates confusion by using strict parallel structure: "the streets in Paris" is balanced by "the streets in any other city." But (B) is better because it saves a word by using "those" instead of repeating "the streets." (C) and (D) only worsen the parallelism.

25. **The correct answer is (C).** The phrase about the "aides" simply supplies extra, parenthetical information. It is not part of the subject, which remains the singular "media advisor." (A), (B), and (D) therefore err in using the plural verb "are." (E) uses the correct singular "is" but reverses the facts—it's the "aides" who "are all in the company" of the "advisor."

answers

26. **The correct answer is (E).** The original is repetitious: if "Lawyers and doctors . . . agree," then "alike" and "both" are superfluous; if there's a "rise in . . . suits," the clause "which are on the increase" is redundant. Only (E) avoids all these errors.

27. **The correct answer is (A).** (B) is wrong because the "if " clause, stating a past condition contrary to fact, requires a past-perfect subjunctive ("had known"). (C) and (D) are wrong because the "possible conclusion" clause requires the perfect form of a modal auxiliary ("would have run"). (E) uses the wrong tense of the subjunctive. (B), (C), and (E) all needlessly add the "if" already implicit in the "had . . . known" construction, which is required in standard written English.

28. **The correct answer is (A).** (B) and (C) confuse "effect" with "affect." (C) and (D) use "than" instead of "from": Things differ "from" one another. (E) uses the singular "that" instead of the plural "those" to refer back to the plural antecedent "findings." Only (A) avoids all these traps.

29. **The correct answer is (D).** (A) is poor on two counts: (1) "the past eight years," or past action continuing into the present, requires the present perfect ("has been") rather than the past tense ("was"); and (2) the two parts of the sentence that should be close for comparative purposes—"shy and awkward" and "powerful and consistent"—are separated. (C) echoes (1) and corrects (2) at the expense of vital information. (B) and (E) echo (2).

30. **The correct answer is (E).** In (A), (C), and (D), "of them" or "of these" is superfluous. In (B), "the latter" is incorrect. Since there are more than two items to refer back to, the correct term is "the last." (If four items were specified, the writer could refer to "the latter two," as distinct from "the former two," but "of all the reasons" implies many more than four.)

Exercise 2: ANSWER KEY AND EXPLANATIONS

1. A	4. B	7. C	10. B	13. B
2. D	5. A	8. D	11. A	14. B
3. A	6. E	9. C	12. B	15. A

1. **The correct answer is (A).** The sentence, with the verb "return," is correct as written. (B), (C), and (D) make unneeded changes that introduce errors into the otherwise correct construction. (E) is incorrect because the verb "returns" is in the wrong case.

2. **The correct answer is (D).** The difficulty with the sentence is the needless verbiage "by it." (C) and (E) also make the needed correction, but they are incorrect because they add something to the sentence to make it awkward.

3. **The correct answer is (A).** The sentence is correct as rendered. (B) changes a properly plural verb to a singular verb, introducing a new error. (C) adds unneeded words, making the sentence awkward. (D) changes the meaning of the sentence slightly. Finally, (E) introduces a new error in usage by changing "so" to "as."

4. **The correct answer is (B).** The difficulty with the sentence is a failure of parallelism. The subject of the sentence is the infinitive "to consider," but the complement is the gerund "is neglecting." One or the other must be changed so that they both have the same form. (B) does this. (D) changes both, so it commits the mirror image of the original error. (C) introduces wording that makes the sentence illogical. (E) introduces a new error, the unacceptable usage of "amounts to."

5. **The correct answer is (A).** The sentence is correct as written. Since the time frame refers to something that occurred in the past and is now over, the verb "would have liked" is correct.

6. **The correct answer is (E).** There is a problem here with verb tense. To express correctly the thought of the sentence, it must be made clear that the erroneous belief preceded the discovery of the new information and that it was ended by that discovery. (E), by using the past perfect "had," correctly places the "belief " as a completed act in the past.

7. **The correct answer is (C).** Again, without getting involved in the intricacies of the subjunctive, because the refusal is not a certainty, to express the doubt we require the "would." Every other choice is wrong because it does not capture the element of doubt expressed by the phrase "out of fear that."

8. **The correct answer is (D).** The original choice of verbs is not logical. The pairing of "could" and "will" in this context doesn't make a meaningful statement. (E) makes an attempt to correct the error but the pairing "would" and "should" is no better than the original.

9. **The correct answer is (C).** The original sentence contains an error that might best be described as the mirror image of the error of the dangling modifier. The introductory phrase is properly placed to modify a subject that is the person or persons who made the discovery. Unfortunately, the impersonal "it" is the wrong subject. (C) corrects this error. (B) fails to correct the original mistake and compounds the problem by substituting an

illogical verb tense. (D) is awkward. Finally, (E) uses the phrase "due to" which cannot be used as a conjunction in Standard Written English.

10. **The correct answer is (B).** The original sentence runs together two distinct ideas. (B) separates the two ideas and does so in such a way that it gives equal weight to both. (C) attempts to separate the ideas, but the resulting sentence does not give them equal weight. (D) makes the same error as (C), plus (D) contains the additional mistake of an inappropriate verb. Finally, (E) subordinates the second idea to the first, but the two ideas should be given equal weight.

11. **The correct answer is (A).** Each of the other choices in some way changes the logical structure or meaning of the original.

12. **The correct answer is (B).** The original sentence is illogical. As written, it implies that one should write to a Congressperson who has an opinion. (B) eliminates this ambiguity. (C) fails to eliminate the ambiguity. (D) is incorrect because the resulting sentence lacks a main clause. (E) is incorrect because it changes the logic of the original sentence (from "is" to "may be") and because it is awkward ("the writing").

13. **The correct answer is (B).** The original sentence is wrong because "they" has no antecedent. (C) is wrong because it is not idiomatic to say "the approaches at curing." (D) contains the same error and makes the additional mistake of using an awkward indirect construction ("by them"). (E) repeats the original mistake and compounds it by using a plural subject "approaches" with a singular verb form "has."

14. **The correct answer is (B).** (A) is incorrect. It is not idiomatic English to say "more on *x* as on *y*." (B) uses the correct idiom, "more on *x* than on *y*." (C) repeats the original error and adds an incorrect verb form, "had been based." (D) corrects the original error but does not follow the sequence of events. It switches from the present tense (*is*) to the past tense (*was*). (E) repeats the original error and introduces a new one, using "where" to mean "in which."

15. **The correct answer is (A).** The sentence is correct as written. (B) makes a slight change in the original, but one that changes the meaning of the original. "Each other" implies that there are only two breeds of dog; "one another" implies that there are several. (C), (D), and (E) make gratuitous changes that result in awkward constructions.

Critical Reasoning

OVERVIEW

- **What does critical reasoning test?**
- **How do you answer critical reasoning questions?**
- **What smart test-takers know**

WHAT DOES CRITICAL REASONING TEST?

As the name implies, critical reasoning tests your reasoning power, and you will learn a lot about reasoning in this chapter. However, the GMAT does not test technical points that are taught in the typical "Introduction to Logic" college course. You would not, for example, be asked to define categorical syllogism or *petitio principii,* but you might be asked to recognize that:

> All whales are mammals.
> All mammals are warm-blooded creatures.
> Therefore, all whales are warm-blooded creatures.

(which, technically speaking, is a categorical syllogism) is a valid argument. And you might be asked to show that you understand that:

> Shakespeare was a better playwright than Shaw. Clearly, Shakespeare's plays are better, so the conclusion that Shakespeare was a better playwright than Shaw is unavoidable.

(which, technically speaking is a *petitio principii)* is a specious argument because it simply begs the question.

GMAT Critical Reasoning Questions

GMAT critical reasoning questions appear in the 75-minute verbal section of the test. Within the section, they are not grouped all together. Instead, they are interspersed with the sentence correction and reading comprehension questions. Critical reasoning questions present brief statements or arguments and ask you to evaluate the form or content of the statement or argument. Each question is constructed from three elements:

chapter 7

Stimulus Material

Stimulus material is the "content" of the item. Stimulus material is an initial paragraph or statement that presents an argument or otherwise states a position. The stimulus material can be about almost anything including a medical breakthrough, a moral dilemma, a scientific theory, a philosophical problem, or a marketing phenomenon. But you don't need any special knowledge. Everything you need to know in terms of item content is right there in the stimulus material.

NOTE

What are the three "building blocks" of critical reasoning?
1. Stimulus
2. Question stem
3. Answer choices
And each has its role to play.

Question Stem

This stem is the "question." It may come in the form of a question, or it may come in the form of an instruction. Either way, the stem tells you what to do with the stimulus material. It may ask you to do any one of the following:

- Identify the conclusion of an argument.
- Point out a premise of an argument.
- Identify strengths or weaknesses in an argument.
- Recognize parallel reasoning.
- Evaluate evidence.
- Draw conclusions and make inferences.

Answer Choices

The answer choices are the possible "responses" to the stem. One of them is the "credited" response or right answer. The wrong answers are known as "distractors" because they are carefully written to distract your attention away from the right answer. In essence, they provide the camouflage in which the test-writers hide the right response.

Here are the directions for GMAT critical reasoning questions, together with a sample question and its explanation.

Anatomy of a Critical Reasoning Item

Directions: The following questions ask you to analyze and evaluate the reasoning in short paragraphs or passages. For some questions, all of the answer choices may conceivably be answers to the question asked. You should select the *best* answer to the question, that is, an answer that does not require you to make assumptions which violate common-sense standards by being implausible, redundant, irrelevant, or inconsistent.

STIMULUS

Officials of the State Industrial Safety Board notified the management of A-1 Ironworks that several employees of the plant had complained about discomfort experienced as a result of the high levels of noise of the factory operations. A-1's management responded by pointing out that the complaints came from the newest employee at the plant and that more experienced workers did not find the factory noise to be excessive. Based on this finding, management concluded that the noise was not a problem and declined to take any remedial action.

(You should notice that management overlooked something: Is there another possible explanation for why complaints came from new employees and not from experienced employees?)

QUESTION STEM

Which of the following, if true, indicates a flaw in A-1's decision not to take remedial action at the plant?

(The stem tells you that management has made a mistake and asks that you identify the error.)

ANSWER CHOICES

(A) Because A-1 is located in an industrial park, no residences are located close enough to the plant to be affected by the noise.

(A distractor. The issue is the effect of noise on employees inside the plant.)

(B) The noise level at the plant varies with activity and is at the highest when the greatest number of employees are on the job.

(A distractor. While this is probably true, it does not address the new employee/experienced employee distinction.)

(C) The experienced employees do not feel discomfort because of significant hearing loss attributable to the high noise level.

(The credited response. Management overlooked this: Experienced employees do not complain because deafness prevents them from hearing the noise.)

(D) Issuing protective ear plugs to all employees would not significantly increase the cost to A-1 of doing business.

(A distractor. If ear plugs would be an effective but inexpensive remedial step, then it would make sense to issue them to employees.)

(E) The State Industrial Safety Board has no independent authority to enforce a recommendation regarding safety procedures.

(A distractor. Irrelevant to the issue at hand.)

TIP

Know the common types of critical reasoning questions:

- Identify the conclusion.
- Point out a premise.
- Identify strengths or weaknesses.
- Recognize parallel reasoning.
- Evaluate evidence.
- Draw a conclusion.

HOW DO YOU ANSWER CRITICAL REASONING QUESTIONS?

Here's a simple, four-step plan that can help you solve critical reasoning questions.

Critical Reasoning: Getting It Right

1. Preview the question stem.
2. Read the stimulus material.
3. Prephrase your answer.
4. Identify the correct answer.

Let's look at these steps in more detail.

1. **Preview the question stem.** There are many things that you could do with the stimulus material. You could attack the conclusion, you could defend the conclusion, you could analyze its structure, you could draw further inferences from it, you could even invent a similar argument, and there are still more things to do. You will be asked to do only one (or, occasionally, two) of these things by the stem. So previewing the stem will help you to focus your thinking.
2. **Read the stimulus material.** This is not as easy at it seems. You are going to have to read more carefully than usual. And this makes sense, since words are the tools of the business manager's trade. The following advertisement will help to make the point. Read it carefully, because there will be a test.

> *Advertisement:* Lite Cigarettes have 50% less nicotine and tar than regular cigarettes. Seventy-five percent of the doctors surveyed said that they would, if asked by patients, recommend a reduced-tar-and-nicotine cigarette for patients who cannot stop smoking.

Pop Quiz

1. Does the ad say that some doctors are encouraging people to start smoking?
2. Does the ad say that some doctors recommend Lite Cigarettes for patients who cannot stop smoking?
3. Does the ad say that most doctors would, if asked by patients, recommend a low-tar-and-nicotine cigarette to patients who cannot stop smoking?

Answers

1. Does the ad say that some doctors are encouraging people to start smoking?

   No. The ad specifically says that the doctors surveyed would recommend a low-tar-and-nicotine cigarette "for patients who cannot stop smoking." That clearly applies only to people who are already smokers.

2. Does the ad say that some doctors recommend Lite Cigarettes for patients who cannot stop smoking?

   No again. The ad specifically says that the doctors surveyed would recommend "a reduced-tar-and-nicotine cigarette." To be sure, Lite Cigarettes apparently fall into that category, but the ad does not say that the doctors surveyed would recommend Lite Cigarettes as opposed to some other reduced-tar-and-nicotine cigarette.

3. Does the ad say that most doctors would, if asked by patients, recommend a low-tar-and-nicotine cigarette for patients who cannot stop smoking?

   No once again. The claim is restricted to "doctors surveyed." No information is given about how many doctors were included in the survey—perhaps only four. Nor does the ad disclose how many surveys were done. Even if the market experts had to conduct ten surveys before they found a group of four doctors to back up their claim, the ad would still be true—though, of course, potentially misleading.

The important point is this: Read carefully and pay attention to detail. This does not mean that you need to tie yourself up in paranoid knots. The GMAT is not out to get you personally. The GMAT is, however, a test that is, in part, designed to separate those who can read carefully and pay attention to detail from those who cannot. So read carefully.

❸ **Prephrase your answer.** Many GMAT problems have answers that go "click" when you find them. They fit in the same way that a well-made key fits a good lock. After you have previewed the stem and then read carefully the stimulus material, try to anticipate what the correct answer will look like. This is particularly true of questions that ask you to attack or defend an argument. (This technique does not work for questions that ask you to identify a parallel line of thinking.)

❹ **Identify the correct answer.** If you have effectively prephrased an answer, then you should be able to identify fairly readily the correct answer. Otherwise, you will have to study the choices carefully. And, again, careful reading means very careful reading. In logical reasoning, each word in the answer choices counts.

Now let's look at some sample GMAT critical reasoning questions. As you read the explanations, think about how the solution process applies.

> The governor claims that the state faces a drought and has implemented new water-use restrictions; but that's just a move to get some free publicity for his reelection campaign. So far this year we have had 3.5 inches of rain, slightly more than the average amount of rain for the same period over the last three years.
>
> Which of the following, if true, would most weaken the conclusion of the argument above?
>
> **(A)** The governor did not declare drought emergencies in the previous three years.
>
> **(B)** City officials who have the authority to mandate water-use restrictions have not done so.
>
> **(C)** The snowmelt that usually contributes significantly to the state's reservoirs is several inches below normal.
>
> **(D)** The amount of water the state can draw from rivers that cross state boundaries is limited by federal law.
>
> **(E)** Water-use restrictions are short-term measures and do little to reduce long-term water consumption.

This question stem asks you to attack the stimulus material. The argument is weak because it depends upon a hidden assumption: Rainfall is the only source of water for the reservoirs. So, your prephrased answer might be "there is another source of water for the reservoirs." (C) fits neatly into this prephrase.

> "Channel One" is a 12-minute school news show that includes two minutes of commercials. The show's producers offer high schools $50,000 worth of television equipment to air the program. Many parents and teachers oppose the use of commercial television in schools, arguing that advertisements are tantamount to indoctrination. But students are already familiar with television commercials and know how to distinguish programming from advertising.
>
> The argument assumes that
>
> **(A)** the effects of an advertisement viewed in a classroom would be similar to those of the same advertisement viewed at home
>
> **(B)** many educators would be willing to allow the indoctrination of students in exchange for new equipment for their schools
>
> **(C)** television advertising is a more effective way of promoting a product to high school students than print advertising
>
> **(D)** high school students are sufficiently interested in world affairs to learn from a television news program
>
> **(E)** a television news program produced especially for high school students is an effective teaching tool

This question stem asks you to identify a hidden assumption of the stimulus material. The argument makes the assumption that television when viewed in the classroom will have a similar effect on children as that when it is viewed at home.

This is a questionable assumption since the teacher/pupil relationship is an authoritative one. So your prephrase might be something like "the two situations are similar," and (A) is a hidden assumption of the argument.

> The spate of terrorist acts against airlines and their passengers raises a new question: should government officials be forced to disclose the fact that they have received warning of an impending terrorist attack? The answer is "yes." The government currently releases information about the health hazards of smoking, the ecological dangers of pesticides, and the health consequences of food.
>
> The argument above relies primarily on
>
> **(A)** circular reasoning
>
> **(B)** generalization
>
> **(C)** authority
>
> **(D)** analogy
>
> **(E)** causal analysis

This question stem asks you to describe the reasoning in the stimulus material. The argument draws an analogy between two situations. So your prephrase would almost surely be "analogy." And the correct answer is (D).

> When it rains, my car gets wet. Since it hasn't rained recently, my car can't be wet.
>
> Which of the following is logically most similar to the argument above?
>
> **(A)** Whenever critics give a play a favorable review, people go to see it; Pinter's new play did not receive favorable reviews, so I doubt that anyone will go to see it.
>
> **(B)** Whenever people go to see a play, critics give it a favorable review; people did go to see Pinter's new play, so it did get a favorable review.
>
> **(C)** Whenever critics give a play a favorable review, people go to see it; Pinter's new play got favorable reviews, so people will probably go to see it.
>
> **(D)** Whenever a play is given favorable reviews by the critics, people go to see it; since people are going to see Pinter's new play, it will probably get favorable reviews.
>
> **(E)** Whenever critics give a play a favorable review, people go to see it; people are not going to see Pinter's new play, so it did not get favorable reviews.

This question stem asks you to parallel the stimulus material. The fallacy in the argument is confusion over necessary and sufficient causes. A sufficient cause is an event that is sufficient to guarantee some effect; a necessary cause is one that is required for some event. (A) exhibits this same fallacy. (Remember that a prephrase will not be possible with this type of question.)

ALERT!

"Parallel" questions can be tricky. The stimulus for a "parallel" question will probably contain an error. Don't fall into the trap of correcting the error. Just find an answer with a similar mistake.

WHAT SMART TEST-TAKERS KNOW

CRITICAL REASONING STIMULUS MATERIAL HAS A LOGICAL STRUCTURE.

Critical reasoning stimulus material is almost always an argument—more statements or assertions one of which, the conclusion, is supposed to follow from the others, the premises. Some arguments are very short and simple:

Premise: No fish are mammals.
Conclusion: No mammals are fish.

Others are extremely lengthy and complex, taking up entire volumes. Some arguments are good, some are bad. Scientists use arguments to justify a conclusion regarding the cause of some natural phenomenon; politicians use arguments to reach conclusions about the desirability of government policies. But even given this wide variety of structures and uses, arguments fall into one of two general categories—deductive and inductive.

A deductive argument is one in which the inference depends solely on the meanings of the terms used:

Premises: All bats are mammals.
All mammals are warm blooded.
Conclusion: Therefore, all bats are warm blooded.

You know that this argument has to be correct just by looking at it. No research is necessary to show that the conclusion follows automatically from the premises.

All other arguments are termed inductive or probabilistic:

Premises: My car will not start; and the fuel gauge reads "empty."
Conclusion: Therefore, the car is probably out of gas.

Notice that here, unlike the deductive argument, the conclusion does not follow with certainty; it is not guaranteed. The conclusion does seem to be likely or probable, but there are some gaps in the argument. It is possible, for example, that the fuel gauge is broken, or that there is fuel in the tank and the car will not start because something else is wrong.

LOCATING THE CONCLUSION IS THE FIRST STEP IN EVALUATING AN ARGUMENT.

The conclusion is the main point of an argument, and locating the conclusion is the first step in evaluating the strength of any argument. In fact, some critical reasoning questions simply ask that you identify the conclusion or main point:

Which of the following is the speaker's conclusion?
Which of the following best summarizes the main point of the argument?
The speaker is attempting to prove that . . .
The speaker is leading to the conclusion that . . .

So, developing techniques for identifying the conclusion of the argument would be important in any case.

Conclusions, however, are important for yet another reason: You cannot begin to look for fallacies or other weaknesses in a line of reasoning or even find the line of reasoning until you have clearly identified the point the author wishes to prove. Any attempt to skip over this important step can only result in misunderstanding and confusion. You have surely had the experience of discussing a point for some length of time only to say finally, "Oh, now I see what you were saying, and I agree with you."

Locating the main point of an argument sometimes entails a bit of work because the logical structure of an argument is not necessarily dependent on the order in which sentences appear. To be sure, sometimes the main point of an argument is fairly easy to find—it is the last statement in the paragraph:

> Since this watch was manufactured in Switzerland, and all Swiss watches are reliable, <u>this watch must be reliable</u>.

Here the conclusion or the point of the line of reasoning is the part that is underlined. The argument also contains two premises: "this watch was manufactured in Switzerland" and "all Swiss watches are reliable." The same argument could be made, however, with the statements presented in a different order:

> <u>This watch must be reliable</u> since it was manufactured in Switzerland and all Swiss watches are reliable.
>
> or
>
> <u>This watch must be reliable</u> since all Swiss watches are reliable and this watch was manufactured in Switzerland.
>
> or
>
> Since this watch was manufactured in Switzerland, <u>it must be reliable</u> because all Swiss watches are reliable.

So you cannot always count on the conclusion of the argument being the last sentence of the paragraph even though sometimes it is. Therefore, it is important to know some techniques for finding the conclusion of an argument.

TIP

Signal words can help you find a conclusion:

- therefore
- hence
- thus
- consequently
- accordingly
- so

THE CONCLUSION OF AN ARGUMENT CAN BE THE FIRST SENTENCE.

It is true that speakers often lead up to the conclusion and make it the grand finale. Sometimes, however, speakers announce in advance where they are going and then proceed to develop arguments in support of their position. So the second most common position for the conclusion of an argument is the first sentence of the stimulus material.

KEY WORDS OFTEN SIGNAL A CONCLUSION.

The stimulus material often uses transitional words or phrases to signal a conclusion, for example, "Ms. Slote has a Master's in Education and she has 20 years of teaching experience, *therefore* she is a good teacher." Other words and phrases to watch include: *hence, thus, so, it follows that, as a result,* and *consequently.*

KEY WORDS OFTEN SIGNAL AN IMPORTANT PREMISE.

In some arguments the premises rather than the conclusion are signaled. Words that signal premises include *since, because,* and *if.*

> *Since* Rex has been with the company 20 years and does such a good job, he will probably receive a promotion.
>
> or
>
> Rex will probably receive a promotion *because* he has been with the company 20 years and he does such a good job.
>
> or
>
> *If* Rex has been with the company 20 years and has done a good job, he will probably receive a promotion.

In each of the three examples just presented, the conclusion is "Rex will probably receive a promotion" and the premise is that "he has been with the company 20 years and does a good job." Of course, many other words can signal premises.

THE CONCLUSION IS THE MAIN POINT OF AN ARGUMENT.

Ask what the author wants to prove. Not all arguments are broken down by the numbers. In such a case, you must use your judgment to answer the question "What is the speaker trying to prove?" For example:

> We must reduce the amount of money we spend on space exploration. Right now, the enemy is launching a massive military buildup, and we need the additional money to purchase military equipment to match the anticipated increase in the enemy's strength.

In this argument there are no key words to announce the conclusion or the premises. Instead, you must ask yourself a series of questions:

> Is the speaker trying to prove that the enemy is beginning a military buildup?

No, because that statement is a premise of the larger argument, so it cannot be the conclusion.

> Is the main point that we must match the enemy buildup?

Again the answer is "no," because that, too, is an intermediate step on the way to some other conclusion.

> Is the speaker trying to prove that we must cut back on the budget for space exploration?

Now the answer is "yes," and that is the author's point.

Things get more complicated when an argument contains arguments within the main argument. The argument about the need for military expenditures might have included this subargument:

> We must reduce the amount of money we spend on space exploration. The enemy is now stockpiling titanium, a metal which is used in building airplanes. And each time the enemy has stockpiled titanium it has launched a massive military buildup. So, right now, the enemy is launching a massive military buildup, and we need the additional money to pur-

chase military equipment to match the anticipated increase in the enemy's strength.

Notice that now one of the premises of the earlier argument is the conclusion of a subargument. The conclusion of the subargument is "the enemy is launching a massive military buildup," which has two explicit premises: "The enemy is now stockpiling titanium" and "a stockpiling of titanium means a military buildup."

No matter how complicated an argument gets, you can always break it down into subarguments. And if it is really complex, those subarguments can be broken down into smaller parts. Of course, the stimulus material on the GMAT cannot be overly complicated because the initial argument will not be much more than a hundred or so words in length. So just keep asking yourself "What is the author trying to prove?"

GMAT CONCLUSIONS ARE CAREFULLY WORDED.

Defining precisely the main point is also an essential step in evaluating an argument. Once the main point of the argument has been isolated, you must take the second step of exactly defining that point. In particular, you should be looking for three things:

1. Quantifiers
2. Qualifiers
3. The author's intention

GMAT CONCLUSIONS ARE CAREFULLY QUANTIFIED.

Quantifiers are words such as *some, none, never, always, everywhere,* and *sometimes.* For example, there is a big difference in the claims:

All mammals live on land.
Most mammals live on land.

The first is false; the second is true. Compare also:

Women in the United States have always had the right to vote.
Since 1920, women in the United States have had the right to vote.

Again, the first statement is false and the second is true. And compare:

It is raining and the temperature is predicted to drop below 32°F; therefore, it will surely snow.
It is raining and the temperature is predicted to drop below 32°F; therefore, it will probably snow.

The first is a much less cautious claim than the second, and if it failed to snow the first claim would have been proved false, though not the second. The second statement claims only that it is probable that snow will follow, not that it definitely will. So someone could make the second claim and defend it when the snow failed to materialize by saying, "Well, I allowed for that in my original statement."

GMAT CONCLUSIONS ARE CAREFULLY QUALIFIED.

Qualifiers play a role similar to that of quantifiers but they are descriptive rather than numerical. As such, they are more concrete and difficult to enumerate. Just make sure that you stay alert for distinctions like this:

> In nations that have a bicameral legislature, the speed with which legislation is passed is largely a function of the strength of executive leadership.

Notice here that the author makes a claim about "nations," so it would be wrong to apply the author's reasoning to states. Further, you should not conclude that the author believes that bicameral legislatures pass different laws from those passed by unicameral legislatures. The author mentions only the "speed" with which the laws are passed, not their content.

> All passenger automobiles manufactured by Detroit auto makers since 1975 have been equipped with seat belts.

TIP

The conclusion is the most important part of the argument. For every critical reasoning question, find the conclusion and read it carefully. The logical structure of the argument should then be clear.

You should not conclude from this statement that all trucks have also been equipped with seat belts since the author makes a claim only about "passenger automobiles," nor should you conclude that imported cars have seat belts, for the author mentions Detroit-made cars only.

> No other major department store offers you a low price and a 75-day warranty on parts and labor on this special edition of the XL 30 color television.

The tone of the ad is designed to create a very large impression on the hearer, but the precise claim made is fairly limited. First, the ad's claim is specifically restricted to a comparison of "department" stores, and "major" department stores at that. It is possible that some non-major department store offers a similar warranty and price; also it may be that another type of retail store, say, an electronics store, makes a similar offer. Second, other stores, department or otherwise, may offer a better deal on the product, say, a low price with a three-month warranty, and still the claim would stand so long as no one else offered exactly a "75-day" warranty. Finally, the ad is restricted to a "special edition" of the television, so, depending on what that means, the ad may be even more restrictive in its claim.

ON THE GMAT, THE AUTHOR'S INTENTION MAY BE CRUCIAL.

The author's intention may also be important. You must be careful to distinguish between claims of fact and proposals of change. Do not assume that an author's claim to have found a problem means the author knows how to solve it. An author can make a claim about the cause of some event without believing that the event can be prevented or even that it ought to be prevented. For example, from the argument:

> Since the fifth ward vote is crucial to Gordon's campaign, if Gordon fails to win over the ward leaders he will be defeated in the election.

you cannot conclude that the author believes Gordon should or should not be elected. The author gives only a factual analysis without endorsing or condemning either possible outcome. Also, from the argument:

> Each year the rotation of the Earth slows a few tenths of a second. In several million years, it will have stopped altogether, and life as we know it will no longer be able to survive on Earth.

you cannot conclude that the author wants to find a solution for the slowing of Earth's rotation. For all we know, the author thinks the process is inevitable, or even desirable.

PREMISES SUPPORT THE CONCLUSION.

A premise is the logical support for a conclusion. The GMAT usually refers to premises as assumptions, but the terminology is not important. It is important not to misunderstand the word *assumption*. Although it is related to the word *assume*, an assumption, as that term is used in logic, does not have the connotation of surmise or guess. In the argument:

> All humans are mortal.
> Socrates is a human.
> Therefore, Socrates is mortal.

the first two statements are assumptions—even though they are obviously true. You can use the words *assumption* and *premise* interchangeably.

EXPLICIT PREMISES ARE SPECIFICALLY STATED.

In the detective novel *A Study in Scarlet* by Sir Arthur Conan Doyle, Sherlock Holmes explains to Dr. Watson that it is possible logically to deduce the existence of rivers and oceans from a single drop of water, though such a deduction would require many intermediate steps. While this may be an exaggeration, it is true that arguments can contain several links. For example:

> Since there is snow on the ground, it must have snowed last night. If it snowed last night, then the temperature must have dropped below 32°F. The temperature drops below 32°F only in the winter. So, since there is snow on the ground, it must be winter here.

It is easy to imagine a Holmesian chain of reasoning that strings additional links in either direction. Instead of starting with "there is snow on the ground," you could have started with "there is a snowman on the front lawn"; and instead of stopping with "it must be winter here," you could have gone on to "so it is summer in Australia." In other words, you could reason from "there is a snowman on the front lawn" to "it is summer in Australia."

IMPLICIT PREMISES ARE NOT STATED.

In practice, arguments do not extend indefinitely in either direction. We begin reasoning at what seems to be a convenient point and stop with the conclusion we had hoped to prove: It must have snowed last night because there is snow on the ground this morning. Now, it should be obvious to you that the strength of an argument depends in a very important way on the legitimacy of its assumptions. And one of the GMAT's favorite tools for building a critical reasoning item is to focus upon an assumption of a special kind: the implicit premise.

Signal words can help you find premises:

- since
- because
- given that
- inasmuch as

Consider some sample arguments:

> Premise: My car's fuel tank is full.
> Conclusion: Therefore, my car will start.

A very effective attack on this argument can be aimed at the first premise—as anyone who has ever had a car fail to start can attest. The battery might be dead or a hundred other things might be wrong. This shows that the argument is not very strong. In logical terms, the argument depends upon an implicit premise:

> Premises: My car's fuel tank is full.
> (The only reason my car might not start is lack of fuel.)
> Conclusion: Therefore, my car will start.

The statement in parentheses is a necessary part of the argument. Otherwise, the conclusion does not follow.

Implicit premises are also called suppressed premises (or assumptions) or hidden premises (or assumptions). You do not have to worry about terminology; you just have to know one when you see it:

Premise:	Edward has less than two years of experience.
Conclusion:	Therefore, Edward is not qualified.
Suppressed Premise:	Only people with at least two years of experience are qualified.
Premise:	This is Tuesday.
Conclusion:	Therefore, the luncheon special is pasta.
Suppressed Premise:	Every Tuesday, the luncheon special is pasta.
Premise:	The committee did not announce its choice by 3:00.
Conclusion:	Therefore, Radu did not get the job.
Suppressed Premise:	Radu gets the job only if the announcement is made by 3:00.

Logical Fallacies

MANY CRITICAL REASONING QUESTIONS TEST FALLACIES.

A fallacy is a mistake in reasoning. Many GMAT questions ask you to demonstrate that you know a mistake when you see one. Of course, there are many different ways to make mistakes, so it is not possible to create an exhaustive list of fallacies; but there are certain fallacies that come up on the GMAT fairly often. If you know what they look like, then they will be easier to spot.

Why do I need to know about fallacies?

If you know what to look for, you're more likely to find it. This section is a checklist of common fallacies used by the GMAT.

Each of the following seven tips spotlights a common GMAT logical fallacy.

EXPLANATIONS OFTEN IDENTIFY THE WRONG CAUSE.

The mistake in reasoning that is tested most often by the GMAT is the fallacy of the wrong cause. An argument that commits this error attributes a causal relationship between two events where none exists or at least the relationship is misidentified. For example:

> Every time the doorbell rings, I find there is someone at the door. Therefore, it must be the case that the doorbell calls these people to my door.

Obviously, the causal link suggested here is backwards. It is the presence of the person at the door which then leads to the ringing of the bell, not vice versa. A more serious example of the fallacy of the false cause is:

> There were more air traffic fatalities in 1979 than there were in 1969; therefore, the airplanes used in 1979 were more dangerous than those used in 1969.

The difficulty with this argument is that it attributes the increase in fatalities to a lack of safety when, in fact, it is probably attributable to an increase in air travel generally. A typical question stem and correct answer for this type of problem might be:

> Which of the following, if true, most undermines the speaker's argument?
>
> (✓) Total airmiles traveled doubled from 1969 to 1979.

ANALOGIES ARE OFTEN FALSE.

A second fallacy that might appear on the GMAT is that of false analogy. This error occurs when a conclusion drawn from one situation is applied to another situation—but the two situations are not very similar. For example:

> People should have to be licensed before they are allowed to have children. After all, we require people who operate automobiles to be licensed.

In this case, the two situations—driving and having children—are so dissimilar that we would probably want to say they are not analogous at all. Having children has nothing to do with driving. A GMAT problem based upon a faulty analogy is likely to be more subtle. For example:

> The government should pay more to its diplomats who work in countries that are considered potential enemies. This is very similar to paying soldiers combat premiums if they are stationed in a war zone.

The argument here relies on an analogy between diplomats in a potentially dangerous country and soldiers in combat areas. Of course, the analogy is not perfect. No analogy can be more than an analogy. So a typical question stem and right answer for this type of problem might be:

> Which of the following, if true, most weakens the argument above?
>
> (✓) Diplomats are almost always evacuated before hostilities begin.

A GENERALIZATION MAY BE WEAK.

A common weakness in an inductive argument is the hasty generalization, that is, basing a large conclusion on too little data. For example:

> All four times I have visited Chicago it has rained; therefore, Chicago probably gets very little sunshine.

ALERT!

Watch out for the common logical fallacies:

- Wrong cause
- False analogy
- Weak generalization
- Ambiguous terms
- Irrelevant evidence
- Circular argument
- *Ad hominem* attack

The rather obvious difficulty with the argument is that it moves from a small sample—four visits—to a very broad conclusion: Chicago gets little sunshine. Of course, generalizing on the basis of a sample or limited experience can be legitimate:

> All five of the buses manufactured by Gutmann which we inspected have defective wheel mounts; therefore, some other buses manufactured by Gutmann probably have similar defects.

Admittedly this argument is not airtight. Perhaps the other uninspected buses do not have the same defect, but this second argument is much stronger than the first. So a typical GMAT stem and correct answer might be:

> Which of the following, if true, would most weaken the argument above?
>
> (✓) The five inspected buses were prototypes built before design specifications were finalized.

SOME ARGUMENTS USE TERMS AMBIGUOUSLY.

A fourth fallacy which the GMAT uses is that of ambiguity. Anytime there is a shifting in the meaning of terms used in an argument, the argument has committed a fallacy of ambiguity. For example:

> The shark has been around for millions of years. The City Aquarium has a shark. Therefore, the City Aquarium has at least one animal that is millions of years old.

The error of the argument is that it uses the word *shark* in two different ways. In the first occurrence, *shark* is used to mean sharks in general. In the second, *shark* refers to one individual animal. Here's another, less playful, example:

> Sin occurs only when a person fails to follow the will of God. But since God is all-powerful, what God wills must actually be. Therefore, it is impossible to deviate from the will of God, so there can be no sin in the world.

The equivocation here is in the word *will.* The first time it is used, the author intends that the will of God is God's wish and implies that it is possible to fail to comply with those wishes. In the second instance, the author uses the word *will* in a way that implies that such deviation is not possible. The argument reaches the conclusion that there is no sin in the world only by playing on these two senses of "will of God." So a representative question stem and correct answer might be:

> The argument above uses which of the following terms in an ambiguous way?
>
> (✓) will

SOME ARGUMENTS USE IRRELEVANT EVIDENCE.

Another fallacy you might encounter in a critical reasoning section is any appeal to irrelevant considerations. For example, an argument that appeals to the popularity of a position to prove the position is fallacious:

> Frederick must be the best choice for chair because most people believe that he is the best person for the job.

That many people hold an opinion obviously does not guarantee its correctness. After all, many people once thought airplanes couldn't fly. A question stem for the argument above plus the correct answer might look like this:

> Which of the following, if true, most weakens the speaker's argument?
>
> (✓) Most people erroneously believe that Frederick holds a Ph.D.

SOME ARGUMENTS ARE CIRCULAR.

A circular argument (begging the question) is an argument in which the conclusion to be proved appears also as a premise. For example:

> Beethoven was the greatest composer of all time, because he wrote the greatest music of any composer, and the one who composes the greatest music must be the greatest composer.

The conclusion of this argument is that Beethoven was the greatest composer of all time, but one of the premises of the argument is that he composed the greatest music, and the other premise states that that is the measure of greatness. The argument is fallacious, for there is really no argument for the conclusion at all, just a restatement of the premise. A typical GMAT stem and correct answer are:

> The argument above is weak because
>
> (✓) it assumes what it hopes to prove.

TIP

Same fallacy, different names. "Circular reasoning," "begging the question," "assuming what's to be proved," and "repeating the premise" are just different ways of naming the same thing.

AD HOMINEM ARGUMENTS ATTACK SOMEONE PERSONALLY.

Yes, *ad hominem* is a Latin phrase, and Latin is not tested on the GMAT. This phrase is just a useful shorthand for this fallacy. Any argument that is directed against the source of the claim rather than the claim itself is an *ad hominem* attack:

> Professor Peters's analysis of the economic impact of the proposed sports arena for the Blue Birds should be rejected, because Professor Peters is a Red Birds fan—most fierce rivals of the Blue Birds.

The suggestion is obviously farfetched. And a representative GMAT stem plus correct answer might look like this:

> The speaker's argument is weak because it
>
> (✓) confuses a person's loyalty to a sports team with the person's ability to offer an expert economic opinion

EXERCISE 1: CRITICAL REASONING

33 Questions • 50 Minutes

Directions: The following questions ask you to analyze and evaluate the reasoning in short paragraphs or passages. For some questions, all of the answer choices may conceivably be answers to the question asked. You should select the *best* answer to the question, that is, an answer that does not require you to make assumptions which violate common-sense standards by being implausible, redundant, irrelevant, or inconsistent.

Example:

Q In an extensive study of the reading habits of magazine subscribers, it was found that an average of between four and five people actually read each copy of the most popular weekly news magazine. On this basis, we estimate that the 12,000 copies of *Poets and Poetry* that are sold each month are actually read by 48,000 to 60,000 people.

The estimate above assumes that

(A) individual magazine readers generally enjoy more than one type of magazine

(B) most of the readers of *Poets and Poetry* subscribe to the magazine

(C) the ratio of readers to copies is the same for *Poets and Poetry* as for the weekly news magazine

(D) the number of readers of the weekly news magazine is similar to the number of readers of *Poets and Poetry*

(E) most readers enjoy sharing copies of their favorite magazines with friends and family members

A **The correct answer is (C).**

1. I. Whenever some of the runners are leading off and all of the infielders are playing in, all of the batters attempt to bunt.

II. Some of the runners are leading off but some of the batters are not attempting to bunt.

Which of the following conclusions can be deduced from the two statements above?

(A) Some of the runners are not leading off.

(B) Some of the batters are attempting to bunt.

(C) None of the infielders is playing in.

(D) All of the infielders are playing in.

(E) Some of the infielders are not playing in.

2. The federal bankruptcy laws illustrate the folly of do-good protectionism at its most extreme. At the debtor's own request, the judge will list all of his debts, take what money the debtor has, which will be very little, and divide that small amount among his creditors. Then the judge declares that those debts are thereby satisfied, and the debtor is free from those creditors. Why, a person could take his credit card and buy a car, a stereo, and a new wardrobe and then declare himself bankrupt! In effect, he will have conned his creditors into giving him all those things for nothing.

   Which of the following adages best describes the author's attitude about a bankrupt debtor?

   (A) "A penny saved is a penny earned."

   (B) "You've made your bed, now lie in it."

   (C) "Absolute power corrupts absolutely."

   (D) "He that governs least governs best."

   (E) "Millions for defense, but not one cent for tribute."

3. MARY: All of the graduates from Midland High School go to State College.

   ANN: I don't know. Some of the students at State College come from North Hills High School.

   Ann's response shows that she has interpreted Mary's remark to mean that

   (A) most of the students from North Hills High School attend State College

   (B) none of the students at State College are from Midland High School

   (C) only students from Midland High School attend State College

   (D) Midland High School is a better school than North Hills High School

   (E) some Midland High School graduates do not attend college

4. Total contributions by individuals to political parties were up 25 percent in this most recent presidential election over those of four years earlier. Hence, it is obvious that people are no longer as apathetic as they were, but are taking a greater interest in politics.

   Which of the following, if true, would considerably weaken the preceding argument?

   (A) The average contribution per individual actually declined during the same four-year period.

   (B) Per capita income of the population increased by 15 percent during the four years in question.

   (C) Public leaders continue to warn citizens against the dangers of political apathy.

   (D) Contributions made by large corporations to political parties declined during the four-year period.

   (E) Fewer people voted in the most recent presidential election than in the one four years earlier.

5. We must do something about the rising cost of our state prisons. It now costs an average of $225 per day to maintain a prisoner in a double-occupancy cell in a state prison. Yet, in the most expensive cities in the world, one can find rooms in the finest hotels which rent for less than $175 per night.

   The argument above might be criticized in all of the following ways EXCEPT

   (A) it introduces an inappropriate analogy

   (B) it relies on an unwarranted appeal to authority

   (C) it fails to take account of costs that prisons have but hotels do not have

   (D) it misuses numerical data

   (E) it draws a faulty comparison

6. As dietitian for this 300-person school, I am concerned about the sudden shortage of beef. It seems that we will have to begin to serve fish as our main source of protein. Even though beef costs more per pound than fish, I expect that the price I pay for protein will rise if I continue to serve the same amount of protein using fish as I did with beef.

   The speaker makes which of the following assumptions?

   (A) Fish is more expensive per pound than beef.

   (B) Students will soon be paying more for their meals.

   (C) Cattle ranchers make greater profits than fishermen.

   (D) Per measure of protein, fish is more expensive than beef.

   (E) Cattle are more costly to raise than fish.

7. New Weight Loss Salons invite all of you who are dissatisfied with your present build to join our Exercise for Lunch Bunch. Instead of putting on even more weight by eating lunch, you actually cut down on your daily caloric intake by exercising rather than eating. Every single one of us has the potential to be slim and fit, so take the initiative and begin losing excess pounds today. Don't eat! Exercise! You'll lose weight and feel stronger, happier, and more attractive.

   Which of the following, if true, would weaken the logic of the argument made by the advertisement?

   (A) Nutritionists agree that it is permissible to skip lunch but it is not a good idea to skip breakfast.

   (B) Most people will experience increased desire for food as a result of the exercise and will lose little weight as a result of enrolling in the program.

   (C) In our society, obesity is regarded as unattractive.

   (D) A person who is too thin is probably not in good health.

   (E) Not everyone is dissatisfied with his or her present build or body weight.

8. Statistics published by the U.S. Department of Transportation show that nearly 80% of all traffic fatalities occur at speeds of under 50 miles per hour and within 25 miles of home. Therefore, you are safer in a car if you are driving at a speed over 50 miles per hour and not within a 25-mile radius of your home.

   Which of the following, if true, most weakens the conclusion of the argument above?

   (A) Teenage drivers are involved in 75% of all traffic accidents resulting in fatalities.

   (B) 80% of all persons arrested for driving at a speed over the posted speed limit are intoxicated.

   (C) 50% of the nation's annual traffic fatalities occur on six weekends that are considered high-risk weekends because they contain holidays.

   (D) The Department of Transportation statistics were based on police reports compiled by the 50 states.

   (E) 90% of all driving time is registered within a 25-mile radius of the driver's home and at speeds less than 50 miles per hour.

9. Usually when we have had an inch or more of rain in a single day, my backyard immediately has mushrooms and other forms of fungus growing in it. There are no mushrooms or fungus growing in my backyard.

   Which of the following would logically complete an argument with the premises given above?

   (A) Therefore, there has been no rain here in the past day.

   (B) Therefore, there probably has been no rain here in the past day.

exercises

(C) Therefore, we have not had more than an inch of rain here in the past day.

(D) Therefore, we probably have not had more than an inch of rain here in the past day.

(E) Therefore, mushroom and fungus will be growing in my backyard tomorrow.

10. Since all swans that I have encountered have been white, it follows that the swans I will see when I visit the Bronx Zoo will also be white.

Which of the following most closely parallels the reasoning of the preceding argument?

(A) Some birds are incapable of flight; therefore, swans are probably incapable of flight.

(B) Every ballet I have attended has failed to interest me; so a theatrical production which fails to interest me must be a ballet.

(C) Since all cases of severe depression I have encountered were susceptible to treatment by chlorpromazine, there must be something in the chlorpromazine that adjusts the patient's brain chemistry.

(D) Because every society has a word for justice, the concept of fair play must be inherent in the biological makeup of the human species.

(E) Since no medicine I have tried for my allergy has ever helped, this new product will probably not work either.

QUESTIONS 11–13

The blanks in the following paragraph mark deletions from the text. For each question, select the phrase that most appropriately completes the text.

Libertarians argue that laws making suicide a criminal act are both foolish and an unwarranted intrusion on individual conscience. With regard to the first, they point out that there is no penalty that the law can assess which inflicts greater injury than the crime itself. As for the second, they argue that it is no business of the state to prevent suicide, for whether it is right to take one's own life is a matter to be addressed to one's own God—the state, by the terms of the Constitution, may not interfere. Such arguments, however, seem to me to be ill-conceived. In the first place, the libertarian makes the mistaken assumption that deterrence is the only goal of the law. I maintain that the laws we have proscribing suicide are___(11)___.

By making it a crime to take any life—even one's own—we make a public announcement of our shared conviction that each person is unique and valuable. In the second place, while it must be conceded that the doctrine of the separation of church and state is a useful one, it need not be admitted that suicide is a crime___(12)___. And here we need not have recourse to the possibility that a potential suicide might, if given the opportunity, repent of the decision. Suicide inflicts a cost upon us all: the emotional cost on those close to the suicide; an economic cost in the form of the loss of production of a mature and trained member of the society which falls on us all; and a cost to humanity at large for the loss of a member of our human community. The difficulty with the libertarian position is that it is an oversimplification. It assesses the evil of___(13)___.

11. **(A)** drafted to make it more difficult to commit suicide

(B) passed by legislators in response to pressures by religious lobbying groups

(C) written in an effort to protect our democratic liberties, not undermine them

(D) important because they educate all to the value of human life

(E) outdated because they belong to a time when church and state were not so clearly divided

12. (A) which does not necessarily lead to more serious crimes
 (B) without a victim
 (C) as well as a sin
 (D) which cannot be prevented
 (E) without motive

13. (A) crimes only in economic terms
 (B) suicide only from the perspective of the person who commits suicide
 (C) laws by weighing them against the evil of the liberty lost by their enforcement
 (D) the mingling of church and state without sufficient regard to the constitutional protections
 (E) suicide in monetary units without proper regard to the importance of life

14. All high-powered racing engines have stochastic fuel injection. Stochastic fuel injection is not a feature which is normally included in the engines of production-line vehicles. Passenger sedans are production-line vehicles.

 Which of the following conclusions can be drawn from these statements?

 (A) Passenger sedans do not usually have stochastic fuel injection.
 (B) Stochastic fuel injection is found only in high-powered racing cars.
 (C) Car manufacturers do not include stochastic fuel injection in passenger cars because they fear accidents.
 (D) Purchasers of passenger cars do not normally purchase stochastic fuel injection because it is expensive.
 (E) Some passenger sedans are high-powered racing vehicles.

15. During New York City's fiscal crisis of the late 1970s, governmental leaders debated whether to offer federal assistance to New York City. One economist who opposed the suggestion asked, "Are we supposed to help out New York City every time it gets into financial problems?"

 The economist's question can be criticized because it

 (A) uses ambiguous terms
 (B) assumes everyone else agrees New York City should be helped
 (C) appeals to emotions rather than using logic
 (D) relies upon second-hand reports rather than first-hand accounts
 (E) completely ignores the issue at hand

16. Some philosophers have argued that there exist certain human or natural rights which belong to all human beings by virtue of their humanity. But a review of the laws of different societies shows that the rights accorded a person vary from society to society and even within a society over time. Since there is no right that is universally protected, there are no natural rights.

 A defender of the theory that natural rights do exist might respond to this objection by arguing that

 (A) some human beings do not have any natural rights
 (B) some human rights are natural while others derive from a source such as a constitution
 (C) people in one society may have natural rights which people in another society lack
 (D) all societies have some institution that protects the rights of an individual in that society
 (E) natural rights may exist even though they are not protected by some societies

QUESTIONS 17 AND 18

The single greatest weakness of American parties is their inability to achieve cohesion in the legislature. Although there is some measure of party unity, it is not uncommon for the majority party to be unable to implement important legislation. The unity is strongest during election campaigns; after the primary elections, the losing candidates all promise their support to the party nominee. By the time the Congress convenes, the unity has dissipated. This phenomenon is attributable to the fragmented nature of party politics. The national committees are no more than feudal lords who receive nominal fealty from their vassals. A member of Congress builds power upon a local base. Consequently, a member is likely to be responsive to local special interest groups. Evidence of this is seen in the differences in voting patterns between the upper and lower houses. In the Senate, where terms are longer, there is more party unity.

17. Which of the following, if true, would most strengthen the author's argument?

(A) On 30 key issues, 18 of the 67 majority party members in the Senate voted against the party leaders.

(B) On 30 key issues, 70 of the 305 majority party members in the House voted against the party leaders.

(C) On 30 key issues, over half the members of the minority party in both houses voted with the majority party against the leaders of the minority party.

(D) Of 30 key legislative proposals introduced by the president, only eight passed both houses.

(E) Of 30 key legislative proposals introduced by a president whose party controlled a majority in both houses, only four passed both houses.

18. Which of the following, if true, would most weaken the author's argument?

(A) Members of Congress receive funds from the national party committee.

(B) Senators vote against the party leaders only two-thirds as often as House members.

(C) The primary duty of an officeholder is to be responsive to a local constituency rather than party leaders.

(D) There is more unity among minority party members than among majority party members.

(E) Much legislation is passed each session despite party disunity.

19. ADVERTISEMENT: When you enroll with Future Careers Business Institute (FCBI), you will have access to our placement counseling service. Last year, 92% of our graduates who asked us to help them find jobs found them. So go to FCBI for your future!

The answer to which of the following questions is potentially the LEAST damaging to the claim of the advertisement?

(A) How many of your graduates asked FCBI for assistance?

(B) How many people graduated from FCBI last year?

(C) Did those people who asked for jobs find ones in the areas for which they were trained?

(D) Was FCBI responsible for finding the jobs or did graduates find them independently?

(E) Was the person reading the advertisement a paid, professional actor?

20. Either you severely punish a child who is bad or the child will grow up to be a criminal. Your child has just been bad. Therefore, you should punish the child severely.

All EXCEPT which of the following would be an appropriate objection to the argument?

(A) What do you consider to be a severe punishment?

(B) What do you mean by the term "bad"?

(C) Isn't your "either-or" premise an oversimplification?

(D) Don't your first and second premises contradict one another?

(E) In what way has this child been bad?

21. Studies recently published in the *Journal of the American Medical Association* say that despite the widespread belief to the contrary, girls are just as likely as boys to have the reading impairment dyslexia. The new studies examined 450 children over a four-year period, from kindergarten through third grade. The research teams found that fewer than half the students referred to them for reading problems actually had them; and although the schools identified four times as many boys as girls as being dyslexic, independent testing by the research teams revealed that the impairment appeared in both sexes with equal frequency. Yet, over the past decades, elaborate research programs have been set up to find the biological basis for the presumed gender difference in developing dyslexia.

Which of the following, if true, best explains the seeming contradiction outlined above between the new research and the conventional sex-linked view of dyslexia?

(A) Many boys who have dyslexia are not identified as suffering any learning disability.

(B) Many girls who do not have any learning impairment are incorrectly identified as having dyslexia.

(C) Earlier research was based entirely on subjects who were diagnosed by teachers as having reading problems.

(D) For years, the incidence of dyslexia has been underreported in school children of both genders.

(E) Learning disabilities are not likely to become evident until a child has reached the fourth grade.

QUESTIONS 22 AND 23

We should abolish the public education system and allow schools to operate as autonomous units competing for students. Students will receive government funds in the form of vouchers which they can then "spend" at the school of their choice. This will force schools to compete for students by offering better and more varied educational services. As in private industry, only the schools that provide customer satisfaction will survive. Since schools that cannot attract students will close, we will see an overall improvement in the quality of education.

22. The argument above rests on which of the following unsupported assumptions?

(A) Maximizing student and parent satisfaction also maximizes student learning.

(B) In order to attract students, all schools will eventually have to offer essentially the same curriculum.

(C) Giving students direct financial aid encourages them to study harder.

(D) Schools should provide only educational services and not additional co-curricular or extra-curricular activities.

(E) All education, both public and private, should be funded either directly or indirectly by government expenditures.

23. Which of the following, if true, would most undermine the argument above?

(A) Schools will make sure that all parents and students are thoroughly informed about the programs offered.

(B) Most students and parents will select a school based upon the convenience of its location.

(C) Students have different interests and different needs that can best be met by a variety of programs.

(D) By forcing schools to operate on a cost-effective basis, a voucher program would actually reduce total educational expenditures.

(E) Financial barriers currently limit the educational choices of students from poorer families.

24. Though I am an amateur athlete—a long-distance runner—I have no love of the Olympic Games. The original purpose was noble, but the games have become a vehicle for politics and money. For example, when the media mention the 1980 winter games at Lake Placid, they invariably show footage of a hockey game. The real story of the 1980 games—Eric Heiden's winning five gold medals in speed skating—is all but forgotten.

The speaker above implies that

(A) Eric Heiden was a better hockey player than speed skater

(B) most people would prefer to watch speed skating over hockey

(C) hockey produces money while speed skating does not

(D) only professional athletes compete in the Olympic Games

(E) amateur athletes are more exciting to watch than professional athletes

25. Some judges are members of the bar. No member of the bar is a convicted felon. Therefore, some judges are not convicted felons.

Which of the following is logically most similar to the argument developed above?

(A) Anyone who jogs in the heat will be sick. I do not jog in the heat, and will therefore likely never be sick.

(B) People who want to avoid jury duty will not register to vote. A person may not vote until age 18. Therefore, persons under 18 are not called for jury duty.

(C) All businesses file a tax return, but many businesses do not make enough money to pay taxes. Therefore, some businesses do not make a profit.

(D) All non-students were excluded from the meeting, but some non-students were interested in the issues discussed. Therefore, some non-students interested in the issues are not allowed in the meeting.

(E) The Grand Canyon is large. The Grand Canyon is in Arizona. Therefore, Arizona is large.

QUESTIONS 26 AND 27

A study published by the Department of Education shows that children in the central cities lag far behind students in the suburbs and the rural areas in reading skills. The report blames this differential on the over-crowding in the classrooms of city schools. I maintain, however, that the real reason that city children are poorer readers than non-city children is that they do not get enough fresh air and sunshine.

26. Which of the following best describes the form of the above argument?

(A) It attacks the credibility of the Department of Education.

(B) It indicts the methodology of the study of the Department of Education.

(C) It attempts to show that central city students read as well as non-city students.

(D) It offers an alternative explanation for the differential.

(E) It argues from analogy.

exercises

27. Which of the following would LEAST strengthen the author's point in the preceding argument?

(A) Medical research that shows a correlation between air pollution and learning disabilities

(B) A report by educational experts demonstrating that there is no relationship between the number of students in a classroom and a student's ability to read

(C) A notice released by the Department of Education retracting that part of their report that mentions overcrowding as the reason for the differential

(D) The results of a federal program that indicates that city students show significant improvement in reading skills when they spend the summer in the country

(E) A proposal by the federal government to fund emergency programs to hire more teachers for central city schools in an attempt to reduce overcrowding in the classrooms

28. Some judges have allowed hospitals to disconnect life-support equipment of patients who have no prospects for recovery. But I say that is murder. Either we put a stop to this practice now, or we will soon have programs of euthanasia for the old and infirm as well as others who might be considered a burden. Rather than disconnecting life-support equipment, we should let nature take its course.

All of the following are valid objections to the above argument EXCEPT

(A) it is internally inconsistent

(B) it employs emotionally charged terms

(C) it presents a false dilemma

(D) it oversimplifies a complex moral situation

(E) it appeals to authority not universally accepted

29. If Paul comes to the party, Quentin leaves the party. If Quentin leaves the party, either Robert or Steve asks Alice to dance. If Alice is asked to dance by either Robert or Steve and Quentin leaves the party, Alice accepts. If Alice is asked to dance by either Robert or Steve and Quentin does not leave the party, Alice does not accept.

If Quentin does not leave the party, which of the following statements can be logically deduced from the information given?

(A) Robert asks Alice to dance.

(B) Steve asks Alice to dance.

(C) Alice refuses to dance with either Robert or Steve.

(D) Paul does not come to the party.

(E) Alice leaves the party.

30. All students have submitted applications for admission. Some of the applications for admission have not been acted upon. Therefore, some more students will be accepted.

The logic of which of the following is most similar to that of the argument above?

(A) Some of the barrels have not yet been loaded on the truck, but all of the apples have been put into barrels. So, some more apples will be loaded onto the truck.

(B) All students who received passing marks were juniors. *X* received a passing mark. Therefore, *X* is a junior.

(C) Some chemicals will react with glass bottles, but not with plastic bottles. Therefore, those chemicals should be kept in plastic bottles and not glass ones.

(D) All advertising must be approved by the Council before it is aired. This television spot for a new cola has not yet been approved by the Council. Therefore, it is not to be aired until the Council makes its decision.

(E) There are six blue marbles and three red marbles in this jar. Therefore, if I blindly pick out seven marbles, there should be two red marbles left to pick.

31. New Evergreen Gum has twice as much flavor for your money as Spring Mint Gum, and we can prove it. You see, a stick of Evergreen Gum is twice as large as a stick of Spring Mint Gum, and the more gum, the more flavor.

Which of the following, if true, would undermine the persuasive appeal of the above advertisement?

(A) A package of Spring Mint Gum contains twice as many sticks as a package of Evergreen Gum.

(B) Spring Mint Gum has more concentrated flavor than Evergreen Gum.

(C) A stick of Evergreen Gum weighs only 50% as much as a stick of Spring Mint Gum.

(D) A package of Evergreen Gum costs twice as much as a package of Spring Mint Gum.

(E) People surveyed indicated a preference for Evergreen Gum over Spring Mint Gum.

32. Judging from the tenor of the following statements and the apparent authoritativeness of their sources, which is the most reasonable and trustworthy?

(A) FILM CRITIC: Beethoven is really very much overrated as a composer. His music is not really that good; it's just very well known.

(B) SPOKESPERSON FOR A MANUFACTURER: The jury's verdict against us for $2 million is ridiculous, and we are sure that the Appeals Court will agree with us.

(C) SENIOR CABINET OFFICER: Our administration plans to cut inefficiency, and we have already begun to discuss plans which we calculate will save the federal government nearly $50 billion a year in waste.

(D) FRENCH WINE EXPERT: The best buy in wines in America today is the California chablis, which is comparable to the French chablis and is available at half the cost.

(E) UNION LEADER: We plan to stay out on strike until management meets each and every one of the demands we have submitted.

33. That it is impossible to foretell the future is easily demonstrated. For if a person should foresee being injured by a mill wheel on the next day, the person would cancel the trip to the mill and remain at home in bed. Since the injury the next day by the mill wheel would not occur, it cannot in any way be said that the future has been foretold.

Which of the following best explains the weakness in this argument?

(A) The author fails to explain how one could actually change the future.

(B) The author uses the word *future* in two different ways.

(C) The author does not explain how anyone could foresee the future.

(D) The argument is internally inconsistent.

(E) The argument is circular.

EXERCISE 2: CRITICAL REASONING

18 Questions • 28 Minutes

Directions: The following questions ask you to analyze and evaluate the reasoning in short paragraphs or passages. For some questions, all of the answer choices may conceivably be answers to the question asked. You should select the *best* answer to the question, that is, an answer that does not require you to make assumptions which violate common-sense standards by being implausible, redundant, irrelevant, or inconsistent.

Example:

Q In an extensive study of the reading habits of magazine subscribers, it was found that an average of between four and five people actually read each copy of the most popular weekly news magazine. On this basis, we estimate that the 12,000 copies of *Poets and Poetry* that are sold each month are actually read by 48,000 to 60,000 people.

The estimate above assumes that

(A) individual magazine readers generally enjoy more than one type of magazine

(B) most of the readers of *Poets and Poetry* subscribe to the magazine

(C) the ratio of readers to copies is the same for *Poets and Poetry* as for the weekly news magazine

(D) the number of readers of the weekly news magazine is similar to the number of readers of *Poets and Poetry*

(E) most readers enjoy sharing copies of their favorite magazines with friends and family members

A **The correct answer is (C).**

1. The Supreme Court's recent decision is unfair. It treats non-resident aliens as a special group when it denies them some rights ordinary citizens have. This treatment is discriminatory, and we all know that discrimination is unfair.

   Which of the following arguments is most nearly similar in its reasoning to the above argument?

   (A) Doing good would be our highest duty under the moral law, and that duty would be irrational unless we had the ability to discharge it; but since a finite creature could never discharge that duty in his lifetime, we must conclude that if there is moral law, the soul is immortal.

   (B) Required core courses are a good idea because students just entering college do not have as good an idea about what constitutes a good education as do the professional educators; therefore, students should not be left complete freedom to select coursework.

   (C) This country is the most free nation on earth largely as a result of the fact that the founding fathers had the foresight to include a Bill of Rights in the Constitution.

   (D) Whiskey and beer do not mix well; every evening that I have drunk both whiskey and beer together, the following morning I have had a hangover.

(E) I know that this is a beautiful painting because Picasso created only beautiful works of art, and this painting was done by Picasso.

2. Creativity must be cultivated. Artists, musicians, and writers all practice, consciously or unconsciously, interpreting the world from new and interesting viewpoints. A teacher can encourage his pupils to be creative by showing them different perspectives for viewing the significance of events in their daily lives.

Which of the following, if true, would most undermine the author's claim?

(A) In a well-ordered society, it is important to have some people who are not artists, musicians, or writers.

(B) A teacher's efforts to show a pupil different perspectives may actually inhibit development of the student's own creative process.

(C) Public education should stress practical skills, which will help a person get a good job, instead of creative thinking.

(D) Not all pupils have the same capacity for creative thought.

(E) Some artists, musicians, and writers "burn themselves out" at a very early age, producing a flurry of great works and then nothing after that.

3. Opponents to the mayor's plan for express bus lanes on the city's major commuter arteries objected that people could not be lured out of their automobiles in that way. The opponents were proved wrong; following implementation of the plan, bus ridership rose dramatically, and there was a corresponding drop in automobile traffic. Nonetheless, the plan failed to achieve its stated objective of reducing average commuting time.

Which of the following would be the most logical continuation of this argument?

(A) The plan's opponents failed to realize that many people would take advantage of improved bus transportation.

(B) Unfortunately, politically attractive solutions do not always get results.

(C) The number of people a vehicle can transport varies directly with the size of the passenger compartment of the vehicle.

(D) Opponents cited an independent survey of city commuters showing that before the plan's adoption only one out of every seven used commuter bus lines.

(E) With the express lanes closed to private automobile traffic, the remaining cars were forced to use too few lanes and this created gigantic traffic tie-ups.

4. Last year, Gambia received $2.5 billion in loans from the International Third World Banking Fund, and its Gross Domestic Product grew by 5%. This year Gambia has requested twice as much money from the ITWBF, and its leaders expect that Gambia's GDP will rise by a full 10%.

Which of the following, if true, would LEAST undermine the expectations of Gambia's leaders?

(A) The large 5% increase of last year is attributable to extraordinary harvests due to unusually good weather conditions.

(B) Gambia's economy is not strong enough to absorb more than $3 billion in outside capital each year.

(C) Gambia does not have sufficient heavy industry to fuel an increase in its GDP of more than 6% per year.

(D) A provision of the charter of the International Third World Banking Fund prohibits the Fund from increasing loans to a country by more than 50% in a single year.

(E) A neighboring country experienced an increase of 5% in its Gross Domestic Product two years ago but an increase of only 3% in the most recent year.

5. Efficiency experts will attempt to improve the productivity of an office by analyzing production procedures into discrete work tasks. They then study the organization of those tasks and advise managers on techniques to speed production, such as rescheduling of employee breaks or relocating various equipment such as the copying machines. I have found a way to accomplish increases in efficiency with much less to do. Office workers grow increasingly productive as the temperature drops, so long as it does not fall below 68°F.

   The passage leads most naturally to which of the following conclusions?

   (A) Some efficiency gains will be short-term only.

   (B) To maintain peak efficiency, an office manager must occasionally restucture office tasks.

   (C) Employees are most efficient when the temperature is at 68°F.

   (D) The temperature-efficiency formula is applicable to all kinds of work.

   (E) Office workers will be equally efficient at 67°F and 69°F.

QUESTIONS 6, 7, AND 8

SPEAKER 1: Those who oppose abortion upon demand make the foundation of their arguments the sanctity of human life, but this seeming bedrock assumption is actually as weak as shifting sand. And it is not necessary to invoke the red herring that many abortion opponents would allow that human life must sometimes be sacrificed for a great good, as in the fighting of a just war. There are counter-examples to the principle of sanctity of life which are even more embarrassing to abortion opponents. It would be possible to reduce the annual number of traffic fatalities to virtually zero by passing federal legislation mandating a nationwide fifteen-mile-per-hour speed limit on *all* roads. You see, implicitly we have always been willing to trade off quantity of human life for quality.

SPEAKER 2: The analogy my opponent draws between abortion and traffic fatalities is weak. No one would propose such a speed limit. Imagine people trying to get to and from work under such a law, or imagine them trying to visit a friend or relatives outside their own neighborhoods, or taking in a sports event or a movie. Obviously such a law would be a disaster.

6. Which of the following best characterizes Speaker 2's response to Speaker 1?

   (A) His analysis of the traffic fatalities case actually supports the argument of Speaker 1.

   (B) His analysis of the traffic fatalities case is an effective rebuttal of Speaker 1's argument.

   (C) His response provides a strong affirmative statement of his own position.

   (D) His response is totally irrelevant to the issue raised by Speaker 1.

   (E) His counter-argument attacks the character of Speaker 1 instead of the merits of Speaker 1's argument.

7. Which of the following represents the most logical continuation of the reasoning contained in Speaker 1's argument?

   (A) Therefore, we should not have any laws on the books to protect human life.

   (B) We can only conclude that Speaker 2 is also in favor of strengthening enforcement of existing traffic regulations as a means to reducing the number of traffic fatalities each year.

(C) So the strongest attack on Speaker 2's position is that he contradicts himself when he agrees that we should fight a just war even at the risk of considerable loss of human life.

(D) Even the laws against contraception are good examples of this tendency.

(E) The abortion question just makes explicit that which for so long has remained hidden from view.

8. Which of the following assumptions are made in the argument of Speaker 1?

(A) The protection of human life is not a justifiable goal of society.

(B) A human fetus should not be considered a "life" for purposes of government protections.

(C) Speed limits and other minor restrictions are an impermissible intrusion by government on human freedom

(D) An appropriate societal decision is made in the balancing of individual lives and the quality of life.

(E) Government may legitimately protect the interests of individuals but has no authority to act on behalf of families or groups.

Some Alphas are not Gammas.

All Betas are Gammas.

9. Which of the following conclusions can be deduced from the two statements above?

(A) Some Alphas are not Betas.

(B) No Gammas are Alphas.

(C) All Gammas are Betas.

(D) All Alphas are Gammas.

(E) Some Alphas are Gammas.

10. I saw Barbara at the race track, and she told me that on the same horse race she made two win bets. She said she bet $10 on Boofer Bear to win at even money, and $5 on Copper Cane to win at odds of 10 to 1. After the race, she went back to the parimutuel window. So one or the other of those two horses must have won the race.

Which of the following is NOT an unstated premise of the reasoning above?

(A) The only bets Barbara made on the race were her win bets on Boofer Bear and Copper Cane.

(B) In the race in question, Boofer Bear and Copper Cane did not finish in a dead heat.

(C) Barbara did not return to the parimutuel window after the race for some reason other than cashing a winning ticket.

(D) Barbara's representation of the bets that she had placed was accurate.

(E) Barbara believed that it was more likely that Boofer Bear would win than Copper Cane.

11. Juana is dining at a Chinese restaurant. She will order either combination platter #2 or combination platter #5, but not both. If she orders combination platter #2, she will eat fried rice. If she orders combination platter #5, she will eat an egg roll. Given the statements above, which of the following must be true?

(A) Juana will eat either fried rice or an egg roll but not both.

(B) If Juana eats an egg roll, then she ordered combination platter #5.

(C) If Juana does not eat an egg roll, then she ordered combination platter #2.

(D) If Juana eats fried rice, then she ordered combination platter #2.

(E) Anyone who orders combination platter #2 eats fried rice.

12. The harmful effects of marijuana and other drugs have been considerably overstated. Although parents and teachers have expressed much concern over the dangers that widespread usage of marijuana and other drugs pose for high school and junior high school students, a national survey of 5,000 students of ages 13 to 17 showed that fewer than 15% of those students thought such drug use was likely to be harmful.

Which of the following is the strongest criticism of the author's reasoning?

(A) The opinions of students in the age group surveyed are likely to vary with age.

(B) Alcohol use among students of ages 13 to 17 is on the rise, and is now considered by many to present greater dangers than marijuana usage.

(C) Marijuana and other drugs may be harmful to users even though the users are not themselves aware of the danger.

(D) A distinction must be drawn between victimless crimes and crimes in which an innocent person is likely to be involved.

(E) The fact that a student does not think a drug is harmful does not necessarily mean he will use it.

13. AL: If an alien species ever visited Earth, it would surely be because they were looking for other intelligent species with whom they could communicate. Since we have not been contacted by aliens, we may conclude that none have ever visited this planet.

AMY: Or, perhaps, they did not think human beings intelligent.

How is Amy's response related to Al's argument?

(A) She misses Al's point entirely.

(B) She attacks Al personally rather than his reasoning.

(C) She points out that Al made an unwarranted assumption.

(D) She ignores the detailed internal development of Al's logic.

(E) She introduces a false analogy.

14. I maintain that the best way to solve our company's present financial crisis is to bring out a new line of goods. I challenge anyone who disagrees with this proposed course of action to show that it will not work.

A flaw in the preceding argument is that it

(A) employs group classifications without regard to individuals

(B) introduces an analogy which is weak

(C) attempts to shift the burden of proof to those who would object to the plan

(D) fails to provide statistical evidence to show that the plan will actually succeed

(E) relies upon a discredited economic theory

15. If quarks are the smallest subatomic particles in the universe, then gluons are needed to hold quarks together. Since gluons are needed to hold quarks together, it follows that quarks are the smallest subatomic particles in the universe.

The logic of the above argument is most nearly paralleled by which of the following?

(A) If this library has a good French literature collection, it will contain a copy of *Les Conquerants* by Malraux. The collection does contain a copy of *Les Conquerants;* therefore, the library has a good French literature collection.

(B) If there is a man-in-the-moon, the moon must be made of green cheese for him to eat. There is a man-in-the-moon, so the moon is made of green cheese.

(C) Either helium or hydrogen is the lightest element of the periodic table. Helium is not the lightest element of the periodic table, so hydrogen must be the lightest element of the periodic table.

(D) If Susan is taller than Bob, and if Bob is taller than Elaine, then if Susan is taller than Bob, Susan is also taller than Elaine.

(E) Whenever it rains, the streets get wet. The streets are not wet. Therefore, it has not rained.

16. In the earliest stages of the common law, a party could have a case heard by a judge only upon the payment of a fee to the court, and then only if the case fit within one of the forms for which there existed a writ. At first the number of such formalized cases of action was very small, but judges invented new forms which brought more cases and greater revenues.

Which of the following conclusions is most strongly suggested by the paragraph above?

(A) Early judges often decided cases in an arbitrary and haphazard manner.

(B) In most early cases, the plaintiff rather than the defendant prevailed.

(C) The judiciary at first had greater power than either the legislature or the executive.

(D) One of the motivating forces for the early expansion in judicial power was economic considerations.

(E) The first common law decisions were inconsistent with one another and did not form a coherent body of law.

17. If Martin introduces an amendment to Evans's bill, then Johnson and Lloyd will both vote the same way. If Evans speaks against Lloyd's position, Johnson will defend anyone voting with him. Martin will introduce an amendment to Evans's bill only if Evans speaks against Johnson's position.

If the above statements are true, each of the following can be true EXCEPT

(A) if Evans speaks against Johnson's position, Lloyd will not vote with Johnson.

(B) if Martin introduces an amendment to Evans's bill, then Evans has spoken against Johnson's position.

(C) if Evans speaks against Johnson's position, Martin will not introduce an amendment to Evans' bill.

(D) if Martin introduces an amendment to Evans's bill, then either Johnson will not vote with Lloyd or Evans did not speak against Johnson's position.

(E) if either Evans did not speak against Lloyd's position or Martin did not introduce an amendment to Evans's bill, then either Johnson did not defend Lloyd or Martin spoke against Johnson's position.

18. Once at a conference on the philosophy of language, a professor delivered a lengthy and tiresome address the central thesis of which was that "yes" and related slang words such as "yeah" can be used only to show agreement with a proposition. At the end of the paper, a listener in the back of the auditorium stood up and shouted in a sarcastic voice, "Oh, yeah?" This constituted a complete refutation of the paper.

The listener argued against the paper by

(A) offering a counter-example

(B) pointing out an inconsistency

(C) presenting an analogy

(D) attacking the speaker's character

(E) citing additional evidence

Exercise 1: ANSWER KEY AND EXPLANATIONS

1. E	8. E	15. E	22. A	29. D
2. B	9. D	16. E	23. B	30. A
3. C	10. E	17. E	24. C	31. E
4. E	11. D	18. C	25. D	32. D
5. B	12. B	19. E	26. D	33. B
6. D	13. B	20. D	27. E	
7. B	14. A	21. C	28. E	

1. **The correct answer is (E).** This item tests logical deduction. Statement I establishes that all batters bunt whenever two conditions are met: Some runners lead off and all infielders play in. Statement II establishes that one of the two conditions is met (some runners are leading off), but denies that all batters are bunting. This can only be because the other condition is not met: It is false that "All infielders are playing in." Recalling our discussion of direct inferences in the instructional overview, we know that this means "Some infielders are not playing in," or answer (E). We cannot conclude (C), that none of the infielders are playing in, only that some are not. Nor can we deduce (D), that all are playing in—for that is logically impossible. Then, recalling our discussion of the meaning of *some* in the Instructional Overview, we eliminate both (A) and (B). Some means "at least one" without regard to the remaining population. That some runners are leading off does not imply that some are not leading off (B). And that some batters are not bunting does not imply that some are bunting.

2. **The correct answer is (B).** The author's attitude toward the bankruptcy law is expressed by his choice of the terms "folly," "protectionism," "conned." The author apparently believes that the debtor who has incurred these debts ought to bear the responsibility for them and that the government should not help the debtor get off the hook. (B) properly expresses this attitude: You have created for yourself a situation by your own actions; now you must accept it. The author may share the view (A) as well, but (A) is not a judgment the author would make about the bankrupt, that is, a person who does not have a penny to save. (C) is completely unrelated to the question at hand; the bankrupt has no power to wield. The author may believe (D), but the question stem asks for the author's attitude about the bankrupt debtor, not the government. (D) would be appropriate to the latter, but it has no bearing on the question at hand. Finally, (E) would be applicable if the government were giving money to pay a ransom to terrorists or some similar situation. The assistance it provides to the bankrupt debtor is not such a program. It does not pay tribute to the debtor.

3. **The correct answer is (C).** Ann's response would be appropriate only if Mary had said, "All of the students at State College come from Midland High." That is why (C) is correct. (D) is wrong, because they are talking about the background of the students, not the reputations of the schools. (E) is wrong, for the question is from where the students at State College come. (B) is superficially

relevant to the exchange, but it, too, is incorrect. Ann would not reply to this statement, had Mary made it, in the way she did reply. Rather, she would have said, "No, there are some Midland students at State College." Finally, Ann would have correctly said (A) only if Mary had said, "None of the students from North Hills attend State College," or "Most of the students from North Hills do not attend State College." But Ann makes neither of these responses, so we know that (A) cannot have been what she thought she heard Mary say.

4. **The correct answer is (E).** If you wanted to determine how politically active people are, what kind of test would you devise? You might do a survey to test political awareness; you might do a survey to find out how many hours people devote to political campaigning each week or how many hours they spend writing letters, etc.; or you might get a rough estimate by studying the voting statistics. The paragraph takes contributions as a measure of political activity. (E) is correct for two reasons. One, the paragraph says nothing about individual activity. It says total contributions were up, not average or per person contributions. Second, (E) cites voting patterns which seem as good as or better an indicator of political activity than giving money. This second reason explains why (A) is wrong. (A) may weaken the argument, but a stronger attack would use voting patterns. (D) confuses individual and corporate contributions, so even if campaign giving were a strong indicator of activity, (D) would still be irrelevant. (B) does not even explain why contributions *in toto* rose during the four years, nor does it tell us anything about the pattern of giving by individual persons. Finally, (C) seems the worst of all the answers, for it hardly constitutes an attack on the author's reasoning. It seems likely that even in the face of increased political activity, public leaders would continue to warn against the dangers of political apathy.

5. **The correct answer is (B).** The chief failing of the argument is that it draws a false analogy. Since prisons are required to feed and maintain as well as house prisoners (not to mention the necessity for security), the analogy to a hotel room is weak at best. (C) focuses on this specific shortcoming. Remember, in evaluating the strength of an argument from analogy it is important to look for dissimilarities which might make the analogy inappropriate. Thus, (A) and (E) are also good criticisms of the argument. They voice the general objection of which (C) is the specification. (D) is also a specific objection—the argument compares two numbers which are not at all similar. So the numerical comparison is a false one. (B) is not a way in which the argument can be criticized, for the author never cites any authority.

6. **The correct answer is (D).** The key phrase in this paragraph is "beef costs more per pound than fish." A careful reading would show that (A) is in direct contradiction to the explicit wording of the passage. (B) cannot be inferred since the dietitian merely says, "I pay." Perhaps the dietitian intends to keep the price of a meal stable by cutting back in other areas. In any event, this is another example of not going beyond a mere factual analysis to generate policy recommendations unless the question stem specifically invites such an extension, e.g., which of the following courses of action would the author recommend? (C) makes an unwarranted inference. From the fact that beef is more costly one would not want to conclude that it is more profitable. (E) is wrong for this reason also. (D) is correct because it focuses on the "per measure of protein,"

which explains why a fish meal will cost the dietitian more than a beef meal, even though fish is less expensive per pound.

7. **The correct answer is (B).** One of the most common patterns to look for with this type of question is the "surprise result," that is, an unanticipated factor that defeats the expected outcome. (B) fits this pattern: you'll be so hungry from the workout that you'll eat more. (Remember that you are told to accept the soundness of each of the answer choices.) The other choices just don't have the same logical "zip." Anyway, (A) seems to strengthen the argument: it's okay to do what the ad suggests. And (C) doesn't focus on the logic of the ad—even though it probably helps to explain why the ad might be effective. (D) and (E) are wrong because they address issues that are not really on the table, so to speak; the ad is not addressing those who are already happy nor those who are overly thin.

8. **The correct answer is (E).** The reasoning in the argument is representative of the fallacy of false cause. Common sense tells you that you are not necessarily safer driving at higher speeds. Moreover, the distance you are from your home does not necessarily make you more or less safe. And it will not do to engage in wild speculation, e.g., people suddenly become more attentive at speeds over 45 miles per hour. The exam is just not that subtle. Rather we should look for a fairly obvious alternative explanation, and we find it in (E). The real reason there are fewer fatalities at speeds over 50 miles per hour and at a distance greater than 25 miles from home is that less driving time is logged under such conditions. Most driving originates at home and proceeds at speeds set for residential areas. (A), (B), and (C) all seem to make plausible statements, but they are irrelevant to the claim made in the stem paragraph. It is difficult to see how they could either weaken or strengthen the argument. (D) has the merit of addressing the statistics used to support the argument, but without further information (D) does not weaken the argument—it merely makes an observation. To be sure, if we knew that states were notoriously bad at gathering statistics, (D) could weaken the argument. But that requires speculation, and we always prefer an obvious answer such as (E).

9. **The correct answer is (D).** The author states that a certain amount of rain in a given time *usually* results in mushrooms growing in his backyard. Both (A) and (B) are wrong for the same reason. From the fact that there has not been the requisite minimum rainfall required for mushrooms, we would not want to conclude that there has been *no* rain at all. (C) overstates the author's case and is for that reason wrong. The author specifically says it "usually" happens this way. Thus, the author would not want to say that the absence of mushrooms and fungus definitely means that the requisite amount of rain has not fallen—only that it seems likely or probable that there has not been enough rain. And (E) would not be supportable without some further premise about rain now. Notice that (D) is a safe conclusion: "probably" and "not more."

10. **The correct answer is (E).** The sample argument is a straightforward generalization: All observed *S* are *P*. *X* is an *S*. Therefore, *X* is *P*. Only (E) replicates this form. The reasoning in (A) is: "Some S are *P*. All *M* are *S*. (All swans are birds, which is a suppressed assumption.) Therefore, all *M* are *P*." That is like saying: "Some children are not well behaved. All little girls are children. Therefore, all little girls are not well behaved." (B), too, contains a suppressed premise. Its structure is: "All *S* are *P*. All *S* are *M*. (All ballets are theatrical productions, which is suppressed.) Therefore, all *M*

are *P*." That is like saying "All little girls are children. All little girls are human. Therefore, all humans are little girls." (C) is not a generalization at all. It takes a generalization and attempts to explain it by uncovering a causal linkage. (D) is simply a *non sequitur*. It moves from the universality of the *concept* of justice to the conclusion that justice is a *physical* trait of humans.

11. **The correct answer is (D).** The author is attempting to argue that laws against suicide are legitimate. The author argues against a simplistic libertarian position which says suicide hurts only the victim. The goal of the law, he argues, is not just to protect the victim from himself. A society passes such a law because it wants to underscore the importance of human life. Reading beyond the blank in the second paragraph makes clear the author's views on the value of human life. (A) flies in the face of the explicit language of the passage. The author does not defend the law as being a deterrent to suicide. (B) might be something the author believes, but it is not something developed in the passage. The author is not concerned here with explaining how the laws came to be on the books, but is concerned only with defending them. If anything, (B) would be more appropriate in the context of an argument against such laws. (C) also is something the author may believe, but the defense of the suicide law is not that it protects liberties—only that it serves a function and does not interfere with constitutional liberties any more than laws that prohibit doing violence to others. (E) is wrong for the same reasons that (B) is wrong. It seems to belong more in the context of an argument against suicide laws.

12. **The correct answer is (B).** With the comments in #11 in mind, it is clear that (B) must be correct. The author wants to make the point that suicide is not a victimless crime; it affects a great many people—even, it is claimed, some who were never personally acquainted with the suicide. Again, reading the whole passage is helpful. (A) is a joke—obviously suicide does not lead to more serious crimes. That is like saying the death penalty is designed to rehabilitate the criminal. (C) simply focuses on the superficial content of the sentence: One, it's talking about church and state, so (C), which mentions sin, is not correct. (D) is wrong because the author is not concerned to defend the laws as deterrents to suicide, as we discussed in #11. Finally, (E) is irrelevant to the point that the entire community is affected by the death of any one of its members.

13. **The correct answer is (B).** This third question, too, can be answered once the comments of #11 are understood. The key word here is "oversimplification." The libertarian oversimplifies matters by imagining that the only function of the law is to protect a person from self-harm. This is oversimplified because it overlooks the fact that such laws also serve the functions of (1) underscoring the value of life, and (2) protecting the community as a whole from the loss of any of its members. (A) is incorrect because the libertarian does not make this error but the related one of evaluating the function of the law only from the perspective of the suicide. (C) is wrong, for the author apparently shares with the libertarian the assumption that a law must not illegitimately interfere with individual liberty. The whole defense of the laws against suicide is that they have a legitimate function. (D) is wrong for the same reasons that (C) of #12 is wrong. Finally, (E) is very much like (A).

14. **The correct answer is (A).** (C) and (D) are wrong because they extrapolate without sufficient information. (E) contradicts the last given statement and so

cannot be a conclusion of it. That would be like trying to infer "all men are mortal" from the premise that "no men are mortal." (B) commits an error by moving from "all *S* are *P*" to "all *P* are *S*." Just because all racing engines have SFI does not mean that all SFIs are in racing engines. Some may be found in tractors and heavy-duty machinery.

15. **The correct answer is (E).** This is a very sticky question, but it is similar to ones that have been on the GMAT. The key here is to keep in mind that you are to pick the BEST answer, and sometimes you will not be very satisfied with any of them. Here (E) is correct by default of the others. (A) has some merit. After all, the economist really isn't very careful in stating the claim. The author says "here we go again" when there is no evidence that we have ever been there before. But there is no particular term the author uses that we could call ambiguous. (B) is wrong because, although the economist assumes some people take that position (otherwise, against whom would the argument be directed), the statement does not imply that the economist alone thinks differently. (C) is like (A), a possible answer, but this interpretation requires additional information. You would have to have said to yourself, "Oh, I see that the economist is against it. He is probably saying this in an exasperated tone and in the context of a diatribe." If there were such additional information, you would be right, and (C) would be a good answer. But there isn't. (E) does not require this additional speculation and so is truer to the given information. (D) would also require speculation. (E) is not perfect, just BEST by comparison.

16. **The correct answer is (E).** The argument assumes that a right cannot exist unless it is recognized by the positive law of a society. Against this assumption, it can be argued that a right may exist even though there is no mechanism for protecting or enforcing it. That this is at least plausible has been illustrated by our own history, e.g., minority groups have often been denied rights. These rights, however, existed all the while—they were just not protected by the government. (A) is incorrect, for the proponent of the theory of natural rights cannot deny that some human beings do not have them. That would contradict the very definition of natural right on which the claim is based. (B) is incorrect because it is not responsive to the argument. Even if (B) is true, the attacker of natural rights still has the argument that there are no universally recognized rights, so there are no universal (natural) rights at all. (C), like (A), is inconsistent with the very idea of a "natural" right. (D) is incorrect because it does not respond to the attacker's claim that no one right is protected universally. Consistency or universality within one society does not amount to consistency or universality across all societies.

17. **The correct answer is (E).** The author is arguing that political parties in America are weak because there is no party unity. Because of this lack of unity, the party is unable to pass legislation. (E) would strengthen this contention. (E) provides an example of a government dominated by a single party (control of the presidency and both houses), yet the party is unable to pass its own legislation. (A) provides little, if any, support for the argument. If there are only 18 defectors out of a total of 67 party members, that does not show tremendous fragmentation. (B) is even weaker by the same analysis: 70 defectors out of a total of 305 party members. (C) is weak because it focuses on the minority party. (D) strengthens the argument less clearly than choice (E) because there are many possible explanations for the failure; for example, a different party controlled the legislature.

18. **The correct answer is (C).** Here we are looking for the argument that will undermine the position taken by the paragraph. Remember that the ultimate conclusion of the paragraph is that this disunity is a weakness and that this prevents legislation from being passed. One very good way of attacking this argument is to attack the value judgment upon which the conclusion is based: Is it good to pass the legislation? The author assumes that it would be better to pass the legislation. We could argue, as in (C), that members of the Congress should not pass legislation simply because it is proposed by the party leadership. Rather, the members should represent the views of their constituents. Then, if the legislation fails, it must be the people who did not want it. In that case, it is better not to pass the legislation. (A) does not undermine the argument. That members receive funding proves nothing about unity after elections. As for (B), this seems to strengthen rather than weaken the argument. The author's thesis argues that there is greater unity in the Senate than in the House. (D) would undermine the argument only if we had some additional information to make it relevant. Finally, (E) does not weaken the argument greatly. That some legislation is passed is not a denial of the argument that more should be passed.

19. **The correct answer is (E).** This advertisement is simply rife with ambiguity. The wording obviously seeks to create the impression that FCBI found jobs for its many graduates and generally does a lot of good for them. But first we should ask how many graduates FCBI had—one, two, three, a dozen, or a hundred. If it had only 12 or so, finding them jobs might have been easy; but if many people enroll at FCBI, they may not have the same success. Further, we might want to know how many people graduated compared with how many enrolled. Do people finish the program, or does FCBI just take their money and then force them out of the program? So (B) is certainly something we need to know in order to assess the validity of the claim. Now, how many of those who graduated came in looking for help in finding a job? Maybe most people had jobs waiting for them (only a few needed help), in which case the job placement assistance of FCBI is not so impressive. Or, perhaps the graduates were so disgusted they did not even seek assistance. So (A) is relevant. (C) is also important. Perhaps FCBI found them jobs sweeping streets—not in business. The ad does not say what jobs FCBI helped its people find. Finally, maybe the ad is truthful—FCBI graduates found jobs—but maybe they did it on their own. So (D) also is a question worth asking. (E), however, is the least problematic. Even if it turns out that the ad was done by a paid, professional actor, so what? That's what you'd expect for an ad.

20. **The correct answer is (D).** The argument commits several errors. One obvious point is that the first premise is very much an oversimplification. Complicated questions about punishment and child rearing are hardly ever easily reduced to "either-or" propositions. Thus, (C) is a good objection. Beyond that, the terms "severely punish" and "bad" are highly ambiguous. It would be legitimate to ask the speaker just what he considered to be bad behavior, (B), and severe punishment, (A). Also, since the speaker has alleged the child has been "bad," and since the term is ambiguous, we can also demand clarification on that score, (E). The one objection it makes no sense to raise is (D). The premises have the very simple logical structure: If a child is bad and not punished, then the child becomes a criminal. Child X is bad. There is absolutely no inconsistency between those two statements.

21. **The correct answer is (C).** Notice that the question gives you some extra guidance here: There is a seeming inconsistency in the reports. On the one hand, much research suggests that dyslexia is a sex-linked problem. On the other hand, the new research suggests it is not. Of course, it is possible that the earlier research was just poorly done, but that wouldn't make a very interesting test answer, e.g., the earlier researchers just added incorrectly. (C) is more representative of the kind of answer you would find on the test: The earlier research was based on data that was biased and no one suspected that fact until now. As for the remaining choices, they hint at various weaknesses in the data on dyslexia, but they do not address the seeming contradiction that is the focus of the question stem.

22. **The correct answer is (A).** Examine each statement. (A) is a hidden assumption of the argument. Under the proposed system, according to the speaker, schools will have to make the customers happy and concludes that this will result in improved education. Thus, a hidden assumption of the argument is the equation between "happy customers" and "improved education." (B) is not an assumption of the argument. Indeed, the speaker implies that in an effort to attract students, schools will try to differentiate themselves from each other. And as for (C), the speaker does not assume that there is any causal connection between "aid" and "study." The speaker expects to see a positive result because schools are doing a better job. That may prompt students to study harder, but the motivating factor then is not "direct financial aid." (D) is apparently a misreading of the paragraph. The speaker says that schools will compete in terms of "educational services," which may be broad enough to include other activities but, in any event, certainly does not preclude offering other activities in the mix. And as for (E), the speaker does not say that there should be no privately funded schools at all—only that the public schools should be funded on a different model.

23. **The correct answer is (B).** The speaker assumes that students and parents will be educated consumers. (Pardon the play on words.) If it turns out that students and parents select a school because it is nearby, then schools don't have any incentive to offer creative educational programs in order to attract students; and a fundamental premise of the plan is proved incorrect. As for (A), this idea actually strengthens the argument for the plan: Schools will make sure that students and parents are educated consumers. (C) too is consistent with the speaker's analysis: Schools will create new programs to attract customers. As for (D), though this idea of cost is not discussed by the speaker, reducing costs would hardly be a disadvantage of a program. Finally, (E) seems to cut in favor of the program, for then the voucher plan seems calculated to ensure that everyone gets a fair opportunity to get an education.

24. **The correct answer is (C).** The speaker contrasts the Olympic sport of hockey, which gets media coverage because it generates revenues, with speed skating, which does not get media coverage. The implication here is that speed skating does not generate revenue. As for (A), this choice confuses the distinction drawn by the speaker. The speaker is contrasting two sports, not an individual's performance in two sports. (B) misconstrues the logical function of the example of speed skating in the argument. Speed skating is offered as an example of a sport which receives little attention even though it produces exciting amateur performances. (In fact, the speaker implies that hockey is more popular than speed skating, at least if one

uses media coverage as a standard.) (D) is an interesting response because it seems at least consistent with the sentiment expressed in the paragraph: Olympic games are really not entirely amateur sports. But (D) overstates the case: All Olympians are professionals. (What about Heiden whom the author mentions favorably?) Finally, (E) goes even further beyond the text. The speaker may or may not hold this opinion.

25. **The correct answer is (D).** Let us use our technique of substituting capital letters for categories. The sample argument can be rendered:

Some *J* are *B*. (Some Judges are Bar members.)

No *B* are *F*. (No Bar members are Felons.)

Therefore, some *J* are not *F*. (Some Judges are not Felons.)

This is a perfectly valid (logical) argument. (D) shares its form and validity:

Some *N* are *I*. (Some Non-students are Interested.)

No *N* are *M*. (No Non-students are Meeting-attenders.)

Therefore, some *I* are not *M*. (Some Interested Non-students are not Meeting-attenders.)

(E) has the invalid argument form:

G is *L*.

G is *A*.

Therefore, *A* is *L*.

(B) and (C) are both set up using more than three categories; therefore, they cannot possibly have the structure of the sample argument that uses only three categories:

(B)—people, people who want to avoid jury duty, people who do not register to vote, persons under 18

(C)—business, entities filing tax returns, business making enough money to pay taxes, business making a profit

Finally, (A) does not parallel the sample argument since it contains the qualification "likely."

26. **The correct answer is (D).** The author's argument is admittedly not a very persuasive one, but the question stem does not ask us to comment on its relative strength. Rather, we are asked to identify the form of argumentation. Here the author suggests an alternative explanation, albeit a somewhat outlandish one. Thus, (D) is correct, (E) is incorrect because the claim about fresh air and the country is introduced as a causal explanation, not an analogy to the city. (C) is wrong for the author accepts the differential described by the report and just tries to explain the existence of the differential in another way. By the same token we can reject both (A) and (B) since the author takes the report's conclusion as a starting point. Although the argument attacks the explanation provided by the *report* published by the Department of Education, it does not attack the *credibility* of the *department* itself. Further, though it disagrees with the *conclusion* drawn by the report, it does not attack the way in which the *study* itself was *conducted*. Rather, it disagrees with the interpretation of the data gathered.

27. **The correct answer is (E).** The question stem asks us to find the one item which will not strengthen the author's argument. That is (E). Remember, the author's argument is an attempt (to be sure, a weak one) to develop an alternative causal explanation. (A) would provide some evidence that the author's claim—which at first glance seems a bit far-fetched—actually has some empirical foundation. While (B) does not add any strength to the author's own expla-

nation of the phenomenon being studied, it does strengthen the author's overall position by undermining the explanation given in the report. (C) strengthens the author's position for the same reason that (B) does: It weakens the position that is attacked. (D) strengthens the argument in the same way that (A) does, by providing some empirical support for the otherwise seemingly far-fetched explanation.

28. **The correct answer is (E).** Perhaps the most obvious weakness in the argument is that it oversimplifies matters. It is like the domino theory arguments adduced to support the war in Vietnam: either we fight Communism now or it will take us over. The author argues, in effect: Either we put a stop to this now, or there will be no stopping it. Like the proponents of the domino theory, the author ignores the many intermediate positions one might take. (C) is one way of describing this shortcoming: The dilemma posed by the author is a false one because it overlooks positions between the two extremes. (B) is also a weakness of the argument: "Cold-blooded murder" is obviously a phrase calculated to excite negative feelings. Finally, the whole argument is also internally inconsistent. The conclusion is that we should allow nature to take its course. How? By prolonging life with artificial means. But the argument doesn't cite an authority, so (E) is the correct answer.

29. **The correct answer is (D).** We can summarize the information, using capital letters to represent each statement:

    If *P*, then *Q*.

    If *Q*, then *R* or *S*.

    If *R* or *S*, and if *Q*, then *A*.

    If *R* or *S* and if not-*Q*, then not-*A*.

    where *P* represents "Paul comes to the party," *Q* represents "Quentin leaves the party," *R* represents "Robert asks Alice to dance," *S* represents "Steve asks Alice to dance," (and conversely *R* represents "Alice is asked by Robert to dance" and *S* represents "Alice is asked by Steve to dance"), and *A* represents Alice accepts. If we have not-*Q*, then we can deduce not-*P* from the first statement; thus, we have (D). (A), (B), and (C) are incorrect since there is no necessity that Robert or Steve ask Alice to dance. (E) is incorrect since this statement is different from our other statements and must be assigned a different letter, perhaps *X*. Notice that "Alice will accept . . . " tells us nothing about whether Alice leaves the party.

30. **The correct answer is (A).** The question stem has the form:

    All *S* are *AP*. (All Students are Applicants.)

    Some *AP* are *AC* (Some Applicants are Accepted.)

    Some *more S* are *AC*. (Some more Students are Accepted.)

    Notice that (A) preserves very nicely the parallel in the conclusion because it uses the word "more." Thus, the error made in the stem argument (that some *more* students will be *accepted*) is preserved in (A): *more* apples will be *loaded*. (B) has a valid argument form (All *S* are *J*; *X* is an *S*; therefore, *X* is a *J*), so it is not parallel to the sample argument. (C) is not similar for at least two reasons. First, its conclusion is a recommendation ("should"), not a factual claim. Second, (C) uses one premise, not two premises as the sample argument does. (D) would have been parallel to the sample argument only if the sample had the conclusion "some more applications must be acted upon." Finally, choice (E) contains an argument that is fallacious, but the fallacy is not similar to that of the question stem.

answers

31. **The correct answer is (E).** The advertisement employs the term "more" in an ambiguous manner. In the context, one might expect the phrase "more flavor" to mean "more highly concentrated flavor," that is, "more flavor per unit weight." What the ad actually says, however, is that the sticks of Evergreen are *larger,* so if they are larger, there must be more *total* flavor. As for (A), it is possible to beat the ad at its own game. If flavor is just a matter of chewing enough sticks, then Spring Mint is as good a deal because, flavor unit for flavor unit, it is no more expensive than Evergreen. Second, (B) would also undermine the ad by focusing on the ambiguity we have just discussed. Finally, (C) also uncovers another potential ambiguity. If the ad is comparing volume rather than weight, Spring Mint may be a better value. After all, who wants to buy a lot of air? As for (A), it is possible to beat the ad at its own game: Want more flavor? Chew more sticks? As for (B), more highly concentrated favor means more flavor per stick, so size is not important. As for (C), a bigger stick doesn't necessarily mean more flavor. And (D), of course, cuts to the heart of the claim: money or value. Choice (E), however, if anything, would add to the appeal of the ad: Do what most people do.

32. **The correct answer is (D).** Again, we remind ourselves that we are looking for the most reliable statement. Even the most reliable, however, will not necessarily be perfectly reliable. Here (D) is fairly trustworthy. We note that the speaker is an expert and so is qualified to speak about wines. In (A), the speaker is making a judgment about something outside the expertise of a film critic. Also, in (D) there is no hint of self-interest—if anything, the speaker is admitting against a possible self-interest that American chablis is a better buy than French chablis. By comparison, (B) and (C), which smack of a self-serving bias, are not so trustworthy. Finally, (E) sounds like a statement made for dramatic effect and so is not to be taken at face value.

33. **The correct answer is (B).** The weakness in the argument is the fallacy of ambiguity. It uses the term "future" in two different ways. In the first instance, it uses the word "future" to mean that which is fixed and definite, that which must occur. But then comes the shift. The author subtly changes usage so that "future" denotes events which might, though not necessarily will, come to pass. As for (A), the author gives a good example of how one might very well be able to change the future. As for (C), the author is concerned to refute the idea of foreseeing future events, so it is not surprising that there is no attempt to explain the mechanism by which such foresight is achieved. (D) and (E) are incorrect because the fallacy is that of ambiguity, not of internal inconsistency (self-contradiction) nor circular reasoning (begging the question).

Exercise 2: ANSWER KEY AND EXPLANATIONS

1. E	5. C	9. A	13. C	17. D
2. B	6. A	10. E	14. C	18. A
3. E	7. E	11. C	15. A	
4. E	8. D	12. C	16. D	

1. **The correct answer is (E).** The argument given in the question stem is circular, that is, it begs the question. It tries to prove that the decision is unfair by claiming that it singles out a group, which is the same thing as discriminating, and then concludes that *since* all discrimination is unfair, so, too, is the court's decision unfair. Of course, the real issue is whether singling out this particular group is unfair. After all, we do make distinctions, e.g., adults are treated differently than children, businesses differently than persons, soldiers differently than executives. The question of fairness cannot be solved by simply noting that the decision singles out some persons. (E) also is circular: It tries to prove this is a beautiful painting because all paintings of this sort are beautiful. (A) is perhaps the second best answer, but notice that it is purely hypothetical in its form: *If* this were true, *then* that would be true. As a consequence, it is not as similar to the question stem as (E), which is phrased in categorical assertions rather than hypothetical statements. (B) moves from the premise that students are not good judges of their needs to a conclusion about the responsibility for planning course work. The conclusion and the premise are not the same so the argument is not circular. (C) is not, technically speaking, even an argument. Remember from our instructional material at the beginning of the book, an argument has premises and a conclusion. These are separate statements. (C) is one long statement, not two short ones. It reads: "*A* because *B*"; not "*A*; therefore *B*." For example, the statement "I am late because the car broke down" is not an inference but a causal statement. In (D), since the premise (everything after the semicolon) is not the same as the conclusion (the statement before the semicolon), the argument is not a circular argument and so does not parallel the stem argument.

2. **The correct answer is (B).** The author's claim depends in a very important way on the assumption that the assistance he advocates will be successful. After all, any proposed course of action that just won't work clearly ought to be rejected. (B) is just this kind of argument: Whatever else you say, your proposed plan will not work; therefore, we must reject it. (A) opens an entirely new line of argument. The author has said only that there is a certain connection between guidance and creativity; he never claims that everyone can or should be a professional artist. Thus, (A) is wrong, as is (E) for the same reason. (C) is wrong for a similar reason. The author never suggests that all students should be professional artists; and, in fact, he may want to encourage students to be creative no matter which practical careers they may choose. (E) is probably the second best answer; it does, to a certain extent, try to attack the workability of the proposal. Unfortunately, it does not address the general connection the author says exists between training and creativity. In other words, (E) does not say the proposal will not work at all; it merely says it may

answers

work too well. Further, (E) is wrong because it does not attribute the "burnout" to the training of the sort proposed by the author.

3. **The correct answer is (E).** What we are looking for here is an intervening causal link that caused the plan to be unsuccessful. The projected train of events was: (1) Adopt express lanes, (2) fewer cars, and (3) faster traffic flow. Between the first and the third steps, however, something went wrong. (E) alone supplies that unforeseen side effect. Since the cars backed up on too few lanes, total flow of traffic was actually slowed, not speeded up. (A) is irrelevant since it does not explain what went wrong *after* the plan was adopted. (B) does not even attempt to address the sequence of events which we have just outlined. Although (C) is probably true and was something the planners likely considered in their projections, it does not explain the plan's failure. Finally, (D) might have been relevant in deciding whether or not to adopt the plan, but given that the plan was adopted, (D) cannot explain why it then failed.

4. **The correct answer is (E).** We have all seen arguments of this sort in our daily lives, and perhaps if we have not been very careful, we have even made the same mistakes made by the leaders of Gambia. For example, last semester, which was fall, I made a lot of money selling peanuts at football games. Therefore, this spring semester I will make even more money. (A), (B), (C), and (D) point out weaknesses in the projections made by Gambia's leaders. (A): Of course, if the tremendous increase in GDP is due to some unique event (my personal income increased last semester when I inherited $2,000 from my aunt), it would be foolish to project a similar increase for a time period during which that event cannot repeat itself. (B): This is a bit less obvious, but the projection is based on the assumption that Gambia will receive additional aid, and will be able to put that aid to use. If they are not in a position to use that aid (I cannot work twice as many hours in the spring), they cannot expect the aid to generate increases in GDP. (C) also is a weakness in the leaders' projections. If there are physical limitations on the possible increases, then the leaders have made an error. Their projections are premised on the existence of physical resources that are greater than those they actually have. And (D) would also undermine the expectation of additional growth: Gambia won't get the whole loan. (E), however, without more, won't weaken the argument, because there is no reason to believe that the experience of a neighbor is applicable to Gambia.

5. **The correct answer is (C).** The conclusion of the paragraph is so obvious that it is almost difficult to find. The author says office workers work better the cooler the temperature—provided the temperature does not drop below 68°. Therefore, we can conclude, the temperature at which workers will be most efficient will be precisely 68°. Notice that the author does not say what happens once the temperature drops below 68° except that workers are no longer as efficient. For all we know, efficiency may drop off slowly or quickly compared with improvements in efficiency as the temperature drops to 68°. So (E) goes beyond the information supplied in the passage. (D) also goes far beyond the scope of the author's claim. His formula is specifically applicable to *office* workers. We have no reason to believe the author would extend his formula to non-office workers. (B) is probably not a conclusion the author would endorse since he claims to have found a way of achieving improvements in efficiency in a different and seemingly per-

manent way. Finally, (A) is not a conclusion the author seems likely to reach since nothing indicates that his formula yields only short-term gains which last as long as the temperature is kept constant. To be sure, the gains will not be repeatable, but then they will not be short-run either.

6. **The correct answer is (A).** Speaker 2 unwittingly plays right into the hands of Speaker 1. Speaker 1 tries to show that there are many decisions regarding human life in which we allow that an increase in the quality of life justifies an increase in the danger to human life. All that Speaker 2 does is to help prove this point. He says the quality of life would suffer if we lowered the speed limits to protect human life. Given this analysis, (B) must be incorrect, for Speaker 2's position is completely ineffective as a rebuttal. Moreover, (C) must be incorrect, for his response is not a strong statement of his position. (D) is incorrect, for while his response is of no value to the position he seeks to defend, it cannot be said that it is irrelevant. In fact, as we have just shown, his position is very relevant to that of Speaker 1's because it supports that position. Finally, (E) is not an appropriate characterization of Speaker 2's position, for he tries, however ineptly, to attack the merits of Speaker 1's position, not the character of Speaker 1.

7. **The correct answer is (E).** Speaker 1 uses the example of traffic fatalities to show that society has always traded the quality of life for the quantity of life. Of course, he says, we do not always acknowledge that is what we are doing, but if we were honest we would have to admit that we were making a trade-off. Thus, (E) is the best conclusion of the passage. Speaker 1's statement amounts to the claim that abortion is just another case in which we trade off one life to make the lives of others better. The only difference is that the life being sacrificed is specifiable and highly visible in the case of abortion, whereas in the case of highway fatalities no one knows in advance on whom the ax will fall. (A) certainly goes far beyond what Speaker 1 is advocating. If anything, he probably recognizes that sometimes the trade-off will be drawn in favor of protecting lives, and thus we need some such laws. (B) must be wrong, first, because Speaker 2 claims this is not his position, and second, because Speaker 1 would prefer to show that the logical consequence of Speaker 2's response is an argument in favor of abortion. (C) is not an appropriate continuation because Speaker 1 has already said this is a weak counter-example and that he has even stronger points to make. Finally, Speaker 1 might be willing to accept contraception, (D), as yet another example of the trade-off, but his conclusion can be much stronger than that; the conclusion of his speech ought to be that abortion is an acceptable practice—not that contraception is an acceptable practice.

8. **The correct answer is (D).** This is a very difficult question. That (D) is an assumption Speaker 1 makes requires careful reading. Speaker 1's attitude about the just war tips us off. He implies that this is an appropriate function of government and, further, that there are even clearer cases. Implicit in his statement is that a trade-off must be made and that it is appropriately a collective decision. (A) is not an assumption of the argument. Indeed, Speaker 1 seems to assume, as we have just maintained, that the trade-off is an appropriate goal of society. Speaker 1 does not assume (B); if anything, he almost states that he accepts that the fetus is a life but it may be traded off in exchange for an increase in the quality of the lives of others. (C) and (E) use language related to the ex-

amples used by Speaker 1 but don't address the logical structure of the argument.

9. **The correct answer is (A).** You might attack this item using a circle diagram. To show the possible relationships of three categories, use three overlapping circles:

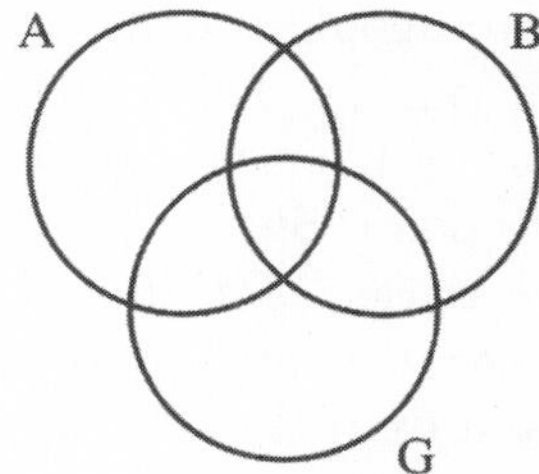

Now enter the information provided by the second statement:

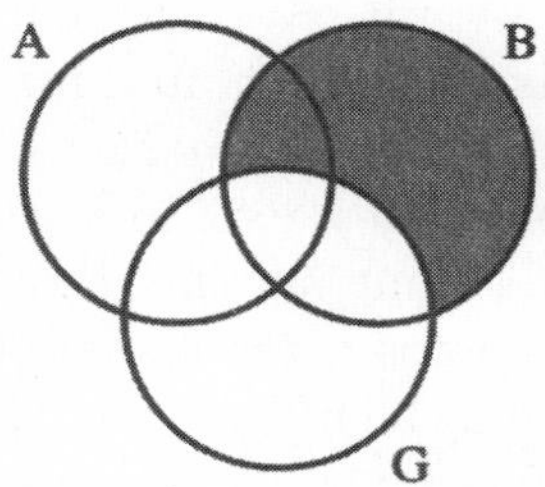

The area that is not logically possible given the second statement is shaded. Now enter the information provided by the first statement:

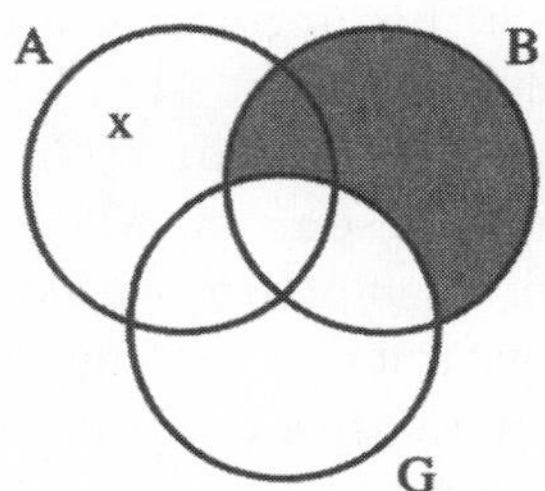

The "x" shows that there is at least one individual which is an Alpha but not a Gamma.

The diagram shows that choice (A) must be true. There is at least one individual that is an Alpha but not a Beta. (B), however, is not necessarily true. The overlap between the Alpha-circle and the Gamma-circle, which represents the possibility that an individual might have both characteristics Alpha and Gamma, is left open. (C) is not necessarily true for a similar reason. There is a portion of the Gamma-circle not contained in the Beta-circle, and this part represents the logical possibility that some individuals could have characteristic Gamma but not characteristic Beta. (D) is shown by the diagram to be false; (E) is shown to be possibly, but not necessarily, true.

10. **The correct answer is (E).** This question asks you to identify hidden assumptions embedded in the speaker's argument. Examine each statement. (A) is an assumption of the argument. Barbara told the speaker about two bets, and the speaker assumes those were the only two she made. (She could have made additional wagers.) (B) is also an assumption of the argument. The speaker concludes that one or the other horse must have won, but that conclusion depends on the assumption that they did not both win. (C) is also an assumption of the argument. The speaker implicitly assumes that the only reason Barbara would return to the parimutuel window is to cash a winning ticket, as opposed to placing another bet. And (D) is also a hidden assumption, similar to (A). (E), however, is not an assumption. Barbara could very well have believed that Copper Cane was more likely to win—indeed, she stood to win more money with that result even though her bet was smaller because of the longer odds.

11. **The correct answer is (C).** It is very important to distinguish what are called necessary conditions from what are called sufficient conditions. A necessary condition is one that must occur for a particular event to take place, e.g., oxygen is a

answers

necessary condition for a fire. A sufficient condition is one that is by itself sufficient to ensure that a certain event occurs, for example, failing the final exam of a course may be sufficient to guarantee a failing mark for the course. This distinction is the key to this item. A statement of the sort "If *X*, then *Y*" (as used here) sets up a sufficient but not a necessary connection. For example, ordering combination #2 guarantees that Juana will eat fried rice, but that may not be the only condition on which she will eat fried rice. For all we know, combination #5 also includes fried rice. Thus, (A), (B), and (D) are wrong. As for (E), the statements that set up the problem talk specifically about Juana, not about people in general.

12. **The correct answer is (C).** If you want to determine whether or not drug use is harmful to high school students, you surely would not conduct a survey of the students themselves. This is why (C) is correct. That a student does not *think* a drug is harmful does not mean that it *is not* actually harmful. (E) misses the point of the argument. The author is not attempting to prove that drug use is not widespread but rather that it is not dangerous. (D) is part of an argument often used in debates over legalization of drugs by proponents of legalization. Here, however, it is out of place. The question is whether the drugs are harmless, that is, whether they are, in fact, victimless. (D) belongs to some other part of the debate. (A) sounds like the start of an argument. One might suggest that students change their minds as they get older, and eventually many acknowledge the danger of such drugs. But (A) does not get that far; and, even if it did, (C) would be stronger for it gives us the final statement up to which that argument would only be leading. Finally, (B) is irrelevant. The question here is the harm of drugs, and that issue can be resolved independent of whether other things are harmful, such as alcohol or drag-racing.

13. **The correct answer is (C).** Amy points out that Al assumes that any extraterrestrial visitors to Earth, seeking intelligent life, would regard human beings here on Earth as intelligent, and therefore contact us. Amy hints that we might not be intelligent enough to interest them in contacting us. This is why (C) is the best answer. (A) is wrong. Amy does not miss Al's point: She understands it very well and criticizes it. (B) is wrong since Amy is not suggesting that Al is any less intelligent than any other human being, just that the aliens might regard us all as below the level of intelligence which they are seeking. (D) is more nearly correct than any other choice save (C). The difficulties with it are threefold: One, there really is not all that much internal development of Al's argument, so (D) does not seem on target; two, in a way she does examine what internal structure there is—she notes there is a suppressed assumption which is unsound; finally, even assuming that what (D) says is correct, it really does not describe the point of Amy's remark nearly so well as (C) does. Finally, (E) is incorrect because Amy does not offer an analogy of any sort.

14. **The correct answer is (C).** The problem with this argument is that it contains no argument at all. Nothing is more frustrating than trying to discuss an issue with someone who will not even make an attempt to prove his case, whose only constructive argument is: "Well, that is my position; if I am wrong, you prove I am wrong." This is an illegitimate attempt to shift the burden of proof. The person who advances the argument naturally has the burden of giving some argument for it. (C) points out this problem. (A) is incorrect because the author uses no group classifications.

(B) is incorrect because the author does not introduce any analogy. (D) is a weak version of (C). It is true that the author does not provide statistical evidence to prove the claim, but then again no kind of argument at all is offered to prove the claim. So if (D) is a legitimate objection to the paragraph (and it is), then (C) must be an even stronger objection. So any argument for answer (D)'s being the correct choice ultimately supports (C) even more strongly. The statement contained in (E) may or may not be correct, but the information in the passage is not sufficient to allow us to isolate the theory upon which the speaker is operating. Therefore, we cannot conclude that it is or is not discredited.

15. **The correct answer is (A).** Let us assign letters to represent the complete clauses of the sentence from which the argument is built. "If quarks . . . universe" will be represented by the letter *P*, the rest of the sentence by *Q*. The structure of the argument is therefore: "If *P* then *Q*. *Q*. Therefore, *P*." The argument is obviously not logically valid. If it were, it would work for any substitutions of clauses for the letters, but we can easily think up a case in which the argument will not work: "If this truck is a fire engine, it will be painted red. This truck is painted red; therefore, it is a fire engine." Obviously, many trucks that are not fire engines could also be painted red. The argument's invalidity is not the critical point. Your task was to find the answer choice that paralleled it—and since the argument first presented was incorrect, you should have looked for the argument in the answer choice that makes the same mistake: (A). It has the form: "If *P*, then *Q*. *Q*. Therefore, *P*." (B) has the form: "If *P*, then *Q*. *P*. Therefore, *Q*," which is both different from our original form and valid to boot. (C) has the form: "*P* or *Q*. Not *P*. Therefore, *Q*." (D) has the form: "If *P*, then *Q*. If *Q*, then *R*. Therefore, if *P*, then *R*." Finally, (E) has the form: "If *P*, then *Q*. Not *Q*. Therefore, not *P*."

16. **The correct answer is (D).** The author explains that the expansion of judicial power by increasing the number of causes of action had the effect of filling the judicial coffers. A natural conclusion to be drawn from this information is that the desire for economic gain fueled the expansion. (A) is not supported by the text since the judges may have made good decisions—even though they were paid to make them. (E) is incorrect for the same reason. (C) is not supported by the text since no mention is made of the other two bodies (even assuming they existed at the time the author is describing). (B) is also incorrect because there is nothing in the text to support such a conclusion.

17. **The correct answer is (D).** As we did in question 15, let us use letters to represent the form of the argument. The first sentence is our old friend: "If *P*, then *Q*." Now we must be careful not to use the same letter to stand for a different statement. No part of the second sentence is also a part of the first one, so we must use a new set of letters: "If *R*, then *S*." Do not be confused by the internal structure of the sentences. Though the second clause of the first sentence speaks about Johnson and Lloyd voting the same way, the second clause of the second sentence speaks about Johnson's defending someone. So the two statements are different ideas and require different letters. The first clause of the third sentence is the same idea as the first clause of the first sentence, so we use letter *P* again, but the second clause is different, *T*. The third sentence uses the phrase "only if," "*P* only if *T*," which can also be written: "If *P*, then *T*."

answers

Our three sentences are translated as:

1. If *P*, then *Q*.
2. If *R*, then *S*.
3. If *P*, then *T*.

Now we can find which of the answers cannot be true.

(A) "If *R*, then not *Q*." That is a possibility. While it cannot be deduced from our three assumptions, nothing in the three assumptions precludes it. So (A) could be true.

(B) "If *P*, then *T*." This is true, a restatement of the final assumption.

(C) "If *T*, then not-*P*." This is possibly true. Sentence 3 tells us, "If *P*, then *T*," which is the same thing as "if not-*T*, then not-*P* "; but it does not dictate consequences when the antecedent clause (the if-clause) is *T*.

(D) "If *P*, then either not-*Q* or not-*T*." This must be false, since sentences 1 and 3 together tell us that from *P* must follow both *Q* and *T*.

(E) "If not-*T* or not-*P*, then either not-*S* or *U*." We have to add a new letter: *U*. In any event, this is possible for the reasons mentioned in (C).

18. **The correct answer is (A).** The listener's comment constitutes a counterexample. It shows by sarcasm that "yeah" can be used to show disagreement. Obviously, the listener does not point out an inconsistency within the speaker's address (even though the listener's remark is inconsistent with the speaker's position). There is no analogy developed by the listener, whose remark is very brief, so (C) is incorrect. The argument is directed against the speaker's contention, not character, so (D) is incorrect. Finally, though the listener's comment is high evidence that the speaker is wrong, the comment itself does not cite evidence, so (E) is incorrect.

SUMMING IT UP:

What You Need to Know About GMAT Verbal Questions

Review these pages the night before you take the GMAT. They will help you do well on GMAT verbal questions.

- The GMAT tests verbal reasoning ability with three question types: reading comprehension, sentence correction, and critical reasoning.
- Questions of all three types are interspersed with each other within the 75-minute Verbal Section of the test.

Reading Comprehension

- GMAT reading comprehension questions ask you to analyze what is stated in a passage and to identify underlying assumptions and implications.
- These steps will help you solve reading comprehension questions.
  1. Preview key sentences.
  2. Read for structure; ignore details.
  3. Do a mental wrap-up.
- All GMAT reading comprehension questions fall into one of six categories:
  1. Main idea
  2. Specific detail
  3. Author's attitude or tone
  4. Logical structure
  5. Inference
  6. Application

Sentence Correction

- Sentence correction questions test your ability to recognize grammatically correct and effective sentences and to choose the best of several suggested revisions.
- These steps will help you solve sentence correction questions.
  1. Read the sentence carefully, trying to identify an error.
  2. If no error is apparent, ask yourself if the sentence is grammatically correct, if it is properly structured, and if it uses correct diction. If you find one or more errors, look for an answer that makes the corrections.

3. If you cannot find an error, read the answer choices. Focus on the *differences* between each choice and the original. Often this will turn up an error that you overlooked.
4. Eliminate choices that contain errors and choose from among those that remain.

- Some sentence correction questions contain multiple errors; others have no mistakes.

Critical Reasoning

- Critical reasoning questions test your reasoning power, not your knowledge of the technical points of formal logic.
- Critical reasoning questions may ask you to do any of the following six tasks:
  1. Identify the conclusion.
  2. Point out a premise.
  3. Identify strengths or weaknesses.
  4. Recognize parallel reasoning.
  5. Evaluate evidence.
  6. Draw a conclusion.
- These steps will help you solve critical reasoning questions.
  1. Preview the question stem.
  2. Read the stimulus material.
  3. Prephrase your answer.
  4. Identify the correct answer.
- Locating the conclusion is the first step in evaluating a critical reasoning argument.
- Key words can signal conclusions or premises.
- Many critical reasoning questions test your ability to recognize one of these seven fallacies:
  1. Wrong cause
  2. False analogy
  3. Weak generalization
  4. Ambiguous terms
  5. Irrelevant evidence
  6. Circular argument
  7. *Ad hominem* attack

PART IV

GMAT QUANTITATIVE QUESTIONS

Problem Solving

OVERVIEW

- **What is problem solving?**
- **How do you answer problem-solving questions?**
- **What smart test-takers know**

WHAT IS PROBLEM SOLVING?

Problem-solving questions are your ordinary, garden-variety math questions—the kind you saw on the SAT. The questions test your mastery of basic mathematical skills and your ability to solve problems using arithmetic, elementary algebra, and geometry. Some problems are strictly math questions such as solving for the value of a variable; the rest will be presented as real-life word problems that require a mathematical solution.

If your basic math skills need work, you'll find plenty of practice in Part VII of this book. That section provides a complete review of arithmetic, algebra, and geometry, along with exercises to build your skills.

GMAT Problem-solving Questions

GMAT problem-solving questions appear in the 75-minute quantitative section. Within the section they are not grouped all together. Instead, they are interspersed with the data sufficiency questions.

Here are the directions for GMAT problem-solving questions and four sample questions together with their explanations.

chapter 8

Anatomy of Problem-solving Questions

Directions: For each of the following questions, select the best of the answer choices.
Numbers: All numbers used are real numbers.
Figures: The diagrams and figures that accompany these questions are for the purpose of providing information useful in answering the questions. Unless it is stated that a specific figure is not drawn to scale, the diagrams and figures are drawn as accurately as possible. All figures are in a plane unless otherwise indicated.

1. $0.2 \times 0.005 =$

(A) 0.0001

(B) 0.001

(C) 0.01

(D) 0.1

(E) 1.0

This is a simple manipulation problem. Manipulation problems, as the name implies, test your knowledge of arithmetic or algebraic manipulations. The correct answer is (B). The item tests whether or not you remember how to keep track of the decimal point in multiplication.

2. If $x + 5 = 8$, then $2x - 1 =$

(A) 25

(B) 12

(C) 5

(D) 4

(E) 0

This manipulation problem tests algebra. The correct answer is (C). Since $x + 5 = 8$, $x = 3$. Then substitute 3 for x in the expression $2x - 1$: $2(3) - 1 = 5$.

3. Joe works two part-time jobs. One week Joe worked 8 hours at one job, earning $150, and 4.5 hours at the other job, earning $90. What were his average hourly earnings for the week?

(A) $8.00

(B) $9.60

(C) $16.00

(D) $19.20

(E) $32.00

This is a practical word problem. Practical word problems go beyond simple manipulations. They require that you use your knowledge of manipulations in practical situations. The correct choice is (D). To find Joe's average hourly earnings, divide the total earnings by the number of hours worked:

$$\frac{150+90}{8+4.5}=\frac{240}{12.5}=19.20$$

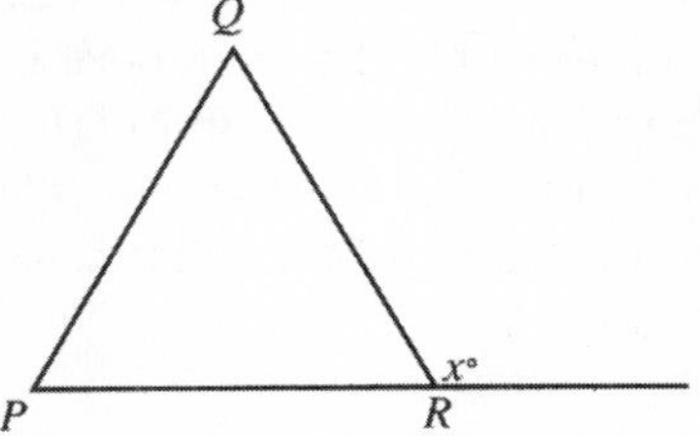

4. In the figure above, $PQ = QR = PR$. What is the value of x?
   - **(A)** 30
   - **(B)** 45
   - **(C)** 60
   - **(D)** 90
   - **(E)** 120

This is obviously a geometry problem. Geometry problems involve the use of basic principles of geometry. The correct answer is (E). This is an equilateral triangle (one having three equal sides), and equilateral triangles also have three equal angles, each 60 degrees. Then *PR*, as extended, forms a straight line. So $x + 60 = 180$, and $x = 120$.

HOW DO YOU ANSWER PROBLEM-SOLVING QUESTIONS?

Here's a simple, four-step plan that can help you answer GMAT problem-solving questions.

Problem Solving: Getting It Right

1. Read the question carefully.
2. Before solving the problem, check the answers.
3. Eliminate choices that are completely off the radar screen.
4. For complex questions, break down the problem.

NOTE

Does the GMAT test college math?

No. All of the topics tested in GMAT math questions are covered in high school math.

Now let's examine each of these steps in more detail.

1. **Read the question carefully.** Some GMAT problems are fairly simple, but others are more complex, particularly practical word problems and more difficult geometry problems. The more complex the question, the easier it is to misread and set off down a wrong track. The importance of this point is illustrated by the following very difficult practical word problem.

> The people eating in a certain cafeteria are either faculty members or students, and the number of faculty members is 15 percent of the total number of people in the cafeteria. After some of the students leave, the total number of persons remaining in the cafeteria is 50 percent of the original total. The number of students who left is what fractional part of the original number of students?
>
> **(A)** $\frac{17}{20}$
>
> **(B)** $\frac{10}{17}$
>
> **(C)** $\frac{1}{2}$
>
> **(D)** $\frac{1}{4}$
>
> **(E)** $\frac{7}{20}$

The correct answer is (B). Let T be the total number of people originally in the cafeteria. Faculty account for 15 percent of T, or $.15T$, and students account for the remaining 85 percent of T, or $.85T$. Then some students leave, reducing the total number of people in the cafeteria to half of what it was originally, or $.5T$. The number of faculty, however, does not change. So the difference between $.5T$ and $.15T$ must be students: $.5T - .15T = .35T$. But this is not yet the answer to the question. The question asks "The number of students who left is what fraction of the original number of students?" Originally there were $.85T$ students; now there are only $.35T$ students, so $.50T$ students left. Now, to complete the solution we set up a fraction: $\frac{50T}{85T} = \frac{10}{17}$.

By this point, you can appreciate that there are several ways to misread the question. Someone might just put $.35T$ over $.85T$ ($\frac{35T}{85T} = \frac{7}{17}$) and choose (D). But this answers the question "The remaining students are what fraction of the original number of students?" That is not the question asked.

Someone might also put $.35T$ over T ($\frac{35T}{T} = \frac{7}{20}$) and select choice (E). But this too answers a different question: "The number of students who remain is what fractional part of the original number of people in the cafeteria?"

There are probably hundreds of other ways to misread the question, but it would be a shame to know how to answer the question and still miss it just because you did not read the question carefully.

❷ **Before solving the problem, check the answers.** As you tackle each problem, start by looking at the answer choices. That way you'll know what form your own solution should take. For example, are the choices all in miles per hour? If so, that's the form your answer must take. Are they all decimals? If so, your solution should be a decimal, not a fraction or a radical.

❸ **Eliminate choices that are completely off the radar screen.** The answer choices are generally arranged in a logical order.

Xxxx xxxxxxx xxxx xxxxxxxxxxx xxxxxxx xxxxxxxxxx xxxx xxxxxxxxxxx xxxx xxxxxxx xxxxxxxxxxx?

(A) 3200
(B) 4800
(C) 12,000
(D) 16,000
(E) 20,000

Notice that the choices in this dummy question are arranged from least to greatest. Occasionally, choices are arranged from greatest to least. And in algebra questions, the choices are arranged logically according to powers and coefficients of variables.

In addition, the wrong choices are not just picked at random. They are usually written to correspond to possible mistakes (misreadings, etc.). This actually helps you. To illustrate this, here is an actual question to go with the dummy answers.

In a certain population, 40 percent of all people have biological characteristic X; the others do not. If 8000 people have characteristic X, how many people do not have X?

(A) 3200
(B) 4800
(C) 12,000
(D) 16,000
(E) 20,000

The correct answer is (C). You can arrive at this conclusion by setting up a proportion:

$$\frac{\text{Percentage with } X}{\text{Number with } X} = \frac{\text{Percentage without } X}{\text{Number without } X}$$

Supplying the appropriate numbers:

$$\frac{40\%}{8000} = \frac{60\%}{x}$$

Cross-multiply: $.40x = .60(8000)$
Solve for x: $x = 12{,}000$

But you can avoid even this little bit of work. A little common sense, when applied to the answer choices, would have eliminated all but (C). In the first place, 40% of

TIP

Look for shortcuts. GMAT problem-solving questions test your math reasoning, not your ability to make endless calculations. If you find yourself mired in calculations, you've missed a shortcut that would have made your work easier.

the people have X, so more people don't have X. If 8,000 people have X, the correct choice has to be greater than 8,000. This eliminates both (A) and (B). Next, we reason that if the correct answer were (D), 16,000, then only about one-third of the people would have X. But we know 40% have X. This allows us to eliminate (D) and also (E).

❹ **For complex questions, break down the problems.** Some practical word problems are fairly complex, and it is easy to get lost. You'll fare better if you break the solution process into separate steps. First, formulate a statement of what is needed; second, find the numbers you need; and third, perform the required calculation.

The enrollments at College X and College Y both grew by 8 percent from 1980 to 1985. If the enrollment at College X grew by 800 and the enrollment at College Y grew by 840, the enrollment at College Y was how much greater than the enrollment at College X in 1985?

(A) 400

(B) 460

(C) 500

(D) 540

(E) 580

The correct choice is (D), but the solution is a good deal more involved than the one needed for the preceding problem, so proceed step by step.

First, isolate the simple question that must be answered:

The enrollments at College X and College Y both grew by 8 percent from 1980 to 1985. If the enrollment at College X grew by 800 and the enrollment at College Y grew by 840, *the enrollment at College Y was how much greater than the enrollment at College X in 1985*?

This can be summarized as follows:

College Y in 1985 – College X in 1985

TIP

The answers line up by size. The quantities in GMAT problem-solving answer choices either go from larger to smaller or the other way around. Remember that when you're trying to eliminate or test answers.

So you know you must find the enrollments at both colleges in 1985. How can you do that? The numbers are there in the question; you just have to figure out how to use them. Take College Y first. You know that enrollments grew by 840 and that this represents an increase of 8%. These numbers will allow you to find the enrollment in 1980:

$$\begin{aligned} \text{8\% of 1980 Total} &= 840 \\ 0.08 \times T &= 840 \\ \text{Solve for } T\text{: } T &= 10{,}500 \end{aligned}$$

This was the enrollment at College Y in 1980, but you need to know the enrollment at College Y in 1985. To do that, just add the increase:

$$\begin{aligned} 1980 + \text{Increase} &= 1985 \\ 10{,}500 + 840 &= 11{,}340 \end{aligned}$$

Now do the same thing for College X:

$$\begin{aligned} 8\% \text{ of 1980 Total} &= 800 \\ 0.08 \times T &= 800 \\ T &= 10{,}000 \\ 1980 + \text{Increase} &= 1985 \\ 10{,}000 + 800 &= 10{,}800 \end{aligned}$$

Now you have the numbers you were looking for. Substitute them back into your original solution statement:

$$\begin{aligned} \text{College } Y \text{ in 1985} - \text{College } X \text{ in 1985} &= \text{Final Answer} \\ 11{,}340 - 10{,}800 &= 540 \end{aligned}$$

This is not the only way of reaching the correct solution, but it is the one most people would be likely to use. And it is very complex. A problem like this illustrates nicely what you should do when you encounter a complex practical word problem.

Now let's look at some more problem-solving questions and their solutions. As you read the solutions, think about how the four-step process would help you find the answers.

Manipulation Problems

Here are five typical GMAT manipulation problems.

1. $0.04 \times 0.25 =$

- **(A)** 0.0001
- **(B)** 0.001
- **(C)** 0.01
- **(D)** 0.1
- **(E)** 1.0

Your approach to a manipulation problem like this one depends upon the degree of difficulty of the manipulation.

The correct answer is (C). The manipulation is very simple, so you should just do the indicated multiplication (keeping careful track of the decimal).

2. $\frac{2}{3} \times \frac{3}{4} \times \frac{4}{5} \times \frac{5}{6} \times \frac{6}{7} \times \frac{7}{8} =$

- **(A)** $\frac{2}{33}$
- **(B)** $\frac{1}{4}$
- **(C)** $\frac{3}{8}$
- **(D)** $\frac{1}{2}$
- **(E)** $\frac{27}{33}$

If the problem seems too difficult, look for a way to simplify things. The test-writers have no interest in determining whether you can do "donkey" math. If a manipulation problem looks to be too difficult, then there is a trick to be discovered. The correct choice is (B). Given enough time, you could work the problem out by multiplying all the numerators, multiplying all the denominators, and then simplifying. But the very fact that this would be time consuming should prompt you to look for an alternative. Try canceling:

$$\frac{2}{\not{3}}\times\frac{\not{3}}{\not{4}}\times\frac{\not{4}}{\not{5}}\times\frac{\not{5}}{\not{6}}\times\frac{\not{6}}{\not{7}}\times\frac{\not{7}}{8}$$

TIP

Don't obsess. If you find yourself stuck on a problem-solving question, don't spend valuable time agonizing over the answer. Since you have to get to the rest of the test, just take your best guess and move on.

3. $(27 \times 34) - (33 \times 27) =$

(A) -1

(B) 1

(C) 27

(D) 33

(E) 918

This time you can simplify matters by factoring:

$$(27 \times 34) - (33 \times 27) = 27(34 - 33) = 27(1) = 27$$

The correct answer is (C).

4. If $3x - 5 = x + 11$, then $x =$

(A) 16

(B) 8

(C) 3

(D) 2

(E) 1

If a problem consists of an equation with just one variable, the solution is almost certainly to solve for the unknown whether it be x or some other variable. The correct answer is (B), and the appropriate method is to solve for x:

	$3x - 5 = x + 11$
Combine terms:	$2x = 16$
Solve for x:	$x = 8$

If a problem presents two equations with two variables, the best strategy is almost certainly to treat them as a system of simultaneous equations.

5. If $x + y = 8$ and $2x - y = 10$, then $x =$

(A) 16

(B) 8

(C) 6

(D) 4

(E) 2

The correct answer is (C), and the correct technique is to treat the two equations simultaneously. First, isolate y from the first equation:

$$x + y = 8$$

So: $$y = 8 - x$$

Next, substitute $8 - x$ into the second equation in place of y:

$$2x - (8 - x) = 10$$

Combine terms: $$3x = 18$$

Solve for x: $$x = 6$$

Practical Word Problems

Here is a typical GMAT word problem.

> $2000 is deposited into a savings account that earns interest at the rate of 10 percent per year, compounded semiannually. How much money will there be in the account at the end of one year?
>
> **(A)** $2105
>
> **(B)** $2200
>
> **(C)** $2205
>
> **(D)** $2400
>
> **(E)** $2600

For complex word problems, break the problem down into smaller parts. First determine what you need to calculate and set up a mathematical expression.

This problem is asking you to calculate the total amount of money in the account at the end of the year. That means you must find the interest earned and add it to the original amount. First, calculate the interest earned during the first six months. To do this, you need to know that the formula for calculating interest is: Principal × Rate × Time = Interest Earned

First Six Months:

Principal	×	Rate	×	Time	=	Interest Earned
$2000	×	10%	×	0.5	=	$100

This $100 is then paid into the account. The new balance is $2100. Now you would calculate the interest earned during the second six months.

Second Six Months:

Principal	×	Rate	×	Time	=	Interest Earned
$2100	×	10%	×	0.5	=	$105

This is then paid into the account. So the final balance is:

$2100 + $105 = $2205

So, the correct answer is (C).

WHAT SMART TEST-TAKERS KNOW

THE GMAT MATH REVIEW IN PART SEVEN OF THIS BOOK CAN POLISH UP RUSTY SKILLS.

If it's been a long time since your last math class, your math skills might need some shoring up. The Math Review in Part VII of this book covers all the basic concepts of arithmetic, elementary algebra, and geometry that you're likely to encounter on the GMAT.

IT'S SMART TO TEST ANSWER CHOICES.

The GMAT is a multiple-choice test, so the correct answer is staring you in the face. Take advantage of this. Solve problems by plugging in the answer choices until you find the one that works.

$5^3 \times 9 =$

(A) 5×27

(B) 15×9

(C) $15 \times 15 \times 5$

(D) 25×27

(E) 125×27

The correct choice is (C), and you learn this by testing each choice to see which one is equivalent to $5^3 \times 9$. The expression $5^3 \times 9 = (5 \times 5 \times 5)\ (3 \times 3) = 15 \times 15 \times 5$.

WHEN TESTING ANSWER CHOICES, IT'S SMART TO START WITH (C).

Remember, the answer is right there in front of you. If you test all the choices, you'll find the right one. However, the smart place to start is with choice (C). Why? Because the quantities in the choices are always arranged in order, either from least to greatest or the other way around. If you start with (C) and it's too great, you'll only have to concentrate on the two lesser choices. That eliminates three of the five choices right away. Here's how this works.

A car dealer who gives a customer a 20 percent discount on the list price of a car still realizes a net profit of 25 percent of cost. If the dealer's cost is $4800, what is the usual list price of the car?

(A) $6000

(B) $6180

(C) $7200

(D) $7500

(E) $8000

You know that one of these five choices must be correct, so all you have to do is test each one until you find the correct one. Start with (C).

If the usual list price is \$7200, what will be the actual selling price after the 20% discount?

Usual List Price – 20% of Usual List Price	=	Final Selling Price
\$7200 – 20% of \$7200	=	Final Selling Price
\$7200 – \$1440	=	\$5760

On that assumption, the dealer's profit would be:

Final Selling Price – Cost	=	Profit
\$5760 – \$4800	=	\$960

Is that a profit of 25%?

\$960/\$4800 is less than $\frac{1}{4}$ and so less than 25%. This proves that (C) is wrong.

Now you need to test another choice, logically either (B) or (D). But which one? Apply a little reasoning to the situation. Assuming a usual cost of \$7200, the numbers worked out to a profit that was too small. Therefore, we need a larger price to generate a larger profit. So try (D).

\$7500 – (.20)(\$7500) = \$6000

If the final selling price is \$6000, that means a profit for the dealer of \$1200. And \$1200/\$4800 = 25%. So (D) must be the correct answer.

Now suppose instead that you had this set of answer choices:

(A) \$4000

(B) \$6000

(C) \$6180

(D) \$7200

(E) \$7500

In this case, you test (C) first and learn that it is incorrect. Then you go to (D) as above. Again, another wrong choice. Does this mean you have to do a third calculation? No! Since the choices are arranged in order, once you have eliminated (C) and (D), you know that (E) must be correct.

YOU CAN ASSUME NUMBER VALUES FOR UNKNOWNS.

Often it is easier to work with numbers than with unknowns. Therefore, when you are faced with a problem like the one below, in which some numbers are presented as variables, try substituting real numbers for each variable.

> At a certain printing plant, each of m machines prints 6 newspapers every s seconds. If all machines work together but independently without interruption, how many minutes will it take to print an entire run of 18,000 newspapers?
>
> **(A)** $\frac{180s}{m}$
>
> **(B)** $\frac{50s}{m}$
>
> **(C)** $50ms$
>
> **(D)** $\frac{ms}{50}$
>
> **(E)** $\frac{300m}{s}$

TIP

Make your life easy. When assuming number values for variables, pick numbers that are easy to work with. Pick small numbers that are simple to manipulate.

Since the information is given algebraically, the letters could stand for any numbers (so long as you don't divide by 0). Pick some values for m and s and see which answer choice works. Start with easy numbers. For purpose of discussion, assume that the plant has 2 machines, so $m = 2$. Also assume that $s = 1$, that is, that each machine produces 6 newspapers each second. On this assumption, each machine prints 360 papers per minute; and with two such machines working, the plant capacity is 720 papers per minute. To find how long it will take the plant to do the work, divide 18,000 by 720.

18,000/720 = 25 minutes

On the assumption that $m = 2$ and $s = 1$, the correct formula should produce the number 25. Test the choices:

(A) $\frac{180s}{m}$ = 180(1)/2 is not equal to 25 (WRONG!)

(B) $\frac{50s}{m}$ = 50(1)/2 is equal to 25 (CORRECT!)

(C) $50ms$ = 50(2)(1) is not equal to 25 (WRONG!)

(D) $\frac{ms}{50}$ = (2)(1)/50 is not equal to 25 (WRONG!)

(E) $\frac{300m}{s}$ = 300(2)/(1) is not equal to 25 (WRONG!)

WHEN NO NUMBERS OR VARIABLES ARE SUPPLIED, YOU CAN PICK YOUR OWN.
When no numbers or variables are supplied, you may find it easier to solve the problem if you assign numerical values to the given information. Pick numbers that are easy to work with.

If the value of a piece of property decreases by 10 percent while the tax rate on the property increases by 10 percent, what is the effect on the taxes?

(A) Taxes increase by 10 percent.

(B) Taxes increase by 1 percent.

(C) There is no change in taxes.

(D) Taxes decrease by 1 percent.

(E) Taxes decrease by 10 percent.

The correct answer is (D). Since no numbers are supplied you are free to supply your own. Assume the piece of property has a value of $1000, and assume further that the original tax rate is 10%. On the basis of those assumptions, the tax bill is originally 10% of $1000 or $100. Now make the specified adjustments. The value of the property drops by 10%, from $1000 to $900, but the tax rate goes up by 10%, from 10% to 11%. The new tax bill is 11% of $900, or $99. The original tax bill was $100; the new tax bill is $99; the net result is a decrease of $1 out of $100, or a 1% decrease.

YOU HAVE TO BE CAREFUL OF YOUR UNITS.
Practical word problems often require you to work with units of measure. Sometimes several different units are involved, so be sure that your answer is expressed in the unit that's asked for.

A certain copy machine produces 13 copies every 10 seconds. If the machine operates without interruption, how many copies will it produce in an hour?

(A) 78

(B) 468

(C) 1800

(D) 2808

(E) 4680

The correct answer is (E). The question stem gives information about copies per 10 seconds, but you must answer in terms of copies per hour. To solve the problem, first convert copies per 10 seconds to copies per minute. This can be done with a proportion:

$$\frac{13 \text{ copies}}{10 \text{ seconds}} = \frac{x \text{ copies}}{60 \text{ seconds}}$$

Solve by cross-multiplication: $13 \times 60 = 10x$
Solve for x: $x = 78$

The correct answer, however, is not 78. A machine that produces 78 copies per minute produces 60 times that in an hour: $60 \times 78 = 4680$.

NOTE

Will I have to know how to convert units of measure?
No. Measurements in problem-solving questions may be given in either English or metric units, but you don't have to know how to convert from one system to the other or from one unit of measure to another. If you need such information, it will be given to you.

THOUGHT-REVERSERS CHANGE THE TERMS.

A thought-reverser is any word such as *not, except,* or *but* which turns a question inside-out. It will determine the solution you're looking for, so you might want to circle it to keep it clearly in mind as you make your calculations.

A survey of 100 people revealed that 72 of them had eaten at restaurant P and that 52 of them had eaten at restaurant Q. Which of the following could not be the number of persons in the surveyed group who had eaten at both P and Q?

(A) 20

(B) 24

(C) 30

(D) 50

(E) 52

The correct answer is (A). Since there are only 100 people in the group, some of them must have eaten at both P and Q. The combined responses for P and Q equal 124, and $124 - 100 = 24$. So 24 is the smallest possible number of people who could have eaten at both P and Q. (The largest possible number would be 52, which is possible if all of those who ate at Q had also eaten at P.)

MOST PROBLEM-SOLVING FIGURES ARE DRAWN TO SCALE.

Most of the problem-solving figures are drawn as accurately as possible. (Note: This is not true of data sufficiency questions.) If a figure is not drawn to scale, it will include the warning: "Note: Figure not drawn to scale."

Unless you are told that a problem-solving figure is not drawn to scale, you may assume that angles and other geometric relationships are as shown. You may also assume that, for example, what looks like a right triangle is a right triangle even if you can't support your assumption with a formal geometric theorem.

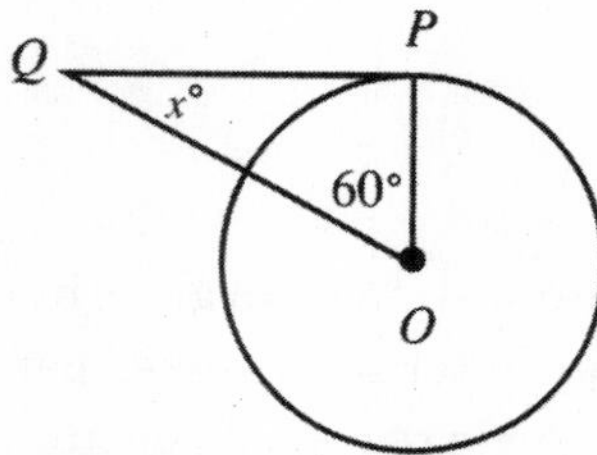

In the figure above, what is the measure of angle x in degrees?

(A) 15°

(B) 30°

(C) 45°

(D) 60°

(E) 90°

The correct answer is (B). To solve the problem, you need to know that angle P is a right angle. Then you have a triangle whose angles measure 60°, 90°, and x°. Since there are 180 degrees in a triangle, x must be 30.

You probably did realize that angle P must be a right angle and not just by looking at it and seeing that it seems to be 90 degrees. Rather your mind's eye probably told you that for some reason or other, angle P had to be 90 degrees.

In fact, angle P must be 90 degrees. PQ is a tangent, and PO is a radius. A tangent intersects a radius at a 90-degree angle. But you do not need to know the "official" justification to answer correctly. Just trust your spatial intuition.

YOU CAN USE MEASURES OF SIMPLE FIGURES TO FIND MEASURES OF MORE COMPLEX ONES.

Many geometry problems involve complex figures. You can often calculate their measures by breaking them up into simpler figures.

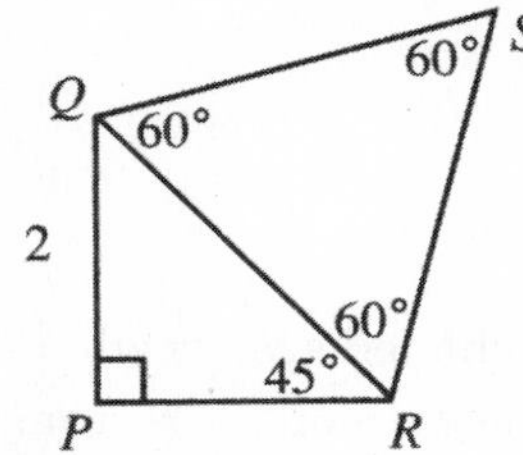

In the figure above, what is the perimeter of triangle QRS?

(A) 12

(B) $6\sqrt{2}$

(C) 6

(D) $3\sqrt{2}$

(E) $2\sqrt{2}$

The correct answer is (B). The trick is to see that QR is not only a side of triangle PQR, but is also a side of triangle QRS. Further, triangle QRS is an equilateral triangle, so if you can find the length of one side, you know the length of the other sides as well.

How can you find the length of QR? Triangle PQR is a 45°-45°-90° triangle. Since QR is 2, PR is also 2. Now you know two legs of the right triangle, and you can use the Pythagorean Theorem to find the hypotenuse:

$$QP^2 + PR^2 = QR^2$$

So:

$$\begin{aligned} 2^2 + 2^2 &= QR^2 \\ 4 + 4 &= QR^2 \\ QR^2 &= 8 \\ QR &= \sqrt{8} \\ QR &= 2\sqrt{2} \end{aligned}$$

Each of the three sides of triangle QRS is equal to $2\sqrt{2}$, so the perimeter of triangle $QRS = 3 \times 2\sqrt{2} = 6\sqrt{2}$.

YOU CAN MEASURE IRREGULAR SHADED AREAS BY RELATING THEM TO FIGURES WITH REGULAR SHAPES.

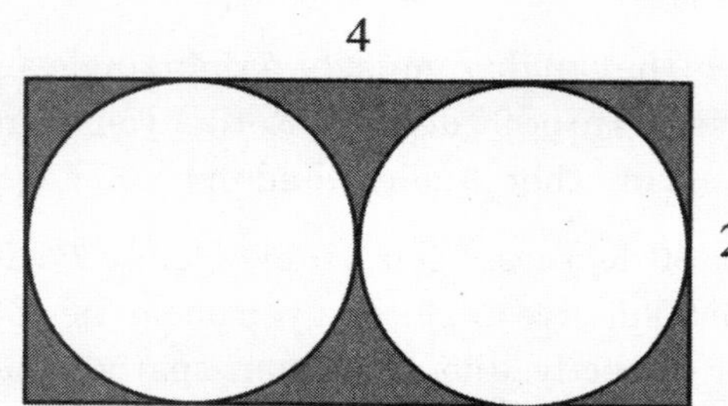

What is the area of the shaded portion of the figure above?

(A) $8 - 8\pi$

(B) $8 - 4\pi$

(C) $8 - 2\pi$

(D) $8 - \pi$

(E) π

The correct answer is (C). The shaded area is what's left over if you take the area of the two circles away from the area of the rectangle:

Rectangle – Two Circles = Shaded Area

First, the area of the rectangle is just $2 \times 4 = 8$. Then, the diameter of the circles is equal to the width of the rectangle. So the diameter of the circles is 2, and the radius is 1. The formula for the area of a circle is πr^2, so each circle has an area of $\pi(1^2) = \pi$. Now we know the area of the shaded part of the diagram:

$$8 - 2(\pi) = 8 - 2\pi$$

TIP

A picture can help. In problem-solving questions, draw a diagram if none is supplied. A diagram is a great way to organize information. Mark it up with the information you're given, and you'll have a better idea of what you're looking for.

BECAUSE A PROBLEM-SOLVING FIGURE IS DRAWN TO SCALE, YOU CAN ESTIMATE MEASURES.

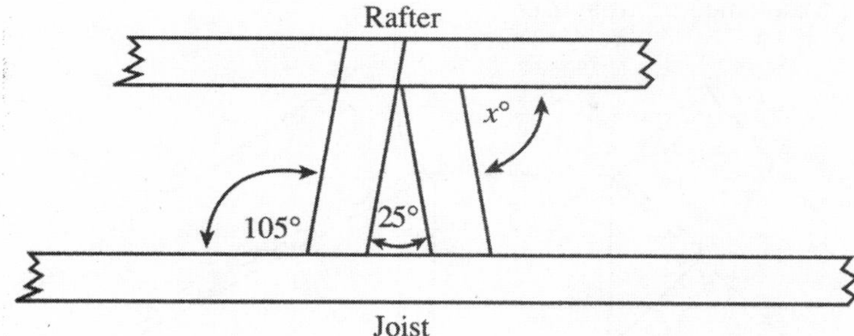

The figure above shows a cross section of a building. If the rafter is parallel to the joist, what is the measure of angle x?

(A) 45

(B) 60

(C) 80

(D) 90

(E) 105

The correct answer is (C), and you can get that without a calculation. Look at the size of x. It is not quite a right angle, so you can eliminate both (D) and (E). Is it as small as 60 degrees? No, so you eliminate (B) and (A) as well. This means that (C) must be the correct answer.

BECAUSE A PROBLEM-SOLVING FIGURE IS DRAWN TO SCALE, YOU CAN MEASURE LENGTHS.

Unless a figure is not drawn to scale, you can use a pencil or other available straight edge as a ruler to measure lengths.

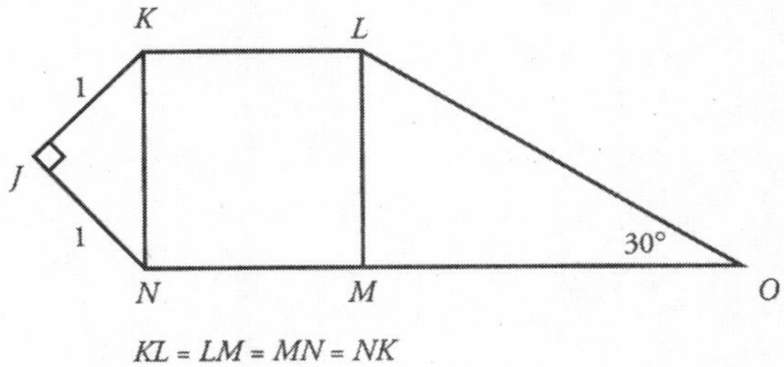

In the figure above, what is the length of LO?

(A) 2

(B) $2\sqrt{2}$

(C) $2\sqrt{3}$

(D) 4

(E) $4\sqrt{2}$

The correct answer is (B).

Take a piece of paper and mark on it the length of *JK*. This distance is 1. Now measure that distance against *LO*.

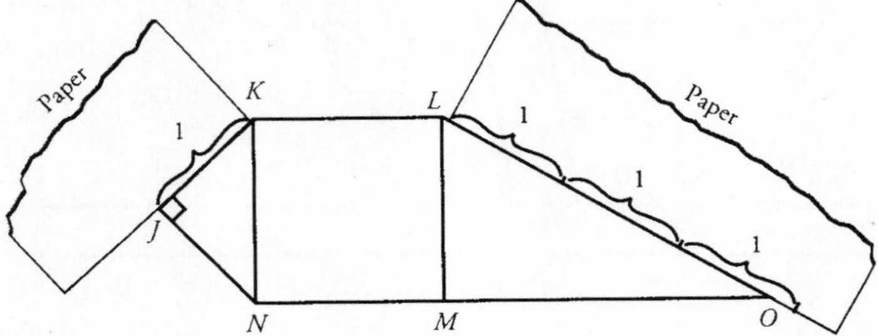

It appears that *LO* is slightly more than 2.5; make it about 2.8. Which answer is closest? The best approximation for $\sqrt{2}$ is 1.4, so (B) is 2(1.4) = 2.8.

EXERCISE 1: PROBLEM SOLVING

50 Questions • 70 Minutes

Directions: For each of the following questions, select the best of the answer choices.
Numbers: All numbers used are real numbers.
Figures: The diagrams and figures that accompany these questions are for the purpose of providing information useful in answering the questions. Unless it is stated that a specific figure is not drawn to scale, the diagrams and figures are drawn as accurately as possible. All figures are in a plane unless otherwise indicated.

1. In a list of numbers, each number after the first is exactly $\frac{1}{3}$ the number immediately preceding it. If the fifth number in the list is 3, what is the second number in the sequence?

(A) $\frac{1}{9}$

(B) $\frac{1}{3}$

(C) 1

(D) 27

(E) 81

2. A merchant sells a certain item for a price that is a whole number of dollars. If the cost of the item to her is \$50, then which of the following could be her profit as a percentage of her cost?

(A) 15%

(B) 25%

(C) $33\frac{1}{3}\%$

(D) 40%

(E) 75%

3. The ratio of x to y is $\frac{1}{2}$. If the ratio of $x + 2$ to $y + 1$ is $\frac{2}{3}$, then what is the value of x?

(A) 6

(B) 4

(C) 3

(D) 2

(E) 1

4. At the Scholarly Text Printing Company, each of n printing presses can produce on the average t books every m minutes. If all presses work without interruption, how many hours will be required to produce a run of 10,000 books?

(A) $\frac{10{,}000(60)mn}{t}$

(B) $\frac{10{,}000(60)tm}{n}$

(C) $\frac{10{,}000mn}{60t}$

(D) $\frac{10{,}000m}{60nt}$

(E) $\frac{10{,}000}{60mnt}$

5. If $\frac{(x-y)^2}{x^2-y^2} = 9$, then $\frac{x+y}{x-y} =$

(A) $\frac{1}{9}$

(B) $\frac{1}{3}$

(C) 1

(D) 3

(E) 9

6. A certain manufacturer has three machines producing the same item. If Machine X produces $\frac{1}{4}$ as many of the item as Machine Y produces in the same time, and Machine Y produces twice as many of the item as Machine Z in the same time, then during a fixed period Machine Z produces what fraction of the total number of items produced?

(A) $\frac{1}{14}$

(B) $\frac{2}{7}$

(C) $\frac{1}{3}$

(D) $\frac{1}{2}$

(E) $\frac{4}{7}$

7. In a certain community, property is assessed at 60% of its appraised value and taxed at the rate of $4.00 per $100 of assessed value. If a taxpayer is assessed $240 per quarter in property taxes, what is the appraised value of the property?

(A) $6,000

(B) $22,500

(C) $24,000

(D) $40,000

(E) $60,000

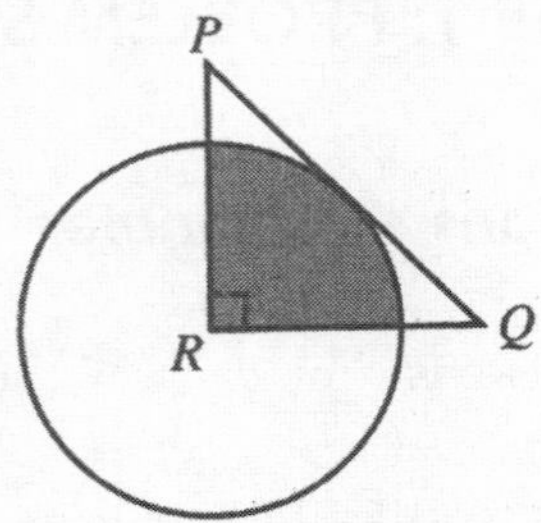

R is the center of the circle.

8. In the figure above, if isosceles right triangle PQR has an area of 4, what is the area of the shaded portion of the figure?

(A) π

(B) 2π

(C) $2\sqrt{2}\pi$

(D) 4π

(E) 8π

9. If cylinder P has a height twice that of cylinder Q and a radius half that of cylinder Q, what is the ratio between the volume of cylinder P and the volume of cylinder Q?

(A) 1:8

(B) 1:4

(C) 1:2

(D) 1

(E) 2:1

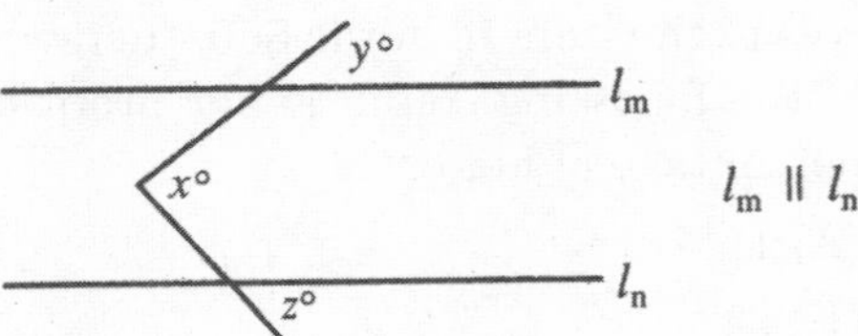

10. In the figure above, which of the following is true?

(A) $y + z = x$

(B) $y = 90°$

(C) $x + y + z = 180$

(D) $y = x + z$

(E) $z = x + y$

exercises

11. If the width of a rectangle is increased by 25% while the length remains constant, the resulting area is what percent of the original area?

(A) 25%

(B) 75%

(C) 125%

(D) 225%

(E) 250%

12. A snapshot measures $2\frac{1}{2}$ inches by $1\frac{7}{8}$ inches. It is to be enlarged so that the longer dimension will be 4 inches. The length of the enlarged shorter dimension will be

(A) $2\frac{1}{2}$ inches

(B) 3 inches

(C) $3\frac{3}{8}$ inches

(D) $2\frac{5}{8}$ inches

(E) none of these

13. From a piece of tin in the shape of a square 6 inches on a side, the largest possible circle is cut out. Of the following, the ratio of the area of the circle to the area of the original square is closest in value to

(A) $\frac{3}{4}$

(B) $\frac{2}{3}$

(C) $\frac{3}{5}$

(D) $\frac{1}{2}$

(E) $\frac{1}{4}$

14. In the Peterson Company, the ratio of upper-management to middle-management personnel is 4:3. If 75% of upper management has experience on the production line, what is the greatest proportion of the total of upper- and middle-management personnel who could have experience on the production line?

(A) $\frac{5}{7}$

(B) $\frac{3}{4}$

(C) $\frac{6}{7}$

(D) $\frac{7}{6}$

(E) $\frac{7}{4}$

15. The function # is defined for any positive whole number N as being the product $\#N = (N-1)(N-2)(N-3)$. What is the sum of #1, #2, #3, and #4?

(A) –10

(B) 6

(C) 12

(D) 60

(E) 256

16. Two crystal spheres of diameter $\frac{x}{2}$ are being packed in a cubic box with a side of x. If the crystal spheres are in the box and the rest of the box is completely filled with packing powder, approximately what proportion of the box is filled with packing powder? (The volume of a sphere of radius r is $\frac{4}{3}\pi r^3$.)

(A) $1\frac{1}{16}$

(B) $\frac{1}{8}$

(C) $\frac{1}{2}$

(D) $\frac{3}{4}$

(E) $\frac{7}{8}$

17. All of the coffee mixtures sold in a certain store contain either Colombian, Jamaican, or Brazilian coffee or some combination of these. Of all the mixtures, 33 contain Colombian coffee, 43 contain Jamaican coffee, and 42 contain Brazilian coffee. Of these, 16 contain at least Colombian and Jamaican coffees, 18 contain at least Jamaican and Brazilian coffees, 8 contain at least Brazilian and Colombian coffees, and 5 contain all three. How many different coffee mixtures are sold in the store?

(A) 71

(B) 81

(C) 109

(D) 118

(E) 165

18. If $x = 3$ and $y = 2$, then $2x + 3y =$

(A) 5

(B) 10

(C) 12

(D) 14

(E) 15

19. If the profit on an item is \$4 and the sum of the cost and the profit is \$20, what is the cost of the item?

(A) \$24

(B) \$20

(C) \$16

(D) \$15

(E) \$12

20. If n is an integer between 0 and 100, then any of the following could be $3n + 3$ EXCEPT

(A) 300

(B) 297

(C) 208

(D) 63

(E) 6

21. A figure that can be folded over along a straight line so that the result is two equal halves which are then lying on top of one another with no overlap is said to have a line of symmetry. Which of the following figures has only one line of symmetry?

(A) square

(B) circle

(C) equilateral triangle

(D) isosceles triangle

(E) rectangle

22. A laborer is paid \$8 per hour for an 8-hour day and $1\frac{1}{2}$ times that rate for each hour in excess of 8 hours in a single day. If the laborer received \$80 for a single day's work, how long did he work on that day?

(A) 6 hr. 40 min.

(B) 9 hr. 20 min.

(C) 9 hr. 30 min.

(D) 9 hr. 40 min.

(E) 10 hr.

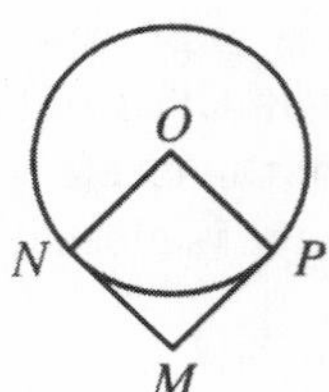

23. The vertex of the square $MNOP$ is located at the center of circle O. If arc NP is 4π units long, then which of the following is the perimeter of the square $MNOP$?

(A) 32

(B) 32π

(C) 64

(D) 64π

(E) 72π

exercises

24. Paul is standing 180 yards due north of point *P*. Franny is standing 240 yards due west of point *P*. What is the shortest distance between Franny and Paul?

(A) 60 yards

(B) 300 yards

(C) 420 yards

(D) 900 yards

(E) 9000 yards

25. If a rectangle has an area of $81x^2$ and a length of $27x$, then what is its width?

(A) $3x$

(B) $9x$

(C) $3x^2$

(D) $9x^2$

(E) $2128x^3$

26. Into how many line segments, each 2 inches long, can a line segment one and one-half yards long be divided?

(A) 9

(B) 18

(C) 27

(D) 36

(E) 48

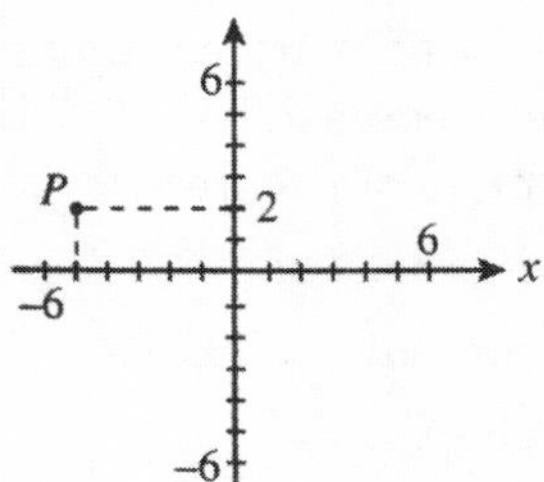

27. In the figure above, the coordinates of point *P* are

(A) (–5, –2)

(B) (–5, 2)

(C) (–2, 5)

(D) (2, –5)

(E) (5, 2)

28. All of the following are prime numbers EXCEPT

(A) 13

(B) 17

(C) 41

(D) 79

(E) 91

29. A girl at point *X* walks 1 mile east, then 2 miles north, then 1 mile east, then 1 mile north, then 1 mile east, then 1 mile north to arrive at point *Y*.

From point *Y*, what is the shortest distance to point *X*?

(A) 7 miles

(B) 6 miles

(C) 5 miles

(D) 2.5 miles

(E) 1 mile

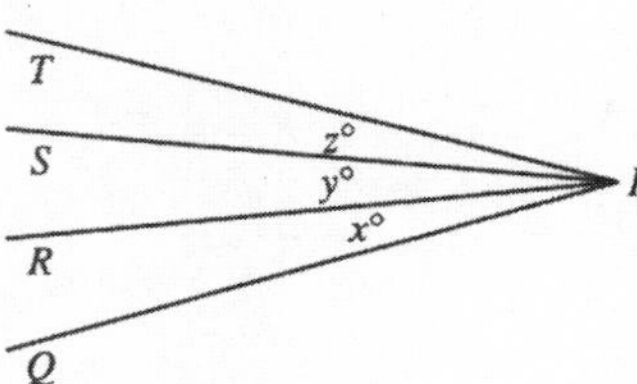

30. In the figure above, the measure of $\angle QPS$ is equal to the measure of $\angle TPR$. Which of the following must be true?

(A) $x = y$

(B) $y = z$

(C) $x = z$

(D) $x = y = z$

(E) $x + y = z$

31. Newtown is due north of Oscarville. Highway *L* runs 31° south of east from Newtown and Highway *M* runs 44° north of east from Oscarville. If *L* and *M* are straight, what is the measure of the acute angle they form at their intersection?

(A) 105°

(B) 89°

(C) 75°

(D) 59°

(E) 46°

32. If an item that ordinarily costs $90 is discounted by 25%, what is the new selling price?

(A) $22.50

(B) $25.00

(C) $45.00

(D) $67.50

(E) $112.50

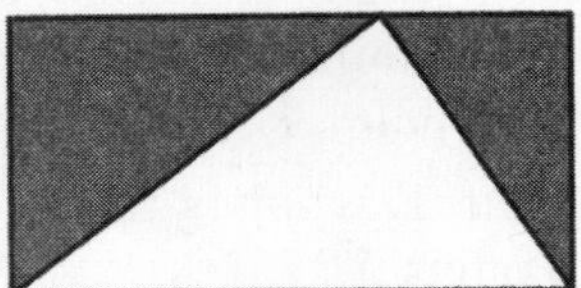

33. In the rectangle above, what is the ratio of $\frac{\text{area of shaded region}}{\text{area of unshaded region}}$?

(A) $\frac{1}{4}$

(B) $\frac{1}{2}$

(C) $\frac{1}{1}$

(D) $\frac{2}{1}$

(E) $\frac{3}{1}$

34. Earl can stuff advertising circulars into envelopes at the rate of 45 envelopes per minute and Ellen requires a minute and a half to stuff the same number of envelopes. Working together, how long will it take Earl and Ellen to stuff 300 envelopes?

(A) 15 minutes

(B) 4 minutes

(C) 3 minutes 30 seconds

(D) 3 minutes 20 seconds

(E) 2 minutes

Distribution	Number in Population
Having X Having Y	25
Having X Lacking Y	10
Lacking X Having Y	25
Lacking X Lacking Y	40

35. The table above gives the distribution of two genetic characteristics, X and Y, in a population of 100 subjects. What is the ratio of $\frac{\text{number of subjects having } X}{\text{number of subjects having } Y}$?

(A) $\frac{7}{5}$

(B) $\frac{1}{1}$

(C) $\frac{5}{7}$

(D) $\frac{7}{10}$

(E) $\frac{1}{4}$

36. If the price of an item is increased by 10% and then decreased by 10%, the net effect on the price of the item is

(A) an increase of 99%

(B) an increase of 1%

(C) no change

(D) a decrease of 1%

(E) a decrease of 11%

37. Lines l_m and l_n lie in the plane x and intersect one another on the perpendicular at point P. Which of the following statements must be true?

(A) A line which lies in plane x and intersects line l_m on the perpendicular at a point other than P does not intersect l_n.

(B) Line segment MN, which does not intersect l_m, does not intersect l_n.

(C) If line l_o lies in plane y and intersects l_m at point P, plane y is perpendicular to plane x.

(D) A circle that lies in plane x and has two points in common with l_m also has two points in common with l_n.

(E) A circle that has exactly one point in common with l_m and one point in common with l_n also lies in plane x.

38. A student conducts an experiment in biology lab and discovers that the ratio of the number of insects in a given population having characteristic X to the number of insects in the population not having characteristic X is 5:3, and that $\frac{3}{8}$ of the insects having characteristic X are male insects. What proportion of the total insect population are male insects having the characteristic X?

(A) $\frac{1}{1}$

(B) $\frac{5}{8}$

(C) $\frac{6}{13}$

(D) $\frac{15}{64}$

(E) $\frac{1}{5}$

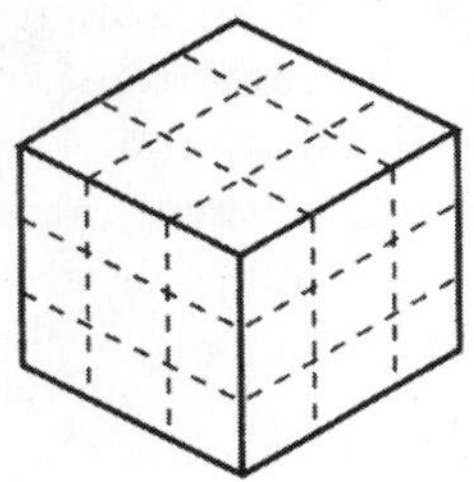

39. The figure above represents a wooden block 3 inches on an edge, all of whose faces are painted black. If the block is cut up along the dotted lines, 27 blocks result, each 1 cubic inch in volume. Of these, how many will have no painted faces?

(A) 1

(B) 3

(C) 4

(D) 5

(E) 7

40. A business firm reduces the number of hours its employees work from 40 hours per week to 36 hours per week while continuing to pay the same amount of money. If an employee earned x dollars per hour before the reduction in hours, how much does the employee earn per hour under the new system?

(A) $\frac{1}{10}$

(B) $\frac{x}{9}$

(C) $\frac{9x}{10}$

(D) $\frac{10x}{9}$

(E) $9x$

41. A painter has painted one-third of a rectangular wall that is ten feet high. When she has painted another 75 square feet of wall, she will be three-quarters finished with the job. What is the length (the horizontal dimension) of the wall?

(A) 18 feet

(B) 12 feet

(C) 10 feet

(D) 9 feet

(E) 6 feet

42. Mr. Johnson grosses $2,000 per month from his mail-order business. If 40 percent of that amount goes for business expenses and 10 percent of the remainder is reinvested in the business, how much of the gross receipts is reinvested in the business?

(A) $80

(B) $100

(C) $110

(D) $120

(E) $200

43. $8^4 \div 2^{10} =$

(A) 4^{-6}

(B) 4

(C) 8

(D) 16

(E) 32

44. $(4 + \sqrt{5})(4 - \sqrt{5})$ is equal to:

(A) –1

(B) 0

(C) 11

(D) 21

(E) $11 + 8\sqrt{5}$

45. A rope 32 feet long was cut into two pieces, one piece 8 feet longer than the other. What is the ratio of the larger piece to the smaller piece?

(A) $\frac{1}{16}$

(B) $\frac{1}{8}$

(C) $\frac{3}{5}$

(D) $\frac{3}{2}$

(E) $\frac{5}{3}$

46. If 3 people working together at the same rate can do a job in $5\frac{1}{3}$ days, what fraction of that job can two of these people do in one day?

(A) $\frac{1}{16}$

(B) $\frac{1}{8}$

(C) $\frac{3}{16}$

(D) $\frac{1}{2}$

(E) $\frac{2}{3}$

47. If interest on a savings account is paid monthly at an annual rate of $6\frac{1}{4}$ percent and if the interest is not reinvested, then in how many years will the total amount of interest earned equal the amount of money saved in the account?

(A) 36

(B) 24

(C) 18

(D) 16

(E) 12

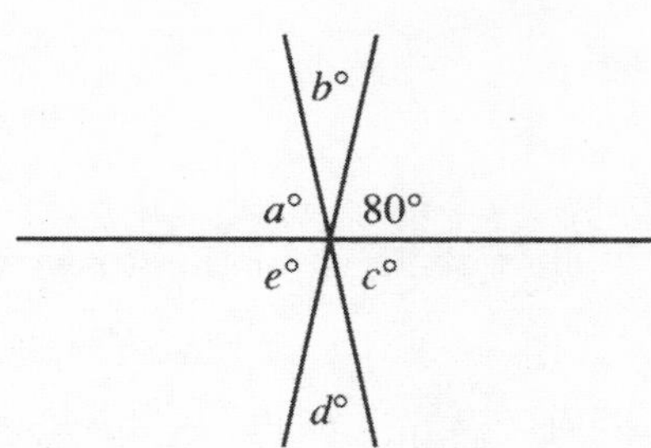

48. In the figure above, if $a = 3d$, $b =$

(A) 25

(B) 35

(C) 75

(D) 800

(E) 100

49. A certain machine produces 8 toys every 4 seconds. If the machine operates without interruption, how many toys will it produce in 2 minutes?

(A) 60

(B) 120

(C) 240

(D) 480

(E) 960

50. If the total sales for a business in a certain year were $150,000, what were sales in June, if June sales were half the monthly average?

(A) $6,250

(B) $12,500

(C) $15,000

(D) $25,000

(E) $48,000

EXERCISE 2: PROBLEM SOLVING

25 Questions • 35 Minutes

Directions: For each of the following questions, select the best of the answer choices.

Numbers: All numbers used are real numbers.

Figures: The diagrams and figures that accompany these questions are for the purpose of providing information useful in answering the questions. Unless it is stated that a specific figure is not drawn to scale, the diagrams and figures are drawn as accurately as possible. All figures are in a plane unless otherwise indicated.

1. A store sells five different kinds of nuts. If it is possible to buy x pounds of the most expensive nuts for $3.20 and x pounds of the cheapest nuts for $1.40, then which of the following could be the cost of purchasing a mixture containing x pounds of each type of nut?

(A) $1.76

(B) $2.84

(C) $3.54

(D) $13.60

(E) $16.00

2. If the result obtained by multiplying a number, x, by a number 1 less than itself is 4 less than multiplying x by itself, then $x=$

(A) 1

(B) 2

(C) 3

(D) 4

(E) 5

3. At a certain party attended by 32 people, 24 of them were students. If 12 of those in attendance were women, and if 6 of the women in attendance were students, then how many of the men who attended the party were NOT students?

(A) 2

(B) 4

(C) 8

(D) 12

(E) 18

4. If $x = 5$, $y = 3$, and $z = 2$, then $\frac{x(y-z)}{y(x+y+z)} =$

(A) $\frac{1}{30}$

(B) $\frac{1}{6}$

(C) 1

(D) 5

(E) 10

5. What is 200% of 0.010?

(A) 0.0002

(B) 0.0005

(C) 0.020

(D) 0.050

(E) 0.20

6. If the average (arithmetic mean) of five different integers is 1, which of the following must be true?

I. 1 is one of the integers.

II. At least one of the integers is negative.

III. 0 is not one of the integers.

(A) I only

(B) II only

(C) I and II only

(D) II and III only

(E) I, II, and III

exercises

7. In a certain school library, 60% of the books are clothbound books. If 30% of those are works of fiction, then what percentage of all books in the library are clothbound works of fiction?

(A) 90%
(B) 30%
(C) 20%
(D) 18%
(E) 2%

8. A traveler has booked a vacation plan with agent X for a total cost of $1,200 and has already paid agent X a nonrefundable deposit equal to 10% of the cost of the vacation plan. She learns that she can purchase the same vacation plan from agent Y for 20% less. If these are the only costs involved, what will be the net result of breaking the contract with agent X, thereby forfeiting the deposit, and then purchasing the plan through agent Y?

(A) An increase in the cost of the vacation of $240
(B) An increase in the cost of the vacation of $120
(C) No change in the cost of the vacation
(D) A decrease in the cost of the vacation of $120
(E) A decrease in the cost of the vacation of $240

9. A gymnast's score for a routine is the average of the scores awarded by ten judges on a scale ranging from 0 to 10. If the first seven judges have awarded the gymnast scores of 7, 8, 7.5, 9, 8.2, 8.5, and 7.8, and she does not receive a score lower than 6 from any of the other judges, then her final score for the routine will be

(A) greater than 8.0
(B) greater than 7.8
(C) greater than or equal to 7.8
(D) between 7.0 and 7.4
(E) greater than or equal to 7.4

10. During a sale, a certain item is sold at a price 40% below its usual selling price. If the dollar savings on the item is $12, then what is its *sale* price?

(A) $30
(B) $24
(C) $18
(D) $15
(E) $6

11. What is 40% of $\frac{10}{7}$?

(A) $\frac{2}{7}$
(B) $\frac{4}{7}$
(C) $\frac{10}{28}$
(D) $\frac{1}{28}$
(E) $\frac{28}{10}$

12. Which of the following is NOT a prime number?

(A) 17
(B) 37
(C) 41
(D) 51
(E) 59

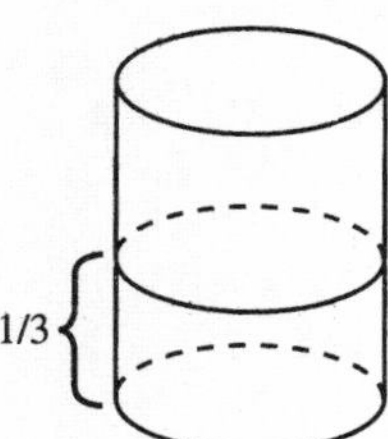

13. As shown in the figure above, a cylindrical oil tank is $\frac{1}{3}$ full. If 3 more gallons are added, the tank will be half full. What is the capacity, in gallons, of the tank?

(A) 15
(B) 16
(C) 17
(D) 18
(E) 19

14. A boy receives grades of 91, 88, 86, and 78 in four of his major subjects. What must he receive in his fifth major subject in order to average 85?

(A) 86
(B) 85
(C) 84
(D) 83
(E) 82

15. If a steel bar is 0.39 feet long, its length in *inches* is

(A) less than 4
(B) between 4 and $4\frac{1}{2}$
(C) between $4\frac{1}{2}$ and 5
(D) between 5 and 6
(E) more than 6

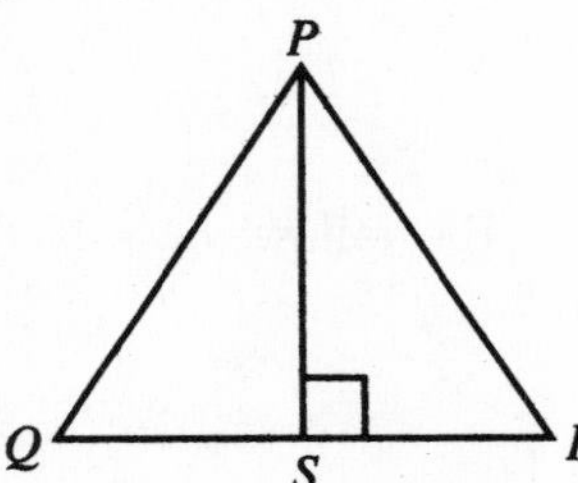

16. In the figure, PS is perpendicular to QR. If $PQ = PR = 26$ and $PS = 24$, then $QR =$

(A) 14
(B) 16
(C) 18
(D) 20
(E) 22

17. A man buys some shirts and some ties. The shirts cost $7 each and the ties cost $3 each. If the man spends exactly $81 and buys the maximum number of shirts possible under these conditions, what is the ratio of shirts to ties?

(A) 5:3
(B) 4:3
(C) 5:2
(D) 4:1
(E) 3:2

18. If a man walks $\frac{2}{5}$ mile in 5 minutes, what is his average rate of walking in miles per hour?

(A) 4
(B) $4\frac{1}{2}$
(C) $4\frac{4}{5}$
(D) $5\frac{1}{5}$
(E) $5\frac{3}{4}$

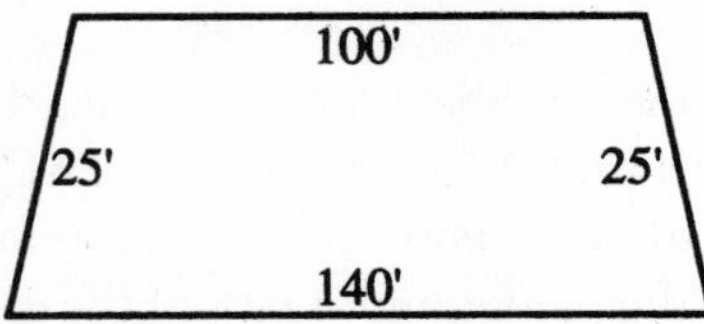

Note: Figure not drawn to scale.

19. One end of a dam has the shape of a trapezoid with the dimensions indicated. What is the dam's area in square feet?

(A) 1,000
(B) 1,200
(C) 1,500
(D) 1,800
(E) Cannot be determined from the information given.

20. If $1 + \frac{1}{t} = \frac{t+1}{t}$, what does t equal?

(A) +2 only
(B) +2 or –2 only
(C) +2 or –1 only
(D) –2 or +1 only
(E) t is any number except 0

21. If R and S are different integers, both divisible by 5, then which of the following is *not necessarily* true?

(A) $R - S$ is divisible by 5.
(B) RS is divisible by 25.
(C) $R + S$ is divisible by 5.
(D) $R^2 + S^2$ is divisible by 5.
(E) $R + S$ is divisible by 10.

22. If a triangle of base 7 is equal in area to a circle of radius 7, what is the altitude of the triangle?

(A) 8π

(B) 10π

(C) 12π

(D) 14π

(E) Cannot be determined from the information given.

23. If the following numbers are arranged in order from the smallest to the largest, what will be their correct order?

I. $\frac{9}{13}$

II. $\frac{13}{9}$

III. 70%

IV. $\frac{1}{.70}$

(A) II, I, III, IV

(B) III, II, I, IV

(C) III, IV, I, II

(D) II, IV, III, I

(E) I, III, IV, II

24. The coordinates of the vertices of quadrilateral $PQRS$ are $P(0, 0)$, $Q(9, 0)$, $R(10, 3)$ and S (1, 3), respectively. The area of $PQRS$ is

(A) $9\sqrt{10}$

(B) $\frac{9}{2}\sqrt{10}$

(C) $\frac{27}{2}$

(D) 27

(E) $27\sqrt{10}$

25. A certain type of siding for a house costs \$10.50 per square yard. What does it cost for the siding for a wall 4 yards wide and 60 feet long?

(A) \$800

(B) \$840

(C) \$2520

(D) \$3240

(E) \$5040

Exercise 1: ANSWER KEY AND EXPLANATIONS

1. E	11. C	21. D	31. C	41. A
2. D	12. B	22. B	32. D	42. D
3. B	13. A	23. A	33. C	43. B
4. D	14. C	24. B	34. B	44. C
5. A	15. B	25. A	35. D	45. E
6. B	16. E	26. C	36. D	46. B
7. D	17. B	27. B	37. A	47. D
8. A	18. C	28. E	38. D	48. A
9. C	19. C	29. C	39. A	49. C
10. A	20. C	30. C	40. D	50. A

1. **The correct answer is (E).** To answer this question, you must work out the sequence, but make sure you work in the correct direction. We know the fifth term, and we want to know the second term. Since each term is $\frac{1}{3}$ the number preceding it in the sequence, the numbers get smaller as the sequence progresses. We are moving backwards, however, so our numbers get larger:

5th	4th	3rd	2nd
3	9	27	81

2. **The correct answer is (D).** Since the question stem has the form "which of the following could be . . . ?", the proper approach is to test choices until you find one that works. Since her cost is \$50, we test (A):

$$\frac{x}{\$50} = .15$$
$$x = \$7.50$$

But a dollar profit or markup of \$7.50 would generate a selling price of \$57.50—not a whole number. (B), (C), and (E) also yield fractional amounts. (D), however, yields a markup of \$20 for a whole dollar selling price of \$70.

3. **The correct answer is (B).** This question is answered by manipulating simultaneous equations:

$$\frac{x}{y} = \frac{1}{2}$$

So: $y = 2x$

And: $\frac{x+2}{y+1} = \frac{2}{3}$

Substituting: $\frac{x+2}{2x+1} = \frac{2}{3}$

Cross-multiplying: $3(x+2) = 2(2x+1)$
$3x + 6 = 4x + 2$

Solving for x: $x = 4$

4. **The correct answer is (D).** This question asks you to express a certain relationship in algebraic notation. Each machine operates at the rate of t books per m minutes or $\frac{t}{m}$. But there are n such machines, so the overall rate of operation will be n times $\frac{t}{m}$ which is $\frac{nt}{m}$. To find the time it will take to produce 10,000 books, we divide that number by the rate of operation:

$$\frac{10{,}000}{\frac{nt}{m}} = 10{,}000 \times \frac{m}{nt} = \frac{10{,}000m}{nt}$$

Finally, we divide that by 60 since there are 60 minutes in every hour: $\frac{10,000m}{60nt}$

5. **The correct answer is (A).** This question tests manipulation of expressions. Begin by factoring the denominator (which is the difference of two squares): $x^2 - y^2 = (x+y)(x-y)$. Since the numerator is $(x-y)(x-y)$, we can divide one $x-y$ with the $x-y$ in the denominator, leaving $\frac{x-y}{x+y}$, so $\frac{x-y}{x+y}$, its reciprocal, is equal to $\frac{1}{9}$.
6. **The correct answer is (B).** Obviously, one way to attack this question is to assign a variable to represent the unknown quantity. But another approach is to assume a concrete value. Let's assume that X produces 100 units in any time period. Machine Y would produce four times that, or 400 units, and Machine Z would produce half of that, or 200 units. On that assumption, the three machines would produce a total of 700 units, of which 200 are produced by Z:
$\frac{200}{700} = \frac{2}{7}$
7. **The correct answer is (D).** First, we find the annual tax bill: $\$240 \times 4 = \$960$. And the rate of taxation is \$4.00/\$100. = 4.0%. So \$960 is equal to 4.0% of the assessed value:

$\$960 = 4.0\%$ of assessed value

$\$960 = 0.04\,AV$

$AV = \frac{\$960}{0.04} = \$24,000$

So the assessed value of the property is \$24,000, but that is only 60% of the appraised value:

Appraised Value $= \frac{\$24,000}{0.60} = \$40,000$
8. **The correct answer is (A).** The shaded area in the question is just a sector of the circle, and since angle R is 90°, the sector is $\frac{1}{4}$ of the whole circle. Once we find the area of the entire circle, we can find the area of the shaded sector, and we can find the area of the circle by determining the length of the radius. How? All we know is that the area of the triangle is 4. Since PR and RQ form a right angle, we can treat them as altitude and base:

$\frac{1}{2}(PR)(RQ) = 4$

But they are equal, so:

$\frac{1}{2}(PR)(PR) = 4$

$PR^2 = 8$

$PR = 2\sqrt{2}$

Now we add a radius and see that it forms a new isosceles right triangle:

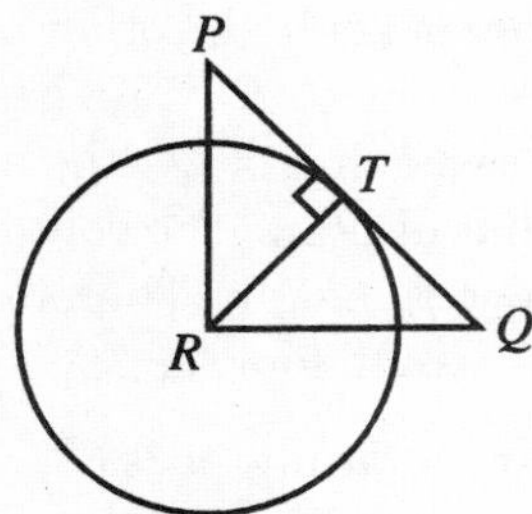

With this type of triangle, the two shorter sides are always equal to half the hypotenuse times $\sqrt{2}$:

$RT = \frac{1}{2}(2\sqrt{2})(\sqrt{2}) = 2$

Now we have the radius. The area of the entire circle is:

$\pi r^2 = \pi(2)^2 = 4\pi$

And the shaded area is $\frac{1}{4}$ of that, or just π.
9. **The correct answer is (C).** Let us begin by assigning letters to the height and radius of each cylinder. Since most people find it easier to deal with whole numbers instead of fractions, let us say that cylinder Q has a radius of $2r$, so that cylinder P can have a radius of r. Then, we assign cylinder Q a height of h so that P can have a height of $2h$. Now, the formula for the volume of a cylinder is $\pi r^2 \times h$. So P and Q have volumes:

answers

Volume $P = \pi(r)^2 \times 2h$

Volume $P = \pi 2r^2h$

Volume $Q = \pi(2r)^2 \times h$

Volume $Q = \pi 4r^2h$

Thus, the ratio of Volume P: Volume Q is $\frac{\pi 2r^2h}{\pi 4r^2h} = \frac{2}{4} = \frac{1}{2}$.

Another way of solving the problem is to use the knowledge that the area of a circle increases with the square of the radius. This means that if P and Q had equal heights, the volume of Q would be *four* times that of P, since the radius of Q is *twice* that of P. On the other hand, if their radii were equal, P would have a volume of only twice that of Q—the height of P is twice that of Q and the volume increases directly with height. Therefore, the ratio must be two to four, or 1:2.

10. **The correct answer is (A).** We begin by extending the lines to give this picture:

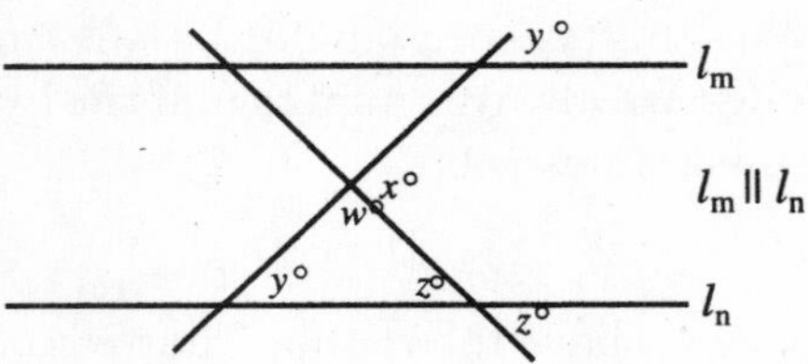

$x + w = 180°$, and we know that $y + z + w = 180°$. So, $x + w = y + z + w$, $x = y + z$.

11. **The correct answer is (C).** Let us begin by drawing the rectangle:

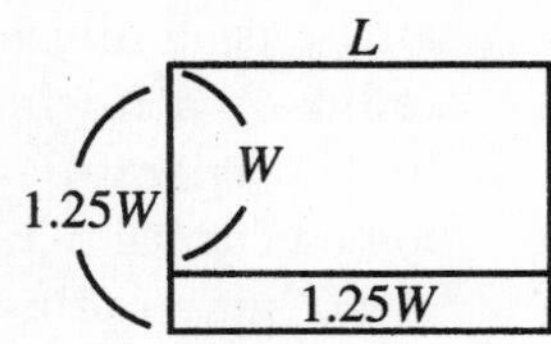

The original area is WL. The width of the new rectangle is $W + .25\% W$, or $1.25W$. So the new area is $1.25WL$. It then follows that the new area is $\frac{1.25WL}{WL}$, or 125% of the old area.

12. **The correct answer is (B).** The proportion to be solved is $2\frac{1}{2} : 4 = 1\frac{7}{8} : x$, where x is the length of the shorter dimension of the enlargement. Solving, we get $x = 3$.

13. **The correct answer is (A).** The area of the circle is π times the square of the radius, or 9π. The area of the square is 36. Thus, the ratio is $\frac{9\pi}{36}$, or $\frac{\pi}{4}$. Approximating π as slightly more than 3, the answer is slightly more than $\frac{3}{4}$.

14. **The correct answer is (C).** First of all, (D) and (E) are impossible on logical grounds since they are greater than 1, and the proportion of something that has a characteristic cannot be greater than 1. That would be like saying, "Five out of three doctors recommend. . . ." We need the total of upper and middle management with production line experience. The ratio 4:3 tells us that the total number of middle- and upper-management personnel in the company can be divided into 7 equal parts, with 4 of them in upper management and 3 in middle management. Of the 4 parts in upper management, 75%, or $\frac{3}{4}$, have experience on the production line. Three-quarters of 4 parts amounts to 3 parts ($\frac{3}{7}$ of the total). You are not told how many of the middle-management personnel have production line experience, but the key word "greatest" tells you that you should consider *all* of the middle-management personnel as having production line experience. This means that there are 3 parts from the upper- management personnel who have production line experience and that there are 3 more parts from the middle-management personnel that are assumed to have production line experience, for a total of 6 parts out of 7, or $\frac{6}{7}$.

15. **The correct answer is (B).** This sort of problem can seem much more difficult than it actually is. The first step is to understand the instructions for doing the

"#" game. For the number $N = 1$, #1 = (1 – 1)(1 – 2)(1 – 3). The key thing to notice is that the first term in this series of terms being multiplied together (1 – 1) is zero. When you multiply by zero, the result is zero no matter what the other numbers are. Not only should this immediately make you realize that you do not need to compute #1, but it should also alert you to the same sort of possibility in at least some of the other # functions with which you are working. In fact, #2 and #3 also come to zero because they also contain terms which equal zeros (2 – 2 and 3 – 3). Thus, only #4 needs to be evaluated: (#4 = (4 – 1)(4 – 2)(4 – 3) = 3 × 2 × 1 = 6).

16. The correct answer is (E). The volume of the powder will be determined by subtracting the volume of the two spheres from the volume of the box. The first thing that you must notice is that the quantity $\frac{x}{2}$, which is given to you to show the size of the spheres, is the *diameter.* Thus $\frac{x}{4}$ is the radius of the spheres. Before calculating the answer, it is probably a good idea to try to visualize the situation.

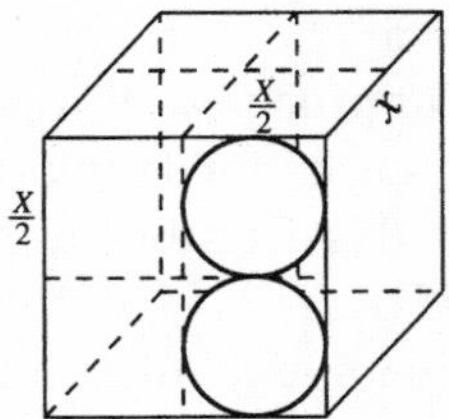

There would be room for 8 spheres in the box if they were placed so that they touched each other. Thus we know that if we divided the box into 8 smaller cubes of side $\frac{x}{2}$, two of them would have spheres in them and the other six would only have packing powder. Having six cubes with only packing powder in them would mean that $\frac{3}{4}$ of the box is completely filled with packing powder, in addition to the powder that is in the two cubes containing the spheres. Thus, (E) is the only possible answer.

By calculation, the volume of one sphere is $V = \left(\frac{4}{3}\right)\pi\left(\frac{x}{4}\right)^3 = \frac{4\pi x^3}{(3)(64)} = \frac{\pi x^3}{48}$. The volume of a cube of side x is x^3, so the volume of the powder will be $x^3 - 2\left(\frac{\pi x^3}{48}\right) = x^3(1 - \frac{\pi}{24})$. If we estimate that π is approximately equal to 3, then we can say that the fraction $\frac{\pi}{24}$ is approximately equal to $\frac{1}{8}$ and the powder makes up approximately $\frac{7}{8}$ of the total volume of the box. You will not often, if ever, need to know the actual value of π; and if you do need to know, it will be sufficient to know that it is slightly more than 3.

17. The correct answer is (B). As with all set problems, the key is to break the situation down into non-overlapping groups. There are three basic coffees (B, J, and C) and these three categories can combine in 7 possible ways: B only, C only, J only, $B + J$ only, $B + C$ only, $J + C$ only, and $B + J + C$. Therefore, your work must start with the information that is given to you in the form of a single category. The only single non-overlapping category that is given is the $B + J + C$ group, of which there are 5 mixtures. The key words, at least, when used to describe the information given about combinations of two coffees, tell you that these numbers describe the number of coffee mixtures containing the two coffees only plus the number of coffee mixtures containing all three coffees. Thus the given information that 16 mixtures contain at least Colombian and Jamaican coffees leads to the conclusion that 16 – 5 = 11 mixtures contain Colombian and Jamaican coffees only; 18 – 5 = 13 mixtures contain Jamaican and Brazilian coffees only; and 8 – 5 = 3 mixtures contain Brazilian and Colombian coffees only.

Perhaps the clearest way of seeing how to do the remaining subtractions is to

answers

draw three overlapping circles, which show all possible combinations. The final breakdown looks like this:

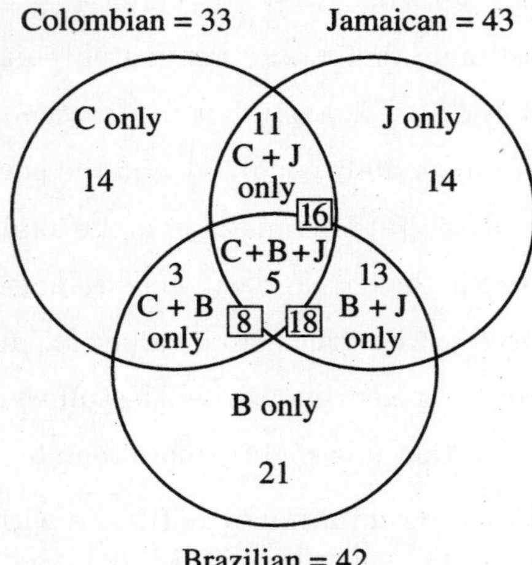

Once the four middle groupings are tied down, then the number of mixtures with only Colombian coffee can be determined by subtraction: 33 – 3 – 5 – 11 = 14; Jamaican only is 43 – 11 – 5 – 13 = 14; and Brazilian only is 42 – 3 – 5 – 13 = 21. Adding the seven categories together gives a total of 81.

Another method of approaching this problem is to consider the total number of inclusions of a coffee into a mixture. There are 43 + 42 + 33 = 118 total inclusions. Fifteen of these are from the five mixtures that include all three coffees. The given information states that there are 16 + 18 + 8 = 42 multiple mentions (at least 2 coffees). Since the multiple mentions can only be two or three coffees, we can see that 15 of the 42 multiple mentions are from the three-coffee blends (counted three times, as shown in the diagram), which leaves 27 double mentions. The number of single mentions can be determined by subtraction: 118 – 3(5) – 2(27) = 49. The total number of mixtures is thus 49 + 5 + 27 = 81. This method is a little more abstract and the first method is therefore preferable for most students.

18. **The correct answer is (C).** This problem simply requires finding the value of the expression $2x + 3y$, when $x = 3$ and $y = 2$: 2(3) + 3(2) = 12.

19. **The correct answer is (C).** You do not need a course in business arithmetic to solve this problem, only the common sense notion that profit is equal to gross revenue less cost. Expressed algebraically, we have $P = GR - C$; then, transposing the C term, we have $C + P = GR$, which is read: cost plus profit (or markup) is equal to gross revenue (or selling price). In this case, P = \$4, GR = \$20: $C + 4 = 20$, so $C = 16$.

20. **The correct answer is (C).** We must test each of the answer choices. The question asks for the one choice in which the answer is not equal to $3n + 3$. In (A), for example, does $300 = 3n + 3$? A quick manipulation will show that there is an integer, n, which solves the equation: $297 = 3n$, so $n = 99$. For (C), however, no integral n exists: $3n + 3 = 208$, $3n = 205$, $n = 68\frac{1}{3}$. So (C) is the answer we want. Another approach is to test each of the answer choices for being divisible by 3 since $3n + 3$ is divisible by 3 when n is an integer. If the sum of all the single digits in a number add up to a number divisible by 3, the number is itself divisible by 3; if not, not (208, for example: 2 + 0 + 8 = 10, is not divisible by 3). Being divisible by 3 does not mean an answer fits the conditions, but not being divisible by 3 means that it doesn't.

21. **The correct answer is (D).** The easiest approach to this problem is to draw the figures, as on the following page.

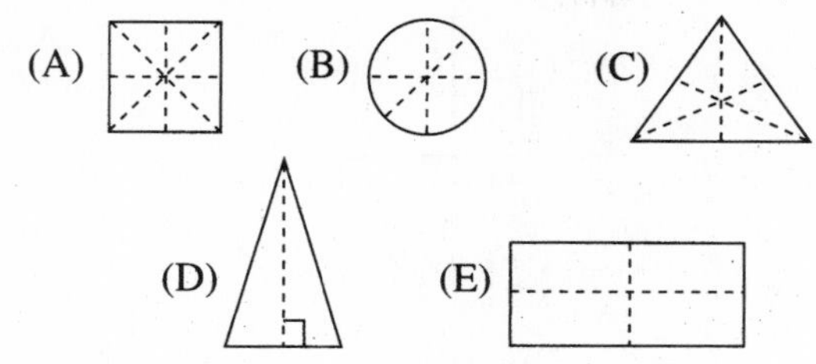

The dotted lines show possible lines of symmetry—that is, these are lines along which a paper cutout of the figure could be folded and the result will be that the two halves exactly match one another. (D) must be our answer, since it is the only figure with but one line of symmetry.

22. **The correct answer is (B).** This problem can, of course, be solved using an equation. We know that the laborer worked 8 hours @ \$8 per hour, but what we need to know is how much overtime he worked. We let x be the number of over-time hours: (8 hrs. × \$8/hr.) + (x hrs. × \$12/hr.) = \$80. The \$12/hr. is the laborer's overtime rate—that is, $\$8 \times 1\frac{1}{2} = \$12$.

    Now it is a fairly simple matter to manipulate the equation:

$$64 + 12x = 80$$
$$12x = 16$$
$$x = \frac{16}{12}$$
$$x = 1\frac{1}{3}$$

    Since $\frac{1}{3}$ of an hour is 20 minutes, the laborer worked 1 hour and 20 minutes of overtime, which, when added to the standard 8 hours, gives a total work day of 9 hours and 20 minutes.

    Now, common-sense reasoning might have gone like this: Well, I know he made \$64 in a regular day. If he made \$80 on a given day, \$16 must have been overtime pay. His overtime rate is time-and-a-half, that is, $1\frac{1}{2}$ times \$8/hr., or \$12/hr. In the first hour of overtime he made \$12, that leaves \$4 more. Since \$4 is one-third of \$12, he has to work another one-third of an hour to make that, which is twenty minutes. So he works 8 hours at standard rates of \$64, one full hour of overtime for another \$12, and another $\frac{1}{3}$ of an overtime hour for \$4. So \$80 represents 9 hours and 20 minutes of work.

23. **The correct answer is (A).** Since $MNOP$ is a square, we know that angle O must be a right angle, that is, 90°. From that we can conclude that arc NP is one-fourth of the entire circle. If arc NP is 4π units long, then the circumference of the circle must be 4 times that long, or 16π units. We are now in a position to find the length of the radius of circle O, and once we have the radius, we will also know the length of the sides of square $MNOP$, since MN and OP are both radii. The formula for the circumference of a circle is $C = 2\pi r$, so:

$$2\pi r = 16\pi$$
$$2r = 16$$
$$r = 8$$

    So the side of the square $MNOP$ must be 8, and its perimeter must be $s + s + s + s$ or 4(8) = 32.

24. **The correct answer is (B).** A quick sketch of the information provided in the problem shows that we need to employ the Pythagorean Theorem:

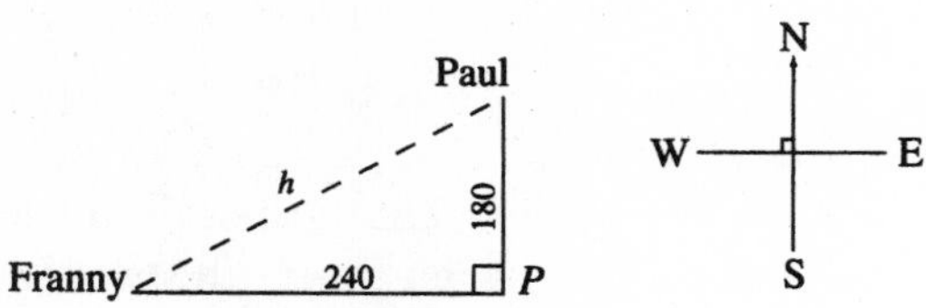

    The shortest distance from Paul to Franny is the hypotenuse of this right triangle:

    $180^2 + 240^2 = h^2$

    It is extremely unlikely that the GMAT would present a problem requiring such a lengthy calculation. So there must be a shortcut available. The key is to recognize that 180 and 240 are multiples of 60—3×60 and 4×60, respectively. This must be a 3,4,5 right triangle, so our hypotenuse must be $5 \times 60 = 300$.

25. **The correct answer is (A).** This problem requires a very simple insight: Area of rectangle = width × length. What makes it difficult is that many students—while they are able to compute the area of any rectangle in which the dimensions are given—"freak out" when dimensions are expressed in terms of a variable rather than real numbers. Those who keep a cool head will say, "Oh, the area is the width times the length." The area here is $81x^2$, the length is $27x$, therefore:

$$(W)(L) = Area$$
$$(W)(27x) = (81x^2)$$

Divide both sides by x:

$$(W)(27) = 81x$$
$$W = 3x$$

26. **The correct answer is (C).** First we must convert $1\frac{1}{2}$ yards into inches. There are 36 inches in a yard, so $1\frac{1}{2}$ yards must contain 36 + 18 or 54 inches. Now, to determine how many two-inch segments there are in 54 inches, we just divide 54 by 2, which equals 27. So there must be 27 two-inch segments in a segment, which is $1\frac{1}{2}$ yards long.

27. **The correct answer is (B).** It is important to remember that the positive x values are to the right of the origin (the intersection between the x- and y-axes), and that the negative values on the x axis are to the left of the origin. Also, the positive y values are above the origin, while the negative y values are below the x-axis.

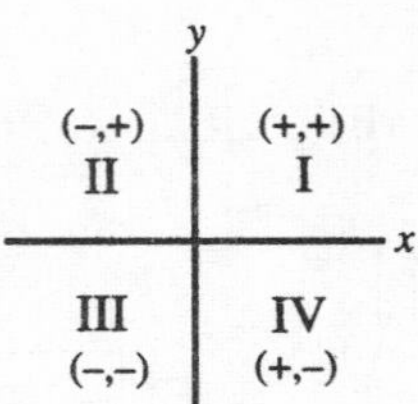

When reading an ordered pair such as (x, y) (called ordered because the first place is always the x-coordinate and the second place is always the y-coordinate), we know the first element is the movement on the horizontal or x-axis (from left to right), while the second element of the pair gives us the vertical distance. In this case, we are five units to the left of the origin, so that gives us an (x) value of negative 5. We are 2 units above the horizontal axis, so that gives us the second value (y) of +2. Thus, our ordered pair is (–5, 2), answer (B).

28. **The correct answer is (E).** Remember that a prime number is an integer which has exactly 2 factors, namely itself and 1. Thus, 13, 17, 41, and 79 are all prime numbers because their only factors are 13 and 1, 17 and 1, 41 and 1, and 79 and 1, respectively. 91, however, is not a prime number since it can be factored by 7 and 13 as well as by 1 and 91.

29. **The correct answer is (C).** The natural starting point here would be to draw the picture:

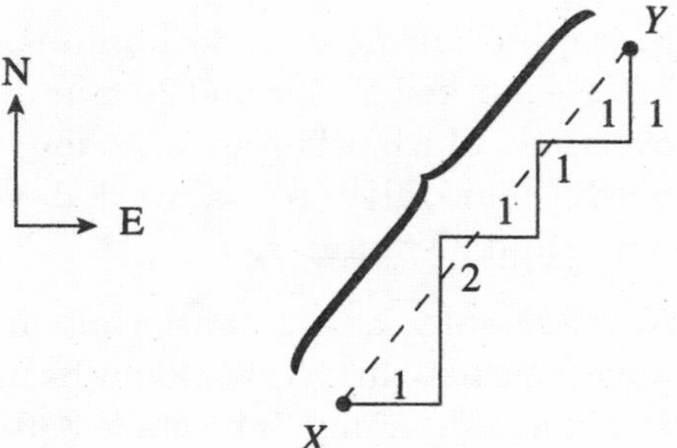

Since directions are perpendicular, we can perform the needed calculation with the Pythagorean Theorem. To simplify things, we can show that the picture above is equivalent to this:

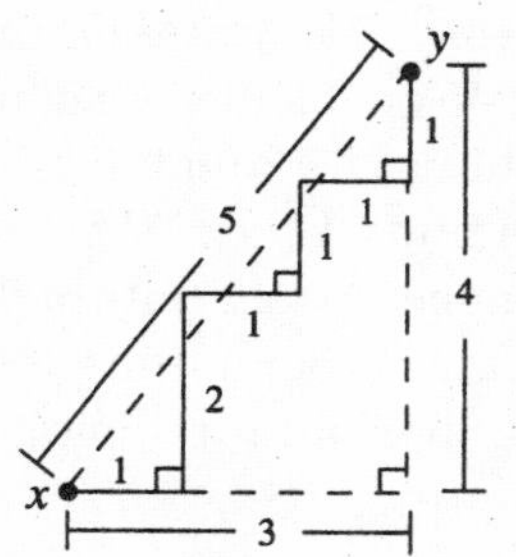

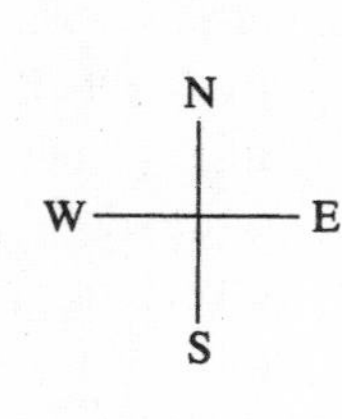

Now we can solve for the distance between X and Y with one use of the Pythagorean Theorem. Since the two legs of the right triangle are 3 and 4, we know that the hypotenuse must be 5. (Remember that 3, 4, and 5, or any multiples thereof, such as 6, 8, and 10, always make a right triangle.)

30. The correct answer is (C). Let us begin by substituting x, y, and z for M$\angle QPS$ and M$\angle TPR$. Since M$\angle QPS$ and M$\angle TPR$ are equal, we know $x + y = z + y$, and since $y = y$, we know that $x = z$. As for (A) and (B), we do not know whether y is equal to x and z; it could be larger or smaller or equal:

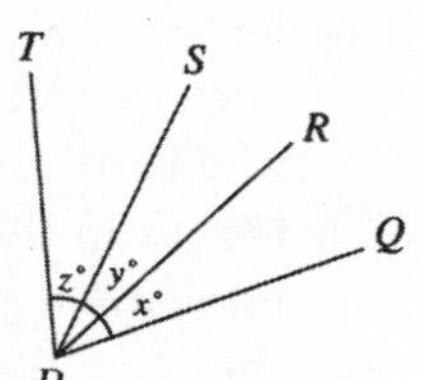

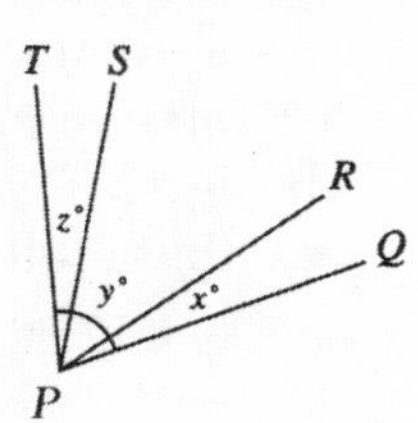

We can also eliminate (D), since we have no information that would lead us to conclude that all three are of equal measure.

31. The correct answer is (C). We must begin by drawing a picture:

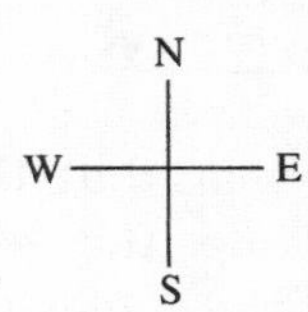

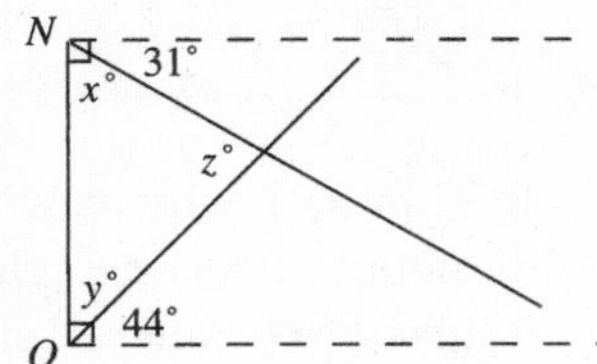

Since the angles at N and O are 90°, we can compute the magnitude of x and y, $x = 90° - 31° = 59°$, and $y = 90° - 44° = 46°$. Then, since x, y, and z are the interior angles of a triangle, we know $x + y + z = 180°$. Substituting for x and y, we have $59° + 46° + z = 180°$, and we solve for z: $z = 75°$. Since z is the angle of intersection between the two highways, our answer must be (C).

32. The correct answer is (D). While it is possible to set up a formula for this problem, Original Price – Discount = Discounted Price, a little common sense is a better attack. The discount is 25% of the original price, and 25% of \$90 is \$22.50. If the item originally cost \$90, and we are getting a discount of \$22.50, the new price will be \$67.50.

33. The correct answer is (C). Let us begin our solution by dropping a perpendicular from the upper vertex of the triangle:

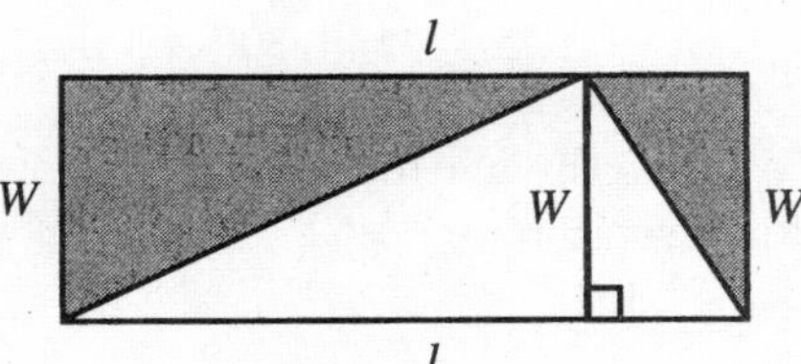

This divides the rectangle into two other rectangles, each with a diagonal running across it:

answers

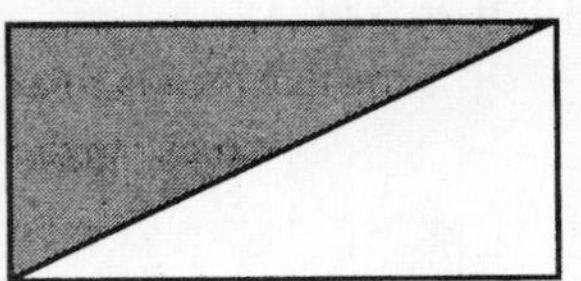

It should be intuitively clear that the diagonal of a rectangle divides the rectangle in half since all sides and angles are equal. Therefore, the left shaded area is equal to the left unshaded area and the right shaded area is equal to the right unshaded area, which means the total shaded area is equal to the total unshaded area. Thus, the triangle has half the area of the rectangle. This is actually the proof of the formula you use to find the area of a triangle—A = (height)(base). Remember this situation since it could easily come up in one problem or another.

34. The correct answer is (B). Since Earl and Ellen will be working together, we add their work rates:

$$\frac{\text{Number of tasks}}{\text{Time}} + \frac{\text{Number of tasks}}{\text{Time}}$$

$$= \frac{\text{Number of tasks together}}{\text{Time}}$$

In this case:

$$\frac{45 \text{ envelopes}}{60 \text{ seconds}} + \frac{45 \text{ envelopes}}{90 \text{ seconds}}$$

$$= \frac{300 \text{ envelopes}}{x \text{ seconds}}$$

Or: $\frac{45}{60} + \frac{45}{90} = \frac{300}{x}$

To make the arithmetic simplify, we reduce fractions:

$\frac{3}{4} + = \frac{300}{x}$

Then we add: $\frac{10}{8} = \frac{300}{x}$

And solve for x: $x = 300(\frac{8}{10}) = 240$ seconds.

Since 240 seconds is equal to 4 minutes, our answer is (B). If you are not comfortable with fractions, you could have kept to minutes.

Another way to approach this problem would be to try to get the rate of each worker in envelopes per minute. Earl is already known to work at 45 envelopes per minute. Ellen takes 1 minutes for the same work. Thus, 45 envelopes are done in three half-minutes. 45 divides by 3 nicely, as we often find on the GMAT, so Ellen does 15 envelopes in $\frac{1}{2}$ minute or 30 envelopes per minute, 45 per minute + 30 per minute = 75 per minute, which means $\frac{300}{75} = 4$ minutes.

35. The correct answer is (D). First, count the number of subjects having characteristic X. The first two categories are those subjects having X(25 which also have Y, 10 which do not have Y but do have X), which is a total of 35. Then count the subjects having Y. These are entered in the first and third categories (25 also have X, 25 have Y but lack X), for a total of 50: Our ratio is $\frac{35}{50}$, which, when simplified by a factor of 5, is equal to $\frac{7}{10}$.

36. The correct answer is (D). Let us logically approach this problem before even trying to calculate it. Although we have a 10% increase and then a 10% decrease, we must always ask ourselves "10% of what?" The increase was 10% of the original price, but the decrease was 10% of the higher price and consequently the decrease is bigger than the increase and the result at the end is less than the starting price, which eliminates answer choices (A), (B), and (C). Similarly, on logical grounds, it is hard to see how a 10% decrease from a 10% higher price could be equal to an 11% decrease from the starting price; that seems too much, which leaves (D) as the answer.

If we wish to compute the answer, let us start by saying that the original price of the item is x. A 10% increase in that price will be one-tenth of x, or $.1x$. When we add the increase to the original price, we find our increased price is $1.1x$. We must then take away 10% of that. Ten percent of $1.1x$ is $.11x$, and subtracting $.11x$ from $1.1x$, we get $.99x$. We started with x; we ended with $.99x$, so we lost $.01x$, which is 1%.

37. **The correct answer is (A).** (A) is necessarily true. Since lines l_m and l_n are perpendicular to one another, a line that intersects l_m on the perpendicular must be parallel to line l_n.

    (B) is not necessarily true. Line segment may fail to intersect l_m simply because it is too short—that is, if extended, for all we know will intersect l_n.

    (C) is not necessarily true. Line l_o may intersect l_m at point P without plane y being perpendicular to plane x. (D) is not necessarily true. The circle might have zero, one (point P), or two points (P and another point) in common with l_n. And (E) is not necessarily true because the circle could lie in a plane other than plane x.

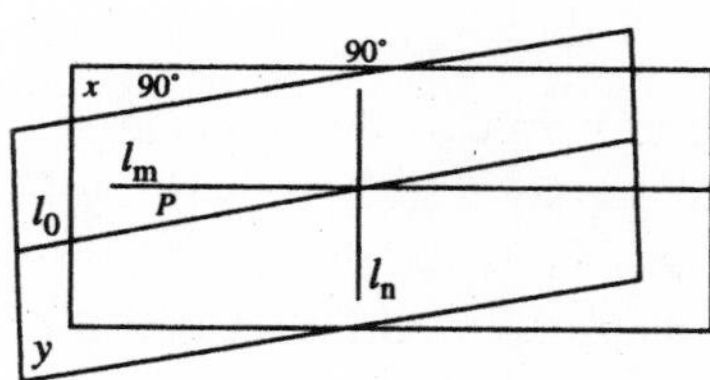

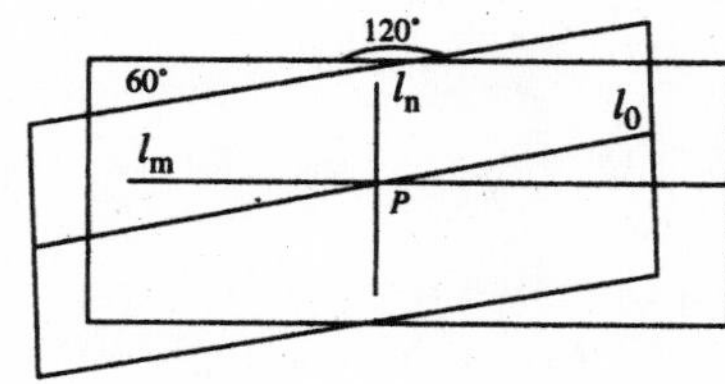

38. **The correct answer is (D).** Since the ratio of insects with X to those without X is 5:3, we know that $\frac{5}{8}$ of the population has X. (There are 8 equal units—5 + 3—5 of which are insects with X.) Then, of those $\frac{5}{8}$, $\frac{3}{8}$ are male. So we take $\frac{3}{8}$ of the $\frac{5}{8}(\frac{3}{8} \times \frac{5}{8})$, and that tells us that $\frac{15}{64}$ of the total population are male insects with X.

39. **The correct answer is (A).** This is an interesting problem in that no formula is going to solve it. Instead, it requires the use of some good old common sense. Perhaps the solution is more easily visualized if we explode the cube.

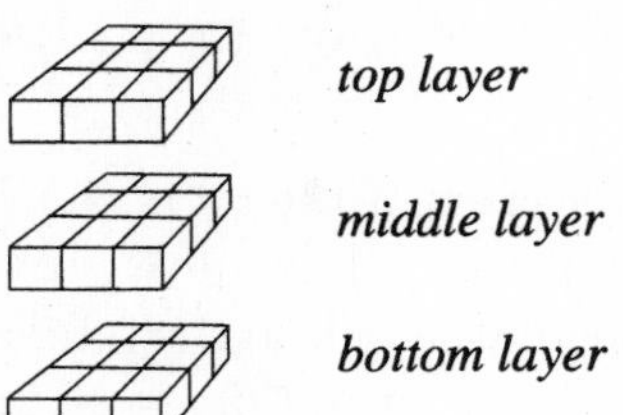

All of the small cubes on the top and the bottom layers will have at least one side painted. In the middle layer, the outer eight smaller cubes encircle the center cube, which is protected on top by the top layer, on the bottom by the bottom layer, and on the remaining four sides by the outside of the sandwich layer.

40. **The correct answer is (D).** Let d stand for the hourly rate under the new system. Since the employee is to make the same amount per week under both systems, it must be the case that:

$$\frac{\$x}{hr} \times 40hrs = \frac{\$d}{hr} \times 36hrs$$

Now we must solve for d:

$$40x = 36d,\ d = \frac{10x}{9}$$

The problem can also be solved in an intuitive way. Since the employee is working less time yet making the same weekly total, the employee must be earning slightly more per hour under the new system than under the old. Answer (A) is just the naked fraction $\frac{1}{10}$, without making reference to monetary units. Answer (B) implies that the employee is making $\frac{1}{9}$ as much per hour under the new system as under the old—that would be a decrease in the hourly rate. Similarly, (C) says that the employee is making only 90% of the old hourly rate and that, too, is a decrease. Finally, (E) says that the employee is making *9 times* the hourly rate under the old system, a figure which is obviously out of line. The only reasonable choice is (D). The moral is: Even if you cannot set up the math in a technically correct way, use a little common sense.

41. **The correct answer is (A).** This problem must be solved in two stages. First, we need to calculate the total area of the wall. The information given in the problem states that $\frac{1}{3}$ of the job plus another 75 square feet equals $\frac{3}{4}$ of the job. In algebraic notation, this is:

$$\frac{1}{3}x + 75 = \frac{3}{4}x$$

$$75 = \frac{3}{4}x - \frac{1}{3}x$$

$$75 = \frac{5}{12}x$$

$$x = 180$$

So the entire wall is 180 square feet—that is, $W \times L = 180$. We know that the height of the wall is 10 feet; so $10 \times L = 180$, and $L = 18$.

42. **The correct answer is (D).** 40 percent of \$2000, or \$800, goes for business expenses. That leaves \$1200. 10 percent of the remaining \$1200, or \$120, is reinvested.

43. **The correct answer is (B).** Since 8 is equal to 2^3, 8^4 is equal to $(2^3)^4$, which is equal to 2^{12}. (To raise a power to a power, you multiply the exponents together to get the new exponent.) 2^{12} divided by $2^{10} = 2^2$, or 4. In a division problem involving exponents on the same base (in this case the base is 2), you must subtract the exponents to obtain the answer.

44. **The correct answer is (C).** Multiplying the binomials together, using FOIL, and remembering that the square root of 5^2 is 5, we obtain $(4 + \sqrt{5})(4 - \sqrt{5}) = 16 + 4(\sqrt{5}) - 4(\sqrt{5}) - 5 = 11$. You may recognize the binomials as the factors of the difference of two squares, and thus see the answer more quickly.

45. **The correct answer is (E).** If the shorter piece is designated by x, then the longer piece must be $x + 8$. The two pieces added together must equal 32 feet, that is, $x + (x + 8) = 32$ or $x = 12$ and $x + 8 = 20$. Thus, the ratio of the larger piece to the smaller piece is $\frac{20}{12}$ or $\frac{5}{3}$.

46. **The correct answer is (B).** If 3 people take $5\frac{1}{3}$ days, then one person would take 3 times as long, or 16 days. Thus one person can do $\frac{1}{16}$ of a job in a day. Two people can do twice as much of a job, or $\frac{1}{8}$, in a day. Alternatively, you may set up the equation $(3)(5\frac{1}{3}) = (2)(x)$, where x is the time it takes 2 workers to complete the job. $x = 8$ days, thus 2 people do $\frac{1}{8}$ of a job in 1 day.

47. **The correct answer is (D).** We simply want to find how long it will take to amass interest equal to 100 percent of the original amount saved. So we must divide 100 percent by the rate of interest per year, $6\frac{1}{4}$ percent, to get the number of years:

$$\frac{100}{6\frac{1}{4}} = 16$$

48. **The correct answer is (A).** In the diagram, the angle opposite e is 80° so e must be 80°. $a + e + d = 180$ (since they sum to a straight angle) and $a = 3d$, so $3d + e + d = 180$. Since $e = 80$, $3d + 80 + d = 180$, or $4d = 100$ and $d = 25$. Since b is opposite d, b also equals 25.

49. **The correct answer is (C).** This question asks about rate: Given a certain rate of operation, how many units will be produced during a certain period? The machine operates at the rate of 8 toys every 4 seconds, or 2 toys every second, which is equal to 120 per minute. Therefore, in 2 minutes, the machine will produce twice that number, or 240 toys.

50. **The correct answer is (A).** This question asks about an average. If yearly sales for the business were $150,000, then the monthly average was $150,000 divided by 12, or $12,500. The question then asks for the June sales, given that sales that month were half the monthly average for the year. Since the monthly average for the year was $12,500 and since June sales were half that, June sales must have been $6,250.

Exercise 2: ANSWER KEY AND EXPLANATIONS

1.	D	6.	B	11.	B	16.	D	21.	E
2.	D	7.	D	12.	D	17.	E	22.	D
3.	A	8.	D	13.	D	18.	C	23.	E
4.	B	9.	E	14.	E	19.	D	24.	D
5.	C	10.	C	15.	C	20.	E	25.	B

1. **The correct answer is (D).** This question can be solved with a little common sense. We know the cost of the most expensive and the least expensive types of nuts. The cost of the other three must be between \$1.40 and \$3.20 for x pounds. What is the least we could expect to pay for x pounds of each type? Well, assume that the other three cost \$1.41 per x pounds: \$1.40 + \$1.41 + \$1.41 + \$1.41 + \$3.20 = \$8.83. This shows that (A), (B), and (C) are incorrect. Next, what is the most you could expect to pay for x pounds of each type? Now assume that the other three cost \$3.19 per x pounds: \$3.20 + \$3.19 + \$3.19 + \$3.19 + \$1.40 = \$14.17. Thus, we eliminate (E). The correct choice is (D) since \$13.60 is in the range between \$8.83 and \$14.17.

2. **The correct answer is (D).** Translated into algebra, the question reads:

$$x(x) - x(x - 1) = 4$$
$$x^2 - x^2 + x = 4$$
$$x = 4$$

3. **The correct answer is (A).** This question can be solved by organizing the information in a table:

	Students	Nonstudents	Total
Women			
Men			
Total			

Entering information:

	Students	Nonstudents	Total
Women	6		12
Men			
Total	24		32

Deducing our further conclusions:

	Students	Nonstudents	Total
Women	6	6	12
Men	18	2	20
Total	24	8	32

The table shows that 2 of the persons at the party were men who were not students.

4. **The correct answer is (B).** This question requires that you evaluate the expression using the numbers given:

$$\frac{x(y-z)}{y(x+y+z)} = \frac{5(3-2)}{3(5+3+2)} = \frac{5}{30} = \frac{1}{6}$$

5. **The correct answer is (C).** One way of solving this problem is to multiply 0.010 by 200% which is just 2.0. Or you might recognize that 200% of any number is twice that number, so 200% of 0.010 must be 0.020.

6. **The correct answer is (B).** As for I, although the average of the five integers is 1, 1 need not be one of the five. For example, the average of –3, –2, 2, 3 and 5 is 1. As for III, 0 could be one of the integers, e.g., the average of –3, –2, –1, 0 and 11 is 1. II, however, is true. Since the five numbers are different integers, at

answers

least one of them must be negative in order to "pull down" the average to 1.

7. **The correct answer is (D).** This question is answered by taking a percentage of a percent. 60% of the books are clothbound, and 30% of those are works of fiction. So, 30% of 60%, or $.30 \times .60 = .18$ or 18% are clothbound works of fiction.

8. **The correct answer is (D).** Here we have a bookkeeping problem. If the traveler breaks her present contract, forfeiting the deposit, she loses 10% of the $1,200 price, or $120. She will then buy the other trip for a cost of 20% less than $1,200: $1,200 – .20($1,200) = $1,200 – $240 = $960. So the total cost will be $960 plus the forfeited deposit of $120: $960 + $120 = $1,080. Still, $1,080 is $120 less than the original price of $1,200.

9. **The correct answer is (E).** The first seven judges have awarded the gymnast a total of 56 points. If she receives nothing lower than a 6 from the other three judges, she will earn from them at least another 18 points, for a total of 74. This means that her average score will be at least 7.4, and it might (or might not) be higher.

10. **The correct answer is (C).** If the item is sold at a 40% discount, then the dollar savings is equal to 40% of the usual price:

$$.40 \times \text{Usual Price} = \$12$$

$$\text{Usual Price} = \frac{\$12}{.40} = \$30$$

This is the usual selling price. The sale price is $12 less, or $18.

11. **The correct answer is (B).**

$$40\% = \frac{2}{5}$$

$$\frac{2}{5} \times \frac{10}{7} = \frac{4}{7}$$

12. **The correct answer is (D).** 51 is divisible by 3 and 17.

13. **The correct answer is (D).** Let C = the capacity in gallons. Then $\frac{1}{3}C + 3 = \frac{1}{2}C$. Multiplying through by 6, we obtain $2C + 18 = 3C$ or $C = 18$.

14. **The correct answer is (E).**

$$\frac{91+88+86+78+x}{5} = 85$$

$$343 + x = 425$$

$$x = 82$$

15. **The correct answer is (C).** $12 \times .39 = 4.68$ inches; that is, between $4\frac{1}{2}$ and 5.

16. **The correct answer is (D).**

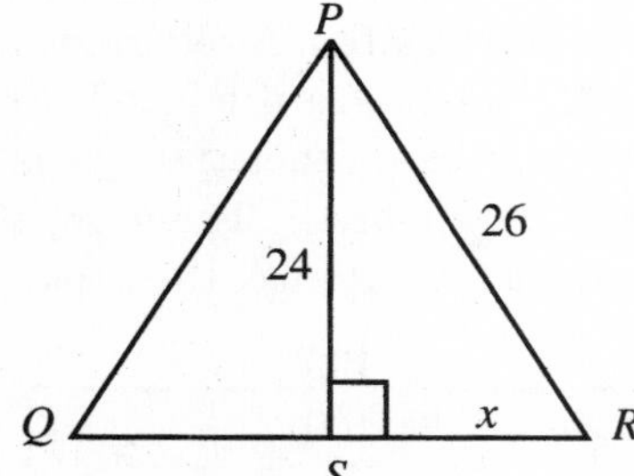

In the figure above, $PS \perp QR$. Then, in right triangle PSR:

$$x^2 + 24^2 = 26^2$$

$$x^2 = 26^2 - 24^2$$

$$x^2 = (26 + 24)(26 - 24)$$

$$x^2 = 50 \times 2 = 100$$

$$x = 10$$

Thus, $QR = 20$.

17. The correct answer is (E). Let s = number of shirts and t = number of ties, where s and t are integers:

Then $7s + 3t = 81$

$$7s = 81 - 3t$$

$$s = \frac{81-3t}{7}$$

Since s is an integer, t must have an integral value such that $81 - 3t$ is divisible by 7. Trial shows that $t = 6$ is the smallest such number, making $s = \frac{81-18}{7} = \frac{63}{7} = 9$. Hence, $s : t = 9:6 = 3:2$.

18. The correct answer is (C).

$$\text{Rate} = \frac{\text{distance}}{\text{time}} =$$

$$\text{rate} = \frac{2}{5} \times \frac{12}{1} = \frac{24}{5} = 4\frac{4}{5} \text{ miles per hour}$$

19. The correct answer is (D). Draw the altitudes indicated. A rectangle and two right triangles are produced. From the figure, the base of each triangle is 20 feet. By the Pythagorean Theorem, the altitude is 15 feet. Hence, the area:

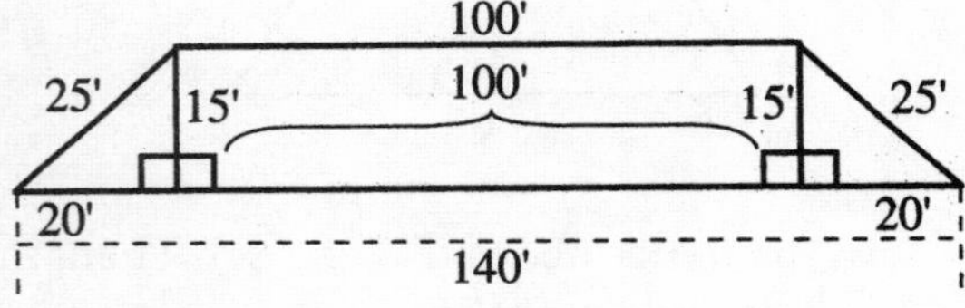

$$K = \frac{1}{2} \cdot 15(100 + 140)$$
$$= \frac{1}{2} \cdot 15 \cdot 240$$
$$= 15 \cdot 120$$
$$= 1800 \text{ square feet}$$

20. The correct answer is (E). If $1 + \frac{1}{t} = \frac{t+1}{t}$, then the right-hand fraction can also be simplified to $1 + \frac{1}{t}$, and we have an identity, which is true for all values of t except 0.

21. The correct answer is (E). Let $R = 5P$ and $S = 5Q$ where P and Q are integers. Then $R - S = 5P - 5Q = 5(P - Q)$ is divisible by 5. $RS = 5P \cdot 5Q = 25PQ$ is divisible by 25. $R + S = 5P + 5Q = 5(P + Q)$ is divisible by 5. $R^2 + S^2 = 25P^2 + 25Q^2 = 25(P^2 + Q^2)$, is divisible by 5. $R + S = 5P + 5Q = 5(P + Q)$, which is not necessarily divisible by 10.

22. The correct answer is (D).

$\frac{1}{2} \cdot 7 \cdot h = \pi \cdot 72$. Dividing both sides by 7, we get $\frac{1}{2}h = 7\pi$, or $h = 14\pi$.

23. The correct answer is (E).

I. $13\overline{)9.00} = .69$; 78; 120; 117

II. $9\overline{)13.00} = 1.44$; 9; 40; 36; 40; 36

III. 70%=.7 IV. $\frac{1}{.70} = \frac{1}{\frac{7}{10}}$

Correct order is $\frac{9}{13}$, 70%, $\frac{1}{70}$, $\frac{13}{9}$ (or I, III, IV, II).

24. The correct answer is (D).

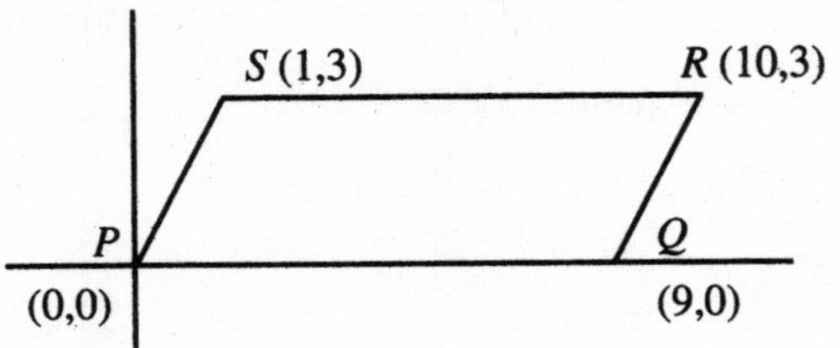

Since PQ and RS are parallel and congruent, the figure is a parallelogram of base = 9 and height = 3. Hence, area = 9 × 3 = 27.

25. The correct answer is (B).

$$\text{Area of wall} = 4 \cdot \frac{60}{3} = 4 \cdot 20 = 80 \text{ sq. yd.}$$

Cost = 80 × \$10.50 = \$840.00.

Data Sufficiency

OVERVIEW

- **What is data sufficiency?**
- **How do you answer data sufficiency questions?**
- **What do the answer choices mean?**
- **What smart test-takers know**

WHAT IS DATA SUFFICIENCY?

Data sufficiency is a unique type of math question created especially for the GMAT. Each data sufficiency question consists of the question itself followed by two numbered statements. Your task is to decide whether the statements—either singly or in combination—provide enough information to answer the question. You must choose:

(A) if statement 1 alone is sufficient to answer the question, but statement 2 alone is not sufficient

(B) if statement 2 alone is sufficient to answer the question, but statement 1 alone is not sufficient

(C) if both statements together are needed to answer the question, but neither statement alone is sufficient

(D) if either statement by itself is sufficient to answer the question

(E) if not enough facts are given to answer the question

Data sufficiency questions are different from the other GMAT math questions because you are not really expected to solve them. Rather, you are asked to determine whether or not a problem can be solved, given certain information.

GMAT Data Sufficiency Questions

On the GMAT, data sufficiency questions appear in the 75-minute quantitative section. Within the section, they are not grouped together. Instead, they are interspersed with problem-solving questions.

Here are the directions for data sufficiency questions, along with some sample questions and explanation.

chapter 9

Anatomy of a Data Sufficiency Item

Directions: Each question below is followed by two numbered facts. You are to determine whether the data given in the statements is sufficient for answering the question. Use the data given, plus your knowledge of math and everyday facts, to choose between the five possible answers.

1. Three packages have a combined weight of 48 pounds. What is the weight of the heaviest package?

(1) One package weighs 12 pounds.

(2) One package weighs 24 pounds.

(A) statement 1 alone is sufficient to answer the question, but statement 2 alone is not sufficient

(B) statement 2 alone is sufficient to answer the question, but statement 1 alone is not sufficient

(C) both statements together are needed to answer the question, but neither statement alone is sufficient

(D) either statement by itself is sufficient to answer the question

(E) not enough facts are given to answer the question

The correct answer is (B). Statement (1) is not sufficient to determine the weight of the heaviest package. It implies only that the combined weight of the other two packages is 36 pounds. (Eliminate (A) and (D).) Statement (2) alone is sufficient for it implies that the combined weight of two of the packages is only 24 pounds. Since the weight of the 24-pound package is equal to the combined weight of the other two packages, the heaviest package must weigh 24 pounds. (Eliminate (C) and (E).) Since statement (2) alone is sufficient to answer the question but statement (1) alone is not, classify this item as (B).

2. How many books are there on a certain shelf?

(1) If four books are removed, the number of books remaining on the shelf will be less than 12.

(2) If three more books are placed on the shelf, the total number of books on the shelf will be more than 17.

(A) statement 1 alone is sufficient to answer the question, but statement 2 alone is not sufficient

(B) statement 2 alone is sufficient to answer the question, but statement 1 alone is not sufficient

(C) both statements together are needed to answer the question, but neither statement alone is sufficient

(D) either statement by itself is sufficient to answer the question

(E) not enough facts are given to answer the question

The correct answer is (C). Neither statement alone is sufficient to answer the question asked. Statement (1) alone implies only that the number of books on the shelf is 15 or fewer, and statement (2) alone implies only that the number of books on the shelf is 15 or more. (Eliminate (A), (B), and (D).) But the two statements taken together are sufficient to answer the question, for they imply that the number of books on the shelf is 15. (15 is the only integer that satisfies both [1] and [2].) Since neither statement alone is sufficient, but the two together are, classify this item as (C).

There are two basic types of GMAT data sufficiency questions:

1. **Numerical value questions.** These questions ask whether it is possible to arrive at an exact numerical solution given certain information:

   What is the value of x?

   What is Joan's salary?

   How many bricks are there in a pile?

2. **"Yes or no" questions.** These questions require only a yes or no answer:

   Is x greater than 1?

   Is Joan's salary more than $10,000 per year?

   Is the total number of bricks in the pile more than 300?

HOW DO YOU ANSWER DATA SUFFICIENCY QUESTIONS?

Here is a simple, four-step plan to help you solve GMAT data sufficiency questions.

Data Sufficiency: Getting It Right

1. Read the question carefully.
2. Pay careful attention to any information provided in the question stem.
3. Consider each statement in isolation.
4. Eliminate choices and, if necessary, guess.

Now let's look at each of these steps in greater detail.

1. **Read the question carefully.** Determine whether it is a "numerical value" or a "yes or no" question. Here is an example:

   How many specially priced boxes of soap powder did a supermarket sell during a day?

   (1) 12% of the customers who came into the supermarket during the day purchased the specially priced soap powder.

   (2) The supermarket had 480 customers that day.

The correct answer is (E). Read the question and statements carefully. The question asks for the number of boxes of the soap powder that were sold. Even

NOTE

Should I do any calculations?

Absolutely not. The question is not "what is the answer"; the question is whether the data are sufficient to answer the question. Look at the following example: What is the value of $x + y$?

(1) $x = \frac{2,427,001}{4.523}$

(2) $y = 0.745\left(\frac{342}{0.917}\right)$

What is the value of $x + y$? Who cares? The right data sufficiency answer is (C). If you know the value of x and the value y, then you know the value of $x + y$.

taking the two statements together, you cannot answer that question. You cannot assume that each person who bought the soap powder purchased exactly one box.

❷ **Pay careful attention to any information provided in the stem.** The following examples illustrate this point:

What is Paul's annual income?

(1) Paul's annual income is $20,000 less than Edna's.

(2) Edna's annual income is 3 times Paul's.

Neither statement alone is sufficient to establish a numerical value for Paul's income. Both taken together, however, work as a system of simultaneous equations to establish that Paul's income is $10,000:

$P = E - 20{,}000$

$E = 3P$

Substituting $3P$ for E:

$P = 3P - 20{,}000$

$-2P = -20{,}000$

$P = 10{,}000$

Since both statements are needed, the correct answer is (C).

Now consider a similar item in which the question stem provides additional information:

Paul and Edna have a combined annual income of $40,000. What is Paul's annual income?

(1) Paul's annual income is $20,000 less than Edna's.

(2) Edna's annual income is 3 times Paul's.

Now, the correct answer is (D). Each statement, by itself, is sufficient to establish that Paul's annual income is $10,000.

What is more important, the question or the statements? They are equally important, and this is something that trips up many test-takers. Most test-takers concentrate on the two statements and tend to overlook the information in the question stem. In more difficult questions, the test-writers will incorporate subtle information into the stem that makes the outcome different.

❸ **Consider each statement in isolation.** Test each statement for sufficiency independently of the other statement.

The trickiest call in data sufficiency is how the two statements work together—so do not go there until you have established that it is necessary to do so. First, determine whether statement (1) is sufficient. Second, determine whether statement (2) is sufficient. Your assessment of each will tell you whether the correct answer is or is not (A), (B), or (D).

If, and only if, you determine that (A), (B), and (D) are not correct should you go on to ask whether the correct answer is (C) or (E). Do not worry about the possible interaction of the two statements until you have determined that a more sophisticated level of analysis is required.

❹ **Eliminate choices and, if necessary, guess.** Even if you are unable to arrive at a complete solution of the problem, you can often eliminate two or three answer choices. The chart below shows how to eliminate choices. A check mark means you have concluded that the statement is sufficient; an ✗ means you have concluded that it is not sufficient; and a question mark indicates doubt:

(1)	✓	
(2)	?	= (A) or (D)
(1)	?	
(2)	✓	= (B) or (D)
(1)	✗	
(2)	?	= (B), (C), or (E)
(1)	?	
(2)	✗	= (A), (C), or (E)

WHAT DO THE ANSWER CHOICES MEAN?

The following pages list twelve examples to illustrate what the answer choices mean for both "numerical value" and "yes or no" data sufficiency questions.

For Numerical Answers: When to Choose (A)

1. What is x?

(1) $x + 2 = 4$

(2) $x^2 = 4$

(1) alone is sufficient to establish the exact value of x as 2. (2), however, is not sufficient. If $x^2 = 4$, x can be either +2 or –2, and that is not sufficient to answer a question that asks "What is x?" The answer is (A).

TIP

When you're sure that Statement 1 is sufficient but you don't know about Statement 2, the answer has to be (A) or (D). Even if you have to guess, you have a 50-50 chance of being correct.

For Numerical Answers: When to Choose (B)

2. What is x?

(1) $x^2 - 1 = 0$

(2) $x = (10)^0$

(2) is sufficient to peg the exact value of x. Since any number to the zero power equals 1, $10^0 = 1$, and x must be 1. (1) is not sufficient. (1) establishes that either $x + 1 = 0$ or $x - 1 = 0$, so that $x = \pm 1$. But knowing that x is one of two possible values is not sufficient to answer a question that asks for the value of x. And the answer is (B).

For Numerical Answers: When to Choose (C)

3. What is the maximum number of cubic blocks of wood that will fit into a box?
   (1) The edge of each block is 2 inches long.
   (2) The box has the shape of a rectangular solid with inner dimensions 20 inches by 40 inches by 16 inches.

To determine exactly how many blocks the box will hold, we need the size and shape of both the blocks and the box. Neither (1) nor (2) alone will give you all of the information you need. (1) gives you the size and shape of the blocks. (2) gives you the size and shape of the box. Both taken together give all of the information you need. And the answer is (C).

For Numerical Answers: When to Choose (D)

4. What is the area of Circle *O*?
   (1) The diameter of Circle *O* is 4.
   (2) The circumference of Circle *O* is 4π.

When you're sure that Statement 2 is sufficient but you don't know about Statement 1, the answer has to be (B)or (D). Even if you have to guess, you have a 50-50 chance of being correct.

(1) is sufficient, for knowing the diameter of the circle allows you to determine the radius, and in turn, the radius gives you the area of the circle by the formula Area = πr^2. (2) also is sufficient. The circumference is 4π. Since the formula for the circumference is $C = 2\pi r$, $4\pi = 2\pi r$, and $r = 2$. So (1) alone is sufficient and (2) alone is sufficient to give the exact value of the area of the circle. And the answer is (D).

For Numerical Answers: When to Choose (E)

5. The total number of employees on the payroll of Corporation *X* was what percent greater on June 30 than it had been on June 1 of the same year?
   (1) During the month of June, 15 employees were dropped from the payroll.
   (2) During the month of June, 37 employees were added to the payroll.

The question asks for the percent increase in the number of employees during June. The two statements together establish that 37 – 15 = 22 people were added to the payroll during June, but that is not sufficient to answer the question asked. And the answer is (E).

For Yes or No Answers: When to Choose (A)

6. If the average height of three people is 68 inches, is the shortest person more than 60 inches tall?

(1) The height of the tallest person is 72 inches.

(2) One of the persons is 70 inches tall.

The answer is (A). (1) is sufficient to answer the question with a definite yes. If x, y, and z represent the three heights, then

$$\frac{x+y+z}{3}=68$$

$$x+y+z=204$$

Then if one of the heights, say z, is 72:

$$x+y=132$$

This means that the sum of the heights of the other two persons must be 132; but we know that neither of them can be as tall as 72 inches, so the shortest person must be taller than 132 – 72 = 60 inches. (2) by itself is not sufficient since it may or may not refer to the tallest person.

For Yes or No Answers: When to Choose (B)

7. Is the product of two numbers greater than 100?

(1) The sum of the two numbers is greater than 50.

(2) Each of the numbers is greater than 10.

The answer is (B). That (1) is not sufficient can be proven by examples. If the two numbers are 30 and 31, their sum is greater than 50 and their product is greater than 100; but if the two numbers are 50 and 1, though their sum is greater than 50, their product is only 50, and less than 100. (2) is sufficient. If both of the numbers are greater than 10, then their product must be greater than 10 × 10, or greater than 100.

For Yes or No Answers: When to Choose (C)

8. Is x a positive integer?

(1) $x > 0$

(2) $x^2 + 16 = 25$

The answer is (C). (1) is not sufficient, for it establishes only that x is positive but has nothing to say as to whether x is an integer. (2) is not sufficient, for it establishes that x is an integer but fails to establish whether x is +3 or –3. Both taken together establish that x = +3, so they answer the question: x is a positive integer.

TIP

When you're sure that Statement 1 is not sufficient but you don't know about Statement 2, the answer must be (B), (C), or (E). Even if you have to guess, you have a one-in-three chance of being correct.

9. Is $a + b > c + d$?

(1) $a > c$

(2) $b > d$

The answer is (C). (1) is not sufficient because we lack information about b and d. Similarly, (2) is not sufficient because we lack information about a and c. Both together are sufficient, for if $a > c$, then adding b to a and d to c will maintain the inequality.

When you're sure that Statement 2 is not sufficient but you don't know about Statement 1, the answer must be (A), (C), or (E). Even if you have to guess, you have a one-in-three chance of being correct.

For Yes or No Answers: When to Choose (D)

10. Is x greater than 0?

(1) x^3 is less than 0.

(2) $3x = -3$

The answer is (D). Statement (1) establishes that $(x)(x)(x)$ is less than 0, so x itself must be a negative number. Statement (1), therefore, is sufficient to establish that the answer to the question is no: x is not greater than 0. Similarly, statement (2) also establishes that x is negative. Watch out! Some test-takers would call this an (E), reasoning (incorrectly) that since the answer to the question is no, the information is not sufficient. In fact, the information is sufficient to give a definite negative answer to the question.

11. Is x a positive number?

(1) $1{,}000{,}001(x)$ is a positive number

(2) $-x$ is a negative number

The answer is (D). (1) establishes that x must be a positive number because 1,000,001, a positive number, multiplied by x is a positive number. (2) also establishes that x is positive, for 1 multiplied by x is negative.

For Yes or No Answers: When to Choose (E)

12. Is a cubic centimeter of substance S heavier than a cubic centimeter of substance T?

(1) A cubic centimeter of S weighs more than 0.25 cubic centimeters of T.

(2) 3 cubic centimeters of T weighs less than 5 cubic centimeters of S.

The answer is (E). (1) establishes only that a cubic unit of S is heavier than 0.25 cubic units of T, but it does not establish how much heavier. (2) works in the same way. Even taking them together, it is not possible to establish which substance is heavier. For example, S and T might even have equal weights.

WHAT SMART TEST-TAKERS KNOW

Common Question Types

IT PAYS TO KNOW THE COMMON PATTERNS.

Finding a single integral value. Some questions provide information that allows you to fix a single integral value.

1. At a clothing store, Fred spent \$130. How many of the articles of clothing that Fred purchased were priced at \$15?

(1) Fred purchased only articles costing \$15 and \$20.

(2) Fred purchased more than two \$20 articles.

At first glance, you might think that the answer to this item is (E). But you should look a little more closely. Although it is true that (1) alone doesn't provide enough information to answer the question, it does narrow the possibilities to two: two \$20 articles plus six \$15 articles, or five \$20 articles and two \$15 articles. And when the information provided in (2) is included, an answer can be obtained. Since the articles of clothing are whole articles (no fractions allowed), Fred purchased exactly two \$15 articles. So, the correct answer is (C).

Determining if a fraction is an integer. If X/M and X/N are integers where both M and N are integers, then X is a multiple of MN.

2. Is $\frac{x}{15}$ an integer?

(1) $\frac{x}{3}$ is an integer.

(2) $\frac{x}{5}$ is an integer.

Neither (1) nor (2) is alone sufficient to answer the question. As for (1), even though x is divisible by 3, x might not be divisible by 15. (For example, if x is 9.) Similarly, (2) is not sufficient. Even though x is divisible by 5, x might not be divisible by 15. (For example, if x is 10.) But both statements taken together are sufficient to answer the question. If x is divisible by both 3 and 5, then x must be divisible by 15. And the correct answer is (C).

TIP

Choices (C) and (E) should be saved for last. You should evaluate each statement independently of the other. That will take care of choices (A), (B), and (D). Only after you have eliminated those possibilities should you begin to worry about the interaction between the statements.

Finding a term in a sequence. To find a particular term in a sequence, you must know the rule for constructing the sequence and the value of a term in the sequence.

3. What is the one-thousandth term in sequence S?

(1) The fifth term in S is 47.

(2) Each term in S following the first term is generated by multiplying the preceding term by 4 and adding 1.

The rule for constructing the sequence is given in (2). And the point of reference is given in (1). There is no need to try to find the value of the thousandth term. You need only recognize that it is possible to do so, so the answer must be (C).

Using fractions, percents, and ratios. Given two quantities, X and Y, knowing any one of the following relationships is sufficient to find the other two relationships:

X is a certain fraction of Y

X is a certain percent of Y

the ratio of X to Y

Thus, if you know that x is $\frac{1}{2}$ of y, you also know that x is 50% of y and that the ratio of x to y is 1:2.

4. If x and y are positive numbers, what percentage is x of y?

(1) The ratio x:y is 5:4.

(2) y is $\frac{4}{5}$ of x

Statement (1) is sufficient. Since the ratio of x to y is 5 to 4, $\frac{x}{y} = \frac{5}{4} = 1.25 = 125\%$. Statement (2) is also sufficient. Since $y = \frac{4}{5}x$, $\frac{x}{y} = \frac{5}{4} = 1.25 = 125\%$. So, the correct answer is (D).

Similarly, if you know fractional, percentage, or ratio relationships between two quantities, you can also determine the reciprocals of those relationships.

Thus, if you know that x is 125% of y, you can deduce that y is 80% of x: $x = 1.25y$, so $x = \frac{5y}{4}$ and $\frac{y}{x} = \frac{4}{5} = 80\%$.

5. If x and y are positive numbers, what percentage is x of y?

(1) y is 50% of x.

(2) The ratio $y : x$ is 1:2.

Each statement is sufficient to establish that x is 200% of y. So the correct answer is (D).

Recognizing the difference between relationships and actual quantities. Fractions, ratios, and percentages do not provide information about the actual quantities, only about the relationship between two quantities.

6. How much money do Peter and Ed have together?

(1) Ed has twice as much money as Peter.

(2) Peter has $2 less than Ed has.

Statement (1) is not sufficient to answer the question. Although you can infer from (1) that Peter has half as much money as Ed, that is not sufficient to answer the question asked. Neither is statement (2) alone sufficient. But both work together to establish that Ed has $4 and Peter has $2. So the correct answer is (C).

Note: A statement about percentage alone does not provide information about actual quantities.

7. Did Diane receive a larger bonus than Claire?

(1) Diane's bonus was 7% of her annual salary.

(2) Claire's bonus was 8% of her annual salary.

To find the actual size of either bonus, you would need to know the dollar amount for the annual of both salaries. As it is, you know only that Claire's bonus was a larger percentage of her salary than that of Diane's bonus. That is not sufficient to answer the question asked, so the correct answer is (E).

Determining relative size. A statement that provides a ratio (or similar relationship) between two quantities is sufficient to establish which is larger.

8. Which of three books, X, Y, or Z, costs the least?

(1) The cost of X is $\frac{2}{3}$ the cost of Y.

(2) The cost of Z is $\frac{5}{4}$ the cost of X.

Neither statement provides the actual cost of any of the three books, but both statements taken together do establish that X is least expensive. (1) establishes that X is less than Y, and (2) establishes that X is less than Z. So the correct answer is (C).

ALERT!

Percents are not quantities. A favorite test-writer strategy is to create questions that invite you to confuse percents with fixed values.

Using percentage of change to find other values. Information about one of the following:

Original Total

New Total

Actual Change

coupled with the percent change in a quantity is sufficient to deduce the other two values.

9. An item is discounted by 15% from its usual selling price. What is the usual selling price?

(1) The dollar value of the discount is \$45.

(2) The discounted price is \$255.

(1) is sufficient, since 15% of the usual selling price is the \$45 value of the discount:

$.15 \text{ Usual Price} = \$45$

$\text{Usual Price} = \frac{\$45}{.15} = \$300$

(2) is also sufficient, for the discounted price is equal to the usual selling price minus the discount; and the discount can be expressed as a percentage of the usual selling price:

$\text{Discount Price} = \text{Usual Price} - (.15 \text{ Usual Price})$

$\text{Discount} = .85 \text{ Usual Price}$

$.85 \text{ Usual Price} = \$255$

$\text{Usual Price} = \$300$

So each statement alone is sufficient, and the correct answer is (D).

Data Sufficiency Math Tips

DATA SUFFICIENCY FIGURES ARE NOT NECESSARILY DRAWN TO SCALE.

For data sufficiency questions, the directions state that the figures will conform to the information given in the question stem. However, they will not necessarily conform to the additional information provided in the numbered statements. So you cannot use a figure alone to estimate an answer. Note that this is contrary to the directions given for problem-solving sections, where figures are drawn to scale unless otherwise noted.

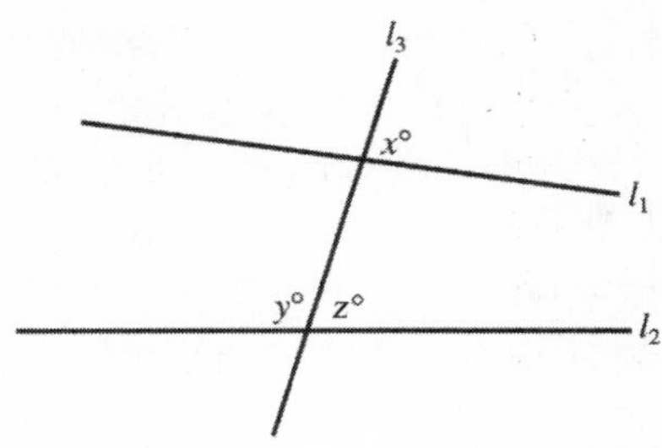

10. In the figure above, are l_1 and l_2 parallel to each other?

(1) $x = z$

(2) $x + y = 180$

The correct answer is (D). Although the lines do not appear to be parallel, you should not conclude on the basis of the figure that they are not parallel. In fact, each statement establishes that they are parallel.

ALERT!

Figures can be deceiving. Figures in the data sufficiency part of the math are not necessarily drawn to scale. Do not be taken in.

THE TRICK IS TO DO AS LITTLE WORK AS POSSIBLE.

The task is to make a judgment about the sufficiency of the additional information. Once you know that the information is sufficient to answer the question, the game is over. You don't need to go further and work out an actual numerical solution.

UNKNOWNS CAN STAND FOR ANY NUMBER.

Unless otherwise indicated, an unknown ranges over the entire number line. It can be 0, 1, a fraction, any other positive number, or any negative number.

11. If $xy \neq 0$, is x greater than y?

(1) $4x = 5y$

(2) $x < 0$

The correct answer is (C). Statement (1) is not, by itself, sufficient to answer the question. If x and y are positive numbers, say $x = 5$ and $y = 4$, then x is greater than y. But if x and y are negative numbers, say $x = -5$ and $y = -4$, then x is less than y. Statement (2) is not alone sufficient to answer the question. But both statements together do answer the question. If $4x = 5y$ and x is less than 0, then x is less than y.

ALERT!

Variables are land mines; tread warily. A variable, unless otherwise restricted, ranges over the whole of the real number system: positive, negative, and zero; fractions and integers. Make sure that you consider all possibilities before you step.

MAY ACT STRANGELY.

Here is an example of a typical data sufficiency trap:

12. Is $xy > 0$?

(1) $xy^2 > 0$

(2) $x^2y^3 < 0$

The correct answer is (C). Any quantity raised to the second power (or other positive even power) generates a positive result. But a quantity raised to the third power (or other positive odd power) may be positive or negative depending on the sign of the original quantity. Thus, statement (1) is not sufficient to establish the sign of xy, but it does establish that x is positive. Statement (2) is not sufficient to establish the sign of xy, but it does establish that y^3, and therefore y, is negative. So both taken together establish that xy is negative.

SOME EQUATIONS HAVE MORE THAN ONE SOLUTION.

An equation with variables raised to a higher power may have more than one solution.

13. What is the value of x?

(1) $x^2 - 9 = 0$

(2) $x > 0$

The correct answer is (C). Statement (1) is not sufficient to fix the value of x. Since $x^2 - 9 = 0$, $x^2 = 9$, and $x = +3$ or $x = -3$. That conclusion coupled with (2), however, is sufficient to answer the question.

SIMULTANEOUS EQUATIONS CAN SOLVE SOME PROBLEMS.

Two variables are always a problem. But you may be able to find values for them if you can set up a system of simultaneous equations.

14. What is the value of x?

(1) $x + y = 12$

(2) $2y = 6$

The correct answer is (C). Neither statement alone is sufficient to fix the value of x. But if you solve for y in the second equation ($y = 3$) and substitute that value for y into the first equation ($x + 3 = 12$), you can find the value of x.

COMPLEX ALGEBRAIC EXPRESSIONS NEED TO BE SIMPLIFIED.

If a data sufficiency item asks for the value of a complex algebraic expression, it may be possible to simplify the expression.

15. If $x + y \neq 0$, what is the value of $\frac{x^2 - y^2}{x + y}$?

(1) $x - y = 2$

(2) $x + y = 2$

The correct answer is (A). Factor the numerator of the expression and simplify:

$$\frac{x^2 - y^2}{x + y} = \frac{(x + y)(x - y)}{x + y} = x - y$$

So statement (1) alone is sufficient to answer the question, but statement (2) is not. So the correct answer is (A).

THE PYTHAGOREAN THEOREM KEEPS POPPING UP.

The Pythagorean Theorem is a GMAT favorite.

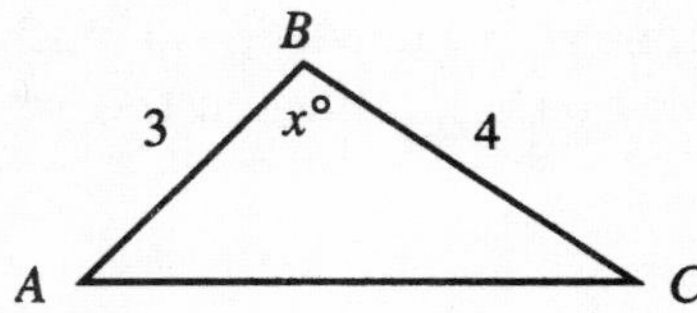

16. What is the value of x in the figure above?

(1) $AC^2 = AB^2 + BC^2$

(2) $AC = 5$

The correct answer is (D). Statement (1), which is the Pythagorean formula, establishes that the sides of the triangle create a right triangle and that AC is the hypotenuse. So $x = 90$. Statement (2) also establishes that the triangle is a right triangle. (It has sides of 3, 4, and 5.) So $x = 90$.

EQUILATERAL FIGURES ARE A GIFT.

If you know one dimension of a regular or equilateral figure, you can deduce everything else about that figure.

For an equilateral triangle, information about any one of the following length of side, perimeter, altitude, or area is sufficient to fix the others.

For a square, information about any one of the following length of a side, the perimeter, the diagonal, or the area is sufficient to fix the others.

For a circle, information about any one of the following length of the radius, length of the diameter, length of the circumference, or the area is sufficient to fix the others.

EXERCISE 1: DATA SUFFICIENCY

30 Questions • 38 Minutes

Directions: Each question below is followed by two numbered facts. You are to determine whether the data given in the statements is sufficient for answering the question. Use the data given, plus your knowledge of math and everyday facts, to choose between the five possible answers. Blacken the oval next to your choice.

1. Is x divisible by 70?

(1) x is divisible by 2 and 5.

(2) x is divisible by 2 and 7.

(A) statement 1 alone is sufficient to answer the question, but statement 2 alone is not sufficient

(B) statement 2 alone is sufficient to answer the question, but statement 1 alone is not sufficient

(C) both statements together are needed to answer the question, but neither statement alone is sufficient

(D) either statement by itself is sufficient to answer the question

(E) not enough facts are given to answer the question

2. Does Bob have more records in his record collection than Linda has in hers?

(1) Christina has more records in her collection than Linda.

(2) Bob has fewer records in his collection than Christina.

(A) statement 1 alone is sufficient to answer the question, but statement 2 alone is not sufficient

(B) statement 2 alone is sufficient to answer the question, but statement 1 alone is not sufficient

(C) both statements together are needed to answer the question, but neither statement alone is sufficient

(D) either statement by itself is sufficient to answer the question

(E) not enough facts are given to answer the question

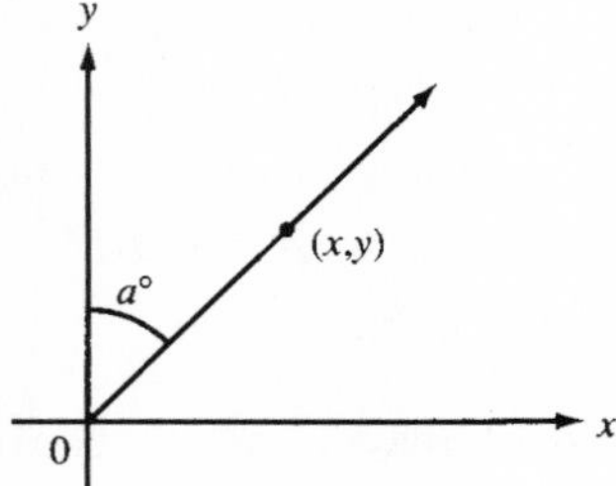

3. In the diagram above, what is the value of a?

(1) $x = 3$

(2) $y = 3$

(A) statement 1 alone is sufficient to answer the question, but statement 2 alone is not sufficient

(B) statement 2 alone is sufficient to answer the question, but statement 1 alone is not sufficient

(C) both statements together are needed to answer the question, but neither statement alone is sufficient

(D) either statement by itself is sufficient to answer the question

(E) not enough facts are given to answer the question

4. Allen and Chris founded a company in 1990. In which year did the company's profits first exceed $100,000?
   (1) In 1990, the company had profits of $15,000, and in every year after that profits were double those of the previous year.
   (2) In 1992, the company had profits of $60,000.
   (A) statement 1 alone is sufficient to answer the question, but statement 2 alone is not sufficient
   (B) statement 2 alone is sufficient to answer the question, but statement 1 alone is not sufficient
   (C) both statements together are needed to answer the question, but neither statement alone is sufficient
   (D) either statement by itself is sufficient to answer the question
   (E) not enough facts are given to answer the question

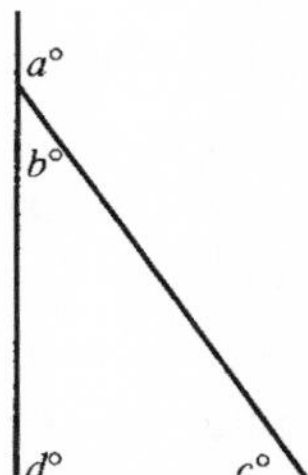

5. In the figure above, what is the value of d?
   (1) $b + c = 90$
   (2) $c + a = 180$
   (A) statement 1 alone is sufficient to answer the question, but statement 2 alone is not sufficient
   (B) statement 2 alone is sufficient to answer the question, but statement 1 alone is not sufficient
   (C) both statements together are needed to answer the question, but neither statement alone is sufficient
   (D) either statement by itself is sufficient to answer the question
   (E) not enough facts are given to answer the question

6. Is x an integer?
   (1) $x > 0$
   (2) $3^2 + 4^2 = x^2$
   (A) statement 1 alone is sufficient to answer the question, but statement 2 alone is not sufficient
   (B) statement 2 alone is sufficient to answer the question, but statement 1 alone is not sufficient
   (C) both statements together are needed to answer the question, but neither statement alone is sufficient
   (D) either statement by itself is sufficient to answer the question
   (E) not enough facts are given to answer the question

7. What is the volume of cube C?
   (1) The total surface area of C is 54 square inches.
   (2) The area of each face of C is 9 square inches.
   (A) statement 1 alone is sufficient to answer the question, but statement 2 alone is not sufficient
   (B) statement 2 alone is sufficient to answer the question, but statement 1 alone is not sufficient
   (C) both statements together are needed to answer the question, but neither statement alone is sufficient
   (D) either statement by itself is sufficient to answer the question
   (E) not enough facts are given to answer the question

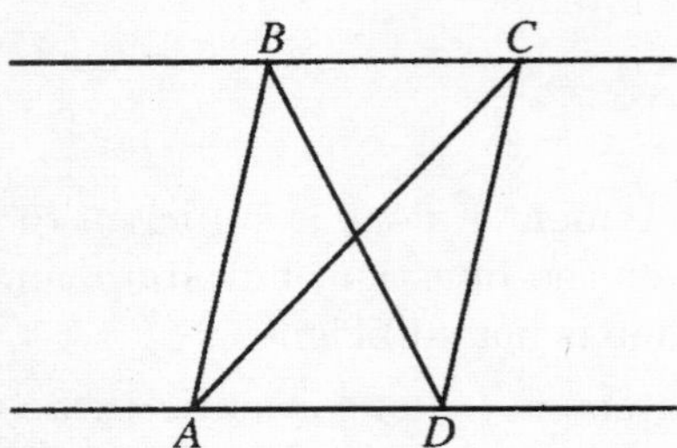

8. In the figure above, what is the ratio

$$\frac{\text{Area of Triangle } ABD}{\text{Area of Triangle } ACD} = ?$$

(1) $AB \parallel CD$

(2) $BC \parallel AD$

(A) statement 1 alone is sufficient to answer the question, but statement 2 alone is not sufficient

(B) statement 2 alone is sufficient to answer the question, but statement 1 alone is not sufficient

(C) both statements together are needed to answer the question, but neither statement alone is sufficient

(D) either statement by itself is sufficient to answer the question

(E) not enough facts are given to answer the question

Budget for Day School D

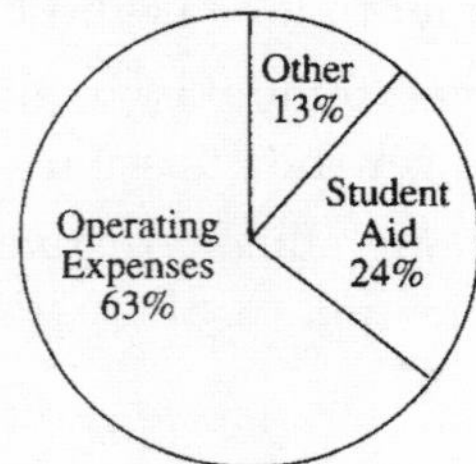

9. How much money did Day School D spend on operating expenses?

(1) The total budget for the school was $9 million.

(2) The school spent $2,160,000 on student aid.

(A) statement 1 alone is sufficient to answer the question, but statement 2 alone is not sufficient

(B) statement 2 alone is sufficient to answer the question, but statement 1 alone is not sufficient

(C) both statements together are needed to answer the question, but neither statement alone is sufficient

(D) either statement by itself is sufficient to answer the question

(E) not enough facts are given to answer the question

10. What is the value of the integer N?

(1) N is an integer multiple of 2, 3, and 6.

(2) $30 < N < 70$

(A) statement 1 alone is sufficient to answer the question, but statement 2 alone is not sufficient

(B) statement 2 alone is sufficient to answer the question, but statement 1 alone is not sufficient

(C) both statements together are needed to answer the question, but neither statement alone is sufficient

(D) either statement by itself is sufficient to answer the question

(E) not enough facts are given to answer the question

11. How much money is saved by buying a box of a dozen donuts instead of 12 donuts singly?

(1) When purchased in a box of 12, the cost of each donut is $0.05 less than if purchased singly.

(2) The price of a box of a dozen donuts is $2.40.

(A) statement 1 alone is sufficient to answer the question, but statement 2 alone is not sufficient

(B) statement 2 alone is sufficient to answer the question, but statement 1 alone is not sufficient

(C) both statements together are needed to answer the question, but neither statement alone is sufficient

(D) either statement by itself is sufficient to answer the question

(E) not enough facts are given to answer the question

12. What is the value of $a^4 - b^4$?

(1) $a^2 + b^2 = 24$

(2) $a^2 - b^2 = 0$

(A) statement 1 alone is sufficient to answer the question, but statement 2 alone is not sufficient

(B) statement 2 alone is sufficient to answer the question, but statement 1 alone is not sufficient

(C) both statements together are needed to answer the question, but neither statement alone is sufficient

(D) either statement by itself is sufficient to answer the question

(E) not enough facts are given to answer the question

13. Daniel invested a total of $10,000 for a period of one year. Part of the money he put into an investment that earned 6 percent simple interest, and the rest of the money into an investment that earned 8 percent simple interest. How much money did he put into the investment that earned 6 percent?

(1) The total interest earned on the $10,000 for the year was $640.

(2) The dollar value of the investment that earned 6 percent was only one-fourth the dollar value of the investment that earned 8 percent.

(A) statement 1 alone is sufficient to answer the question, but statement 2 alone is not sufficient

(B) statement 2 alone is sufficient to answer the question, but statement 1 alone is not sufficient

(C) both statements together are needed to answer the question, but neither statement alone is sufficient

(D) either statement by itself is sufficient to answer the question

(E) not enough facts are given to answer the question

14. Is x greater than y?

(1) $3x = 4y$

(2) $x = \frac{k}{3}$, $y = \frac{k}{4}$, and $k > 0$

(A) statement 1 alone is sufficient to answer the question, but statement 2 alone is not sufficient

(B) statement 2 alone is sufficient to answer the question, but statement 1 alone is not sufficient

(C) both statements together are needed to answer the question, but neither statement alone is sufficient

(D) either statement by itself is sufficient to answer the question

(E) not enough facts are given to answer the question

15. Is the perimeter of a rectangular yard greater than 60 meters?

(1) The two shorter sides of the yard are each 15 meters long.

(2) The length of the yard is 3 meters longer than the width of the yard.

(A) statement 1 alone is sufficient to answer the question, but statement 2 alone is not sufficient

(B) statement 2 alone is sufficient to answer the question, but statement 1 alone is not sufficient

(C) both statements together are needed to answer the question, but neither statement alone is sufficient

(D) either statement by itself is sufficient to answer the question

(E) not enough facts are given to answer the question

exercises

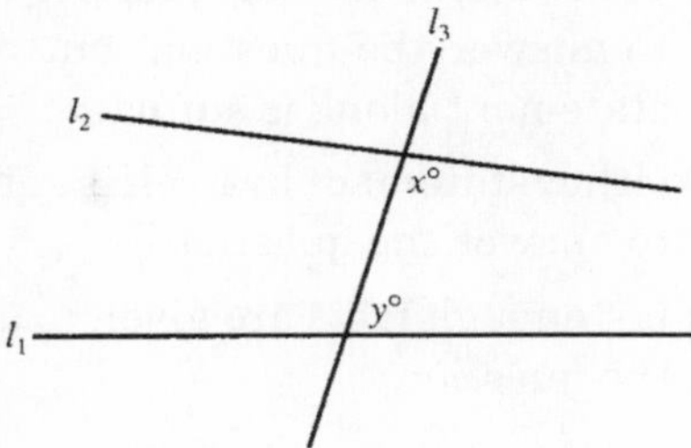

16. In the figure above, l_1 and l_2 intersect l_3. Do l_1 and l_2 intersect to the right of l_3?
    (1) $x > y$
    (2) $x + y < 180$
    (A) statement 1 alone is sufficient to answer the question, but statement 2 alone is not sufficient
    (B) statement 2 alone is sufficient to answer the question, but statement 1 alone is not sufficient
    (C) both statements together are needed to answer the question, but neither statement alone is sufficient
    (D) either statement by itself is sufficient to answer the question
    (E) not enough facts are given to answer the question

17. What is the value of $(p + q)(r + s)$?
    (1) $p(r + s) = 5$ and $q(r + s) = 3$
    (2) $(p + q) = (r + s)$
    (A) statement 1 alone is sufficient to answer the question, but statement 2 alone is not sufficient
    (B) statement 2 alone is sufficient to answer the question, but statement 1 alone is not sufficient
    (C) both statements together are needed to answer the question, but neither statement alone is sufficient
    (D) either statement by itself is sufficient to answer the question
    (E) not enough facts are given to answer the question

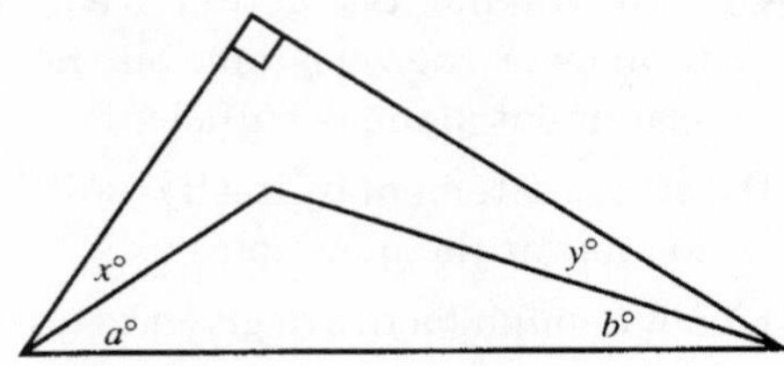

18. In the figure above, what is the value of $x + y$?
    (1) $a = 2b$
    (2) $a + b = 45$
    (A) statement 1 alone is sufficient to answer the question, but statement 2 alone is not sufficient
    (B) statement 2 alone is sufficient to answer the question, but statement 1 alone is not sufficient
    (C) both statements together are needed to answer the question, but neither statement alone is sufficient
    (D) either statement by itself is sufficient to answer the question
    (E) not enough facts are given to answer the question

19. Can a circle be drawn so that its circumference includes all four vertices of quadrilateral Q?
    (1) All four sides of Q are equal in length.
    (2) Each of the interior angles of Q measures 90°.
    (A) statement 1 alone is sufficient to answer the question, but statement 2 alone is not sufficient
    (B) statement 2 alone is sufficient to answer the question, but statement 1 alone is not sufficient
    (C) both statements together are needed to answer the question, but neither statement alone is sufficient
    (D) either statement by itself is sufficient to answer the question
    (E) not enough facts are given to answer the question

20. If Patty is five years older than Rod, how old is Rod?

(1) Fifteen years ago, Patty was twice as old as Rod.

(2) Five years ago, the sum of Patty's age and Rod's age was 35.

(A) statement 1 alone is sufficient to answer the question, but statement 2 alone is not sufficient

(B) statement 2 alone is sufficient to answer the question, but statement 1 alone is not sufficient

(C) both statements together are needed to answer the question, but neither statement alone is sufficient

(D) either statement by itself is sufficient to answer the question

(E) not enough facts are given to answer the question

21. How many hours long is time period T?

(1) T begins at 12:01 A.M. on Friday and ends at 12:01 A.M. on Wednesday.

(2) T is exactly 5 days long.

(A) statement 1 alone is sufficient to answer the question, but statement 2 alone is not sufficient

(B) statement 2 alone is sufficient to answer the question, but statement 1 alone is not sufficient

(C) both statements together are needed to answer the question, but neither statement alone is sufficient

(D) either statement by itself is sufficient to answer the question

(E) not enough facts are given to answer the question

22. A shipment of 70 items is to be divided into three lots. How many pieces are in the largest of the three lots?

(1) The number of items in the largest lot is equal to the sum of the number of items of the other two lots.

(2) The smallest lot contains 10 items.

(A) statement 1 alone is sufficient to answer the question, but statement 2 alone is not sufficient

(B) statement 2 alone is sufficient to answer the question, but statement 1 alone is not sufficient

(C) both statements together are needed to answer the question, but neither statement alone is sufficient

(D) either statement by itself is sufficient to answer the question

(E) not enough facts are given to answer the question

23. If $N > 0$, is N a whole number?

(1) $3 \times N$ is an odd number.

(2) $2 \times N$ is an even number.

(A) statement 1 alone is sufficient to answer the question, but statement 2 alone is not sufficient

(B) statement 2 alone is sufficient to answer the question, but statement 1 alone is not sufficient

(C) both statements together are needed to answer the question, but neither statement alone is sufficient

(D) either statement by itself is sufficient to answer the question

(E) not enough facts are given to answer the question

24. A swimming pool is supplied water by two pipes, P and Q. If pipe P operating alone can fill the pool in 12 hours, how long will it take pipe Q operating alone to fill the pool?

(1) Operating together, pipes P and Q can fill the pool in 4 hours.

(2) Pipe P supplies water at the rate of 520 gallons per hour, and 6240 gallons are required to fill the pool.

(A) statement 1 alone is sufficient to answer the question, but statement 2 alone is not sufficient

(B) statement 2 alone is sufficient to answer the question, but statement 1 alone is not sufficient

(C) both statements together are needed to answer the question, but neither statement alone is sufficient

(D) either statement by itself is sufficient to answer the question

(E) not enough facts are given to answer the question

25. What is the 999th term of the series S?

(1) The first four terms of S are $(1 + 1)^2$, $(2 + 1)^2$, $(3 + 1)^2$, and $(4 + 1)^2$.

(2) For every x, the xth term of S is $(x + 1)^2$.

(A) statement 1 alone is sufficient to answer the question, but statement 2 alone is not sufficient

(B) statement 2 alone is sufficient to answer the question, but statement 1 alone is not sufficient

(C) both statements together are needed to answer the question, but neither statement alone is sufficient

(D) either statement by itself is sufficient to answer the question

(E) not enough facts are given to answer the question

26. If x and y are integers, is x less than y?

(1) The cube of x is less than the cube of y.

(2) The square of x is less than the square of y.

(A) statement 1 alone is sufficient to answer the question, but statement 2 alone is not sufficient

(B) statement 2 alone is sufficient to answer the question, but statement 1 alone is not sufficient

(C) both statements together are needed to answer the question, but neither statement alone is sufficient

(D) either statement by itself is sufficient to answer the question

(E) not enough facts are given to answer the question

27. When one piece of fruit is taken at random from a fruit bowl, what is the chance that it is an apple?

(1) There are half as many apples as oranges in the fruit bowl.

(2) A third of the fruit in the fruit bowl are oranges.

(A) statement 1 alone is sufficient to answer the question, but statement 2 alone is not sufficient

(B) statement 2 alone is sufficient to answer the question, but statement 1 alone is not sufficient

(C) both statements together are needed to answer the question, but neither statement alone is sufficient

(D) either statement by itself is sufficient to answer the question

(E) not enough facts are given to answer the question

28. How many chocolate bars 2 inches wide and 4 inches long can be packed into carton Q?

(1) The inside dimensions of carton Q are 8 inches by 8 inches by 12 inches.

(2) The width of carton Q is equal to the height and $\frac{3}{4}$ of the length.

(A) statement 1 alone is sufficient to answer the question, but statement 2 alone is not sufficient

(B) statement 2 alone is sufficient to answer the question, but statement 1 alone is not sufficient

(C) both statements together are needed to answer the question, but neither statement alone is sufficient

(D) either statement by itself is sufficient to answer the question

(E) not enough facts are given to answer the question

29. Is K greater than L?

(1) K is greater than $2L$.

(2) The difference $K - L$ is positive.

(A) statement 1 alone is sufficient to answer the question, but statement 2 alone is not sufficient

(B) statement 2 alone is sufficient to answer the question, but statement 1 alone is not sufficient

(C) both statements together are needed to answer the question, but neither statement alone is sufficient

(D) either statement by itself is sufficient to answer the question

(E) not enough facts are given to answer the question

30. A piece of wood 7 feet long is cut into three pieces. What is the length of each of the pieces?

(1) The length of the longest piece is equal to the sum of the lengths of the other two pieces.

(2) The length of the shortest piece is 6 inches.

(A) statement 1 alone is sufficient to answer the question, but statement 2 alone is not sufficient

(B) statement 2 alone is sufficient to answer the question, but statement 1 alone is not sufficient

(C) both statements together are needed to answer the question, but neither statement alone is sufficient

(D) either statement by itself is sufficient to answer the question

(E) not enough facts are given to answer the question

EXERCISE 2: DATA SUFFICIENCY

15 Questions • 19 Minutes

Directions: Each question below is followed by two numbered facts. You are to determine whether the data given in the statements is sufficient for answering the question. Use the data given, plus your knowledge of math and everyday facts, to choose between the five possible answers.

1. A company's profit was $600,000 in 1980. What was its profit in 1981?

(1) There was a 20 percent increase in income in 1981.

(2) There was a 25 percent increase in costs in 1981.

(A) statement 1 alone is sufficient to answer the question, but statement 2 alone is not sufficient

(B) statement 2 alone is sufficient to answer the question, but statement 1 alone is not sufficient

(C) both statements together are needed to answer the question, but neither statement alone is sufficient

(D) either statement by itself is sufficient to answer the question

(E) not enough facts are given to answer the question

2. If x is an integer, is x an odd number?

(1) x^3 is not negative.

(2) x is either a negative number or an odd number, but not both.

(A) statement 1 alone is sufficient to answer the question, but statement 2 alone is not sufficient

(B) statement 2 alone is sufficient to answer the question, but statement 1 alone is not sufficient

(C) both statements together are needed to answer the question, but neither statement alone is sufficient

(D) either statement by itself is sufficient to answer the question

(E) not enough facts are given to answer the question

3. What is the average speed of an automobile as it travels the 300 miles between city A and city B?

(1) The automobile averages 50 miles per hour for the first three hours.

(2) The automobile averages 45 miles per hour for the last three hours.

(A) statement 1 alone is sufficient to answer the question, but statement 2 alone is not sufficient

(B) statement 2 alone is sufficient to answer the question, but statement 1 alone is not sufficient

(C) both statements together are needed to answer the question, but neither statement alone is sufficient

(D) either statement by itself is sufficient to answer the question

(E) not enough facts are given to answer the question

4. If the ratio of boys to girls attending school S in 1980 was $\frac{1}{2}$, what was the ratio of boys to girls attending school S in 1981?

(1) 50 more boys were attending school S in 1981 than in 1980.

(2) 50 more girls were attending school S in 1981 than in 1980.

(A) statement 1 alone is sufficient to answer the question, but statement 2 alone is not sufficient

(B) statement 2 alone is sufficient to answer the question, but statement 1 alone is not sufficient

(C) both statements together are needed to answer the question, but neither statement alone is sufficient

(D) either statement by itself is sufficient to answer the question

(E) not enough facts are given to answer the question

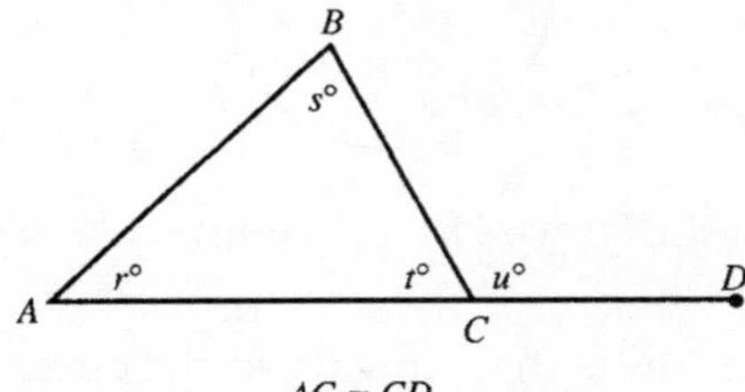

AC = CD

5. In the figure above, does $r = t$?

(1) The length of AB plus the length of AC equals the length of BC plus the length of CD.

(2) $u = s + t$.

(A) statement 1 alone is sufficient to answer the question, but statement 2 alone is not sufficient

(B) statement 2 alone is sufficient to answer the question, but statement 1 alone is not sufficient

(C) both statements together are needed to answer the question, but neither statement alone is sufficient

(D) either statement by itself is sufficient to answer the question

(E) not enough facts are given to answer the question

6. How many of the three different positive integers a, b, and c are divisible by 7?

(1) The product of a, b, and c is divisible by 3, but only c is divisible by 21.

(2) Each of the three positive integers is divisible by 3, but only c is divisible by 21.

(A) statement 1 alone is sufficient to answer the question, but statement 2 alone is not sufficient

(B) statement 2 alone is sufficient to answer the question, but statement 1 alone is not sufficient

(C) both statements together are needed to answer the question, but neither statement alone is sufficient

(D) either statement by itself is sufficient to answer the question

(E) not enough facts are given to answer the question

7. A stock returned what percent of its cost in a dividend at the end of the year?

(1) The amount of the dividend was less than 10 percent of the cost of the stock.

(2) The amount of dividend paid on each share was $1.20; and the stock cost $60 per share.

(A) statement 1 alone is sufficient to answer the question, but statement 2 alone is not sufficient

(B) statement 2 alone is sufficient to answer the question, but statement 1 alone is not sufficient

(C) both statements together are needed to answer the question, but neither statement alone is sufficient

(D) either statement by itself is sufficient to answer the question

(E) not enough facts are given to answer the question

8. What is the average (arithmetic mean) of the ages of Mark, Paul, Edward, Maxine, and Linda?

(1) The average (arithmetic mean) of the ages of Mark, Paul, and Edward is 20 years.

(2) The average (arithmetic mean) of the ages of Maxine and Linda is 25 years.

(A) statement 1 alone is sufficient to answer the question, but statement 2 alone is not sufficient

(B) statement 2 alone is sufficient to answer the question, but statement 1 alone is not sufficient

(C) both statements together are needed to answer the question, but neither statement alone is sufficient

(D) either statement by itself is sufficient to answer the question

(E) not enough facts are given to answer the question

9. Peter, Mary, and Edna took the same examination. Which of them received the highest score?

(1) There was a 10-point gap between Peter's score and Mary's score.

(2) There was an 8-point gap between Edna's score and Peter's score.

(A) statement 1 alone is sufficient to answer the question, but statement 2 alone is not sufficient

(B) statement 2 alone is sufficient to answer the question, but statement 1 alone is not sufficient

(C) both statements together are needed to answer the question, but neither statement alone is sufficient

(D) either statement by itself is sufficient to answer the question

(E) not enough facts are given to answer the question

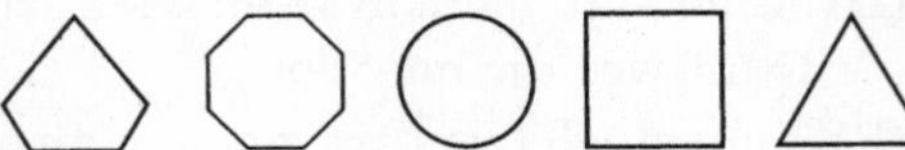

10. Each of the figures above is a different color: green, red, blue, orange, or yellow. Which is the green figure?

(1) The green figure is between the blue and the orange figures.

(2) The green figure is between the red and the yellow figures.

(A) statement 1 alone is sufficient to answer the question, but statement 2 alone is not sufficient

(B) statement 2 alone is sufficient to answer the question, but statement 1 alone is not sufficient

(C) both statements together are needed to answer the question, but neither statement alone is sufficient

(D) either statement by itself is sufficient to answer the question

(E) not enough facts are given to answer the question

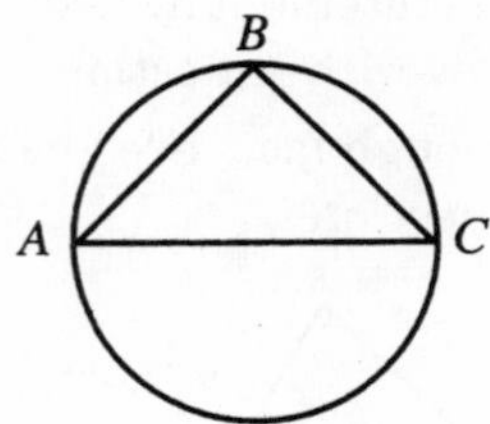

11. In the figure above, is angle ABC a right angle?

(1) AC is the diameter of the circle.

(2) $AB = BC$

(A) statement 1 alone is sufficient to answer the question, but statement 2 alone is not sufficient

(B) statement 2 alone is sufficient to answer the question, but statement 1 alone is not sufficient

(C) both statements together are needed to answer the question, but neither statement alone is sufficient

(D) either statement by itself is sufficient to answer the question

(E) not enough facts are given to answer the question

12. If a car is driven 150 miles, the fuel tank is filled to what percent of capacity at the end of the trip?

(1) The car averaged 15 miles per gallon for the trip.

(2) The tank was filled to 75 percent of capacity at the start of the trip.

(A) statement 1 alone is sufficient to answer the question, but statement 2 alone is not sufficient

(B) statement 2 alone is sufficient to answer the question, but statement 1 alone is not sufficient

(C) both statements together are needed to answer the question, but neither statement alone is sufficient

(D) either statement by itself is sufficient to answer the question

(E) not enough facts are given to answer the question

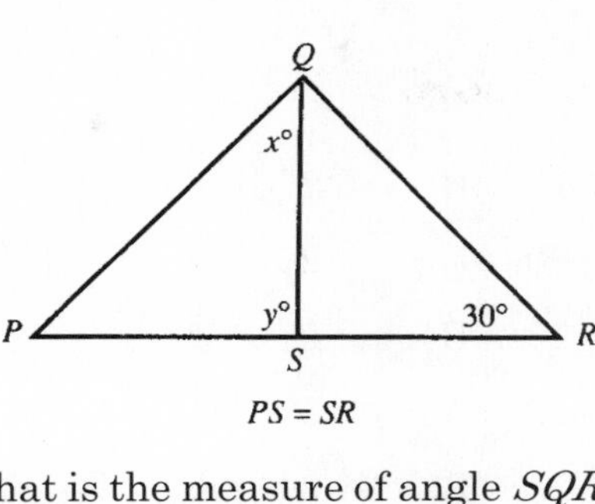

13. What is the measure of angle SQR in the figure above?

 (1) $x = 40°$

 (2) $y = 80°$

 (A) statement 1 alone is sufficient to answer the question, but statement 2 alone is not sufficient

 (B) statement 2 alone is sufficient to answer the question, but statement 1 alone is not sufficient

 (C) both statements together are needed to answer the question, but neither statement alone is sufficient

 (D) either statement by itself is sufficient to answer the question

 (E) not enough facts are given to answer the question

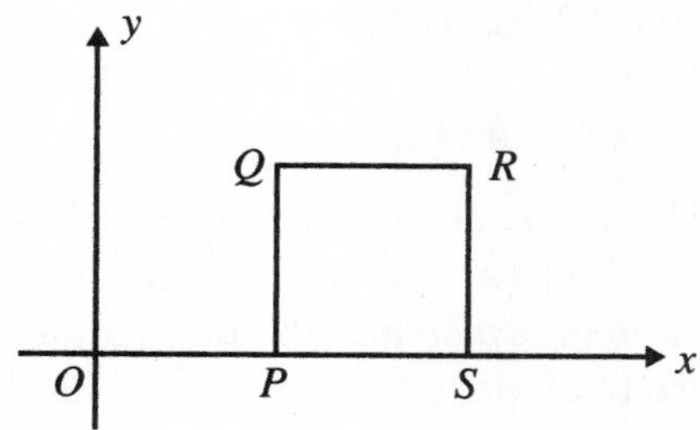

14. In the figure above, $PQRS$ is a square the base of which is situated on the x-axis. What is the perimeter of the square?

 (1) The y-coordinate for point Q is 6.

 (2) The x-coordinate for point P is 4.

 (A) statement 1 alone is sufficient to answer the question, but statement 2 alone is not sufficient

 (B) statement 2 alone is sufficient to answer the question, but statement 1 alone is not sufficient

 (C) both statements together are needed to answer the question, but neither statement alone is sufficient

 (D) either statement by itself is sufficient to answer the question

 (E) not enough facts are given to answer the question

15. A rectangular plot of land is represented on a map. What are the actual dimensions of the plot of land?

 (1) The length of the rectangular figure on the map representing the actual plot of land is twice as long as the width.

 (2) The map is drawn so that each inch on the map represents an actual distance of 10 feet.

 (A) statement 1 alone is sufficient to answer the question, but statement 2 alone is not sufficient

 (B) statement 2 alone is sufficient to answer the question, but statement 1 alone is not sufficient

 (C) both statements together are needed to answer the question, but neither statement alone is sufficient

 (D) either statement by itself is sufficient to answer the question

 (E) not enough facts are given to answer the question

Exercise 1: ANSWER KEY AND EXPLANATIONS

1. C	7. D	13. D	19. B	25. B
2. E	8. B	14. B	20. D	26. A
3. C	9. D	15. A	21. B	27. C
4. A	10. E	16. B	22. A	28. E
5. A	11. A	17. A	23. B	29. B
6. B	12. B	18. B	24. A	30. C

1. **The correct answer is (C).** Statement (1) alone is not sufficient to answer the question. Statement (1) implies that x is divisible by 10 ($2 \times 5 = 10$), but a number can be divisible by 10 without being divisible by 70. Similarly, (2) alone is insufficient. (2) implies that x is divisible by 14 ($2 \times 7 = 14$), but a number can be divisible by 14 without being divisible by 70. Both statements taken together are sufficient to answer the question, for together they imply that x is divisible by 70 ($2 \times 5 \times 7 = 70$).

2. **The correct answer is (E).** Neither (1) nor (2) alone can be sufficient, because neither provides a basis for comparing the number of records in Bob's collection with the number in Linda's collection. Nor are the two together sufficient. Although the two statements establish that both Bob and Linda have fewer records than Christina, that information is not sufficient to answer the question asked.

3. **The correct answer is (C).** Neither statement alone is sufficient to determine the angle at which the line intersects the y-axis, but both taken together contain sufficient information to determine that the angle is 45°:

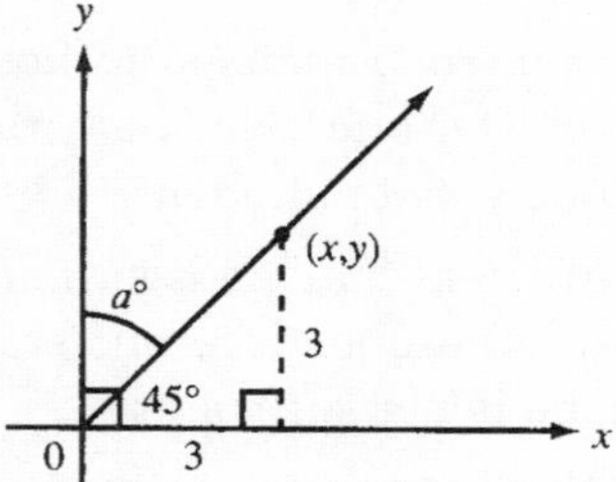

4. **The correct answer is (A).** Statement (1) is sufficient to answer the question. In 1991, profits were $30,000; in 1992, $60,000; and in 1993, $120,000. Therefore, it was in 1993 that profits first exceeded $100,000. Statement (2), however, is not sufficient to answer the question. Since (1) alone is sufficient to answer but (2) is not, this item should be classified as (A).

5. **The correct answer is (A).** Statement (1) alone is sufficient. Since the sum of the degree measures of the interior angles of a triangle is 180, $b + c + d = 180$. Then, given that $b + c = 90$,

$$(b + c) + d = 180$$
$$90 + d = 180$$
$$d = 90$$

(2), however, is not sufficient to answer the question. $a + b = 180$, so $b = 180 - a$. This in turn implies

$$d + c + (180 - a) = 180$$
$$c - a + d = 180$$

But $c - a$ is not equal to $c + a$, so information about $c + a$ does not answer the question.

6. **The correct answer is (B).** (1) alone is not sufficient to answer the question, for (1) implies only that x is a positive number, not that x is an integer. (2) alone, however, is sufficient to answer the question.

7. **The correct answer is (D).** Statement (1) alone is sufficient to answer the question. The surface area of a cube is composed of six equal faces, and each of those faces is a square. (1) implies that the edge of the cube has a length of 3:

$$54 = 6 \times \text{edge} \times \text{edge}$$
$$9 = \text{edge}^2$$
$$\text{edge} = 3$$

(2) also is sufficient, for it too implies that the length of the edge is 3:

$$\text{area} = \text{edge} \times \text{edge}$$
$$9 = \text{edge}^2$$
$$\text{edge} = 3$$

8. **The correct answer is (B).** Since the triangles share a common base, they will have the same area if, and only if, they have altitudes of equal length. That (1) alone is not sufficient to answer the question can be demonstrated by distorting the figure:

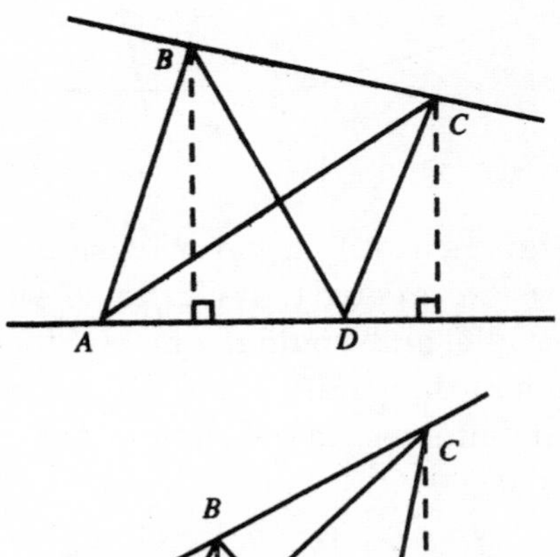

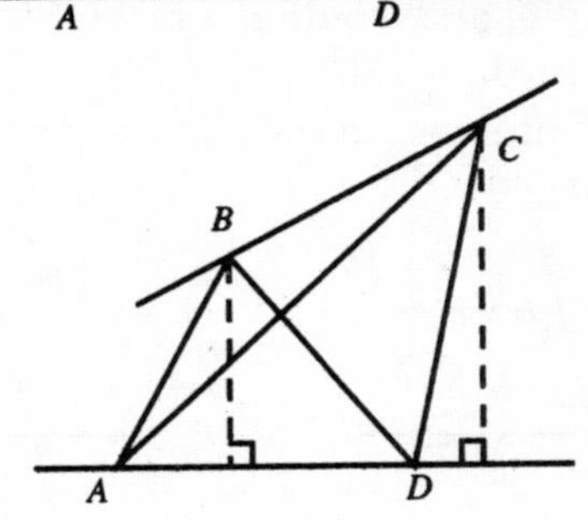

Even though $AB \| CD$ in each of the figures, the lengths of the altitudes of the two triangles may or may not be equal. (2), however, is sufficient to answer the question, for (2) implies that the two altitudes have the same length:

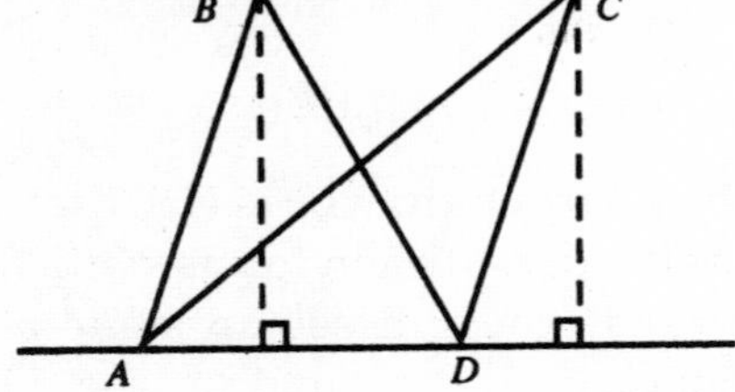

9. **The correct answer is (D).** Statement (1) alone is sufficient to answer the question. Operating expenses were 63% of \$9,000,000 = \$5,670,000. Statement (2) is also sufficient, for (2) implies that the total budget was \$9,000,000:

$$63\% \text{ of Total} = \$5{,}670{,}000$$
$$0.63T = \$5{,}670{,}000$$
$$T = \$9{,}000{,}000$$

And as shown above, that information, when coupled with the data provided by the chart, is sufficient to answer the question.

10. **The correct answer is (E).** Neither (1) nor (2) alone is sufficient to answer the question, and even taken together they do not provide enough information to answer it. Although (1) implies that N must be a multiple of 6, there are six numbers between 30 and 70 that are divisible by 6.

11. **The correct answer is (A).** Statement (1) alone is sufficient to answer the question. (1) implies that buying a box of a dozen donuts results in a cost savings of $12 \times \$0.05 = \$0.60$. Statement (2), however, is not sufficient, because (2) provides no information about the cost of donuts when purchased one at a time.

12. **The correct answer is (B).** The expression $a^4 - b^4$ is the difference between two squares and can be factored:

$$a^4 - b^4 = (a^2 + b^2)(a^2 - b^2)$$

Statement (1) alone is not sufficient to fix the value of the expression, but (2) is. If $a^2 - b^2 = 0$:

$$a^4 - b^4 = (a^2 + b^2)(0) = 0$$

13. **The correct answer is (D).** Statement (1) alone is sufficient to answer the question, for you can set up simultaneous equations. Let x stand for the amount invested at 6 percent and y for the amount invested at 8 percent. Since a total of \$10,000 was invested at both rates,

$$x + y = \$10{,}000$$

Then, $(x)(0.06)$ plus $(y)(0.08)$ is the total amount of interest earned:

$$0.06x + 0.08y = \$640$$

Using the first equation, redefine y in terms of x:

$$y = \$10{,}000 - x$$

And substitute this value for y in the second equation:

$$\begin{aligned} 0.06x + 0.08(\$10{,}000 - x) &= \$640 \\ 0.06x + \$800 - 0.08x &= \$640 \\ 0.02x &= \$160 \\ x &= \$8{,}000 \end{aligned}$$

Statement (2) is also sufficient. Again, let x stand for the amount that earned 6 percent and y for the amount that earned 8 percent. (2) implies:

$$x = 4y$$

Given that $x + y = \$10{,}000$,

$$\begin{aligned} 4y + y &= \$10{,}000 \\ 5y &= \$10{,}000 \\ y &= \$2{,}000 \end{aligned}$$

So $x = \$10{,}000 - \$2{,}000 = \$8{,}000$

14. **The correct answer is (B).** Statement (1) alone is not sufficient. If x and y are positive, then given that $3x = 4y$, x is greater than y. But if x and y are negative, then given that $3x = 4y$, y is greater than x. (For example, x might be –4 and y, –3.) Statement (2), however, is sufficient to answer the question. Since $x = \frac{k}{3}$, $3x = k$, and since $y = \frac{k}{4}$, $4y = k$. This implies that $3x = 4y$. And here it is stipulated that k is positive, which means that both x and y must also be positive. Therefore, (2) implies that x is greater than y.

15. **The correct answer is (A).** Statement (1) is sufficient to answer the question. The sum of the lengths of the two shorter sides must be less than half of the perimeter of the rectangle. Since 15 + 15 = 30, the total perimeter of the yard must be more than twice 30. (2), however, is not sufficient to answer the question, for (2) provides no information about the actual length of either side.

16. **The correct answer is (B).** Statement (1) is not sufficient, as the following figures make clear:

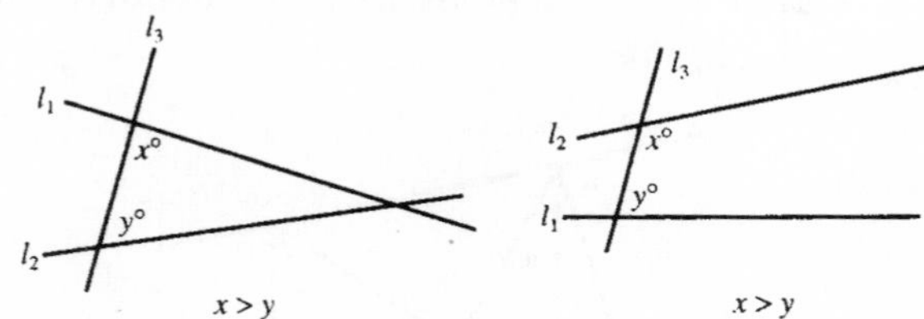

Statement (2), however, is sufficient. If $x + y$ were equal to 180°, l_1 and l_2 would be parallel and would not meet. Since $x + y$ is less than 180°, l_1 and l_2 must eventually intersect to the right of l_3:

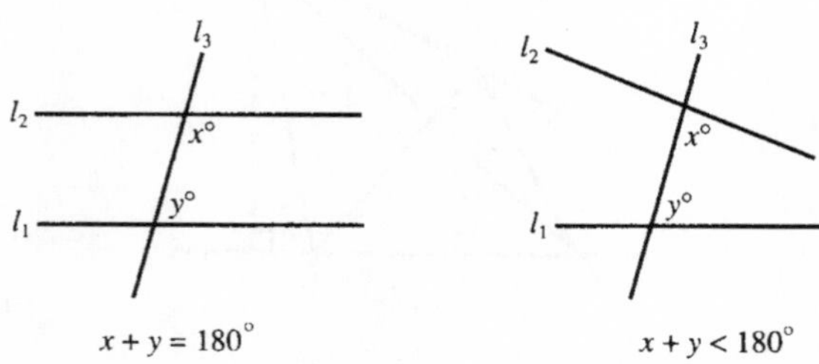

17. **The correct answer is (A).** First, perform the indicated operation:

$(p + q)(r + s) = pr + ps + qr + qs$

Statement (1) alone is sufficient to answer the question:

$p(r + s) = pr + ps$
$q(r + s) = qr + qs$

So the value of the expression in the question stem is $5 + 3 = 8$. Statement (2), however, is not sufficient to answer the question. The fact that the two terms are equal implies nothing about the product of those terms.

18. **The correct answer is (B).** Statement (1) is not sufficient to answer the question, for (1) provides no information about the size of x and y. Statement (2), however, is sufficient. Since the figure is a triangle,

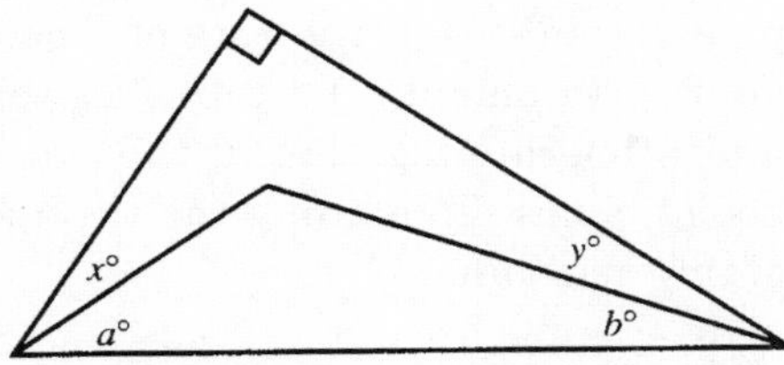

$$90^\circ + (a + x) + (b + y) = 180^\circ$$
$$(a + x) + (b + y) = 90^\circ$$
$$a + b + x + y = 90^\circ$$

Since $a + b = 45^\circ$,

$$45^\circ + x + y = 90^\circ$$
$$x + y = 45^\circ$$

19. **The correct answer is (B).** Statement (1) is not sufficient to answer the question. If Q is a square, it can be inscribed in a circle:

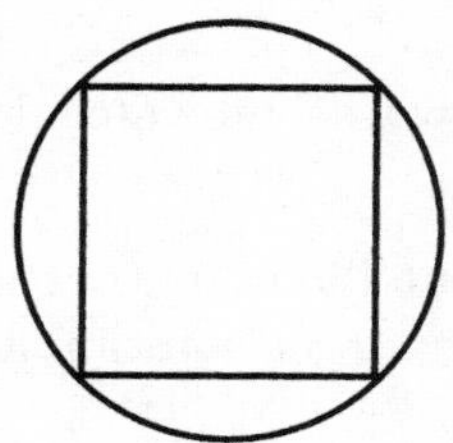

But a quadrilateral with four equal sides need not be a square:

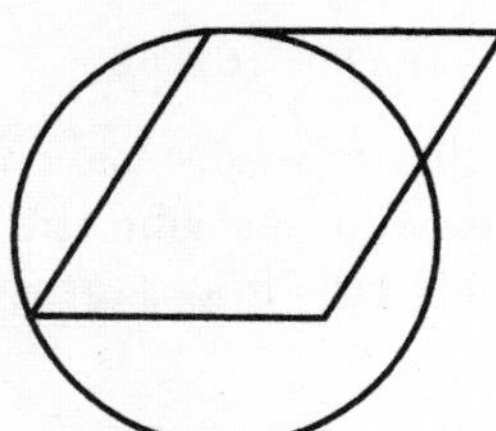

Statement (2), however, is sufficient to answer the question. A quadrilateral with four 90° angles is a rectangle. The diagonal of a rectangle creates two right triangles, and any right triangle can be inscribed in a semicircle:

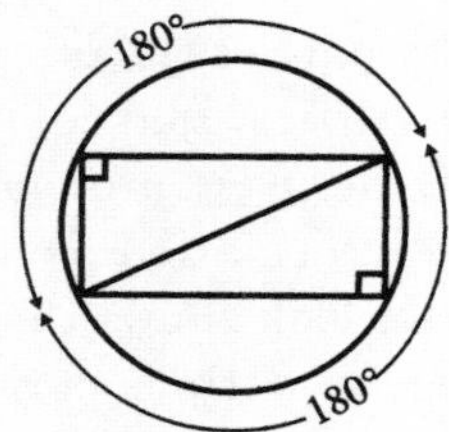

20. **The correct answer is (D).** Statement (1) is sufficient to answer the question. Let P and R represent the present ages of Patty and Rod, respectively. The question stem establishes

$P = R + 5$

And statement (1) establishes

$P - 15 = 2(R - 15)$

We now have two equations and only two variables:

$$P = R + 5$$
$$P - 15 = 2(R - 15)$$

Solve for R:

$$(R + 5) - 15 = 2(R - 15)$$
$$R - 10 = 2R - 30$$
$$R = 20$$

A similar line of reasoning shows that statement (2) is also sufficient. Using P

and R again, we represent the information provided by (2) as follows:

$$(P-5)+(R-5)=35$$
$$P+R=45$$

Couple this new equation with the one used above to describe the information contained in the question stem and solve for R:

$$P+R=45$$
$$(R+5)+R=45$$
$$2R=40$$
$$R=20$$

21. **The correct answer is (B).** Statement (2) is quite clearly enough to answer the question. A time period that is exactly 5 days long is 120 hours long.

The tricky part of the question is statement (1). At first glance, it might seem that statement (1) provides essentially the same information as statement (2), but a closer look shows that is incorrect. Just because a time period begins on Friday and ends on Wednesday does not mean the period is exactly 5 days long. It could be 12 days, or 19 days, or even longer.

22. **The correct answer is (A).** Statement (2) is not enough to answer the question. To know the size of the smallest lot is not enough to fix the size of the largest lot.

Statement (1), however, does fix the size of the largest lot. What statement (1) is really saying is that the largest lot is exactly $\frac{1}{2}$ of the total shipment. (It is equal to the sum of the other two, so it must be half.) Since it is half of the shipment, and since the shipment contains 70 items, the largest lot contains 35 items.

Of course, statement (1) alone does not fix the size of each of the other two lots, but that is not important. The question asks only for the number of items in the largest lot.

23. **The correct answer is (B).** This question illustrates the importance of considering all possibilities. At first, you might think that statement (1) is sufficient, reasoning (erroneously) that for $3N$ to be an odd number N must be an integer. But this is incorrect. If $N=\frac{1}{3}$, then $3N=1$, and N is in that case a fraction, not a whole number. So statement (1) is not enough.

Statement (2), however, is sufficient to establish that N is a whole number. The smallest even (positive) number is 2. So the least N could be, given statement (2), is 1—a whole number. And for any even number larger than 2, N would still have to be a whole number.

24. **The correct answer is (A).** Statement (1), when coupled with the information given in the stem, is sufficient to answer the question. The stem establishes that pipe P operates at the rate of 1 pool/12 hours. Statement (1) establishes that P and Q operate together at the rate of 1 pool/4 hours. Combining the two pieces of information:

$$\frac{1\text{ pool}}{12\text{ hours}}+Q\text{'s rate}=\frac{1\text{ pool}}{4\text{ hours}}$$

Then you could solve for Q. (Note: It is not necessary to do so, but for practice here is how it is done.)

$$\frac{1}{12}+\frac{1}{x}=\frac{1}{4}$$
$$\frac{1}{x}=\frac{1}{4}-\frac{1}{12}$$
$$\frac{1}{x}=\frac{2}{12}=\frac{1}{6}$$
$$x=6$$

In other words, pipe Q could do the job in 6 hours.

Statement (2) is neither sufficient nor necessary to the solution just given.

25. **The correct answer is (B).** (2) is sufficient because it gives a rule for calculating any term of the series. (1) looks good, but does not actually tell us that the series continues in the same manner beyond the terms listed; thus it is not sufficient.

26. **The correct answer is (A).** (1) is sufficient because the cube of a number retains the same sign as the original number or base, e.g., $(-2)^3 = -8$; $(+2)^3 = +8$. However, the square of a number is always positive, and thus x and y might be negative without changing the relationship between their squares. If $x = -2$ and $y = +3$, (2) is true; but (2) is also true if $x = +2$ and $y = -3$.

27. **The correct answer is (C).** In order to know the chances of taking an apple, it is necessary to know the fraction of apples in the fruit bowl. It is not necessary to know the fractions of all of the fruits in the fruit bowl. (1) only tells the relationship between oranges and apples, but there may be other fruits. (2) only tells the fraction of oranges. Together they permit the calculation that one-sixth of the fruits in the fruit bowl are apples.

28. **The correct answer is (E).** To know the number of chocolate bars that can be packed into the carton, you need to know at least the three dimensions of the chocolate bars and the three dimensions of the carton. Only two dimensions of the chocolate bar are given in the initial information and the third dimension is never supplied, hence (E). The two propositions do give the three dimensions of the carton, but that is not enough.

29. **The correct answer is (B).** In (1), if $K > 2L$, K could equal 3 and L could equal 0 ($K > L$); or K could equal -4 and L could equal -3 ($K < L$). In (2), if $K - L$ is positive, then $K - L > 0$ and $K > L$ (adding L to both sides in $K - L > 0$), so (2) is sufficient to answer the question.

30. **The correct answer is (C).** In this problem there are three unknown quantities. In order to determine them, you need three equations. From the given conditions you can write $x + y + z = 7$ feet, where x, y, and z represent the lengths of each of the three pieces. From (1) you can write $x = y + z$. These two equations are not sufficient to answer the question. From (2) you can write $y = 6$ or $z = 6$. Now, with both (1) and (2), there is sufficient information to arrive at an answer (3 equations and 3 unknowns). You need not solve the equations, but the longest piece is 3 feet 6 inches long, the shortest piece is 6 inches long, and the other piece is 3 feet long.

Exercise 2: ANSWER KEY AND EXPLANATIONS

1. E	4. E	7. B	10. C	13. B
2. C	5. D	8. C	11. A	14. A
3. E	6. B	9. E	12. E	15. E

1. **The correct answer is (E).** Profit = Income – Costs, so we need to know income and costs. Neither proposition by itself will allow us to compute the 1981 costs and income. The information in (1) and (2) together gives us only percentage increases. Without the actual 1980 income and cost numbers, we cannot calculate 1981 income and costs. If the percentage increases for costs and income had been the same, then you could have computed the new profit. For example, if both costs and income had increased by 50 percent, then the profit would also have increased by 50 percent. With the given information, it is not enough. For example, if in 1980 income were \$1,000,000 and the costs were \$400,000 (for a 1980 profit of \$600,000), the 1981 income would be \$1,200,000 and the 1981 costs would be \$500,000, for a 1981 profit of \$700,000. If the 1980 figures were \$10,000,000 – \$9,400,000 = \$600,000, then 1981 would be \$12,000,000 – \$11,750,000 = \$250,000. This shows that you don't even know whether the profit is larger or smaller in 1981.

2. **The correct answer is (C).** (1) tells us that x must be positive or zero, since the cube of any negative number is negative. From (2) we know that x is negative or odd, but not both. Thus, given (1) and (2), x must be odd.

3. **The correct answer is (E).** In order to find the average speed for the whole trip, we will at least need to have information about all of the miles of the trip. Traveling at 50 miles per hour for the first three hours and 45 miles per hour for the last three hours, the car will have gone $(50 \times 3) + (45 \times 3) = 285$ miles. We do not know how long it took to travel the remaining 15 miles, and so cannot calculate the average speed for the entire trip.

4. **The correct answer is (E).** The question can be analyzed algebraically by expressing each statement as an equation. Letting x represent the number of boys attending S in 1980 and y the number of girls for the same year, we have:
$$\frac{x}{y} = \frac{1}{2} \quad \frac{x+50}{y+50} = z$$
where z is the ratio of boys to girls for 1981. Even if we treat these two algebraic statements as simultaneous equations, we still have three variables, x, y and z, and there is no way to eliminate two of three to solve for any one variable.

Alternatively, you should be able to see that neither statement alone is sufficient to answer the question. Then you can prove that the correct answer is (E) by using the test-taking tactic of picking concrete numbers. Assuming the number of boys in 1980 to be 25 and the number of girls in 1980 to be 50 (a ratio of 1:2), the ratio of boys to girls in 1981 would be:
$$\frac{25+50}{50+50} = \frac{75}{100} = \frac{3}{4}$$

But assuming the number of boys in 1980 to be 250 and the number of girls to be 500 (again, the 1:2 ratio stipulated by the question stem), the ratio for 1981 would be:
$$\frac{250+50}{500+50} = \frac{300}{550} = \frac{6}{11}$$

So the ratio for 1981 depends on the actual number of students attending S in

answers

1980 and not just on the ratio for 1980. Neither statement, however, gives us any information about the actual number of students in attendance in 1980.

5. **The correct answer is (D).** Since AC and CD are equal, (1) means that $AB = BC$, triangle ABC is isosceles, and $r = t$. (2) tells us that $u = s + t$. u also equals $s + r$ since it is an exterior angle to triangle ABC. Therefore, $s + r = s + t$ or $r = t$.

6. **The correct answer is (B).** (1) means that there is at least one factor of 3 in the three integers, but two or all three could be divisible by 3. The fact that only one of the three is divisible by 21 means that only one is divisible by *both* 3 and 7. However, the question concerns merely the divisibility of the three integers by 7 alone. It is certainly possible to be divisible by 7 and not by 21. For example, satisfying (1), the three integers could be 2, 5 and 21, in which case only one of the three is divisible by 7; but it is also possible that the three integers are 2, 7 and 21, in which case two of the three are divisible by 7. Thus, (1) is not sufficient. (2) is sufficient since any integer divisible by 3 and 7 is divisible by 21. Therefore, since only c is divisible by 21, only c can be divisible by 7.

7. **The correct answer is (B).** Statement (1) only gives a limit on the percentage the question asks about. (2) does give the information needed to compute the percentage of the stock's cost which the dividend represents.

8. **The correct answer is (C).** In order to determine the average of all five of the persons mentioned in the problem, the total of the five ages is needed. Knowing the averages of the three men and of the two women will permit this calculation. The only thing that you need to check carefully is that all of the persons are included in the two averages and that there is no overlap.

9. **The correct answer is (E).** The key to this problem is the insight that there is no information given about which of the scores is at the higher end of the gap and which at the lower end of the gap. Thus, neither of the propositions gives adequate, or indeed helpful, information.

10. **The correct answer is (C).** This is really a logic problem, not a mathematics problem. Whatever is being asked for, the answer will be found by ordinary reasoning rather than some esoteric formula. Each proposition by itself merely establishes that the green figure is not at the ends since it must be between two other figures. Taking them together shows that the green figure must be the central figure; there must be two figures to the left of the green figure and two figures to the right of it.

11. **The correct answer is (A).** Angle ABC is an angle inscribed in a semicircle. An inscribed angle intercepts an arc with twice the degree measure of the angle. If the angle intercepts a semicircle, whose arc measures 180°, the angle is a right angle. Thus, (1) is sufficient. That (2) is not sufficient is shown by the following figures:

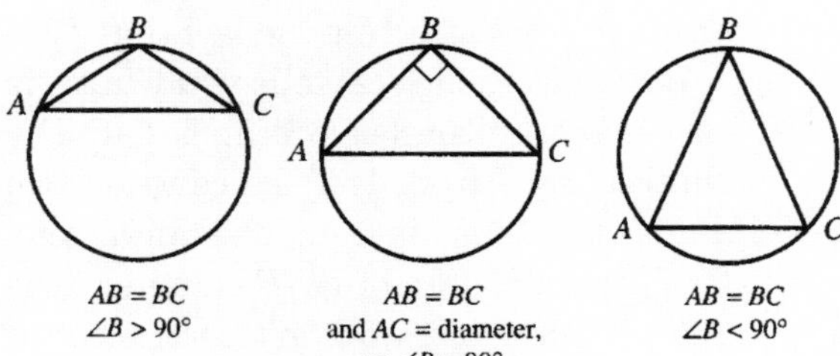

12. **The correct answer is (E).** This is the sort of problem in which it is particularly important to analyze what sort of information would be required to answer the question before doing any computation or detailed analysis. Since the original information gives data about the length of the trip and asks about the percentage of capacity to which the tank is filled, you

will need to link these two ideas in order to answer the question. In order to know what percentage of the tank is full, you will need to know the amount of gas in the tank and the total capacity of the tank. Nowhere in the problem is there the slightest information that gives you the total capacity of the tank. Nor is there any information that would allow you to deduce the final percentage of the starting percentage, though (2) does take one step along that path. (1) allows the calculation that the tank contains 10 gallons less ($\frac{150}{15}$) at the end of the trip than at the beginning, but since the original amount of gas is unknown, the answer to the final percentage filled is unobtainable.

13. **The correct answer is (B).** In order to find the measure of angle *SQR,* either the whole of the measure of angle *PQR* must be found so that x can be subtracted from it to give the desired answer, or the measure of angle *QSR* must be found so that the three angles of the right-hand triangle can be added together to make 180°, thus permitting the calculation of angle *SQR.* Although $PS = SR$, there is no reason to believe that *QS* is perpendicular to *PR.* Point *Q* could be moved up and down line *QR* (*QR* could be lengthened or shortened) without affecting the fact that $PS = SR$. However, once (2) tells you what y is the measure of angle *QSR* can be found by subtracting y from 180°, since those two angles together make up a straight line. Once the measure of *QSR* is found (it is 100°, though you wouldn't even need to compute it), the measure of *SQR* can be found from $\angle QSR + \angle SQR + 30° = 180°$. Thus, (2) is sufficient by itself. (1) by itself does not address either of the two issues identified at the beginning of this discussion. Knowing just a part of the measure of angle *PQR* does not permit the calculation of the other part without further information. Thus, (1) is not sufficient by itself. Identifying at the beginning the kind of information that is most likely to help would direct your attention to (2) first and reduce your chances of mistakenly calling this a (C).

14. **The correct answer is (A).** In order to find the perimeter of a square, you need to know the length of a side. In a coordinate geometry situation, some information is known from the conventions of the graph. For instance, the x-axis, part of which forms one of the sides of the square, has a y-coordinate of 0. Furthermore, since the figure is a square, *QP* is perpendicular to the x-axis. As a vertical line, every point on it will have the same x-coordinate, and the distance along the line can be found directly from the y-coordinate. (1) is sufficient because knowing that the y-coordinate of *P* is 0 from the diagram and the y-coordinate of *Q* is 6 from the proposition permits the deduction that the length of *PQ* is 6. *PQRS* is then a square with a side of 6, whose perimeter would be (6)(4) or 24. (2) is not sufficient because knowing how far the square is from the y-axis is of no help in determining the length of a side.

15. **The correct answer is (E).** The question asks for the actual dimensions of the land itself. Given that the land is rectangular, knowing the width and length would be sufficient to answer the question. Neither statement alone nor both statements together provide this information. (1) is clearly insufficient since it does not give us the actual measurement of either the length or the width. (2) alone is insufficient since it does not tell us the length or width of the figure on the map. Even using both together, we are still lacking a critical piece of information: the length and width (either of the figure or the plot of land).

SUMMING IT UP:

What You Need to Know About GMAT Quantitative Questions

Review this page the night before you take the GMAT. It will help you do well on the quantitative questions.

- The GMAT tests quantitative reasoning skills with two question types: problem solving and data sufficiency.
- On the test, questions of both types are interspersed with each other within the 75-minute Quantitative Section.

Problem Solving

- GMAT problem-solving questions test your ability to solve problems using arithmetic, elementary algebra, and geometry.
- Some problem-solving questions are strictly calculations; others are word problems requiring a mathematical solution.
- These steps will help you answer problem-solving questions.
  1. Read the question carefully.
  2. Before solving the problem, check the answers.
  3. Eliminate choices that are completely off the radar screen.
  4. For complex questions, break down the problem.
- It's smart to test answer choices, and when testing choices, it's smart to start with (C).
- Most problem-solving figures are drawn to scale.

Data Sufficiency

- For data sufficiency questions, the task is to decide whether two statements—either singly or in combination—provide enough information to answer a question.
- For data sufficiency questions, you don't actually have to calculate an answer.
- These steps can help you solve data sufficiency questions:
  1. Read the question carefully.
  2. Pay careful attention to any information provided in the question stem.
  3. Consider each statement in isolation.
  4. Eliminate choices and guess.
- In data sufficiency questions, figures are not necessarily drawn to scale.
- A statement about percentage alone does not provide information about actual quantities.
- You must consider every possibility for unknowns.

PART V

GMAT ANALYTICAL WRITING ASSESSMENT

Analytical Writing Assessment

chapter 10

OVERVIEW

- **What is the analytical writing assessment?**
- **How is the assessment graded?**
- **How do you handle the analytical writing assessment?**
- **What smart test-takers know**

WHAT IS THE ANALYTICAL WRITING ASSESSMENT?

The Analytical Writing Assessment (AWA) is a test of your ability to write essays under timed conditions. At first, this task may seem daunting; but once you become more familiar with what is required, it will seem less so.

One recent development in graduate study in management has been the growing awareness on the part of educators that effective communication is an important quality of a good manager. The Analytical Writing Assessment, or essay component, of the GMAT was designed to help admissions officers identify those applicants who have effective writing skills.

The Analytical Writing portion of the test requires essay responses on two topics (called "prompts"). Each response must be written within a 30-minute time limit. One of the prompts will be an "issue" topic and the other an "argument" topic. Given the severe time constraints, the Analytical Writing Assessment is obviously a fairly crude measure, and schools are cautioned against placing too much emphasis on small differences in scores. Admissions officers are reminded that candidate responses are at best first drafts written under difficult circumstances.

Since the GMAT is now given on computer, you will have to "keyboard" your essay or type it in. Is that a big deal? Apparently not. The studies done by the GMAT test-makers indicate that the results are pretty much the same regardless of whether a candidate hand writes or types the essay. If anything, for people with handwriting that is difficult to read, the computer-based version of the AWA may be an advantage.

HOW IS THE ASSESSMENT GRADED?

Both essays are graded according to the same criteria, and it is a good idea to know what counts and what does not count in the grading system. Essays are graded on content, organization, and mechanics. Contrast the following descriptions of an "Outstanding" essay (a "6" on the scale of 0 to 6) and a "Seriously Flawed" essay (a "2"):

Outstanding (6)

- Explores ideas and develops a position on the issue with insightful reasons and/or persuasive examples
- Is clearly well organized
- Demonstrates superior facility with the conventions of Standard Written English but may have minor flaws

Seriously Flawed (2)

- Is unclear or seriously limited in presenting or developing a position on the issue and provides few, if any, relevant examples
- Is disorganized
- Contains numerous errors in grammar, usage, or mechanics that interfere with meaning

On page 301 are the directions for the Analytical Writing Assessment "Analysis of an Issue" and "Analysis of an Argument" essays, along with some sample prompts.

Anatomy of the Analytical Writing Assessment

ANALYSIS OF AN ISSUE

Directions: In this part, you will be required to analyze the issue outlined below and explain your views on it. The "question" has no "correct" or "incorrect" answer. Rather, you should take into account a variety of perspectives as you develop your theme.

Read the statement and the explanation following it. Type in your response using the keyboard.

> "Every business decision is based on the profit motive. Even charity has as its ultimate goal generating good will for the person or group doing the charity."

Assuming that the term "business decision" is broad enough to include the decisions of any decision-making authority—an individual, a family, a small business, or a large corporation—explain whether you think that this point is valid. In your discussion, use reasons and/or examples drawn from your own experiences, observations, or readings.

ANALYSIS OF AN ARGUMENT

Directions: In this part, you are asked to write an analysis of an argument. You are not asked to present your personal views on the topic. Rather, you are asked to evaluate the argument by identifying any questionable assumptions that underlie the reasoning, possible alternative explanations and/or counter- examples that might weaken its conclusion, or what type of evidence might be useful in attacking or defending the argument.

Read the argument and the instructions that follow it. Type in your response using the keyboard.

The following appeared in the editorial section of a newspaper.

> Most public schools recess for two to three months during the summer. The traditional summer vacation was first adopted to permit schoolchildren to help raise and harvest crops, but schoolchildren no longer engage in these activities. Ironically, then, a policy that was intended to result in greater productivity now results in wasted time.

Discuss how well reasoned you think this argument is. In your discussion analyze the logic of the argument and the evidence offered in support of the conclusion. You can also discuss what additional evidence, if any, would be useful in strengthening or weakening the argument.

HOW DO YOU HANDLE THE ANALYTICAL WRITING ASSESSMENT?

Here is a simple, four-step plan to help you succeed on the GMAT Analytical Writing Assessment.

Analytical Writing Assessment: Getting It Right

1. Read the topic and decide what position you want to take.
2. Outline your thinking using the scratch paper that is provided.
3. Type your essay.
4. Proofread your essay.

WHAT SMART TEST-TAKERS KNOW

What You Should NOT Do

Given the objective of the exercise and the limitations of the Analytical Writing Assessment, there are several things you should not do.

YOU SHOULD NEVER WRITE ON A TOPIC OTHER THAN THE ONES YOU ARE GIVEN. The directions are very clear on this score, and the readers are specifically instructed to assign a grade of zero (the lowest possible) to any response that is written on a different topic.

The prompts are specifically designed to provide candidates with an opportunity to write. To work, then, they must be topics that are accessible to everyone. For this reason, the topics do not presuppose any special knowledge.

YOU SHOULD NOT TRY TO MAKE THE SUBJECT OF THE PROMPT MORE IMPORTANT THAN IT IS. Many candidates imagine that their essays will be considerably improved if they make clear to the reader that they feel passionately about the topic or that they consider the topic to be of very grave concern. Unfortunately, extreme passion or grave concern is usually simply out of place. For example, suppose you began your response to the argument topic on school recess as follows:

> Requiring schoolchildren to remain in classes during the summer would prevent them from learning about the beauties of nature. Year-round schooling would be a violation of a child's fundamental Constitutional right to life, liberty, and the pursuit of happiness.

Well, perhaps. But an argument to make those conclusions persuasive is surely going to require more time and space than is available for the response to the prompt.

YOU SHOULD NOT TRY TO DO TOO MUCH.

The severe time constraints have yet another consequence for your approach to this part of the test. A half hour is not a lot of time to read a prompt, generate a few ideas, organize those ideas into a coherent essay (perhaps jotting down a brief outline), write three or four paragraphs, and proofread and correct the final product.

In this case, more is not necessarily better. It is preferable to write a shorter essay that is complete than to aspire to write a magnum opus only to run out of time with the project only started.

What You Should Do

The content of your essays will obviously depend on the wording of the prompts. However, rest assured that the topics do not presuppose that you have any special knowledge. In fact, the topics themselves are designed to suggest ideas that you can include in your essay.

YOU SHOULD USE THE PROMPT TO GENERATE IDEAS FOR YOUR ESSAY.

You can find several ideas that can be included in an essay in the language of the prompt itself. For example, you might approach the "issue" topic above by considering the issue from the perspective of a large corporation, then from the perspective of a small business, and then from the perspective of an individual. You might theorize that the larger and more impersonal the organization, the less likely it is to act for altruistic reasons.

YOU SHOULD ILLUSTRATE YOUR IDEAS WITH EXAMPLES.

Another way of generating ideas for your essay is to think about the topic concretely rather than abstractly. In fact, "use of examples" figures prominently in the scoring analysis set out above. An important feature of the "outstanding" essay is the use of "persuasive examples," and a noticeable weakness of the "seriously flawed" essay is the use of "few, if any, relevant examples."

Consider a point that you might make about the "argument" topic above:

> Summer vacations now serve a useful even though different function. They provide time for families to spend together that they otherwise wouldn't have.

The point has considerable intuitive plausibility just as written, but it could be strengthened by adding a "for instance":

> Summer vacations now serve a useful even though different function. They provide time for families to spend together that they otherwise wouldn't have. This is especially true for people working in essential services such as firefighters, police officers, and hospital workers. Only a handful of such workers can be released from their duties at any given time. If the only

> scheduled breaks in the school year were those for holidays such as Thanksgiving or the New Year, then many such families would hardly ever have a chance to be together.

YOU SHOULD ORGANIZE THE ESSAY BY USING THE "THREE MAIN POINTS" APPROACH.

This "three main points" approach results in a four- or five-paragraph essay:

Paragraph 1: Introduction.

Paragraph 2: First point.

Paragraph 3: Second point.

Paragraph 4: Third point.

Paragraph 5: Conclusion. (Optional)

Using this template, an adequate or even strong essay naturally emerges almost without effort. For example:

> The argument regarding summer vacation is flawed in three respects. First, it assumes that schoolchildren do not work during the summer. Second, it presupposes that schoolchildren do not otherwise use their summer vacation productively. Finally, it suggests that year-round schooling would be efficient.
>
> First, the argument assumes, without proof, that schoolchildren no longer work during the summer vacation. While it may be true that schoolchildren are no longer routinely employed in agriculture, it is surely wrong that schoolchildren as a rule do not work. Many older children fill seasonal positions, such as lifeguards.
>
> Second, the argument presupposes that schoolchildren who do not work are not using their time productively. But working at a job is not the only way of using time productively. For example, summer travel or reading would hardly be a waste of time.
>
> Finally, the argument implies that year-round schooling would be effective, but this assumes that schoolchildren are more like adults who don't need a fairly long break in their routine. Research into the question might very well show that a two- to three-month break actually makes the educational process more efficient.
>
> So the difficulty with the argument, as presented, is that it makes several unwarranted assumptions. For that reason, the conclusion does not follow logically from the premises.

YOU SHOULD FOLLOW THE RULES OF STANDARD WRITTEN ENGLISH.

According to the analysis of the grading scheme provided above, a good essay may have minor flaws but in general will observe the conventions of standard written English. Now, as luck would have it, you have already studied materials as part of your review for the GMAT that will help you in this regard: sentence correction. Sentence correction is the question type that has long been used by the GMAT to test writing skills, but sentence correction is really an editing exercise rather than a writing exercise. This is one reason for the addition of the Analytical Writing Assessment. Still, the chapter on sentence correction will help you make sure that you have correctly executed your essay.

YOU SHOULD PROOFREAD YOUR ESSAY USING A CHECKLIST OF COMMON ERRORS.

As you proofread your essay, consciously ask the following questions:

- Does each sentence have a main verb?
- Does the verb agree with its subject?
- Does each pronoun have a referent (antecedent)?
- Are all of the elements of each series presented in the same form? (Are the elements parallel?)
- Does each sentence say what it means to say? (Have you avoided misplaced modifiers and faulty comparisons?)
- Is each sentence properly organized and punctuated? (Simpler sentence structures are less likely to result in errors than complex ones.)

If the issues raised by the questions in this list are not clear to you, be sure to review the chapter on sentence correction.

SUMMING IT UP:

What You Need to Know About the Analytical Writing Assessment

Review this page the night before you take the GMAT. It will help you do well on the Analytical Writing Assessment.

- The Analytical Writing Assessment requires essay responses to two topics ("prompts"): an "issue" topic and an "argument" topic.
- Essays are graded on a scale of 0 to 6 for content, organization, and mechanics.
- These steps can help you handle the Analytical Writing Assessment:
    1. Read the topic and decide what position you want to take.
    2. Outline your thinking using the scratch paper that is provided.
    3. Type your essay.
    4. Proofread your essay.
- You should always write on the given topic.
- You should illustrate your ideas with examples.
- You should organize each essay by using the "three main points" approach.

PART VI

FIVE PRACTICE TESTS

Practice Test 1

ANALYTICAL WRITING ASSESSMENT

I. Analysis of an Issue

Time—30 Minutes

Directions: In this section you will have 30 minutes to analyze and explain your views on the topic presented below. Read the statement and directions carefully. An essay on a topic other than the one assigned will automatically be assigned a grade of 0.

Note: On the CAT version, you will keyboard your essay. For this exercise, allow yourself three sides of regular $8\frac{1}{2} \times 11$- inch paper for each essay response.

> People who live in the suburbs but make a daily commute into a central city to their places of employment often express wonder at how people are able to reside in the central city. The suburbanites mention the seemingly higher crime rate of the central city and the cramped living quarters. On the other hand, people who live and work in the central city say that they prefer their arrangement because they avoid the necessity of a lengthy commute and have readily available a variety of cultural amenities such as theaters and restaurants that suburbanites do not.

Which position do you find more compelling? Explain your position using reasons and/or examples drawn from your personal experience, observations, or readings.

II. Analysis of an Argument
Time—30 Minutes

Directions: In this section you will have 30 minutes to write a critique of the argument presented below. Read the argument and directions carefully. Write only on the topic given. An essay on a topic other than the one assigned will automatically be assigned a grade of 0.

Note: On the CAT version, you will keyboard your essay. For this exercise, allow yourself three sides of regular $8\frac{1}{2} \times 11$- inch paper for each essay response.

> At present, water usage in the city is metered, and property owners are billed quarterly according to usage. This system, however, requires the use of meter readers who must check each meter on a quarterly basis. If property owners were billed on the basis of "frontage," that is, according to the size of their property, bills could be generated automatically and the cost of the meter readers could be saved.

How persuasive do you find this argument? Explain your point of view by analyzing the line of reasoning and the use of evidence in the argument. Discuss also what, if anything, would make the argument more persuasive or would help you better to evaluate its conclusion.

VERBAL SECTION

41 Questions • 75 Minutes

Directions: For each of the following questions, choose the correct answer. To simulate the experience of taking the CAT, answer each question in order. Do not skip any questions, and do not go back to any questions you have already answered.

For Sentence Correction questions: In questions of this type, either part or all of a sentence is underlined. The sentence is followed by five ways of writing the underlined part. Choice (A) repeats the original; the other answer choices vary. If you think that the original phrasing is the best, choose (A). If you think one of the other answer choices is the best, select that choice.

Sentence Correction questions test your ability to recognize correct and effective expression. Follow the requirements of Standard Written English: grammar, choice of words, and sentence construction. Choose the answer that results in the clearest, most exact sentence, but does not change the meaning of the original sentence.

practice test

Example:

Q The possibility of massive earthquakes <u>are regarded by most area residents with</u> a mixture of skepticism and caution.

(A) are regarded by most area residents with
(B) is regarded by most area residents with
(C) is regarded by most area residents as
(D) is mostly regarded by area residents with
(E) by most area residents is regarded with

A The correct answer is (C).

For Critical Reasoning questions: Questions of this type ask you to analyze and evaluate the reasoning in short paragraphs or passages. For some questions, all of the answer choices may conceivably be answers to the question asked. You should select the *best* answer to the question, that is, an answer that does not require you to make assumptions that violate common-sense standards by being implausible, redundant, irrelevant, or inconsistent.

Example:

Q In an extensive study of the reading habits of magazine subscribers, it was found that an average of between four and five people actually read each copy of the most popular weekly news magazine. On this basis, we estimate that the 12,000 copies of *Poets and Poetry* that are sold each month are actually read by 48,000 to 60,000 people.

The estimate above assumes that

(A) individual magazine readers generally enjoy more than one type of magazine
(B) most of the readers of *Poets and Poetry* subscribe to the magazine
(C) the ratio of readers to copies is the same for *Poets and Poetry* as for the weekly news magazine
(D) the number of readers of the weekly news magazine is similar to the number of readers of *Poets and Poetry*
(E) most readers enjoy sharing copies of their favorite magazines with friends and family members

A The correct answer is (C).

For Reading Comprehension questions: Each passage is followed by questions or incomplete statements about the passage. Each statement or question is followed by lettered words or expressions. Select the word or expression that most satisfactorily completes each statement or answers each question in accordance with the meaning of the passage.

1. During the summer of 1981, when it looked like parts of New York and New Jersey were going to run short of water, many businesses and homes were affected by the stringent restrictions on the use of water.
   (A) it looked like parts of New York and New Jersey were going to run
   (B) it looked as if parts of New York and New Jersey would have run
   (C) it appeared that parts of New York and New Jersey would run
   (D) appearances were that parts of New York and New Jersey would run
   (E) it was the appearance that parts of New York and New Jersey would be running

2. The books of W.E.B. DuBois before World War I constituted as fundamental a challenge to the accepted ideas of race relations that, two generations later, will be true of the writings of the radical writers of the 1960s.
   (A) that, two generations later, will be true of
   (B) that, two generations later, would be true of
   (C) as, two generations later, would be true of
   (D) as, two generations later, would
   (E) just in the way that, two generations later, did

3. For the reason that gasoline was relatively cheap and twenty-five cents per gallon in the 1960s, the average American came to view unfettered, inexpensive driving as a right rather than a lucky privilege.
   (A) For the reason that gasoline was relatively cheap and
   (B) Because gasoline was relatively cheap and
   (C) Due to the fact that gasoline was a relatively inexpensive
   (D) In that gasoline was a relatively inexpensive
   (E) Because gasoline was a relatively cheap

QUESTIONS 4 AND 5

On his first trip to the People's Republic of China, a young U.S. diplomat of very subordinate rank embarrassed himself by asking a Chinese official how it was that Orientals managed to be so inscrutable. The Chinese official smiled and then gently responded that he preferred to think of the inscrutability of his race in terms of a want of perspicacity in Occidentals.

4. Which of the following best describes the point of the comment made by the Chinese official?
   (A) It is not merely the Chinese, but all Oriental people who are inscrutable.
   (B) Most Americans fail to understand Chinese culture.
   (C) What one fails to perceive may be attributable to carelessness in observation rather than obscurity inherent in the object.
   (D) Since the resumption of diplomatic relations between the United States and communist China, many older Chinese civil servants have grown to distrust the Americans.
   (E) If the West and the East are ever to truly understand one another, there will have to be considerable cultural exchange between the two.

5. Which of the following best characterizes the attitude and response of the Chinese official?
   (A) Angry
   (B) Fearful
   (C) Emotional
   (D) Indifferent
   (E) Compassionate

6. The political masters of the health care system have not listened to professional health planners because it has not been profitable for them to do that thing.
   (A) has not been profitable for them to do that thing
   (B) has not been profitable for them to do so
   (C) has been unprofitable for them to do that thing
   (D) has been unprofitable for them to do so
   (E) doing so had not been profitable for them

7. People waste a surprising amount of money on gadgets and doodads that they hardly ever use. For example, my brother spent $25 on an electric ice-cream maker two years ago, but he has used it on only three occasions. Yet, he insists that regardless of the number of times he actually uses the ice-cream maker, the investment was a good one because ________.

   Which of the following best completes the thought of the paragraph?
   (A) the price of ice cream will go up in the future
   (B) he has purchased the ice-cream maker for the convenience of having it available if and when he needs it
   (C) in a society that is oriented toward consumer goods, one should take every opportunity to acquire things
   (D) today $25 is not worth what it was two years ago on account of the inflation rate
   (E) by using it so infrequently he has conserved a considerable amount of electrical energy

8. William Blake was once asked to interpret a particularly obscure passage in one of his poems. He responded, "When I wrote that verse, only God and I knew the meaning of that passage. Now, only God knows."

   What is the point of Blake's response?
   (A) God is infinitely wiser than human beings.
   (B) Most people are unable to understand poetry.
   (C) Poets rarely know the source of their own creative inspiration.
   (D) A great poem is inspired by the muse.
   (E) He has forgotten what he had originally meant by the verse.

9. Because of the efforts of Amory Lovins and other advocates of the "soft" path of solar energy, the economics of nuclear power are being more closely examined now than ever before.
   (A) being more closely examined now than ever before
   (B) being attacked more vigorously than ever before
   (C) open to closer examination than they ever were before
   (D) more closely examined than before
   (E) more examined than they ever were before now

practice test

10. Most bacterial populations grown in controlled conditions will quickly expand to the limit of the food supply, produced toxic waste products that inhibit further growth, and reached an equilibrium state within a relatively short time.

(A) produce toxic waste products that inhibit further growth, and reached an equilibrium state within a relatively short time

(B) will have produced toxic waste products that inhibit further growth and also will reach an equilibrium state within a relatively short time

(C) will then produce a toxic waste product that inhibits further growth and thus reached an equilibrium state in a very short time

(D) produce toxic waste products that inhibit further growth, and reach equilibrium

(E) produce toxic waste products that inhibit further growth, and reach an equilibrium state in a fairly prompt way

11. A little-known danger of potent hallucinogens such as lysergic acid diethylamide-25 is that not only is the user immediately disoriented, but also he will experience significant ego suppression for a period of three weeks as well.

(A) but also he will experience significant ego suppression for a period of three weeks as well

(B) but also he will experience significant ego suppression for a period of three weeks

(C) but also there will be a three-week period of ego suppression as well

(D) but the ego is suppressed for a period of three weeks as well

(E) but the user's ego is suppressed for a period of three weeks in addition

QUESTIONS 12–18

War has escaped the battlefield and now can, with modern guidance systems on missiles, touch virtually every square yard of the earth's surface. It no longer involves only the military profession, but engulfs also entire civilian populations. Nuclear weapons have made major war unthinkable. We are forced, however, to think about the unthinkable because a thermonuclear war could come by accident or miscalculation. We must accept the paradox of maintaining a capacity to fight such a war so that we will never have to do so.

War has also lost most of its utility in achieving the traditional goals of conflict. Control of territory carries with it the obligation to provide subject peoples certain administrative, health, education, and other social services; such obligations far outweigh the benefits of control. If the ruled population is ethnically or racially different from the rulers, tensions and chronic unrest often exist which further reduce the benefits and increase the costs of domination. Large populations no longer necessarily enhance state power and, in the absence of high levels of economic development, can impose severe burdens on food supply, jobs, and the broad range of services expected of modern governments. The noneconomic security reasons for the control of territory have been progressively undermined by the advances of modern technology. The benefits of forcing another nation to surrender its wealth are vastly outweighed by the benefits of persuading that nation to produce and exchange goods and services. In brief, imperialism no longer pays.

Making war has been one of the most persistent of human activities in the 80 centuries since men and women settled in cities and became thereby "civilized," but the modernization of the past 80 years has fundamentally changed the role and function of war. In pre-modernized societies, successful warfare brought significant material rewards, the most obvious of which were the stored wealth of the defeated. Equally important was human labor—control over people as slaves or levies for the victor's army—and the productive capacity of agricultural lands and mines. Successful warfare also produced psychic benefits. The removal or destruction of a threat brought a sense of security, and power gained over others created pride and national self-esteem. Warfare was also the most complex, broad-scale and demanding activity of pre-modernized people. The challenges of leading men into battle, organizing, moving and supporting armies, attracted the talents of the most vigorous, enterprising, intelligent and imaginative men in the society. "Warrior" and "statesman" were usually synonymous, and the military was one of the few professions in which an able, ambitious boy of humble origin could rise to the top. In the broader cultural context, war was accepted in the pre-modernized society as a part of the human condition, a mechanism of change, and an unavoidable, even noble, aspect of life. The excitement and drama of war made it a vital part of literature and legends.

12. The primary purpose of the passage is to

(A) theorize about the role of the warrior-statesman in pre-modernized society

(B) explain the effects of war on both modernized and pre-modernized societies

(C) contrast the value of war in a modernized society with its value in pre-modernized society

(D) discuss the political and economic circumstances which lead to war in pre-modernized societies

(E) examine the influence of the development of nuclear weapons on the possibility of war

13. According to the passage, leaders of pre-modernized society considered war to be

(A) a valid tool of national policy

(B) an immoral act of aggression

(C) economically wasteful and socially unfeasible

(D) restricted in scope to military participants

(E) necessary to spur development of unoccupied lands

14. The author most likely places the word "civilized" in quotation marks (line 45) in order to

(A) show dissatisfaction at not having found a better word

(B) acknowledge that the word was borrowed from another source

(C) express irony that war should be a part of civilization

(D) impress upon the reader the tragedy of war

(E) raise a question about the value of war in modernized society

15. The author mentions all of the following as possible reasons for going to war in a pre-modernized society EXCEPT

(A) possibility of material gain

(B) promoting deserving young men to higher positions

(C) potential for increasing the security of the nation

(D) desire to capture productive farming lands

(E) need for workers to fill certain jobs

16. The author is primarily concerned with discussing how

(A) political decisions are reached

(B) economic and social conditions have changed

(C) technology for making war has improved

(D) armed conflict has changed

(E) war lost its value as a policy tool

17. Which of the following best describes the tone of the passage?

(A) Outraged and indignant

(B) Scientific and detached

(C) Humorous and wry

(D) Fearful and alarmed

(E) Concerned and optimistic

18. With which of the following statements about a successfully completed program of nuclear disarmament would the author most likely agree?

(A) Without nuclear weapons, war in modernized society would have the same value it had in pre-modernized society.

(B) In the absence of the danger of nuclear war, national leaders could use powerful conventional weapons to make great gains from war.

(C) Eliminating nuclear weapons is likely to increase the danger of an all-out, worldwide military engagement.

(D) Even without the danger of a nuclear disaster, the costs of winning a war have made armed conflict on a large scale virtually obsolete.

(E) War is caused by aggressive instincts, so if nuclear weapons were no longer available, national leaders would use conventional weapons to reach the same end.

19. A recent survey by the economics department of an Ivy League university revealed that increases in the salaries of preachers are accompanied by increases in the nationwide average of rum consumption. From 1965 to 1970 preachers' salaries increased on the average of 15% and rum sales grew by 14.5%. From 1970 to 1975 average preachers' salaries rose by 17% and rum sales by 17.5%. From 1975 to 1980 rum sales expanded by only 8% and average preachers' salaries also grew by only 8%.

Which of the following is the most likely explanation for the findings cited in the paragraph?

(A) When preachers have more disposable income, they tend to allocate that extra money to alcohol.

(B) When preachers are paid more, they preach longer; and longer sermons tend to drive people to drink.

(C) Since there were more preachers in the country, there were also more people; and a larger population will consume greater quantities of liquor.

(D) The general standard of living increased from 1965 to 1980, which accounts for both the increase in rum consumption and preachers' average salaries.

(E) A consortium of rum importers carefully limited the increases in imports of rum during the test period cited.

20. Since all four-door automobiles I have repaired have eight-cylinder engines, all four-door automobiles must have eight-cylinder engines.

The author argues on the basis of

(A) special training

(B) generalization

(C) syllogism

(D) ambiguity

(E) deduction

21. Two women, one living in Los Angeles, the other living in New York City, carried on a lengthy correspondence by mail. The subject of the exchange was a dispute over certain personality traits of Winston Churchill. After some two dozen letters, the Los Angeles resident received the following note from her New York City correspondent: "It seems you were right all along. Yesterday I met someone who actually knew Sir Winston, and he confirmed your opinion."

The two women could have been arguing on the basis of all of the following EXCEPT

(A) published biographical information

(B) old news film footage

(C) direct personal acquaintance

(D) assumption

(E) third-party reports

22. Many people mistakenly believe that the body's nutritional requirements remain the same irregardless of the quantity and form of other nutrients ingested, physical activity, and emotional state.

(A) irregardless of the quantity and form of other nutrients ingested, physical activity, and emotional state

(B) irregardless of the other nutrients, physical activity, and emotional state

(C) regardless of the quantity of nutrients or physical exercise or emotional excitation

(D) regardless of the quantity or form of nutrients or physical exercise and emotional statement

(E) regardless of the quantity or form of other nutrients ingested, physical activity, or emotional state

23. Measuring the brain waves of human beings while they are engaged in different types of thought hopefully will enable neuropsychologists better to understand the relationship between the structures of the brain and thinking.

(A) hopefully will enable

(B) hopefully might enable

(C) will, it is hoped, enable

(D) would hopefully enable

(E) will, it is to be hoped by all, enable

24. It appears from a study of the detailed grammar of the Hopi Indians that their system of assigning tenses is very different from that of English or other European languages.

(A) It appears from a study of the detailed grammar of the Hopi Indians that their system

(B) It seems that study of the Hopi Indians indicates that their system

(C) A detailed study of the grammar of the Hopi Indian language indicates that its system

(D) Detailed study of Hopi Indians reveals that their system

(E) The Hopi Indians have a system

25. The protection of the right of property by the Constitution is tenuous at best. It is true that the Fifth Amendment states that the government may not take private property for public use without compensation, but it is the government that defines private property.

Which of the following is most likely the point the author is leading up to?

(A) Individual rights that are protected by the Supreme Court are secure against government encroachment.

(B) Private property is neither more nor less than that which the government says is private property.

(C) The government has no authority to deprive an individual of his liberty.

(D) No government that acts arbitrarily can be justified.

(E) The keystone of American democracy is the Constitution.

practice test

26. *Daily Post* newspaper reporter Roger Nightengale let it be known that Andrea Johnson, the key figure in his award-winning series of articles on prostitution and drug abuse, was a composite of many persons and not a single, real person, and so he was the subject of much criticism by fellow journalists for having failed to disclose that information when the articles were first published. But these were the same critics who voted Nightengale a prize for his magazine serial *General,* which was a much dramatized and fictionalized account of a Korean War military leader whose character was obviously patterned closely after that of Douglas MacArthur.

In which of the following ways might the critics mentioned in the paragraph argue that they were NOT inconsistent in their treatment of Nightengale's works?

(A) Fictionalization is an accepted journalistic technique for reporting on sensitive subject matter such as prostitution.

(B) Critic disapproval is one of the most important ways members of the writing community have for ensuring that reporting is accurate and to the point.

(C) Newspaper reporters usually promise confidentiality to their sources and have an obligation to protect their identities.

(D) There is a critical difference between dramatizing events in a piece of fiction and presenting distortions of the truth as actual fact.

(E) Well-known personalities are public figures whose personal lives are acceptable material for journalistic investigations.

27. Why pay outrageously high prices for imported sparkling water when there is now an inexpensive water carbonated and bottled here in the United States at its source—Cold Springs, Vermont. Neither you nor your guests will taste the difference, but if you would be embarrassed if it were learned that you were serving a domestic sparkling water, then serve Cold Springs Water—but serve it in a leaded crystal decanter.

The advertisement rests on which of the following assumptions?

(A) It is not difficult to distinguish Cold Springs Water from imported competitors on the basis of taste.

(B) Most sparkling waters are bottled at the source, but additional carbonation is added to make them more active.

(C) Import restrictions and customs duties that are passed on to consumers artificially inflate the price of imported waters.

(D) Sparkling waters taste best when they are decanted from their bottles into another container for service.

(E) Some people may purchase an imported sparkling water over a domestic one as a status symbol.

QUESTIONS 28–34

Until Josquin des Prez, 1440–1521, Western music was liturgical, designed as an accompaniment to worship. Like the intricately carved gargoyles perched atop medieval cathedrals beyond sight of any human, music was composed to please God before anybody else; its dominant theme was reverence. Emotion was there, but it was the grief of Mary standing at the foot of the Cross, the joy of the faithful hailing Christ's resurrection. Even the secular music of the Middle Ages was tied to predetermined patterns that sometimes seemed to stand in the way of individual expression.

While keeping one foot firmly planted in the divine world, Josquin stepped with the other into the human. He scored magnificent masses, but also newly expressive motets such as the lament of David over his son Absalom or the "Deploration d'Ockeghem," a dirge on the death of Ockeghem, the greatest master before Josquin, a motet written all in black notes, and one of the most profoundly moving scores of the Renaissance. Josquin was the first composer to set psalms to music. But alongside *Benedicite omnia opera Domini Domino* ("Bless the Lord, all ye works of the Lord") he put *El Grillo* ("The cricket is a good singer who manages long poems") and *Allegez moy* ("Solace me, sweet pleasant brunette"). Josquin was praised by Martin Luther, for his music blends respect for tradition with a rebel's willingness to risk the horizon. What Galileo was to science, Josquin was to music. While preserving their allegiance to God, both asserted a new importance for man.

Why then should Josquin languish in relative obscurity? The answer has to do with the separation of concept from performance in music. In fine art, concept and performance are one; both the art lover and the art historian have thousands of years of paintings, drawings and sculptures to study and enjoy. Similarly with literature: Poetry, fiction, drama, and criticism survive on the printed page or in manuscript for judgment and admiration by succeeding generations. But musical notation on a page is not art, no matter how lofty or excellent the composer's conception; it is, crudely put, a set of directions for producing art. Being highly symbolic, musical notation requires training before it can even be read, let alone performed. Moreover, because the musical conventions of other days are not ours, translation of a Renaissance score into modern notation brings difficulties of its own. For example, the Renaissance notation of Josquin's day did not designate the tempo at which the music should be played or sung. It did not indicate all flats or sharps; these were sounded in accordance with musicianly rules, which were capable of transforming major to minor, minor to major, diatonic to chromatic sound, and thus affect melody, harmony, and musical expression. A Renaissance composition might include several parts—but it did not indicate which were to be sung, which to be played, nor even whether instruments were to be used at all.

Thus, Renaissance notation permits of several interpretations and an imaginative musician may give an interpretation that is a revelation. But no matter how imaginative, few modern musicians can offer any interpretation of Renaissance music. The public for it is small, limiting the number of musicians who can afford to learn, rehearse, and perform it. Most of those who attempt it at all are students organized in *collegia musica* whose memberships have a distressing habit of changing every semester, thus preventing directors from maintaining the year-in, year-out continuity required to achieve excellence of performance. Finally, the instruments used in Renaissance times—drummhorns, recorders, rauschpfeifen, shawms, sackbuts, organettos—must be specially procured.

28. The primary purpose of the passage is to

(A) introduce the reader to Josquin and account for his relative obscurity

(B) describe the main features of medieval music and show how Josquin changed them

(C) place Josquin's music in an historical context and show its influence on later composers

(D) enumerate the features of Josquin's music and supply critical commentary

(E) praise the music of Josquin and interest the reader in further study of medieval music

29. The passage contains information that would help answer all of the following questions EXCEPT

(A) What are the titles of some of Josquin's secular compositions?

(B) What are the names of some Renaissance musical instruments?

(C) Who was the greatest composer before Josquin?

(D) Where might it be possible to hear Renaissance music performed?

(E) What are the names of some of Josquin's most famous students?

30. The passage implies that all of the following are characteristics of modern musical notation EXCEPT

(A) The tempo at which a composition is to be played is indicated in the notation.

(B) Whether a note is a sharp or a flat is indicated in the notation.

(C) The notation indicates which parts of the music are to be played by which instruments.

(D) Whether a piece is in a major or minor key is clearly indicated.

(E) The notation leaves no room for interpretation by the musician.

31. The author would most likely agree with which of the following statements?

(A) Music is a more perfect art form than painting or sculpture.

(B) Music can be said to exist only when it is being performed.

(C) Josquin was the greatest composer of the Middle Ages.

(D) Renaissance music is superior to music produced in modern times.

(E) Most people dislike Josquin because they do not understand his music.

32. The passage leads most logically to a proposal to

(A) establish more collegia musica

(B) study Josquin's compositional techniques in greater detail

(C) include Renaissance music in college studies

(D) provide funds for musicians to study and play Josquin

(E) translate Josquin's music into modern notation

33. The author cites all of the following as reasons for Josquin's relative obscurity EXCEPT

(A) the difficulty one encounters in attempting to read his musical notation

(B) the inability of modern musicians to play instruments of the Renaissance

(C) the difficulty of procuring unusual instruments needed to play the music

(D) the lack of public interest in Renaissance music

(E) problems in finding funding for the study of Renaissance music

34. The author's attitude toward Galileo (lines 37–38) can best be described as

(A) admiring

(B) critical

(C) accepting

(D) analytical

(E) noncommittal

35. Choose the best completion of the following paragraph.

Parochial education serves the dual functions of education and religious instruction, and church leaders are justifiably concerned to impart important religious values regarding relationships between the sexes. Thus, when the administrators of a parochial school system segregate boys and girls in separate institutions, they believe they are helping to keep the children pure by removing them from a source of temptation. If the administrators realized, however, that children would be more likely to develop the very attitudes they seek to engender in the company of the opposite sex, they would ________.

(A) put an end to all parochial education

(B) no longer insist upon separate schools for boys and girls

(C) abolish all racial discrimination in the religious schools

(D) stop teaching foolish religious tripe, and concentrate instead on secular educational programs

(E) reinforce their policies of isolating the sexes in separate programs

36. Professor Branch, who is chair of the sociology department, claims she saw a flying saucer the other night. But since she is a sociologist instead of a physicist, she cannot possibly be acquainted with the most recent writings of our finest scientists that tend to discount such sightings, so we can conclude her report is unreliable.

Which of the following would be the most appropriate criticism of the author's analysis?

(A) The author makes an irrelevant attack on Professor Branch's credentials.

(B) The author may not be a physicist, and therefore may not be familiar with the writings cited.

(C) Even the U.S. Air Force cannot explain all of the sightings of UFOs which are reported to them each year.

(D) A sociologist is sufficiently well educated to read and understand scientific literature in a field other than her own.

(E) It is impossible to get complete agreement on matters such as the possibility of life on other planets.

37. While everyone continues to hope for their survival, it is unlikely that the astronauts <u>could have made it back to the shelter before the power plant exploded</u>.

(A) could have made it back to the shelter before the power plant exploded

(B) were making it back to the shelter before the power plant exploded

(C) were able to make it back to the shelter before the power plant explodes

(D) have been able to make it back to the shelter before the power plant will explode

(E) could have made it to the shelter before the power plant explosion would have destroyed them

38. By the time peace and happiness <u>will have come to the planet, many lives will be wasted</u>.

(A) will have come to the planet, many lives will be wasted

(B) come to the planet, many lives will have been wasted

(C) will have come to the planet, many lives will have been wasted

(D) shall have come to the planet, many lives shall be wasted

(E) would have come to the planet, many lives would have been wasted

39. INQUISITOR: Are you in league with the devil?

VICTIM: Yes.

INQUISITOR: Then you must be lying, for those in league with the "Evil One" never tell the truth. So you are not in league with the devil.

The inquisitor's behavior can be described as paradoxical because he

(A) charged the victim with being in a league with the devil but later recanted

(B) relies on the victim's answer to reject the victim's response

(C) acts in accordance with religious law but accuses the victim of violating that law

(D) questions the victim about his ties with the devil but does not himself believe there is a devil

(E) asked the question in the first place, but then refused to accept the answer that the victim gave

practice test

40. "Whom did you pass on the road?" the King went on, holding his hand out to the messenger for some hay.

"Nobody," said the messenger.

"Quite right," said the King. "This young lady saw him, too. So, of course, Nobody walks slower than you."

The King's response shows that he believes

(A) the messenger is a very good messenger

(B) "Nobody" is a person who might be seen

(C) the young lady's eyesight is better than the messenger's

(D) the messenger is not telling him the truth

(E) there was no person actually seen by the messenger on the road

41. It could be argued that the most significant virtue of a popular democracy is not the right to participate in the selection of leaders, <u>but rather that it affirms</u> our importance in the scheme of things.

(A) but rather that it affirms

(B) but rather its affirmation of

(C) but rather it's affirmation in terms of

(D) but instead of that, its affirming that

(E) affirming rather

QUANTITATIVE SECTION

37 Questions • 75 Minutes

Directions: For each of the following questions, Choose the correct answer. To simulate the experience of taking the CAT, answer each question in order. Do not skip any questions, and do not go back to any questions you have already answered.
Numbers: All numbers used are real numbers.
Figures: The diagrams and figures that accompany these questions are for the purpose of providing information useful in answering the questions. Unless it is stated that a specific figure is not drawn to scale, the diagrams and figures are drawn as accurately as possible. All figures are in a plane unless otherwise indicated.
For Data Sufficiency questions: Each question is followed by two numbered facts. You are to determine whether the data given in the statements are sufficient for answering the question. Use the data given, plus your knowledge of math and everyday facts, to choose between the five possible answers.

Example:

Q Which copy machine, *X* or *Y*, makes copies at the faster rate?

(1) Machine *X* makes 90 copies per minute.

(2) In three minutes, *X* makes 1.5 more copies than *Y*.

(A) statement 1 alone is sufficient to answer the question, but statement 2 alone is not sufficient

(B) statement 2 alone is sufficient to answer the question, but statement 1 alone is not sufficient

(C) both statements together are needed to answer the question, but neither statement alone is sufficient

(D) either statement by itself is sufficient to answer the question

(E) not enough facts are given to answer the question

A **The correct answer is (B).**

1. If w, x, y, and z are real numbers, each of the following equals $w(x+y+z)$ EXCEPT

   (A) $wx + wy + wz$

   (B) $(x + y + z)w$

   (C) $wx + w(y + z)$

   (D) $3w + x + y + z$

   (E) $w(x + y) + wz$

2. A carpenter needs four boards, each 2 feet 10 inches long. If wood is sold only by the foot, what is the minimum length, in feet, of wood the carpenter must buy?

   (A) 9

   (B) 10

   (C) 11

   (D) 12

   (E) 13

3. What is the value of x?

(1) $x^2 + x = 2$

(2) $x^2 + 2x - 3 = 0$

(A) statement 1 alone is sufficient to answer the question, but statement 2 alone is not sufficient

(B) statement 2 alone is sufficient to answer the question, but statement 1 alone is not sufficient

(C) both statements together are needed to answer the question, but neither statement alone is sufficient

(D) either statement by itself is sufficient to answer the question

(E) not enough facts are given to answer the question

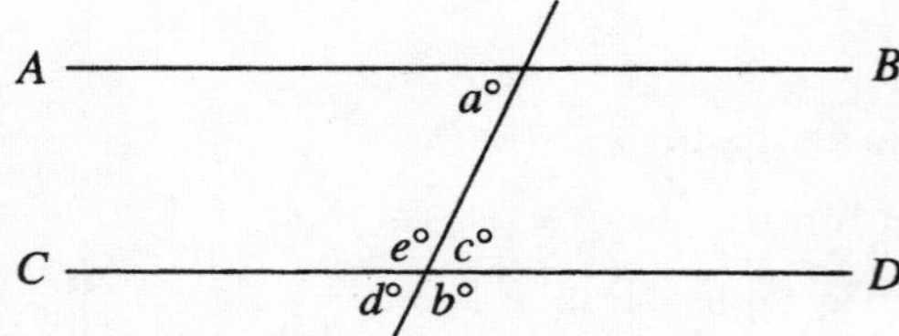

4. Is AB parallel to CD?

(1) $a + b = 180°$

(2) $a + c + d + e = 360°$

(A) statement 1 alone is sufficient to answer the question, but statement 2 alone is not sufficient

(B) statement 2 alone is sufficient to answer the question, but statement 1 alone is not sufficient

(C) both statements together are needed to answer the question, but neither statement alone is sufficient

(D) either statement by itself is sufficient to answer the question

(E) not enough facts are given to answer the question

5. A, B, and C are three consecutive even integers (not necessarily in order). Which has the greatest value?

(1) $A + B = C$

(2) C is a positive number.

(A) statement 1 alone is sufficient to answer the question, but statement 2 alone is not sufficient

(B) statement 2 alone is sufficient to answer the question, but statement 1 alone is not sufficient

(C) both statements together are needed to answer the question, but neither statement alone is sufficient

(D) either statement by itself is sufficient to answer the question

(E) not enough facts are given to answer the question

6. If x and y are non-negative, is $(x + y)$ greater than xy?

(1) $x = y$

(2) $x + y$ is greater than $x^2 + y^2$

(A) statement 1 alone is sufficient to answer the question, but statement 2 alone is not sufficient

(B) statement 2 alone is sufficient to answer the question, but statement 1 alone is not sufficient

(C) both statements together are needed to answer the question, but neither statement alone is sufficient

(D) either statement by itself is sufficient to answer the question

(E) not enough facts are given to answer the question

7. What is the weight of one of three identical bricks?
   (1) Two bricks weigh as much as three 6-lb. weights.
   (2) Three bricks weigh as much as one brick plus 18 lbs.
   (A) statement 1 alone is sufficient to answer the question, but statement 2 alone is not sufficient
   (B) statement 2 alone is sufficient to answer the question, but statement 1 alone is not sufficient
   (C) both statements together are needed to answer the question, but neither statement alone is sufficient
   (D) either statement by itself is sufficient to answer the question
   (E) not enough facts are given to answer the question

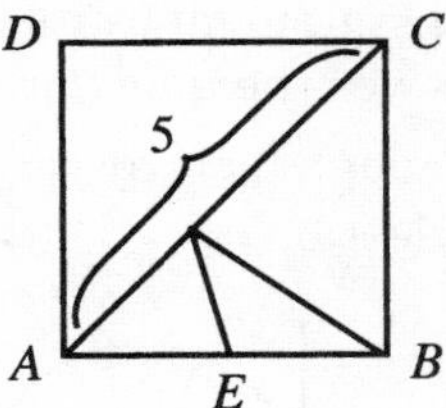

8. In the diagram, find the length of *AB.*
   (1) *ABCD* is a rectangle.
   (2) $AC - AE = AB + BE$
   (A) statement 1 alone is sufficient to answer the question, but statement 2 alone is not sufficient
   (B) statement 2 alone is sufficient to answer the question, but statement 1 alone is not sufficient
   (C) both statements together are needed to answer the question, but neither statement alone is sufficient
   (D) either statement by itself is sufficient- to answer the question
   (E) not enough facts are given to answer the question

9. If $2x + y = 7$ and $x - y = 2$, then $x + y =$
   (A) 6
   (B) 4
   (C) $\frac{3}{2}$
   (D) 0
   (E) –5

10. A girl rode her bicycle from home to school, a distance of 15 miles, at an average speed of 15 miles per hour. She returned home from school by walking at an average speed of 5 miles per hour. What was her average speed for the round trip if she took the same route in both directions?
    (A) 7.5 miles per hour
    (B) 10 miles per hour
    (C) 12.5 miles per hour
    (D) 13 miles per hour
    (E) 25 miles per hour

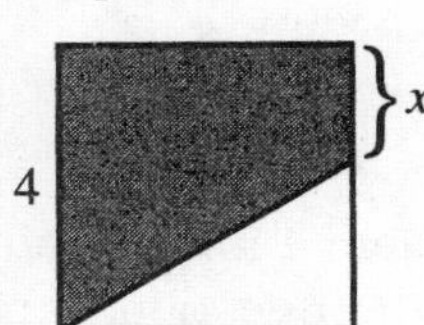

11. In the square above with side 4, the ratio $\frac{\text{area of shaded region}}{\text{area of unshaded region}} =$
    (A) $\frac{2+x}{4}$
    (B) $\frac{4+x}{8}$
    (C) 2
    (D) $\frac{4+x}{4-x}$
    (E) $2x$

12. Ned is two years older than Mike, who is twice as old as Linda. If the ages of the three total 27 years, how old is Mike?
    (A) 5 years
    (B) 8 years
    (C) 9 years
    (D) 10 years
    (E) 12 years

practice test

13. What is the side of a square if its area is $36x^2$?

(A) 9

(B) $9x$

(C) $6x^2$

(D) 6

(E) $6x$

14. If Susan has \$5 more than Tom, and if Tom has \$2 more than Ed, which of the following exchanges will ensure that each of the three has an equal amount of money?

(A) Susan must give Ed \$3 and Tom \$1.

(B) Tom must give Susan \$4 and Susan must give Ed \$5.

(C) Ed must give Susan \$1 and Susan must give Tom \$1.

(D) Susan must give Ed \$4 and Tom must give Ed \$5.

(E) Either Susan or Ed must give Tom \$7.

15. What is the value of p?

(1) $p = 4q$

(2) $q = 4p$

(A) statement 1 alone is sufficient to answer the question, but statement 2 alone is not sufficient

(B) statement 2 alone is sufficient to answer the question, but statement 1 alone is not sufficient

(C) both statements together are needed to answer the question, but neither statement alone is sufficient

(D) either statement by itself is sufficient to answer the question

(E) not enough facts are given to answer the question

16. A perfect number is one which is equal to the sum of all its positive factors that are less than the number itself. Which of the following is a perfect number?

(A) 1

(B) 4

(C) 6

(D) 8

(E) 10

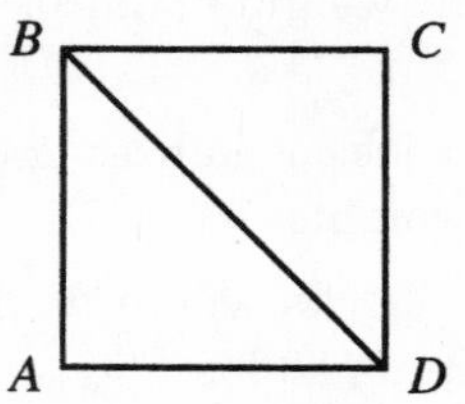

17. Is $ABCD$ a square?

(1) AB is parallel to CD.

(2) ΔBCD is an equilateral triangle.

(A) statement 1 alone is sufficient to answer the question, but statement 2 alone is not sufficient

(B) statement 2 alone is sufficient to answer the question, but statement 1 alone is not sufficient

(C) both statements together are needed to answer the question, but neither statement alone is sufficient

(D) either statement by itself is sufficient to answer the question

(E) not enough facts are given to answer the question

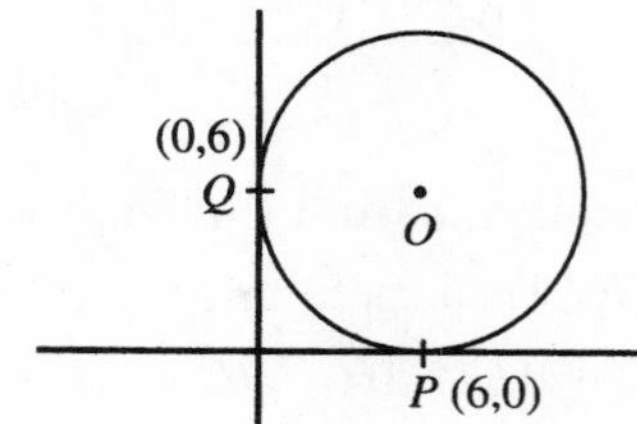

18. In the figure above, the coordinates of points P and Q are (6,0) and (0,6), respectively, What is the area of the circle O?

(A) 36π

(B) 12π

(C) 9π

(D) 6π

(E) 3π

19. A cylinder has a radius of 2 feet and a height of 5 feet. If it is already 40% filled with a liquid, how many more cubic feet of liquid must be added to completely fill it?

(A) 6π

(B) 8π

(C) 10π

(D) 12π

(E) 16π

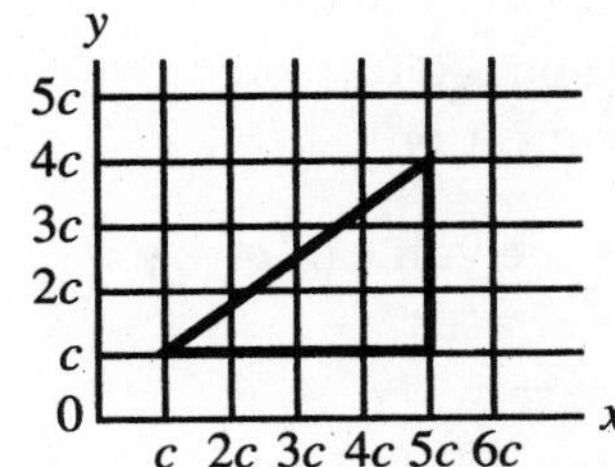

20. If the area of the above triangle is 54, then $c =$

(A) 3

(B) 6

(C) 10

(D) 12

(E) 15

21. In the same amount of time a new production assembly robot can assemble 8 times as many transmissions as an old assembly line. If the new robot can assemble x transmissions per hour, how many transmissions can the new robot and the old assembly line produce together in five days of round-the-clock production?

(A) $\frac{45x}{8}$

(B) $15x$

(C) $\frac{135x}{8}$

(D) $135x$

(E) $1080x$

22. A carpenter is building a frame for a wall painting. The painting is in the shape of a rectangle. If the sides of the rectangle are in the ratio of 3:2 and the shorter side has a length of 15 inches, how many inches of framing material does the carpenter need to frame the painting?

(A) 12

(B) $22\frac{1}{2}$

(C) $37\frac{1}{2}$

(D) 50

(E) 75

23. A marathon runner running along a prescribed route passes through neighborhoods *J, K, L,* and *M,* not necessarily in that order. How long does it take to run from *J* to *M*?

(1) The runner averages 8 miles per hour on the route from *J* to *M.*

(2) *M* is 4 miles from *K* and 12 miles from *L,* but *J* is 15 miles from *K.*

(A) statement 1 alone is sufficient to answer the question, but statement 2 alone is not sufficient

(B) statement 2 alone is sufficient to answer the question, but statement 1 alone is not sufficient

(C) both statements together are needed to answer the question, but neither statement alone is sufficient

(D) either statement by itself is sufficient to answer the question

(E) not enough facts are given to answer the question

practice test

24. Mary has qualified to become a police officer. Has Albert qualified to become a police officer?

(1) If Albert qualifies to become a police officer, then Mary will qualify to become a police officer.

(2) If Albert does not qualify to become a police officer, then Mary will not qualify to become a police officer.

(A) statement 1 alone is sufficient to answer the question, but statement 2 alone is not sufficient

(B) statement 2 alone is sufficient to answer the question, but statement 1 alone is not sufficient

(C) both statements together are needed to answer the question, but neither statement alone is sufficient

(D) either statement by itself is sufficient to answer the question

(E) not enough facts are given to answer the question

25. Is $\frac{x}{5}$ an integer?

(1) $\frac{x}{12{,}345}$ is an integer.

(2) $\frac{x}{336}$ is an integer.

(A) statement 1 alone is sufficient to answer the question, but statement 2 alone is not sufficient

(B) statement 2 alone is sufficient to answer the question, but statement 1 alone is not sufficient

(C) both statements together are needed to answer the question, but neither statement alone is sufficient

(D) either statement by itself is sufficient to answer the question

(E) not enough facts are given to answer the question

26. What is the volume of cube X?

(1) The diagonal of one of the faces of X is $\sqrt{6}$.

(2) The diagonal of the cube from the upper rear left corner to the lower front right corner is 3.

(A) statement 1 alone is sufficient to answer the question, but statement 2 alone is not sufficient

(B) statement 2 alone is sufficient to answer the question, but statement 1 alone is not sufficient

(C) both statements together are needed to answer the question, but neither statement alone is sufficient

(D) either statement by itself is sufficient to answer the question

(E) not enough facts are given to answer the question

27. What is the value of $p^8 - q^8$?

(1) $p^7 + q^7 = 127$

(2) $p - q = 0$

(A) statement 1 alone is sufficient to answer the question, but statement 2 alone is not sufficient

(B) statement 2 alone is sufficient to answer the question, but statement 1 alone is not sufficient

(C) both statements together are needed to answer the question, but neither statement alone is sufficient

(D) either statement by itself is sufficient to answer the question

(E) not enough facts are given to answer the question

28. Is x a negative number?

(1) $4x + 24 > 0$

(2) $4x - 24 < 0$

(A) statement 1 alone is sufficient to answer the question, but statement 2 alone is not sufficient

(B) statement 2 alone is sufficient to answer the question, but statement 1 alone is not sufficient

(C) both statements together are needed to answer the question, but neither statement alone is sufficient

(D) either statement by itself is sufficient to answer the question

(E) not enough facts are given to answer the question

29. In 1972, country X had a population of P and M cases of meningitis, for a per capita rate of meningitis of $\frac{M}{P}$. If, over the next ten years, the number of cases of meningitis decreased by 50% and the population of country X increased by 50%, what is the percentage change in the per capita rate of meningitis over the ten-year period?

(A) $33\frac{1}{3}$% increase

(B) no change

(C) $33\frac{1}{3}$% decrease

(D) 50% decrease

(E) $66\frac{2}{3}$% decrease

30. A slot machine in a Las Vegas casino has an average profit of \$600 for each 8-hour shift for the five days Sunday through Thursday, inclusive. If the average per-shift profit on Friday and Saturday is 25% greater than on the other days of the week and the slot machine is in operation every hour of every day, what is the total weekly profit that the casino makes from the slot machine?

(A) \$4500

(B) \$9000

(C) \$13,500

(D) \$15,500

(E) \$27,000

31. An apartment dweller pays \$125 per quarter for theft insurance. The policy will cover the loss of cash and valuables during the course of a year in excess of \$350 by reimbursing 75% of the value of the loss above \$350. During the course of a certain year, the apartment dweller suffers the theft of \$1250 in cash—but no other losses—by theft. What is the difference between the combined amount paid in theft insurance and unreimbursed losses for that year, and the amount that would have been lost if the apartment dweller had not had any insurance?

(A) \$125

(B) \$175

(C) \$225

(D) \$350

(E) \$675

32. If $x + 6 = 3$, then $x + 3 =$

(A) –9

(B) –3

(C) 0

(D) 3

(E) 9

33. A person is standing on a staircase. He walks down 4 steps, up 3 steps, down 6 steps, up 2 steps, up 9 steps, and down 2 steps. Where is he standing in relation to the step on which he started?

(A) 2 steps above

(B) 1 step above

(C) the same place

(D) 1 step below

(E) 4 steps above

34. A class begins at 1:21 P.M. and ends at 3:36 P.M. the same afternoon. How many minutes long was the class?

(A) 457

(B) 215

(C) 150

(D) 135

(E) 75

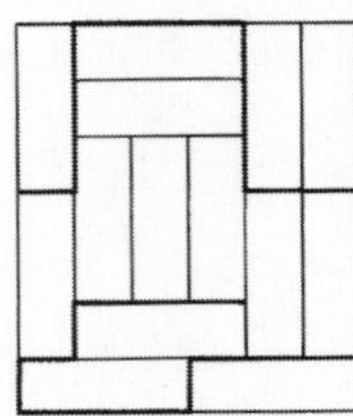

35. In the figure above, a rectangle is divided into smaller rectangles of the same shape and size. What is the area of the large rectangle?

(1) The length of the darkened path at the top of the diagram is 45.

(2) The length of the darkened path at the bottom of the diagram is 39.

(A) statement 1 alone is sufficient to answer the question, but statement 2 alone is not sufficient

(B) statement 2 alone is sufficient to answer the question, but statement 1 alone is not sufficient

(C) both statements together are needed to answer the question, but neither statement alone is sufficient

(D) either statement by itself is sufficient to answer the question

(E) not enough facts are given to answer the question

36. A sales representative will receive a 15% commission on a sale of $2800. If she has already received an advance of $150 on that commission, how much more is she due on the commission?

(A) $120

(B) $270

(C) $320

(D) $420

(E) $570

37. Does $(x + y)^2 + (x - y)^2$ equal 170?

(1) $x^2 + y^2 = 85$

(2) $x = 7$ and $y = 6$

(A) statement 1 alone is sufficient to answer the question, but statement 2 alone is not sufficient

(B) statement 2 alone is sufficient to answer the question, but statement 1 alone is not sufficient

(C) both statements together are needed to answer the question, but neither statement alone is sufficient

(D) either statement by itself is sufficient to answer the question

(E) not enough facts are given to answer the question

answers

ANSWER KEY AND EXPLANATIONS

Verbal Section

1. C	9. A	17. B	25. B	33. B	41. B
2. D	10. D	18. D	26. D	34. A	
3. E	11. B	19. D	27. E	35. B	
4. C	12. C	20. B	28. A	36. A	
5. E	13. A	21. C	29. E	37. A	
6. B	14. C	22. E	30. E	38. B	
7. B	15. B	23. C	31. B	39. B	
8. E	16. E	24. C	32. D	40. B	

1. **The correct answer is (C).** A future possibility of this sort is not expressed by "like." "Looked like" should not be used to mean "appeared." (B) errs in saying "would have" since it is a simple future idea not requiring that construction. (C) correctly uses "appeared" and "would" without the "have." (D) is not so much wrong as an unnecessary change in the sentence structure. (E) similarly is unnecessary and too wordy.

2. **The correct answer is (D).** The first part of the sentence sets up a comparison through the use of "as . . . as," and the original as well as (B) and (E) fail to carry it out. The "be true of " part of the sentence in (C) is not needed since it is implied in the "as . . . as" construction by the fact that DuBois's work was a fundamental challenge.

3. **The correct answer is (E).** The original fails because the "for the reason" construction is poor, and also the "cheap and" fails to make it clear that the price was cheap, which the sentence intends. (B) fails to correct the "and" and (C) and (D) fail to improve the "for the reason that."

4. **The correct answer is (C).** The point of the Chinese official's comment is that the Chinese may appear to some Westerners to be "inscrutable" because those Westerners simply do not pay very careful attention to what is directly before them. Thus, (C) is the best answer. (A) is misleading. The Chinese official refers to Occidentals in general, but he never mentions Orientals in general. Even so, (A) misses the main point of the anecdote. (B) is better than (A) since it is at least generally related to the point of the Chinese official, but the precise point is not that Americans (rather than Occidentals) fail to understand Chinese culture, but rather that they suffer from a more specific myopia: They find they are not able to penetrate the motivations of the Chinese. In any event, the point of the passage is not just that there is such a failure, but that such failure is attributable to the lack of insight of Westerners—not any real inscrutability of the Chinese. (E) mentions the problem of understanding, but the difficulty described in the passage is one way only. Nowhere is it suggested that the Chinese have difficulty in understanding Westerners. Finally, (D) would be correct only if the passage had contained some key word to qualify the official's response, such as *hesitatingly* or *cautiously*.

5. **The correct answer is (E).** Once it is seen that the passage is humorous, this question is fairly easy. The official

"smiles" and he "gently" responds. Further, the scenario is set by the first sentence: A *junior* official *embarrassed* himself. This shows the situation is uncomfortable for the American, but it is not a serious international incident. And the Chinese official's response is kind—not angry (A), not fearful (B), not indifferent (D). (C) requires an assumption of malice on the part of the Chinese official. By comparison, "compassion" better fits the description of the official's action—smiling and gentle.

6. **The correct answer is (B).** (A) fails because "that thing" refers to a diffuse idea in the sentence better expressed by (B). (C) and (D) allege that it was *un*profitable, while only a lack of profit was stated. (E) has an unneeded change of tense.

7. **The correct answer is (B).** Here the problem is to make sense out of the brother's claim that a device he rarely used and may never use again is still a good investment. It is not land, a work of art, or some similar thing, so it does not appear as though it will appreciate in value. The advantage, then, of owning must come from merely being able to possess it. Thus, (B), which cites the convenience of having the item to use if and when he should decide to do so, is best. (A) can be disregarded because the brother regards the investment as a good one *even if* he never again uses the device. To save money on ice cream, he would have to use it. (C) is highly suggestive—is the brother saying that it is a good idea to have things around in case one needs them? If so, then (C) sounds a bit like (B). But (C) is not nearly so direct as (B), and it requires some work to make it into (B). (D) is wrong because saving money by having purchased earlier would be worthwhile only if the item is actually needed. After all, a great deal you made by buying a ton of hay is not a great deal just because the price of hay is going up—you need an elephant (or a horse, or a plan to resell, or something) to make it worthwhile. Just buying hay because it's a "bargain" is no bargain at all. (E) is fairly silly. It is like saying: "The bad news is that someone stole your car; the good news is that the price of gasoline went up by 25¢ a gallon this morning." The point is that you will avoid some trivial injury or cost at the expense of something more serious.

8. **The correct answer is (E).** Again, the passage is somewhat lighthearted. The poet is saying that the poem is obscure: When he wrote it only he and the Almighty could understand it, and now (it is so difficult) even he has forgotten the point of the verse. (A) is somewhat attractive because the passage does state that God knows what humans do not. Of course, once one understands the point of the passage, (A) can be discarded. Even so, there is something about (A) that lets you know it is wrong—"infinitely." One might infer from the poet's comments that humans are not as wise as God, but it is not possible to conclude, on the basis of the one example, that God is infinitely wiser than humans. (B) is also attractive, for the poet is saying that it is difficult to understand this particular poem. But (B) is wrong because he is not saying that humans cannot understand poetry in general. (C) and (D) are distractions. They play on the term "God" in the paragraph. The poet cites God as the one who understands the verse—not the one who inspired it.

9. **The correct answer is (A).** The original is correct. (B) introduces the new idea of attack, which is not in the original. (C) and (D) lose the idea of "now." (E) trades the idea of the closeness of the examination for one of quantity, which changes the meaning.

10. **The correct answer is (D).** The three verbs in parallel are: "will expand," "(will) produce," and "(will) reached." This shows the original error. Also, the adverb "quickly" will carry forward to all three verbs. (B) fails for introducing a "have" for "produced." (C) fails to correct the "reached" and adds a gratuitous "then." (E)'s addition of "fairly prompt way" is an error, for level of usage. (D) corrects the "reached" and drops the unneeded time of equilibrium, and the redundant "state."

11. **The correct answer is (B).** "Not only" requires "but also"; hence (D) and (E) fail. "Not only" already includes the idea of an additional item, so the "as well" of the original and (C) are wrong.

12. **The correct answer is (C).** This is a main idea question, and the task is to find a choice which expresses the main thesis of the passage without being too narrow or too broad. (A) is too narrow, since this is but a minor feature of the discussion. (E) can be eliminated on the same grounds, since the possibility of nuclear destruction is but one important difference between war in a modernized society and war in a pre-modernized society. (B) is an attractive choice, but it is not the main thesis of the passage. The author does indeed discuss some of the effects of war on both modernized and pre-modernized societies, but this discussion is subordinate to a larger goal: to show that because of changing circumstance (effects are different), the value of war has changed. (D) is incorrect because it misses this main point and because the author discusses more than just pre-modernized societies.

13. **The correct answer is (A).** The second paragraph describes the attitude of pre-modernized society toward war: accepted, even noble, necessary. Coupled with the goals of war in pre-modernized societies, described in the first paragraph, we can infer that leaders of pre-modernized society regarded war as a valid policy tool. On this ground we select (A), eliminating (B) and (C). As for (D), although this can be inferred to have been a feature of war in pre-modernized society, (D) is not responsive to the question: What did the leaders think of war, that is, what was their attitude? (E) can be eliminated on the same ground and on the further ground that "necessity" for war was not that described in (E).

14. **The correct answer is (C).** The author is discussing war, a seemingly uncivilized activity. Yet, the author argues that war, at least in pre-modernized times, was the necessary result of certain economic and social forces. The use of the term "civilized" is ironic. Under other circumstances, the explanations offered by (A) and (B) might be plausible, but there is nothing in this text to support either of those. (D), too, might under other circumstances be a reason for placing the word in quotation marks, but it does not appear that this author is attempting to affect the reader's emotions; the passage is too detached and scientific for that. Finally, (E) does articulate one of the author's objectives, but this is not the reason for putting the one word in quotations. The explanation for that is something more specific than an overall idea of the passage.

15. **The correct answer is (B).** This is an explicit idea question, and (A), (C), (D), and (E) are all mentioned at various points in the passage as reasons for going to war. (B), too, is mentioned, but it is mentioned as a feature of the military establishment in pre-modernized society—not as a reason for going to war.

16. **The correct answer is (E).** This is another main idea question, and (B), (C), and (D) can be eliminated as too narrow. It is true the author mentions that economic and social conditions, technology, and armed conflict have all changed, but

this is not the ultimate point to be proved. The author's main point is that *because* of such changes, the value of war has changed. (A) is only tangentially related to the text. Though we may learn a bit about how decisions are made, in part, this is not the main burden of the argument.

17. **The correct answer is (B).** We have already mentioned that the tone of the passage is neutral—scientific and detached. As for the remaining choices, (A) and (D) can be eliminated as overstatements. To be sure, the author seems to deplore the destruction which might result from a nuclear war, but that concern does not rise to the status of outrage, indignation, fear, or alarm. (E) is a closer call. While it is true that the author expresses concern about the ability of modernized society to survive war, and while there is arguably a hint of optimism or hope, it cannot be said that these are the *defining* features of the passage. A better description of the prevailing tone is offered by (B). As for (C), the one ironic reference ("civilized") does not make the entire passage humorous.

18. **The correct answer is (D).** This is an application question and we must take the information from the passage and apply it to a new situation. The author offers two reasons for the conclusion that war is no longer a viable policy tool: (1) the danger of world-wide destruction and (2) the costs after victory outweigh the benefits to be won. We can conclude that even in the absence of nuclear weapons, war will still lack its traditional value, as argued by the author in the fourth paragraph. Thus, we can eliminate (A) and (B) on the grounds that they are contradicted by the author's thinking. (E) can be eliminated for the same reason and because no such "instincts" are discussed in the text. A close look at (C) shows that it is not in agreement with the author's view, since the author believes that though nuclear weapons deter nuclear war, war is obsolete for other reasons as well.

19. **The correct answer is (D).** You must always be careful of naked correlations. Sufficient research would probably turn up some sort of correlation between the length of skirts and the number of potatoes produced by Idaho, but such a correlation is obviously worthless. Here, too, the two numbers are completely unrelated to one another at any concrete cause-and-effect level. What joins them is the very general movement of the economy. The standard of living increases; so, too, does the average salary of a preacher, the number of vacations taken by factory workers, the consumption of beef, the number of color televisions, and the consumption of rum. (D) correctly points out that these two are probably connected only this way. (A) is incorrect for it is inconceivable that preachers, a small portion of the population, could account for so large an increase in rum consumption. (B) is wildly implausible. (C), however, is more likely. It strives for that level of generality of correlation achieved by (D). The difficulty with (C) is that it focuses upon *total* preachers, not the *average* preacher; and the passage correlated not *total* income for preachers with rum consumption, but *average* income for preachers with consumption of rum. (E) might be arguable if only one period had been used, but the paragraph cites three different times during which this correlation took place.

20. **The correct answer is (B).** This is a relatively easy question. The argument is similar to "All observed instances of S are P; therefore, all S must be P." (All swans I have seen are white; therefore, all swans must be white.) There is little to suggest the author is a mechanic or a factory worker in an automobile plant; therefore, (A) is incorrect—and would be

so even if the author were an expert because the author does not argue using that expertise. A syllogism is a formal logical structure such as: "All *S* are *M*; all *M* are *P*; therefore, all *S* are *P*," and the argument about automobiles does not fit this structure—so (C) is wrong. By the same token, (E) is wrong since the author generalizes—the author does not deduce, as by logic, anything. Finally, (D) is incorrect because the argument is not ambiguous, and one could hardly argue on the basis of ambiguity anyway.

21. **The correct answer is (C).** The key phrase here—and the problem is really just a question of careful reading—is "who actually knew." This reveals that neither of the two knew the person whom they were discussing. There are many ways, however, of debating about the character of people with whom one is not directly acquainted. We often argue about the character of Napoleon or even fictional characters such as David Copperfield. When we do, we are arguing on the basis of indirect information. Perhaps we have read a biography of Napoleon (A), or maybe we have seen a news film of Churchill (B). We may have heard from a friend, or a friend of a friend, that so and so does such and such (E). Finally, sometimes we just make more or less educated guesses, (D). In any event, the two people described in the paragraph could have done all of these things. What they could not have done—since they finally resolved the problem by finding someone who actually knew Churchill—was to have argued on the basis of their own personal knowledge.

22. **The correct answer is (E).** "Irregardless" is not an English word, eliminating the original and (B). (C) and (D) carelessly drop the term "ingested," which changes the meaning. (E) also correctly uses "or" as a connector since the intended meaning of the sentence is to refer to these ideas severally and not as a single group.

23. **The correct answer is (C).** "Hopefully" is not acceptable in Standard Written English. The correct phrase is "it is hoped" as in (C). (E)'s phrase denies the fact of the hope expressed by the original sentence.

24. **The correct answer is (C).** There is a lack of coordination between the underlined part's reference to the system of the Hopis and the other part's reference to the system of certain languages. (C) corrects that error. In addition, it seems more likely that it is a detailed study that is at issue than a detailed grammar studied at some unknown depth.

25. **The correct answer is (B).** Here we have a question that asks us to draw a conclusion from a set of premises. The author points out that the Constitution provides that the government may not take private property. The irony, according to the author, is that government itself defines what it will classify as private property. We might draw an analogy to a sharing practice among children: You divide the cake and I will choose which piece I want. The idea behind this wisdom is that this ensures fairness to both parties. The author would say that the Constitution is set up so that the government not only divides (defines property), it chooses (takes what and when it wants). (A) is contradicted by this analysis. (C) is wide of the mark since the author is discussing property rather than liberty. While the two notions are closely connected in the Constitution, this connection is beyond the scope of this argument. (D) is also beyond the scope of the argument. It makes a broad and unqualified claim that is not supported by the text. (E) is really vacuous and, to the extent that we try to give it content, it must fail for the same reason as choice (A).

26. The correct answer is (D). The insight required to solve this problem is that the apparent contradiction can be resolved by observing that the two cases are essentially different. The one is supposed to be a factual story; the other is a fictional account. (B) misses the point of the problem: the task is to reconcile the seemingly conflicting positions of the critics, not to explain what role critics fill. (A), (C), and (E) are full of possibilities. For example, you might argue anyone of these points in defense of the journalist—but that's not what the question stem asks for. You're supposed to explain away the seeming inconsistency in the position of the critics. And in the testing environment, to the extent that you want to argue that one or more of these choices might help to make an argument to support (D), then you'd have to choose (D) as the better answer just because it makes the point most directly.

27. The correct answer is (E). The main point of the advertisement is that you should not hesitate to buy cold Springs Water, even though it is not imported. (A) would weaken the appeal of the ad: if your guests can taste the difference, then the subterfuge (even though introduced only as a dramatic device) would not be effective. As for (B), while it may be true that even "naturally carbonated" waters are further carbonated at the time of bottling, this idea is not relevant. (C) has some merit in the real world, but it is not an assumption of this speaker: why the imports are more costly is not relevant. And (D) is wrong because the subterfuge suggestion is not to be taken literally but only as a suggestion to make the point dramatically. (E) is an assumption of the argument—status counts.

28. The correct answer is (A). This is a main idea question. The passage actually makes two points: Who is Josquin, and why have we never heard of him? (A) correctly mentions both of these. (B) is incorrect for the main focus is not to describe medieval music at all. Rather, the author focuses on Josquin, a man of the Renaissance. (C) is incorrect because the author is more concerned to introduce the reader to Josquin than to place Josquin into a context. And in any event, though the author mentions some ways in which Josquin broke with his predecessors, this is not a discussion of his "influence on later composers." (D) is incorrect, for the enumeration of features of Josquin's music is incidental to the task of introducing the reader to Josquin. The author praises Josquin's music but does not offer critical commentary. Finally, (E) is incorrect because it fails to refer to the second major aspect of the passage: Why is Josquin not better known?

29. The correct answer is (E). This is an explicit idea question. (A) is answered in paragraph 2 ("Solace me, . . . "). (B) is answered in the final paragraph (sackbut). (C) is answered in the second paragraph (Ockeghem). An answer to (D) is suggested in the final paragraph. (E) must be the correct answer, since the author never makes reference to any students.

30. The correct answer is (E). This is an inference question. In the third paragraph the author lists certain difficulties in reading a Renaissance score: no tempo specified, missing flats and sharps, no instrument/voice indication, and no instruction as to whether a piece is written in a major or a minor key. Since these are regarded as deficiencies of Renaissance scoring, we may infer that modern music notation contains all of these. But (E) overstates the case. Although modern notation provides more guidance, the author does not say that it literally leaves no room for individual interpretation.

31. The correct answer is (B). This is an application question. The support for (B) is found in paragraph 3, where the author discusses the distinction between concept and performance. The author states that music does not exist as printed notes. The notation is just a set of instructions for producing music. So the author would agree with (B). As for (A), it is conceivable that the author might endorse this statement—though it is also possible that the author would reject it. It is clear, however, that as between the statement in (B) and that in (A) we can be sure that the author would endorse (B). So (B), rather than (A), must be correct. (C) is incorrect because Josquin belongs to the Renaissance, not the Middle Ages. (D) fails for the same reason that (A) fails. Finally, there is no support for the statement in (E).

32. **The correct answer is (D).** Here, too, we have an application question. There is some merit to each of the choices, but we are looking for the one answer that is most closely connected with the text. Since the author discusses the lack of funding as one important reason for Josquin's obscurity, an obscurity the author deplores, the argument might be used to support a proposal for funds to promote Josquin's music. That is (D). (A) is less clearly supported by the text. To the extent that it is read as a device to promote Josquin's music, it would be less effective than (D) since the author states that *collegia musica* have a high turnover of students. Establishing yet another one would not do as much to bring Josquin's music to more people as (D). As for (B) and (E), these do not tie in with the idea of publicizing Josquin's music. Finally, (C) has some plausibility, but (D) has a connection with the passage which (C) lacks.

33. **The correct answer is (B).** This is an explicit idea question. (C), (D), and (E) are mentioned in the final paragraph. (A) is mentioned in the third paragraph. (B) is never mentioned. The author states that musicians who read modern notation have difficulty reading Renaissance notation—not that these musicians lack talent.

34. **The correct answer is (A).** This is a tone question. The author compares Josquin to Galileo in order to praise Josquin. This must mean that the author has a very high opinion of Galileo. So (D) and (E) can be eliminated because they are merely neutral. (B) can be eliminated because of its negative connotations. And (C) can be eliminated as being lukewarm, when the author is clearly enthusiastic about Josquin and therefore Galileo as well.

35. **The correct answer is (B).** Careful reading of the paragraph shows that the author believes that the insistence on instruction in religious values is *justifiable;* the author disagrees, however, on the question of how best to inculcate those values. The author believes that the proper attitude toward relations between the sexes could best be learned by children in the company of the other sex. Thus, (E) is diametrically opposite to the policy the author would recommend. (A) and (D) must be wrong because the passage clearly indicates that the author supports parochial schools and the religious instruction they provide. (C) is a distraction. It plays on the association of segregation and racial discrimination. Racial segregation is not the only form of segregation. The word *segregation* means generally to separate or to keep separate.

36. **The correct answer is (A).** In this story, the identity of the person who reports the incident is irrelevant. So long as it is not someone with a special infirmity (very poor eyesight, for example) or poor credibility (an inveterate liar), the person is quite capable of reporting what she saw—or what she thought she saw. The most serious weakness of the analysis presented is that it attacks Professor Branch's credentials. To be sure, one

might want to question the accuracy of the report: At what time did it occur? What were the lighting conditions? Had the observer been drinking or smoking? But these can be asked independently of attacking the qualifications of the source. Thus, (D) must be wrong, for special credentials are just not needed in this case, so the wrong way to defend Professor Branch is to defend those. By the same token, it makes no sense to defend Branch by launching a counter-*ad hominem* attack on her attacker, so (B) is incorrect. (C) and (E) may or may not be true, but they are surely irrelevant to the question of whether this particular sighting is to be trusted.

37. **The correct answer is (A).** The original is correct. (B) changes the meaning to a discussion of what they were doing rather than one of their possible success. (C) and (D) change the time of the explosion for no good reason. (E) erroneously has both a "would" and a "could." One of these is sufficient to give the idea of uncertainty.

38. **The correct answer is (B).** The future perfect should be used to refer to an event between the present and some future reference point. In the original it refers to the future reference point, thus (A) is wrong. In (C) and (D) it is used for both the future reference point (time peace . . . comes) and the intermediate point (lives . . . wasted). This is wrong. The use of "shall" is without meaning here. (E) uses "would have," which introduces an uncertainty not present in the original. (B) does everything correctly.

39. **The correct answer is (B).** The inquisitor's behavior is paradoxical—that is, internally inconsistent or contradictory. The victim tells him that he is in league with the devil, so the inquisitor refuses to believe him because those in league with the devil never tell the truth. In other words, the inquisitor refuses to believe the victim because he accepts the testimony of the victim. Thus, (B) is correct. (A) is incorrect because the inquisitor does not *withdraw* anything he has said; in fact, he lets everything he has said stand, and that is how he manages to contradict himself. (E) is a bit more plausible, but it is incomplete. In a certain sense, the inquisitor does not accept the answer, but the real point of the passage is that his basis for *not* accepting the answer is that he *does* accept the answer: He believes the victim when he says he is in league with the devil. (C) and (D) find no support in the paragraph. Nothing suggests that the inquisitor is violating any religious law, and nothing indicates that the inquisitor does not himself believe in the devil.

40. **The correct answer is (B).** The key here is that the word "nobody" is used in a cleverly ambiguous way and, as many of you probably know, the "young lady" in the story is Lewis Carroll's Alice. This is fairly representative of his word play. (E) must be incorrect since it misses completely the little play on words: "I saw Nobody," encouraging a response such as "Oh, is he a handsome man?" (D) is beside the point, for the King is not interested in the messenger's veracity. He may be interested in his reliability (A); but, if anything, we should conclude the King finds the messenger unreliable since "nobody walks slower" than the messenger. (C) is wrong because the question is not a matter of eyesight. The King does not say, "If you had better eyes, you might have seen Nobody."

41. **The correct answer is (B).** Parallelism is the issue here. The parallel creating elements are "not . . . but rather" and the parts after those two must be similar in construction. After the "not" we have a noun, and that is what we should have after "but rather" as well. (E) drops the "but," and (C) and (D) add unneeded words.

ANSWER KEY AND EXPLANATIONS

Quantitative Section

1. D	8. B	15. C	22. E	29. E	36. B
2. D	9. B	16. C	23. E	30. C	37. D
3. C	10. A	17. B	24. B	31. B	
4. A	11. D	18. A	25. A	32. C	
5. C	12. D	19. D	26. D	33. A	
6. B	13. E	20. A	27. B	34. D	
7. D	14. A	21. D	28. E	35. D	

1. **The correct answer is (D).** By multiplying out the given expression, we learn $w(x + y + z) = wx + wy + wz$, which shows that (A) is an equivalent expression. Second, given that it does not matter in multiplication in which order the elements are listed (i.e., $2 \times 3 = 3 \times 2 = 6$), we can see that (B) is also an equivalent expression. From $wx + wy + wz$, we can factor the w's from the first two terms: $w(x + y) + wz$, which shows that (E) is an equivalent expression. Finally, we could also factor the w's from the last two terms: $wx + w(y+z)$, which shows that (C) is an equivalent expression. (D) is not, however, equivalent: $w + w + w + x + y + z$. The 3 should make you suspicious of (D).

2. **The correct answer is (D).** The problem requires you to find the amount of wood that is needed and then find the number of whole feet that will give you the wood that is needed. In this particular problem there is no question about trying to fit different lengths together, as there might be if, for instance, the wood were only available in 5-foot sections. To find the total wood needed, you must multiply 2 feet, 10 inches by 4. Two feet times 4 is 8 feet. Ten inches times 4 is 40 inches, which is between 3 feet (36 inches) and 4 feet (48 inches). There is no way to get 40 inches of wood out of 3 feet. You should round up, so that there is enough wood and the answer is thus 8 feet plus 4 feet = 12 feet.

3. **The correct answer is (C).** From equation (1), x may be either 1 or –2. From equation (2), x may be 1 or –3. Thus, if both are true, $x = 1$.

4. **The correct answer is (A).** $b = e$, $a + e = 180°$, which means is parallel to . Equation (2) shows us only that $a = b$, which makes the two lines parallel only where $a = b = 90°$.

5. **The correct answer is (C).** There are three possible combinations fulfilling (1): $-2 + (-4) = (-6)$; $-2 + 2 = 0$; and $2 + 4 = 6$. Of these, only the last satisfies property (2).

6. **The correct answer is (B).** (1) does not work by itself since $x = y = 0$ and $x = y = 1$ give different answers. (2) means that either x or y are both fractions between 0 and 1, since that is the only way squaring can reduce the result. Adding a fraction $(x + y)$ increases the result, but multiplying by a fraction (xy) decreases it. Thus, $x + y > xy$ under (2). Checking for zero gives a compatible result.

7. **The correct answer is (D).** Since there is only one unknown, the weight of a brick, you only need a single equation to

give you sufficient information. Each of the propositions (1) and (2) give an equation, so each is sufficient. You should not bother to calculate the actual weight of the brick, though it is 9 pounds.

8. **The correct answer is (B).** It is tempting to leap to an answer saying that both propositions are needed, but although (1) is clearly not sufficient by itself because it leaves open the issue of the relative proportions of the sides of the rectangle, (2) must be evaluated separately. As it happens, (2) is sufficient. Taking equation (2) and adding AE to both sides, we have: $AC = AB + BE + AE$. Since $BE + AE = AB$, $AC = 2AB$, so $AB = 2\frac{1}{2}$.

9. **The correct answer is (B).** Here we need to solve the simultaneous equations. Though there are different methods, one way to find the values of x and y is first to redefine x in terms of y. Since $x - y = 2$, $x = 2 + y$. We can now use $2 + y$ as the equivalent of x and substitute $2 + y$ for x in the other equation:

$$2(2 + y) + y = 7$$

$$4 + 2y + y = 7$$

$$3y = 3$$

$$y = 1$$

Once we have a value of y, we substitute that value into either of the equations. Since the second is a bit simpler, we may prefer to use it:

$x - 1 = 2$, so $x = 3$. Now we can determine that $x + y$ is $3 + 1$, or 4.

Another approach would be to add the two equations together so that the y terms will cancel themselves out:

$$\begin{array}{r} 2x + y = 7 \\ \underline{+ (x - y = 2)} \\ 3x = 9, \quad \text{thus } x = 3 \end{array}$$

Find y by substituting 3 for x in either equation.

10. **The correct answer is (A).** Average speed requires total distance divided by total time. Therefore it is incorrect to average the two speeds together, for, after all, the girl moved at the slower rate for three times as long as she moved at the faster rate, so they cannot be weighted equally. The correct way to solve the problem is to reason that the girl covered the 15 miles by bicycle in 1 hour. She covered the 15 miles by walking in 3 hours. Therefore, she traveled a total of 30 miles in a total of 4 hours. 30 miles/4 hours = 7.5 miles per hour.

11. **The correct answer is (D).** While we know by inspection that the shaded area is larger—the diagonal of a rectangle divides the rectangle in half—the answer choices tell us more is needed, though (C) is eliminated. We begin by noting that the area which is left unshaded is a triangle with a 90° angle. This means that we have an altitude and a base at our disposal. Then we note that the shaded area is the area of the square minus the area of the triangle. So we are in a position to compute the area of the square, the triangle, and the shaded part of the figure. In the first place, the base of the triangle—which is the unshaded area of the figure—is equal to the side of the square, 4. The altitude of that triangle is four units long less the unknown distance x, or $4 - x$. So the area of the triangle, $\frac{1}{2}ab$, is $\frac{1}{2}(4 - x)(4)$. The area of the square is 4×4, or 16, so the shaded area is 16 minus the triangle, which we have just determined is $\frac{1}{2}(4 - x)(4)$. Let us first pursue the area of the triangle:

$$\frac{1}{2}(4 - x)(4) = (4 - x)(2) = 8 - 2x$$

Substituting in the shaded portion:

$$16 - (8 - 2x) = 8 + 2x$$

Now we complete the ratio, $8 + 2x$ is the numerator, since that is the shaded area, and $8 - 2x$ is the denominator, since that is the unshaded area: $\frac{8+2x}{8-2x}$. And we simplify by 2 to yield $\frac{4+x}{4-x}$.

12. **The correct answer is (D).** Since Linda is the youngest and the other ages are derived from hers, let us assign the value x for Linda's age. In that case Mike will be $2x$ years old, since he is twice as old as Linda. Finally, Ned will be $2x + 2$ since he is two years older than Mike. Our three ages are: Linda, x; Mike, $2x$; and Ned, $2x + 2$. We know that these three ages total 27. Hence, $x + 2x + 2x + 2 = 27$. And now we solve for x:

$$5x + 2 = 27$$
$$5x = 25$$
$$x = 5$$

So Linda is 5 years old. Then, if Linda is 5, Mike must be 10 years old.

If Mike is used as a basis, $M = y$, $L = \frac{y}{2}$, $N = y + 2$. Thus, $y + \frac{y}{2} + (y + 2) = 27$; $2\frac{1}{2}y = 25$; $y = 10$.

13. **The correct answer is (E).** We know that the formula for the area of a square is s^2 = area. So $s^2 = 36x^2$, and, taking the square root of both sides, we learn $s = 6x$. (Note: There is no question here of a negative solution, since geometrical distances are always positive.)

14. **The correct answer is (A).** Since we do not know how much money Ed has, we must assign that amount the value of x. We now establish that Tom has x + \$2 since he has \$2 more than Ed; and we know that Susan has (x + \$2) + \$5, which is x + \$7, since she has \$5 more than Tom. We want to divide this money equally. The natural thing to do, then, is to add up all the money and divide it by 3. The total held by all three individuals is: $x + (x + 2) + (x + 2 + 5) = 3x + 9$. Dividing that by 3, we want everyone to have $x + 3$. Ed has x, so he needs to receive 3. Tom has $x + 2$, so he needs to receive 1. Susan has $x + 7$, so she needs to rid herself of 4. Susan gets rid of this 4 by giving 1 to Tom and 3 to Ed, giving us answer choice (A).

Some shortcutting is possible by considering that Susan has the most money, and then Tom and then Ed. Therefore, any answer which has Ed give up money cannot result in equal shares, eliminating (C) and (E). Furthermore, since Susan has the most, she must give up the most. In (D) Tom gives more than Susan, so this is eliminated. In (B), Susan gives out more than Tom, but she also receives from Tom, so her net giving out is only \$1, compared to Tom's \$4, so this is also wrong, which leaves (A).

15. **The correct answer is (C).** On one level, this is an easy problem. There are two unknowns in the situation, p and q. There are two different equations without any squares or exponents, so there is enough information using both equations. If you try to actually solve the problem, which is not really necessary, you may have some difficulty since it appears insoluble at first. Since we are interested in p, substitute from equation (2) into (1), getting $p = 4(4p)$; $p = 16p$, which seems impossible. However, there is one value of p that will work, and that is zero. Thus p is determined by the two equations.

16. **The correct answer is (C).** Do not let the term "perfect number" throw you. Accept the definition of any such oddball term and apply it to the problem. Since the factors of 6 less than 6 itself are 1, 2, and 3, 6 is the perfect number ($1 + 2 + 3 = 6$). 1 is not a perfect number since there are no factors of 1 less than itself. 4 is not a perfect number since the factors of 4 less than 4 are 1 and 2 and $1 + 2 \neq 4$. Nor is 8 a perfect number since the factors of 8 that are less than 8 itself are 1, 2, and 4, and those total 7, not 8. Finally, 10 is not a perfect number since the key factors here are 1, 2, and 5, which total 8, not 10.

17. **The correct answer is (B).** This is one of the rare problems in which you are asked a "yes/no" question, and the answer is "no." (1) is nice, but not enough by itself. (2) makes it impossible for *ABCD* to be a square since the diagonal of a square is not equal to its sides. Some suspicion that this might be a "no" question is raised by the fact that equilateral triangles have nothing to do with squares.

18. **The correct answer is (A).** By connecting *Q* and *O* or *P* and *O*, it can be seen that the radius of circle *O* is 6 units. (Remember, when a circle is named after a point, that point is the center of the circle.) The formula for the area of a circle is πr^2, so the area of circle *O* is: $\pi(6)^2 = 36\pi$.

19. **The correct answer is (D).** We begin by computing the capacity of the cylinder, which is πr^2 times height. Since the radius is 2 and the height is 5, the capacity of this cylinder is $\pi(2)^2 \times 5 = 20\pi$ cu. ft. It is already 40% full, which means that 60% of the capacity is left. 60% of 20π cu. ft. = 12π cu. ft.

20. **The correct answer is (A).** We are seeking *c*, but the given information is about the area of the triangle, while *c* is a distance. However, the formula for the area of triangles connects distance to area, so we should compute the area in terms of *c*. We know that we have a right angle in the lower right-hand corner of the figure. So this gives us an altitude and a base. The altitude is $3c$ units long and the base is $4c$ units long. So, the area is $\frac{1}{2}ab$ or $\frac{1}{2}(3c)(4c) = \frac{1}{2}(12c^2) = 6c^2$. And this is equal to 54. $6c^2 = 54$; so $c^2 = 9$ and $c = 3$.

21. **The correct answer is (D).** In order to find out the total production for the five days of round-the-clock production, you first need to know the rate of production for some time period and the number of that time period in the five days. To find the rate of production, add the rate of production of the new machine ($\frac{x}{\text{hour}}$) to the rate of production of the old machine, which is $\frac{1}{8}$ as much ($\frac{x}{8}$ per hour). Adding these two together you get a total production rate of $x + \frac{x}{8} = (\frac{9}{8})x$ per hour. This must be multiplied by the number of hours in five days (5)(24) to give the total production: $\frac{(9)(x)(5)(24)}{8} = 135x$ transmissions.

22. **The correct answer is (E).** Since the shorter side of the rectangle is 15 inches, the statement that the sides of the rectangle have the ratio of 3:2 means that the long side is found by the equation $\frac{3}{2} = \frac{x}{15}$, which becomes $45 = 2x$ by cross-multiplication, leading to the result that the long side of the rectangle is $22\frac{1}{2}$ inches long. Since a rectangle has two pairs of sides (the two lengths and the two widths), it is necessary only to refer to the sides in terms of two different sizes. Once the length and width of the rectangle have been calculated, the length of framing needed will be found by computing the perimeter of the rectangle by $2(22\frac{1}{2}) + 2(15) = \text{perimeter} = 45 + 30 = 75$ inches. Answer choice (C) is the result of adding only one set of sides. Choice (D) is reached through the error of considering the side of 15 to be the longer side.

23. **The correct answer is (E).** In order to know how long a moving object takes, you need to know the distance traveled and the rate of speed: Neither is given in the original information. The rate is given in (1), but that is not enough by itself; nor is (2). The question then comes down to whether (2) actually gives the distance between *J* and *M*. Note that the order of the neighborhoods along the marathon route is not necessarily in alphabetic order. (2) is not sufficient because the order of the neighborhoods could be ei-

ther with K between J and M, or with J between K and M. Thus, the distance is not specified and the answer is (E).

24. **The correct answer is (B).** Both of the given propositions establish a definite relationship between the officerships of Albert and Mary. Since the original information gives us the actual officership status of Mary (she is qualified), the temptation is to say that both propositions are sufficient. (1), however is not sufficient by itself. It leaves open the question of what happens if Albert does not qualify, because Mary may still qualify even if Albert doesn't. (2) is sufficient because it tells us that if Albert did not qualify, then it is certain that Mary did not qualify. Since Mary did qualify, we must know that Albert must also have qualified.

25. **The correct answer is (A).** The issue is whether 5 is an integral factor of x. According to (1), x can be divided by 12,345 and yield an integer. Since the last digit of 12,345 is 15, it has a factor of 5, and thus x must have a factor of 5 in order to be divisible by 12,345. (2) is not enough because 336 does not have a factor of 5, so that we cannot say for certain that $x/5$ is an integer; although it is still possible [suppose $x = (12{,}345)(336)$].

26. **The correct answer is (D).** A cube is a highly structured figure. All the edges must, by definition, be equal to each other and all the opposite faces parallel, and all the other symmetries of a cube maintained no matter what size the cube may be. Therefore, in principle, if you know any well-defined line in the cube—any edge or any diagonal of a side, or the diagonal of the whole cube—you can compute the lengths of any other line, the area of the sides, or the volume of the cube. Thus, in principle, both statement (1) and statement (2) are sufficient to permit the computation of the volume of the cube. On the actual test, you would leave it there, choice (D), and go on to the next problem. For instructional purposes only, we include a brief description of the way in which each statement could be used.

Statement (1): Each face of a cube is a square. Since the diagonal of a square forms a 45-45-90 right triangle with two of the sides, the length of the diagonal can be computed as $\sqrt{2}$ times the length of a side using the Pythagorean Theorem, or from your knowledge of right triangles. Once an edge of the cube is known, the volume of the cube can be computed as the third power (or cube) of the edge.

Statement (2): The diagonal of the cube forms a right triangle with the diagonal of a face and one of the edges, as shown below. By the same process described in the explanation of statement (1), the length of a diagonal is $\sqrt{2}$ times the length of an edge. Thus the Pythagorean Theorem equation for the triangle which includes the diagonal of the whole cube is $d^2 = (\sqrt{2}\,s)^2 + (s)^2$, and thus the diagonal $= \sqrt{3}$ times the length of the side. Therefore, knowing the length of the diagonal permits calculation of the length of an edge and of the volume of the cube.

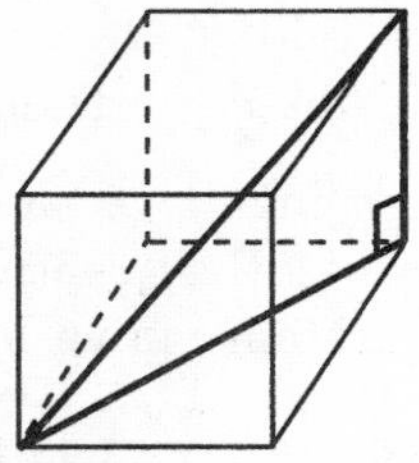

27. **The correct answer is (B).** Since the p and q terms are to the eighth power, simply having two equations for two unknowns is not sufficient. Usually, it is a good idea to try and factor polynomials if they are not easy to deal with in their original form. In this case, we can factor $p^8 - q^8$ into the difference between squares

since the square of something to the fourth power is the same base to the eighth power. Thus:

$$p^8 - q^8 = (p^4 - q^4)(p^4 + q^4).$$

This in turn factors to

$$(p^2 - q^2)(p^2 + q^2)(p^4 + q^4),$$

which factors to

$$(p - q)(p + q)(p^2 + q^2)(p^4 + q^4).$$

This gives us something that we can use since $(p - q)$ is stated in proposition (2) and is equal to zero. If $p - q$ is equal to zero, then anything multiplied by zero is equal to zero and the whole thing is equal to zero.

A shorter method would be to note that (2) transforms into $p = q$, which means that $p^8 = q^8$, which means that $p^8 - q^8 = 0$. The factoring approach might be needed if the propositions referred to $p^2 + q^2 = 0$ or to some other intermediate factor.

28. **The correct answer is (E).** Manipulating (1) to get x alone, we get:

$4x + 24 > 0$
$4x > -24$ (subtract +24 from both sides)
$x > -6$ (divide both sides by +4)

Manipulating (2), we get:

$4x - 24 < 0$
$4x < +24$ (add +24 to both sides)
$x < +6$ (divide both sides by +4)

Each statement allows for the possibility that x may be either positive or negative, and the question cannot be answered.

29. **The correct answer is (E).** Since the number of cases is the numerator of the fraction that represents the per capita rate of meningitis and the population is the denominator, both a decrease in the number of cases and an increase in the population will tend to lower the rate. Since we have both, and both changes are substantial, we may expect a substantial decrease in the rate. Thus, (A) and (B) may be eliminated on logical grounds. The new rate is found by computing $\frac{50\%M}{150\%P} = \frac{1M}{3P}$, which is $\frac{1}{3}$ of the original rate of $\frac{M}{P}$. If the new rate is $\frac{1}{3}$ of the old rate, then the percentage change is a decrease of $1 - \frac{1}{3} = \frac{2}{3}$, or $66\frac{2}{3}\%$.

30. **The correct answer is (C).** The total profit is the sum of the profit for the five-day period and the profit for the two-day period Friday and Saturday. You must also remember that there are 24 hours in a day, and thus the profit per 8-hour shift must be multiplied by 3 in order to get the daily profit. For the five-day period, the profit is \$600 (per shift) × 3 (shifts per day) × 5 (days) = \$9000. The profit per shift for the other days is 25% greater and is thus \$600 + $\frac{1}{4}$(\$600) = \$600 + \$150 = \$750. The total profit for the two-day period is calculated as \$750 (per shift) × 3 (shifts per day) × 2 (days) = \$4500. The total profit for the week is \$9000 + \$4500 = \$13,500.

31. **The correct answer is (B).** When a question is as convoluted as this one, the issue must assuredly be the unraveling of just what is being asked for. Thinking backward is a good approach. We are asked for the difference between two numbers: (cost of insurance + unreimbursed losses) – (loss if no insurance) = answer. The cost of the insurance is \$125 per quarter, which means that the annual cost is 4 × \$125 = \$500. That is the first number in our equation. The unreimbursed losses consist of two items. First, there is the deductible, that is, the amount of loss that must be sustained before any reimbursement is made. Here, the first \$350 of loss is not reimbursed, so that is one part of the unreimbursed loss. In addition, even when reimbursement is made, it is only made for 75%, or $\frac{3}{4}$ of

the value of the loss above \$350. The total loss was \$1250, \$900 above the \$350 deductible. Three-quarters of \$900 is \$675, but that is the portion of the \$900 that *is* reimbursed; so $\frac{1}{4} \times \$900 = \$225$ is the portion that is *not* reimbursed. Thus the total non-reimbursed amount is \$350 + 225 = \$575, which is the second figure we needed for our computation. The third figure is the total amount of the loss, since without insurance it would all have been a loss; this is \$1250. We thus can compute (\$500 + \$575) – \$1250 = –\$175. But the negative sign is irrelevant because the difference is all that is asked, not whether one is greater than the other.

32. The correct answer is (C). Since $x + 6 = 3$, $x = -3$. Then, substituting –3 for x in the second expression, $x + 3$ is $-3 + 3 = 0$.

33. The correct answer is (A). Probably the easiest way to solve this problem is just to count the steps on your fingers, but the same process can be expressed mathematically. Let those steps he walks down be assigned negative values, and those steps he walks up be positive. We then have: $-4 + 3 - 6 + 2 + 9 - 2 = +2$. So the person comes to rest two steps above where he started.

34. The correct answer is (D). This is a problem which is most easily solved directly. From 1:21 to 2:21 is 60 minutes. From 2:21 to 3:21 is 60 minutes. So far we have a total of 120 minutes. Then, from 3:21 to 3:36 is 15 minutes, for a total of 135 minutes.

35. The correct answer is (D). In order to find the area of the large rectangle, you need to find its length and width. The only measures of those dimensions that the problem gives you are the small rectangles. Since the only information that is given is that all of the small rectangles are the same shape and size, the first place to look for additional understanding is to the ways that the small rectangles build up into the large rectangle. In addition, the fact that both of the statements concern paths made up of pieces of small rectangles should also focus your attention on the small rectangles. Since the small rectangles are rectangles, their length and width are the key dimensions. Since all of the small rectangles are the same shape and size, the fact that three widths equal one length gives you the proportions of the small rectangles. This is shown in the following details from the diagram:

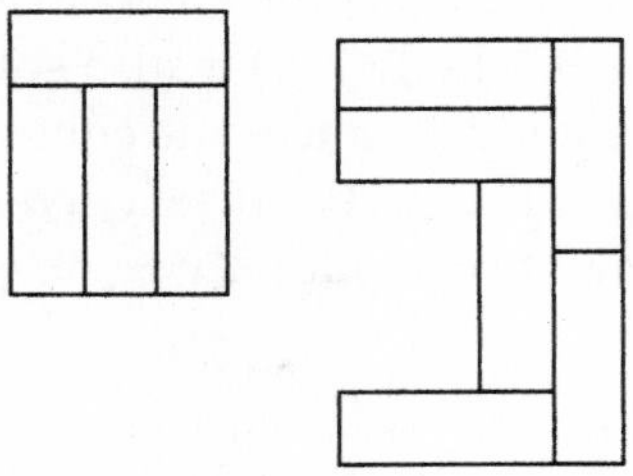

Once you know that three widths of a small rectangle is equal to one length, the information given in the propositions becomes very useful. The upper path referred to in proposition (1) is composed of four lengths and three widths, which is equal to 15 widths (or 5 lengths). Since the proposition gives the value of this path as 45, you can calculate that one width is equal to 45 divided by 15 or 3. Knowing the value of a width of the small rectangle allows you to calculate the value of the length of the small rectangle and thus its area and the area of the large rectangle. You could also directly calculate the length and width of the large rectangle 21 (7 small rectangle widths) and 18 (6 small rectangle widths), respectively. Similarly, the lower path is equivalent to 13 small rectangle widths and knowing its length as 39 permits the area of the large rectangle to be calculated.

36. The correct answer is (B). First, we must compute the total commission that will be owed: 15% of \$2800 = \$420. Then we must take into account the fact that the sales representative has already received \$150 of that sum. So she is now owed: \$420 – \$150 = \$270.

37. **The correct answer is (D).** As usual with polynomials, when they are not helpful in one form, rename them as the other form. Here they are in factors, but the expanded form will be most useful.

$(x^2 + y^2) + (x^2 - y^2) = x^2 + 2xy + y^2 + x^2 - 2xy + y^2 = 2x^2 + 2y^2 = 2(x^2 + y^2)$

(2) is certainly sufficient by itself; the only issue is whether (1) is also sufficient. As the simplification of the equation shows, (1) is sufficient because it gives the value needed to compute $2(x^2 + y^2)$.

Practice Test 2

ANALYTICAL WRITING ASSESSMENT

I. ANALYSIS OF AN ISSUE

Time—30 Minutes

Directions: In this section you will have 30 minutes to analyze and explain your views on the topic presented below. Read the statement and directions carefully. Write only on the topic given. An essay on a topic other than the one assigned will automatically be assigned a grade of 0.

Note: On the CAT version, you will keyboard your essay. For this exercise, allow yourself three sides of regular $8\frac{1}{2} \times 11$- inch paper for each essay response.

> A 90-year-old farmer was asked what technological advance in the past 125 years has done the most to improve the quality of life. The farmer answered, "Electricity, because it makes so many chores easier and faster to do." A 35-year-old business executive was asked the same question and responded, "Electricity, because it makes so many chores easier and faster to do."

Which position do you find more compelling? Explain your position using reasons and/or examples drawn from your personal experience, observations, or readings.

II. ANALYSIS OF AN ARGUMENT

Time—30 Minutes

Directions: In this section you will have 30 minutes to write a critique of the argument presented below. Read the argument and directions carefully. Write only on the topic given. An essay on a topic other than the one assigned will automatically be assigned a grade of 0.
Note: On the CAT version, you will keyboard your essay. For this exercise, allow yourself three sides of regular $8\frac{1}{2} \times 11$- inch paper for each essay response.

> In order to qualify for a hunting license to take wild deer with a rifle, a state resident need only fill out a short form giving name and address and pay a $10 annual fee. The state should also require hunters to attend a safety course. A one-day course covering the safe use of fire arms and behavior in the woods would virtually ensure that shooting accidents during hunting season would be eliminated.

How persuasive do you find this argument? Explain your point of view by analyzing the line of reasoning and the use of evidence in the argument. Discuss also what, if anything, would make the argument more persuasive or would help you better to evaluate its conclusion.

VERBAL SECTION

41 Questions • 75 Minutes

Directions: For each of the following questions, choose the correct answer. To simulate the experience of taking the CAT, answer each question in order. Do not skip any questions, and do not go back to any questions you have already answered.

For Sentence Correction questions: In questions of this type, either part or all of a sentence is underlined. The sentence is followed by five ways of writing the underlined part. Choice (A) repeats the original; the other answer choices vary. If you think that the original phrasing is the best, choose (A). If you think one of the other answer choices is the best, select that choice.

Sentence Correction questions test your ability to recognize correct and effective expression. Follow the requirements of standard written English: grammar, choice of words, and sentence construction. Choose the answer that results in the clearest, most exact sentence, but does not change the meaning of the original sentence.

Example:

Q The possibility of massive earthquakes <u>are regarded by most area residents with</u> a mixture of skepticism and caution.

(A) are regarded by most area residents with

(B) is regarded by most area residents with

(C) is regarded by most area residents as

(D) is mostly regarded by area residents with

(E) by most area residents is regarded with

A The correct answer is (B).

For Critical Reasoning questions: Questions of this type ask you to analyze and evaluate the reasoning in short paragraphs or passages. For some questions, all of the answer choices may conceivably be answers to the question asked. You should select the *best* answer to the question, that is, an answer that does not require you to make assumptions that violate common-sense standards by being implausible, redundant, irrelevant, or inconsistent.

Example:

Q In an extensive study of the reading habits of magazine subscribers, it was found that an average of between four and five people actually read each copy of the most popular weekly news magazine. On this basis, we estimate that the 12,000 copies of *Poets and Poetry* that are sold each month are actually read by 48,000 to 60,000 people.

The estimate above assumes that

(A) individual magazine readers generally enjoy more than one type of magazine

(B) most of the readers of *Poets and Poetry* subscribe to the magazine

(C) the ratio of readers to copies is the same for *Poets and Poetry* as for the weekly news magazine

(D) the number of readers of the weekly news magazine is similar to the number of readers of *Poets and Poetry*

(E) most readers enjoy sharing copies of their favorite magazines with friends and family members

A The correct answer is (B).

For Reading Comprehension questions: Each passage is followed by questions or incomplete statements about the passage. Each statement or question is followed by lettered words or expressions. Select the word or expression that most satisfactorily completes each statement or answers each question in accordance with the meaning of the passage.

1. If they would have found the receipt by mid-April, they would have paid less tax.
   (A) If they would have found the receipt by mid-April, they would have paid less tax.
   (B) If they would have found the receipt by mid-April, they had paid less tax.
   (C) If they had found the receipt by mid-April, they would have paid fewer tax.
   (D) If they had found the receipt by mid-April, they would have paid less tax.
   (E) If they find the receipt by mid-April, they will pay less tax.

2. The libraries with the Corinthian columns that contain almost a million volumes opened last evening.
   (A) with the Corinthian columns that contain almost a million volumes
   (B) with the Corinthian columns that contained almost a million volumes
   (C) with the Corinthian columns that contains almost a million volumes
   (D) with the Corinthian columns and which contain almost a million volumes
   (E) which contain almost a million volumes with the Corinthian columns

3. The Russian scientists who have been studying the remnants of an ancient Siberian city feel that its residents devote more time to making pottery than they have to learning survival skills.
   (A) devote more time to making pottery than they have to
   (B) devote more time to making pottery than they do to
   (C) devoted more time to making pottery than they did to
   (D) devote more time to the making of their pottery than to
   (E) devoted more time to making pottery than they do to

4. Which of the following activities would depend upon an assumption which is inconsistent with the judgment that you cannot argue with taste?
   (A) A special exhibition at a museum
   (B) A beauty contest
   (C) A system of garbage collection and disposal
   (D) A cookbook filled with old New England recipes
   (E) A movie festival

5. If George graduated from the University after 1974, he was required to take Introductory World History.

   The statement above can be logically deduced from which of the following?
   (A) Before 1974, Introductory World History was not a required course at the University.
   (B) Every student who took Introductory World History at the University graduated after 1974.
   (C) No student who graduated from the University before 1974 took Introductory World History.
   (D) All students graduating from the University after 1974 were required to take Introductory World History.
   (E) Before 1974, no student was not permitted to graduate from the University without having taken Introductory World History.

6. The leader of the Neanderthal tribe rarely hunted for food, and because of it was never acknowledged as a great hunter.

(A) The leader of the Neanderthal tribe rarely hunted for food, and because of it

(B) Because the leader of the Neanderthal tribe rarely hunted for food, he

(C) In that he rarely hunted for food, the leader of the Neanderthal tribe was

(D) Rarely hunting for food was the reason that the leader of the Neanderthal tribe

(E) Hunts were rare, and because of this the leader of the Neanderthal tribe

7. Largemouth bass are usually found living in shallow waters near the lake banks wherever minnows are found. There are no largemouth bass living on this side of the lake.

Which of the following would logically complete an argument with the preceding premises given?

(A) Therefore, there are no minnows on this side of the lake.

(B) Therefore, there are probably no minnows on this side of the lake.

(C) Therefore, there will never be any minnows on this side of the lake.

(D) Therefore, largemouth bass are not found in the shallow water of rivers unless minnows are also present.

(E) Therefore, lakes that contain minnows are the only habitat where largemouth bass are found.

8. TOMMY: That telephone always rings when I am in the shower and can't hear it.

JUANITA: But you must be able to hear it; otherwise you couldn't know that it was ringing.

Juanita's response shows that she presupposes that

(A) the telephone does not ring when Tommy is in the shower

(B) Tommy's callers never telephone except when he is in the shower

(C) Tommy's callers sometimes hang up thinking he is not at home

(D) Tommy cannot tell that the telephone has rung unless he actually heard it

(E) the telephone does not always function properly

9. The physicians explained that had the patient known the warning signs of cancer, he would have come in earlier for a check-up.

(A) had the patient known the warning signs of cancer, he would have come in earlier

(B) if the patient had known the warning signs of cancer, he would have come in earlier

(C) if the patient knew the warning signs of cancer, he would have come in earlier

(D) had the patient known the warning signs of cancer, he would come in earlier

(E) if the patient would have known the warning signs of cancer, he would have come in earlier

10. The general's hopes for success in battle were dashed as a result of the willingness of the native population to cooperate with the enemy.

(A) as a result of the willingness of the native population to cooperate with the enemy.

(B) because the native population was willing to cooperate with the enemy.

(C) insofar as the native population was willing to cooperate with the enemy.

(D) because the native population would have a willingness to cooperate with enemy.

(E) by the native population's apparent willingness to cooperate with the enemy.

11. <u>The marines who landed on the beaches of Iwo Jima effected the rescue of several prisoners of war whose assault took the enemy by surprise.</u>

    (A) The marines who landed on the beaches at Iwo Jima effected the rescue of several prisoners of war whose assault took the enemy by surprise.

    (B) The marines effected the rescue of several prisoners of war who had landed on the beaches at Iwo Jima and whose assault had taken the enemy by surprise.

    (C) The marines who landed on the beaches at Iwo Jima effected the rescue of several prisoners of war whose assault had taken the enemy by surprise.

    (D) The marines who landed on the beaches at Iwo Jima affected the rescue of several prisoners of war whose assault had taken the enemy by surprise.

    (E) The marines who landed on the beaches at Iwo Jima, and whose assault took the enemy by surprise, effected the rescue of several prisoners of war.

QUESTIONS 12–18

Under existing law, a new drug may be labeled, promoted, and advertised only for those conditions in which safety and effectiveness have been demonstrated and of which the Food and Drug Administration (FDA) has approved, or so-called "approved uses." Other uses have come to be called "unapproved uses" and cannot be legally promoted. In a real sense, the term "unapproved" is a misnomer because it includes in one phrase two categories of marketed drugs that are very different: drugs which are potentially harmful and will never be approved, and already approved drugs that have "unapproved" uses. It is common for new research and new insights to demonstrate valid new uses for drugs already on the market. Also, there are numerous examples of medical progress resulting from the serendipitous observations and therapeutic innovations of physicians, both important methods of discovery in the field of therapeutics. Before such advances can result in new indications for inclusion in drug labeling, however, the available data must meet the legal standard of substantial evidence derived from adequate and well-controlled clinical trials. Such evidence may require time to develop, and, without initiative on the part of the drug firm, it may not occur at all for certain uses. However, because medical literature on new uses exists and these uses are medically beneficial, physicians often use these drugs for such purposes prior to FDA review or changes in labeling. This is referred to as "unlabeled uses" of drugs.

A different problem arises when a particular use for a drug has been examined scientifically and has been found to be ineffective or unsafe, and yet physicians who either are uninformed or who refuse to accept the available scientific evidence continue to use the drug in this way. Such use may have been reviewed by the FDA and rejected, or, in some cases, the use may actually be warned against in the labeling. This subset of uses may be properly termed "disapproved uses."

Government policy should minimize the extent of unlabeled uses. If such uses are valid—and many are—it is important that scientifically sound evidence supporting them be generated and that the regulatory system accommodate them into drug labeling. Continuing rapid advances in medical care and the complexity of drug usage, however, makes it impossible for the government to keep drug labeling up to date for every conceivable situation. Thus, when a particular use of this type appears, it is also important, and in the interest of good medical care, that no stigma be attached to "unapproved usage" by practitioners while the formal evidence is assembled between the time of discovery and the time the new use is included in the labeling. In the case of "disapproved uses," however, it is proper policy to warn against these in the package insert. Whether use of a drug for these purposes by the uninformed or intransigent physician constitutes a violation of the current Federal Food, Drug, and Cosmetic Act is a matter of debate that involves a number of technical and legal issues. Regardless of that, the inclusion of disapproved uses in the form of contraindications, warnings and other precautionary statements in package inserts is an important practical deterrent to improper use. Except for clearly disapproved uses, however, it is in the best interests of patient care that physicians not be constrained by regulatory statutes from exercising their best judgment in prescribing a drug for both its approved uses and any unlabeled uses it may have.

12. The author is primarily concerned with

(A) refuting a theory

(B) drawing a distinction

(C) discrediting an opponent

(D) describing a new development

(E) condemning an error

13. According to the passage, an unlabeled use of a drug is any use that

(A) has been reviewed by the FDA and specifically rejected

(B) is medically beneficial despite the fact that such use is prohibited by law

(C) has medical value but has not yet been approved by FDA for inclusion as a labeled use

(D) is authorized by the label as approved by the FDA on the basis of scientific studies

(E) is made in experiments designed to determine whether a drug is medically beneficial

14. It can be inferred from the passage that the intransigent physician (lines 76–77)

(A) continues to prescribe a drug even though he knows it is not in the best interests of the patient

(B) refuses to use a drug for an unlabeled purpose out of fear that he may be stigmatized by its use

(C) persists in using a drug for disapproved uses because he rejects the evidence of its ineffectiveness or dangers

(D) experiments with new uses for tested drugs in an attempt to find medically beneficial uses for the drugs

(E) should be prosecuted for violating the Federal Food, Drug, and Cosmetic Act in using drugs for disapproved uses

15. All of the following are mentioned in the passage as reasons for allowing unlabeled uses of drugs EXCEPT

(A) the increased cost to the patient of buying an FDA-approved drug

(B) the medical benefits which can accrue to the patient through unlabeled use

(C) the time lag between initial discovery of a medical use and FDA approval of that use

(D) the possibility that a medically beneficial use may never be clinically documented

(E) the availability of publications to inform physicians of the existence of such uses

16. With which of the following statements about the distinction between approved and unlabeled uses would the author most likely agree?

(A) Public policy statements have not adequately distinguished between uses already approved by the FDA and medically beneficial uses which have not yet been approved.

(B) The distinction between approved and unlabeled uses has been obscured because government regulatory agencies approve only those uses which have been clinically tested.

(C) Practicing physicians are in a better position than the FDA to distinguish between approved and unlabeled uses because they are involved in patient treatment on a regular basis.

(D) The distinction between approved and unlabeled uses should be discarded so that the patient can receive the full benefits of any drug use.

(E) The practice of unlabeled uses of drugs exists because of the time lag between discovery of a beneficial use and the production of data needed for FDA approval.

17. The author regards the practice of using drugs for medically valid purposes before FDA approval as

(A) a necessary compromise

(B) a dangerous policy

(C) an illegal activity

(D) an unqualified success

(E) a short-term phenomenon

18. Which of the following statements best summarizes the point of the passage?

(A) Patients have been exposed to needless medical risk because the FDA has not adequately regulated unlabeled uses as well as disapproved uses.

(B) Physicians who engage in the practice of unlabeled use make valuable contributions to medical science and should be protected from legal repercussions of such activity.

(C) Pharmaceutical firms develop and test new drugs which initially have little or no medical value but later are found to have value in unlabeled uses.

(D) Doctors prescribe drugs for disapproved purposes primarily because they fail to read manufacturers' labels or because they disagree with the clinical data about the value of drugs.

(E) The government should distinguish between unlabeled use and disapproved use of a drug, allowing the practice of unlabeled use and condemning disapproved uses.

19. ADVERTISEMENT: You cannot buy a more potent pain-reliever than RELIEF without a prescription.

Which of the following statements is inconsistent with the claim made by the advertisement?

(A) RELIEF is not the least expensive non-prescription pain-reliever one can buy.

(B) Another non-prescription pain-reliever, TOBINE, is just as powerful as RELIEF.

(C) Some prescription pain-relievers are not as powerful as RELIEF.

(D) An experimental pain reliever more powerful than RELIEF is available free-of-charge to subjects who participate in a study.

(E) A non-prescription pain-reliever more powerful than any other, including RELIEF, is available for purchase without a prescription.

QUESTIONS 20 AND 21

A behavioral psychologist interested in animal behavior noticed that dogs who are never physically disciplined (e.g., with a blow from a rolled-up newspaper) never bark at strangers. She concluded that the best way to keep a dog from barking at strange visitors is to not punish the dog physically.

20. The psychologist's conclusion is based on which of the following assumptions?

(A) Striking a dog with a newspaper or other object is an inappropriate method for conditioning canine behavior.

(B) Dogs that are never physically disciplined grow up more well-adjusted than dogs that have been subjected to such discipline.

(C) There were no instances of an unpunished dog barking at a stranger that had not been observed.

(D) Dogs normally bark only at strangers who have previously been physically abusive or threatening.

(E) Human children who are physically disciplined are more likely to react negatively to strangers than those who are not.

21. Suppose the psychologist decides to pursue her project further, and she studies 25 dogs that are known to bark at strangers. Which of the following possible findings would undermine her original conclusion?

(A) Some of the owners of the dogs studied did not physically punish the dog when it barked at a stranger.

(B) Some of the dogs studied were never physically punished.

(C) The owners of some of the dogs studied believe that a dog which barks at strangers is a good watchdog.

(D) Some of the dogs barked at people who were not strangers.

(E) None of the dogs was disciplined by the method of a rolled-up newspaper.

22. Unafraid of neither lightning nor thunder during a storm, Mr. Jones enjoyed walking in the park during heavy downpours.

(A) Unafraid of neither lightning nor thunder

(B) Afraid of both lightning and thunder

(C) Unafraid of neither lightning or thunder

(D) Unafraid of either lightning or thunder

(E) Afraid of either lightning or thunder

23. Should we be told that our recommendations pertinent to the kind of use made of our vehicles have been accepted, we will gladly cooperate with the ultimate plan.

(A) Should we be told that our recommendations pertinent to the kind of use made of our vehicles have been accepted, we will

(B) If we are told that recommendations about use of our vehicles has been accepted, we will

(C) Should we be told that our recommendations for the use of our vehicles have been accepted, we will

(D) Our being told of the acceptance of our recommendations pertinent to use made of our vehicles should cause us to

(E) Our being told of all recommendations about the use of our vehicles being accepted will cause us to

practice test

24. Authors of the seventeenth century used alliteration to both refine their writing and increase a listener's pleasure.

(A) Authors of the seventeenth century used alliteration to both refine their writing and increase

(B) Authors of the seventeenth century utilized alliteration both to refine their writing and to increase

(C) Seventeenth-century authors utilized alliteration both to refine their writing and to increase

(D) Seventeenth-century authors used alliteration both to refine their writing and to increase

(E) Seventeenth-century authors used alliteration to refine their writing, and also to increase

25. Everything a child does is the consequence of some prior experience. Therefore, a child psychologist must study the personal history of each patient.

The author's conclusion logically depends upon the premise that

(A) everything that a child is doing that child has already done before

(B) every effect is causally generated by some previous effect

(C) studying a child's personal history is the best way to learn about that child's parents

(D) a child will learn progressively more about the world because experience is cumulative

(E) it is possible to ensure that a child will grow up to be a mature, responsible adult

26. It is sometimes argued that we are reaching the limits of the earth's capacity to supply our energy needs with fossil fuels. In the past ten years, however, as a result of technological progress making it possible to extract resources from even marginal wells and mines, yields from oil and coal fields have increased tremendously. There is no reason to believe that there is a limit to the earth's capacity to supply our energy needs.

Which of the following statements most directly contradicts the conclusion drawn above?

(A) Even if we exhaust our supplies of fossil fuel, the earth can still be mined for uranium for nuclear fuel.

(B) The technology needed to extract fossil fuels from marginal sources is very expensive.

(C) Even given the improvements in technology, oil and coal are not renewable resources; so we will eventually exhaust our supplies of them.

(D) Most of the land under which marginal oil and coal supplies lie is more suitable to cultivation or pasturing than to production of fossil fuels.

(E) The fuels that are yielded by marginal sources tend to be high in sulfur and other undesirable elements which aggravate the air pollution problem.

27. Some sociologists believe that religious sects such as the California-based Waiters, who believe the end of the world is imminent and seek to purify their souls by, among other things, abstaining completely from sexual relations, are a product of growing disaffection with modern, industrialized and urbanized living. As evidence, they cite the fact that there are no other active organizations of the same type which are more than 50 or 60 years old. The evidence, however, fails to support the conclusion for __________.

Which of the following is the most logical completion of the passage?

(A) the restrictions on sexual relations are such that the only source of new members is outside recruitment, so such sects tend to die out after a generation or two

(B) it is simply not possible to gauge the intensity of religious fervor by the length of time the religious sect remains viable

(C) the Waiters group may actually survive beyond the second generation of its existence

(D) there are other religious sects that emphasize group sexual activity which currently have several hundred members

(E) the Waiters are a California-based organization and have no members in the Northeast, which is even more heavily urban and industrialized than California

QUESTIONS 28–34

The existence of both racial and sexual discrimination in employment is well documented, and policy makers and responsible employers are particularly sensitive to the plight of the black female employee on the theory that she is doubly the victim of discrimination. That there exist differences in income be-tween white and black people is clear, but it is not so clear that these differences are solely the result of racial discrimination in employment. The two groups differ in productivity, so basic economics dictates that their incomes will differ.

To obtain a true measure of the effect of racial discrimination in employment it is necessary to adjust the gross black/white income ratio for these productivity factors. White women in urban areas have a higher educational level than black women and can be expected to receive larger incomes. Moreover, state distribution of residence is important because blacks are over-represented in the South where wage rates are typically lower than elsewhere and where racial differentials in income are greater. Also, black people are over-represented in large cities; incomes of black people would be greater if black people were distributed among cities of different sizes in the same manner as white people.

After standardization for these productivity factors, the income of black urban women is estimated to be between 108 and 125 percent of the income of white women. This indicates that productivity factors more than account for the actual white/black income differential for women. Despite their greater education, white women's *actual* median income is only 2 to 5 percent higher than that of black women in the North. Unlike the situation of men, the evidence indicates that the money income of black urban women was as great as, or greater than, that of whites of similar productivity in the North, and probably in the United States as a whole. For men, however, the adjusted black/white income ratio is approximately 80 percent.

At least two possible hypotheses may explain why the adjustment for productivity more than accounts for the observed income differential for women, whereas the income differential persists for men. First, there may be more discrimination against black men than against black women. The different occupational structures for men and women give some indication why this could be the case, and institutionalized considerations—for example, the effect of unionization in cutting competition—may also contribute. Second, the data are consistent with the hypothesis that the intensity of discrimination against women differs little between white and black people. Therefore, racial discrimination adds little to the effects of existing sex discrimination.

These findings suggest that a black woman does not necessarily suffer relatively more discrimination in the labor market than does a white woman. Rather, for women, the effects of sexual discrimination are so pervasive that the effects of racial discrimination are negligible. Of course, this is not to say that the more generalized racial discrimination of which black women, like black men, are victims does not disadvantage black women in their search for work.

After all, one important productivity factor is level of education, and the difference between white and black women on this scale is largely the result of racial discrimination.

28. The primary purpose of the passage is to

(A) explain the reasons for the existence of income differentials between men and women

(B) show that racial discrimination against black women in employment is less important than sexual discrimination

(C) explore the ways in which productivity factors such as level of education influence the earning power of black workers

(D) sketch a history of racial and sexual discrimination against black and female workers in the labor market

(E) offer some suggestions as to how public officials and private employers can act to solve the problem of discrimination against black women

29. According to the passage, the gross black/white income ratio is not an accurate measure of discrimination in employment because the gross ratio

(A) fails to include large numbers of black workers who live in the large cities and in the South

(B) must be adjusted to reflect the longer number of hours and greater number of days worked by black employees

(C) represents a subjective interpretation by the statistician of the importance of factors such as educational achievement

(D) is not designed to take account of the effects of the long history of racial discrimination

(E) includes income differences attributable to real economic factors and not to discrimination

30. Which of the following best describes the relationship between the income level of black women and that of black men?

(A) In general, black men earn less money than do black women.

(B) On the average, black women in the South earn less money than do black men in large northern cities.

(C) Productivity factors have a greater dollar value in the case of black women.

(D) Black men have a higher income level than black women because black men have a higher level of education.

(E) The difference between income levels for black and white women is less than that for black and white men.

31. Which of the following best describes the logical relationship between the two hypotheses presented in lines 53–58?

(A) The two hypotheses may both be true since each phenomenon could contribute to the observed differential.

(B) The two hypotheses are contradictory, and if one is proved to be correct, the other is proved incorrect.

(C) The two hypotheses are dependent on each other, and empirical disconfirmation of the one is disconfirmation of the other.

(D) The two hypotheses are logically connected, so that proof of the first entails the truth of the second.

(E) The two hypotheses are logically connected, so that it is impossible to prove either one to be true without also proving the other to be true.

32. Which of the following best describes the tone of the passage?

(A) Confident and overbearing

(B) Ill-tempered and brash

(C) Objective and critical

(D) Tentative and inconclusive

(E) Hopeful and optimistic

33. If the second hypothesis mentioned by the author (lines 66–72) is correct, a general lessening of the discrimination against women should lead to

(A) a higher white/black income ratio for women

(B) a lower white/black income ratio for women

(C) lower female/male income ratio

(D) an increase in the productivity of women

(E) an increase in the level of education of women

34. The author's attitude toward racial and sexual discrimination in employment can best be described as one of

(A) apology

(B) concern

(C) indifference

(D) indignation

(E) anxiety

QUESTIONS 35 AND 36

In recent years, unions have begun to include in their demands at the collective bargaining table requests for contract provisions, which give labor an active voice in determining the goals of a corporation. Although it cannot be denied that labor leaders are highly skilled administrators, it must be recognized that their primary loyalty is and must remain to their membership, not to the corporation. Thus, labor participation in corporate management decisions makes about as much sense as __________.

35. Which of the following represents the best continuation of the passage?

(A) allowing inmates to make decisions about prison security

(B) a senior field officer asking the advice of a junior officer on a question of tactics

(C) a university's asking the opinion of the student body on the scheduling of courses

(D) Chicago's mayor inviting the state legislators for a ride on the city's subway system

(E) the members of a church congregation discussing theology with the minister

36. The author's reasoning leads to the further conclusion that

(A) the authority of corporate managers would be symbolically undermined if labor leaders were allowed to participate in corporate planning

(B) workers have virtually no idea of how to run a large corporation

(C) workers would not derive any benefit from hearing the goals of corporate management explained to them at semiannual meetings

(D) the efficiency of workers would be lowered if they were to divide their time between production line duties and management responsibilities

(E) allowing labor a voice in corporate decisions would involve labor representatives in a conflict of interest

37. Married women raising young children do not respond to social stresses as poorly as unmarried women do.

(A) as poorly as unmarried women do.

(B) as much as unmarried women do.

(C) as poorly as unmarried women.

(D) as much as unmarried women have.

(E) as well as unmarried women.

38. Your incessant meddling in my affairs, your obnoxious ridiculing of my suggestions and sudden departure prevented our conference from yielding significant results.

(A) and sudden departure prevented

(B) and your suddenness of departure prevented

(C) and your sudden departing prevented

(D) and your sudden departing caused the prevention of

(E) plus your sudden departure prevented

practice test

39. Which of the following arguments contains circular reasoning?

(A) The Bible must be accepted as the revealed word of God, for it is stated several times in the Bible that it is the one, true word of God. And since the Bible is the true word of God, we must accept what it says as true.

(B) It must be possible to do something about the deteriorating condition of the nation's interstate highway system. But the repairs will cost money. Therefore, it is foolish to reduce federal appropriations for highway repair.

(C) The Learner Commission's Report on Pornography concluded that there is a definite link between pornography and sex crimes. But no one should accept that conclusion because the Learner Commission was funded by the Citizens' Committee Against Obscenity, which obviously wanted the report to condemn pornography.

(D) People should give up drinking coffee. Of ten people who died last year at City Hospital from cancer of the pancreas, eight of them drank three or more cups of coffee a day.

(E) Guns are not themselves the cause of crime. Even without firearms crimes would be committed. Criminals would use knives or other weapons.

40. Any truthful auto mechanic will tell you that your standard 5,000-mile checkup can detect only one-fifth of the problems which are likely to go wrong with your car. Therefore, such a checkup is virtually worthless and a waste of time and money.

Which of the following statements, if true, would LEAST weaken the conclusion of the argument above?

(A) Those problems which the 5,000-mile checkup will turn up are the ten leading causes of major engine failure.

(B) For a new car, a 5,000-mile checkup is required to protect the owner's warranty.

(C) During a 5,000-mile checkup the mechanic also performs routine maintenance which is necessary to the proper functioning of the car.

(D) During a 5,000-mile checkup of a vehicle, a mechanic can detect incipient problems that might later lead to major difficulties.

(E) A manufacturer's review of reports based on 5,000-mile checkups shows that the checkups found problems in less than of 1 percent of the cars checked.

41. Breeding and education <u>establishes the rules of behavior for any person, as does</u> occupation and income.

(A) establishes the rules of behavior for any person, as does

(B) establish the rules of behavior for any person, as does

(C) establish the rules of behavior for any person, and so does

(D) establish the rules of behavior for any person, as do

(E) establishes the rules of behavior for any person, and so does

QUANTITATIVE SECTION

37 Questions • 75 Minutes

Directions: For each of the following questions, choose the correct answer. To simulate the experience of taking the CAT, answer each question in order. Do not skip any questions, and do not go back to any questions you have already answered.
Numbers: All numbers used are real numbers.
Figures: The diagrams and figures that accompany these questions are for the purpose of providing information useful in answering the questions. Unless it is stated that a specific figure is not drawn to scale, the diagrams and figures are drawn as accurately as possible. All figures are in a plane unless otherwise indicated.
For Data Sufficiency questions: Each question is followed by two numbered facts. You are to determine whether the data given in the statements are sufficient for answering the question. Use the data given, plus your knowledge of math and everyday facts, to choose between the five possible answers.

Example:

Q Which copy machine, X or Y, makes copies at the faster rate?

(1) Machine X makes 90 copies per minute.
(2) In three minutes, X makes 1.5 more copies than Y.

(A) statement 1 alone is sufficient to answer the question, but statement 2 alone is not sufficient
(B) statement 2 alone is sufficient to answer the question, but statement 1 alone is not sufficient
(C) both statements together are needed to answer the question, but neither statement alone is sufficient
(D) either statement by itself is sufficient to answer the question
(E) not enough facts are given to answer the question

A **The correct answer is (B).**

1. From the time 6:15 P.M. to the time 7:45 P.M. of the same day, the minute hand of a standard clock describes an arc of

(A) 30°
(B) 90°
(C) 180°
(D) 540°
(E) 910°

2. Which of the following fractions is the LEAST?

(A) $\frac{7}{8}$
(B) $\frac{7}{12}$
(C) $\frac{8}{9}$
(D) $\frac{1}{2}$
(E) $\frac{6}{17}$

3. If the area of a rectangle is 20, what is its perimeter?
   (1) The length of the rectangle is 5.
   (2) The width of the rectangle is 1 unit less than its length.
   (A) statement 1 alone is sufficient to answer the question, but statement 2 alone is not sufficient
   (B) statement 2 alone is sufficient to answer the question, but statement 1 alone is not sufficient
   (C) both statements together are needed to answer the question, but neither statement alone is sufficient
   (D) either statement by itself is sufficient to answer the question
   (E) not enough facts are given to answer the question

4. Is the average of ten integers greater than 10?
   (1) Half of the integers are greater than 10.
   (2) Half of the integers are less than 10.
   (A) statement 1 alone is sufficient to answer the question, but statement 2 alone is not sufficient
   (B) statement 2 alone is sufficient to answer the question, but statement 1 alone is not sufficient
   (C) both statements together are needed to answer the question, but neither statement alone is sufficient
   (D) either statement by itself is sufficient to answer the question
   (E) not enough facts are given to answer the question

5. Is $A > B$?
   (1) $AX > BX$
   (2) $X < 0$
   (A) statement 1 alone is sufficient to answer the question, but statement 2 alone is not sufficient
   (B) statement 2 alone is sufficient to answer the question, but statement 1 alone is not sufficient
   (C) both statements together are needed to answer the question, but neither statement alone is sufficient
   (D) either statement by itself is sufficient to answer the question
   (E) not enough facts are given to answer the question

6. What is the length of the diagonal of a certain rectangle?
   (1) The area of the rectangle is 16.
   (2) The perimeter of the rectangle is 16.
   (A) statement 1 alone is sufficient to answer the question, but statement 2 alone is not sufficient
   (B) statement 2 alone is sufficient to answer the question, but statement 1 alone is not sufficient
   (C) both statements together are needed to answer the question, but neither statement alone is sufficient
   (D) either statement by itself is sufficient to answer the question
   (E) not enough facts are given to answer the question

7. If Tim weighs X, where X is a whole number, what is Tim's weight?
   (1) If Tim gains 6 pounds, he will weigh less than 186 pounds.
   (2) If Tim gains 8 pounds, he will weigh more than 186 pounds.
   (A) statement 1 alone is sufficient to answer the question, but statement 2 alone is not sufficient
   (B) statement 2 alone is sufficient to answer the question, but statement 1 alone is not sufficient
   (C) both statements together are needed to answer the question, but neither statement alone is sufficient
   (D) either statement by itself is sufficient to answer the question
   (E) not enough facts are given to answer the question

8. Is the integer T divisible by 15?
   (1) The sum of the digits of T equals 15.
   (2) The units digit of T is a 3.
   (A) statement 1 alone is sufficient to answer the question, but statement 2 alone is not sufficient
   (B) statement 2 alone is sufficient to answer the question, but statement 1 alone is not sufficient
   (C) both statements together are needed to answer the question, but neither statement alone is sufficient
   (D) either statement by itself is sufficient to answer the question
   (E) not enough facts are given to answer the question

9. A truck departed from Newton at 11:53 A.M. and arrived in Far City, 240 miles away, at 4:41 P.M. on the same day. What was the approximate average speed of the truck on this trip?
   (A) 20 mph
   (B) 34 mph
   (C) 50 mph
   (D) 54 mph
   (E) 72 mph

10. If m, n, o and p are real numbers, each of the following expressions equals $m(nop)$ EXCEPT
   (A) $(op)(mn)$
   (B) $ponm$
   (C) $p(onm)$
   (D) $(mp)(no)$
   (E) $(mn)(mo)(mp)$

ABCD is a square

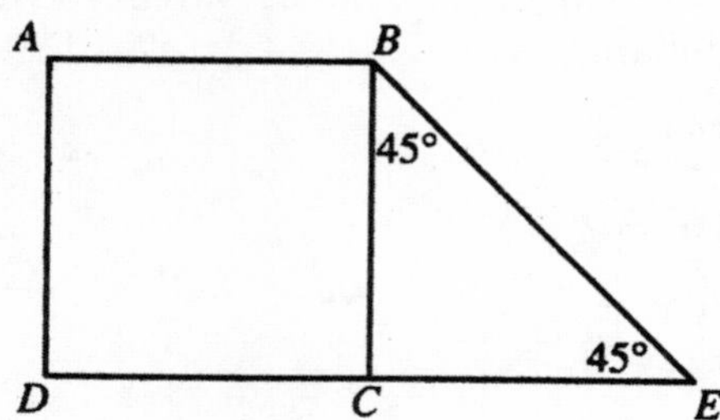

11. If the area of the triangle BCE is 8, what is the area of the square $ABCD$?
   (A) 16
   (B) $8\sqrt{2}$
   (C) 8
   (D) 4
   (E) $2\sqrt{2}$

12. The diagonal of the floor of a rectangular closet is $7\frac{1}{2}$ feet. The shorter side of the closet is $4\frac{1}{2}$ feet. What is the area of the closet in square feet?
   (A) 37
   (B) 27
   (C) $\frac{54}{4}$
   (D) $\frac{21}{4}$
   (E) 5

13. Which of the following fractions expressed in the form $\frac{P}{Q}$ is most nearly approximated by the decimal, $.PQ$, where P is the tenths' digit and Q is the hundredths' digit?
   (A) $\frac{1}{8}$
   (B) $\frac{2}{9}$
   (C) $\frac{3}{4}$
   (D) $\frac{4}{5}$
   (E) $\frac{8}{9}$

14. If b books can be purchased for d dollars, how many books can be purchased for m dollars?

(A) $\frac{bm}{d}$

(B) bdm

(C) $\frac{d}{bm}$

(D) $\frac{b+m}{d}$

(E) $\frac{b-m}{d}$

15. What is the length of the diagonal of a cube?

(1) The sides of the cube have length 1.

(2) The diagonals of the faces of the cube have length $\sqrt{2}$.

(A) statement 1 alone is sufficient to answer the question, but statement 2 alone is not sufficient

(B) statement 2 alone is sufficient to answer the question, but statement 1 alone is not sufficient

(C) both statements together are needed to answer the question, but neither statement alone is sufficient

(D) either statement by itself is sufficient to answer the question

(E) not enough facts are given to answer the question

16. If a square $MNOP$ has an area of 16, then its perimeter is

(A) 4

(B) 8

(C) 16

(D) 32

(E) 64

17. How long did a round trip take?

(1) The outward journey took 1 hour longer than the return journey.

(2) The return journey was 75 miles.

(A) statement 1 alone is sufficient to answer the question, but statement 2 alone is not sufficient

(B) statement 2 alone is sufficient to answer the question, but statement 1 alone is not sufficient

(C) both statements together are needed to answer the question, but neither statement alone is sufficient

(D) either statement by itself is sufficient to answer the question

(E) not enough facts are given to answer the question

18. John has more money than Mary but less than Bill. If the amounts held by John, Mary, and Bill are x, y, and z respectively, which of the following is true?

(A) $z < x < y$

(B) $x < z < y$

(C) $y < x < z$

(D) $y < z < x$

(E) $x < y < z$

19. 10% of 360 is how much more than 5% of 360?

(A) 5

(B) 9

(C) 18

(D) 36

(E) 48

20. If $x^2 + 3x + 10 = 1 + x^2$, then $x^2 =$

(A) 0

(B) 1

(C) 4

(D) 7

(E) 9

21. Which of the following must be true?

I. Any of two lines which are parallel to a third line are also parallel to each other.

II. Any two planes which are parallel to a third plane are parallel to each other.

III. Any two lines which are parallel to the same plane are parallel to each other.

(A) I only

(B) II only

(C) I and II only

(D) II and III only

(E) I, II, and III

22. An item costs 90% of its original price. If 90¢ is added to the discount price, the cost of the item will be equal to its original price. What is the original price of the item?

(A) $.09

(B) $.90

(C) $9.00

(D) $9.90

(E) $9.99

23. Points *R, S, T* and *U* are on line *RU* as shown. Which is greater, *TU* or *ST*?

(1) *RU* is 15 units long.

(2) Points *S* and *T* trisect line segment *RU*.

(A) statement 1 alone is sufficient to answer the question, but statement 2 alone is not sufficient

(B) statement 2 alone is sufficient to answer the question, but statement 1 alone is not sufficient

(C) both statements together are needed to answer the question, but neither statement alone is sufficient

(D) either statement by itself is sufficient to answer the question

(E) not enough facts are given to answer the question

24. John, Peter, and Paul together have ten marbles. If each has at least one marble, how many marbles does each boy have?

(1) John has 5 more than Paul.

(2) Peter has half as many as John.

(A) statement 1 alone is sufficient to answer the question, but statement 2 alone is not sufficient

(B) statement 2 alone is sufficient to answer the question, but statement 1 alone is not sufficient

(C) both statements together are needed to answer the question, but neither statement alone is sufficient

(D) either statement by itself is sufficient to answer the question

(E) not enough facts are given to answer the question

25. Is x positive?

(1) $x^2 - 1 = 0$

(2) $x^3 + 1 = 0$

(A) statement 1 alone is sufficient to answer the question, but statement 2 alone is not sufficient

(B) statement 2 alone is sufficient to answer the question, but statement 1 alone is not sufficient

(C) both statements together are needed to answer the question, but neither statement alone is sufficient

(D) either statement by itself is sufficient to answer the question

(E) not enough facts are given to answer the question

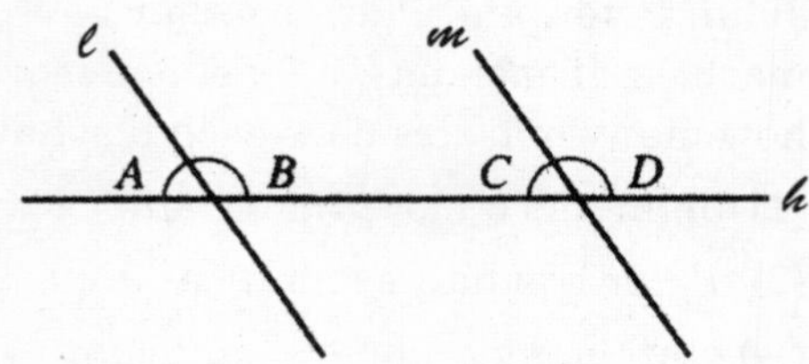

26. l, m, and h are straight lines with $l \parallel m$. Is $\angle b$ equal to 90°?
   (1) $\angle A = 55°$
   (2) $\angle D > 90°$
   (A) statement 1 alone is sufficient to answer the question, but statement 2 alone is not sufficient
   (B) statement 2 alone is sufficient to answer the question, but statement 1 alone is not sufficient
   (C) both statements together are needed to answer the question, but neither statement alone is sufficient
   (D) either statement by itself is sufficient to answer the question
   (E) not enough facts are given to answer the question

27. A rectangle is 40 inches long. What is its area?
   (1) Its perimeter is 140 inches.
   (2) The length of the diagonal is 50 inches.
   (A) statement 1 alone is sufficient to answer the question, but statement 2 alone is not sufficient
   (B) statement 2 alone is sufficient to answer the question, but statement 1 alone is not sufficient
   (C) both statements together are needed to answer the question, but neither statement alone is sufficient
   (D) either statement by itself is sufficient to answer the question
   (E) not enough facts are given to answer the question

28. What are the values of A and B?
   (1) $2A - 3B = 17$
   (2) $6B - 4A = -34$
   (A) statement 1 alone is sufficient to answer the question, but statement 2 alone is not sufficient
   (B) statement 2 alone is sufficient to answer the question, but statement 1 alone is not sufficient
   (C) both statements together are needed to answer the question, but neither statement alone is sufficient
   (D) either statement by itself is sufficient to answer the question
   (E) not enough facts are given to answer the question

29. If $mp + nq = 12mq$, and $mq > 0$, then $\frac{p}{q} + \frac{n}{m} = ?$
   (A) 12
   (B) $12mn$
   (C) $12m + 12q$
   (D) 0
   (E) $mp + nq$

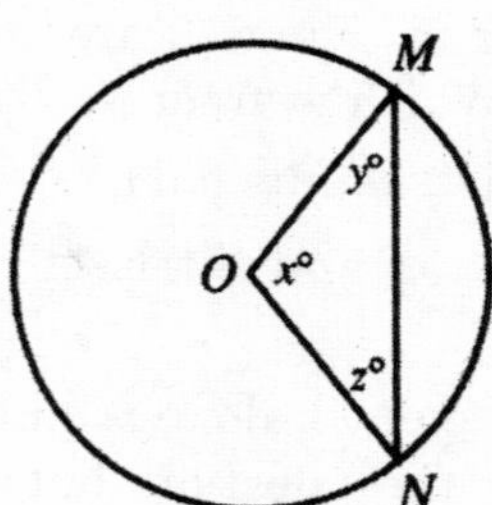

30. In circle O above, $MN > NO$. All of the following must be true EXCEPT
   (A) $MN < 2MO$
   (B) $x > y$
   (C) $z = y$
   (D) $x = y + z$
   (E) $x > 60°$

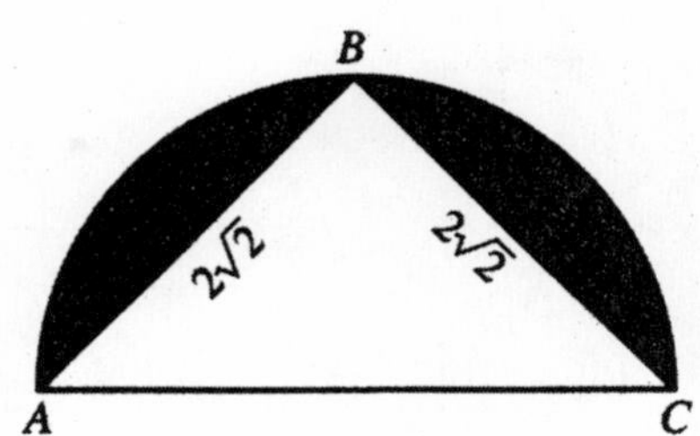

31. Triangle *ABC* is inscribed in a semicircle. What is the area of the shaded region above?

(A) $2\pi - 2$

(B) $2\pi - 4$

(C) $4\pi - 4$

(D) $8\pi - 4$

(E) $8\pi - 8$

32. The * of any number is defined as the result obtained by adding the square of the number to twice the number. What number is the * of 12?

(A) 12

(B) 168

(C) 1728

(D) 1752

(E) 2024

33. In the figure, $AB = BC$ and angles *BAD* and *BCD* are right angles. Which one of the following conclusions may be drawn?

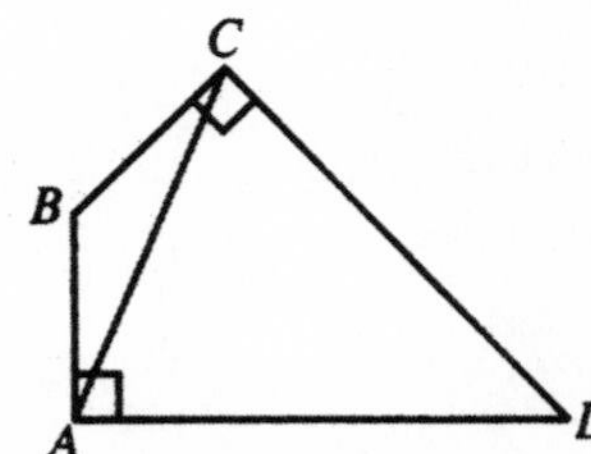

(A) measure of angle *BCA* = measure of angle *CAD*

(B) measure of angle *B* is greater than the measure of angle *D*

(C) $AC = CD$

(D) $AD = CD$

(E) *BC* is shorter than *CD*

34. A merchant sells a radio for $80, thereby making a profit of 25% of the cost. What is the ratio of cost to selling price?

(A) $\frac{4}{5}$

(B) $\frac{3}{4}$

(C) $\frac{5}{6}$

(D) $\frac{2}{3}$

(E) $\frac{3}{5}$

35. Is $A > B$?

(1) *A* is positive.

(2) $(A + B)^2$ is positive.

(A) statement 1 alone is sufficient to answer the question, but statement 2 alone is not sufficient

(B) statement 2 alone is sufficient to answer the question, but statement 1 alone is not sufficient

(C) both statements together are needed to answer the question, but neither statement alone is sufficient

(D) either statement by itself is sufficient to answer the question

(E) not enough facts are given to answer the question

36. How many degrees are between the hands of a clock at 3:40?

(A) 150°

(B) 140°

(C) 130°

(D) 125°

(E) 120°

practice test

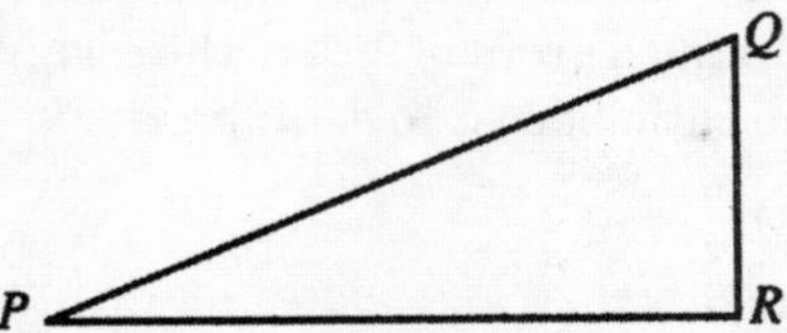

37. Is triangle PQR a right triangle?

(1) $\angle P < \angle Q$

(2) $\angle P + \angle Q = \angle R$

(A) statement 1 alone is sufficient to answer the question, but statement 2 alone is not sufficient

(B) statement 2 alone is sufficient to answer the question, but statement 1 alone is not sufficient

(C) both statements together are needed to answer the question, but neither statement alone is sufficient

(D) either statement by itself is sufficient to answer the question

(E) not enough facts are given to answer the question

ANSWER KEY AND EXPLANATIONS

Verbal Section

1. D	10. B	19. E	28. B	37. A
2. D	11. E	20. C	29. E	38. C
3. C	12. B	21. B	30. E	39. A
4. B	13. C	22. D	31. A	40. E
5. D	14. C	23. C	32. C	41. D
6. B	15. A	24. D	33. A	
7. B	16. E	25. B	34. B	
8. D	17. A	26. C	35. A	
9. A	18. E	27. A	36. E	

1. **The correct answer is (D).** (A) is incorrect because the "if" clause, expressing past condition contrary to fact, requires the past-perfect subjunctive ("had found"). (B) is wrong because the "possible conclusion" clause requires the perfect form of a modal auxiliary ("would have paid"). (C) fails because "fewer" refers to items that can be counted; tax, as a collective quantity, requires "less." (E) changes the meaning.

2. **The correct answer is (D).** (D) is not elegant but at least it is unambiguous and correct. Poor phrasing in (A) and (E) results in ambiguities: Do the columns contain volumes? Do the volumes have columns? (B) changes the tense and hence the overall meaning. (C) errs in agreement of subject and verb: the plural noun "libraries" must take the plural verb "contain."

3. **The correct answer is (C).** When seen from the context of the present, activities of ancient peoples should be described in the past (or past perfect) tenses. (A), (B), (D), and (E) put one or both of the ancient activities in the present or present perfect tenses. (D) also errs in adding three superfluous words. Only (C) is completely correct.

4. **The correct answer is (B).** The proposition that you cannot argue with taste says that taste is relative. Since we are looking for an answer choice inconsistent with that proposition, we seek an answer choice that argues that taste, or aesthetic value, is absolute, or at least not relative—that there are standards of taste. (B) is precisely that.

   (C) and (D) are just distractions, playing on the notion of taste in the physical sense and the further idea of the distasteful; but these superficial connections are not strong enough.

   (A), (B), and (E) are all activities in which there is some element of aesthetic judgment or appreciation. In (A), the holding of an exhibition, while implying some selection principle and thus some idea of a standard of taste, does not truly purport to judge aesthetics in the way that (B), precisely a beauty *contest*, does. The exhibition may be of historical or biographical interest, for example. (E) also stresses more of the exhibition aspect than the judging aspect. You should not infer that all movie festivals are contests, since the word "festival" does not require this interpretation and, in fact, there are festivals at which the judging aspect is minimal or non-existent. The Cannes Film Festival, while perhaps the best known, is not the only type of movie festival there is. The questions are not tests of your knowledge of the movie industry.

5. **The correct answer is (D).** Note the question stem carefully: We are to find the answer choice *from which* we can deduce the sample argument. You must pay careful attention to the question stem in every problem. (D) works nicely as it gives us the argument structure: "All post-1974 students are required. . . . George is a post-1974 student. Therefore, George is required. . . ." Actually, the middle premise is phrased in the conditional (with an "if"), but our explanation is close enough, even if it is a bit oversimplified. (A) will not suffice, for while it describes the situation before 1974, it just does not address itself to the post-1974 situation. And George is a post-1974 student. (B) also fails. From the fact that all of those who took the course graduated after 1974, we cannot conclude that George was one of them (any more than we can conclude from the proposition that all airline flight attendants lived after 1900 and that Richard Nixon, who lived after 1900, was one of them). (C) fails for the same reason that (A) fails. (E) is a bit tricky because of the double negative. It makes the sentence awkward. The easiest way to handle such a sentence is to treat the double negative as an affirmative. The negative cancels the negative, just as in arithmetic a negative number times a negative number yields a positive number. So (E) actually says that before 1974 the course was not required. That is equivalent to (A) and must be wrong for the same reason.

6. **The correct answer is (B).** (A), (C), and (D) require 14 words each to say what (B) says, more gracefully, in 12. (E) changes the meaning.

7. **The correct answer is (B).** (B) is the only one of the three which is completely supported by the argument. (C) is easily dismissed. That there are no minnows on this side of the lake now surely does not mean that there will never be any, any more than the fact that there are no children in the park now means that there never will be any children in the park. (A) is very close to (B) and differs only in the qualification introduced by the word "probably," but that is an important qualification. The author states specifically that bass are *usually* found wherever there are minnows. So where there are no bass, he *expects* to find no minnows. But, of course, he cannot be certain. Perhaps there are other reasons for the absence of bass: The water is too cold or too shallow or too muddy for bass, though not for minnows. So (A) overstates the case. The author apparently allows that you may find minnows without bass—but not usually. (D) cannot be deduced from the premises since no information is provided about rivers (as opposed to lakes). And (E) is not inferable, since the information about lakes does not preclude the possibility that largemouth bass are found elsewhere.

8. **The correct answer is (D).** Juanita wonders how Tommy knows the phone has rung if he couldn't hear it because of the shower. She overlooks the possibility that he learned the phone had rung without actually hearing it himself. Perhaps someone else lives with him who heard it; perhaps Tommy has an answering machine and later learned that the phone rang while he was in the shower, maybe the caller calls back and tells Tommy he called earlier and Tommy says "Oh, I must have been in the shower and didn't hear it." Juanita overlooks these possibilities. (A) is incorrect because Juanita apparently assumes the phone does ring and that Tommy can hear it ringing. (C)

and (E) may or may not be true, but they do not address themselves to Juanita's statement. (B) could only underlie Juanita's objection to Tommy's remarks if hearing calls were the only possible way in which Tommy could learn of the call. But as we show, there are other possibilities.

9. **The correct answer is (A).** (C) and (E) are incorrect because the clause expressing past condition contrary to fact requires past-perfect subjunctive ("had known"). (D) is incorrect because the clause stating a possible conclusion requires the perfect form of a modal auxiliary ("would have come"). (A) and (B) both use the correct verb forms in both clauses but (B) adds "if "; this word is superfluous and alters the word order required by Standard Written English.

10. **The correct answer is (B).** (A) requires 15 words, and (C) 12, to say what (B) says in 11. (D) and (E) change the meaning.

11. **The correct answer is (E).** (A), (B), (C), and (D) are obviously confused: men whose landing and assault surprised the enemy could not have been prisoners at the time. (D) also confuses "affected" with "effected."

12. **The correct answer is (B).** This is a main idea question. In the very first paragraph the author presents the distinction between unlabeled and prohibited uses and then proceeds to develop the important implications of the distinction. (B) correctly describes this form of argument. (A) must be incorrect since no theory is cited for refutation. (C) is incorrect since no opponent is mentioned. (D) can be eliminated since there is no evidence that the practice of unlabeled uses is a recent development. (E) can be eliminated for either of two reasons. First, if one interprets "error" here to mean the practice of forbidden uses, then that is not the main point of the argument. Or if one interprets "error" to mean the confusing of unlabeled with prohibited uses, then (E) is eliminated because "condemn" is inappropriate. The author may wish to correct a misconception, but that is not the wording of (E). Moreover, the method used to accomplish that end is drawing a distinction. Thus, (B) stands as correct.

13. **The correct answer is (C).** This is an explicit idea question. The reference we need is to be found in the first paragraph. There the author explains that the term "unlabeled use" is used to refer to any medically valuable use of any already approved drug that has not yet been specifically recognized by the FDA. (A) is incorrect because this is a prohibited use, as that term is used in the text. (B) is incorrect because an unlabeled use is one that was not considered when the drug was originally labeled; it is one discovered later, not one proposed, tested and rejected. (D) is incorrect because this use the author would term a labeled use. Finally, (E) is incorrect since this refers to research designed to determine whether a drug has labeled uses because it meets the legal standard of substantial evidence of such uses.

14. **The correct answer is (C).** This is an inference question that requires that we collate information from two parts of the passage. In paragraph two the author refers to physicians who persist in prohibited use for one of two reasons: ignorance or refusal to accept evidence. Then, in the third paragraph, the author refers to physicians who use drugs in violation of labeling instructions as either uninformed or intransigent. The parallelism here tells us that the intransigent physician is the one who rejects the evidence that the drug is ineffective. This is neatly captured by (C). (A) is incorrect since the intransigent physician prescribes the drug in violation of the labeling provision because he believes that the drug is effec-

answers

tive. (B) is incorrect, for this would be a physician who is anything but intransigent. As for (D), an intransigent physician might take such actions, but this is not the defining characteristic of an intransigent physician. Finally, (E) can be eliminated since the author specifically expresses reservations as to whether such behavior is illegal.

15. **The correct answer is (A).** Here we have an explicit detail question, with a thought reverser. Four of the five choices will be incorrect because they are mentioned in the passage. The remaining choice will be correct because it is the one *not* explicitly mentioned. (B) can be eliminated since the medical benefits of an unlabeled usage are specifically mentioned in both the first and final paragraphs. (C) is incorrect since the time lag that might delay application of a new usage is mentioned in the first paragraph as a reason for permitting that usage, even though that usage has not been formally approved. (D), too, must be incorrect since the possibility that a manufacturer might not incur the expenses to secure formal approval of a new usage is explicitly mentioned in the first paragraph. Finally, (E) can be eliminated since the first paragraph also points out that literature is available to ensure that doctors are familiar with the limitations of the unlabeled use. (A) must be the correct answer, for nowhere in the passage is the cost to the consumer mentioned as a reason for allowing unlabeled usage.

16. **The correct answer is (E).** This is an application, and we must find the statement that is most likely to be acceptable to the author. (E) would likely be embraced by the author since it is in agreement with the first paragraph of the passage, which explains that unlabeled uses are created by the time lag between the discovery of the use and the accumulation of data needed to prove that use effective. (A) is an attractive answer, but it fails upon careful reading. The distinction referred to there is that between approved and unlabeled uses. The distinction which the author attempts to draw is between two types of unapproved uses: unlabeled and prohibited. This is the distinction which has been blurred, says the author, not the distinction between approved and unlabeled. (B) is incorrect for the same reason. The blurred distinction is between unlabeled and prohibited uses (both types of unapproved uses), not between approved and unlabeled uses. (C) is incorrect since the distinction between unlabeled and approved uses is a matter of practice, not categorization. The unlabeled use exists because a physician *uses* the drug in a beneficial but not yet approved way, not because the physician or government decides that the use is unlabeled versus approved. (D) is incorrect since the author calls for caution in unlabeled use in the final paragraph.

17. **The correct answer is (A).** This is a tone question. What is the author's attitude toward unlabeled usage? In the passage, the author notes benefits to be derived from unlabeled usages, but the author also points out some dangers in such usage. Unlabeled usage, then, in the author's view, can best be described as a compromise necessitated by economic and perhaps social (governmental) factors. Thus, (A) is correct. (B) is incorrect for it states the case too strongly. The author recognizes both the dangers and the benefits of unlabeled usages. (D) is incorrect for overstating the case in the other direction. The author mentions not only advantages but disadvantages to the policy. (C) can be eliminated for it does not describe the author's attitude. Unlabeled uses are arguably (but only arguably, see final paragraph) illegal,

but that is not the defining characteristic of the author's attitude toward the *policy* of tolerating the unlabeled usages. Finally, (E) is incorrect for two reasons. One, it, like (C), is not responsive to the question, that is, (E) is not descriptive of the author's attitude. Two, if anything, the passage supports the conclusion that the practice of unlabeled usage is not short-term but inherent in the licensing process.

18. **The correct answer is (E).** This is a main idea question, and the main idea of this passage, already discussed at some length, is neatly summarized by (E). Answer (B) is surely the second best answer, but (B) must fail by comparison with (E) because it is too narrow. To be sure, one point the author makes is that the physician who prescribes unlabeled uses should not be subject to legal liability. But that is only part of the argument. That recommendation depends on the distinction between the two types of unapproved uses. (E) makes reference to this additional point. Notice also that in a way (B) is included in (E), so (E) is broad enough to describe the overall point of the author. (A) is incorrect since the author is cautioning against overzealous enforcement of laws against unlabeled uses. (C) is incorrect because it is never mentioned in the passage. Finally, (D) is incorrect because this is at best a minor part of the argument.

19. **The correct answer is (E).** (A) is not inconsistent with the advertisement since the ad is touting the strength of the pain-reliever, not its price. (C), too, can easily be seen not to be inconsistent. The ad speaks of non-prescription pain-relievers, but (C) brings up the irrelevant matter of prescription pain-relievers. (B) is not inconsistent because RELIEF does not claim to be the strongest pain-reliever, only that no other non-prescription pain-reliever is stronger. (D) is not inconsistent because it does not talk about sales but about medicine given "free of charge" in a study. (E), however, directly contradicts the ad.

20. **The correct answer is (C).** (C) is an assumption of the psychologist. She observed the dogs for a certain period of time, and found that each time a stranger approached they kept silent. From those observed instances she concluded that the dogs never barked at strangers. Obviously her theory would be disproved (or at least it would have to be seriously qualified) if, when she was not watching, the dogs barked their heads off at strangers. (A) is not an assumption because the speaker makes no value judgment about how dogs ought to be treated. (B) is similar in that no such broad conclusion about "better adjusted" is implied. (D) and (E) are simply confused readings of the speaker's thinking.

21. **The correct answer is (B).** (B) would undermine the psychologist's thesis that "only a beaten dog barks." It cites instances in which the dog was not beaten and still barked at strangers. This would force the psychologist to reconsider her conclusion about the connection between beating and barking. (A) is not like (B). It does not state the dogs were never beaten; it states only that the dogs were not beaten when they barked at strangers. It is conceivable that they were beaten at other times. If they were, then even though they might bark at strangers (and not be beaten at that moment), they would not be counter-examples to the psychologist's theory. (C) is not an assumption of the psychologist, as we saw in the preceding question, so denying it does not affect the strength of her argument. The psychologist is concerned with the factual connection between beating a dog and its barking; information about the owners' feelings can hardly be relevant to the factual issue. (D) is an inter-

esting choice, but the fact that some of the dogs also barked at non-strangers doesn't address the connection between discipline and barking at strangers: so they also barked at non-strangers, so what? And (E) is wrong because the analysis depends not on the particular object used, but on the notion of physical discipline.

22. **The correct answer is (D).** Context indicates Jones is not afraid of bad weather; all that is required is a single negative. (A) uses a double negative ("Un-" and "neither . . . nor"). (C) incorrectly mixes the "either . . . or" and "neither . . . nor" constructions. (B) and (E) change the meaning.

23. **The correct answer is (C).** (A) requires 22 words to say what (C) says in 18. (B), (D), and (E) all change the meaning of the original; (B) also uses the singular verb "has" with the plural noun "recommendations."

24. **The correct answer is (D).** (A) is wordier than need be, fails to repeat "to" in the parallel structure ("to refine . . . to increase"), and misplaces the modifier "both." (B) and (C) needlessly substitute "utilized" for the short, simple "used." (E) uses a loose "also" instead of the tight "both" construction and incorrectly adds a comma.

25. **The correct answer is (B).** Here the author must assume that every effect which is part of the child's experience has been generated by a cause which was also a part of the child's experience, but that is possible only on the assumption that the cause, which is an effect itself, is the result of some previous cause. In other words, every effect flows from some earlier effect. Now, admittedly, that seems to lead to a pretty absurd conclusion: Therefore, there could be no beginning of experience for the child—it must stretch back infinitely. But the question stem does not ask us to critique the argument, only to analyze it and uncover its premises. (A) is wrong because the author does not say all experiences are alike, only that the one today has its roots in the one yesterday. For example, sometimes the presence of moisture in the atmosphere causes rain, sometimes snow. (C) oversimplifies matters in two respects. One, while the author may agree that a child's experiences may tell us *something* about the parents (assuming the child is in intimate contact with them), we surely would not want to conclude that is the *best* way to learn about the parents. Two, the parents are not the only source of experience the child has, so the later effects would be the result of non-parental causes as well. (D) is incorrect because the author need not assume that experience is cumulative. In some cases, the cause-and-effect sequence may only reiterate itself so that experience is circular rather than cumulative. Finally, (E) is another example of going too far—of extending a simple factual statement beyond the scope the author originally gave it. Here the author says that experience causes experience, but never suggests that we are in a position to use this principle practically, to manipulate the input to mold the child.

26. **The correct answer is (C).** The author claims that we have unbounded resources, and tries to prove this by showing that we are getting better and better at extracting those resources from the ground. But that is like saying, "I have found a way to get the last little bit of toothpaste out of the tube; therefore, the tube will never run out." (C) calls our attention to this oversight. (A) does not contradict the author's claim. In fact, it seems to support it. The author might suggest, "Even if we run out of fossil fuels, we still have uranium for nuclear power." (B) is an attack on the author's general stance, but it does not really

contradict the particular conclusion drawn. The author says, "We have enough." (B) says, "It is expensive." Both could very well be true, so they cannot contradict one another. (D) is similar to (B). Yes, you may be correct, the technology is expensive, or in this case wasteful, but it will still get us the fuel we need. Finally, (E) is incorrect for pretty much these same reasons. Yes, the energy will have unwanted side effects, but the author claimed only that we could get the energy. The difficulty with (B), (D), and (E) is that though they attack the author's general *position* they do not *contradict* the author's *conclusion*.

27. **The correct answer is (A).** The author's position is in opposition to the position of the sociologists cited. Because the author claims an alternative interpretation of the evidence, the most logical continuation of the passage will be the one which explains why such sects are not a recent phenomenon even though there are no old ones around. (A) does this neatly. Since the members abstain from sexual relations, they will not reproduce members and the sect will tend to die out. This explains why there are none more than 50 or 60 years old. (C), if anything, supports the position of the sociologists, for it implicitly gives up trying to explain the evidence differently and also undercuts the explanation the author might have given. (B) is irrelevant because intensity of religious fervor is irrelevant to the length of the sect's existence; it cannot possibly help the author explain away the evidence of the sociologists. (D) is irrelevant for another reason. The author needs to explain why the sects are all relatively young without having recourse to the thesis of the sociologists that they are a recent phenomenon. That there are other organizations which encourage sexual relations of whatever kind cannot help the author explain a phenomenon such as the Waiters. Finally, (E) is a distraction, picking up as it does on a minor detail. The author needs to explain the short-livedness of groups of which the Waiters is only an example.

28. **The correct answer is (B).** This is a main idea question. The author begins by acknowledging that there exists an actual differential between the earnings of whites and blacks, but then the author moves quickly to block the automatic presupposition that this is attributable to discrimination *in employment*. The author then examines the effect of various productivity variables on the differentials between black and white men and between black and white women, with particular emphasis on the latter. The conclusion of the argument is that there is little difference in the adjusted earnings of black and white women, and the reason for this is the overpowering influence of sexual discrimination. (B) captures this analysis. (A) is incorrect since the author's primary focus is the black woman. Black female workers are studied by comparing them with white female workers. The differentials between men and women generally are only incidentally related to this analysis. (C) fails because this is a subordinate level of argumentation. The author introduces productivity factors to adjust actual earnings merely to evaluate better the effects of discrimination. (D) is incorrect since no history is offered aside from casual references to the distribution of workers. Finally, (E) is incorrect since the author makes no such recommendations.

29. **The correct answer is (E).** This is an explicit idea question, the answer to which is found in paragraphs one and two. There the author states that the actual ratio is not an accurate measure of discrimination *in employment* because it fails to take account of productivity factors. (A) is incorrect because of the word "in-

clude"—the gross ratio fails to *adjust* for distribution. (B) is not mentioned and so cannot be an answer to a question that begins with the phrase "According to the passage . . ." (C), too, is never mentioned in the passage, and so it fails for the same reason, as does (D).

30. **The correct answer is (E).** This is an explicit detail question and our needed reference is the third paragraph, which gives us comparisons, or ratios, of the earnings of black men to the earnings of white men and of the earnings of black women to the earnings of white women. Notice that the comparisons are relative. We never get actual dollar amounts, nor do we get comparisons between women and men. (E) recognizes that the only conclusion that can be drawn on this basis is that the differential between black and white women is less than the differential between black and white men. The first is a difference of only 2 to 5 percent (before adjustment for productivity factors), while the second is about 20 percent (before adjustment). (A), (C), and (D) can be eliminated on the ground that no such male/female comparison is possible. (B) can be eliminated since no such information is supplied.

31. **The correct answer is (A).** This is a logical structure question. The author states that there are two explanations to be considered: (1) black men are found in jobs characterized by greater racial discrimination, and (2) sexual discrimination in the case of women renders insignificant the racial discrimination against black women. But each of these could be true since both could contribute to the phenomenon being studied. There is only an empirical, not a logical, connection between the two, that is, the extent to which each does have explanatory power as a matter of fact. On this ground we can eliminate every other answer choice.

32. **The correct answer is (C).** This is a tone question, and the best description of the treatment of the subject matter is provided by (C). (A) can be eliminated for the treatment, while confident, is not offensive. (B) can be eliminated for that reason as well. (D) is incorrect since there is nothing tentative or inconclusive about the treatment. To acknowledge that one is unable to determine which of two competing theories is preferable is not to be inconclusive or tentative. Finally, though some readers may find in the author's discussion reason for hope or optimism, we cannot say that the author actually shows us these attitudes.

33. **The correct answer is (A).** This is an application question. What would happen if sexual discrimination against women were no longer a factor? On the assumption that the second hypothesis is correct, racial discrimination against women is not a significant factor because it is overpowered by sexual discrimination. The author acknowledges the existence of the racial discrimination, so elimination of the sexual discrimination should result in the manifestation of increased racial discrimination against black women (on the assumption that the second theory is correct). The result should be a greater disparity between white and black female workers, with white female workers enjoying the higher end of the ratio. This is articulated by (A). (B) is contradicted by this analysis and must be incorrect. (C) is irrelevant since male earning levels are not being explained. Finally, there is nothing to suggest that (D) or (E) would occur.

34. **The correct answer is (B).** This is a tone question. Notice that this question asks not about the tone of the presentation but about the author's attitude toward a particular subject. We must take our cue from the first paragraph, where the author refers to the efforts of "respon-

sible employers." This indicates that the author is sympathetic to the situation of workers who are victims of discrimination. (B) is the best way of describing this attitude. (E) is much too strong, for concern is not anxiety. Further, (C) is much too weak, for the reference to responsible employers indicates the author is not indifferent. (D), like (E), overstates the case. Finally, (A) is incorrect since the author offers no apology.

35. **The correct answer is (A).** Here we are looking for the most perfect analogy. Keep in mind, first, that the author opposes the move, and second, all of the features of the union-management situation in particular that they are adversaries. (A) captures both elements. The relationship between prison administrators and inmates is adversarial, and the suggestion that inmates make decisions on security is outrageous enough that it captures also the first element. (B) fails on both counts. First, the two are not on opposites of the fence; second, the senior officer is *asking* for advice—not deferring to the opinion of his junior officer. (C) is very similar. First, the administration of the university and the student body are not necessarily adversaries; at least, although they may disagree on the best means for advancing the goals of the university, there is often agreement about those goals. Second, the administration is, as with (B), *asking* advice, not abdicating responsibility for the decision. In (D) we lack both elements; the mayor need not be an adversary of the state legislators (he may be seeking their assistance), nor is he giving them his authority to make decisions. Finally, (E) lacks both elements as well; the minister is a leader, not an adversary, who is discussing questions, not delegating authority.

36. **The correct answer is (E).** The author's reason for rejecting the notion of labor participation in management decisions is that the labor leaders first have a responsibility to the people they represent and that the responsibility would color their thinking about the needs of the corporation. This thinking is reflected in the adage: No man can serve two masters. (B) is incorrect for the author is referring to the labor *leaders*, not the rank-and-file; and it is specifically mentioned that the leaders are skilled administrators. (D) is incorrect because it, too, fails to respect the distinction between union leader and union member. (A) is a distraction. The notion that the authority would be "symbolically undermined" is edifying but finds no support in the paragraph. In any event, it entirely misses the main point of the paragraph as we have explained it. (C) also fails to observe the distinction between leader and worker, not to mention also that it is only remotely connected with the discussion.

37. **The correct answer is (A).** (B), (D), and (E) change the meaning. (C) omits the "do" needed to focus the contrast with married women who "do not."

38. **The correct answer is (C).** In its first two phrases, the original sentence establishes a pattern of parallelism ("Your . . . meddling, your . . . ridiculing"). (A), (B), and (E) fail to continue the pattern. Both (C) and (D) do continue it ("your . . . departing"), but (D) adds three unnecessary words, leaving (C) as the best version.

39. **The correct answer is (A).** (A) is circular. It is like saying, "I never tell a lie; and you must believe that because, as I have just told you, I never tell a lie." So (A) is the answer. (E) might seem circular: Guns do not cause crimes, people do. But it is not. The point is that these crimes would be committed anyway, and the author explains how they would be committed. (C) is an *ad hominem* attack. It rejects the conclusion of the argument not because the argument is illogical but because it comes from a particular source.

Remember, not all *ad hominem* are illegitimate. It is perfectly all right to inquire into possible biases of the source, and that is just what occurs here. (D) is a fairly weak argument. It takes a handful of observed instances and generalizes to a strong conclusion. But even though it may be weak, it does fit the description "generalization." (B) is just left over and fits none of the descriptions.

40. **The correct answer is (E).** The conclusion of the speaker is that the checkup has *no* value, so anything which suggests the checkup does have value will undermine the conclusion. (A) shows a possible advantage of having the checkup. It says, in effect, while the checkup is not foolproof and will not catch everything, it does catch some fairly important things. (B) also gives us a possible reason for having a 5,000-mile checkup. Even if it won't keep our car in running order, it is necessary if we want to take advantage of our warranty. Finally, (C) also gives us a good reason to have a checkup: The mechanic will make some routine adjustments. (D) weakens the argument on the theory that "A ounce of prevention is worth a pound of cure." Choice (E), however, actually seems to strengthen the argument: the policy prevents very few problems.

41. **The correct answer is (D).** Choices (A), (B), (C), and (E) each contain one or two errors in agreement of subject and verb. Plural subject "breeding and education" requires plural verb "establish," just as plural subject "occupation and income" requires "do."

answers

ANSWER KEY AND EXPLANATIONS

Quantitative Section

1. D	9. C	17. E	25. B	33. D
2. E	10. E	18. C	26. D	34. A
3. D	11. A	19. C	27. D	35. E
4. E	12. B	20. E	28. E	36. C
5. C	13. E	21. C	29. A	37. B
6. C	14. A	22. C	30. D	
7. C	15. D	23. B	31. B	
8. B	16. C	24. C	32. B	

1. **The correct answer is (D).** The minute hand will make one complete circle of the dial by 7:15. Then it will complete another half circle by 7:45. Since there are 360° in a circle, the arc traveled by the minute hand will be one full 360° plus half of another full 360°, yielding 360° + 180° = 540°.

2. **The correct answer is (E).** One way of solving this problem would be to rename each of the fractions as a decimal or find a common denominator so that a direct comparison can be made. This is too time-consuming. Instead, anytime the GMAT asks a question similar to this one, the student can be confident that there is very likely some shortcut available. Here the shortcut is to recognize that every answer choice, except for (E), is either equal to or greater than $\frac{1}{2}$, $\frac{7}{8}$ and $\frac{8}{9}$ are clearly much larger than $\frac{1}{2}$, $\frac{7}{12}$ must be greater than $\frac{1}{2}$ since $\frac{6}{12}$ is equal to $\frac{1}{2}$. But $\frac{6}{17}$ is less than $\frac{1}{2}$. So (E) is the least of the fractions. Even if the shortcut had eliminated only two or three answers, it would have been worthwhile.

3. **The correct answer is (D).** The area of a rectangle equals its length times its width, and the perimeter of a rectangle is the sum of its sides, or twice the sum of its length and its width. From (1) you can find the width of the rectangle:

$$5W = 20$$
$$W = 4$$

You can then find the perimeter of the rectangle:

$$2(L + W) = P$$
$$2(5 + 4) = P = 18$$

From (2) you can also determine the length and width of the rectangle by setting up an equation with one unknown $x(x - 1) = 20$, where x equals the length and $(x - 1)$ equals the width. Then, solving for x:

$$x^2 - x - 20 = 0$$
$$(x - 5)(x + 4) = 0$$

$x = 5$ or $x = -4$. Since a negative length is impossible, the length, x, is 5, and the width, $x - 1$, is 4. Thus the perimeter is $2(5 + 4) = 18$. To answer the question, it is not necessary to solve the equations and actually find the perimeter using (1) and (2) separately. It is sufficient (the name of the section is Data Sufficiency) to know that the length and width can be found by each of the two statements separately.

4. **The correct answer is (E).** From (1) or (2) separately, you know that the average can be either greater than 10 or less than 10; just think of groups of numbers that yield averages both less than 10 and greater than 10. For example, five 11's and five 1's yield an average of 6, but five 9's and five 15's yield an average of 12. Using (1) and (2) together will not produce an answer to the question either; the same two groups above can be used to answer the question either "yes" or "no."

5. **The correct answer is (C).** If $AX > BX$, $A > B$ if X is positive, but $A < B$ if X is negative because multiplying or dividing both sides of an inequality by the same negative number changes the direction of the inequality, but multiplying or dividing by a positive number does not change the direction. (2) by itself tells you nothing about A or B. (1) and (2) together, however, tell you that $A < B$. Thus the answer to the question is "no."

6. **The correct answer is (C).** If the area of the rectangle is 16, the length and width are variable, e.g., 4 and 4, 8 and 2, 16 and 1, and thus the length of the diagonal is variable. If the perimeter is 16, the length and width are also variable, e.g., 1 and 7, 2 and 6, 3 and 5, and thus the length of the diagonal is also variable. If (1) and (2) are both used, then the length must be 4 and the width must be 4, so that the diagonal, according to the Pythagorean Theorem, is $4\sqrt{2}$. Using (1) and (2) together gives two equations with two unknowns, an area equation and a perimeter equation, enabling you to determine the length and width of the rectangle and, therefore, the length of the diagonal by means of the Pythagorean Theorem.

7. **The correct answer is (C).** (1) tells you that $X + 6 < 186$ and $X < 180$ (subtracting 6 from both sides), which is not sufficient to answer the question. (2) tells you that $X + 8 > 186$ and $X > 178$ (subtracting 8 from both sides), which is not sufficient to answer the question. Both (1) and (2) together tell you that $178 < X < 180$ (X is greater than 178 and less than 180), which implies that X is 179 (since X must be a whole number).

8. **The correct answer is (B).** If (1) is true, then T may or may not be divisible by 15; for example, T could be 555, which is divisible by 15 (divisible means that the result of dividing is an integer with no remainder, or an integer rather than an integer plus a proper fraction), or T could be 348, which is not divisible by 15. (2) tells you that T is definitely not divisible by 15, because in order for an integer to be divisible by 15 it must also be divisible by 5 (since 5 is a factor of 15). An integer divisible by 5 must have a 5 or 0 as its last digit. Since in (2) the units digit is 3 (not 5 or 0), the integer is not divisible by 5 and hence not by 15. Thus, given (2) only, the answer to the question is "no."

9. **The correct answer is (C).** Average speed is nothing more than miles traveled over the time taken: rate speed = $\frac{\text{distance}}{\text{time}}$. The elapsed time here is 4 hours and 48 minutes. 48 minutes is $\frac{4}{5}$ hours. Our formula then will be: $\frac{240}{4\frac{4}{5}}$. We attack the problem by renaming the denominator as an improper fraction: $4\frac{4}{5} = \frac{24}{5}$ and then we multiply by the reciprocal of the divisor:

$$\frac{240 \text{ miles}}{4\frac{4}{5}} = \frac{240}{\frac{24}{5}} = \frac{5 \times \cancel{240}^{10}}{\cancel{24}} = 50 \text{ miles/hr.}$$

Notice that setting up the problem in this way avoids a lot of needless arithmetic.

This is characteristic of the GMAT. Most problems do not require a lengthy calculation. Usually the numbers used in constructing the questions are selected in a way that will allow for dividing like factors, factoring, or other shortcut devices. On the test, fractions are usually easier to work with than decimals.

10. **The correct answer is (E).** Multiplication is both associative and commutative. By associative, we mean that the grouping of the elements is not important—for example, $(5 \times 6) \times 7 = 5 \times (6 \times 7)$. By commutative we mean that the order of the elements is unimportant—for example, $5 \times 6 = 6 \times 5$. So (A), (B), (C), and (D) are all alternative forms for m(nop), but (E) is not: $(mn)(mo)(mp) = m^3nop$.

11. **The correct answer is (A).** There is an easy and a more complicated way to handle this question. The more complex method is to begin with the formula for the area of a triangle: Area = $\frac{1}{2}$(altitude)(base). Since angle *CBE* is equal to angle *CEB*, *BC* is equal to *CE*, and the altitude and the base are equal. So:

$$8 = \frac{1}{2}(BC)(CE)$$
$$16 = (BC)(BC)$$
$$BC = 4$$

And, of course, *BC* is also the side of the square, so the area of the square is $4 \times 4 = 16$.

Now, an easier method of solving the problem is to recognize that *BC* and *CE* are equal to sides of the square *ABCD*, so the area of triangle *BCE* is simply half that of the square. So the square must be double the triangle, or 16. A 45-45-90 right triangle is half of a square, and its hypotenuse is the diagonal of the square.

12. **The correct answer is (B).** Although some students will be able to solve this problem without the use of a diagram, for most drawing the floor plan of the closet is the logical starting point:

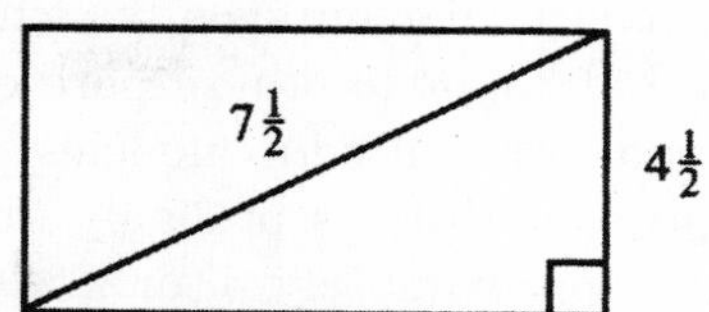

Now it becomes clear that the Pythagorean Theorem is the key to solving this problem. Once the dimensions are renamed as improper fractions, the problem is simplified further: the triangle is a 3-4-5 right triangle ($\frac{9}{2}$, $\frac{12}{2}$, $\frac{15}{2}$). The two legs of the right triangle are simultaneously the width and length of the rectangle. So the area of the closet is:

$$\frac{9}{2} \times 6 = \frac{54}{2} = 27$$

13. **The correct answer is (E).** This is an unusual problem, one which requires careful reading rather than some clever mathematical insight. The question asks us to compare the fractions in the form with the decimal *.PQ*. For example, we rename the fraction $\frac{1}{8}$ as the decimal .18 for purposes of comparison and ask how closely the second approximates the first. Since $\frac{1}{8}$ is .125, we see that the fit is not a very precise one. Similarly, with $\frac{2}{9}$, the corresponding decimal we are to compare is .29, but the actual decimal equivalent of $\frac{2}{9}$ is .222. The equivalent for $\frac{3}{4}$ is .34, not even close to the actual decimal equivalent of .75. Similarly, for $\frac{4}{5}$, the artificially derived .45 is not very close to the actual decimal equivalent of .80; but for $\frac{8}{9}$ we use the decimal .89, and this is fairly close—the closest of all the fractions listed—to the actual decimal equivalent of , which is .888.

If you have difficulties in finding the decimals for fractions, try to relate the fractions to percentages, which are in hundredths, or to other, more common decimal-fraction equivalencies. For example, one-third is probably known to you as approximately .33 or 33%. A ninth is one-third of a third; hence a ninth is approximately $\frac{33\%}{3} = 11\%$ or .11. Eight-ninths is thus 8(11%) = 88%.

14. **The correct answer is (A).** If a problem seems a bit too abstract to handle using algebraic notation, a sometimes useful technique is to try to find a similar, more familiar situation. For example, virtually everyone could answer the following question: Books cost $5 each; how many books can be bought for $100? The calculation goes: $\frac{1 \text{ book}}{\$5} \times \$100 = 20$ books. So, too, here the number of books which can be purchased per d dollars must be multiplied by the number of dollars to be spent, or m: $\frac{b}{d} \times m$, or $\frac{bm}{d}$. Pursuing this line of attack, it might be worthwhile to point out that substitution of real numbers in problems like this is often an effective way of solving the problem. Since the variables and the formulas are general—that is, they do not depend upon any given number of books or dollars—the correct answer choice must work for all possible values. Suppose we assume, therefore, 2(b) books can be purchased for $5($d$), and that the amount to be spent is $50($m$). Most people can fall back onto common sense to calculate the number of books that can be purchased with $50: 20 books. But of the five formulas offered as answer choices, only (A) gives the number 20 when the values are substituted: For $b = 2$, $d = 5$ and $m = 50$, (A) $= \frac{(2)(50)}{5} = 20$, (B) = (2)(5)(50) = 500, (C) $= \frac{5}{(2)(50)} = \frac{1}{20}$, (D)$= \frac{2+50}{5} = \frac{52}{5}$, (E) $= \frac{2-50}{5} = \frac{-48}{5}$. Substitution will take longer than a direct algebraic approach, but it is much better than simply guessing if you have the time and can't get the algebra to work right.

15. **The correct answer is (D).** (1) by itself fixes the size of the cube completely and is therefore sufficient to answer the question (the answer is $\sqrt{3}$). Likewise, (2) by itself fixes the size of the cube completely, because from the length of the diagonals of the faces you can deduce that the sides are of length 1, and it is therefore sufficient to answer the question.

16. **The correct answer is (C).** The formula for the area of a square is side times side. Since the square has an area of 16, we know $s \times s = 16$, $s^2 = 16$, so side = 4. Then we compute the perimeter of the square as the sum of the lengths of its four sides: 4 + 4 + 4 + 4 = 16.

17. **The correct answer is (E).** (1) tells you nothing about the time the return journey took. Using (1) by itself, you can conclude only that the round trip took more than one hour. (2) by itself tells you nothing about how long the return journey or the round trip took. (1) and (2) together likewise tell you nothing about the length of time that any portion of the trip took.

18. **The correct answer is (C).** Since John has more money than Mary, we note that x is greater than y. Then, John has less money than Bill has, so x is less than z. This gives us $x > y$ or $y < x$ and $x < z$. Thus (C), $y < x < z$.

19. **The correct answer is (C).** There are several ways of running the calculation for this problem. One way is to reason: 10% of 360 is 36. Since 5% is one half of 10%, 5% of 360 is one half of 36, or 18. Since 10% of 360 is 36, and since 5% of 360 is 18, the difference between the two is 36 – 18 = 18.

20. **The correct answer is (E).** Again, perhaps the most natural starting point for

a solution is working on the expression, rearranging by grouping like terms. $x^2 + 3x + 10 = 1 + x^2$. By transposing (subtracting from both sides) the x^2 term, we see that the x^2 is eliminated:

$3x + 10 = 1$, so $3x = -9$, and $x = -3$

Although the x^2 term was eliminated from our initial expression, we know the value of x. It is now a simple matter to substitute -3 for x in the expression x^2, and we learn $x^2 = 9$.

21. **The correct answer is (C).** Proposition I is true. It is the geometry theorem that two lines parallel to a third must be parallel to each other.

l_1 l_2 l_3

$l_1 \parallel l_2$
$l_3 \parallel l_2$
$\therefore l_1 \parallel l_3$

Proposition II is also necessarily true. Just as with lines, if two planes are parallel to a third plane, they must likewise be parallel to each other.

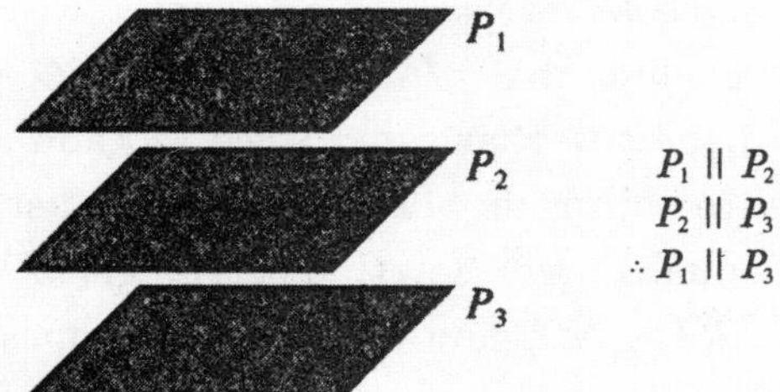

Proposition III, however, is not necessarily true. Two lines might be drawn in a plane parallel to another plane and yet intersect one another:

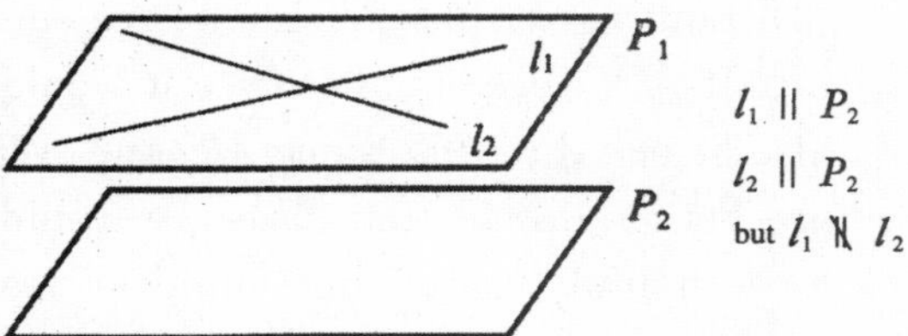

22. **The correct answer is (C).** We all know the simple formula that price minus discount equals discounted price—that much is just common-sense arithmetic. What we sometimes overlook, however, is the fact that the discounted price can be expressed either in monetary terms, e.g., \$5.00 or 37¢, or in percentage terms, e.g., 50% of the original price. In this case, the discount is given as a percentage of the original price. So we have original price −90¢ = 90% of original price; or, using x for the original price: $x - \$.90 = .9x$. This is an equation with only one variable, so we proceed to solve for x: $.1x = \$.90$, so $x = \$9.00$.

23. **The correct answer is (B).** If (1) is true, you cannot answer the question without knowing the relative positions of points S and T. (Remember that geometric figures in the Data Sufficiency section are not necessarily drawn to scale, i.e., the lengths or sizes may not be what they appear to be.) If (2) is true, then the lengths of TU, ST, and RS are equal to each other, and therefore the answer to the question is "neither."

24. **The correct answer is (C).** If John has 5 more than Paul, there are two possible combinations: Paul could have 1 and John 6, or Paul could have 2 and John 7. Note that 3 and 8 are impossible since the total number of marbles is only 10. So (1) is not sufficient to answer the question. If Peter has half as many as John, there are three possible combinations: Peter could have 1 and John 2, Peter could have 2 and John 4, or Peter could have 3 and John 6. Again, (2) is not sufficient by itself. If both conditions are known, the only possibility is that Paul has 1, John has 6 and Peter has 3.

25. **The correct answer is (B).** (1) tells you that x equals 1 or −1, so (1) is insufficient to answer the question. (2) tells you that x equals −1, so (2) by itself is sufficient to answer the question.

26. **The correct answer is (D).** In (1), if $\angle A = 55°$, then $\angle B = 180° - 55° = 125°$. Therefore, (1) is sufficient to answer the question. In (2), if $\angle D > 90°$, then $\angle B$ is also greater than 90° because $\angle B$ and $\angle D$ are corresponding angles with respect to parallel lines l and m and are therefore equal. So the answer to the question is "no" and (2) is sufficient.

27. **The correct answer is (D).** The area of a rectangle equals its length times its width. The length is given as 40. The perimeter (twice the sum of the length and the width) is given in (1), so the width can be found as follows:

$$2(L + W) = 140$$
$$2(40 + W) = 140$$
$$40 + W = 70$$
$$W = 30$$

Now you know the length and the width which are sufficient to find the area. In (2) you are given the length of the diagonal. By using the Pythagorean Theorem you can find the width as follows:

$$40^2 + W^2 = 50^2$$
$$W = 30$$

Now the area can also be found.

28. **The correct answer is (E).** If you divide both sides of the second equation by –2, the result is the equation in (1). Therefore, equation (2) is equivalent to equation (1). There are many solutions to equation (1)—and equation (2). For example, $A = 0$ and $B = \frac{-17}{3}$, and $A = 1$ and $B = -5$.

29. **The correct answer is (A).** This problem is particularly elusive since there is no really clear starting point. One way of getting a handle on it is to manipulate the expression $\frac{p}{q}+\frac{n}{m}$. If we add the two terms together using the common denominator of my, we have $\frac{mp+nq}{mq}$. We can see that this bears a striking similarity to the first equation given in the problem: $mp + nq = 12mq$. If we manipulate that equation by dividing both sides by mq, we have $\frac{mp+nq}{mq} = 12$. But since $\frac{p}{q}+\frac{n}{m}$ is equivalent to $\frac{mp+nq}{mq}$, we are entitled to conclude that $\frac{p}{q}+\frac{n}{m}$ is also equal to 12.

30. **The correct answer is (D).** This problem, too, is fairly difficult. The difficulty stems from the fact that its solution requires several different formulas. For example, we can conclude that (A) is necessarily true. MN is not a diameter. We know this since a diameter passes through the center of the circle. So whatever the length of MN, it is less than that of the diameter (the diameter is the longest chord which can be drawn in a circle). Since $2MO$ would be equal to a diameter (twice the radius is the diameter), and since MN is less than a diameter, we can conclude that MN is less than $2MO$. We also know that $z = y$. Since MO and NO are both radii of circle O, they must be equal. So we know that in triangle MNO, $MO = NO$; and since angles opposite equal sides are equal, we conclude that $z = y$. (B) requires still another line of reasoning. Since MN is greater than NO, the angle opposite MN, which is x, must be greater than the angle opposite NO, which is y. So x is greater than y. Finally, (E) requires yet another line of reasoning. If MN were equal to NO, it would also be equal to MO, since MO and NO are both radii. In that case, we would have an equilateral triangle and all angles would be 60°. Since MN is greater than MO and NO, the angle opposite MN, which is x, must be greater than 60°. So

(D) must be the correct answer. A moment's reflection will show that it is not necessarily true that $x = y + z$. This would be true only in the event that MNO is a right triangle, but there is no information given in the problem from which we are entitled to conclude that $x° = 90°$.

31. The correct answer is (B). To solve this problem, you must recognize that angle ABC is a right angle. This is because the triangle is inscribed in a semicircle (the vertex of the triangle is situated on the circumference of the circle), and an inscribed angle intercepts twice the arc. For example:

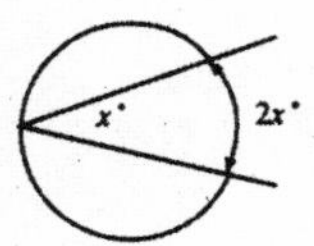

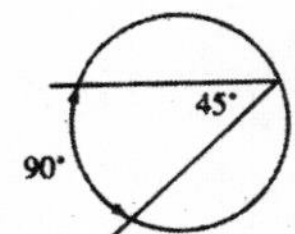

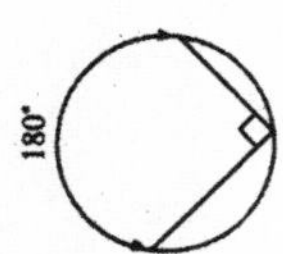

Once it is recognized that ABC is a right triangle, the shaded area can be computed by taking the area of the triangle from the area of the semicircle, or expressed in pictures:

Line AC is the hypotenuse of triangle of ABC, so its length is:

$$AC^2 = (2\sqrt{2})^2 + (2\sqrt{2})^2$$
$$AC^2 = 8+8$$
$$AC = 4$$

AC is also the diameter of the circle, so the radius of the entire circle is 2 (radius is one-half diameter). We are now in a position to compute the area of the semicircle. Since the area of the entire circle would be πr^2 the area of the semicircle is:

$$\frac{\pi r^2}{2} = \frac{\pi(2)^2}{2} = 2\pi$$

Then we compute the area of the triangle. The area of a triangle is $\frac{ab}{2}$, and in any right triangle either of the two sides will serve as the altitude, the other serving as the base. For example:

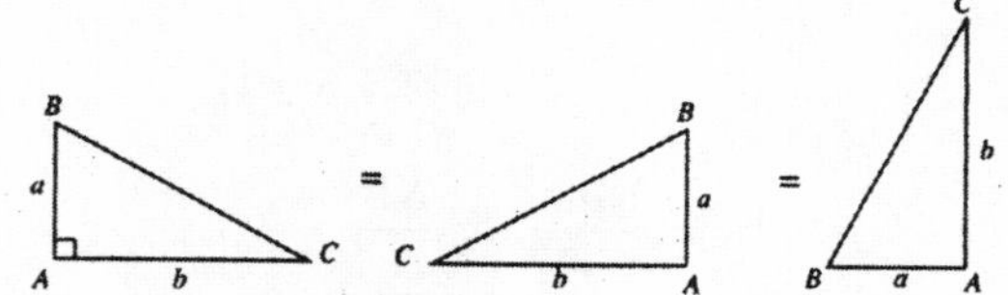

In this case, we have area $= \frac{1}{2}(2\sqrt{2})(2\sqrt{2}) = 4$. Referring to our pictorial representation of the problem:

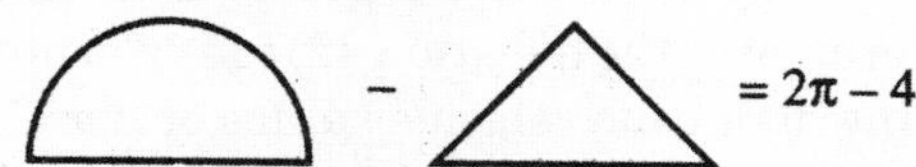

32. The correct answer is (B). This problem does not actually need to be calculated. The symbol * is standing for a set of instructions. These instructions start with the square of the number and then add twice the number, which could be symbolized by * of $x = x^2 + 2x$. Since 12 squared is 144, the answer must be something in that general neighborhood, and the only answer that is close is (B), 168. The calculation would be $12^2 + 2 \times 12 = 144 + 24 = 168$.

33. The correct answer is (D). If angles BAD and BCD are right angles, they are equal. Measure of angle BAC equals measure of angle BCA, since they are base angles of an isosceles triangle. Subtracting equals from equals, angle DAC equals angle DCA. Therefore, triangle ACD is an isosceles triangle, and $AD = CD$.

answers

34. The correct answer is (A). Let x = the cost.

Then
$$x + \frac{1}{4}x = 80$$
$$4x + x = 320$$
$$5x = 320$$
$$= \$64 \text{ (cost)}$$
$$\frac{Cost}{S.P.} = \frac{64}{80}$$
$$= \frac{4}{5}$$

35. The correct answer is (E). (1) gives no information about B, so (1) is insufficient to answer the question. (2) tells you nothing about the relative values of A and B, but only that the square of $(A + B)$ is positive, so (2) is also insufficient.

36. The correct answer is (C).

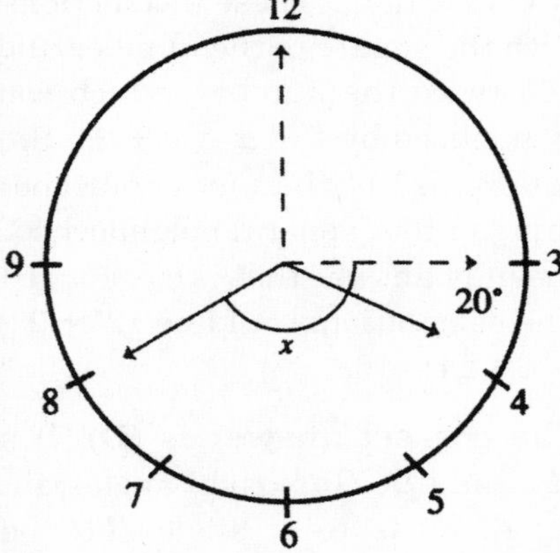

At 3:00, large hand is at 12 and small hand is at 3. During the next 40 minutes, large hand moves to 8 and small hand moves $\frac{40}{60} = \frac{2}{3}$ of the distance between 3 and 4. Since there is 30° between two numbers on a clock, $\angle x = 5(30°) - 20° = 150° - 20° = 130°$.

37. The correct answer is (B). If $\angle P < \angle Q$, it is possible for any one of the three angles to be a right angle, which would make the triangle a right triangle, or it is possible for none of the three angles to be a right angle, so (1) by itself is insufficient to answer the question. (2) tells you that $\angle R$ is a right angle ($\angle R = 90°$), since the sum of the three angles is 180°: $\angle P + \angle Q + \angle R = 180°$; $\angle P + \angle Q = \angle R$; $\angle R + \angle R = 180°$ (by substituting $\angle R$ for $\angle P + \angle Q$ in $\angle P + \angle Q + \angle R = 180°$); $2\angle R = 180°$; therefore $\angle R = 90°$ (by dividing both sides of the equation by 2). Thus, (2) is sufficient to answer the question.

Practice Test 3

ANALYTICAL WRITING ASSESSMENT

I. Analysis of an Issue

Time—30 Minutes

Directions: In this section you will have 30 minutes to analyze and explain your views on the topic presented below. Read the statement and directions carefully. Write only on the topic given. An essay on a topic other than the one assigned will automatically be assigned a grade of 0.

Note: On the CAT version, you will keyboard your essay. For this exercise, allow yourself three sides of regular $8\frac{1}{2} \times 11$- inch paper for each essay response.

> Football enthusiasts insist that their sport, more than any other, epitomizes the character of the American people. They say that its rough and tumble style and aggressive play on a large field are reminiscent of the pioneer era of America's history. Other people say that no sporting contest, which is confined to a particular time and played by a strict set of rules, can truly epitomize a nation's character.

Which position do you find more compelling? Explain your position using reasons and/or examples drawn from your personal experience, observations, or readings.

practice test 3

II. Analysis of an Argument

Time—30 Minutes

Directions: In this section you will have 30 minutes to write a critique of the argument presented below. Read the argument and directions carefully. Write only on the topic given. An essay on a topic other than the one assigned will automatically be assigned a grade of 0.

Note: On the CAT version, you will keyboard your essay. For this exercise, allow yourself three sides of regular $8\frac{1}{2} \times 11$- inch paper for each essay response.

In the garden of the art museum are several unique sculptures. To protect these pieces, the museum should install a security system that includes infrared motion detectors and video surveillance cameras. A comprehensive security system would virtually eliminate the danger that any of these pieces would be stolen.

How persuasive do you find this argument? Explain your point of view by analyzing the line of reasoning and the use of evidence in the argument. Discuss also what, if anything, would make the argument more persuasive or would help you better to evaluate its conclusion.

VERBAL SECTION

41 Questions • 75 Minutes

Directions: For each of the following questions, choose the correct answer. To simulate the experience of taking the CAT, answer each question in order. Do not skip any questions, and do not go back to any questions you have already answered.
For Sentence Correction questions: In questions of this type, either part or all of a sentence is underlined. The sentence is followed by five ways of writing the underlined part. Choice (A) repeats the original; the other answer choices vary. If you think that the original phrasing is the best, choose (A). If you think one of the other answer choices is the best, select that choice.

Sentence Correction questions test your ability to recognize correct and effective expression. Follow the requirements of Standard Written English: grammar, choice of words, and sentence construction. Choose the answer that results in the clearest, most exact sentence, but does not change the meaning of the original sentence.

Example:

Q The possibility of massive earthquakes are regarded by most area residents with a mixture of skepticism and caution.

(A) are regarded by most area residents with

(B) is regarded by most area residents with

(C) is regarded by most area residents as

(D) is mostly regarded by area residents with

(E) by most area residents is regarded with

A The correct answer is (B).

For Critical Reasoning questions: Questions of this type ask you to analyze and evaluate the reasoning in short paragraphs or passages. For some questions, all of the answer choices may conceivably be answers to the question asked. You should select the *best* answer to the question, that is, an answer that does not require you to make assumptions that violate common-sense standards by being implausible, redundant, irrelevant, or inconsistent.

Example:

Q In an extensive study of the reading habits of magazine subscribers, it was found that an average of between four and five people actually read each copy of the most popular weekly news magazine. On this basis, we estimate that the 12,000 copies of *Poets and Poetry* that are sold each month are actually read by 48,000 to 60,000 people.

The estimate above assumes that

(A) individual magazine readers generally enjoy more than one type of magazine

(B) most of the readers of *Poets and Poetry* subscribe to the magazine

(C) the ratio of readers to copies is the same for *Poets and Poetry* as for the weekly news magazine

(D) the number of readers of the weekly news magazine is similar to the number of readers of *Poets and Poetry*

(E) most readers enjoy sharing copies of their favorite magazines with friends and family members

A The correct answer is (C).

For Reading Comprehension questions: Each passage is followed by questions or incomplete statements about the passage. Each statement or question is followed by lettered words or expressions. Select the word or expression that most satisfactorily completes each statement or answers each question in accordance with the meaning of the passage.

1. It has been <u>said that to be afraid of the dark is being afraid</u> of all those things we cannot comprehend and, therefore, instinctively fear.

(A) said that to be afraid of the dark is being afraid

(B) said, that to be afraid of the dark, is being afraid

(C) said being afraid of the dark is to be afraid

(D) said that to be afraid of the dark is to be afraid

(E) said that to be being afraid of the dark is to be being afraid

2. <u>Hurtling through space, Anna saw a shooting star and was transfixed by the rare beauty of this sight.</u>

(A) Hurtling through space, Anna saw a shooting star and was transfixed by the rare beauty of this sight.

(B) Anna saw a shooting star and was transfixed by the rare beauty of this sight hurtling through space.

(C) Anna saw a shooting star hurtling through space and was transfixed by the rare beauty of this sight.

(D) Anna saw, hurtling through space, a shooting star and was transfixed by the rare beauty of this sight.

(E) Transfixed by the rare beauty of this sight, Anna saw a shooting star hurtling through space.

3. A study on the therapeutic value of pets as companions for the elderly has shown that cats <u>are more superior than dogs as far as household companions are concerned.</u>

(A) are more superior than dogs as far as household companions are concerned.

(B) are superior to dogs as household companions.

(C) are superior to dogs as far as household companions are concerned.

(D) are more superior to dogs as household companions.

(E) are superior household companions than dogs.

4. Children in the first three grades who attend private schools spend time each day working with a computerized reading program. Public schools have very few such programs. Tests prove, however, that public-school children are much weaker in reading skills when compared to their private-school counterparts. We conclude, therefore, that public-school children can be good readers only if they participate in a computerized reading program.

The author's initial statements logically support his conclusion only if which of the following is also true?

(A) All children can learn to be good readers if they are taught by a computerized reading program.

(B) All children can learn to read at the same rate if they participate in a computerized reading program.

(C) Better reading skills produce better students.

(D) Computerized reading programs are the critical factor in the better reading skills of private-school students.

(E) Public-school children can be taught better math skills.

5. Is your company going to continue to discriminate against women in its hiring and promotion policies?

The question above might be considered unfair because it

(A) fails to mention that other companies might have similar practices

(B) assumes that the interviewee agrees with the policies of the company

(C) reveals a bias on the part of the questioner

(D) contains a hidden presupposition that the responder might wish to contest

(E) shifts the focus of attention from the person interviewed to the company

6. Tibetan rugs are so expensive because <u>the weaver still pursues his art as they have</u> for centuries, by hand-dyeing all their wool and then knotting each thread individually to achieve a unique pattern for every piece.

(A) the weaver still pursues his art as they have

(B) the weaver still pursues his art as he has

(C) weavers still pursue their art as they have

(D) weavers still pursue their art as was done

(E) the weaver still pursues his art as has been done

QUESTIONS 7 AND 8

Ms. Evangeline Rose argued that money and time invested in acquiring a professional degree are totally wasted. As evidence supporting her argument, she offered the case of a man who, at considerable expense of money and time, completed his law degree and then married and lived as a house-husband, taking care of their children and working part time at a day care center so his wife could pursue her career.

7. Ms. Rose makes the unsupported assumption that

(A) an education in the law is useful only in pursuing law-related activities

(B) what was not acceptable 25 years ago may very well be acceptable today

(C) wealth is more important than learning

(D) professional success is a function of the quality of one's education

(E) only the study of law can be considered professional study

8. The logical reasoning of Ms. Rose's argument is closely paralleled by which of the following?

(A) A juvenile delinquent who insists that his behavior should be attributable to the fact that his parents did not love him.

(B) A senator who votes large sums of money for military equipment, but who votes against programs designed to help the poor.

(C) A conscientious objector who bases his draft resistance on the premise that there can be no moral wars.

(D) When a policeman is found guilty of murdering his wife, an opponent of police brutality who says, "That's what these people mean by law and order."

(E) A high school senior who decides that rather than go to college he will enroll in a vocational training program to learn to be an electrician.

9. A number of prominent educators question <u>whether the decreasing</u> enrollment of students in colleges and universities is a reversible trend and fear that if the numbers do not go up, many institutions of higher learning will simply go out of business.

(A) whether the decreasing

(B) decreased

(C) that the decreasing

(D) if the decreasing

(E) the decreased

practice test

10. <u>If I was President, I would call an immediate halt</u> to the development of all nuclear weapons.

(A) If I was President, I would call an immediate halt

(B) If President, I would call an immediate halt

(C) If I was President, I would immediately call a halt

(D) As President, I would call an immediate halt

(E) If I were President, I would call an immediate halt

11. A survey of American business schools concludes that <u>female students are more concerned about job discrimination than male students.</u>

(A) female students are more concerned about job discrimination than male students.

(B) female students are more concerned about job discrimination than male students are.

(C) female students, as opposed to male students, are more concerned about job discrimination.

(D) female students are more concerned about job discrimination than male students are concerned.

(E) female students are more concerned about job discrimination than their male counterparts.

QUESTIONS 12–18

Although it is now possible to bring most high blood pressure under control, the causes of essential hypertension remain elusive. Understanding how hypertension begins is at least partly a problem of understanding when in life it begins, and this may be very early—perhaps within the first few months of life. Since the beginning of the century, physicians have been aware that hypertension may run in families, but before the 1970s, studies of the familial aggregation of blood pressure treated only populations 15 years of age or older. Few studies were attempted in younger persons because of a prevailing notion that blood pressures in this age group were difficult to measure and unreliable and because essential hypertension was widely regarded as a disease of adults.

In 1971, a study of 700 children, ages 2 to 14, used a special blood pressure recorder which minimizes observer error and allows for standardization of blood pressure readings. Before then, it had been well established that the blood pressure of adults aggregates familially, that is, the similarities between the blood pressure of an individual and his siblings are generally too great to be explained by chance. The 1971 study showed that familial clustering was measurable in children as well, suggesting that factors responsible for essential hypertension are acquired in childhood. Additional epidemiological studies demonstrated a clear tendency for the children to retain the same blood pressure patterns, relative to their peers, four years later. Thus, a child with blood pressure higher or lower than the norm would tend to remain higher or lower with increasing age.

Meanwhile, other investigators uncovered a complex of physiologic roles—including blood pressure—for a vasoactive system called the kallikrein-kininsystem. Kallikreins are enzymes in the kidney and blood plasma which act on precursors called kininogens to produce vasoactive peptides called kinins. Several different kinins are produced, at least three of which are (powerful blood vessel dilators. Apparently, the kallikrein-kinin system normally tends to offset the elevations in arterial pressure that result from the secretion of salt-conserving hormones such as aldosterone on the one hand and from activation of the sympathetic nervous system (which tends to constrict blood vessels) on the other hand.

It is also known that urinary kallikrein excretion is abnormally low in subjects with essential hypertension. Levels of urinary kallikrein in children are inversely related to the diastolic blood pressures of both children and their mothers. Children with the lowest kallikrein levels are found in the families with the highest blood pressures. In addition, black children tend to show somewhat lower urinary kallikrein levels than white children, and blacks are more likely to have high blood pressure. There is a great deal to be learned about the biochemistry and physiologic roles of the kallikrein-kinin system. But there is the possibility that essential hypertension will prove to have biochemical precursors.

12. The author is primarily concerned with

(A) questioning the assumption behind certain experiments involving children under the age of 15

(B) describing the new scientific findings about high blood pressure and suggesting some implications

(C) describing two different methods for studying the causes of high blood pressure

(D) revealing a discrepancy between the findings of epidemiological studies and laboratory studies on essential hypertension

(E) arguing that high blood pressure may be influenced by familial factors

13. Which of the following is mentioned as a factor that initially discouraged the study of hypertension in children?

(A) An expectation that high blood pressure in children was untreatable

(B) Repeated unsuccessful attempts to treat hypertension in adults

(C) The belief that blood pressure in adults aggregates familially

(D) The belief that it was difficult or impossible to measure accurately blood pressures in children

(E) Ignorance of important differences in the physical constitution of ethnic subgroups

14. The argument in the passage leads most naturally to which of the following conclusions?

(A) A low output of urinary kallikrein is a likely cause of high blood pressure in children.

(B) The kallikrein-kinin system plays an important role in the regulation of blood pressure.

(C) Essential hypertension may have biochemical precursors which may be useful predictors in children.

(D) The failure of the body to produce sufficient amounts of kinins is the cause of essential hypertension.

(E) It is now possible to predict high blood pressure by using familial aggregations and urinary kallikrein measurement.

15. The author refers to the somewhat lower urinary kallikrein levels in black children (lines 71–75) in order to

(A) support the thesis that kallikrein levels are inversely related to blood pressure

(B) highlight the special health problems involved in treating populations with high concentrations of black children

(C) offer a causal explanation for the difference in urinary kallikrein levels between black and white children

(D) suggest that further study needs to be done on the problem of high blood pressure among black adults

(E) prove that hypertension can be treated if those persons likely to have high blood pressure can be found

practice test

16. The author states that the kallikrein-kinin system may affect blood pressure by

(A) directly opposing the tendency of the sympathetic nervous system to constrict blood vessels

(B) producing kinins, which tend to dilate blood vessels

(C) suppressing the production of hormones such as aldosterone

(D) controlling the levels of kallikrein in the urine

(E) compensating for cross-subgroup differentials

17. The evidence that a child with blood pressure higher or lower than the norm would tend to retain the same blood pressure pattern with increasing age (lines 40–43) is introduced by the author in order to

(A) suggest that essential hypertension may have biochemical causes

(B) show that high blood pressure can be detected in children under the age of 15

(C) provide evidence that factors affecting blood pressure are already present in children

(D) propose that increased screening of children for high blood pressure should be undertaken

(E) refute arguments that blood pressure in children cannot be measured reliably

18. The author's argument is presented primarily by

(A) contrasting two methods of doing scientific research

(B) providing experimental evidence against a conclusion

(C) presenting new scientific findings for a conclusion

(D) analyzing a new theory and showing its defects

(E) criticizing scientific research on blood pressure done before 1971

19. A cryptographer has intercepted an enemy message that is in code. He knows that the code is a simple substitution of numbers for letters. Which of the following would be the least helpful in breaking the code?

(A) Knowing the frequency with which the vowels of the language are used

(B) Knowing the frequency with which two vowels appear together in the language

(C) Knowing the frequency with which odd numbers appear relative to even numbers in the message

(D) Knowing the conjugation of the verb *to be* in the language on which the code is based

(E) Knowing every word in the language that begins with the letter *R*

20. One way of reducing commuting time for those who work in the cities is to increase the speed at which traffic moves in the heart of the city. This can be accomplished by raising the tolls on the tunnels and bridges connecting the city with other communities. This will discourage auto traffic into the city and will encourage people to use public transportation instead.

Which of the following, if true, would LEAST weaken the argument above?

(A) Nearly all of the traffic in the center of the city is commercial traffic which will continue despite toll increases.

(B) Some people now driving alone into the city would choose to car-pool with each other rather than use public transportation.

(C) Any temporary improvement in traffic flow would be lost because the improvement itself would attract more cars.

(D) The numbers of commuters who would be deterred by the toll increases would be insignificant.

(E) The public transportation system is not able to handle any significant increase in the number of commuters using the system.

21. An independent medical research team recently did a survey at a mountain retreat founded to help heavy smokers quit or cut down on their cigarette smoking. Eighty percent of those persons smoking three packs a day or more were able to cut down to one pack a day after they began to take End-Smoke with its patented desire suppressant. Try End-Smoke to help you cut down significantly on your smoking.

Which of the following, if true, offers the strongest criticism of the advertisement?

(A) Heavy smokers may be psychologically as well as physically addicted to tobacco smoking.

(B) Of the 20 percent who failed to achieve significant results, most were addicted to other substances as well.

(C) The independent medical research team included several members who were experts in the field of nicotine addiction.

(D) A survey conducted at a mountain retreat to aid smokers may yield different results than one would expect under other circumstances.

(E) The overall percentage of the general population who smoke regularly has not declined dramatically over the past 20 years.

22. The revelation that Shakespeare wrote certain of his plays expressly for Queen Elizabeth I lends credence to the theory that the dark lady of the sonnets was <u>not Shakespeare's mistress nor any other woman the playwright had romanced</u> but, in fact, the Queen herself.

(A) not Shakespeare's mistress nor any other woman the playwright had romanced

(B) neither Shakespeare's mistress or any other woman the playwright had romanced

(C) neither Shakespeare's mistress nor any other woman the playwright had romanced

(D) not Shakespeare's mistress or any other woman the playwright had romanced

(E) not Shakespeare's mistress neither any other woman he had romanced

23. The recent drop in the prime interest rate probably results from the Federal Reserve Bank's tight money policy and <u>its effect on lending institutions rather than to the drop in the overall</u> rate of inflation.

(A) its effect on lending institutions rather than to the drop in the overall

(B) its affect on lending institutions, as opposed to the drop in the overall

(C) it's effect on lending institutions, rather than from the drop in the overall

(D) its effect on lending institutions rather than from the drop in the overall

(E) the effect on lending institutions, rather than to the drop in the overall

24. Before they will sit down and resume bargaining, the strikers demand that management halt legal proceedings, including current court actions aimed at incarcerating demonstrators, <u>and releases all strike leaders who have already been jailed.</u>

(A) and releases all strike leaders who have already been jailed.

(B) and releasing all strike leaders who have already been placed in jailed.

(C) and release all strike leaders who have already been jailed.

(D) in addition to releasing all presently jailed strike leaders.

(E) but release all strike leaders who have already been jailed.

25. JOCKEY: Horses are the most noble of all animals. They are both loyal and brave. I knew of a farm horse which died of a broken heart shortly after its owner died.

VETERINARIAN: You're wrong. Dogs can be just as loyal and brave. I had a dog who would wait every day on the front steps for me to come home, and if I did not arrive until midnight, he would still be there.

All of the following are true of the claims of the jockey and the veterinarian EXCEPT

(A) both claims assume that loyalty and bravery are characteristics which are desirable in animals.

(B) both claims assume that the two most loyal animals are the horse and the dog.

(C) both claims assume that human qualities can be attributed to animals.

(D) both claims are supported by only a single example of animal behavior.

(E) neither claim is supported by evidence other than the opinions and observations of the speakers.

26. Rousseau assumed that human beings in the state of nature are characterized by a feeling of sympathy toward their fellow humans and other living creatures. In order to explain the existence of social ills, such as the exploitation of some human beings by other human beings, Rousseau maintained that our natural feelings are crushed under the weight of unsympathetic social institutions. Rousseau's argument described above would be most strengthened if it could be explained how

(A) creatures naturally characterized by feelings of sympathy for all living creatures could create unsympathetic social institutions

(B) we can restructure our social institutions so that they will foster our natural sympathies for one another

(C) modern reformers might lead the way to a life which is not inconsistent with the ideals of the state of nature

(D) non-exploitative conduct could arise in conditions of the state of nature

(E) a return to the state of nature from modern society might be accomplished

27. Every element on the periodic chart is radioactive, though the most stable elements have half-lives which are thousands and thousands of years long. When an atom decays, it splits into two or more smaller atoms. Even considering the fusion taking place inside of stars, there is only a negligible tendency for smaller atoms to transmute into larger ones. Thus, the ratio of lighter to heavier atoms in the universe is increasing at a measurable rate.

Which of the following sentences provides the most logical continuation of this paragraph?

(A) Without radioactive decay of atoms, there could be no solar combustion and no life as we know it.

(B) Therefore, it is imperative that scientists begin developing ways to reverse the trend and restore the proper balance between the lighter and the heavier elements.

(C) Consequently, it is possible to use a shifting ratio of light to heavy atoms to calculate the age of the universe.

(D) Therefore, there are now more light elements in the universe than heavy ones.

(E) As a result, the fusion taking place inside stars has to produce enough atoms of the heavy elements to offset the radioactive decay of large atoms elsewhere in the universe.

QUESTIONS 28–34

Many critics of the current welfare system argue that existing welfare regulations foster family instability. They maintain that those regulations, which exclude most poor husband-and-wife families from Aid to Families with Dependent Children assistance grants, contribute to the problem of family dissolution. Thus, they conclude that expanding the set of families eligible for family assistance plans or guaranteed income measures would result in a marked strengthening of the low-income family structure. If all poor families could receive welfare, would the incidence of instability change markedly? The answer to this question depends on the relative importance of three categories of potential welfare recipients. The first is the "cheater"—the husband who is reported to have abandoned his family, but in fact disappears only when the social caseworker is in the neighborhood. The second consists of a loving husband and devoted father who, sensing his own inadequacy as a provider, leaves so that his wife and children may enjoy the relative benefit provided by public assistance. There is very little evidence that these categories are significant.

The third category is the unhappily married couple who remain together out of a sense of economic responsibility for their children, because of the high costs of separation, or because of the consumption benefits of marriage. This group is numerous. The formation, maintenance and dissolution of the family is in large part a function of the relative balance between the benefits and costs of marriage as seen by the individual members of the marriage. The major benefit generated by the creation of a family is the expansion of the set of consumption possibilities. The benefits from such a partnership depend largely on the relative dissimilarity of the resources or basic endowments each partner brings to the marriage. Persons with similar productive capacities have less economic "cement" holding their marriage together. Since the family performs certain functions society regards as vital, a complex network of social and legal buttresses has evolved to reinforce marriage. Much of the variation in marital stability across income classes can be explained by the variation in costs of dissolution imposed by society, e.g., division of property, alimony, child support, and the social stigma attached to divorce.

Marital stability is related to the costs of achieving an acceptance agreement on family consumption and production and to the prevailing social price of instability in the marriage partners' social-economic group. Expected AFDC income exerts pressures on family instability by reducing the cost of dissolution. To the extent that welfare is a form of government-subsidized alimony payments, it reduces the institutional costs of separation and guarantees a minimal standard of living for wife and children. So welfare opportunities are a significant determinant of family instability in poor neighborhoods, but this is not the result of AFDC regulations that exclude most intact families from coverage. Rather, welfare-related instability occurs because public assistance lowers both the benefits of marriage and the costs of its disruption by providing a system of government-subsidized alimony payments.

28. The author's primary concern is to

(A) interpret the results of a survey

(B) discuss the role of the father in low-income families

(C) analyze the causes of a phenomenon

(D) recommend reforms in the welfare system

(E) change public attitude toward welfare recipients

29. Which of the following would provide the most logical continuation of the final paragraph?

(A) Paradoxically, any liberalization of AFDC eligibility restrictions is likely to intensify, rather than mitigate, pressures on family stability.

(B) Actually, concern for the individual recipients should not be allowed to override considerations of sound fiscal policy.

(C) In reality, there is virtually no evidence that AFDC payments have any relationship at all to problems of family instability in low-income marriages.

(D) In the final analysis, it appears that government welfare payments, to the extent that the cost of marriage is lowered, encourage the formation of low-income families.

(E) Ultimately, the problem of low-income family instability can be eliminated by reducing welfare benefits to the point where the cost of dissolution equals the cost of staying married.

30. All of the following are mentioned by the author as factors tending to perpetuate a marriage EXCEPT

(A) the stigma attached to divorce

(B) the social class of the partners

(C) the cost of alimony and child support

(D) the loss of property upon divorce

(E) the greater consumption possibilities of married people

31. Which of the following best summarizes the main idea of the passage?

(A) Welfare restrictions limiting the eligibility of families for benefits do not contribute to low-income family instability.

(B) Contrary to popular opinion, the most significant category of welfare recipients is not the "cheating" father.

(C) The incidence of family dissolution among low-income families is directly related to the inability of families with fathers to get welfare benefits.

(D) Very little of the divorce rate among low-income families can be attributed to fathers' deserting their families so that they can qualify for welfare.

(E) Government welfare payments are at present excessively high and must be reduced in order to slow the growing divorce rate among low-income families.

32. The tone of the passage can best be described as

(A) confident and optimistic

(B) scientific and detached

(C) discouraged and alarmed

(D) polite and sensitive

(E) callous and indifferent

33. With which of the following statements about marriage would the author most likely agree?

(A) Marriage is an institution that is largely shaped by powerful but impersonal economic and social forces.

(B) Marriage has a greater value to persons in higher income brackets than to person in lower income brackets.

(C) Society has no legitimate interest in encouraging people to remain married to one another.

(D) Marriage as an institution is no longer economically viable and will gradually give way to other forms of social organization.

(E) The rising divorce rate across all income brackets indicates that people are more self-centered and less concerned about others than before.

34. The passage would most likely be found in a

(A) pamphlet on civil rights

(B) basic economics text

(C) book on the history of welfare

(D) religious tract on the importance of marriage

(E) scholarly journal devoted to public policy questions

QUESTIONS 35 AND 36

SPEAKER: The great majority of people in the United States have access to the best medical care available anywhere in the world.

OBJECTOR: There are thousands of poor in this country who cannot afford to pay to see a doctor.

35. Which of the following is true of the objector's comment?

(A) It uses emotionally charged words.

(B) It constitutes a hasty generalization on few examples.

(C) It is not necessarily inconsistent with the speaker's remarks.

(D) It cites statistical evidence which tends to confirm the speaker's points.

(E) It overlooks the distinction the speaker draws between a cause and its effect.

36. A possible objection to the speaker's comments would be to point to the existence of

(A) a country that has more medical assistants than the United States

(B) a nation where medical care is provided free of charge by the government

(C) a country in which the people are given better medical care than Americans

(D) government hearings in the United States on the problems poor people have getting medical care

(E) a country that has a higher hospital-bed-per-person ratio than the United States

37. Since they shared so much when they were growing up, Elizabeth and Sarah have cultivated a very special friendship and even now confide their most intimate thoughts only <u>to one another.</u>

(A) to one another.

(B) one with the other.

(C) one with another.

(D) each to the other.

(E) to each other.

38. Henrik Ibsen's plays posed as great a challenge to middle-class Scandinavians' expectations of the drama <u>that almost a century later Edward Albee will offer</u> to theatergoers in America.

(A) that almost a century later Edward Albee will offer

(B) that, almost a century later, Edward Albee would offer

(C) as, almost a century later, Edward Albee did offer

(D) just as, almost a century later, Edward Albee offered

(E) as, almost a century later, Edward Albee would offer

QUESTIONS 39 AND 40

The blanks in the following paragraph indicate deletions from the text. For questions 39 and 40, select the completion that is most appropriate.

I often hear smokers insisting that they have a *right* to smoke whenever and wherever they choose, as though there are no conceivable circumstances in which the law might not legitimately prohibit smoking. This contention is obviously indefensible. Implicit in the development of the concept of a right is the notion that one person's freedom of action is circumscribed by the _____(39)_____. It requires nothing more than common sense to realize that there are situations in which smoking presents a clear and present danger: in a crowded theater, around flammable materials, during take-off in an airplane. No one would seriously deny that the potential harm of smoking in such circumstances more than outweighs the satisfaction a smoker would derive from smoking. Yet, this balancing is not unique to situations of potential catastrophe. It applies equally as well to situations where the potential injury is small, though in most cases, as for example a person's table manners, the injury of the offended person is so slight we automatically strike the balance in favor of the person acting. But once it is recognized that a balance of freedoms must be struck, it follows that a smoker has a *right* to smoke only when and where _____(40)_____.

39. **(A)** Constitution of our nation

(B) laws passed by Congress and interpreted by the Supreme Court

(C) interest of any other person to not be injured or inconvenienced by that action

(D) rights of other persons not to smoke

(E) rights of non-smoking persons not to have to be subjected to the noxious fumes of tobacco smoking

40. **(A)** the government chooses to allow smoking

(B) the smoker finally decides to light up

(C) the smoker's interest in smoking outweighs the interests of other persons in his not smoking

(D) the smoker can ensure that no other persons will be even slightly inconvenienced by the smoke

(E) there are signs which explicitly state that smoking is allowed in that area

41. <u>Although Bill Tilden was perhaps the greatest tennis player of all time, his real accomplishments were overshadowed for many years by rumors about his personal life.</u>

(A) Although Bill Tilden was perhaps the greatest tennis player of all time, his real accomplishments were overshadowed for many years by rumors about his personal life.

(B) Perhaps the greatest tennis player of all time, Bill Tilden's real accomplishments were nevertheless overshadowed for many years by rumors about his personal life.

(C) Perhaps the greatest tennis player of all time, rumors about his personal life overshadowed Bill Tilden's real accomplishments for many years.

(D) For many years Bill Tilden's real accomplishments were overshadowed by rumors about his personal life, despite being perhaps the greatest tennis player of all time.

(E) Although Bill Tilden's real accomplishments were overshadowed for many years by rumors about his personal life, perhaps he was the greatest tennis player of all time.

QUANTITATIVE SECTION

37 Questions • 75 Minutes

Directions: For each of the following questions, choose the correct answer. To simulate the experience of taking the CAT, answer each question in order. Do not skip any questions, and do not go back to any questions you have already answered.
Numbers: All numbers used are real numbers.
Figures: The diagrams and figures that accompany these questions are for the purpose of providing information useful in answering the questions. Unless it is stated that a specific figure is not drawn to scale, the diagrams and figures are drawn as accurately as possible. All figures are in a plane unless otherwise indicated.
For Data Sufficiency questions: Each question is followed by two numbered facts. You are to determine whether the data given in the statements are sufficient for answering the question. Use the data given, plus your knowledge of math and everyday facts, to choose between the five possible answers.

Example:

Q Which copy machine, X or Y, makes copies at the faster rate?

(1) Machine X makes 90 copies per minute.

(2) In three minutes, X makes 1.5 more copies than Y.

(A) statement 1 alone is sufficient to answer the question, but statement 2 alone is not sufficient

(B) statement 2 alone is sufficient to answer the question, but statement 1 alone is not sufficient

(C) both statements together are needed to answer the question, but neither statement alone is sufficient

(D) either statement by itself is sufficient to answer the question

(E) not enough facts are given to answer the question

A **The correct answer is (B).**

1. A certain machine processes 8 quarts of milk every 6 seconds. How many gallons of milk can the machine process in 3 minutes?

(A) 18

(B) 20

(C) 60

(D) 75

(E) 120

2. During a half-price sale, Ms. Baker bought a toothbrush for the usual price and a second toothbrush for one-half the usual price. If she paid $1.80 for the two toothbrushes, what was the usual price of a toothbrush?

(A) $.50

(B) $.60

(C) $.90

(D) $1.20

(E) $2.40

3. 149 people were aboard Flight 222 when it arrived at Los Angeles from New York City with Chicago as the only intermediate stop. How many people first boarded the flight in Chicago?

(1) 170 people were aboard the flight when it left New York City.

(2) 23 people from the flight deplaned in Chicago and did not reboard.

(A) statement 1 alone is sufficient to answer the question, but statement 2 alone is not sufficient

(B) statement 2 alone is sufficient to answer the question, but statement 1 alone is not sufficient

(C) both statements together are needed to answer the question, but neither statement alone is sufficient

(D) either statement by itself is sufficient to answer the question

(E) not enough facts are given to answer the question

4. The total number of active members in a college fraternity is $12\frac{1}{2}$ percent higher this year than last year. How many active members does the fraternity have this year?

(1) Last year, 23 members of the fraternity graduated.

(2) Last year, there were 56 active members in the fraternity.

(A) statement 1 alone is sufficient to answer the question, but statement 2 alone is not sufficient

(B) statement 2 alone is sufficient to answer the question, but statement 1 alone is not sufficient

(C) both statements together are needed to answer the question, but neither statement alone is sufficient

(D) either statement by itself is sufficient to answer the question

(E) not enough facts are given to answer the question

5. Is p a positive number?

(1) $5p$ is a positive number

(2) $-p$ is a negative number

(A) statement 1 alone is sufficient to answer the question, but statement 2 alone is not sufficient

(B) statement 2 alone is sufficient to answer the question, but statement 1 alone is not sufficient

(C) both statements together are needed to answer the question, but neither statement alone is sufficient

(D) either statement by itself is sufficient to answer the question

(E) not enough facts are given to answer the question

6. Is 15 the average (arithmetic mean) of x, y, and 15?
   (1) $x + y = 30$
   (2) $x - y = 4$
   (A) statement 1 alone is sufficient to answer the question, but statement 2 alone is not sufficient
   (B) statement 2 alone is sufficient to answer the question, but statement 1 alone is not sufficient
   (C) both statements together are needed to answer the question, but neither statement alone is sufficient
   (D) either statement by itself is sufficient to answer the question
   (E) not enough facts are given to answer the question

7. Mary, Paul, and Susan all played in a summer softball league, and each hit at least one home run during the season. Which of the three players hit the most home runs?
   (1) Paul hit $\frac{4}{5}$ as many home runs as Mary.
   (2) Mary hit $\frac{5}{4}$ as many home runs as Susan.
   (A) statement 1 alone is sufficient to answer the question, but statement 2 alone is not sufficient
   (B) statement 2 alone is sufficient to answer the question, but statement 1 alone is not sufficient
   (C) both statements together are needed to answer the question, but neither statement alone is sufficient
   (D) either statement by itself is sufficient to answer the question
   (E) not enough facts are given to answer the question

8. What is the perimeter of a rectangle if the ratio of its width to its length is 3 to 4?
   (1) The width of the rectangle is 6.
   (2) The area of the rectangle is 48.
   (A) statement 1 alone is sufficient to answer the question, but statement 2 alone is not sufficient
   (B) statement 2 alone is sufficient to answer the question, but statement 1 alone is not sufficient
   (C) both statements together are needed to answer the question, but neither statement alone is sufficient
   (D) either statement by itself is sufficient to answer the question
   (E) not enough facts are given to answer the question

9. For which of the following lengths of a side of a square would the perimeter be divisible by both 4 and 7?
   (A) 3
   (B) 4
   (C) 5
   (D) 6
   (E) 7

10. On a certain day, a news vendor began the day with P papers. Between opening and noon, he sold 40 percent of the papers, and between noon and closing, he sold 60 percent of the papers which remained. What percent of the original P papers did he sell?
   (A) 0%
   (B) 20%
   (C) 24%
   (D) 76%
   (E) 100%

11. The value of a certain office machine depreciates in such a way that its value at the end of each year is $\frac{4}{5}$ of its value at the beginning of the same year. If the initial value of the machine is \$5,000, what is its value at the end of 3 years?

(A) \$4,750.25

(B) \$4,000.00

(C) \$2,560.00

(D) \$2,000.00

(E) \$640.00

12. In a certain year, corporation X produced 40 percent of the total world production of a certain drug. If corporation X produced 18 kilograms of the drug, how many kilograms were produced by producers other than corporation X?

(A) 22

(B) 27

(C) 36

(D) 40

(E) 45

13. If $x < 0$, which of the following is NOT necessarily true?

(A) $\frac{1}{x^2} > 0$

(B) $x^2 > x^3$

(C) $x^5 < x^4$

(D) $x^2 + x^3 > 0$

(E) $x^3 < 0$

14. In a certain year, the income of an individual from her investments amounted to 45 percent of her total income. If municipal bonds accounted for $\frac{2}{3}$ of her investment income, then the ratio of income derived from municipal bonds to total *noninvestment* income was

(A) $\frac{2}{3}$

(B) $\frac{6}{11}$

(C) $\frac{3}{10}$

(D) $\frac{3}{11}$

(E) $\frac{3}{20}$

15. Was Mark's average running speed for the first hour of his 26-mile marathon 11 miles per hour?

(1) He ran the entire 26 miles in 2.5 hours.

(2) He ran the last 15 miles in 1.5 hours.

(A) statement 1 alone is sufficient to answer the question, but statement 2 alone is not sufficient

(B) statement 2 alone is sufficient to answer the question, but statement 1 alone is not sufficient

(C) both statements together are needed to answer the question, but neither statement alone is sufficient

(D) either statement by itself is sufficient to answer the question

(E) not enough facts are given to answer the question

16. For a certain concert, 560 tickets were sold for a total of \$2,150. If an orchestra seat sold for twice the balcony seat price of \$2.50, how many of the tickets sold were balcony seat tickets?

(A) 235

(B) 260

(C) 300

(D) 325

(E) 358

17. If $p > 0$, what percent is p of q?
   (1) $q = 2p$
   (2) $p + q = 36$
   (A) statement 1 alone is sufficient to answer the question, but statement 2 alone is not sufficient
   (B) statement 2 alone is sufficient to answer the question, but statement 1 alone is not sufficient
   (C) both statements together are needed to answer the question, but neither statement alone is sufficient
   (D) either statement by itself is sufficient to answer the question
   (E) not enough facts are given to answer the question

18. A certain liquid fertilizer contains 10 percent mineral X by volume. If a farmer wishes to treat a crop with $\frac{3}{4}$ of a liter of mineral X per acre, how many acres can he treat with 300 liters of the liquid fertilizer?
   (A) 40
   (B) 24
   (C) 18
   (D) 16
   (E) 12

19. At the beginning of a class, a classroom has 3 empty chairs and all students are seated. No student leaves the classroom, and additional students equal to 20 percent of the number of students already seated enter the class late and fill the empty chairs. What is the total number of chairs in the classroom?
   (A) 18
   (B) 15
   (C) 10
   (D) 6
   (E) 3

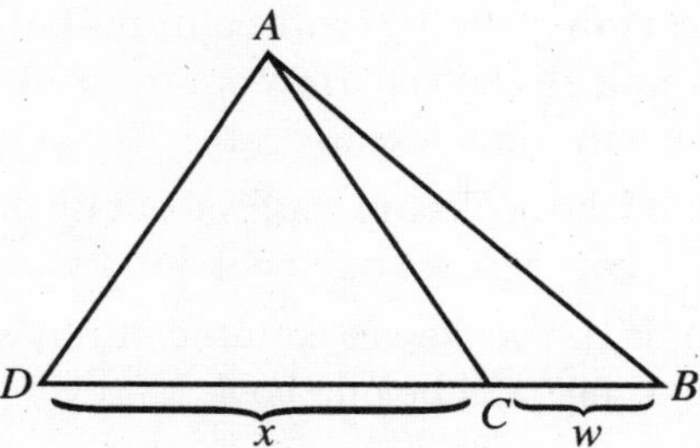

20. In the figure above, the ratio $\frac{w}{x}$ is $\frac{1}{3}$. What is the ratio $\frac{area\ \Delta ABC}{area\ \Delta ACD}$?
   (A) $\frac{1}{6}$
   (B) $\frac{1}{3}$
   (C) $\frac{3}{1}$
   (D) $\frac{6}{1}$
   (E) $\frac{9}{1}$

21. In a certain shipment, x out of every y items were found to be defective. If 10 defective items were found in the shipment, what was the total number of items in the shipment?
   (A) $\frac{10y}{x}$
   (B) $\frac{10x}{y}$
   (C) 10y
   (D) $\frac{10y}{y-x}$
   (E) $\frac{10y}{x-y}$

22. Four cylindrical cans each with a radius of 2 inches are placed on their bases inside an open square pasteboard box. If the four sides of the box bulge slightly, which of the following could be the internal perimeter of the base of the box, expressed in inches?
   (A) 64
   (B) 32
   (C) 30
   (D) 20
   (E) 16

practice test

23. A certain packing crate contains between 50 and 60 books. How many books are there in the packing crate?

(1) If the books are counted out by threes, there will be one book left over.

(2) If the books are counted out by sixes, there will be one book left over.

(A) statement 1 alone is sufficient to answer the question, but statement 2 alone is not sufficient

(B) statement 2 alone is sufficient to answer the question, but statement 1 alone is not sufficient

(C) both statements together are needed to answer the question, but neither statement alone is sufficient

(D) either statement by itself is sufficient to answer the question

(E) not enough facts are given to answer the question

24. If x, y, and z are the lengths of three sides of a triangle, is $z > 8$?

(1) $x + y = 8$

(2) $x = 6$

(A) statement 1 alone is sufficient to answer the question, but statement 2 alone is not sufficient

(B) statement 2 alone is sufficient to answer the question, but statement 1 alone is not sufficient

(C) both statements together are needed to answer the question, but neither statement alone is sufficient

(D) either statement by itself is sufficient to answer the question

(E) not enough facts are given to answer the question

25. If N and P denote the nonzero digits of a four-digit number $NNPP$, is $NNPP$ divisible by 4?

(1) NPP is divisible by 8.

(2) NPP is divisible by 4.

(A) statement 1 alone is sufficient to answer the question, but statement 2 alone is not sufficient

(B) statement 2 alone is sufficient to answer the question, but statement 1 alone is not sufficient

(C) both statements together are needed to answer the question, but neither statement alone is sufficient

(D) either statement by itself is sufficient to answer the question

(E) not enough facts are given to answer the question

26. A supermarket sells both a leading brand of laundry powder and its own brand of laundry powder. On all sizes of the leading brand it makes a profit of 15 percent of cost per box. On all sizes of its own brand it makes a profit of 10 percent of cost per box. For a certain month, from the sales of which of the two brands does the supermarket realize the greater profit?

(1) Ounce for ounce, the supermarket pays a higher wholesale price for the leading brand than it does for its own brand.

(2) Ounce for ounce, the supermarket sells 25 percent more of its own brand than of the leading brand.

(A) statement 1 alone is sufficient to answer the question, but statement 2 alone is not sufficient

(B) statement 2 alone is sufficient to answer the question, but statement 1 alone is not sufficient

(C) both statements together are needed to answer the question, but neither statement alone is sufficient

(D) either statement by itself is sufficient to answer the question

(E) not enough facts are given to answer the question

27. If x and y are positive integers, is $x > y$?

(1) $x^2 < y$

(2) $\sqrt{x} < y$

(A) statement 1 alone is sufficient to answer the question, but statement 2 alone is not sufficient

(B) statement 2 alone is sufficient to answer the question, but statement 1 alone is not sufficient

(C) both statements together are needed to answer the question, but neither statement alone is sufficient

(D) either statement by itself is sufficient to answer the question

(E) not enough facts are given to answer the question

28. Machine M can produce x units in $\frac{3}{4}$ of the time it takes machine N to produce x units. Machine N can produce x units in $\frac{2}{3}$ the time it takes machine O to produce x units. If all three machines are working simultaneously, what fraction of the total output is produced by machine N?

(A) $\frac{1}{2}$

(B) $\frac{1}{3}$

(C) $\frac{4}{13}$

(D) $\frac{8}{29}$

(E) $\frac{6}{33}$

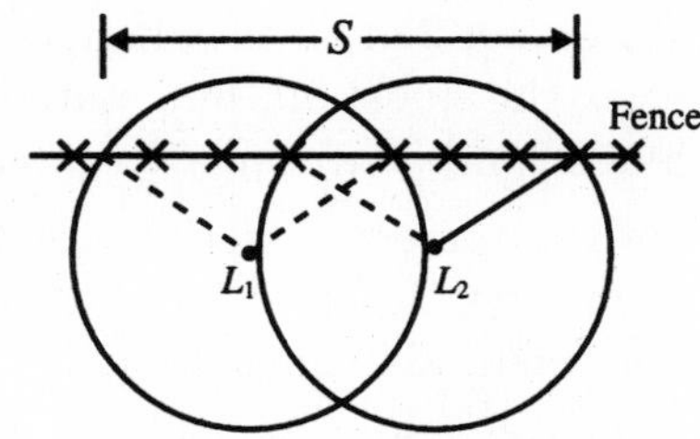

29. In the figure above, two security lights, L_1 and L_2, are located 100 feet apart. Each illuminates an area of radius 100 feet, and both are located 60 feet from a chain-link fence. What is the total length s of fence, in feet, illuminated by the two lights?

(A) 260

(B) 240

(C) 220

(D) 200

(E) 180

30. $(3508)^2 - (3510 \times 3508) =$

(A) 7020

(B) 0

(C) –2

(D) –3508

(E) –7016

31. A fruit seller bought 2000 quarts of berries at 80 cents per quart. If $\frac{1}{4}$ of the berries become too ripe for sale, what should be the selling price per quart of the remainder so that the gross profit will be 20 percent of the total cost?

(A) $0.25

(B) $0.80

(C) $1.00

(D) $1.10

(E) $1.28

32. Charlene spent $\frac{2}{5}$ of her income for January for rent, and $\frac{3}{4}$ of the remainder on other expenses. If she put the remaining $180 in her savings account, how much was her income in January?

(A) $1,000

(B) $1,200

(C) $1,400

(D) $1,600

(E) $1,800

practice test

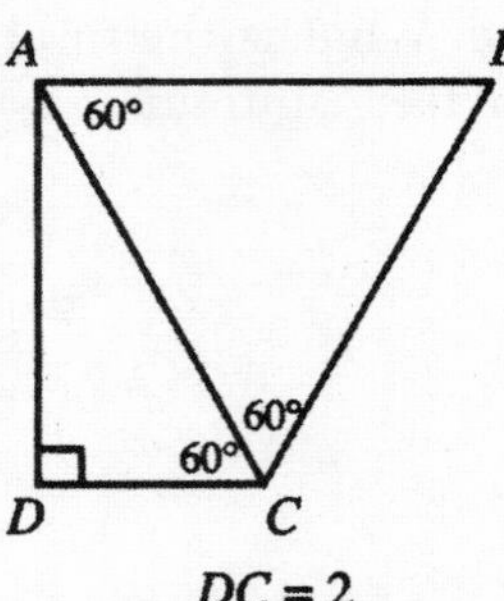

33. In the figure above, what is the area of triangle *ABC?*

(A) $8\sqrt{3}$

(B) $8\sqrt{2}$

(C) 8

(D) $4\sqrt{3}$

(E) $2\sqrt{3}$

34. If the numerator of a fraction is decreased 25 percent and the denominator of that fraction is increased 25 percent, then the difference between the resulting and the original fractions represents what percentage decrease?

(A) 40%

(B) 45%

(C) 50%

(D) 60%

(E) 75%

35. If the number of square units in the area of a circle is *A* and the number of linear units in the circumference is *C,* what is the radius of the circle?

(1) $\frac{A}{C} = \frac{3}{2}$

(2) $A > C + 3$

(A) statement 1 alone is sufficient to answer the question, but statement 2 alone is not sufficient

(B) statement 2 alone is sufficient to answer the question, but statement 1 alone is not sufficient

(C) both statements together are needed to answer the question, but neither statement alone is sufficient

(D) either statement by itself is sufficient to answer the question

(E) not enough facts are given to answer the question

36. A racetrack bounded by two concentric circles, one with a diameter of 160 yards and the other with a diameter of 140 yards, is to covered with asphalt. If the asphalt layer is to be 1 foot deep, how many cubic yards of asphalt will be needed?

(A) 75π

(B) 90π

(C) 500π

(D) 1500π

(E) 2000π

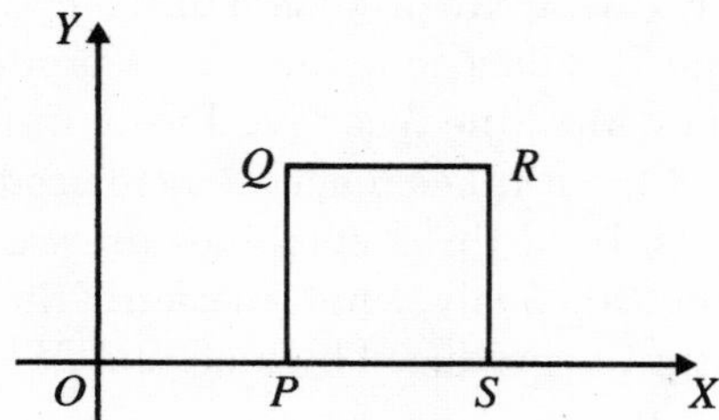

37. In the figure above, *P* and *S* are points on the *x*-axis. What is the area of square *PQRS*?

(1) The coordinates of point *P* are (2, 0).

(2) The coordinates of point *R* are (6, 4).

(A) statement 1 alone is sufficient to answer the question, but statement 2 alone is not sufficient

(B) statement 2 alone is sufficient to answer the question, but statement 1 alone is not sufficient

(C) both statements together are needed to answer the question, but neither statement alone is sufficient

(D) either statement by itself is sufficient to answer the question

(E) not enough facts are given to answer the question

ANSWER KEY AND EXPLANATIONS

Verbal Section

1. D	10. E	19. C	28. C	37. E
2. C	11. B	20. B	29. A	38. E
3. B	12. B	21. D	30. B	39. C
4. D	13. D	22. C	31. A	40. C
5. D	14. C	23. D	32. B	41. A
6. C	15. A	24. C	33. A	
7. A	16. B	25. B	34. E	
8. D	17. C	26. A	35. C	
9. A	18. C	27. C	36. C	

1. **The correct answer is (D).** (D) is correct because it expresses the two things being compared in like grammatical forms: "to be afraid of . . . is to be afraid of" (infinitives). (A), (B), and (C) fail because they compare unlike forms: "to be afraid" (infinitive) with "being afraid" (gerund). (E) uses the same form for both parts, but is an unnecessary combination of the two possibilities. (B) also uses commas incorrectly. Using the gerund form in both parts would also be correct.

2. **The correct answer is (C).** The problem is raised by placement of the modifier "hurtling through." Who or what is hurtling, Anna [(A), (D)], the sight (B), or the shooting star [(C), (E)]? Of the two clearest statements—(C) and (E)—(C) presents the facts in a better order.

3. **The correct answer is (B).** (A) errs in three ways: "superior" is already a comparative adjective and does not need the comparative form "more"; the idiom is "superior to," not "superior than"; and the "far as . . . concerned" phrase embodies an unneeded repetition. (C), (D) and (E) each make one of these errors; (E) also is awkward in its word order.

4. **The correct answer is (D).** The author's recommendation that public schools should have computerized reading programs depends upon the correctness of the explanation of the present deficiency in reading skills in the public schools. The contrast with private-school students shows that the author thinks the deficiency can be attributed to the lack of such a program in the public schools. So, one of the author's assumptions, and that is what the question stem is asking about, is that the differential in reading skills is a result of the availability of a computerized program in the private-school system and the lack thereof in the public-school system. (E) is, of course, irrelevant to the question of *reading* skills. (C) tries to force the author to assume a greater burden than the author has undertaken. The author claims that the reading skills of public-school children could be improved by a computerized reading program. The author does not argue the merits of having good reading skills. (A) and (B) are wrong for the same reason. The author's claim must be interpreted to mean "of children who are able to learn, all would benefit from a comput-

erized reading program." When the author claims that "public-school children can be good readers," the author is not implying that all children can learn to be good readers nor that all can learn to read equally well.

5. **The correct answer is (D).** The question contains a hidden presupposition that the company has discriminatory practices in the first place. This rhetorical strategy is also called a complex question or, pejoratively, a loaded question. (B) is not a correct description of the question, but the questioner doesn't make such an assumption. The other choices describe features of the question, but not ones that would be considered unfair, as the question stem asks.

6. **The correct answer is (C).** (A) is incorrect because it switches from the singular ("weaver," "his") to the plural ("they"). Changing this segment to all singular, as in (B), would not tie in with "their wool" later in the sentence. So it is better to change all references to the plural, as in (C). (D) and (E) unpleasantly switch from the personal active to the impersonal passive.

7. **The correct answer is (A).** There are two weaknesses in Ms. Rose's argument. One will be treated in the explanation of the following question—she reaches a very general conclusion on the basis of one example. We are concerned for the moment with the second weakness. Even if Rose had been able to cite numerous examples like the case she mentions, her argument would be weak because it overlooks the possibility that an education may be valuable even if it is not used to make a living. Importantly, Rose may be correct in her criticism of the man she mentions—we need make no judgment about that—but the assumption is nonetheless *unsupported* in that she gives no arguments to support it. (B) plays on the superficial detail of the paragraph—the inversion of customary role models. But that is not relevant to the structure of the argument; the form could have been as easily shown using a woman with a law degree who decided to become a sailor, or a child who studied ballet but later decided to become a doctor. (D) also is totally beside the point. Rose never commits herself to so specific a conclusion. She simply says professional education is a waste; she never claims success is related to quality of education. (E) is wrong because Rose is making a general claim about professional education—the man with the law degree was used merely to illustrate her point. (C) is perhaps the second-best answer, but it is still not nearly as good as (A). The author's objection is that the man she mentions did not use his law degree in a law-related field. She never suggests that such a degree should be used to make money. She might not have objected to his behavior if he had used the degree to work in a public interest capacity.

8. **The correct answer is (D).** As we noted at the beginning of our discussion of question 7, there is another weakness in Rose's argument: She takes a single example and from it draws a very general conclusion. (D) exemplifies this weakness. Here, too, we have a person who rests his claim on a single example, and obviously this makes the claim very weak. (E) mentions education, but here education is a detail of the argument. The form of the argument—a foolish generalization—is not restricted to education. (A), (B), and (C) are all wrong because they do not reflect the form of the argument, a generalization on a single example.

9. **The correct answer is (A).** (C), (B), and (E) change the meaning; in (B) and (E) the result is gibberish. (D) would make sense but would not be Standard Written English: the required conjunction in such an indirect question is "whether."

10. **The correct answer is (E).** Since the writer talks of a condition contrary to fact (he is not President), he should use the subjunctive form "I were," as in (E). "I was," as in (A) and (C), would be acceptable in informal speech but not in Standard Written English. (B) is too elliptical. (C) and (D) slightly change the meaning: (C) makes the "halt" the President's very first action; (D) implies he has a realistic chance of being President.

11. **The correct answer is (B).** (A) and (E) err in being ambiguous: They could mean that females are more concerned about discrimination than about males. (D) goes further than it has to by repeating the full phrase "are concerned." All that is necessary is the key word "are," as in (B). (C) is not incorrect, but it is less graceful and too wordy.

12. **The correct answer is (B).** This is a main idea question. As correctly described by (B), the author explains the results of some studies and suggests some implications of new findings for detecting high blood pressure. (E) is incorrect since it is but a minor aspect of the passage. The author notes that there is such a correlation, but is not primarily concerned with proving the existence of such a relationship. (C) can be eliminated because the main point is not to describe the epidemiological and clinical studies from a methodological point of view. Rather, the author is concerned with the findings of these studies. (D) can be eliminated on similar ground, for the author indicates that both methods of study point to the existence of a familial connection. (A) can be eliminated since the author does not criticize, but rather relies on, these experiments.

13. **The correct answer is (D).** This is a specific detail (explicit idea) question, so the main task is to find the right part of the passage. In the last sentence of the first paragraph, the author explicitly states that a factor that initially discouraged the study of hypertension in children was the unfounded belief that it was difficult to measure blood pressure in children. (A), (B), and (E) are just not mentioned anywhere. The idea suggested by (C) is mentioned, but in the second paragraph, so you know it can't be an answer to this question.

14. **The correct answer is (C).** This question asks us to make a further application of the arguments given in the passage, and the greatest danger may be the temptation to overstate the case. This is the difficulty with answer (E). The author's remarks are qualified in the closing sentences. It may be "possible," but it is never asserted that it is now possible to do this. (D) also overstates the case. The author states that these chemical deficiencies are associated with high blood pressure, not that such deficiencies *cause* high blood pressure. And to the extent that one wants to argue that such deficiencies *contribute* to high blood pressure (based on paragraph three), that is not sufficient to support the causal statement expressed in (D). As for (A), the author notes that the low output of urinary kallikrein is associated with high blood pressure, that is, it may be another symptom of whatever physiological disorder causes high blood pressure, but that means it is an effect of the underlying cause and not the cause itself. Finally, (B) can be eliminated because it is not a further conclusion of the passage. To the extent that (B) reiterates what is stated already—and note that (B) states the kallikrein-kinin system is important in determining blood pressure, not that the system *causes* high blood pressure—it is not appropriate as a further statement based on arguments presented. (C) is, however, a natural extension of the argument. Remember, the author begins by noting that it is important to determine when high blood pressure begins, and

then suggests that it may begin as early as infancy.

15. **The correct answer is (A).** This is a logical detail question. In essence, the question stipulates that the author does introduce such evidence and then asks for what reason. In the final paragraph the author is discussing the connection between low urinary kallikrein excretion and high blood pressure. By noting that black children often show this and that black people often have high blood pressure, the author hopes to provide further evidence for the connection. As for (B), though this may be an incidental effect of the reference, it cannot be said that this is the logical function of the argument in the overall development of the passage. (C) is incorrect since the author is not asserting a causal connection but only a correlation. (D) is incorrect for a reason similar to that which eliminates (B). Though this might be a further application for the point, it is not the reason the author incorporates the data into the argument of this passage. Finally, (E) is one of the main themes of the passage, but it does not explain why the author introduced the particular point at the particular juncture in the argument.

16. **The correct answer is (B).** This is an explicit detail question. In the third paragraph, the author mentions that the kallikrein-kinin system produces chemicals which operate to dilate blood vessels. As for (A) and (C), the author does not state that the kallikrein-kinin system interferes directly with either the sympathetic nervous system or the production of aldosterone—only that it *offsets* the effects of those actions. As for (D), the reference to kallikrein levels in urine comes in the last paragraph, the wrong place for an answer to this question. And whatever (E) is saying, it just doesn't answer the question.

17. **The correct answer is (C).** This is a logical detail question: Why does the author introduce this information? In the second paragraph the author is describing new research done on children, which suggests that the factors related to high blood pressure are already detectable in children. (A) is incorrect since the author has not yet begun to discuss the biochemical research, only epidemiological surveys. (B) is incorrect since it is not a correct response to the question. The author does state that such research is actually possible, but does not cite the results of the study in order to prove the study was possible. Rather, the author cites the results to prove the further conclusion outlined in (C). (D) is incorrect because it is not a response to the question. To be sure, one might use the results of the study cited to support the recommendation articulated in (D), but that is not the author's motivation for introducing it in argument. As for (E), this fails for the same reason that (B) fails.

18. **The correct answer is (C).** This is a logical structure question. The argument is developed primarily by describing findings and supporting a conclusion. As for (A), though two types of research, epidemiological studies and clinical studies, are mentioned, they are not contrasted. (B) is incorrect since the author's main purpose is to support a conclusion, and, whatever refutation is offered in the passage (e.g., against the position that blood pressure in children cannot be measured accurately), it is offered in the service of a greater point. (E) must fail for a similar reason. And (D) fails for this reason as well: The author is supporting a position, not refuting it.

19. **The correct answer is (C).** To break the code, the cryptographer needs information about the language which the code conceals. (A), (B), (D), and (E) all

provide such information. (C), however, says nothing about the underlying language. The code could even use all even or all odd numbers for the symbol substitutions without affecting the information to be encoded.

20. **The correct answer is (B).** The question is one which tests the validity or strength of a causal inference. Often such arguments can be attacked by finding intervening causal linkages, that is, variables which might interfere with the predicted result. (A) cites such a variable. If the traffic problem is created by commercial traffic which will not be reduced by toll increases, then the proposed increases will not solve the problem. (C), too, is such a variable. It suggests that the proposal is essentially self-defeating. (D) undermines the claim by arguing that the deterrent effect of a price increase is simply not significant, so the proposal will have little, if any, effect. (E) attacks the argument on a different ground. The ultimate objective of the plan is to reduce commuting time. Even assuming a drop in auto traffic because some commuters use public transportation, no advantage is gained if the public transportation system cannot handle the increase in traffic. (B), however, does very little to the argument. In fact, it could be argued that (B) is one of the predicted results of the plan: a drop in the number of autos because commuters begin to car-pool.

21. **The correct answer is (D).** The exam frequently uses arguments based on analogy, and often the correct answer is one that points out that two situations are not necessarily similar. That's a good way of describing this item: maybe it was the mountain retreat location rather than the medicine that was the deciding factor. (A) is wrong because even granting the point, there is still a physical addiction to be addressed. (B) and (E) are typical wrong answers for an item like this: interesting, but which way does this idea cut? Since neither clearly weakens the ad, neither could be the correct answer. Finally, (C), if anything, seems to strengthen the ad by suggesting that the study was authoritative.

22. **The correct answer is (C).** In Standard Written English, the negative correlative conjunctions "neither . . . nor" function together, as in (C). If one of them appears in a negating construction like (A), (B), or (E), the other should also appear, but in the appropriate order of "neither . . . nor." In (D), "or" is wrong because when it is used as a correlative conjunction, it appears only with "either," which would be contrary to the meaning here.

23. **The correct answer is (D).** (D) is correct because it extends the structure begun with "results from" by repeating the "from" at the crucial point. The others are incorrect. (A) used "to" where "from" is needed; (B) confuses "affect" with "effect" and fails to extend the "results from" structure; (C) makes two errors in punctuation—neither the apostrophe nor the comma is used correctly; (E) repeats (A)'s error with an unnecessary comma.

24. **The correct answer is (C).** (C) is correct because after a verb like "demand" the action called for must be expressed in the subjunctive mood, e.g., "that management halt . . . and release. . . ."(B) uses the correct verb form but the wrong conjunction: "but" violates the meaning. (A), (B), and (D) all violate the parallelism required. (D) also creates an awkward final phrase.

25. **The correct answer is (B).** Notice that there is much common ground between the jockey and the veterinarian. The question stem asks you to uncover the areas on which they are in agreement, by asking which of the answer choices is NOT a shared assumption. Note that the excep-

tion can be an area neither has as well as an area only one has. Examine the dialogue. Both apparently assume that human emotions can be attributed to animals since they talk about them being loyal and brave (C), and both take those characteristics as being noble—that is, admirable (A). Neither speaker offers scientific evidence; each rests content with an anecdote (E) and (D). As for (B), though each speaker defends his choice for the first (*most* loyal), neither speaker takes a position on the second most loyal animal. For example, the jockey might believe that horses are the most loyal animals and that goldfish are the second most loyal animals.

26. **The correct answer is (A).** Although we do not want to argue theology, perhaps a point taken from that discipline will make this question more accessible: "If God is only good, from where does evil come?" Rousseau, at least as far as his argument is characterized here, faced a similar problem. If humans are by nature sympathetic, what is the source of their nonsympathetic social institutions? (A) poses this critical question. The remaining choices each commit the same fundamental error. Rousseau *describes* a situation. The paragraph never suggests that he proposed a *solution.* Perhaps Rousseau considered the problem of modern society irremediable.

27. **The correct answer is (C).** The last sentence of the paragraph is very important. It tells us that the proportion of light atoms in the universe is increasing (because heavy ones decay into light ones, but the reverse process does not occur) and that this trend can be measured. By extrapolation back into time on the basis of present trends, scientists can find out when it all began. (B) and (E) are incorrect for the same reason. The author describes a physical phenomenon occurring on a grand scale. There is no hint that it will be possible for scientists to reverse it (B). Further, (E) is in direct contradiction with information given in the paragraph: The ratio is not stable because the stars do not produce enough heavy atoms to offset the decay. (D) cannot be inferred from the passage. Although the *ratio* of light to heavy atoms is increasing, we should not conclude that the ratio is greater than 1:1. And, in any event, this would not be nearly so logical a conclusion to the passage as (C). Finally, (A) is a distraction. It picks up on a minor detail in the passage and inflates that into a conclusion. Moreover, the passage clearly states that the process which keeps the stars going is fusion, not decay.

28. **The correct answer is (C).** This is a main idea question. The main point of the passage is that those who believe AFDC restrictions contribute to family dissolution are in error. It is not the restrictions on aid but the aid itself, according to the author, that contributes to the dissolution of low-income families. So the primary purpose of the passage is to analyze the causes of a phenomenon. (A) is incorrect, for any such results are mentioned only obliquely and are only incidental to the main development. (B) describes something that is integral to the argument but is not the main point of the argument. As for (D), the author offers no such recommendation. While an argument for reform might use the argument in the passage for such recommendations, we cannot attribute any proposal for reform to the author. Finally, (E) describes what may be a result of the argument, but changing the attitude of the public, as opposed to engaging in scholarly debate, does not appear to be the objective of the text.

29. **The correct answer is (A).** As we noted above, the author argues that it is not the restrictions on aid that create pressures

on low-income families; it is the aid itself. We can apply this reasoning to answer this question. The analysis in the text can be used to predict that an increase in the availability of aid would tend to increase pressures on the family unit. Thus, reducing restrictions, because it would result in an increase in aid availability, would actually tend to create more pressure for divorce. This would have the exact opposite effect predicted by those who call for welfare reforms such as eliminating restrictions. (A) is nice also because of the word "paradoxically," which opens the statement, for the result would be paradoxical from the standpoint of the reformer. (C) and (D) can be eliminated because they are contradicted by the analysis given in the passage. (B) is eliminated because the author never addresses questions of fiscal policy. Finally, (E) goes too far in two respects. First, it overstates the author's case. The author does not suggest that the only factor operating in the dissolution of low-income families is welfare, and therefore, would not likely suggest that the problem could be entirely controlled by manipulating benefit levels. Further, it is not clear that the author advocates any particular policy. The scholarly tone of the article suggests that the author may or may not believe public policy on welfare should take into account the problem of divorce.

30. **The correct answer is (B).** This is an explicit idea question. In discussing the costs of divorce in the third paragraph (costs meaning both economic and social costs), the author mentions (A), (C), and (D) as encouraging people to stay married. Earlier in that same paragraph, the author mentions consumption possibilities as a factor tending to hold a marriage together. (B) is never mentioned in this respect. Although primarily interested in low-income family stability, the author never states that social or economic class is a factor in perpetuating a marriage. And to the extent that one mounts an argument to the effect that the pressures described in paragraph three (costs of divorce and greater consumption possibilities) would naturally tend to operate more powerfully for lower-income families, the author is applying that reasoning to a new situation. So that argument, since it is new, cannot be a factor mentioned by the author in this passage and cannot, therefore, be an answer to the question asked.

31. **The correct answer is (A).** This is obviously a main idea question, and we have already analyzed the main point of the passage. It is nicely stated by (A). (B) is not the main idea but only an incidental feature of the argument. (C) is incorrect since this is in direct contradiction to the main point of the passage. (D) fails for the same reason that (B) fails. Finally, (E) is incorrect because there is no warrant in the passage to support the conclusion that the author would make such a recommendation. The author argues in a very scholarly and neutral fashion; thus we cannot attribute to the author any attitude about the wisdom of welfare policy.

32. **The correct answer is (B).** As we have just noted, the scholarly treatment of the passage is best described as scientific and detached. As for (A), though the author may be confident, there is no hint of optimism. (C) can be eliminated for a similar reason: There is no hint of alarm or discouragement. As for (D), to the extent that it can be argued that the author's treatment is scholarly, and therefore polite and sensitive, (B) is a better description of the overall tone. The defining elements of a scholarly treatment are those set forth in (B). Those elements suggested by (D) would be merely incidental to, and parasitic upon, the main features of scientific neutrality and de-

tachment. Finally, though the author's treatment is detached, it would be wrong to say that the author is callous and indifferent—any more than we would want to say that the doctor who analyzes the causes of a disease in clinical terms is therefore callous and indifferent.

33. **The correct answer is (A).** With an application question of this sort, we must be careful not to overstate the strength of the author's case. This is the reason (D) is incorrect. Though the author points out that there are economic pressures on families which tend to encourage divorce, it would go beyond that analysis to attribute to the author the statement in choice (D). (E), too, overstates the case. Though the author prefers to analyze family stability primarily in economic terms, the text will not support the judgment that people are getting more self-centered. If anything, a rising divorce rate would be analyzed by the author in broad social and economic terms, rather than in personal terms as suggested by (E). (B) is incorrect because it takes us too far beyond the analysis given in paragraph three. While it is conceivable that further analysis would generate the conclusion in (B), (A) is much closer to the actual text. This is not to say that (B) is necessarily a false statement. Rather, this is to accept the structure of the question: Would the author *most likely* agree. Finally, (C) attributes to the author a value judgment which has no support in the text.

34. **The correct answer is (E).** This, too, is an application question. And, as just pointed out, we are looking for the most likely source. It is not impossible that the passage was taken from a basic economics text or a book on the history of welfare. It could conceivably be one of several readings included in such books, but it seems more likely, given the scholarly tone and the particular subject, that (E) is the correct answer. It seems unlikely that this would have appeared in (A) or (D).

35. **The correct answer is (C).** It is important to pay careful attention to the ways in which a speaker qualifies her claims. In this case, the speaker has said only that the *great majority* of people can get medical care—she does not claim that *all* can. Thus, built into the claim is the implicit concession that some people may not have access to medical care. Thus, the objector's response fails to score against the speaker. The speaker could just respond, "Yes, I realize that and that is the reason why I qualified my remarks." (A) is incorrect for the only word in the objector's statement which is the least bit emotional is "poor," and it seems rather free from emotional overtones here. It would have been a different case had the objector claimed, "There are thousands of poor and starving people who have no place to live. . . . " (D) is wrong for two reasons. First, the evidence is really not statistical; it is only numerical. Second, and more important, the evidence, if anything, cuts against the speaker's claim—not that it does any damage given the speaker's qualifications but it surely does not strengthen the speaker's claim. Finally, inasmuch as the speaker does not offer a cause-effect explanation, (E) must be wrong.

36. **The correct answer is (C).** There are really two parts to the speaker's claim. First, she maintains that the majority of Americans can get access to the medical care in this country; and, second, that the care they have access to is the best in the world. As for the second, good medical care is a function of many variables: number and location of facilities, availability of doctors, quality of education, etc. (A) and (E) may both be consistent with the speaker's claim. Even though we have fewer assistants (A) than some

other country, we have more doctors, and that more than makes up for the fewer assistants. Or, perhaps, we have such good preventive medicine that people do not need to go into the hospital as frequently as the citizens of other nations, (E). (B) is wrong for a similar reason. Although it suggests there is a country in which people have greater access to the available care, it does not come to grips with the second element of the speaker's claim: that the care we get is the best. (C), however, does meet both because it cites the existence of a country in which people are *given* (that is the first element) *better* (the second element) care. (D) is not in opposition to the speaker's claim since she has implicitly conceded that some people do not have access to the care.

37. **The correct answer is (E).** In Standard Written English, "each other" is the reciprocal pronoun for two persons, "one another" for more than two. Hence, (E) is the only correct answer. In informal speech, (A) would be acceptable.

38. **The correct answer is (E).** (A) errs in three ways: it uses "as . . . that" instead of "as . . . as," which is required in comparing things to an equal degree; it fails to put "almost a century later" in commas, required since the phrase is nonessential; and it uses "will offer" where, in the sequence of tenses after the past verb "posed," the past form of "will" ("would offer") is required. (B) and (C) each correct only two of the three errors; (D), only one; (E) is entirely correct.

39. **The correct answer is (C).** Note the word *right* is italicized in the first sentence of the paragraph. The author is saying that this idea of a right can be only understood as the outcome of a balancing of demands. The smoker has an interest in smoking; the nonsmoker has an interest in being free from smoke; so the question of which one actually has a *right* to have that *interest* protected depends upon which of those interests is considered to be more important. In some cases the balance is easily struck; in other cases it is difficult; but in all cases, the weighing, implicitly or explicitly, occurs. (C) captures the essence of this thought. In the case of smoking, the interests of both parties must be taken into account. (A) is a distraction. It is true the passage treats "rights," and it is also true that our Constitution protects our rights; but the connection suggested by (A) is a spurious one. It fails to address itself to the logic of the author's argument. The same objections can be leveled against (B). The wording of (D) makes it wrong. The passage is concerned with the demands of the nonsmoker *to be free from* the smoke of others, not with whether someone chooses to smoke. (E) is premature. At this juncture the author is merely laying the foundation for the argument. The conclusion with regard to smoking is reached only at the end of the paragraph. (See discussion of the following question.) (E) is wrong also because it mentions the "rights" of non- smoking persons. The whole question the author is addressing is whether the non-smoking person has a *right* as opposed to an interest or a mere claim.

40. **The correct answer is (C).** Here is where the author makes the general discussion of the balancing of interests to determine rights specifically applicable to the question of smoking. A smoker will have a *right* to smoke when and where the smoker's interests outweigh the interests of those who object, and (C) provides a pretty clear statement of this conclusion. (A) overstates the author's case. While it may be true that ultimately it will be some branch of the government which strikes the balance of interests, the phrase "chooses to allow" does not do justice to the author's concept of the balancing. The government is not simply choosing; it is weighing. Of course,

since the balance may or may not be struck in favor of the smoker, (B) is incorrect. (E) confuses the problem of enforcement with the process of balancing. The passage leads to the conclusion that the balance must be struck. How that decision is later enforced is a practical matter the author is not concerned to discuss in this passage. Finally, (D), like (A), overstates the case. The smoker has an interest in being allowed to smoke, just as much as the non-smoker has an interest in being free from the smoke. A balance must be struck by giving proper weight to both. The author never suggests that the interest of the smokers can be completely overridden. Thus, for example, a smoker may have a more powerful interest in smoking than a non-smoker has in his being free from smoke, if the non-smoker can—with some small inconvenience—protect himself from the smoke.

41. **The correct answer is (A).** The original is best because it relates the circumstances in the most logical, most dramatic order, and without error. (B) and (C) leave their opening phrase dangling: (B) links "the greatest player" not to Tilden, but to his "accomplishments"; and (C), to the "rumors"! (C), (D), and (E) fail to arrange the facts as effectively as (A) does; (D) is especially awkward.

ANSWER KEY AND EXPLANATIONS

Quantitative Section

1. C	9. E	17. A	25. D	33. D
2. D	10. D	18. A	26. E	34. A
3. C	11. C	19. A	27. A	35. A
4. B	12. B	20. B	28. B	36. C
5. D	13. D	21. A	29. A	37. B
6. A	14. B	22. C	30. E	
7. C	15. C	23. B	31. E	
8. D	16. B	24. A	32. B	

1. **The correct answer is (C).** This question can be analyzed in several ways, all of them acceptable, but it is obviously important to make the proper conversions: quarts to gallons and seconds to minutes. We recommend that once you have analyzed a question such as this, you make a marginal notation in your test booklet of the final form the answer must assume; gal/3 min. This will remind you to do the needed conversions.

   Some students will analyze this as a rate problem:

   output = rate × time

   The rate at which the machine processes milk is 8 qt/6 sec, which is equal to 2 gal/6 sec or 1 gal/ 3 sec. Then the running time is 3 minutes, or 180 seconds. Substituting into the rate formula:

   output = 1 gal/3 sec × 180 sec = 60 gal

   Other students will prefer to use a proportion. Since output varies directly with running time (the longer the running time, the greater the output), we can set up a direct proportion. Let R stand for running time and O for output, and we will use subscripts 1 and 2 to designate the shorter (6 second) and longer (3 minute) running times, respectively. Using these notational devices, we can set up the direct proportion in any of four different ways:

   $$\frac{O_1}{O_2}=\frac{R_1}{R_2} \quad \frac{O_2}{O_1}=\frac{R_2}{R_1} \quad \frac{R_1}{O_1}=\frac{R_2}{O_2} \quad \frac{O_1}{R_1}=\frac{O_2}{R_2}$$

   Each of these formulas is a mathematical summary for a statement such as, "The output in case 1 *is to* the output in case 2 as the running time in case 1 *is to* the running time in case 2." That is, the ratio of the two outputs is the same as the ratio of the two running times. Taking the first formula (as a matter of arbitrary selection) and substituting numbers, we have:

   $$\frac{2 \text{ gal}}{x \text{ gal}}=\frac{6 \text{ sec}}{180 \text{ sec}}$$

   Cross-multiplying:

   $$360 = 6x$$
   $$x = 60$$

2. **The correct answer is (D).** We begin by recognizing that Ms. Baker spent $1.80 and that this $1.80 represents, in a sense, two separate purchases at two different prices (one item at full price and a second item at half price). We do not know the usual price, so we use x to designate this unknown. Then we relate the second price to x. If x is the full price, then the sale price is one-half of that, or $\frac{1}{2}x$. When

answers

added, these two equal $1.80, so we have:

$$x + \frac{1}{2}x = \$1.80$$

Solving for x,

$$\frac{3}{2}x = 1.80$$
$$x = 1.80\left(\frac{2}{3}\right)$$
$$x = 1.20$$

It is also possible to answer this question by testing each of the answer choices. Since it is characteristic of the exam that choices are arranged in order of magnitude (least to greatest or vice versa), we test (C) first. If the regular price were $.90, then the sale price for the second item would be $\frac{1}{2}$($.90), or $.45, for a total price of $1.35. But the question stem tells us that Ms. Baker paid a total of $1.80, not $1.35. This tells us that (C) is not the correct answer, and it also tells us that the usual price is more than $.90 (otherwise, she would not have paid so much for both combined). So we test (D) next. If the usual price is $1.20, then the price for the second item is $.60, and the combined total is $1.80, which confirms that (D) is correct. Suppose the answer choices had been arranged differently, for example, (C) $.50, (D) $.90, (E) $1.20. We would have tested (C) and (D) and found them to be incorrect. That would have proved (by the process of elimination) that (E) was correct. There would have been no need then to test (E).

3. **The correct answer is (C).** We are asked to determine how many people first boarded the flight in Chicago. (1) is not sufficient by itself. Though we know that 149 people were aboard the plane when it arrived in Los Angeles and (1) specifies the number on board when it left New York City, we cannot assume that those people on the plane when it arrived in Los Angeles were originally on board when the flight left New York City because the flight stopped in Chicago. Nor is (2) sufficient by itself, for we need to know how many passengers were on board when the flight left New York City. Both statements together, however, are sufficient. If we know how many people were on board when the flight left New York City, how many got off in Chicago, and how many arrived in Los Angeles, simple arithmetic will tell us how many first boarded in Chicago (though, of course, there is no reason to do the arithmetic).

4. **The correct answer is (B).** We are asked to determine the number of active members in the fraternity this year. Statement (1) is not sufficient since it does not tell us anything about the number of active members last year or this year, only something about the number of active members lost upon graduation. (2), however, is sufficient. If we know the number last year, and the percentage increase in membership, a simple calculation will give us the number of active members this year: Number of Active Members Last Year × $112\frac{1}{2}$ percent = Number of Active Members This Year. Since we are concerned only about the number of active members and not about where they went or where they came from, (1) is not needed for this calculation.

5. **The correct answer is (D).** We are asked a very limited question: Is p positive, not what is the value of p? This question will give a yes or no answer. (1) is sufficient. Since 5 is positive and the product of 5 times p is positive, p must be positive. So the answer to the question is, "Yes, p is positive." That shows that (1) is sufficient to answer the question posed. Similarly, (2) is sufficient. Since $-p$ is equivalent to -1 times p and since the product of that multiplication is negative, p must be positive.

6. **The correct answer is (A).** Here we are asked a yes or no question. Is 15 the average of x, y, and 15? What does this

mean? This is asking whether $\frac{x+y+15}{3}$ = 15. A quick manipulation shows that this is asking whether $x + y = 30$. (1) answers that question in the affirmative, so statement (1), by itself, establishes that the answer to the question is yes. (2), however, is not sufficient to establish anything about the *sum* of x and y (as opposed to the *difference* between x and y). To be sure, if we wanted to find exact values for x and y, both (1) and (2) would be needed, but that is not necessary for this particular question.

7. **The correct answer is (C).** We need only establish the identity of the player who hit the most home runs. It is not necessary to rank the other two players. (1) is not sufficient since it establishes only that Paul hit fewer home runs than Mary. (2) is not sufficient since it establishes only that Mary hit more home runs than Susan. Both together establish that Mary hit more home runs than either of the other two players. This establishes the identity of the number one home run hitter, so both statements taken together are sufficient to answer the question.

8. **The correct answer is (D).** Here we must establish the perimeter of the rectangle. Remember that knowing width and length will give us the perimeter. When coupled with the information provided in the question stem about the ratio between width and length, (1) is sufficient to answer the question about the perimeter. We could calculate the length (it is 8) and compute the perimeter (it is 28). That (2) is also sufficient is perhaps a little more difficult to see. (2) tells us that width times length equals 48; this is an equation with two unknowns. But since we know that $\frac{\text{width}}{\text{length}} = \frac{3}{4}$, we can express one of the two variables in terms of the other. For example, $w = \frac{3}{4}(l)$. Substituting this value for w in the equation for area, we have $\frac{3}{4}(l)(l) = 48$. Although the equation gives us two solutions ($l^2 = 64$, so $l = +8$ or -8), since we are dealing with distance, only one value, the positive value, is possible. So (2) also is sufficient by itself.

9. **The correct answer is (E).** This is a problem in which it is essential to keep in mind that the array of answer choices dictates your attack on the question. After all, there is an infinite number of squares the perimeters of which are divisible by both 4 and 7, e.g., 28, 56, 112, etc.—in other words, any square the perimeter of which is divisible by 28 (4×7). The most efficient way of attacking this question is to test each choice. (A), (B), (C), and (D) have perimeters of 12, 16, 20, and 24, respectively, numbers that are not divisible by both 4 and 7. (E), however, has a perimeter of 28, divisible by both 4 and 7, and that is the correct choice.

10. **The correct answer is (D).** This problem is largely a matter of bookkeeping—that is, making sure you keep straight the difference between what was sold and what remained. We can attack the question by using P to designate the number of papers the vendor started with. He sold 40 percent of this, or $.4P$, which left $.6P$ newspapers. In the afternoon, he sold 60 percent of this $.6P$, or $.36P$, which left $.24P$ papers. So the vendor sold $.76P$ out of a total of P papers, or 76 percent of all the papers. You can arrive at the same conclusion by arbitrarily picking a number to use instead of P. Since the problem does not specify the actual number of papers at the beginning of the day, the conditions are valid for any number—provided we do not wind up with fractions of papers. To avoid this problem, we pick a number large enough to avoid fractions of papers, yet not so large as to be cumbersome, say, 100 papers. If the vendor started with 100 papers and sold 40 percent in the morning, he had 60 papers for the afternoon. He sold 60 percent of those, or 36 papers,

leaving 24 papers at the end of the day. This means he sold 76 out of 100 papers, or 76 percent of the papers he had at the beginning of the day.

11. **The correct answer is (C).** One way of attacking this question is to compute $\frac{1}{5}$ of the value of the machine at the beginning of a year and subtract that from the total value of the machine at the beginning of the year. For example, the machine is valued at $5,000 in the first year, so it depreciates by $\frac{1}{5}$, or $1,000, leaving a value at the end of the year of $4,000. Then you would repeat this process two more times to get the value at the end of the third year. A simpler attack is to recognize that at the end of the year the machine has only $\frac{4}{5}$, or .8, of its value at the beginning of the year. So at the end of the first year, the machine has the value .8 × $5,000 = $4,000. At the end of the second year, it has the value .8 × $4,000 = $3,200. At the end of the third year, its value is .8 × $3,200 = $2,560.

12. **The correct answer is (B).** Again, there are several valid approaches to the problem. Some students will first want to determine the total amount of the drug produced. Using T to designate the total amount, we set the equation:

    40 percent of $T = 18$. So,
    $.4T = 18$
    $T = 45$

    Since 45 is the total amount produced, and since corporation X accounted for 18, the others produced 27.

    Another way of attacking the question is to set up a proportion:

    $$\frac{40\%}{18} = \frac{60\%}{x}$$

    Notice that we use 60 percent since that is the proportion of the total produced by all other producers. To solve the proportion, you cross-multiply and solve for x.

    Finally, if you were unable to solve the problem using a mathematical formula, you could always fall back on the technique of testing each choice. You would select (C) to test first. Assuming other producers produced 36 kilos of the drug, this would give total production of 36 plus 18, or 54 kilos. But $\frac{18}{54}$ is equal to $\frac{1}{3}$ which is only $33\frac{1}{3}$ percent, so other producers did not produce as much as 36 kilos. Next you would test (B), and a quick calculation would prove (B) to be the correct choice.

13. **The correct answer is (D).** For this question, there really is no substitute for testing each answer choice. (D) is the correct answer, for it makes a statement which is NOT necessarily true. If x is –1, the value of $x^2 + x^3$ is exactly 0. Again, if x is –2, then the value of the statement is $(-2)^2 + (-2)^3$, which is –4. As for (A), since x^2 will always be positive, $\frac{1}{x^2}$ must be positive, and the statement is always true. Similar reasoning shows (B) to be necessarily true. x^2 will always be positive while x^3 will always be negative. (C) is proved true by the same reasoning. Any even-numbered power of a negative value will be positive, and any odd-numbered power will be negative. Finally, (E) makes a true statement since x^3 will always be negative.

14. **The correct answer is (B).** This question is largely a matter of careful reading. We are looking for the ratio "municipal bond income: noninvestment income." Municipal bonds accounted for $\frac{2}{3}$ of 45 percent of total income, or 30 percent of the total. Noninvestment income was 55 percent of the total. So the ratio we need is: $\frac{30\% \text{ of total}}{55\% \text{ of total}} = \frac{6}{11}$. You will notice that this ratio will be 6:11 regardless of the total amount of income. So we do not need to

know the actual dollar value of income to solve the problem.

15. The correct answer is (C). We are asked a yes or no question: Was the speed 11 mph for the first hour? (1) is not sufficient, for we cannot assume that Mark maintained a constant pace for the entire 2.5 hours. (2) is not sufficient, for it gives us Mark's running speed for the last 15 miles and for the last 1.5 hours. Both statements taken together, however, answer the question. From (1) we learn that the total running time was 2.5 hours. From (2) we learn that the last 15 miles were covered in 1.5 hours. This means that the first 11 miles were covered in the first hour. This is sufficient to answer the question posed. Incidentally, the answer to the question is yes, but that is a step we do not have to take within the Data Sufficiency format.

16. The correct answer is (B). One way of attacking this question is to use simultaneous equations. Let x be the number of balcony tickets sold and y the number of orchestra tickets sold. How many tickets were sold in total? The answer is 560, the sum of the number of balcony and the number of orchestra tickets: $x + y = 560$. How much money was taken in? $2,150. Where did it come from? It came from x tickets at $2.50 and y tickets at $5.00: $2.50x + 5.00y = 2150$. Now, both of the statements are true:

$$x + y = 560$$
$$2.5x + 5y = 2150$$

And that it is why we call these statements simultaneous equations—both are true at the same time. Now, we use algebraic techniques to solve for x:

Isolating y: $y = 560 - x$

Substituting for y:

$$2.5x + 5(560 - x) = 2150$$

Solving for x:

$$2.5x + 2800 - 5x = 2150$$
$$-2.5x = -650$$
$$x = 260$$

For the "mathophobes," this question can be attacked by testing answer choices. Begin with (C). Assume that 300 tickets were sold at $2.50 each. How many tickets were then sold at $5.00? 260. So what would be total revenues? (300 @ $2.50) + (260 @ $5.00) = $2,050. But that is not equal to $2,150; it is $100 short. So, did we assume too few or too many cheap tickets? Obviously, we assumed too many cheap tickets, so you would test the next smaller answer, (B). A quick calculation will show that (B) is the correct answer.

17. The correct answer is (A). Since the question stipulates that p is greater than 0, to determine what percent p is of q, we need only to know the ratio between p and q. (1) gives us this. It establishes that $p = \frac{1}{2}q$, which means 50 percent of q. (2), however, does not do the trick. Knowing the sum of two numbers, in and of itself, will not allow us to say anything about the ratio between those two numbers.

18. The correct answer is (A). The key to this question is keeping track of the interrelationships between the pieces of information. One way of attacking the problem is first to determine what volume of mineral X the farmer has in 300 liters of the fertilizer. Since the fertilizer is 10 percent mineral X, 300 liters of the fertilizer will contain 30 liters of mineral X.

Then, we want to put $\frac{3}{4}$ of a liter on each acre. So we need to divide:

$$\frac{30 \text{ liters}}{\frac{3}{4} \text{ liters / acre}}$$

To divide, we multiply by the reciprocal of the divisor:

$$30 \text{ liters} \times \frac{4 \text{ acres}}{3 \text{ liters}} = 40 \text{ acres}$$

answers

Notice that just as we used the reciprocal of the numerical fraction, so too we converted the units "fraction": liter per acre to acre per liter. Then, we had the unit "liter" in the numerator (30 liters) and the unit "liter" in the denominator ($\frac{\text{acres}}{\text{liters}}$), and just as numbers divide out, so do units divide out. This left only one type of unit in the problem, "acres," and that unit was in the numerator. In other words, our answer was 40 acres, and this little bookkeeping device confirms that we did the problem correctly. Notice that if you attempt to multiply 30 liters by $\frac{3}{4}$ liter per acre (rather than dividing), you will have two units of "liters" in the numerator and the unit "acres" in the denominator. Your answer would then read so many liters^2 per acre; and that is obviously not an answer to the question "How many acres . . . ?"

19. **The correct answer is (A).** As with many problems on the test, there is more than one line of attack that can be used. One way of approaching this question is to set up an algebraic statement. Let x designate the number of students already seated at the beginning of class; then the three additional late-comers are equal to 20 percent of that.

So: $.20x = 3$

And: $x = 15$

The number of students originally seated was 15. But the question asks not about the number originally seated, but about the total number of chairs in the classroom. So we must add in the three late-comers, and 15 + 3 = 18.

20. **The correct answer is (B).** To find the area of a triangle, we will need an altitude:

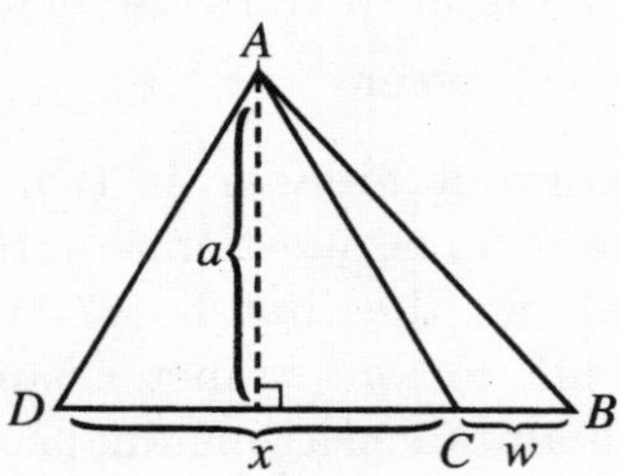

You will observe that our altitude is the altitude not only for D *ADC* but also the altitude for D *ABC*. Using a for altitude, we set up the ratio required:

$$\frac{\frac{1}{2}aw}{\frac{1}{2}ax} = \frac{w}{x} = \frac{1}{3}$$

Notice that the $\frac{1}{2}$ in the numerator and the $\frac{1}{2}$ in the denominator divide out, as does the a, leaving only the ratio w/x, which is stipulated in the problem to be 1:3.

21. **The correct answer is (A).** This question can be answered using a proportion.

$$\frac{x}{y} = \frac{10}{T}$$

This asserts that the ratio of 10 defective items to total (T) items shipped is $x{:}y$. Cross-multiplying, we have:

$$Tx = 10y$$

and dividing by x,

$$T = \frac{10y}{x}$$

22. **The correct answer is (C).** A sketch of the bottom of the box may be helpful:

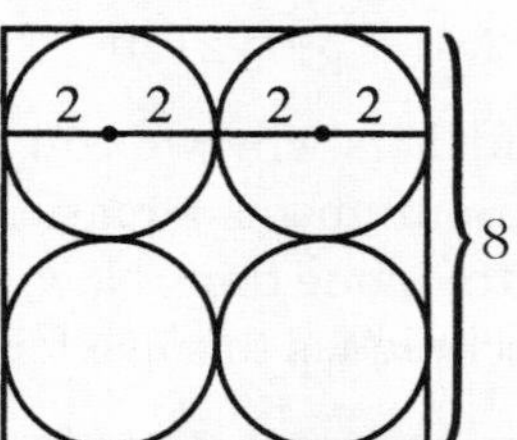

Since the radius of each can is 2, the diameter of each can is 4. If the cans fit exactly into the box, the box would have a side of 8 and a perimeter of 32. But we

answers

are told the box bulges slightly, so the inside perimeter must be slightly less than 32.

23. The correct answer is (B). Here the question is really asking whether we can pinpoint one integer between 50 and 60. (1) is not sufficient since it establishes that the number of books is 52, 55, or 58. (2), however, is sufficient. There is only one number between 50 and 60 which is one greater than a number divisible by 6. That number is 55 (54 divided by 6 = 9, then adding 1 makes the number 55). So (2) alone is sufficient to establish the exact number of books in the crate, but (1) alone is not sufficient.

24. The correct answer is (A). To answer the question, is $z > 8$, you may want to sketch a triangle:

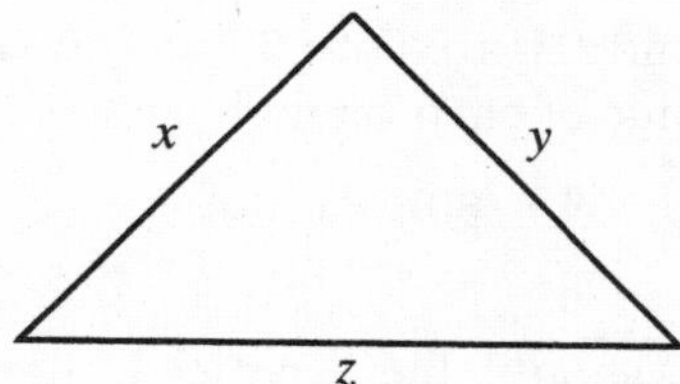

(1) is sufficient to establish that z is not greater than 8. If $x + y = 8$, then z cannot be greater than 8, for then x, y, and z could not be the lengths of three sides of a triangle. This is because the length of any one side of a triangle must always be less than the sum of the lengths of the remaining two sides. (2), however, is not sufficient to answer the question. Knowing that $x = 6$ leaves open the possibility that z is greater than, less than, or even equal to 8.

25. The correct answer is (D). The question asks whether *NNPP* is divisible by 4. We can analyze the problem as follows. (1) is sufficient for the following reason: What is the difference between *NPP* and *NNPP*? Obviously, the extra *N* on the left of the number. But what does that mean? Since it is located in the fourth place to the left of the decimal point, it means "$N \times 1000$." Therefore, $NPP + (N \times 1000) = NNPP$. We are told in (1) that *NPP* is divisible by 8, so *NNPP* will be divisible by 8 provided that $N \times 1000$ is also divisible by 8. Since 1000 is divisible by 8, $N \times 1000$ will be divisible by 8, so *NNPP* must also be divisible by 8. And if a number is divisible by 8, it must be divisible by 4 as well. So (1) is sufficient. The same reasoning can be used to show that (2) is sufficient. Since $N \times 1000$ is divisible by 4 and since *NPP* is divisible by 4, $NPP + (N \times 1000)$ or *NNPP*, must also be divisible by 4.

26. The correct answer is (E). The question requires that we determine which brand accounted for the greater dollar profit. It should be fairly clear that (1) will not do the trick because it does not tell us how much of each was sold. (2) also is insufficient since it does not establish the wholesale price, and without that we cannot compute the dollar profit per item. The question is now whether both statements together answer the question. A moment's reflection will show the answer is no. (1), coupled with information provided in the stem, establishes that the monetary profit is higher on the name-brand items. But how much greater? If we sell enough of the generic brand, we will make more money on the generic brand. But how much is enough? That will depend on the difference in the per item profit. And that critical piece of information is missing.

27. The correct answer is (A). This question is a bit easier. Is $x > y$? (1) establishes that the answer to this question is no. Since x and y are both positive integers (as stipulated in the stem), x must be less than x^2, and if x^2 is less than y, then x must be less, not greater, than y. (2), however, is not sufficient. That the square root of x is less than y does not establish anything about x and y. For example, if x

is 4 and y is 3, then the square root of x, which is 2, is less than y; and yet x is greater than y. On the other hand, if x is 4 and y is 5, then both x and the square root of x are less than y.

28. The correct answer is (B). To answer this question, we must find a way of relating all three rates to each other. Since M is given in terms of N, and N in terms of O, let us use N as our standard. If N operates at rate r, then at what rate does M operate? Since M can produce x units in $\frac{3}{4}$ the time it takes N to produce x units, M is operating at $\frac{4}{3}r$. Then, since N takes only $\frac{2}{3}$ the time to produce x units as machine O requires, O is operating at only $\frac{2}{3}r$. If all three machines are operating together, the total rate will be the sum of all three individual rates:

$$\frac{4}{3}r + r + \frac{2}{3}r = 3r$$

The total rate of output for all three machines working together is $3r$, of which r is being contributed by N. So N is producing $\frac{1}{3}$ of the total units.

You can reach the same conclusion by using concrete numbers. Assume that machine N produces 10 units per minute (or whatever time unit). Then, M produces 10 units per $\frac{3}{4}$ minute. How many units is that per minute?

$$\frac{10 \text{ units}}{\frac{3}{4} \text{ min.}} = \frac{40}{3} \text{ units per minute}$$

Then, O will produce only $\frac{2}{3}$ of 10 units, or $\frac{20}{3}$ units, per minute. So our three machines operate at $\frac{40}{3}$, $\frac{30}{3}$, and $\frac{20}{3}$ units per minute, respectively. If all three machines are operating together, how many units will they produce totally in one minute? $\frac{90}{3}$, or 30 units per minute. And how many of those are produced by N? 10! So N produced $\frac{1}{3}$ of the total output.

29. The correct answer is (A). Here we have a geometry problem. Since this is a standardized test, you know there must be some key to the question, some insight that is required. Here it is useful to sketch some additional lines:

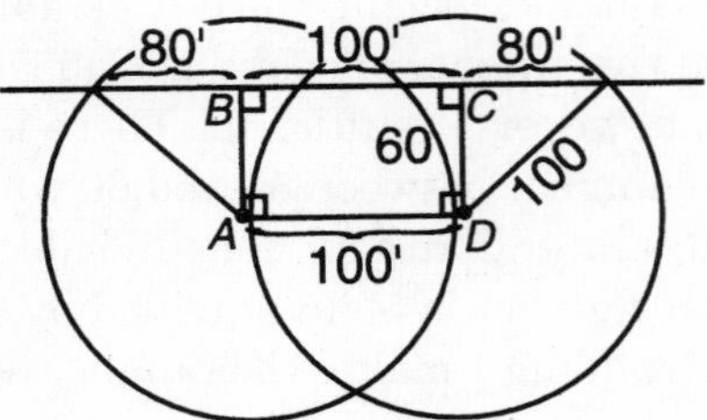

For convenience, we letter the points as shown. Now, $ABCD$ is a rectangle. Since the two lights are 100 feet apart, BC is also 100. Then, we observe that and are sides of right triangles, the hypotenuses of which are radii and equal to 100. Since AB and CD are both 60, the one remaining side of each triangle is:

$$x^2 + (60)^2 = (100)^2$$
$$x = 80$$

(You should have noticed the 3, 4, 5 relationship.) So the total length is 80 + 100 + 80 = 260.

There is actually an easier way to solve the problem. Unless otherwise indicated, figures for problem-solving questions are drawn to scale. Why not measure the distance? Use the edge of your answer sheet as a straight edge. Measure the distance between the two lights, making light pencil marks to indicate the distance. That distance represents 100 feet on the map. Now measure the length of the fence. You should find that it is slightly over $2\frac{1}{2}$ of those lengths, or slightly over 250 feet. So the correct answer must be (A).

answers

30. **The correct answer is (E).** In a problem such as this, which appears to involve considerable arithmetic, always look for a shortcut. If you recognize that 3510×3508 is the same as $(3508 + 2)(3508)$, which equals $(3508 \times 3508) + (3508 \times 2)$, the problem becomes much easier. We then have $(3508)^2 - (3510 \times 3508) = (3508 \times 3508) - [(3508 \times 3508) + (2 \times 3508)] = -(2 \times 3508) = -7016$.

31. **The correct answer is (E).** First we need to find the cost of the berries. 2000 quarts × 80 cents per quart is \$1600. The gross profit must be 20 percent of that amount, or (.20)(\$1600) = \$320. The total selling price of the berries must be \$1600 + \$320 = \$1920. One-quarter of the berries cannot be sold, that is, $\frac{3}{4}$ of the berries can be sold. $\frac{3}{4}$ of 2000 is 1500 quarts. The selling price per quart must be \$1920/(1500 quarts), or \$1.28 per quart.

32. **The correct answer is (B).** Let us call Charlene's income for January x. She spent $\frac{2}{5}x$ on rent, leaving $\frac{3}{5}x$. $\frac{3}{4}$ of the remainder was spent on other expenses, leaving $(\frac{1}{4})(\frac{3}{5})x$ or $\frac{3}{20}x$. That must equal the remaining \$180, so $\frac{3}{20}x = \$180$, and $x = \$1200$.

33. **The correct answer is (D).** Triangle ABC is an equilateral triangle, since its third angle must also be 60°. If we can find the side of this triangle, we can then find its area. Triangle ACD is a 30-60-90 right triangle, so AC, which is the hypotenuse, must be twice as long as the shorter leg, DC; thus, it is 4. Now that we have the side, we may calculate the area of equilateral triangle ABC. The altitude a of the triangle makes two 30-60-90 triangles as illustrated in the diagram below. Note that this altitude will bisect the base AC.

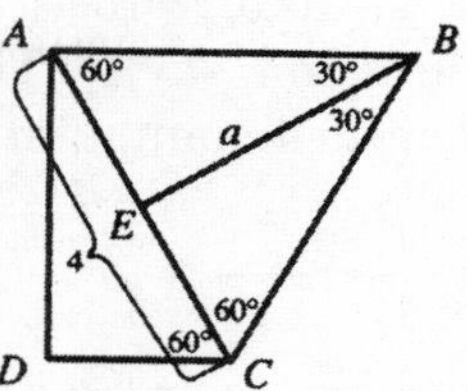

Triangle ABE is the 30-60-90 triangle which allows us to find the needed altitude. The small leg of triangle ABE (side AE) is half of AC, that is, 2. Thus the longer leg (side BE) is $\sqrt{3}$ times that, or $2\sqrt{3}$. The area of ABC can now be found to be $(\frac{1}{2})$(base)(height) = $(\frac{1}{2})(4)(2\sqrt{3}) = 4\sqrt{3}$.

34. **The correct answer is (A).** Let us for convenience call the original fraction $\frac{a}{b}$. Then the numerator of the new fraction (being decreased by 25 percent, which is $.25a$) must be $a - .25a$, or $.75a$. The new denominator, being increased by 25 percent, must be $b + .25b$, or $1.25b$. The new fraction is, therefore, $\frac{.75a}{1.25b}$. Percentage decrease is found by taking the difference of the two fractions and dividing by the original fraction. In this case the difference is $\frac{a}{b} - \frac{.75a}{1.25b}$. Factoring out the $\frac{a}{b}$ we have $\frac{a}{b}(1 - \frac{.75}{1.25})$. Since .75 is equal to $\frac{3}{4}$ and 1.25 is equal to $1\frac{1}{4}$, or $\frac{5}{4}$, the expression inside the parenthesis is $1 - \frac{\frac{3}{4}}{\frac{5}{4}}$ or $1 - \frac{3}{5}$, which equals $\frac{2}{5}$. So the difference is $(\frac{2}{5})(\frac{a}{b})$. The percentage increase is now found to be $(\frac{2}{5})(\frac{a}{b})$ divided by the old fraction, $\frac{a}{b}$, yielding an answer of $\frac{2}{5}$ = 40 percent.

Or, as a test-taking practice, you might pick any fraction, say, $\frac{1}{1}$. Then you perform the needed manipulations:

$$\frac{1-(.25 \times 1)}{1+(.25 \times 1)} = \frac{.75}{1.25} = \frac{3}{5}$$

So the decrease, expressed as a percent, was:

$$\frac{1-\frac{3}{5}}{1} = \frac{2}{5} = 40 \text{ percent}$$

35. The correct answer is (A). We determine whether we have sufficient information to determine the radius of the circle. Using (1), we have $\frac{\pi r^2}{2\pi r} = \frac{3}{2}$ We simplify the left-hand fraction by both π and by r. Cross-multiplying and solving for r, we learn $r = 3$. So (1) is sufficient. (2), however, does not contain enough information. It establishes only that the number of square units in the area is more than 3 greater than the number of linear units in the circumference. But an infinite number of radii will satisfy that statement.

36. The correct answer is (C). We must first find the area of the racetrack, which we may then multiply by the depth of the asphalt layer to find the volume of asphalt needed. From the diagram below it should be clear that the area of the track is found by calculating the area of the large circle and the area of the small circle, then subtracting the latter from the former.

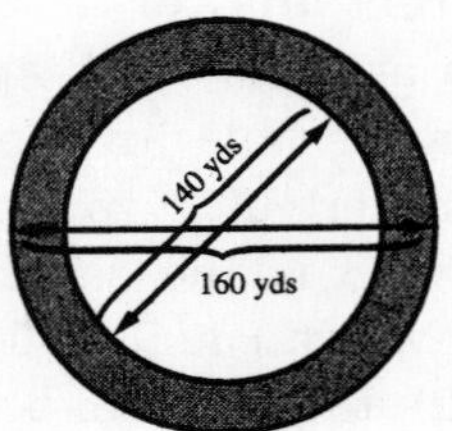

The larger circle has a diameter of 160 yards, thus a radius of 80 yards and an area of π times $(80)^2$, or 6400π square yards. The smaller has a diameter of 140 yards, thus a radius of 70 yards and an area of π times $(70)^2$, or 4900π square yards. Subtracting the smaller area from the larger, we obtain the 6400π – 4900π = 1500π as the area of the track. Since the asphalt layer is to be 1 foot, or $\frac{1}{3}$ yard, deep, we must multiply 1500π by $\frac{1}{3}$, getting 500π cubic yards as the answer.

37. The correct answer is (B). To answer this question, we need only find one side of the square, for all sides are equal and the area of the square is computed by the formula: side × side. (1) is not sufficient to establish any conclusion about the length of the sides of the figure. (1) proves only that P is located on the x-axis (which is stipulated in the stem also) and that P is two units to the right of the origin (O). (2), however, gives more information. Knowing that R has a y-coordinate of 4, tells us that the distance from R to S is four units. This gives us the one side of the square we need.

Practice Test 4

ANALYTICAL WRITING ASSESSMENT

I. Analysis of an Issue

Time—30 Minutes

> **Directions:** In this section you will have 30 minutes to analyze and explain your views on the topic presented below. Read the statement and directions carefully. Write only on the topic given. An essay on a topic other than the one assigned will automatically be assigned a grade of 0.
>
> Note: On the CAT version, you will keyboard your essay. For this exercise, allow yourself three sides of regular $8\frac{1}{2} \times 11$- inch paper for each essay response.

In regions that have four distinct seasons, some people would say that the autumn is the best time of year. The season offers beautiful foliage, brisk weather, and a bountiful harvest. Others would say that spring is the best time of year because it is the rebirth of nature and signals warming temperatures.

Which position do you find more compelling? Explain your position using reasons and/or examples drawn from your personal experience, observations, or readings.

II. Analysis of an Argument

Time—30 Minutes

Directions: In this section you will have 30 minutes to write a critique of the argument presented below. Read the argument and directions carefully. Write only on the topic given. An essay on a topic other than the one assigned will automatically be assigned a grade of 0.

Note: On the CAT version, you will keyboard your essay. For this exercise, allow yourself three sides of regular $8\frac{1}{2} \times 11$- inch paper for each essay response.

> The dietitians of our public schools supervise the ordering, preparation, and serving of lunches and sometimes breakfasts to school children. The state should implement a program of continuing education for these people. If dietitians were required to attend a three-day workshop each year, covering topics such as recent developments in nutritional theory and new methods of food preservation, as a condition of employment, the quality of the food eaten by school children would be greatly improved.

How persuasive do you find this argument? Explain your point of view by analyzing the line of reasoning and the use of evidence in the argument. Discuss also what, if anything, would make the argument more persuasive or would help you better to evaluate its conclusion.

VERBAL SECTION

41 Questions • 75 Minutes

Directions: For each of the following questions, choose the correct answer. To simulate the experience of taking the CAT, answer each question in order. Do not skip any questions, and do not go back to any questions you have already answered.
For Sentence Correction questions: In questions of this type, either part or all of a sentence is underlined. The sentence is followed by five ways of writing the underlined part. Choice (A) repeats the original; the other answer choices vary. If you think that the original phrasing is the best, choose (A). If you think one of the other answer choices is the best, select that choice.

Sentence Correction questions test your ability to recognize correct and effective expression. Follow the requirements of Standard Written English: grammar, choice of words, and sentence construction. Choose the answer that results in the clearest, most exact sentence, but does not change the meaning of the original sentence.

practice test

Example:

Q The possibility of massive earthquakes <u>are regarded by most area residents with</u> a mixture of skepticism and caution.

(A) are regarded by most area residents with

(B) is regarded by most area residents with

(C) is regarded by most area residents as

(D) is mostly regarded by area residents with

(E) by most area residents is regarded with

A The correct answer is (B).

For Critical Reasoning questions: Questions of this type ask you to analyze and evaluate the reasoning in short paragraphs or passages. For some questions, all of the answer choices may conceivably be answers to the question asked. You should select the *best* answer to the question, that is, an answer that does not require you to make assumptions that violate common-sense standards by being implausible, redundant, irrelevant, or inconsistent.

Example:

Q In an extensive study of the reading habits of magazine subscribers, it was found that an average of between four and five people actually read each copy of the most popular weekly news magazine. On this basis, we estimate that the 12,000 copies of *Poets and Poetry* that are sold each month are actually read by 48,000 to 60,000 people.

The estimate above assumes that

(A) individual magazine readers generally enjoy more than one type of magazine

(B) most of the readers of *Poets and Poetry* subscribe to the magazine

(C) the ratio of readers to copies is the same for *Poets and Poetry* as for the weekly news magazine

(D) the number of readers of the weekly news magazine is similar to the number of readers of *Poets and Poetry*

(E) most readers enjoy sharing copies of their favorite magazines with friends and family members

A The correct answer is (C).

For Reading Comprehension questions: Each passage is followed by questions or incomplete statements about the passage. Each statement or question is followed by lettered words or expressions. Select the word or expression that most satisfactorily completes each statement or answers each question in accordance with the meaning of the passage.

1. The former First Lady continued her efforts on behalf of the mentally retarded, raising funds, visiting hospitals, <u>and she was speaking out for their rights.</u>

(A) and she was speaking out for their rights.

(B) and their rights were spoken out for by her.

(C) and to speak out for their rights.

(D) also in speaking out for their rights.

(E) and speaking out for their rights.

2. The number of adults in the United States who are illiterate is <u>rising, but it is probably only temporary.</u>

(A) rising, but it is probably only temporary.

(B) rising, but it is only temporary.

(C) rising, but it is temporary only.

(D) rising, but the increase is probably only a temporary one.

(E) rising, although the increase may only be temporarily.

3. Although most physicians agree that exercise is necessary for physical and mental well-being, <u>they caution against doing too much too soon.</u>

(A) they caution against doing too much too soon.

(B) doing too much too soon is cautioned against by them.

(C) but cautioning against doing too much too soon.

(D) yet caution against doing too much too soon.

(E) it is cautioned against to do too much too soon.

4. All effective administrators are concerned about the welfare of their employees, and all administrators who are concerned about the welfare of their employees are liberal in granting time off for personal needs; therefore, all administrators who are not liberal in granting time off for their employees' personal needs are not effective administrators.

If the argument above is valid, then it must be true that

(A) no ineffective administrators are liberal in granting time off for their employees' personal needs

(B) no ineffective administrators are concerned about the welfare of their employees

(C) some effective administrators are not liberal in granting time off for their employees' personal needs

(D) all effective administrators are liberal in granting time off for their employees' personal needs

(E) all time off for personal needs is granted by effective administrators

5. CLYDE: You shouldn't drink so much wine. Alcohol really isn't good for you.

GERRY: You're wrong about that. I have been drinking the same amount of white wine for 15 years, and I never get drunk.

Which of the following responses would best strengthen and explain Clyde's argument?

(A) Many people who drink as much white wine as Gerry does, get very drunk.

(B) Alcohol does not always make a person drunk.

(C) Getting drunk is not the only reason alcohol is not good for a person.

(D) If you keep drinking white wine, you may find in the future that you are drinking more and more.

(E) White wine is not the only drink that contains alcohol.

6. Transcendentalism was seen as a somewhat pantheistic philosophy <u>and opposed by orthodox Christians.</u>

(A) and opposed by orthodox Christians.

(B) and orthodox Christians opposed them.

(C) that orthodox Christians opposed it.

(D) being opposed by orthodox Christians.

(E) and orthodox Christians oppose it.

7. In considering the transportation needs of our sales personnel, the question of the relative cost of each of our options is very important. The initial purchase outlay required for a fleet of diesel autos is fairly high, though the operating costs for them will be low. This is the mirror image of the cost picture for a fleet of gasoline-powered cars. The only way, then, of making a valid cost comparison is on the basis of________.

Which of the following best completes the above paragraph?

(A) projected operating costs for both diesel- and gasoline-powered autos

(B) the average costs of both fleets over the life of each fleet

(C) the purchase cost for both diesel-powered and gasoline-powered autos

(D) the present difference in the operating costs of the two fleets

(E) the relative amount of air pollution that would be created by the one type of car compared with the other

8. The Dormitory Canteen Committee decided that the prices of snacks in the Canteen vending machines were already high enough, so they told Vendo Inc., the company holding the vending machine concession for the Canteen, either to maintain prices at the then current levels or to forfeit the concession. Vendo, however, managed to thwart the intent of the Committee's instructions without actually violating the letter of those instructions.

Which of the following is probably the action taken by Vendo referred to in the above paragraph?

(A) The president of Vendo met with the university's administration, and they ordered the Committee to rescind its instructions.

(B) Vendo continued prices at the prescribed levels but reduced the size of the snacks vended in the machines.

(C) Vendo ignored the Committee's instructions and continued to raise prices.

(D) Vendo decided it could not make a fair return on its investment if it held the line on prices, so it removed its machines from the Dormitory Canteen.

(E) Representatives of Vendo met with members of the Dormitory Canteen Committee and offered them free snacks to influence other members to change the Committee's decision.

9. Although the consensus reaction to initial marketing surveys was not favorable, the growing acceptance by consumers seem to indicate that the product will ultimately be very popular.

(A) seem to indicate that the product will ultimately be very popular.

(B) seems to indicate the ultimate popularity of the product.

(C) seems to indicate that the product will ultimately be very popular.

(D) are indicating that the product will ultimately be very popular.

(E) seems to be an indication as to the ultimately popularity of the product.

10. Unlike Edgar Allan Poe, whose works were ignored in his native country, the works of Hawthorne were read and appreciated by the public and by contemporary critics.

(A) Edgar Allan Poe, whose works were ignored in his native country, the

(B) Edgar Allan Poe whose native country ignored his work, the

(C) the works of Edgar Allan Poe, ignored in his native country, the

(D) the works of Edgar Allan Poe which were ignored in his native country, the

(E) the works of Edgar Allan Poe having been ignored in his native country, the

11. Jockeys at most racetracks become familiar with the horses by riding them in early morning workouts which keeps both the jockeys and the horses in good condition.

(A) become familiar with the horses by riding them in early morning workouts which

(B) become familiar with the horses and also ride them in early morning workouts which

(C) become familiar with the horses by riding them in early morning workouts, a practice which

(D) ride horses to become familiar with them in early morning workouts which

(E) ride horses in early morning workouts and become familiar with them which

QUESTIONS 12–18

Desertification in the arid United States is flagrant. Groundwater supplies beneath vast stretches of land are dropping precipitously. Whole river systems have dried up; others are choked with sediment washed from denuded land. Hundreds of thousands of acres of previously irrigated cropland have been abandoned to wind or weeds. Several million acres of natural grassland are eroding at unnaturally high rates as a result of cultivation or overgrazing. All told, about 225 million acres of land are undergoing severe desertification.

Federal subsidies encourage the exploitation of arid land resources. Low-interest loans for irrigation and other water delivery systems encourage farmers, industry, and municipalities to mine groundwater. Federal disaster relief and commodity programs encourage arid-land farmers to plow up natural grassland to plant crops such as wheat and, especially, cotton. Federal grazing fees that are well below the free-market price encourage overgrazing of the commons. The market, too, provides powerful incentives to exploit arid land resources beyond their carrying capacity. When commodity prices are high relative to the farmer's or rancher's operating costs, the return on a production-enhancing investment is invariably greater than the return on a conservation investment. And when commodity prices are relatively low, arid land ranchers and farmers often have to use all of their available financial resources to stay solvent.

The incentives to exploit arid land resources are greater today than ever. The government is now offering huge new subsidies to produce synfuel from coal or oil shale as well as alcohol fuel from crops. Moreover, commodity prices are on the rise; and they will provide farmers and agribusiness with powerful incentive to overexploit arid land resources. The existing federal government cost-share programs designed to help finance the conservation of soil, water, and vegetation pale in comparison to such incentives.

In the final analysis, when viewed in the national perspective, the effects on agriculture are the most troublesome aspect of desertification in the United States, for it comes at a time when we are losing over a million acres of rain-watered crop and pasture land per year to "higher uses"—shopping centers, industrial parks, housing developments, and waste dumps—heedless of the economic need of the United States to export agricultural products or of the world's need for U.S. food and fiber. Today the arid West accounts for 20% of the nation's total agricultural output. If the United States is, as it appears, well on its way toward overdrawing the arid land resources, then the policy choice is simply to pay now for the appropriate remedies or pay far more later, when productive benefits from arid land resources have been both realized and largely terminated.

12. The author is primarily concerned with

(A) discussing a solution

(B) describing a problem

(C) replying to a detractor

(D) finding a contradiction

(E) defining a term

13. The passage mentions all of the following as effects of desertification EXCEPT

(A) increased sediment in rivers

(B) erosion of land

(C) overcultivation of arid land

(D) decreasing groundwater supplies

(E) loss of land to wind or weeds

14. The author most likely encloses the phrase "higher uses" (line 59) in quotations marks in order to

(A) alert the reader to the fact that the term is very important

(B) minimize the importance of desertification in non-arid land

(C) voice his support for expansion of such programs

(D) express concern over the extent of desertification

(E) indicate disagreement that such uses are more important

15. The passages mentions all of the following as economic factors tending to contribute to desertification EXCEPT

(A) price incentives for farmers to use arid lands to produce certain commodities

(B) artifically low government fees for use of public grazing lands

(C) government subsidies for fuels that are manufactured from a variety of crops

(D) worldwide demand for the food and fiber produced in the United States

(E) lack of effective government financial incentives to conserve soil, water, and vegetation

16. According to the passage, the most serious long-term effect of desertification would be the reduced ability of

(A) the United States to continue to export agricultural products

(B) municipalities to supply water to meet the needs of residents

(C) farmers to cover the cost of producing crops

(D) the United States to meet the food needs of its own people

(E) the United States to produce sufficient fuel for energy from domestic sources

17. The passage leads most logically to discussion of a proposal for

(A) reduced agricultural output in the United States

(B) direct government aid to farmers affected by desertification

(C) curtailing the conversion of land to shopping centers and housing

(D) government assistance to develop improved farming methods to increase exploitation of arid land

(E) increased government assistance to finance the conservation of arid land

18. The author's attitude toward desertification can best be described as one of

(A) alarm

(B) optimism

(C) understanding

(D) conciliation

(E) concern

19. The president of the University tells us that a tuition increase is needed to offset rising costs. That is simply not true. Weston University is an institution approximately the same size as our own University, but the president of Weston University has announced that they will not impose a tuition increase on their students.

The author makes his point primarily by

(A) citing new evidence

(B) proposing an alternative solution

(C) pointing out a logical contradiction

(D) drawing an analogy

(E) clarifying an ambiguity

20. Only White Bear gives you all-day deodorant protection and the unique White Bear scent.

If this advertising claim is true, which of the following cannot also be true?

(A) Red Flag deodorant gives you all-day deodorant protection.

(B) Open Sea deodorant is a more popular deodorant than White Bear.

(C) White Bear aftershave lotion uses the White Bear scent.

(D) All Day deodorant provides all-day protection and uses a scent with a similar chemical composition to that of White Bear.

(E) Lost Horizons deodorant contains a scent with the same chemical composition as that of White Bear and gives all-day deodorant protection.

21. Clara prefers English Literature to Introductory Physics. She likes English Literature, however, less than she likes Basic Economics. She actually finds Basic Economics preferable to any other college course, and she dislikes Physical Education more than she dislikes Introductory Physics.

All of the following statements can be inferred from the information given above EXCEPT

(A) Clara prefers Basic Economics to English Literature.

(B) Clara likes English Literature better than she likes Physical Education.

(C) Clara prefers Basic Economics to Advanced Calculus.

(D) Clara likes World History better than she likes Introductory Physics.

(E) Clara likes Physical Education less than she likes English Literature.

22. In addition to the revised curriculum requested last semester, the students are now demanding that a new grading system be instituted.

    (A) In addition to the revised curriculum requested last semester, the students are now demanding that a new grading system be instituted.

    (B) In addition to the revised curriculum that had been requested last semester, the students are now demanding that a new grading system be instituted.

    (C) The students are now demanding that a new grading system be instituted in addition to the revised curriculum they requested last semester.

    (D) Added to the revised curriculum that was requested last semester by the students, they are now demanding the institution of a new grading system.

    (E) Added to the new curriculum requested last semester, the students have now demanded the institution of a new grading system.

23. Her lecture was unsuccessful not so much because of her lack of preparation but instead because of her inability to organize her material.

    (A) but instead because of

    (B) as

    (C) so much as

    (D) than

    (E) rather than

24. A private house in New York City is a building owned by an individual or individuals having less than eight units and no commercial space.

    (A) a building owned by an individual or individuals having less than eight units and no commercial space.

    (B) one that an individual or individuals own with fewer than eight units and no commercial space.

    (C) a building with fewer than eight units, no commercial space, and is owned by an individual or individuals.

    (D) one that has fewer than eight units, no commercial space and it is owned by an individual or individuals.

    (E) one that has fewer than eight units, is owned by an individual or individuals, and has no commercial space.

25. In *The Adventure of the Bruce-Partingon Plans,* Sherlock Holmes explained to Dr. Watson that the body had been placed on the top of the train while the train paused at a signal.

    "It seems most improbable," remarked Watson.

    "We must fall back upon the old axiom," continued Holmes, "that when all other contingencies fail, whatever remains, however improbable, must be the truth."

    Which of the following is the most effective criticism of the logic contained in Holmes' response to Watson?

    (A) You will never be able to obtain a conviction in a court of law.

    (B) You can never be sure you have accounted for all other contingencies.

    (C) You will need further evidence to satisfy the police.

    (D) The very idea of putting a dead body on top of a train seems preposterous.

    (E) You still have to find the person responsible for putting the body on top of the train.

26. PROFESSOR: Under the rule of primogeniture, the first male child born to a man's first wife is always first in line to inherit the family estate.

STUDENT: That can't be true; the Duchess of Warburton was her father's only surviving child by his only wife and she inherited his entire estate.

The student has misinterpreted the professor's remark to mean which of the following?

(A) Only men can father male children.

(B) A daughter cannot be a firstborn child.

(C) Only sons can inherit the family estate.

(D) Illegitimate children cannot inherit their father's property.

(E) A woman cannot inherit her mother's property.

27. All of the following conclusions are based upon accurate expense vouchers submitted by employees to department heads of a certain corporation in 1995. Which of them is LEAST likely to be weakened by the discovery of additional 1995 expense vouchers?

(A) The accounting department had only 15 employees and claimed expenses of at least $500.

(B) The sales department had at least 25 employees and claimed expenses of at least $35,000.

(C) The legal department had at least 2 employees and claimed no more than $3,000 in expenses.

(D) The public relations department had no more than 1 employee and claimed no more than $200 in expenses.

(E) The production department had no more than 500 employees and claimed no more than $350 in expenses.

QUESTIONS 28–34

According to legend, Aesculapius bore two daughters, Panacea and Hyegeia, who gave rise to dynasties of healers and hygienists. The schism remains today, in clinical training and in practice; and because of the imperative nature of medical care and the subtlety of health care, the former has tended to dominate. Preventive medicine has as its primary objective the maintenance and promotion of health. It accomplishes this by controlling or manipulating environmental factors that affect health and disease. For example, in California presently there is serious suffering and substantial economic loss because of the failure to introduce controlled fluoridation of public water supplies. Additionally, preventive medicine applies prophylactic measures against disease by such actions as immunization and specific nutritional measures. Third, it attempts to motivate people to adopt healthful lifestyles through education.

For the most part, curative medicine has as its primary objective the removal of disease from the patient. It provides diagnostic techniques to identify the presence and nature of the disease process. While these may be applied on a mass basis in an attempt to "screen" out persons with preclinical disease, they are usually applied after the patient appears with a complaint. Second, it applies treatment to the sick patient. In every case, this is, or should be, individualized according to the particular need of each patient. Third, it utilizes rehabilitation methodologies to return the treated patient to the best possible level of functioning.

While it is true that both preventive medicine and curative medicine require cadres of similarly trained personnel such as planners, administrators, and educators, the underlying delivery systems depend on quite distinctive professional personnel. The requirements for curative medicine call for clinically trained individuals who deal with patients on a one-to-one basis and whose training is based primarily on an understanding of the biological, pathological, and psychological processes that determine an individual's health and disease status. The locus for this training is the laboratory and clinic. Preventive medicine, on the other hand, calls for a very broad spectrum of professional personnel, few of whom require clinical expertise. Since their actions apply either to environmental situations or to population groups, their training takes place in a different type of laboratory or in a community not necessarily associated with the clinical locus.

The economic differences between preventive medicine and curative medicine have been extensively discussed, perhaps most convincingly by Winslow in the monograph *The Cost of Sickness and the Price of Health.* Sickness is almost always a negative, nonproductive and harmful state. All resources expended to deal with sickness are therefore fundamentally economically unproductive. Health, on the other hand, has a very high value in our culture. To the extent that healthy members of the population are replaced by sick members, the economy is doubly burdened. Nevertheless, the per capita cost of preventive measures for specific diseases is generally far lower than the per capita cost of curative medicine applied to treatment of the same disease. Prominent examples are dental caries, poliomyelitis and phenylketonuria.

There is an imperative need to provide care for the sick person within a single medical care system, but there is no overriding reason why a linkage is necessary between the two components of a health care system, prevention and treatment. A national health and medical care program composed of semi- autonomous systems for personal health care and medical care would have the advantage of clarifying objectives and strategies and of permitting a more equitable division of resources between prevention and cure.

28. The author's primary concern is to

(A) refute a counterargument

(B) draw a distinction

(C) discuss a dilemma

(D) isolate causes

(E) describe new research

29. The author mentions which of the following as differences between curative and preventive medicine?

I. Curative medicine is aimed primarily at people who are already ill, whereas preventive medicine is aimed at healthy people.

II. Curative medicine is focused on an individual patient, whereas preventive medicine is applied to larger populations.

III. The per capita cost of curative medicine is generally much higher than the per capita cost of preventive medicine.

(A) I only

(B) II only

(C) I and II

(D) II and III only

(E) I, II, and III

30. It can be inferred that the author regards a program of controlled fluoridation of public water supplies as

(A) an unnecessary government program that wastes economic resources

(B) a potentially valuable strategy of preventive medicine

(C) a government policy that has relatively little effect on the health of a population

(D) an important element of curative medicine

(E) an experimental program the health value of which has not been proved

31. Which of the following best explains the author's use of the phrase "doubly burdened" (line 81)?

(A) A person who is ill not only does not contribute to production; treatment consumes economic resources.

(B) The per capita cost of preventive measures is only one-half of the per capita cost of treatment.

(C) The division between preventive medicine and curative medicine requires duplication of administrative expenses.

(D) The individual who is ill must be rehabilitated after the cure has been successful.

(E) The person who is ill uses economic resources that could be used to finance prevention rather than treatment programs.

32. It can be inferred that the author regards Winslow's monograph (lines 70–73) as

(A) ill-conceived

(B) incomplete

(C) authoritative

(D) well organized

(E) highly original

33. The author cites dental caries, poliomyelitis, and phenylketonuria in order to prove that

(A) some diseases can be treated by preventive medicine

(B) some diseases have serious consequences if not treated

(C) preventive medicine need not be linked to treatment

(D) the cost of preventing some diseases is less than the cost for treatment

(E) less money is allocated to prevention of some diseases than to treating them

34. The main reason the author advocates separating authority for preventive medicine from that for curative medicine is

(A) the urgency of treatment encourages administrators to devote more resources to treatment than to prevention

(B) the cost of treating a disease is often much greater than the cost of programs to prevent the disease

(C) the professionals who administer preventive health care programs must be more highly trained than ordinary doctors

(D) curative medicine deals primarily with individuals who are ill, whereas preventive medicine is applied to healthy people

(E) preventive medicine is a relatively recent development, whereas curative medicine has a long history

35. Mr. Mayor, when is the city government going to stop discriminating against its Hispanic residents in the delivery of critical municipal services?

The form of the question above is most nearly paralleled by which of the following?

(A) Mr. Congressman, when is the Congress finally going to realize that defense spending is out of hand?

(B) Madam Chairperson, do you anticipate the committee will take luncheon recess?

(C) Dr. Greentree, what do you expect to be the impact of the Governor's proposals on the economically disadvantaged counties of our state?

(D) Gladys, since you're going to the grocery store anyway, would you mind picking up a quart of milk for me?

(E) Counselor, does the company you represent find that its affirmative action program is successful in recruiting qualified minority employees?

36. The main ingredient in this bottle of Dr. John's Milk of Magnesia is used by nine out of ten hospitals across the country as an antacid and laxative.

If this advertising claim is true, which of the following statements must also be true?

(A) Nine out of ten hospitals across the country use Dr. John's Milk of Magnesia for some ailments.

(B) Only one out of ten hospitals in the country does not treat acid indigestion and constipation.

(C) Only one out of ten hospitals across the country does not recommend Dr. John's Milk of Magnesia for patients who need a milk of magnesia.

(D) Only one of ten hospitals across the country uses a patent medicine other than Dr. John's Milk of Magnesia as an antacid and laxative.

(E) Nine out of ten hospitals across the country use the main ingredient in Dr. John's Milk of Magnesia as an antacid and laxative.

37. Kate Chopin, an American writer of the last century, <u>and a feminist, writing about strong independent women before such a movement existed.</u>

(A) and a feminist writing about strong independent women before such a movement existed.

(B) was a feminist before such a movement existed, and she wrote about strong independent women.

(C) wrote about strong, independent women and was a feminist before such a movement existed.

(D) was writing about strong independent women and was feminist before the existence of such a movement.

(E) a feminist before such a movement existed and writing about strong independent women before such a movement existed.

38. <u>Although severely damaged by the collision and already sinking,</u> the coast guard arrived at the freighter in time to save the crew.

(A) Although severely damaged by the collision and already sinking,

(B) Although it had been severely damaged by the collision and was already sinking,

(C) Although the freighter had been severely damaged in the collision and was already sinking,

(D) Although the freighter was severely damaged in the collision and it was also already sinking,

(E) Severely damaged in the collision, and although sinking,

QUESTIONS 39 AND 40

I. All wheeled conveyances that travel on the highway are polluters.

II. Bicycles are not polluters.

III. Whenever I drive my car on the highway, it rains.

IV. It is raining.

39. If the above statements are all true, which of the following statements must also be true?

(A) Bicycles do not travel on the highway.

(B) Bicycles travel on the highway only if it is raining.

(C) If my car is not polluting, then it is not raining.

(D) I am now driving on the highway.

(E) My car is not a polluter.

practice test

40. The conclusion "my car is not polluting" could be logically deduced from statements I–IV if statement

(A) II were changed to: "Bicycles are polluters."

(B) II were changed to: "My car is a polluter."

(C) III were changed to: "If bicycles were polluters, I would be driving my car on the highway."

(D) IV were changed to: "Rainwater is polluted."

(E) IV were changed to: "It is not raining."

41. According to recent studies, <u>the median income of women is still only equal to two thirds of men.</u>

(A) the median income of women is still only equal to two thirds of men.

(B) women's median income is still two-thirds of men only.

(C) the median income of women is still only two-thirds that of men.

(D) women's median income is still two-thirds of only that of men.

(E) the median income of women is still only two-thirds of a man's.

QUANTITATIVE SECTION

37 Questions • 75 Minutes

Directions: For each of the following questions, choose the correct answer. To simulate the experience of taking the CAT, answer each question in order. Do not skip any questions, and do not go back to any questions you have already answered.
Numbers: All numbers used are real numbers.
Figures: The diagrams and figures that accompany these questions are for the purpose of providing information useful in answering the questions. Unless it is stated that a specific figure is not drawn to scale, the diagrams and figures are drawn as accurately as possible. All figures are in a plane unless otherwise indicated.
For Data Sufficiency questions: Each question is followed by two numbered facts. You are to determine whether the data given in the statements are sufficient for answering the question. Use the data given, plus your knowledge of math and everyday facts, to choose between the five possible answers.

Example:

Q Which copy machine, X or Y, makes copies at the faster rate?

(1) Machine X makes 90 copies per minute.

(2) In three minutes, X makes 1.5 more copies than Y.

(A) statement 1 alone is sufficient to answer the question, but statement 2 alone is not sufficient

(B) statement 2 alone is sufficient to answer the question, but statement 1 alone is not sufficient

(C) both statements together are needed to answer the question, but neither statement alone is sufficient

(D) either statement by itself is sufficient to answer the question

(E) not enough facts are given to answer the question

A **The correct answer is (B).**

1. Which of the following could be the measures of the sides of a single triangle?

I. 3, 4, 5

II. 5, 12, 18

III. 3, 3, 3

(A) I only
(B) II only
(C) III only
(D) I and II only
(E) I and III only

2. A deck of cards is 1.5 centimeters thick. If each of the cards is 0.03 centimeters thick, how many cards are in the deck?

(A) 45
(B) 50
(C) 450
(D) 500
(E) 1500

3. Exactly how many of the 18 persons on a college's debating team are seniors?

   (1) There are more than 14 seniors on the debating team.

   (2) The number of persons on the debating team who are not seniors is 3.

   (A) statement 1 alone is sufficient to answer the question, but statement 2 alone is not sufficient

   (B) statement 2 alone is sufficient to answer the question, but statement 1 alone is not sufficient

   (C) both statements together are needed to answer the question, but neither statement alone is sufficient

   (D) either statement by itself is sufficient to answer the question

   (E) not enough facts are given to answer the question

4. What percent is x of y?

   (1) $3x = 5y$

   (2) y is 60% of x.

   (A) statement 1 alone is sufficient to answer the question, but statement 2 alone is not sufficient

   (B) statement 2 alone is sufficient to answer the question, but statement 1 alone is not sufficient

   (C) both statements together are needed to answer the question, but neither statement alone is sufficient

   (D) either statement by itself is sufficient to answer the question

   (E) not enough facts are given to answer the question

5. Which point, point P or point Q, is farther from the center of circle O?

   (1) Point P is inside circle O.

   (2) Point Q is outside circle O.

   (A) statement 1 alone is sufficient to answer the question, but statement 2 alone is not sufficient

   (B) statement 2 alone is sufficient to answer the question, but statement 1 alone is not sufficient

   (C) both statements together are needed to answer the question, but neither statement alone is sufficient

   (D) either statement by itself is sufficient to answer the question

   (E) not enough facts are given to answer the question

6. The population of County X was 25,000 on January 1, 1976. During what year did its population reach 250,000?

   (1) The population doubled each year.

   (2) The population was 800,000 on January 1, 1981.

   (A) statement 1 alone is sufficient to answer the question, but statement 2 alone is not sufficient

   (B) statement 2 alone is sufficient to answer the question, but statement 1 alone is not sufficient

   (C) both statements together are needed to answer the question, but neither statement alone is sufficient

   (D) either statement by itself is sufficient to answer the question

   (E) not enough facts are given to answer the question

7. Marshall bought a set of encyclopedias on the installment plan. How much money does he still owe on the encyclopedias?

   (1) He has already paid \$384.

   (2) He still owes 12 monthly payments of \$36 dollars each.

   (A) statement 1 alone is sufficient to answer the question, but statement 2 alone is not sufficient

   (B) statement 2 alone is sufficient to answer the question, but statement 1 alone is not sufficient

   (C) both statements together are needed to answer the question, but neither statement alone is sufficient

   (D) either statement by itself is sufficient to answer the question

   (E) not enough facts are given to answer the question

8. What time will a watch show at noon on Wednesday if it loses x seconds every y hours?

   (1) $x = 6$

   (2) $y = 24$

   (A) statement 1 alone is sufficient to answer the question, but statement 2 alone is not sufficient

   (B) statement 2 alone is sufficient to answer the question, but statement 1 alone is not sufficient

   (C) both statements together are needed to answer the question, but neither statement alone is sufficient

   (D) either statement by itself is sufficient to answer the question

   (E) not enough facts are given to answer the question

9. Of a certain group of 100 people, 40 graduated from High School *X*, 65 graduated from College *Y*, and 30 live in City *Z*. What is the greatest possible number of people in this group who did *not* graduate from High School *X*, did *not* graduate from College *Y*, *and* do *not* live in City *Z*?

   (A) 5

   (B) 15

   (C) 35

   (D) 65

   (E) 85

10. If $(x - 6)(2x + 1) = 0$, and $x > 0$, then $x =$

   (A) 6

   (B) 3

   (C) 2

   (D) $\frac{1}{2}$

   (E) $\frac{1}{6}$

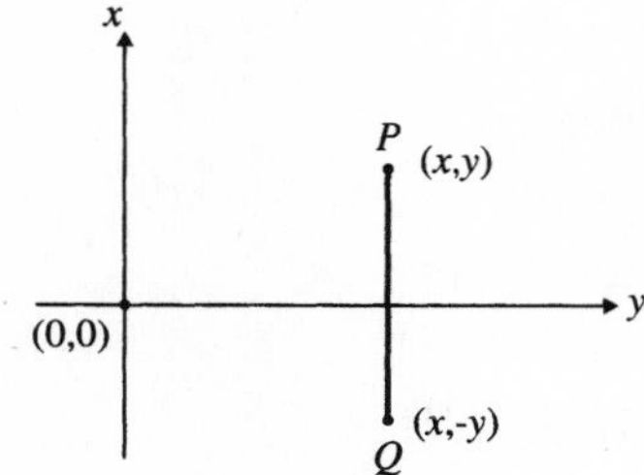

11. In the figure above, what are the coordinates of the midpoint of *PQ*?

   (A) (x, y)

   (B) $(x, 0)$

   (C) $(0, 0)$

   (D) $(0, y)$

   (E) $(-x, -y)$

12. At the beginning of a certain job, the counter on a photocopy machine read 1254. At the end of the job, the counter read 2334. If the running time for the job was 30 minutes, then what was the average operating speed of the machine in copies per *second*?

   (A) .6

   (B) 1.1

   (C) 6

   (D) 36

   (E) 2160

practice test

13. A merchant makes a profit of \$10 on a certain item. If the dollar cost of the item is a whole number, then which of the following could NOT represent her profit as a percentage of her cost?

(A) 10%

(B) 20%

(C) 25%

(D) 40%

(E) 80%

14. If x is an even number, which of the following must be odd?

I. $3x + 1$

II. $(5x)^2 + 2$

III. $(x + 1)^2$

(A) I only

(B) III only

(C) I and II only

(D) I and III only

(E) I, II, and III

15. What is the value of the integer x?

(1) x is an integral multiple of 3, 4, and 5

(2) $50 < x < 70$

(A) statement 1 alone is sufficient to answer the question, but statement 2 alone is not sufficient

(B) statement 2 alone is sufficient to answer the question, but statement 1 alone is not sufficient

(C) both statements together are needed to answer the question, but neither statement alone is sufficient

(D) either statement by itself is sufficient to answer the question

(E) not enough facts are given to answer the question

16. A salesclerk is paid a minimum weekly salary of \$210 plus a commission equal to 10% of the value of sales she makes in excess of \$3,000 for the week. If the salesclerk wishes to earn at least \$370 for a week, what is the minimum value of sales she must make for that week?

(A) \$1,600

(B) \$3,700

(C) \$4,600

(D) \$6,700

(E) \$6,910

17. A sealed tank is constructed so that liquid can be added to the tank only through pipe X and taken from the tank only through pipe Y. If the tank contains 10,000 gallons of liquid, how long will it take to reduce the amount of liquid to 1200 gallons?

(1) Pipe Y removes liquid from the tank 8 times faster than pipe X adds liquid to the tank.

(2) Pipe X adds 50 gallons of liquid to the tank per minute while pipe Y removes 400 gallons of liquid from the tank per minute.

(A) statement 1 alone is sufficient to answer the question, but statement 2 alone is not sufficient

(B) statement 2 alone is sufficient to answer the question, but statement 1 alone is not sufficient

(C) both statements together are needed to answer the question, but neither statement alone is sufficient

(D) either statement by itself is sufficient to answer the question

(E) not enough facts are given to answer the question

18. On Monday, a depositor withdraws funds from his savings account equal to 10% of the amount on deposit, and on Friday he deposits $140. If there were no other transactions, and if the amount in the account following Friday's transaction was 125% of the original amount, how much money was originally in the account?

(A) $125

(B) $175

(C) $400

(D) $500

(E) $540

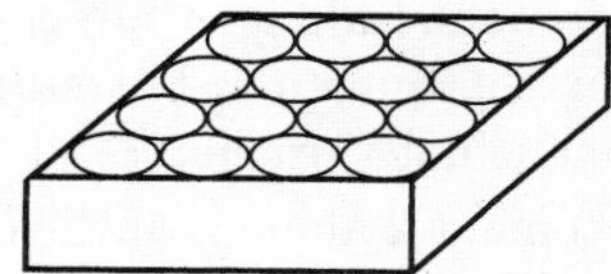

19. Sixteen cylindrical cans, each with a radius of 1 inch, are placed inside a rectangular cardboard box as shown above. If the cans touch adjacent cans and/or the walls of the box as shown, which of the following could be the interior area of the bottom of the box, expressed in square inches?

(A) 16

(B) 32

(C) 64

(D) 128

(E) 256

20. In a certain shipment of 120 new cars, $\frac{2}{3}$ of the cars are equipped with radios and $\frac{2}{5}$ are equipped with air conditioners. If 20 of the cars are equipped with neither a radio nor with an air conditioner, how many cars in the shipment are equipped with both a radio and an air conditioner?

(A) 20

(B) 28

(C) 32

(D) 58

(E) 76

Y
(2,y) (x,y)
(0,0) X

21. If the figure above is a rectangle, then what is the area of the figure, expressed in terms of x and y?

(A) xy

(B) $4xy$

(C) xy^2

(D) $y(x - 2)$

(E) $x(y - 2)$

22. Mr. Williams invested a total of $12,000 for a one-year period. Part of the money was invested at 5% simple interest, and the rest was invested at 12% simple interest. If he earned a total of $880 in interest for the year, how much of the money was invested at 12%?

(A) $1,920

(B) $4,000

(C) $4,800

(D) $7,200

(E) $8,000

23. How long will it take machine M to fill an order for x widgets if the machine operates at a constant rate and operation is not interrupted?

(1) The machine produces 150 widgets per minute.

(2) At the end of 2 hours, the machine has produced 40% of the widgets needed to fill the order.

(A) statement 1 alone is sufficient to answer the question, but statement 2 alone is not sufficient

(B) statement 2 alone is sufficient to answer the question, but statement 1 alone is not sufficient

(C) both statements together are needed to answer the question, but neither statement alone is sufficient

(D) either statement by itself is sufficient to answer the question

(E) not enough facts are given to answer the question

24. What is the total weight of four crates?

(1) The average weight of the four crates is 200 pounds.

(2) The total weight of two of the crates is exactly three times the total weight of the other two crates.

(A) statement 1 alone is sufficient to answer the question, but statement 2 alone is not sufficient

(B) statement 2 alone is sufficient to answer the question, but statement 1 alone is not sufficient

(C) both statements together are needed to answer the question, but neither statement alone is sufficient

(D) either statement by itself is sufficient to answer the question

(E) not enough facts are given to answer the question

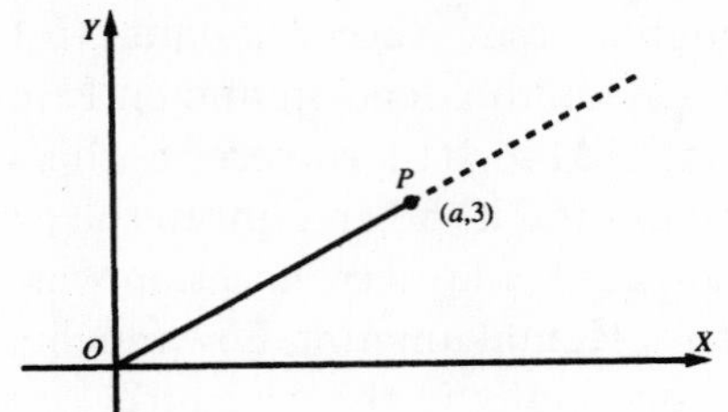

25. Line OP is drawn on the coordinate axes as shown. What is the value of a?

(1) $OP = 6$

(2) The angle formed by OP and the x-axis is 30°.

(A) statement 1 alone is sufficient to answer the question, but statement 2 alone is not sufficient

(B) statement 2 alone is sufficient to answer the question, but statement 1 alone is not sufficient

(C) both statements together are needed to answer the question, but neither statement alone is sufficient

(D) either statement by itself is sufficient to answer the question

(E) not enough facts are given to answer the question

26. A rectangular piece of carpet of 200 square yards is cut into two pieces, and the smaller piece is sold. What is the perimeter of the remaining piece?

(1) The area of the remaining piece is 120 square yards.

(2) The following figure is a diagram of the remaining piece.

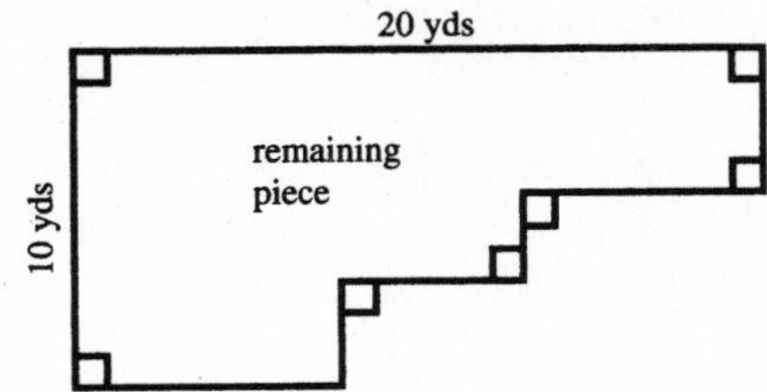

(A) statement 1 alone is sufficient to answer the question, but statement 2 alone is not sufficient

(B) statement 2 alone is sufficient to answer the question, but statement 1 alone is not sufficient

(C) both statements together are needed to answer the question, but neither statement alone is sufficient

(D) either statement by itself is sufficient to answer the question

(E) not enough facts are given to answer the question

27. What is the value of $\frac{1}{x} + \frac{1}{y} + \frac{1}{z}$?

(1) $\frac{xy + xz + yz}{xyz} = 4$

(2) $x + y = 3$

(A) statement 1 alone is sufficient to answer the question, but statement 2 alone is not sufficient

(B) statement 2 alone is sufficient to answer the question, but statement 1 alone is not sufficient

(C) both statements together are needed to answer the question, but neither statement alone is sufficient

(D) either statement by itself is sufficient to answer the question

(E) not enough facts are given to answer the question

28. A candy bar originally costs x cents per y ounces. If the size of the candy bar is reduced by 1 ounce and the price is increased by 10%, what is the new cost of the candy bar, expressed in cents per ounce?

(A) $\frac{x-y}{10}$

(B) $\frac{11(x-y)}{10}$

(C) $\frac{11x}{10y}$

(D) $\frac{11x}{10(y-1)}$

(E) $\frac{11x}{1-y}$

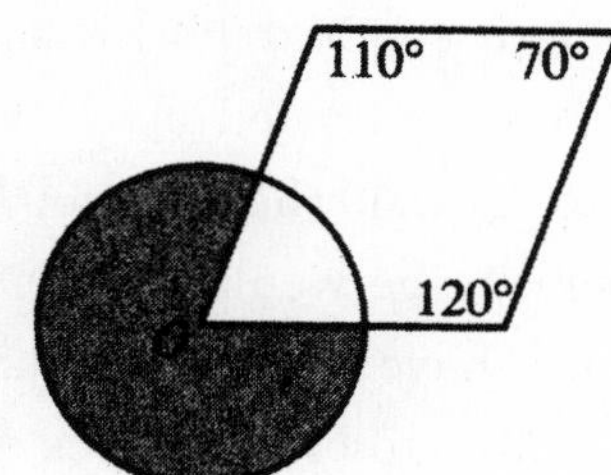

29. In the figure above, the circle O has a radius of 6. What is the area of the shaded portion of the figure?

(A) $\frac{\pi}{2}$

(B) $\frac{5\pi}{2}$

(C) 12π

(D) 18π

(E) 30π

30. If $\frac{1}{x} = 6$ and $\frac{1}{y} = \frac{1}{3}$, then $\frac{x}{y} =$

(A) $\frac{1}{18}$

(B) $\frac{1}{2}$

(C) 1

(D) 2

(E) 18

31. If during a one-year period, the dividend paid on a certain share of stock was equal to $8\frac{3}{8}$% of the par value of the stock, then the dividend paid was what fraction of the par value of the stock?

(A) $\frac{32}{800}$

(B) $\frac{67}{800}$

(C) $\frac{32}{100}$

(D) $\frac{67}{100}$

(E) $\frac{72}{100}$

32. From March 1 to March 31 the price of a certain commodity fell by $\frac{1}{4}$, and from April 1 to April 30 the price fell by $\frac{1}{3}$. By what percentage would the price of the commodity have to increase during the month of May to bring it back up to the level of March 1?

(A) $14\frac{2}{7}$%

(B) 25%

(C) 50%

(D) $66\frac{2}{3}$%

(E) 100%

33. If a machine consumes $\frac{k}{5}$ kilowatts of power every t hours, how much power will three such machines consume in 10 hours?

(A) $\frac{6t}{k}$

(B) $\frac{t}{k}$

(C) $30kt$

(D) $\frac{k}{t}$

(E) $\frac{6k}{t}$

34. Machine P can produce x widgets in 10 hours, Machine Q can produce x widgets in 6 hours, and Machine R can produce $2x$ widgets in 15 hours. If the three machines work together but independently, without interruption, how much time, expressed in hours, will be needed for them to produce $5x$ widgets?

(A) $7\frac{2}{3}$

(B) 8

(C) $10\frac{2}{3}$

(D) 12

(E) $23\frac{1}{2}$

35. How many times does Mary get paid in a certain year X?

(1) Mary is paid every Friday.

(2) The year X is a leap year.

(A) statement 1 alone is sufficient to answer the question, but statement 2 alone is not sufficient

(B) statement 2 alone is sufficient to answer the question, but statement 1 alone is not sufficient

(C) both statements together are needed to answer the question, but neither statement alone is sufficient

(D) either statement by itself is sufficient to answer the question

(E) not enough facts are given to answer the question

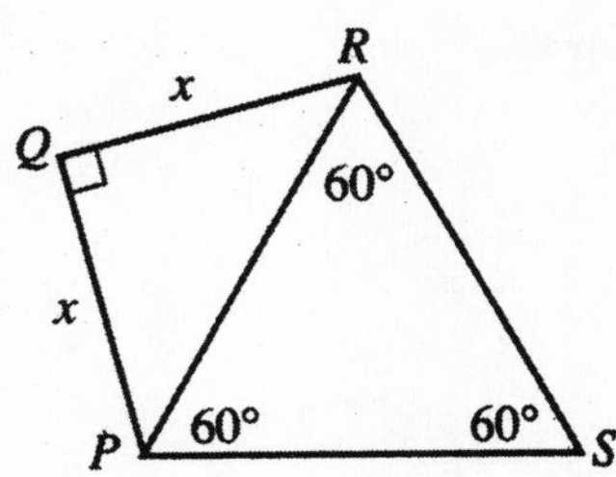

36. If $QR = 2$, then what is the perimeter of quadrilateral $PQRS$ in the figure above?

(A) $6\sqrt{2} + 4$

(B) $4\sqrt{2} + 4$

(C) $4\sqrt{2} + 2$

(D) $2\sqrt{2} + 2$

(E) $3\sqrt{2}$

37. How many of the 60 applicants for a job passed neither the physical nor the written exam?

(1) Of the 60 applicants, exactly 10% passed both the physical and the written exams.

(2) Of the 60 applicants, exactly 50% passed the physical exam, and exactly 20% passed the written exam.

(A) statement 1 alone is sufficient to answer the question, but statement 2 alone is not sufficient

(B) statement 2 alone is sufficient to answer the question, but statement 1 alone is not sufficient

(C) both statements together are needed to answer the question, but neither statement alone is sufficient

(D) either statement by itself is sufficient to answer the question

(E) not enough facts are given to answer the question

ANSWER KEY AND EXPLANATIONS

Verbal Section

1. E	9. C	17. E	25. B	33. D	41. C
2. D	10. D	18. E	26. C	34. A	
3. A	11. C	19. D	27. B	35. A	
4. D	12. B	20. E	28. B	36. E	
5. C	13. C	21. D	29. E	37. C	
6. A	14. E	22. A	30. B	38. C	
7. B	15. D	23. B	31. A	39. A	
8. B	16. A	24. E	32. C	40. E	

1. **The correct answer is (E).** The original sentence contains an error of faulty parallelism. You need a form to parallel raising funds and visiting hospitals. (B) and (C) fail to correct the error. (D) has the merit of using the *-ing* form of "to speak" (making it parallel in that respect), but the gratuitous "in" is not idiomatic and also destroys the parallelism.

2. **The correct answer is (D).** The problem is that the "it" has no clear antecedent. Only (D) and (E) correct the error. (E) is incorrect, however, because it introduces a new error—"temporarily" is an adverb and cannot describe "increase."

3. **The correct answer is (A).** (B) is wrong because it uses a clumsy indirect expression (the passive voice). (C) is wrong because it is a fragment without a main verb. (D) is incorrect because the additional conjunction (yet) is not needed, and because the resulting clause lacks a subject. (E) is incorrect because "it" is singular and cannot have as its antecedent, "physicians."

4. **The correct answer is (D).** Let us use letters to represent the categories. "All effective administrators" will be *A*. "Concerned about welfare" will be *C*. "Are liberal" will be *L*. The three propositions can now be represented as:

   1. All *A* are *W*.
   2. All *W* are *L*.
   3. All non-*L* are not *A*.

   Proposition # 3 is equivalent to "all *A* are not non-*L*," and that is in turn equivalent to "all *A* are *L*." Thus, (D) follows fairly directly as a matter of logic. (A) is incorrect, for while we know that "all *A* are *L*," we would not want to conclude that "No *L* are *A*"—there might be some ineffective administrators who grant time off. They could be ineffective for other reasons. (B) is incorrect for the same reason. Even though all effective administrators are concerned about their employees' welfare, this does not mean that ineffective administrators could not be concerned. They might be concerned but ineffective for another reason. (C) is clearly false given our propositions; we know that all effective administrators are liberal. Finally, (E) is not inferable. Just because all effective administrators grant time off does not mean that all the time granted off is granted by effective administrators.

5. **The correct answer is (C).** The weakness in Gerry's argument is that he assumes, incorrectly, that getting drunk is the only harm Clyde has in mind. Clyde could respond very effectively by pointing to some other harms of alcohol. (A) would not be a good response for Clyde since he is

concerned with Gerry's welfare. The fact is that other people get drunk when Gerry does not is hardly a reason for Gerry to stop drinking. (B) is also incorrect. That other people do or do not get drunk is not going to strengthen Clyde's argument against Gerry. He needs an argument that will impress Clyde, who apparently does not get drunk. (D) is perhaps the second best answer, but the explicit wording of the paragraph makes it unacceptable. Gerry has been drinking the same quantity for 15 years. Now, admittedly, it is possible he will begin to drink more heavily, but that *possibility* would not be nearly so strong a point in Clyde's favor as the *present* existence of harm (other than inebriation). Finally, (E) is irrelevant, since it is white wine that Gerry does drink.

6. **The correct answer is (A).** The original sentence contains a correct elliptical construction. The second verb, "opposed," implicitly relies on the verb "was." (B) introduces a new error. "Them" is a plural pronoun and cannot be used to refer to "Transcendentalism," which is singular. (C) and (D) disrupt the parallel construction of the sentence. (E) introduces a new error (the illogical choice of verb tense).

7. **The correct answer is (B).** The point of the passage is that a meaningful comparison between the two systems is going to be difficult since the one is cheap in the short run but expensive in the long run, while the other is expensive in the short run and cheap in the long run. The only appropriate way of doing the cost comparison is by taking account of both costs—which is what (B) does. To take just the long-run costs would be to ignore the short-run costs involved, so (A) is wrong; and taking the short-run costs while ignoring the long-run costs is no better, so (C) is wrong. If (A) is wrong, then (D) also has to be wrong, and the more so because it is not even projecting operating costs. Finally, (E) is a distraction—the connection between diesel fuel and air pollution is irrelevant in a paragraph which is concerned with a cost comparison.

8. **The correct answer is (B).** One way of "making more money" other than raising the price of a product is to decrease the size or quality of the product. This is what Vendo must have done. By doing so, Vendo accomplished the equivalent of a price increase without actually raising the price. (C) contradicts the paragraph which states that Vendo did not violate the letter of the instructions—that is, the literal meaning—though they did violate the intention. (D) also contradicts the paragraph. Had Vendo forfeited the franchise, that would have been within the letter of the "either-or" wording of the instructions. (A) and (E) require much speculation beyond the information given, and you should not indulge yourself in imaginative thinking when there is an obvious answer such as (B) available.

9. **The correct answer is (C).** The original sentence is incorrect because the verb "seem" does not agree with its subject "acceptance." (D) changes the verb but fails to correct the error. (B) and (E) correct the error in the original but use unidiomatic phrases ("indicate the popularity" and "as to").

10. **The correct answer is (D).** This sentence is wrong because it incorrectly compares Edgar Allan Poe (the person) with the works of Hawthorne. (B) contains the same error. (C) contains an ambiguity. It is not clear whether it was Poe or his works that were ignored. (E) uses an incorrect verb tense "having been."

11. **The correct answer is (C).** The original sentence is wrong because "which" has no antecedent. Only (C) solves the problem (by adding a noun, "practice"). In addition, (B) changes the meaning of the sentence because it no longer says that the jockey rides in order to become

familiar with the horses. (E) commits the same error.

12. **The correct answer is (B).** This is a main idea question. The author's primary concern is to discuss the problem of desertification. So choice (B) is correct. A natural extension of the discussion would be a proposal to slow the process of desertification, but that is not included in the passage as written, so (A) must be incorrect. (C), (D), and (E) are each incorrect because we find no elements in the passage to support those choices. Even admitting that the author intends to define, implicitly, the term "desertification," that is surely not the main point of the passage. The author also dwells at length on the causes of the problem.

13. **The correct answer is (C).** This is an explicit idea question. In the first paragraph, the author mentions (A), (B), (D), and (E) as features of desertification. (C), however, is one of the *causes* of desertification mentioned in the second paragraph.

14. **The correct answer is (E).** This is an inference question. The author places the phrase "higher uses" in quotation marks. In essence, this is similar to prefacing the phrase with the disclaimer "so called." This impression is reinforced by the final entry in the list of examples of "higher uses": waste dumps. This is not to say that the author would argue that such uses are not important. Rather, this is to say that the author does not believe that those uses are more important than agricultural uses. (A) is incorrect since this term is no more important than other terms used in the passage. (B) is incorrect since the author is talking about the conversion of non-arid land to higher uses. (C) is incorrect since the author is clearly opposed to such expansion. Finally, (D) is a sentiment expressed in the passage, but that is not the reason for placing this phrase in quotation marks.

15. **The correct answer is (D).** This is a specific detail (explicit idea) question with a thought-reverser. The correct answer is (D). The author mentions world demand for U.S. products in the final paragraph, but "mention" alone does not make this a correct answer to the question. The right answer to a specific detail question must not only be mentioned; it must also answer the question asked. In this case, global need is mentioned as a reason to avoid desertification (feeding people is important) and not as a cause. The other choices are mentioned as causes: (A) and (B) in paragraph 2; (C) and (E) in paragraph 3.

16. **The correct answer is (A).** This is an explicit idea question, and the answer is found in the last paragraph. There the author states that the most serious long-term effect of desertification will be on the United States' ability to export agricultural products. This will be harmful to the United States economically and to the rest of the world in terms of meeting the demand for food and fiber. As for (B) and (C), though these are plausible as effects of desertification, the author does not mention them specifically, and he certainly does not describe them as the most serious effects of desertification. (D) is incorrect because the author's concern is over the ability of the United States to continue to export agricultural products, not the ability of the United States to meet domestic demand. Finally, (E) fails for the same reason that (B) and (C) are incorrect. Though it might arguably be one result of desertification (and that is an issue we need not address), the author never mentions it as a possible effect.

17. **The correct answer is (E).** This is an application question. In the passage the author indicates that government programs which encourage exploitation of arid land are in large measure responsible for the rapid rate of desertification. A

natural extension of the discussion would be a proposal for government spending to conserve arid lands. And this receives specific support in the third paragraph, where the author mentions that government conservation incentives are inadequate. With regard to (A), the author seems to believe that it is necessary for the United States to continue to export agricultural products to meet the world demand. (B) is surely incorrect, for the author argues that aid to farmers is one cause of the rapid rate of desertification. (D) is incorrect for the same reason. As for (C), the conversion of land to "higher uses" is mentioned as a factor complicating the process of desertification. It is not a cause of desertification. The most natural extension of the passage would be a discussion of how to combat desertification.

18. **The correct answer is (E).** This is a tone question. We can surely eliminate (B), (C), and (D) as not expressing the appropriate element of worry. Then, between (A) and (E), (A) overstates the case. The author says we solve the problem now or we solve it later (at a higher cost). But that is an expression of concern, not alarm.

19. **The correct answer is (D).** The author introduces the example of the second university without explaining why we should consider that case similar to the one we are arguing about (except for size). This shows that the author is introducing an analogy—though not a very strong one. (A) is perhaps the second best answer. But it would be correct only if there were a *contention* that the author had introduced new evidence in support of the argument. The author does not articulate a contention and then adduce evidence for it. (B) is wrong because the author offers no solution to the problem and argues that the problem does not exist. Finally, (C) and (E) must be wrong because the author neither mentions a logical contradiction nor points to any ambiguity in an opponent's argument.

20. **The correct answer is (E).** Another deodorant might also give all-day protection. The ad claims that White Bear is the only deodorant that gives you *both* protection and scent—a vacuous enough claim since White Bear is probably the only deodorant with the White Bear scent. Of course, (C) is not affected by this point, since the White Bear Company may put its unique scent into many of its products. (B) is also not inconsistent with the ad—that another product is more popular does not say that it has the features the ad claims for the White Bear deodorant. (D) is not inconsistent because the chemical composition is merely "similar." But (E) is inconsistent: the same protection and the same scent.

21. **The correct answer is (D).** The easiest way to set this problem up is to draw a relational line:

PE IP EL BE
Dislikes ⟶ Likes

We note that Clara likes Basic Economics better than anything else, which means she must like it better than Advanced Calculus. So even though Advanced Calculus does not appear on our line, since we know that Basic Economics is the maximum, Clara must like Advanced Calculus less than Basic Economics. So (C) can be inferred. But we do not know where World History ranks on the preference line, and since Introductory Physics is not a maximal or a minimal value, we can make no judgment regarding it and an unplaced course. Quick reference to the line will show that (A), (B), and (E) are inferable.

22. **The correct answer is (A).** (B) uses an incorrect verb tense "had been requested." (C) is wordy and also changes the logic of the sentence by saying that the grading system is somehow to be added to the

answers

curriculum. (E) commits the same error. (D) is awkward and needlessly uses the passive voice.

23. **The correct answer is (B).** (A) is incorrect because it is unidiomatic to say "not so much as *x* but instead because of *y*." The correct idiom is "not so much *x* as *y*."

24. **The correct answer is (E).** The original sentence commits an error of logic. It actually says that it is the individual or individuals who have eight units and no commercial space. (B) runs together several logically separate ideas. (C) and (D) do separate the ideas, but the ideas are not rendered in parallel forms.

25. **The correct answer is (B).** We have seen examples before of the form of argument Holmes has in mind: "*P* or *Q*; not-*P*; therefore, *Q*." Here, however, the first premise of Holmes' argument is more complex: "*P* or *Q* or *R* . . . *S*," with as many possibilities as he can conceive. He eliminates them one by one until no single possibility is left. The logic of the argument is perfect, but the weakness in the form is that it is impossible to guarantee that all contingencies have been taken into account. Maybe one was overlooked. Thus, (B) is the correct answer. (A), (C), and (E) are wrong for the same reason. Holmes' method is designed to answer a particular question—in this case, "Where did the body come from?" Perhaps the next step is to apply the method to the question of the identity of the murderer, as (E) suggests, but at this juncture he is concerned with the preliminary matter of how the murder was committed. In any event, it would be wrong to assail the logic of Holmes' deduction by complaining that it does not prove enough. Since (A) and (C) are even more removed from the particular question raised, they, too, must be wrong. Finally, (D) is nothing more than a reiteration of Watson's original comment, and Holmes has already responded to it.

26. **The correct answer is (C).** Notice that the student responds to the professor's comment by saying, "That can't be true," and then uses the Duchess of Warburton as a counter-example. The Duchess would only be a counter-example to the professor's statement had the professor said that women cannot inherit the estates of their families. Thus, (C) must capture the student's misinterpretation of the professor's statement. What has misled the student is that he has attributed too much to the professor. The professor has cited the general rule of primogeniture—the eldest male child inherits—but he has not discussed the special problems that arise when no male child is born. In those cases, presumably a non-male child will have to inherit. (E) incorrectly refers to inheriting from a mother in discussing a case in which the woman inherited her father's estate. (D) is wrong, for the student specifically mentions the conditions that make a child legitimate: born to the wife of her father. (A) was inserted as a bit of levity: Of course, only men can *father* children of either sex. Finally, firstborn or not, a daughter cannot inherit as long as there is any male child to inherit, so (B) must be incorrect.

27. **The correct answer is (B).** This question requires careful attention to the quantifiers in each claim. An additional expense voucher might indicate additional expenses for an already identified employee or expenses incurred by an additional employee. A claim that states only that there are "at least so many employees" and that they incurred "at least this in expenses" cannot be contradicted by a revision upward in any number. A claim that states "there were exactly so many employees" or that states "there were at most so many employees" is contradicted by the discovery of another employee. The same reasoning ap-

plies to expenses. An "at least" claim is not contradicted by an upward revision, but the other claims are. (A) can be contradicted by an upward revision in the number of employees. (C) can be contradicted by an upward revision in the amount of expenses claimed. (D) and (E) can be contradicted on both grounds. (B) cannot be contradicted by any new finding.

28. **The correct answer is (B).** This is a main-idea question. The author draws a distinction between preventive health care and curative health care and suggests that there should be established separate authorities for each. So the primary method of developing the argument is the drawing of a distinction, as correctly stated by (B). (A) is incorrect since the author does not cite any counterarguments to his position. (C) is incorrect, for a dilemma is a "damned if you do and damned if you don't" argument. To draw a distinction is not necessarily to set up a dilemma. (D) is incorrect, for whatever causes of poor health are discussed in the passage are not the main focus of the discussion. (E) is incorrect for a similar reason. Whatever new research we may try to read into the passage, e.g., the Winslow monograph, is surely not the main point of the passage.

29. **The correct answer is (E).** This is an explicit-idea question. In the first sentence of the second paragraph, the author notes that treatment is aimed at a patient already ill, but we have been told in the first paragraph that preventive care is just that, aimed at people who are healthy in order to keep them that way. So statement I is part of the correct answer. Similarly, statement II is supported by the first two paragraphs, particularly the sentence of the second paragraph that reads, "While these may be applied on a mass basis . . . , they are usually applied after the patient appears with a complaint," thus distinguishing preventive care from curative care. Finally, per capita differences in cost care are discussed in paragraph 4.

30. **The correct answer is (B).** This is an inference question. In the first paragraph, the author discusses the basic strategy of preventive medicine and then states that in California there is needless suffering and economic harm due to the failure of authorities to implement controlled fluoridation. The development of the argument leads us to conclude that the author regards the failure of the authorities to fluoridate water as a failure to implement a preventive health care program. (B) explains this reasoning. (A) is incorrect since the author holds a positive attitude about fluoridation. (C) is incorrect because the author cites the failure to fluoridate as an example of a failure to adopt a potentially valuable preventive strategy. (D) is incorrect because fluoridation is a preventive, rather than a treatment, strategy. Finally, (E) is incorrect since the author recommends the fluoridation of water as a valuable preventive strategy.

31. **The correct answer is (A).** This is an inference question. In paragraph 4, the author remarks that expenditure of resources on treatment is an expenditure that is lost, that is, produces nothing positive (eliminating the negative is not regarded as producing a positive result). Then, the sick person is also not contributing anything positive while he or she is sick. So the economy is doubly disadvantaged because of the burden on or drain on resources to cure an ill person and because production is lost. (A) neatly captures this idea. (B) is incorrect because the author never quantifies the cost difference between the two types of care, saying only that prevention is less costly than treatment. (C) is incorrect because the author eventually will support such a division on the ground that

answers

the two activities are sufficiently dissimilar to warrant a division of authority. (D) is incorrect since both rehabilitation and cure belong to curative medicine, so that will not explain why the economy is doubly burdened. Finally, (E) is attractive because it is at least consistent with the general theme of the passage. But (E) is not responsive to the question. It does not explain why the economy is doubly burdened by the person who requires treatment.

32. **The correct answer is (C).** This is an attitude, or tone, question. Two clues support answer choice (C). First, the author refers to the monograph and then continues to make points made by Winslow. This indicates that the author agrees with Winslow. Second the author refers to the analysis by Winslow as "convincing." (A) and (B) can be eliminated because of the negative connotations associated with both terms. (D) can be eliminated because style is not relevant to the point under discussion. Finally, (E) is the second best answer. We eliminate (E) because the author states that the economics of prevention have been widely discussed, indicating that the uniqueness of Winslow's contribution is not necessarily originality. Further, the reference to the persuasiveness of Winslow's analysis makes (C) a better descriptive phrase to apply to the author's attitude than (E).

33. **The correct answer is (D).** This is a logical detail question. The author introduces these three diseases in the paragraph discussing the economics of prevention, and following the statement that the cost of prevention is less than the cost of treatment when averaged out on a per capita basis. (D) makes this point. (A) is incorrect, for while this is a statement the author would surely accept, it is not the reason for introducing the examples. (B) is incorrect for a similar reason. This may very well be true, but it is not an answer to the question. (C) must be wrong, for though this is one of the main points of the discussion, it will not answer this particular question. Finally, (E) is also a statement which the author could accept, but it is not responsive to the question.

34. **The correct answer is (A).** This is a question about the logical structure of the argument. The author mentions several differences between preventive and curative medicines: cost, personnel, and persons addressed. But these differences are not compelling reasons for creating a division of authority. The need to separate authority for the two strategies is discussed in the first and last paragraphs. The value of the division will be to clarify objectives and redress the inequitable division of resources. These are problems, so says the first paragraph, because "the imperative nature of medical care" will allow it to dominate health care. In other words, the urgency of treatment attracts attention. This is the explanation provided in (A). And for this reason it is not cost, (B); personnel, (C); or persons addressed, (D), which is the important difference. Finally, (E) is directly contradicted by the opening sentences of the passage.

35. **The correct answer is (A).** The question stem contains a hidden assumption: It is a loaded question. It presupposes that the person questioned agrees that the city is discriminating against its Hispanic residents. (A) is a good parallel. The questioner assumes that the Congressman agrees that defense spending is out of hand, which may or may not be true. (B) makes no such assumption. It can be answered with a simple yes if the chairperson plans to take a luncheon recess; otherwise a no will do the job. (C) requires more than a yes or no answer, but it still contains no presuppositions. Since the question asks "what," the speaker may respond by saying much, little, or none at all. (D) may be said to make a presuppositi-

tion—Gladys is going to the store—but here the presupposition is not concealed. It is made an explicit condition of the answer. Finally, (E) is a little like (B) in that a simple yes or no can communicate the counselor's opinion. It might be objected that (E) presupposes that the company has an affirmative action program, and that this makes it similar to the question stem. Two responses can be made. First, (E) is in this way like (D): The assumption—if there is one—is fairly explicit. Second, (E) does not have the same loaded tone as (A) does, so by comparison (A) is a better choice.

36. The correct answer is (E). The ad is a little deceptive. It tries to create the impression that if hospitals are using Dr. John's Milk of Magnesia, people will believe it is a good product. But what the ad actually says is that Dr. John uses the same *ingredient* that hospitals use (milk of magnesia is a simple suspension of magnesium hydroxide in water). The ad is something like an ad for John's Vinegar that claims it has "acetic acid," which is vinegar. (A), (B), (C), and (D), in various ways, fall into the trap of the inviting wording, and those statements are not conclusions that can be logically inferred. Statement (E), however, is logically inferable: from 9 of 10 X use Y, you can infer that it is true that Y is used by 9 out of 10 X.

37. The correct answer is (C). The sentence has no main verb. (E) fails to correct the error. (B) is incorrect because (by using a new independent clause) it changes the logic of the sentence. (D) uses an incorrect verb tense, "was writing."

38. The correct answer is (C). The original sentence contains a misplaced modifier. It says that the coast guard was severely damaged and already sinking. (B) fails to correct the error. The "it" still "wants" to refer to the coast guard because of the proximity of the modifier to that noun. (E) too fails to correct the error. (D) corrects the problem of the misplaced modifier but makes an error of faulty parallelism.

39. The correct answer is (A). Statements I and II combine to give us (A). If all wheeled conveyances that travel on the highway are polluters, and a bicycle does not travel on the highway, then a bicycle cannot be a polluter. If (A) is then correct, (B) must be incorrect because bicycles do not travel on the highways at all. (C) and (D) make the same mistake. III must be read to say, "If I am driving, it is raining," not "If it is raining, I am driving." (E) is clearly false since my car is driven on the highway. Don't make the problem harder than it is.

40. The correct answer is (E). Picking up on our discussion of (C) and (D) in the previous question, III must read, "If I am driving, then it is raining." Let that be: "If P, then Q." If we then had not-Q, we could deduce not-P. (E) gives us not-Q by changing IV to "It is not raining." Changing I or II or even both is not going to do the trick, for they don't touch the relationship between my driving my car and rain—they deal only with pollution and we need the car to be connected. Similarly, if we change III to make it deal with pollution, we have not adjusted the connection between my driving and rain, so (C) must be wrong. (D) is the worst of all the answers. Whether rainwater is polluted or not has nothing to do with the connection between my driving and rain. Granted, there is the unstated assumption that my car only pollutes when I drive it, but this is OK.

41. The correct answer is (C). This sentence contains a logical error. It compares the median income of women to men and not to the income of men. (B) and (D) contain the same error. (E) is wrong because it changes the logic of the original sentence. (E) makes a comparison between the median income of women and the median income of *a* man (which man?).

ANSWER KEY AND EXPLANATIONS

Quantitative Section

1. E	9. C	17. B	25. D	33. E
2. B	10. A	18. C	26. B	34. D
3. B	11. B	19. C	27. A	35. E
4. D	12. A	20. B	28. D	36. B
5. C	13. E	21. D	29. E	37. C
6. A	14. D	22. B	30. A	
7. B	15. C	23. B	31. B	
8. E	16. C	24. A	32. E	

1. **The correct answer is (E).** As for 1, a triangle could have sides of 3, 4, and 5 and would be the special case of the right triangle. And the numbers given in III could also form a triangle, an equilateral triangle. But no triangle could have the sides given in II, for the largest side would be longer than the sum of the other two sides.

2. **The correct answer is (B).** This problem is solved simply by division—but make sure you keep track of your decimal point: 1.5 ÷ 0.03 = 50.

3. **The correct answer is (B).** (1) is not sufficient, even with the information provided by the question stem. Although we learn from the stem that there are 18 people on the team, (1) leaves us with the possibilities of 15, 16, 17, or 18 seniors. (2), however, is sufficient. The dichotomy seniors-not-seniors is exhaustive; that is, a member must fall into one of the two categories. Therefore, knowing that the number of not-seniors is 3, coupled with the information provided in the stem that the total is 18, tells us that the number of seniors is 15. Of course, it was not necessary to carry the analysis to this final step. It was sufficient to recognize that sufficient information is provided by (2).

4. **The correct answer is (D).** A percentage is nothing but a fraction expressed in a special way, e.g., $\frac{1}{5} = .20 = 20\%$, or $\frac{1}{2} = .50 = 50\%$. So if we can find the appropriate fraction, i.e., the appropriate ratio, then we can rename that fraction ratio as a percentage. So this question really asks, "What is $\frac{x}{y}$?" (1), by manipulation, gives $\frac{x}{y} = \frac{5}{3}$. Though we do not need to carry through the calculation, this tells us that x is $166\frac{2}{3}$ percent of y. Similarly, (2) is expressed mathematically as: $y = .6x$, which can be rewritten as, $\frac{x}{y} = \frac{1}{.6} = 166\frac{2}{3}$ percent. But we stress that there is no reason to do the conversion. Once you see that you have the ratio of $\frac{x}{y}$ you can stop.

5. **The correct answer is (C).** The question stem provides no information other than that there are two points and a circle. The question is whether P or Q is farther from the center. (1) establishes that P is in the circle, but where is Q? (2) establishes that Q is outside the circle, but where is P? This shows that neither alone is sufficient. Both (1) and (2) together are sufficient. Since a circle is defined as the location of all points equidistant from the center (take a fixed length of string, tie a crayon to one end

and nail down the other end, then draw a circle), the point inside the circle must be closer to the center than any point either on the circle or, in this case, outside the circle.

6. **The correct answer is (A).** This question reminds us of the importance of considering each statement independently of the other. (1) is sufficient. If we know the starting date and the population on that date, since (1) gives us the rate of growth, we know when the population reaches a certain mark. (2) alone will not do the trick. This proves that the correct choice is (A). You may also have noted that (2) is actually deducible from (1) coupled with the question stem. As we have pointed out in our instructional overview, the two statements will never contradict each other. In this case, (2) is a conclusion that could be reached on the basis of the other information given in the problem. (2) presents information that could be obtained from (1), so the answer must be either (A) or (D).

7. **The correct answer is (B).** This question is slightly different from the preceding question. In the preceding question the second statement was redundant, that is, already contained in the stem and (1). So there the choice had to be either (A) or (D). Here, however, (1) not only cannot establish an answer, in and of itself, but it is also irrelevant to the question since the total price is not given. (2), on the other hand, is sufficient to answer the question, since it tells us how much is owed.

8. **The correct answer is (E).** (1) and (2) are interesting in that they tell us how much time the watch will lose every hour, but what does the question ask? Not how much time will be lost but what the watch will read. For that we would need to know the reading at the starting point of the relevant period and also the length of the relevant period. As it is, the watch could read anything.

9. **The correct answer is (C).** We want the greatest possible number of people who do not fall into at least one of the three categories. We find the theoretical maximum by concentrating as many persons as possible in the three categories, leaving as many as possible "free" from the three categories. So if we assume that the 40 people who graduated from High School *X* are among the 65 who graduated from College *Y*, we leave 35 persons free of both categories (100 – 65 = 35). Then we assume that the 30 who live in City *Z* also belong to the group of 65, though just what other characteristics they share does not concern us. We are still left with a maximum of 35 people who fall into none of the three categories.

10. **The correct answer is (A).** This question shows an equation in the stage just prior to solving for the two roots (the two possible values of x). The equation can be read as saying either $(x - 6)$ is equal to 0 or $(2x + 1) = 0$. This means the two possible values of x are +6 and $-\frac{1}{2}$. Since the question stem stipulates that $x > 0$, we want the positive root, which is +6. As an alternative to this reasoning, you might simply have substituted choices back into the equation, starting with (A), until you found one that worked:

$$(+6 - 6)(2(6) + 1) = 0\ (13) = 0$$

which demonstrates that +6 works. So (A) must be the correct choice.

11. **The correct answer is (B).** This questions tests your familiarity with the coordinate system. A basic problem many people have is remembering which is the up-down axis and which is the side-to-side axis. The first number given in the pair is always the x-coordinate and represents location from side to side; the second number is the y-coordinate and represents location on the up-and-down axis. The line shown on the graph runs in an up-down direction, with no change

answers

from side to side. This means that the x-coordinate is the same for every point on that line. So the correct solution will look like this: $(x, ?)$. Then, if we look for a point that is midway between y and $-y$, that will have to be 0, and the coordinates of the midpoint are $(x, 0)$.

12. **The correct answer is (A).** This is a fairly straightforward problem asking you to compute rate. The only trick is to make sure your final choice is expressed in copies per second. You find the total number of copies produced by subtracting: 2334 – 1254 = 1080. That number was produced in 30 minutes, or 1800 seconds (30 × 60 = 1800). So the rate per second is $\frac{1080}{1800}$ = 0.6 copies per second.

13. **The correct answer is (E).** Notice the presence of the word *NOT* in the question. We are looking for the one choice that is not possible, given that the dollar cost of the item is a whole number. To express profit as a percentage of cost, you would create a fraction profit/cost, which would then be renamed as a percentage. So profit/cost × 100 gives profit as a percentage of cost. Since profit is $10, the calculation for this particular question must be $10/cost × 100 is equal to percent profit:

    $10/cost × 100 = x%

    This we can rewrite as:

    $10(100)/$x$% = cost

    Or as:

    $10/$x$ = cost

    where x now represents the decimal equivalent of a percentage. So to determine whether an answer choice is possible, you need only substitute the decimal equivalent in for x. For example, (A):

    $10/.10 = $100

    which says that a profit of $10 on top of a cost of $100 would be a 10% profit. Since the $100 is a whole dollar amount, (A) is possible.

    The correct choice is (E):

    $$\frac{\$10}{.80} = \$12.50$$

    But $12.50 is not a whole dollar value.

14. **The correct answer is (D).** This question tests properties of odd and even numbers and can be solved either by substituting some values for x into each statement or by thinking about the characteristics of such numbers in a more abstract way. Thinking in the more general way, we reason as follows.

    As for I, since x is even, $3x$ must also be even, and $3x + 1$ an odd number.

    As for II, since x is even, $5x$ must be even; and since $5x$ is even, $5x$ times $5x$ is even, and an even number plus 2 is still even.

    As for III, since x is even, $x + 1$ is odd and $x + 1$ times $x + 1$ is also an odd number.

15. **The correct answer is (C).** It should be obvious that neither (1) nor (2), in and of itself, is sufficient. The question, then, is whether we have a (C) or an (E) question. We can only have a (C) answer if both statements serve to define a single precise value for x. This must be checked by calculation. The least common multiple of x will be 3 × 4 × 5 = 60. The next greatest multiple of x will be 120. So (2), with (1), proves that $x = 60$.

16. **The correct answer is (C).** The main trick here is to figure out how the accounting procedure takes account of the specific numbers. First, if the clerk wishes to earn at least $370 for a week, then in addition to her base salary of $210, she must earn at least $160 in commissions. Since her commission is 10% of sales, sales of $1,600 will earn her the $160. But she earns commissions only on those sales in excess of $3,000, so she must sell $1,600 more than $3,000, or at least $4,600.

17. **The correct answer is (B).** For this question, it is important to pay attention

to the question and to observe that (1) is redundant of (2). First, the question asks *how long* it will take to reduce the amount of liquid to 1200 gallons. Since we are given the total in the tank at the start, (2) is sufficient; you just take the difference between the two rates to find how much liquid will disappear during a certain time. Then (1) is not sufficient, since it does not give an absolute number—for example, one could fill at the rate of 1 gallon a minute and the other empty at the rate of 8 gallons a minute.

18. **The correct answer is (C).** The transactions can be described algebraically as follows:

$$OT - .1OT + \$140 = 1.25OT$$

where OT represents "original total." Translated into ordinary English, the algebra reads "The original total minus 10% of the original total plus another 140 dollars is equal to 125% of the original total." Solving for OT:

$$OT - .1OT + 140 = 1.25OT$$
$$.9OT + 140 = 1.25OT$$
$$140 = .35OT$$
$$OT = \frac{140}{.35}$$
$$OT = 400$$

You can check the result of this algebraic manipulation by using \$400 as the original total. Take away 10% of that, or \$40, leaving \$360 in the account. Then add back in \$140, bringing the total to \$500. And \$500 is 25% more than \$400.

19. **The correct answer is (C).** A picture should make clear the solution to the problem:

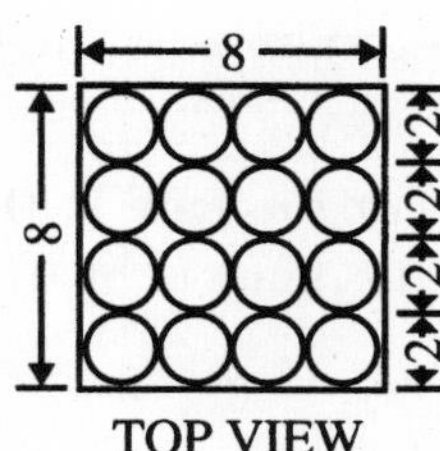

The box has inside dimensions of 8 and 8, so the area is $8 \times 8 = 64$ square inches.

20. **The correct answer is (B).** The solution to this question requires you to see the relationship between two overlapping categories or sets:

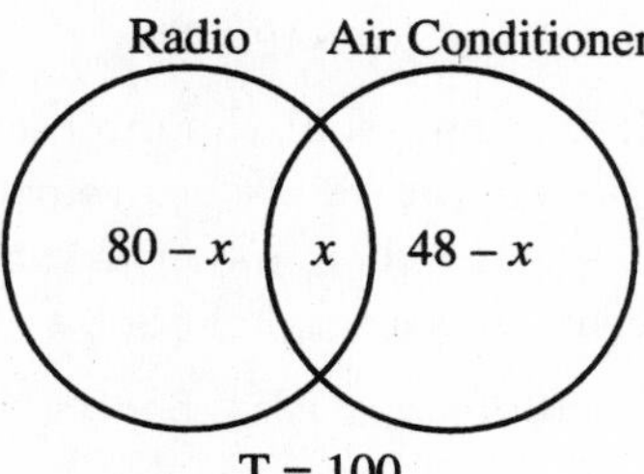

The x in the overlapping area indicates that we do not know how many cars belong to both categories. Then, the part of the circle labeled "Radio" that does not belong to the overlap has $80 - x$ cars ($\frac{2}{3}$ of the 120 cars have radios). Similarly, the part of the circle labeled "Air Conditioner" that does not belong to the overlap has $48 - x$ cars ($\frac{2}{3}$ of the 120 cars have air conditioners). And the total of all three areas is 100 (since 20 cars have no radio or air conditioner, $120 - 20 = 100$). So we add the three areas together:

$$(80 - x) + x + (48 - x) = 100$$
$$128 - x = 100$$
$$x = 28$$

So the number of cars with both radios and air conditioners is 28.

21. **The correct answer is (D).** Here is another question testing your understanding of the coordinate graph. To find the area of the rectangle, we must express the dimensions using x and y. The width of the rectangle is simply y, because the point (x, y) is located y units above the x-axis. The length of the rectangle is $x - 2$ because it runs from point 2 to point x, parallel to the x-axis. Since width is y and length is $x - 2$, the area must be $y(x - 2)$.

answers

22. The correct answer is (B). This question can be solved using simultaneous equations. For example, let x be the amount of money invested at 5% and let y be the amount of money invested at 12%. Using those symbols, since the total amount invested was \$12,000, we write:

$$x + y = \$12{,}000$$

Next, we know that the interest earned on x (at the rate of 5% per year) plus the interest earned on y (at the rate of 12% per year) was a total of \$880 in interest:

$$x(.05) + y(.12) = \$880$$

So we have two equations:

$$x + y = 12{,}000$$
$$.05x + .12y = 880$$

We can solve for each variable by the following method. First, since $x + y = 12{,}000$, $x = 12{,}000 - y$. We substitute that value of x into the second equation:

$$.05\ (12{,}000 - y) + .12y = 880$$
$$600 - .05y + .12y = 880$$
$$.07y = 280$$
$$y = 4{,}000$$

So the amount invested at 12% was \$4,000.

23. The correct answer is (B). (2) is sufficient. If we know that the machine produces 40% of x in 2 hours, then, assuming a constant rate of production (as stipulated by the question stem), the machine will produce x (or the entire order) in 5 hours. (1) is not sufficient by itself, nor is it needed for this calculation.

24. The correct answer is (A). If we know the average of a group and the number of items or members in the group, then we must also know the total for the group. So statement (1) tells us that the total weight is $200 \times 4 = 800$. Statement (2) is not sufficient by itself since for it to be sufficient we would need some other numbers (for example, the weight of two smaller crates).

25. The correct answer is (D). Here we must see the possibility of using the Pythagorean Theorem. Since we are dealing with a coordinate system, we can add the following line to make a right triangle:

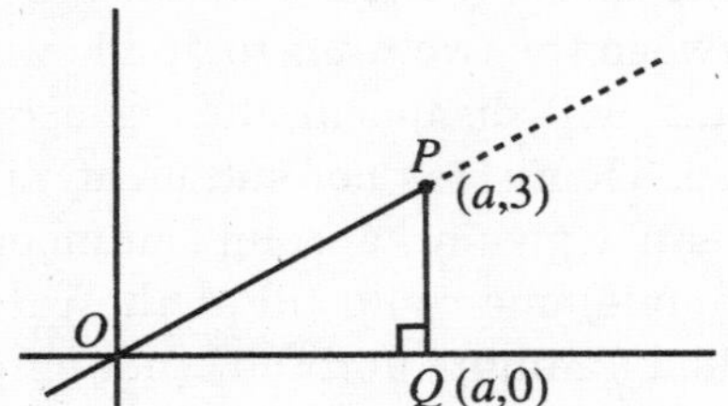

Since line PQ is parallel to the y-axis, point Q must have the same x-coordinate as point P. And since Q is on the x-axis, it has a y-coordinate of 0. This means that $PQ = 3$. The conclusion can be reached either by common reasoning or by the distance formula. By common reasoning, the only distance covered from P to Q is the vertical distance from 0 on the y-axis to a value of 3 on the y-axis. So the line is 3 units long. For those who prefer to use the distance formula:

$$d = \sqrt{(x_2 - x_1)^2 + (y_2 - y_1)^2}$$

which is really nothing but a special case of the Pythagorean Theorem. So:

$$d = \sqrt{(a-a)^2 + (3-0)^2}$$
$$d = \sqrt{3^2} = 3$$

Thus, (1) is sufficient, for we have one leg of the right triangle as 3 (PQ), and the hypotenuse as 6 [by (1)], so we could use the Pythagorean Theorem to find the length of . And that length will be equal to the x-coordinate, a. Similarly, (2) allows us to determine that triangle OPQ is a 30°-60°-90° triangle, and, using the special properties of that triangle, we can also determine the length of and the value of a.

26. The correct answer is (B). (1) is not sufficient as shown by the following drawings.

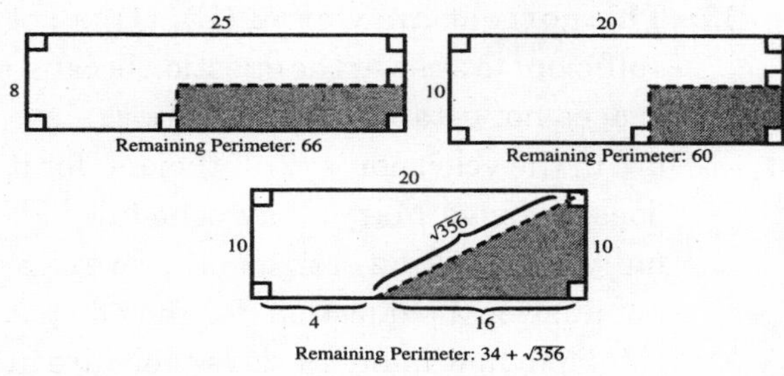

(1) does not assert that the cut used right angles. (2), however, does assert it, and that is sufficient to answer the question regarding the perimeter:

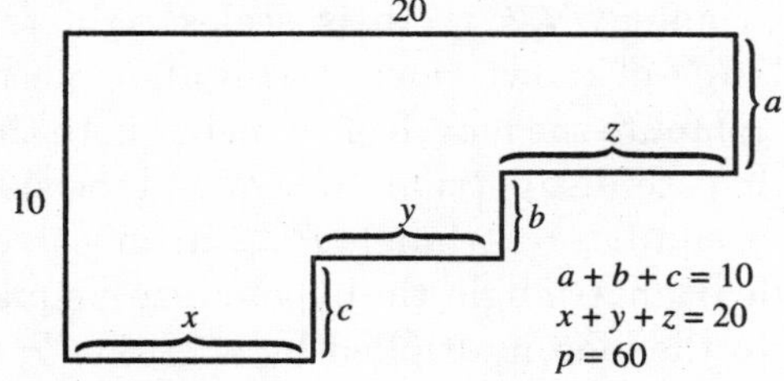

27. The correct answer is (A). (1) is sufficient. The expression $\frac{1}{x} + \frac{1}{y} + \frac{1}{z} = \frac{y+x}{xy} + \frac{1}{z} = \frac{xy + xz + yz}{xyz}$ and (1) establishes that this has the value of 4, answering the question. (2) is not sufficient. Breaking into the addition (at the point where we have $\frac{y+x}{xy} + \frac{1}{z}$) with the information that $x + y = 3$, gives the expression $\frac{3}{xy} + \frac{1}{z}$, but that is insufficient to establish a value for the expression.

28. The correct answer is (D). This question asks that you express the changes described in an algebraic formula. The original cost per ounce is x cents per ounce. One change is the increase in price of 10%, from x cents to $\frac{11}{10}x$ cents. But the size of the candy bar is reduced by 1 ounce. So instead of the new price being $\frac{11}{10}x$ cents per ounce, it is now $\frac{11}{10}x$ cents per $y - 1$ ounces. So the correct formula is $\frac{11x}{10(y-1)}$.

29. The correct answer is (E). The key here is to see that the shaded area is what is left over after the unshaded portion of the circle is taken away from the entire area of the circle:

Shaded Area = Area of Circle minus Unshaded Wedge

First, the area of the entire circle is πr^2 or 36π. Next, the angle at the center of the circle belongs to the quadrilateral. The sum of the interior angles of a quadrilateral is 360°, so the missing angle must be 60°. And 60° is $\frac{1}{6}$ of the total number of degrees in a circle, so the unshaded wedge is $\frac{1}{6}$ the area of the circle, or $\frac{1}{6}$ of 36π, which is 6π. Substituting into our solution statement:

Shaded Area = 36π minus $6\pi = 30\pi$

30. The correct answer is (A). A quick way to answer the question is to recognize that each of the equations can be turned upside down. In other words, $\frac{1}{x} = 6$, then $x = \frac{1}{6}$.
And $\frac{1}{y} = \frac{1}{3}$, then $y = 3$. So $\frac{x}{y} = \frac{\frac{1}{6}}{3} = \frac{1}{18}$.

31. The correct answer is (B). For all of the distracting business about stock and par value and so on, this question really just requires that you rename a mixed fraction as a proper fraction. The question asks "the dividend was what fraction of the par value?" We are told that the dividend was $8\frac{3}{8}$% of the par value. So we set up a fraction:

$$8\frac{3}{8}\% = \frac{8\frac{3}{8}}{100} = \frac{\frac{67}{8}}{100} = \frac{67}{800}$$

32. The correct answer is (E). One way of answering the question is to assign an arbitrary number to represent the price of the commodity on March 1. Let us assume it was \$100. First, the price falls by $\frac{1}{4}$, from \$100 to \$75. Then it falls another $\frac{1}{3}$ to \$50. To return to its original level, the price must increase by \$50, and \$50 is 100% of \$50.

33. The correct answer is (E). Here we are asked to express a relationship using an algebraic formula. We reason as follows. First, a single machine consumes $\frac{k}{5}$ kilowatts every t hours, which is a rate of $\frac{\frac{k}{5}}{t}$, or $\frac{k}{5t}$. Next, we have three such machines, and they will consume at three times the rate of one machine: $\frac{3k}{5t}$. Finally, a direct proportion will show us how much is consumed in 10 hours:

$$\frac{3k}{5t} = \frac{x}{10}$$

Cross-multiply: $30k = (x)5t$

Divide by *5t:* $\frac{30k}{5t} = x$

$$\frac{6k}{t} = x$$

So three such machines operating for 10 hours will consume $\frac{6k}{t}$.

34. The correct answer is (D). Here we have a problem asking us to calculate a combined rate of operation—with the additional twist that the rates are expressed in terms of an x. We proceed in the usual fashion:

Rate (1) + Rate (2) + Rate (3) = Rate Combined

Amount: $\frac{x}{10}+\frac{x}{6}+\frac{2x}{15}=\frac{5x}{y}$
Time:

(where y is the unknown time needed to answer the question).

Add: $\frac{3x+5x+4x}{30} = \frac{5x}{y}$

Fractions: $\frac{12x}{30} = \frac{5x}{y}$

Cross-multiply: $y(12x) = 150x$

Divide by $12x$: $y=\frac{150x}{12x} = 12.5$ hours

35. The correct answer is (E). (1) is not sufficient to answer the question because it does not establish how many Fridays are in the year, nor is (2) sufficient, for it does not give Mary's pay schedule. Finally, even taking both together we cannot answer the question, for they do not establish how many Fridays there are in the particular leap year. $\frac{366}{4} = 91$ with remainder 2. So there could be 91 or 92 paydays for Mary.

36. The correct answer is (B). Notice that triangle *PQR* is an isosceles right triangle of known sides, 2. This allows us to compute the length of , which is both the hypotenuse of triangle *PQR* and the side of equilateral triangle *PRS.* In an isosceles right triangle, the hypotenuse is equal to the side multiplied by $\sqrt{2}$. So $PR = 2\sqrt{2}$, and and have the same length. So the entire perimeter is:

$$PQ + QR + RS + SP = \text{Perimeter } PQRS$$

$$2 + 2 + 2\sqrt{2} + 2\sqrt{2} = \text{Perimeter } PQRS$$

$$4 + 2(2\sqrt{2}) = \text{Perimeter } PQRS$$

$$4 + 4\sqrt{2} = \text{Perimeter } PQRS$$

37. The correct answer is (C). That (1) is insufficient to answer the question can be shown by a diagram:

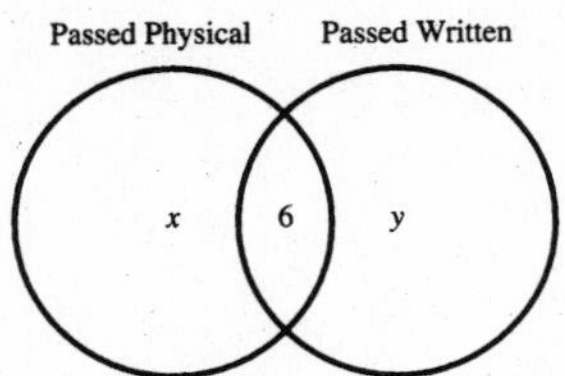

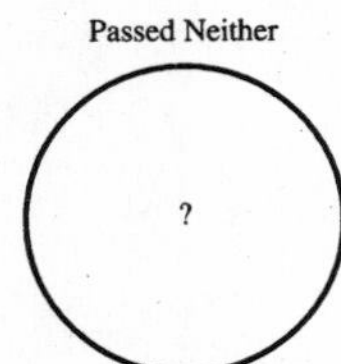

(1) does not tell us how many persons are in *x* and *y*. That (2) is not sufficient can be shown by a similar diagram:

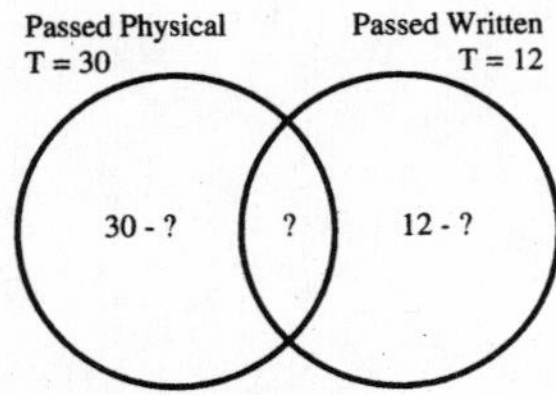

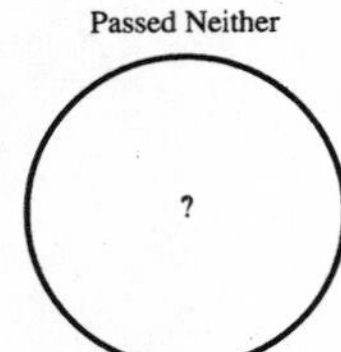

(2) does not establish how many applicants passed both exams, and that is needed; the question stem asks how many passed neither. Both taken together will do the trick:

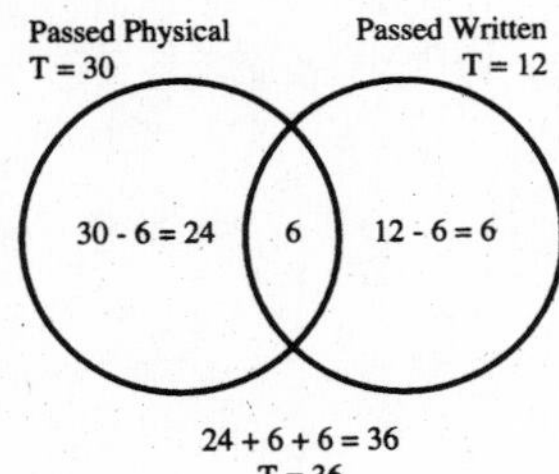

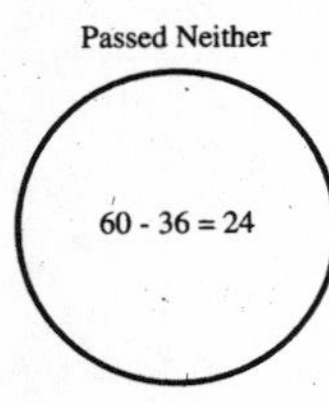

Practice Test 5

ANALYTICAL WRITING ASSESSMENT

I. Analysis of an Issue

Time—30 Minutes

Directions: In this section you will have 30 minutes to analyze and explain your views on the topic presented below. Read the statement and directions carefully. Write only on the topic given. An essay on a topic other than the one assigned will automatically be assigned a grade of 0.

Note: On the CAT version, you will keyboard your essay. For this exercise, allow yourself three sides of regular $8\frac{1}{2} \times 11$- inch paper for each essay response.

> Some people long for the "good old days" when schools emphasized the "three r's" of "reading, writing, and arithmetic." They maintain that school curriculums of today are watered-down versions of sounder ones and therefore less effective. Other people defend the curriculum of today's schools pointing out that students must be exposed to a greater variety of material and to material that is more complex.

Which position do you find more compelling? Explain your position using reasons and/or examples drawn from your personal experience, observations, or readings.

II. Analysis of an Argument

Time—30 Minutes

Directions: In this section you will have 30 minutes to write a critique of the argument presented below. Read the argument and directions carefully. Write only on the topic given. An essay on a topic other than the one assigned will automatically be assigned a grade of 0.

Note: On the CAT version, you will keyboard your essay. For this exercise, allow yourself three sides of regular $8\frac{1}{2} \times 11$- inch paper for each essay response.

The rescue squad, which provides ambulance service to a substantial portion of the county, is staffed entirely by volunteers who train and serve for no monetary compensation. The rescue squad receives an annual equipment budget from the county government but has to submit special requests for unusual pieces of equipment. The county should give the rescue squad funds to purchase a defibrilator, an electronic device used to regularize the heartbeat of patients who have suffered a heart attack. With a defibrilator, the rescue squad could ensure that county residents will have an excellent chance of surviving a heart attack.

How persuasive do you find this argument? Explain your point of view by analyzing the line of reasoning and the use of evidence in the argument. Discuss also what, if anything, would make the argument more persuasive or would help you better to evaluate its conclusion.

VERBAL SECTION

41 Questions • 75 minutes

Directions: For each of the following questions, choose the correct answer. To simulate the experience of taking the CAT, answer each question in order. Do not skip any questions, and do not go back to any questions you have already answered. ***For Sentence Correction questions:*** In questions of this type, either part or all of a sentence is underlined. The sentence is followed by five ways of writing the underlined part. Choice (A) repeats the original; the other answer choices vary. If you think that the original phrasing is the best, choose (A). If you think one of the other answer choices is the best, select that choice.

Sentence Correction questions test your ability to recognize correct and effective expression. Follow the requirements of Standard Written English: grammar, choice of words, and sentence construction. Choose the answer that results in the clearest, most exact sentence, but does not change the meaning of the original sentence.

Example:

Q The possibility of massive earthquakes <u>are regarded by most area residents with</u> a mixture of skepticism and caution.

- **(A)** are regarded by most area residents with
- **(B)** is regarded by most area residents with
- **(C)** is regarded by most area residents as
- **(D)** is mostly regarded by area residents with
- **(E)** by most area residents is regarded with

A **The correct answer is (B).**

For Critical Reasoning questions: Questions of this type ask you to analyze and evaluate the reasoning in short paragraphs or passages. For some questions, all of the answer choices may conceivably be answers to the question asked. You should select the *best* answer to the question, that is, an answer that does not require you to make assumptions that violate common-sense standards by being implausible, redundant, irrelevant, or inconsistent.

Example:

 In an extensive study of the reading habits of magazine subscribers, it was found that an average of between four and five people actually read each copy of the most popular weekly news magazine. On this basis, we estimate that the 12,000 copies of *Poets and Poetry* that are sold each month are actually read by 48,000 to 60,000 people.

The estimate above assumes that

(A) individual magazine readers generally enjoy more than one type of magazine

(B) most of the readers of *Poets and Poetry* subscribe to the magazine

(C) the ratio of readers to copies is the same for *Poets and Poetry* as for the weekly news magazine

(D) the number of readers of the weekly news magazine is similar to the number of readers of *Poets and Poetry*

(E) most readers enjoy sharing copies of their favorite magazines with friends and family members

A **The correct answer is (C).**

For Reading Comprehension questions: Each passage is followed by questions or incomplete statements about the passage. Each statement or question is followed by lettered words or expressions. Select the word or expression that most satisfactorily completes each statement or answers each question in accordance with the meaning of the passage.

1. After reading two different poems, she could not decide which poem was the most beautiful, since each had their own unique features.

   (A) she could not decide which poem was the most beautiful, since each had their own

   (B) she could not decide which poem was the more beautiful, since each had their own

   (C) she could not decide which poem was the most beautiful, since each had its own

   (D) she could not decide which poems were the most beautiful, since each had their own

   (E) she could not decide which poem was the more beautiful, since each had its own

2. The exclusive French restaurant has been popular with business customers because of its excellent service, responsive management, and because its parking facilities are extensive.

   (A) because of its excellent service, responsive management, and because its parking facilities are extensive.

   (B) because of its excellent service, responsive management, and because their parking facilities are extensive.

   (C) because of its service, which is excellent, management, which is responsive, and because of parking facilities which are extensive.

   (D) because of its excellent service, responsive management, and extensive parking facilities.

   (E) because of its excellent service, responsive management, and its extensive parking facilities.

3. Men's interest in developing a cure for cancer have promoted the rapid advances in the abstruse field now known as Genetic Engineering.

   (A) Men's interest in developing a cure for cancer have promoted

   (B) Men's interest in developing a cure for cancer has promoted

   (C) That men are interested in developing a cure for cancer have promoted

   (D) Interest in developing a cure for cancer has promoted

   (E) Men's interest in developing a cure for cancer has promoted

QUESTIONS 4 AND 5

Roberts is accused of a crime, and Edwards is the prosecution's key witness.

I. Roberts can be convicted on the basis of Edwards' testimony against him.

II. Edwards' testimony would show that Edwards himself participated in Roberts' wrongdoing.

III. The crime of which Roberts is accused can only be committed by a person acting alone.

IV. If the jury learns that Edwards himself committed some wrong, they will refuse to believe any part of his testimony.

4. If propositions I, II, and III are assumed to be true and IV false, which of the following best describes the outcome of the trial?

   (A) Both Edwards and Roberts will be convicted of the crime of which Roberts is accused.

   (B) Both Edwards and Roberts will be convicted of some crime other than the one with which Roberts is already charged.

   (C) Roberts will be convicted while Edwards will not be convicted.

   (D) Roberts will not be convicted.

   (E) Roberts will testify against Edwards.

5. If all four propositions are taken as a group, it can be pointed out that the scenario they describe is

(A) a typical situation for a prosecutor

(B) impossible because the propositions are logically inconsistent

(C) unfair to Edwards, who may have to incriminate himself

(D) unfair to Roberts, who may be convicted of the crime

(E) one which Roberts' attorney has created

6. Delegates to the Republican Party convention chose their candidate and was able to ratify all aspects of his campaign platform at the convention in Denver.

(A) chose their candidate and was able

(B) chose their candidate and were able

(C) chose its candidate and were able

(D) chose its candidate and was able

(E) had chosen their candidate and was able

QUESTIONS 7 AND 8

There is a curious, though nonetheless obvious, contradiction in the suggestion that one person ought to give up his life to save the life of the one other person who is not a more valuable member of the community. It is true that we glorify the sacrifice of the individual who throws herself in front of the attacker's bullets saving the life of her lover at the cost of her own. But here is the ____(7)____: Her life is as important as his. Nothing is gained in the transaction; not from the community's viewpoint, for one life was exchanged for another equally as important; not from the heroine's viewpoint, for she is ____(8)____; and not from the rescued lover's perspective, for he would willingly have exchanged places.

7. **(A)** beauty of human love

(B) tragedy of life

(C) inevitability of death

(D) defining characteristic of human existence

(E) paradox of self-sacrifice

8. **(A)** dying

(B) in love

(C) dead

(D) a heroine

(E) a faithful companion

9. For the reason that the university's senior tenured faculty is still quite young and therefore many years away from retirement, it seems unlikely that the junior faculty will be able to easily achieve tenure in the foreseeable future.

(A) For the reason that

(B) Because

(C) Being that

(D) On account of

(E) In that

10. Just as William Shakespeare was the preeminent poet of England, so Robert Frost was the preeminent poet of the United States.

(A) Just as William Shakespeare was the preeminent poet of England, so Robert Frost

(B) Just like William Shakespeare was the preeminent poet of England, so Robert Frost

(C) As William Shakespeare was the preeminent poet of England, Robert Frost

(D) Just as England's preeminent poet was William Shakespeare, Robert Frost

(E) As William Shakespeare was the preeminent poet of England, in the same manner Robert Frost

11. Jonas Salk, an American physician whose careful studies demonstrated a means of providing lasting immunity to polio.

    (A) Jonas Salk, an American physician whose careful studies demonstrated a means of providing lasting immunity to polio.

    (B) Providing lasting immunity to polio was demonstrated by Jonas Salk, an American physician with careful studies.

    (C) Jonas Salk was an American physician who had careful studies which demonstrated a means of providing lasting immunity to polio.

    (D) Jonas Salk was an American physician whose careful studies demonstrated a means of providing lasting immunity to polio.

    (E) Jonas Salk, whose careful studies demonstrated a means of providing lasting immunity to polio, an American physician.

QUESTIONS 12–18

In the art of the Middle Ages, we never encounter the personality of the artist as an individual; rather it is diffused through the artistic genius of centuries embodied in the rules of religious art. Art of the Middle Ages is first a sacred script, the symbols and meanings of which were well settled. The circular halo placed vertically behind the head signifies sainthood, while the halo impressed with a cross signifies divinity. By bare feet, we recognize God, the angels, Jesus Christ and the apostles, but for an artist to have depicted the Virgin Mary with bare feet would have been tantamount to heresy. Several concentric, wavy lines represent the sky, while parallel lines water or the sea. A tree, which is to say a single stalk with two or three stylized leaves, informs us that the scene is laid on earth. A tower with a window indicates a village, and, should an angel be watching from the battlements, that city is thereby identified as Jerusalem. Saint Peter is always depicted with curly hair, a short beard, and a tonsure, while Saint Paul has always a bald head and a long beard.

A second characteristic of this iconography is obedience to a sacred mathematics. "The Divine Wisdom," wrote Saint Augustine, "reveals itself everywhere in numbers," a doctrine attributable to the neo-Platonists who revived the genius of Pythagoras. Twelve is the master number of the Church and is the product of three, the number of the Trinity, and four, the number of material elements. The number seven, the most mysterious of all numbers, is the sum of four and three. There are the seven ages of man, seven virtues, seven planets. In the final analysis, the seven-tone scale of Gregorian music is the sensible embodiment of the order of the universe. Numbers also require a symmetry. At Chartres, a stained glass window shows the four prophets, Isaiah, Ezekiel, Daniel, and Jeremiah, carrying on their shoulders the four evangelists, Matthew, Mark, Luke and John.

A third characteristic of this art is to be a symbolic language, showing us one thing and inviting us to see another. In this respect, the artist was called upon to imitate God, who had hidden a profound meaning behind the literal and wished nature itself to be a moral lesson to man. Thus, every painting is an allegory. In a scene of the final judgment, we see the foolish virgins at the left hand of Jesus and the wise at his right, and we understand that this symbolizes those who are lost and those who are saved. Even seemingly insignificant details carry hidden meaning: The lion in a stained glass window is the figure of the Resurrection.

These, then, are the defining characteristics of the art of the Middle Ages, a system within which even the most mediocre talent was elevated by the genius of the centuries. The artists of the early Renaissance broke with tradition at their own peril. When they are not outstanding, they are scarcely able to avoid insignificance and banality in their religious works, and, even when they are great, they are no more than the equals of the old masters who passively followed the sacred rules.

12. The primary purpose of the passage is to
    - **(A)** theorize about the immediate influences on art of the Middle Ages
    - **(B)** explain why artists of the Middle Ages followed the rules of a sacred script
    - **(C)** discuss some of the important features of art of the Middle Ages
    - **(D)** contrast the art of the Middle Ages with that of the Renaissance
    - **(E)** explain why the Middle Ages had a passion for order and numbers

13. It can be inferred that a painting done in the Middle Ages is most likely to contain
    - **(A)** elements representing the numbers three and four
    - **(B)** a moral lesson hidden behind the literal figures
    - **(C)** highly stylized buildings and trees
    - **(D)** figures with halos and bare feet
    - **(E)** a signature of the artist and the date of execution

14. Which of the following best describes the attitude of the author toward art of the Middle Ages?
    - **(A)** The author understands and admires it.
    - **(B)** The author regards it as the greatest art of all time.
    - **(C)** The author prefers the music of the period to its painting.
    - **(D)** The author realizes the constraints placed on the artist and is disappointed that individuality is never evident.
    - **(E)** The author regards it generally as inferior to the works produced during the period preceding it.

15. The author refers to Saint Augustine in order to
    - **(A)** refute a possible objection
    - **(B)** ridicule a position
    - **(C)** present a suggestive analogy
    - **(D)** avoid a contradiction
    - **(E)** provide proof by illustration

16. All of the following are mentioned in the passage as elements of the sacred script EXCEPT
    - **(A)** abstract symbols such as lines to represent physical features
    - **(B)** symbols such as halos and crosses
    - **(C)** clothing used to characterize individuals
    - **(D)** symmetrical juxtaposition of figures
    - **(E)** use of figures to identify locations

17. The passage would most likely be found in a
    - **(A)** sociological analysis of the Middle Ages
    - **(B)** treatise on the influence of the Church in the Middle Ages
    - **(C)** scholarly analysis of art in the Middle Ages
    - **(D)** preface to a biography of Saint Augustine
    - **(E)** pamphlet discussing religious beliefs

18. By the phrase "diffused through the artistic genius of centuries," the author most likely means
    - **(A)** the individual artists of the Middle Ages did not have serious talent
    - **(B)** great works of art from the Middle Ages have survived until now
    - **(C)** an artist who faithfully followed the rules of religious art was not recognized during his lifetime
    - **(D)** the rules of religious art, developed over time, left little freedom for the artist
    - **(E)** religious art has greater value than the secular art of the Renaissance

19. There are no lower bus fares from Washington, D.C., to New York City than those of Flash Bus Line.

Which of the following is logically inconsistent with the above advertising claim?

(A) Long Lines Airways has a Washington, D.C., to New York City fare that is only one-half that charged by Flash.

(B) Rapid Transit Bus Company charges the same fare for a trip from Washington, D.C., to New York City as Flash charges.

(C) Cherokee Bus Corporation has a lower fare from New York City to Boston than does Flash.

(D) Linea Rapida Bus Company has a New York City to Washington, D.C. fare that is less than the corresponding fare of Flash Bus Lines.

(E) Birch Bus Lines offers a late-night fare from Washington, D.C., to New York City that is two-thirds the price of the corresponding fare of Flash Bus Line.

20. It is a well-documented fact that for all teenage couples who marry, the marriages of those who do not have children in the first year of their marriage survive more than twice as long as the marriages of those teenage couples in which the wife does give birth within the first 12 months of marriage. Therefore, many divorces could be avoided if teenagers who marry were encouraged to seek counseling on birth control as soon after marriage as possible.

The evidence regarding teenage marriages supports the author's conclusion only if

(A) in those couples to which a child was born within the first 12 months, there is not a significant number in which the wife was pregnant at the time of marriage

(B) the children born during the first year of marriage to those divorcing couples lived with the teenage couple

(C) the child born into such a marriage did not die at birth

(D) society actually has an interest in determining whether or not people should be divorced if there are not children involved

(E) encouraging people to stay married when they do not plan to have any children is a good idea

21. CLARENCE: Mary is one of the most important executives at the Trendy Cola Company.

PETER: How can that be? I know for a fact that Mary drinks only Hobart Cola.

Peter's statement implies that

(A) Hobart Cola is a subsidiary of Trendy Cola

(B) Mary is an unimportant employee of Hobart Cola

(C) all cola drinks taste pretty much alike

(D) an executive uses only that company's products

(E) Hobart is a better-tasting cola than Trendy

22. The selection in the free-agent draft was based less on the player's availability <u>and more on</u> his willingness to accept a low salary.

(A) and more on

(B) than

(C) but more on

(D) as on

(E) than on

23. The winding roads of San Jacinto Hill <u>were less in number than El Capitan.</u>

(A) were less in number than El Capitan.

(B) were less in number than those of El Capitan.

(C) were fewer in number than that of El Capitan.

(D) were fewer in number than those of El Capitan.

(E) were less than El Capitan.

24. <u>The nurse told me that the doctor's office closes at 5:00 P.M.</u>

(A) The nurse told me that the doctor's office closes at 5:00 P.M.

(B) The nurse told me that the doctor's office closed at 5:00 P.M.

(C) The nurse had told me that the doctor's office had closed at 5:00 P.M.

(D) The nurse told me that the doctor's office had closed at 5:00 P.M.

(E) The nurse told me that the doctor's office would have to close at 5:00 P.M.

25. ERIKA: Participation in intramural competitive sports teaches students the importance of teamwork, for no one wants to let teammates down.

NICHOL: That is not correct. The real reason students play hard is that such programs place a premium on winning and no one wants to be a member of a losing team.

Which of the following comments can most reasonably be made about the exchange between Erika and Nichol?

(A) If fewer and fewer schools are sponsoring intramural sports programs now than a decade ago, Erika's position is undermined.

(B) If high schools and universities provide financial assistance for the purchase of sports equipment, Nichol's assertion about the importance of winning is weakened.

(C) If teamwork is essential to success in intramural competitive sports, Erika's position and Nichol's position are not necessarily incompatible.

(D) Since the argument is one about motivation, it should be possible to resolve the issue by taking a survey of deans at schools that have intramural sports programs.

(E) Since the question raised is about hidden psychological states, it is impossible to answer it.

26. Clark must have known that his sister Janet and not the governess pulled the trigger, but he silently stood by while the jury convicted the governess. Any person of clear conscience would have felt terrible for not having come forward with the information about his sister, and Clark lived with that information until his death 30 years later. Since he was an extremely happy man, however, I conclude that he must have helped Janet commit the crime.

Which of the following assumptions must underlie the author's conclusion of the last sentence?

(A) Loyalty to members of one's family is conducive to contentment.

(B) Servants are not to be treated with the same respect as members of the peer-age.

(C) Clark never had a bad conscience over his silence because he was also guilty of the crime.

(D) It is better to be a virtuous man than a happy one.

(E) It is actually better to be content in life than to behave morally toward one's fellow humans.

27. Current motion pictures give children a distorted view of the world. Animated features depict animals as loyal friends, compassionate creatures, and tender souls, while "spaghetti Westerns" portray men and women as deceitful and treacherous, cruel and wanton, hard and uncaring. Thus, children are taught to value animals more highly than other human beings.

Which of the following, if true, would weaken the author's conclusion?

(A) Children are not allowed to watch "spaghetti Westerns."

(B) The producers of animated features do not want children to regard animals as higher than human beings.

(C) Ancient fables, such as Androcles and the Lion, tell stories of the cooperation between humans and animals, and they usually end with a moral about human virtue.

(D) Children are more likely to choose to watch animated presentations with characters such as animals than those with people as actors.

(E) Animals often exhibit affection, loyalty, protectiveness, and other traits that are considered desirable characteristics in humans.

QUESTIONS 28–34

The most damning thing that can be said about the world's best-endowed and richest country is that it is not only not the leader in health status, but that it is so low in the ranks of the nations. The United States ranks 18th among nations of the world in male life expectancy at birth, 9th in female life expectancy at birth, and 12th in infant mortality. More importantly, huge variations are evident in health status in the United States from one place to the next and from one group to the next.

The forces that affect health can be aggregated into four groupings that lend themselves to analysis of all health problems. Clearly the largest aggregate of forces resides in the person's environment. His own behavior, in part derived from his experiences with his environment, is the next greatest force affecting his health. Medical care services, treated as separate from other environmental factors because of the special interest we have in them, make a modest contribution to health status. Finally, the contributions of heredity to health are difficult to judge. We are templated at conception as to our basic weaknesses and strengths, but many hereditary attributes never become manifest because of environmental and behavioral forces that act before the genetic forces come to maturity and other hereditary attributes are increasingly being palliated by medical care.

No other country spends what we do per capita for medical care. The care available is among the best technically, even if used too lavishly and thus dangerously, but none of the countries which stand above us in health status have such a high proportion of medically disenfranchised persons. Given the evidence that medical care is not that valuable and access to care not that bad, it seems most unlikely that our bad showing is caused by the significant proportion who are poorly served. Other hypotheses have greater explanatory power: excessive poverty, both actual and relative, and excessive affluence.

Excessive poverty is probably more prevalent in the United States than in any of the countries that have a better infant mortality rate and female life expectancy at birth. This is probably true also for all but four or five of the countries with a longer male life expectancy. In the notably poor countries that exceed us in male survival, difficult living conditions are a more accepted way of life, and, in several of them, a good basic diet, basic medical care, basic education and lifelong employment opportunities are an everyday fact of life. In the United States a national unemployment level of 10 percent may be 40 percent in the ghetto, while less than 4 percent elsewhere. The countries that have surpassed us in health do not have such severe or entrenched problems. Nor is such a high proportion of their people involved in them.

Excessive affluence is not so obvious a cause of ill health, but, at least until recently, few other nations could afford such unhealthful ways of living. Excessive intake of animal protein and fats, dangerous imbibing of alcohol, use of tobacco and drugs (prescribed and proscribed), and dangerous recreational sports and driving habits are all possible only because of affluence. Our heritage, desires, opportunities and our macho, combined with the relatively low cost of bad foods and speedy vehicles, make us particularly vulnerable to our affluence. And those who are not affluent try harder. Our unacceptable health status, then, will not be improved appreciably by expanded medical resources nor by their redistribution so much as a general attempt to improve the quality of life for all.

28. Which of the following would be the most logical continuation of the passage?

(A) Suggestions for specific proposals to improve the quality of life in America

(B) A listing of the most common causes of death among male and female adults

(C) An explanation of the causes of poverty in America, both absolute and relative

(D) A proposal to ensure that residents of central cities receive more and better medical care

(E) A study of the overcrowding in urban hospitals serving primarily the poor

29. All of the following are mentioned in the passage as factors affecting the health of the population EXCEPT

(A) the availability of medical care services

(B) the genetic endowment of individuals

(C) overall environmental factors

(D) the nation's relative position in health status

(E) an individual's own behavior

30. The author is primarily concerned with

(A) condemning the United States for its failure to provide better medical care to the poor

(B) evaluating the relative significance of factors contributing to the poor health status in the United States.

(C) providing information which the reader can use to improve his or her personal health

(D) comparing the general health of the U.S. population with world averages

(E) advocating specific measures designed to improve the health of the U.S. population

31. The passage best supports which of the following conclusions about the relationship between per capita expenditures for medical care and the health of a population?

(A) The per capita expenditure for medical care has relatively little effect on the total amount of medical care available to a population.

(B) The genetic makeup of a population is a more powerful determinant of the health of a population than the per capita expenditure for medical care.

(C) A population may have very high per capita expenditures for medical care and yet have a lower health status than other populations with lower per capita expenditures.

(D) The higher the per capita expenditure on medical care, the more advanced is the medical technology; the more advanced the technology, the better is the health of the population.

(E) Per capita outlays for medical care devoted to adults are likely to have a greater effect on the status of the population than outlays devoted to infants.

32. The author refers to the excessive intake of alcohol and tobacco and drug use in order to

(A) show that some health problems cannot be attacked by better medical care

(B) demonstrate that use of tobacco and intoxicants is detrimental to health

(C) cite examples of individual behavior which have adverse consequence for health status

(D) refute the contention that poor health is related to access to medical care

(E) illustrate ways in which affluence may contribute to poor health status

33. The passage provides information to answer which of the following questions?

(A) What is the most powerful influence on the health status of a population?

(B) Which nation in the world leads in health status?

(C) Is the life expectancy of males in the United States longer than that of females?

(D) What are the most important genetic factors influencing the health of an individual?

(E) How can the United States reduce the incidence of unemployment in the ghetto?

34. In discussing the forces that influence health, the author implies that medical care services are

(A) the least important of all

(B) a special aspect of an individual's environment

(C) a function of an individual's behavior pattern

(D) becoming less important as technology improves

(E) too expensive for most people

35. There is something irrational about our system of laws. The criminal law punishes a person more severely for having successfully committed a crime than it does a person who fails in his attempt to commit the same crime—even though the same evil intention is present in both cases. But under the civil law a person who attempts to defraud his victim but is unsuccessful is not required to pay damages.

Which of the following, if true, would most weaken the author's argument?

(A) Most persons who are imprisoned for crimes will commit another crime if they are ever released from prison.

(B) A person is morally culpable for his evil thoughts as well as for his evil deeds.

(C) There are more criminal laws on the books than there are civil laws on the books.

(D) A criminal trial is considerably more costly to the state than a civil trial.

(E) The goal of the criminal law is to punish the criminal, but the goal of the civil law is to compensate the victim.

36. In his most recent speech, my opponent, Governor Smith, accused me of having distorted the facts, misrepresenting his own position, suppressing information, and deliberately lying to the people.

Which of the following possible responses by this speaker would be LEAST relevant to his dispute with Governor Smith?

(A) Governor Smith would not have begun to smear me if he did not sense that his own campaign was in serious trouble.

(B) Governor Smith apparently misunderstood my characterization of his position, so I will attempt to state more clearly my understanding of it.

(C) At the time I made those remarks, certain key facts were not available, but new information uncovered by my staff does support the position I took at that time.

(D) I can only wish Governor Smith had specified those points he considered to be lies so that I could have responded to them now.

(E) With regard to the allegedly distorted facts, the source of my information is a Department of Transportation publication entitled "Safe Driving."

37. It has been shown through extensive physical and statistical testing that domestic cars <u>accelerate like foreign cars do.</u>

(A) accelerate like foreign cars do.

(B) can accelerate like foreign cars do.

(C) accelerate as foreign cars.

(D) accelerate as foreign cars do.

(E) will accelerate as foreign cars.

practice test

38. Results of the recent study make it mandatory that the Surgeon General rejects implementation of the experimental procedure.

(A) rejects

(B) should reject

(C) reject

(D) must reject

(E) will reject

39. Politicians are primarily concerned with their own survival; artists are concerned with revealing truth. Of course, the difference in their reactions is readily predictable. For example, while the governmental leaders wrote laws to ensure the triumph of industrialization in Western Europe, artists painted, wrote about, and composed music in response to the horrible conditions created by the Industrial Revolution. Only later did political leaders come to see what the artists had immediately perceived, and then only through a glass darkly. Experience teaches us that ________.

Which of the following represents the most logical continuation of the passage?

(A) artistic vision perceives in advance of political practice

(B) artists are utopian by nature while governmental leaders are practical

(C) throughout history political leaders have not been very responsive to the needs of their people

(D) the world would be a much better place to live if only artists would become kings

(E) history is the best judge of the progress of civilization

40. A parent must be constant and even-handed in the imposition of burdens and punishments and the distribution of liberties and rewards. In good times, a parent who too quickly bestows rewards creates an expectation of future rewards that he may be unable to fulfill during bad times. In bad times, a parent who waits too long to impose the punishment gives the impression that his response was forced, and the child may interpret this as ________.

Which of the following represents the most logical continuation of the passage?

(A) a signal from his parent that the parent is no longer interested in the child's welfare

(B) a sign of weakness in the parent that he can exploit

(C) indicating a willingness on the part of the parent to bargain away liberties in exchange for the child's assuming some new responsibilities.

(D) an open invitation to retaliate

(E) a symbol of his becoming an adult

41. Fidel Castro found it simple to seize power, but maintaining it difficult.

(A) maintaining it difficult.

(B) its maintenance difficult.

(C) difficult to maintain it.

(D) difficulty was experienced in maintaining it.

(E) difficult inasmuch as maintaining it was concerned.

QUANTITATIVE SECTION

37 Questions • 75 Minutes

Directions: For each of the following questions, choose the correct answer. To simulate the experience of taking the CAT, answer each question in order. Do not skip any questions, and do not go back to any questions you have already answered.
Numbers: All numbers used are real numbers.
Figures: The diagrams and figures that accompany these questions are for the purpose of providing information useful in answering the questions. Unless it is stated that a specific figure is not drawn to scale, the diagrams and figures are drawn as accurately as possible. All figures are in a plane unless otherwise indicated.
For Data Sufficiency questions: Each question is followed by two numbered facts. You are to determine whether the data given in the statements are sufficient for answering the question. Use the data given, plus your knowledge of math and everyday facts, to choose between the five possible answers.

Example:

Q Which copy machine, X or Y, makes copies at the faster rate?

(1) Machine X makes 90 copies per minute.

(2) In three minutes, X makes 1.5 more copies than Y.

(A) statement 1 alone is sufficient to answer the question, but statement 2 alone is not sufficient

(B) statement 2 alone is sufficient to answer the question, but statement 1 alone is not sufficient

(C) both statements together are needed to answer the question, but neither statement alone is sufficient

(D) either statement by itself is sufficient to answer the question

(E) not enough facts are given to answer the question

A **The correct answer is (B).**

1. If the average of x, y, and 30 is 10, then the average of x and y is

(A) 0

(B) 5

(C) $7\frac{1}{2}$

(D) 10

(E) 30

2. All of the 120 seniors in Coolidge High School are members of the chess club, the pep club, or both. If 90 seniors are in the pep club and 70 seniors are in the chess club, how many seniors are in both clubs?

(A) 10

(B) 20

(C) 30

(D) 40

(E) 50

3. Exactly how many pennies are there in Jean's piggy bank?
   (1) There are more than 7 pennies in the bank.
   (2) There are fewer than 9 pennies in the bank.
   (A) statement 1 alone is sufficient to answer the question, but statement 2 alone is not sufficient
   (B) statement 2 alone is sufficient to answer the question, but statement 1 alone is not sufficient
   (C) both statements together are needed to answer the question, but neither statement alone is sufficient
   (D) either statement by itself is sufficient to answer the question
   (E) not enough facts are given to answer the question

4. Joe bought a $2,400 microcomputer on a monthly payment plan. How much money does Joe still owe on the computer?
   (1) He has made six payments.
   (2) He still owes ten payments of $150 each.
   (A) statement 1 alone is sufficient to answer the question, but statement 2 alone is not sufficient
   (B) statement 2 alone is sufficient to answer the question, but statement 1 alone is not sufficient
   (C) both statements together are needed to answer the question, but neither statement alone is sufficient
   (D) either statement by itself is sufficient to answer the question
   (E) not enough facts are given to answer the question

5. Does $x = 15$?
   (1) The average of x, y, and z is 5.
   (2) $y = -z$
   (A) statement 1 alone is sufficient to answer the question, but statement 2 alone is not sufficient
   (B) statement 2 alone is sufficient to answer the question, but statement 1 alone is not sufficient
   (C) both statements together are needed to answer the question, but neither statement alone is sufficient
   (D) either statement by itself is sufficient to answer the question
   (E) not enough facts are given to answer the question

6. How far is gas station X from gas station Z?
   (1) Gas station Y is 5 miles from gas station Z.
   (2) Gas station X is 3 miles from gas station Y.
   (A) statement 1 alone is sufficient to answer the question, but statement 2 alone is not sufficient
   (B) statement 2 alone is sufficient to answer the question, but statement 1 alone is not sufficient
   (C) both statements together are needed to answer the question, but neither statement alone is sufficient
   (D) either statement by itself is sufficient to answer the question
   (E) not enough facts are given to answer the question

7. What was the annual interest earned on a savings account of $3,000?
   (1) The rate of interest on the account was $5\frac{1}{4}$% annual simple interest.
   (2) The account was maintained for 10 years.
   (A) statement 1 alone is sufficient to answer the question, but statement 2 alone is not sufficient
   (B) statement 2 alone is sufficient to answer the question, but statement 1 alone is not sufficient
   (C) both statements together are needed to answer the question, but neither statement alone is sufficient
   (D) either statement by itself is sufficient to answer the question
   (E) not enough facts are given to answer the question

8. Is Susan taller than Jill?

(1) Susan is taller than Beth.

(2) Beth is shorter than Jill.

(A) statement 1 alone is sufficient to answer the question, but statement 2 alone is not sufficient

(B) statement 2 alone is sufficient to answer the question, but statement 1 alone is not sufficient

(C) both statements together are needed to answer the question, but neither statement alone is sufficient

(D) either statement by itself is sufficient to answer the question

(E) not enough facts are given to answer the question

9. If a and b are positive integers and $a^3b^2 = 72$, then $a + b =$

(A) 36

(B) 17

(C) 8

(D) 6

(E) 5

10. $\frac{.250}{.333}$ divided by $\frac{.125}{.167}$ is most nearly

(A) 10

(B) 5

(C) 1

(D) .667

(E) .500

11. Which of the following fractions is closest to 1 given that $a > b > 1$?

(A) $\frac{a}{b}$

(B) $\frac{(a+2)}{(b+2)}$

(C) $\frac{(a+1)}{(b+1)}$

(D) $\frac{(a+1)}{b}$

(E) $\frac{(a-1)}{(b-1)}$

12. In an office with 21 staff members, $\frac{1}{3}$ are men and $\frac{2}{3}$ are women. To obtain a staff in which $\frac{1}{4}$ are men, how many women should be hired?

(A) 7

(B) 5

(C) 3

(D) 2

(E) 1

13. In college X, 40 percent of the women and 20 percent of the men are taking courses in mathematics. If 55 percent of the students at college X are women, what percent of all college X students take mathematics courses?

(A) 35

(B) 31

(C) 30

(D) 26

(E) 25

14. If cylinder A has three times the height and one-third the diameter of cylinder B, what is the ratio of the volume of A to the volume of B?

(A) 3:1

(B) 1:1

(C) 1:3

(D) 1:9

(E) 1:27

practice test

15. What is the 57th number in a series of numbers?

(1) Each number in the series is 3 more than the preceding number.

(2) The tenth number in the series is 29.

(A) statement 1 alone is sufficient to answer the question, but statement 2 alone is not sufficient

(B) statement 2 alone is sufficient to answer the question, but statement 1 alone is not sufficient

(C) both statements together are needed to answer the question, but neither statement alone is sufficient

(D) either statement by itself is sufficient to answer the question

(E) not enough facts are given to answer the question

16. A jogger desires to run a certain course in $\frac{1}{4}$ less time than she usually takes. By what percent must she increase her average running speed to accomplish this goal?

(A) 20%

(B) 25%

(C) $33\frac{1}{3}\%$

(D) 50%

(E) 75%

17. John took a test composed of 125 questions. What percent of all the questions on the test did John answer correctly?

(1) He left 20 of the questions blank.

(2) He answered 53 of the questions correctly.

(A) statement 1 alone is sufficient to answer the question, but statement 2 alone is not sufficient

(B) statement 2 alone is sufficient to answer the question, but statement 1 alone is not sufficient

(C) both statements together are needed to answer the question, but neither statement alone is sufficient

(D) either statement by itself is sufficient to answer the question

(E) not enough facts are given to answer the question

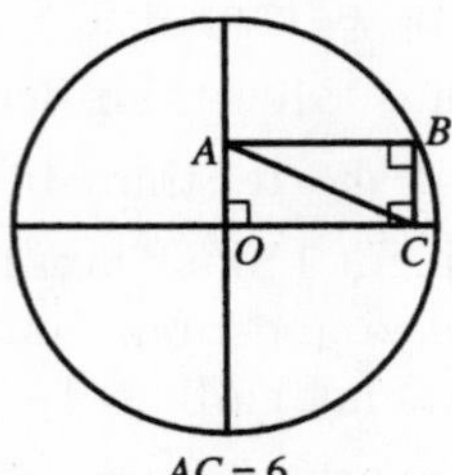

18. What is the area of circle O above?

(A) 24π

(B) 36π

(C) 48π

(D) 64π

(E) 72π

19. A magazine costs $1.00 per copy to produce. If $20,000 was taken in for advertising in the magazine, how many copies at 75 cents per copy must be sold to make a profit of exactly $10,000?

(A) 10,000

(B) 20,000

(C) 25,000

(D) 35,000

(E) 40,000

20. If a is a positive integer and if remainders of 4 and 6 are obtained when 89 and 125, respectively, are divided by a, then $a =$

(A) 7

(B) 9

(C) 15

(D) 17

(E) 19

21. A pen-and-pencil set costs $12, the same as when the items are bought separately. If the pen costs $11 more than the pencil, what is the cost of the pencil?

(A) $0.50

(B) $1.00

(C) $1.50

(D) $6.00

(E) $11.00

22. A salesman makes a commission of x percent on the first \$2,000 worth of sales in any given month and y percent on all further sales during that month. If he makes \$700 from \$4,000 of sales in October and he makes \$900 from \$5,000 of sales in November, what is the value of x?

(A) 2%

(B) 5%

(C) 10%

(D) 15%

(E) 20%

23. What percent of the selling price of item X was profit?

(1) The profit was \$20 less than the selling price of item X.

(2) The cost of the item was $\frac{3}{4}$ of the selling price.

(A) statement 1 alone is sufficient to answer the question, but statement 2 alone is not sufficient

(B) statement 2 alone is sufficient to answer the question, but statement 1 alone is not sufficient

(C) both statements together are needed to answer the question, but neither statement alone is sufficient

(D) either statement by itself is sufficient to answer the question

(E) not enough facts are given to answer the question

24. If a is a positive integer, what is the value of 75 percent of $\frac{b}{a}$?

(1) $a = 2$

(2) $b = 4a$

(A) statement 1 alone is sufficient to answer the question, but statement 2 alone is not sufficient

(B) statement 2 alone is sufficient to answer the question, but statement 1 alone is not sufficient

(C) both statements together are needed to answer the question, but neither statement alone is sufficient

(D) either statement by itself is sufficient to answer the question

(E) not enough facts are given to answer the question

25. What are the chances that a die will come up six on the fifth roll?

(1) It is a normal six-sided die which is unbiased and always comes up either one, two, three, four, five, or six.

(2) The first four rolls came up six.

(A) statement 1 alone is sufficient to answer the question, but statement 2 alone is not sufficient

(B) statement 2 alone is sufficient to answer the question, but statement 1 alone is not sufficient

(C) both statements together are needed to answer the question, but neither statement alone is sufficient

(D) either statement by itself is sufficient to answer the question

(E) not enough facts are given to answer the question

26. How old is Robert now?

(1) The product of his age now and his age five years from now is 24.

(2) Six years from now he will be three times as old as he is now.

(A) statement 1 alone is sufficient to answer the question, but statement 2 alone is not sufficient

(B) statement 2 alone is sufficient to answer the question, but statement 1 alone is not sufficient

(C) both statements together are needed to answer the question, but neither statement alone is sufficient

(D) either statement by itself is sufficient to answer the question

(E) not enough facts are given to answer the question

27. How many square floor tiles with each side x will it take to cover a rectangular kitchen floor?

(1) The width of the kitchen floor is $10x$.

(2) The length of the kitchen floor is $30x$.

(A) statement 1 alone is sufficient to answer the question, but statement 2 alone is not sufficient

(B) statement 2 alone is sufficient to answer the question, but statement 1 alone is not sufficient

(C) both statements together are needed to answer the question, but neither statement alone is sufficient

(D) either statement by itself is sufficient to answer the question

(E) not enough facts are given to answer the question

28. A magician wants to ship a magic wand to the location of his next show. The rectangular box he has available for this purpose measures 6 inches wide by 8 inches long by 10 inches high. What is the longest cylindrical wand of negligible diameter that can be shipped in this box?

(A) 10 inches

(B) $8\sqrt{2}$ inches

(C) $8\sqrt{3}$ inches

(D) $10\sqrt{2}$ inches

(E) $10\sqrt{3}$ inches

29. The price of a left-handed widget increased 20 percent in 1981 and 10 percent in 1982. By approximately what percent would the price at the end of 1982 have to be decreased to restore the price of the widget to its pre-1981 price?

(A) 40%

(B) 35%

(C) 30%

(D) 26%

(E) 24%

30. Patricia invested a sum of money at an annual simple interest rate of $10\frac{1}{2}$%. At the end of 4 years the amount invested plus interest earned was $781.00. What was the dollar amount of the original investment?

(A) $231.84

(B) $318.16

(C) $550.00

(D) $750.00

(E) $781.84

31. If a taxicab charges x cents for the first $\frac{1}{9}$ mile and $\frac{x}{5}$ cents for each additional $\frac{1}{9}$ mile or fraction thereof, what is the charge, in cents, for a ride of y miles, where y is a whole number?

(A) $x + \frac{xy - x}{45}$

(B) $x - \frac{xy - x}{45}$

(C) $\frac{2x + 9y}{5}$

(D) $x + \frac{9x - y}{5}$

(E) $x + \frac{9xy - x}{5}$

32. The formula for calculating the final velocity of a body, initially at rest, that undergoes a constant acceleration is $v^2 = 2ad$; where v is final velocity, a is acceleration, and d is distance traveled. If a body initially at rest is subjected to a constant acceleration of 10 meters/second^2 until it reaches a velocity of 20 meters/second, how far, expressed in meters, has the body traveled?

(A) 200

(B) 100

(C) 40

(D) 20

(E) 10

33. Two mail sorters, P and Q, work at constant rates. If P can sort x letters in 60 minutes and Q can sort x letters in 30 minutes, how long will it take (expressed in minutes) for both sorters, working together but independently, to sort x letters?

(A) 45

(B) 20

(C) 15

(D) 10

(E) 3

34. If 20 liters of chemical X are added to 80 liters of a mixture that is 10% chemical X and 90% chemical Y, then what percentage of the resulting mixture is chemical X?

(A) 15%

(B) 28%

(C) $33\frac{1}{3}\%$

(D) 40%

(E) 60%

35. What is the height of a cylindrical condensed milk can with a diameter of 4 inches?

(1) The number of cubic inches in the volume of the can is 10π times the radius of the can.

(2) The can holds 2 pounds of milk.

(A) statement 1 alone is sufficient to answer the question, but statement 2 alone is not sufficient

(B) statement 2 alone is sufficient to answer the question, but statement 1 alone is not sufficient

(C) both statements together are needed to answer the question, but neither statement alone is sufficient

(D) either statement by itself is sufficient to answer the question

(E) not enough facts are given to answer the question

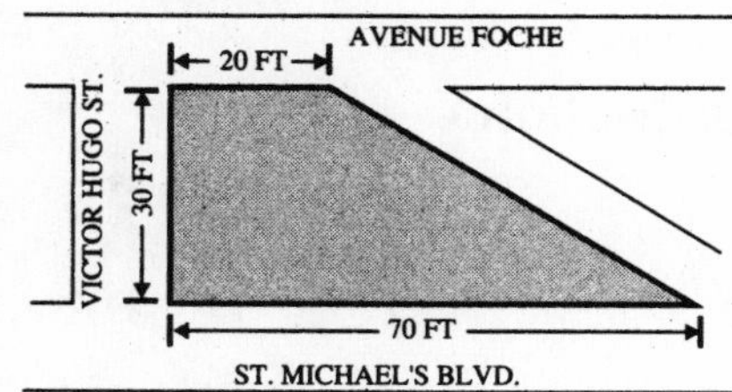

36. In the figure above, all streets run in straight lines. If the angle of intersection of Avenue Foche and Victor Hugo Street is 90° and Avenue Foche is parallel to St. Michael's Boulevard, then what is the area of the shaded portion of the figure (expressed in square feet)?

(A) 600

(B) 750

(C) 1350

(D) 2400

(E) 3750

37. If $a + b + c = 50$, what is the value of a?

(1) $c = 4a - b$

(2) The average of b and c is $2a$.

(A) statement 1 alone is sufficient to answer the question, but statement 2 alone is not sufficient

(B) statement 2 alone is sufficient to answer the question, but statement 1 alone is not sufficient

(C) both statements together are needed to answer the question, but neither statement alone is sufficient

(D) either statement by itself is sufficient to answer the question

(E) not enough facts are given to answer the question

ANSWER KEY AND EXPLANATIONS

Verbal Section

1. E	10. A	19. E	28. A	37. D
2. D	11. D	20. A	29. D	38. C
3. D	12. C	21. D	30. B	39. A
4. D	13. B	22. E	31. C	40. B
5. B	14. A	23. D	32. E	41. C
6. B	15. E	24. A	33. A	
7. E	16. D	25. C	34. B	
8. C	17. C	26. C	35. E	
9. B	18. D	27. A	36. A	

1. **The correct answer is (E).** The original sentence contains two errors. First, when comparing only two items, we must use the comparative degree of the adjective (the *-er* form for most adjectives). Thus the sentence should use "more" rather than "most." Second, the pronoun "their" is plural, but its antecedent or referent is "each," a singular pronoun. This error can be eliminated by changing "their" to "its." (B) and (C) each correct one error but not both. (D) fails to make either correction and commits the additional sin of introducing an illogical change in the number of the subject. Only (E) makes the needed, and only the needed, changes.

2. **The correct answer is (D).** The error in this sentence is one of faulty parallelism. When presenting elements in a series, you should remember to make sure those elements are of similar type, e.g., all clauses, all phrases, all infinitives, all gerunds. Here, the first two elements are noun phrases (. . . service, . . . management). To preserve the parallelism, the third element should have the same form: . . . service, . . . management, . . . facilities. Both (D) and (E) make the required change. (D) is preferable to (E), however, because (E) includes a second—and gratuitous—"its," disrupting the parallelism.

3. **The correct answer is (D).** The sentence contains two errors. First, the phrasing "Men's interest . . . " is both awkward and incorrect. The sentence could be changed to read "Man's interest," but even that is unnecessary. The sentence can be more concisely written as rendered by (D)—and conciseness is important on the test. Second, there is a failure of agreement between subject and verb. The subject of the sentence is "interest," which must take a singular verb; (D) does this by changing "have" to the singular "has."

4. **The correct answer is (D).** We take the first three propositions together and ignore the fourth since we are to assume it is false. Roberts cannot be convicted without Edwards' testimony (I), but that testimony will show that Edwards participated in the crime (II). But if Edwards participated in the crime, Roberts cannot be convicted of it because he is accused of a crime that can be committed only by a person acting alone (III). Either Edwards will testify or Edwards will not

testify—that is a tautology (logically true). If Edwards testifies, according to our reasoning, Roberts cannot be convicted. If Edwards does not testify, Roberts cannot be convicted (I). Either way, Roberts will not be convicted. (E) cannot be correct since we have no way of knowing, as a matter of logic, whether Edwards will or will not testify. We know only that *if* he does, certain consequences will follow, and *if* he does not, other consequences will follow. (A) can be disregarded since the crime is one that only a solo actor can commit (III). (C) is incorrect because we have proved that, regardless of Edwards' course of action, Roberts cannot be convicted. Finally, (B) is a logical *possibility,* which is not precluded by the given information, but we cannot logically deduce it from the information given.

5. **The correct answer is (B).** Examine carefully the connection between II and IV. Suppose Edwards testifies. His testimony will show he too has committed some wrong (II); but when the jury learns this, they will not believe any part of that testimony (IV), which means that they will not believe Edwards committed the wrong—a contradiction. Since II and IV cannot both be true at the same time, the scenario they describe is an impossible one—like saying a circle is a square. The remaining answers are all distractions.

6. **The correct answer is (B).** The error here is a failure of agreement between subject and verb. The subject of the sentence is "delegates," so the verb should be the plural "were." The pronoun "their" is correct as written, so any choice which fails to correct the error or gratuitously changes the number of "their" is incorrect.

7. **The correct answer is (E).** In the very first sentence, the author remarks that this is "curious" and a "contradiction," so the only correct answer choice will be one that follows up on this idea as (E) does when it speaks of *paradox.* Nothing that precedes the blank suggests that the author is speaking of "beauty" or "tragedy," so (A) and (B) can be disregarded. As for (C), the passage does speak about death, but not of death's inevitability; rather it dwells on death under certain circumstances that may not be inevitable. As for (D), while death may characterize human existence, the kind of death mentioned—self-sacrifice—is not indicated to be an inherent part of all human life.

8. **The correct answer is (C).** The author shows, from three different perspectives, why the sacrifice is meaningless. The community does not win, because both lives were equally important. The lover who is saved does not profit, and that is shown by the fact that he would be perfectly willing to do the transaction the other way. If he has no preference (or even prefers the alternative outcome, his death), it cannot be said that he benefited from the exchange of lives. Finally, the need to prove that the action has no value to the heroine: The author says she does not benefit because she is not in a position to enjoy or savor, or whatever, her heroism. The reason for that is that she is *dead* (C), not dying (A), for dying would leave open the possibility that her sacrifice would bring her joy in her last minutes, and then the author's contention that the transaction has *no* value would be weakened. (D) is wrong, for it is specifically stated that she is a heroine, so it is an inappropriate *completion* of the sentence. (B) and (E) may both be true, but they do not explain why the action has no value to anyone.

9. **The correct answer is (B).** The construction "For the reason that" is just not acceptable usage. (C), (D), and (E) are also unacceptable constructions in Standard Written English. In general, as a matter of test-taking tactics, choose a simple and direct construction.

answers

10. The correct answer is (A). The sentence contains no error. (B) introduces an error by changing "as" to "like," substituting a preposition for a conjunction, but the sentence needs a conjunction to join the two clauses. (D) introduces an error in parallelism by changing the order of the subject and the predicate complement. (E) introduces an awkward phrasing in the main clause. (C) is a bit more subtle. First, the changes made by (C) alter slightly the meaning of the sentence. Second, (C) makes changes which are not required, and, as a matter of tactics, you should make no change unless you have a justification for that change. The justification need not be couched in formal terms, but it should be more than "I just don't like it." You should be able to pinpoint an error, explain in informal terms why it is an error, and then find a sentence that corrects the error before you make any change.

11. The correct answer is (D). The sentence is not really a sentence at all, only a sentence fragment, for the original phrasing contains no verb for which "Jonas Salk" is the subject. (E) suffers from the same defect. (B) and (C) have the merit of introducing a verb, but both (B) and (C) are incorrect because of awkward and, in (C)'s case, incorrect structure.

12. The correct answer is (C). This is obviously a main idea question. The author discusses three important characteristics of art of the Middle Ages—the sacred script, the sacred mathematics, and sacred symbolic language. In the final paragraph, the author mentions in passing the Renaissance, primarily as a way of praising the art of the Middle Ages. (C) does a fair job of describing this development. (A) can be eliminated because the discussion focuses on the art of the Middle Ages, not on the art preceding the Middle Ages. And a mention of what might be called influences, e.g., the revival of certain views of Pythagoras, is done only in passing. (D) is incorrect for the same sort of reason. The closing reference to art of the Renaissance cannot be considered the overall theme of the passage. Finally, (B) and (E) are incorrect because the author never takes on the "why."

13. The correct answer is (B). This is an inference question. In essence, the question is asking which of the five features listed was most likely to be found in a painting. (E) can be eliminated since that is inconsistent with the idea of the artist who recedes into the background of the sacred rules. As for (A), the author's only example of numbers was their use in music. This does not lead us to conclude that numbers might not be important in painting as well, but we cannot conclude on the other hand that every painting was likely to use the numbers three or four. (C) and (D) are mentioned as characteristics of certain subjects, but the author does not imply that the subjects were treated in every painting. (B), however, has the specific support of paragraph 3. There the author states that "every painting is an allegory." So, though the specific content of paintings of the period would vary from work to work, the technique of a literal image and a hidden meaning pervaded the work of the period.

14. The correct answer is (A). The tone of the passage is clearly one of appreciation—in the sense that the author both understands the art and admires it. This is further supported by the contrast between art of the Middle Ages and religious art of the Renaissance at the end of the passage. (B) overstates the case. The author is only discussing the one period, with only casual reference to the period following it. We cannot conclude from this discussion of art of the Middle Ages that the author considers this art the greatest of all art. (C) cannot be deduced from the passage, for the reference to music will not support such a judgment. (D) is inconsistent with the author's opening and closing remarks. Finally, (E), too, must be incorrect given the generally approving treatment of the passage.

15. **The correct answer is (E).** This is a question about a logical detail: Why does the author quote Saint Augustine? At that point, the author has just asserted that the art of the Middle Ages also is characterized by a passion for numbers. Then the author quotes a statement from Augustine which makes that very point. The reason for the quotation must be to give an example of the general attitude toward numbers. Answer choice (E) describes this move. (A) is incorrect since no objection is mentioned. (B) is incorrect for the same reason, and for the further reason that "ridicule" is inconsistent with the tone of the passage. (C) is incorrect because the author is not attempting to demonstrate the similarities between two things. Finally, (D) is incorrect since it does not appear that the author is in any danger of falling into a contradiction.

16. **The correct answer is (D).** This is an explicit idea question. Each of the incorrect answers is mentioned in the first paragraph as an element of the sacred script. As for (A), lines may be used to represent water or the sky. As for (B), these indicate sainthood or divinity. As for (C), shoes are mentioned as an identifying characteristic. And (E) also is mentioned (a tree represents earth). (D), however, is not mentioned as an element of the sacred script. Symmetry is discussed in conjunction with numbers, and that has to do with another characteristic altogether.

17. **The correct answer is (C).** This is an application question. Of course, we do not know where the passage actually appeared, and the task is to pick the most likely source. We stress this because it is always possible to make an argument for any of the answer choices to a question of this sort. But the fact that a justification is possible does not make that choice correct. The strongest possible justification makes the correct choice correct. (C) is the most likely source. The passage focuses on art and is scholarly in tone. (A) can be eliminated because the passage casts no light on social conditions of the period. (B) can be eliminated for a similar reason. The author treats art in and of itself, not as a social force. And certainly we cannot conclude that by discussing religious art the author wants to discuss the Church. (D) is incorrect because the reference to Saint Augustine is incidental and illustrative only. (E) is incorrect because it is inconsistent with the scholarly and objective tone of the passage.

18. **The correct answer is (D).** This is an inferred idea question, one asking for an interpretation of a phrase. The idea of the first paragraph is that the rules of art in the Middle Ages place constraints on the artist so that his artistic effort had to be made within certain conventions. As a result, painting was not individualistic. This is most clearly expressed by (D). (A) is incorrect since the author is saying that the artist's talent just did not show as individual talent. (B) is incorrect, for though this is a true statement, it is not a response to the question. (C) is perhaps the second best answer because it at least hints at what (D) says more clearly. But the author does not mean to say the artist was not recognized in his lifetime. Perhaps he was. What the author means to say is that we do not now see the personality of the artist. Finally, (E) is just a confused reading of a part of the passage not relevant here.

19. **The correct answer is (E).** This question is primarily a matter of careful reading. The phrase "no lower bus fares" must not be read to mean that Flash uniquely

has the lowest fare; it means only that no one else has a fare lower than that of Flash. It is conceivable that several companies share the lowest fare. So (B) is not inconsistent with the claim made in the advertisement. (C) is not inconsistent since it mentions the New York City to Boston route, and it is the Washington, D.C., to New York City route that is the subject of the ad's claim. (A) is not inconsistent since it speaks of an *air* fare and the ad's language carefully restricts the claim to *bus* fares. (D) is a bit tricky, but the ad cites only the D.C. to New York trip—(D) talks about the New York to D.C. trip. So there is no contradiction. (E) is clearly a contradiction, and this is a good time to remind you to read all of the choices before selecting one. You might have bitten on (D), but when you see (E), you know that it is a better answer.

20. **The correct answer is (A).** The main point of the passage is that pregnancy and a child put strain on a young marriage, and so such marriages would have a higher survival rate without the strain of children. It would seem, then, that encouraging such couples not to have children would help them stay married; but that will be possible only if they have not already committed themselves, so to speak, to having a child. If the wife is already pregnant at the time of marriage, the commitment has already been made, so the advice is too late. (B) and (C) are wrong for similar reasons. It is not only the continued presence of the child in the marriage that causes the stress but the very pregnancy and birth. So (B) and (C) do not address themselves to the *birth* of the child, and that is the factor to which the author attributes the dissolution of the marriage. (D) is wide of the mark. Whether society does or does not have such an interest, the author has shown us a causal linkage, that is, a mere fact of the matter. The author states: If this, then fewer divorces. The author may or may not believe there should be fewer divorces. (E) is wrong for this reason also, and for the further reason that it says "do not *plan*" to have children. The author's concern is with children during the early part of the marriage. There is no suggestion that couples should never have children.

21. **The correct answer is (D).** Peter's surprise is over the fact that an important executive of a company would use a competitor's product, hence (D). (B) is wrong because Peter's surprise is not that Mary is unimportant; rather he knows Mary is important, and that is the reason for surprise. (E) is irrelevant to the exchange, for Peter imagines that regardless of taste, Mary ought to consume the product she is responsible in part for producing. The same reasoning can be applied to (C). Finally, (A) is a business distraction. It has business overtones, but it is important to always keep in mind that this section, like all sections of the GMAT, tests reasoning and reading abilities—not knowledge of business.

22. **The correct answer is (E).** The error in the sentence is an illogical construction. As written, the sentence reads "less on . . . and more on. . . . " The sentence means to say "less on . . . than on. . . . " (E) makes the needed change.

23. **The correct answer is (D).** The sentence contains two errors. First, there is a faulty comparison. As constructed, the sentence makes an attempt to compare the number of winding roads of San Jacinto Hill with El Capitan. But the comparison should be between "roads" and "roads." Second, when referring to discrete quantities, items that can be counted, we use the words "fewer" and "fewest" rather than "less" and "least."

24. **The correct answer is (A).** The sentence is correct as written. The only question is whether the present tense of the

verb is correct. In this case, the sentence uses the present tense, "closes," to assert that this is the usual practice of the doctor. Each alternative answer choice changes the meaning of the sentence. Thus, each alternative choice is incorrect, because it makes a gratuitous change from the original and in so doing, changes the intent of the original sentence.

25. **The correct answer is (C).** The dispute here is over the motivation to compete seriously in intramural sports. Erika claims it is a sense of responsibility to one's fellows; Nichol argues it is a desire to win. But the two may actually support one another. In what way could one possibly let his fellows down? If the sport was not competitive, it would seem there would be no opportunity to disappoint them. So the desire to win contributes to the desire to be an effective member of the team. Nothing in the exchange presupposes anything about the structure of such programs beyond the fact that they are competitive, that is, that they have winners and losers. How many such programs exist, how they are funded, and similar questions are irrelevant, so both (A) and (B) are incorrect. (D) is close to being correct, but it calls for a survey of *deans.* The dean is probably not in a position to describe the motivation of the *participants.* Had (D) specified participants, it too would have been a correct answer. Of course, only one answer can be correct on the GMAT. Finally, (E) must be wrong for the reason cited in explaining (D); it should be possible to find out about the motivation.

26. **The correct answer is (C).** Clark was unhappy if he had a clear conscience but knew, or Clark was happy if he knew but had an unclear conscience. It is not the case that Clark was unhappy, so he must have been happy. Since he knew, however, his happiness must stem from an unclear conscience. (A), (D), and (E) are incorrect because they make irrelevant value judgments. As was just shown, the author's point can be analyzed as a purely logical one. (B) is just distraction, playing on the connection between "governess" and "servant," which, of course, are not the same thing.

27. **The correct answer is (A).** The author's point depends on the *assumption* that children see both animated features and "spaghetti Westerns." Obviously, if that assumption is untrue, he cannot claim that his conclusion follows. It may be true that children get a distorted picture of the world from other causes, but the author has not claimed that. He claims only that it comes from their seeing animated features and "spaghetti Westerns." Presumably, the two different treatments cause the inversion of values. The intention of the producers in making the films is irrelevant since an action may have an effect not intended by the actor. Hence, (B) would not touch the author's point. Further, that there are other sources of information that present a proper view of the world does not prove that the problem cited by the author does not produce an inverted view of the world. So (C) would not weaken his point. (D) reminds us of the importance of careful reading. You might want to interpret (D) to say the same thing as (A), but then you'd have to choose (A) because it makes the telling point more forcefully and directly. Finally, (E) is irrelevant to the author's conclusion: children learn to value animals more than people. Of course, as an exercise in debate, you might argue that this is a good thing, but that is not what (E) says.

28. **The correct answer is (A).** This is an application question. As we have noted before, application questions tend to be difficult because the correct answer can be understood as correct only in context. With an explicit idea question, for ex-

ample, an answer can be understood as right or wrong—either the author said it or he did not. With a question such as this, the *most logical continuation* depends on the choices available. Here the best answer is (A). The author concludes the discussion of the causes of our poor showing on the health status index by asserting that the best way to improve this showing is a general improvement in the quality of life. That is an intriguing suggestion, and an appropriate follow-up would be a list of proposals that might accomplish this. As for (B), this could be part of such a discussion, but a listing of the most common causes of death would not, in and of itself, represent an extension of the development of the argument. (C), too, has some merit. The author might want to talk about the causes of poverty as a way of learning how to improve the quality of life by eliminating the causes. But this argument actually cuts in favor of (A), for the justification for (C) then depends on (A)—that is, it depends on the assumption that the author should discuss the idea raised in (A). (D) is incorrect because the author specifically states in closing that redistribution of medical resources is not a high priority. (E) can be eliminated on the same ground.

29. **The correct answer is (D).** This is an explicit idea question, and we find mention of (A), (B), (C), and (E) in the second paragraph. (D), too, is mentioned, but (D) is not a "factor affecting the health of the population." (D) is a measure of, or an effect of, the health of the population, not a factor causing it.

30. **The correct answer is (B).** This is a main idea question. (A) can be eliminated because the author actually minimizes the importance of medical care as a factor affecting the health of a population. (C) can be eliminated because this is not the author's objective. To be sure, an individual may use information supplied in the passage to improve in some way his or her health, but that is not why the author wrote the passage. (D) is incorrect because this is a small part of the argument, a part which is used to advance the major objective outlined in (B). Finally, (E) is incorrect since the author leaves us with a pregnant suggestion but no specific recommendations. (B), however, describes the development of the passage. The author wishes to explain the causes of the poor health status of the United States. It is not, she argues, lack of medical care or even poor distribution of medical care, hypotheses which, we can infer from the text, are often proposed. She then goes on to give two alternative explanations: affluence and poverty.

31. **The correct answer is (C).** This is an application question. (C) is strongly supported by the text. In the third paragraph, the author specifically states that we have the highest per capita expenditure for medical care in the world. Yet, as she notes in the first paragraph, we rank rather low in terms of health. (A) is not supported by the arguments given in the passage. Though medical care may not be the most important determinant of health, the author never suggests that expenditure is not correlated with overall availability. (B) is incorrect and specifically contradicted by the second paragraph, where the author states that genetic problems may be covered over by medical care. (D) is incorrect since the author minimizes the importance of technology in improving health. Finally, (E) is simply not supported by any data or argument given in the passage.

32. **The correct answer is (E).** This is a logical detail question. The author refers to excess consumption to illustrate the way in which affluence, one of her two hypotheses, could undermine an individual's health. As for (A), while it is

true that such problems may not be susceptible to medical treatment, the author does not introduce them to prove that. She introduces them at the particular point in the argument to prove that affluence can undermine health. (B) is incorrect for a similar reason. The author does not introduce the examples to prove that drinking and smoking are unhealthful activities; she presupposes her readers know that already. Then, on the assumption that the reader already believes that, the author can say, "See, affluence causes smoking and drinking, which we all know to be bad." (C) must fail for the same reason. Finally, (D) is incorrect since this is not the reason for introducing the examples. Although the author does argue that medical care and health are not as tightly linked as some people might think, this is not the point she is working on when she introduces smoking and drinking. With a logical detail question of this sort, we must be careful to select an answer that explains why the author makes the move she does at the particular juncture in the argument. Neither general reference to the overall idea of the passage (e.g., to prove a main point) nor a reference to a collateral argument will do the trick.

33. **The correct answer is (A).** The answer to the question posed in answer choice (A), environment, is explicitly provided in the second paragraph. As for (B), though some information is given about the health status of the United States, no other country is mentioned by name. As for (C), though some statistics are given about life expectancies in the United States, no comparison of male and female life expectancies is given. As for (D), though genetic factors are mentioned generally in the second paragraph, no such factors are ever specified. Finally, the author offers no recommendations, so (E) must be incorrect.

34. **The correct answer is (B).** This is an inferred idea question based on a specific reference. In the second paragraph the author lists four groups of factors that influence health. In referring to medical services, she says they are treated separately from environmental factors because of our special interest in them. This implies that she would actually consider them to be just another, although important, factor in the environment. As for (A), the least important group of factors is specifically stated to be genetic factors. As for (C), there is no support for such a conclusion in that paragraph. The same reason allows us to eliminate both (D) and (E).

35. **The correct answer is (E).** The point of the passage is that there is a seeming contradiction in our body of laws. Sometimes a person pays for his attempted misdeeds, and other times he does not pay for them. If there could be found a good reason for this difference, then the contradiction could be explained away. This is just what (E) does. It points out that the law treats the situations differently because it has different goals: Sometimes we drive fast because we are in a hurry; other times we drive slowly because we want to enjoy the scenery. (B) would not weaken the argument, for it only intensifies the contradiction. (D) makes an attempt to reconcile the seemingly conflicting positions by hinting at a possible goal of one action that is not a goal of the other. But, if anything, it intensifies the contradiction because one might infer that we should not try persons for attempted crimes because criminal trials are expensive, yet we should allow compensation for attempted frauds because civil trials are less expensive. (C) and (A) are just distractions. Whether there are more of one kind of law than another on the books has nothing to do with the seeming contradiction. And

whether persons are more likely to commit a second crime after they are released from prison does not speak to the issue of whether an unsuccessful attempt to commit a crime should be a crime in the first place.

36. **The correct answer is (A).** The question stem asks us to focus on the "dispute" between the two opponents. What will be relevant to it will be those items that affect the merits of the issues, or perhaps those that affect the credibility of the parties. (C) and (E) both mention items—facts and their sources—that would be relevant to the substantive issues. (B) and (D) are legitimate attempts to clarify the issues and so are relevant. (A) is not relevant to the issues, nor is it relevant to the credibility (e.g., where did the facts come from) of the debaters. (A) is the least relevant because it is an *ad hominem* attack (an attack on the person and not on an argument).

37. **The correct answer is (D).** The error in the sentence is its use of the preposition "like." Since "like" is intended to join a clause, we need a conjunction such as "as." (C) and (E) make the needed correction, but (C) introduces a slight ambiguity through its needless change and (E) alters the meaning of the sentence somewhat.

38. **The correct answer is (C).** This is an example of a verb in the subjunctive tense. The subjunctive is used to express a wish, a command or a statement contrary to fact and is indicated by the use of the opposite verb tense. So, whereas "Surgeon General" would normally take the singular verb "rejects," because the question involves a command in the subjunctive tense, the opposite—or plural—verb "reject" is correct.

39. **The correct answer is (A).** The point of the passage is that artists see things as they really are, whereas politicians see things as they want them to be. (B) is wrong, for, if anything, it is the politicians who see things through rose-colored glasses, whereas the artists see the truth of a stark reality. (C) can be overruled, for the passage implies that political leaders are responsive to the needs of people—it is just that they are a little late. Moreover, the point of the passage is to draw a contrast between artists and politicians; and even if the conclusion expressed in (C) is arguably correct, it is not as good an answer choice as (A), which *completes* the comparison. (D) has no ground in the passage. Be careful not to move from an analysis of facts—artists saw the problems earlier than the politicians did—to a conclusion of value or policy—therefore we should turn out the politicians. The author may very well believe that as sad as these circumstances are, nothing can be done about them, e.g., things are bad enough with the politicians in charge, but they would be much worse with artists running things. (E) also finds no ground in the passage.

answers

40. **The correct answer is (B).** The argument for consistency is that it avoids the danger that actions will be misinterpreted. If a parent is overly generous, a child will think the parent will always be generous, even when generosity is inappropriate. By the same token, if a parent does not draw the line until pushed to do so, the child will believe that he *forced* the parent's response. A parent, so goes the argument, should play it safe and leave himself a cushion. (D) makes an attempt to capture this thought but overstates the case. The author implies only that this may show weakness, not that the child will necessarily exploit that weakness and certainly not that the child will exploit it violently. And if the author had intended that thought he surely would not have used the word *retaliate,* which implies a *quid pro quo.* Both (A) and (E) have no basis in the passage, and neither is relevant to the idea of rewards and punishments. (C) does treat the general idea of the passage, but if confuses the idea of weakness with the more specific notion of willingness to bargain.

41. **The correct answer is (C).** Here the sentence suffers from faulty parallelism. The sentence should read "to seize power, . . . to maintain it."

ANSWER KEY AND EXPLANATIONS

Quantitative Section

1. A	9. E	17. B	25. A	33. B
2. D	10. C	18. B	26. D	34. B
3. C	11. B	19. E	27. C	35. A
4. B	12. A	20. D	28. D	36. C
5. C	13. B	21. A	29. E	37. D
6. E	14. C	22. D	30. C	
7. A	15. C	23. B	31. E	
8. E	16. C	24. B	32. D	

1. **The correct answer is (A).** We may express the given information as $\frac{x+y+30}{3} = 10$. Thus, $x + y + 30 = 30$, $x + y = 0$, and $\frac{x+y}{2} = 0$, so the average of x and y is 0. Since $x + y = 0$, $x = -y$ (and $y = -x$), which means that of x and y, one term must be positive and the other negative (e.g., +3 and –3).

2. **The correct answer is (D).** This is a problem of intersecting sets, and can be diagrammed with circles, as below. The total number of seniors is 120. Letting x be the number of seniors in both clubs, $70 - x$ seniors must be in the chess club only and $90 - x$ seniors must be in the pep club only. The sum of those three quantities must be the total number of seniors. Thus, $x + (70 - x) + (90 - x) = 120$ and $x = 40$.

3. **The correct answer is (C).** According to (1) there are more than 7 pennies in the bank, and according to (2) there are fewer than 9 pennies in the bank. The only integer greater than 7 but less than 9 is 8, so that must be the number of pennies in the bank. If this situation did not refer to pennies (or something else that had to occur in integral values), there would not be sufficient information to answer the question since 7.5, 8.6, etc., might then be acceptable.

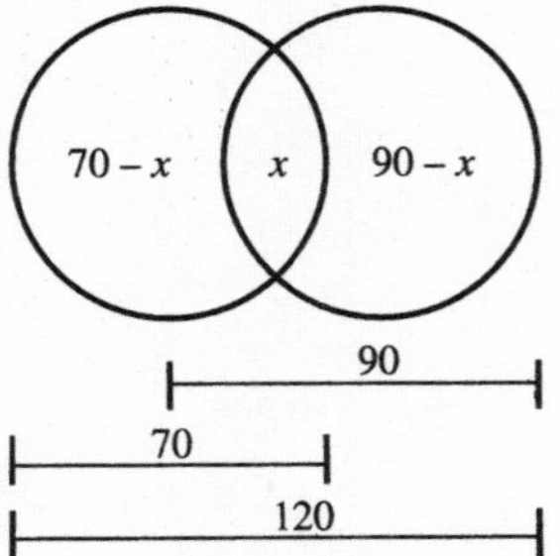

4. **The correct answer is (B).** (1) does not tell us how much is still owed. It doesn't even tell us, by itself, how much Joe has paid since (1) does not tell us the amount of the monthly payments. (2), however, is sufficient by itself, since it allows us to compute his indebtedness: $150 × 10 = $1,500.

5. **The correct answer is (C).** (1) tells us that $\frac{x+y+z}{3} = 5$, which is not sufficient by itself to determine x. However, if we also know (2), we may substitute $-z$ for y in the equation from (1), getting $\frac{x+(-z)+z}{3} = 5$, or $\frac{x}{3} = 5$ and $x = 15$.

6. **The correct answer is (E).** We do not know how the three gas stations are ordered, or even if they all fall on the same straight line, so, even knowing (1) and (2), it is impossible to calculate the distance from gas station X to gas station Z.

7. **The correct answer is (A).** To find interest earned, we need to have the amount of principal, the rate of interest and the time period. The original information gives us the principal and the time period (annual). Thus (1), which gives the interest rate, is sufficient to obtain an answer (by finding $5\frac{1}{4}\%$ of \$3,000, which is $.0525 \times \$3{,}000 = \$157.50$). (2) is irrelevant since annual interest income, not total income, is asked for. Also, (2) does not provide us with the interest rate for the period during which the account was maintained.

8. **The correct answer is (E).** Since both statements are merely comparative (*-er*) and they do not compare the two items we are asked to compare, neither is sufficient by itself. Combining both pieces of information tells us that Beth is shorter than either Susan or Jill (thus, she is the shortest), but we have no information relating Susan and Jill to each other and thus cannot tell who is the tallest.

9. **The correct answer is (E).** This problem has a certain trial-and-error aspect to it. We need to find a pair of factors of 72 such that one of them is a perfect square and the other is a perfect cube. 72 is 9×8, and 9 is 3 squared and 8 is 2 cubed, so a is 3 and b is 2. Thus, $a + b$ is 5.

10. **The correct answer is (C).** The solution to this problem is greatly facilitated if fractional equivalents of the decimal expressions are used, since there are convenient equivalents for each of the decimals in the problem. .250 is $\frac{1}{4}$, .333 is about $\frac{1}{3}$, .125 is $\frac{1}{8}$, and .167 is about $\frac{1}{6}$. (If you did not notice this immediately, a review of the percentage equivalents provided in the math refresher section is indicated.) The problem now becomes:

$$\frac{\frac{\frac{1}{4}}{\frac{1}{3}}}{\frac{\frac{1}{8}}{\frac{1}{6}}} = \frac{\frac{1}{4} \times \frac{3}{1}}{\frac{1}{8} \times \frac{6}{1}} = \frac{\frac{3}{4}}{\frac{3}{4}} = 1$$

11. **The correct answer is (B).** This is an example of a problem whose exact nature is not fully known until the answer choices are examined. Here, a simplifying approach is to choose convenient values for a and b and then evaluate the fractions, picking the fraction nearest to 1 as the answer. Let us work with $a = 3$ and $b = 2$, since a must be greater than b. Then answer choice (A) becomes $\frac{3}{2}$, or $1\frac{1}{2}$. (B) becomes $\frac{5}{4}$, or $1\frac{1}{4}$. (C) becomes $\frac{4}{3}$, or $1\frac{1}{3}$. (D) becomes $\frac{4}{2}$, or 2. Finally, (E) becomes $\frac{2}{1}$, or 2. All of the answer choices are greater than one, and (B), which is the least of them, is therefore closest to 1.

12. **The correct answer is (A).** If the office has 21 staff members and $\frac{1}{3}$ are men, then there are $21 \times \frac{1}{3}$ or 7 men on the staff. Since the problem does not specify the hiring of any more men, the 7 men must be $\frac{1}{4}$ of the new staff total. So $\frac{1}{4}x = 7$ where x is the total number of staff after hiring. Hence $x = 28$, and subtracting from this total the 21 current staff members yields 7 women who must be hired.

13. **The correct answer is (B).** Answering this question involves finding percentages of percentages. If 40% of the women students take mathematics courses and 55% of the students are women, then 40% of 55% of the students are women enrolled in mathematics courses. This is (.40)(.55) = .22 = 22%. Similarly, since 100 – 55 = 45% of all students are men, then 20% of 45% of the students are men taking mathematics courses. This is equal to (.20)(.45) = .09 = 9%. The total percentage taking mathematics courses is found by adding the two computed percentages together: 22% + 9% = 31%.

14. **The correct answer is (C).** The volume of a cylinder is $\pi r^2 h$ where r is the radius of the base and h is the height of the cylinder. Letting this represent the volume of cylinder *B,* we can then find what the volume of cylinder *A* would be. If the height of cylinder *B* is h, then the height of cylinder *A* is $3h$. If the radius of cylinder *B* is r, then the radius of cylinder *A* is $\frac{1}{3}r$. Therefore, the volume of cylinder *A* must be $\pi\left(\frac{1}{3}r\right)^2 3h = \pi \times \frac{1}{9}r^2 \times 3h = \frac{1}{3}\pi r^2 h$. The ratio of the volume of *A* to that of *B,* which is what the question asks for, must be $\frac{\frac{1}{3}\pi r^2 h}{\pi r^2 h} = \frac{1}{3}$, by division of common factors.

15. **The correct answer is (C).** (1) does give us a lot of information about the series, but it does not tell us where the series starts, and a series does not have to start with 1. Thus, (1) is not sufficient by itself. (2) clearly does not suffice by itself since there is no way to connect the 10th number in the series to the 57th. Knowing (1) and (2) together, we could count forward by threes from the 10th number, 29, to the 57th number. Alternatively, we could write an equation: 57th number in the series = 29 + (57 – 10)(3). This is a perfect example of a problem that you should absolutely *NOT* solve numerically. Once you know that there is enough information, that's the end of it.

16. **The correct answer is (C).** Let us call the jogger's original rate r_1 and her increased rate r_2. If the original time is t, then the new time would be $\frac{3}{4}t$. Since the distance is the same in both cases, $D = r_1 t = r_2\left(\frac{3}{4}t\right)$, or $r_2 = \frac{4}{3}r_1$. The increase in speed would be $\frac{4}{3}r_1 - r_1 = \frac{1}{3}r_1$. Dividing this by the old total gives us the percentage increase:

$$\frac{\frac{1}{3}r_1}{r_1} = \frac{1}{3} = 33\frac{1}{3}\%$$

17. **The correct answer is (B).** To compute the percentage asked for, we need the number correctly answered and the total number of questions. The total is given in the original information, so all that is needed is the number correctly answered. (1) reveals the number of questions left blank but says nothing about the number of questions answered correctly or incorrectly. (2) is sufficient since the required percentage would be $\frac{53 \text{ correct}}{125} \times 100$.

18. **The correct answer is (B).** This question is basically an "insight" problem in the sense that solving it is quite easy if one sees a key relationship in the problem. Here we are given the length of a diagonal of *ABCO, AC* = 6. *ABCO* is a rectangle, so its diagonals are equal in length. The other diagonal of *ABCO, OB,* is also a radius of circle *O,* and also has a length of 6. Thus the area of circle *O,* π times radius squared, is π times 6^2 or 36π. If the "insight" escaped you, there was one further tactic you could have employed: measure. In this section, unless otherwise indicated, drawings are to

scale. You could have used the edge of your answer sheet to measure the known quantity and then have compared that to the radius of the circle. The radius of the circle would have measured 6.

19. **The correct answer is (E).** Profit = Income – Cost = \$10,000. Income is here made up of two parts, advertising income and sales income. Advertising income is \$20,000, and sales income is the number of copies sold times the price per copy, or (\$0.75)(x), where x is the number of copies sold. Income is thus ($.75x + 20{,}000$) dollars. Total cost is cost per copy times the number of copies, or ($1.00x$) dollars. So the desired equation is $(.75x + 20{,}000) - 1.00x = 10{,}000$ or $-.25x = -10{,}000$ or $x = 40{,}000$ copies.

20. **The correct answer is (D).** If a remainder of 4 is obtained when 89 is divided by a, then a must divide $89 - 4 = 85$ evenly. Similarly, if a remainder of 6 is obtained when 125 is divided by a, then a must divide $125 - 6 = 119$ evenly. 85 is 17×5 and 119 is 17×7. The only integer that divides both numbers evenly is 17, so that is the correct answer.

21. **The correct answer is (A).** It is easy to misread this problem. It states that the pen costs \$11 more than the pencil, not that the pen costs \$11. Letting x = the cost of the pen and y = the cost of the pencil, we can write two equations: $x + y = 12$ and $x - y = 11$. Subtracting the second equation from the first we get $2y = 1$ and $y = .50$.

22. **The correct answer is (D).** The information given in this problem again allows us to set up two equations with two unknowns. The October commission can be expressed as $\left(\frac{x}{100}\right)(2000) + \left(\frac{y}{100}\right)(4000 - 2000)$ which must equal 700. This simplifies to $20x + 20y = 700$. The November commission can be written as $\left(\frac{x}{100}\right)(2000) + \left(\frac{y}{100}\right)(5000 - 2000) = 900$, which simplifies to $20x + 30y = 900$. Subtracting the first equation from the second, we get $10y = 200$ or $y = 20$. Substituting for y in the first equation we get $20x + (20)(20) = 700$, $20x = 300$ or $x = 15$.

23. **The correct answer is (B).** The requested percentage is a fraction in which the profit is the numerator and the selling price is the denominator. Another way to look at the question is that we need to be able to link the profit and the selling price paid into a fraction or ratio or percentage. We might also be asked to use the everyday idea of profit as the difference between cost and selling price. (1) allows us to link the profit and selling price in the form: profit = selling price – \$20. However, that is a linkage based on addition and subtraction and does not permit a firm conclusion about the ratio we have been asked to determine. For example, the selling price could be \$520 and the profit \$500, or the selling price could be \$30 and the profit \$10. (2) tells us that $\frac{1}{4}$ of the selling price is profit (since $\frac{3}{4}$ of the selling price was the cost of the item and the cost plus the profit equals the selling price). Don't confuse yourself by worrying about different types of costs.

24. **The correct answer is (B).** Since (1) tells us nothing about b, it cannot be sufficient. By dividing each side of the equation in (2) by a, we obtain $\frac{b}{a} = 4$, and 75 percent of 4 is 3, so (2) is sufficient. This is a good example of a question in which you could easily leap ahead to a (C) answer choice without sufficient consideration of each proposition by itself.

25. **The correct answer is (A).** From (1) we know that there are six different, equally likely outcomes of any throw of the die. The probability of the die coming up six is thus one out of six. However, each roll is

totally independent, and thus the fate of previous rolls does not affect the chances for the current roll. Thus (2) is irrelevant.

26. **The correct answer is (D).** (1) gives us the equation $x(x + 5) = 24$, where x is Robert's age now. This equation has a positive root, 3, and a negative root, –8. Although you can find these roots by solving the quadratic equation $x^2 + 5x - 24 = 0$, it is quicker to just consider what the factors of 24 are and select the ones that satisfy the conditions. Even more efficient would be an approach of trying out potential ages and seeing which ones work. The only advantage to knowing the quadratic formulation is that you will more quickly appreciate that there is only one positive root; since Robert cannot be –8 years old, he must be 3 years old and thus (1) is sufficient. (2) yields the equation $x + 6 = 3x$, and again $x = 3$.

27. **The correct answer is (C).** We need the area of one tile and the area of the floor. A square floor tile of side x has an area of x^2. From (1) and (2) the area of the kitchen floor can be calculated as $(10x)(30x) = 300x^2$. The number of tiles needed to cover the floor must then be the area of the floor divided by the area per tile, that is, $\frac{300x^2}{x^2}$ or 300.

28. **The correct answer is (D).** The longest straight-line distance in a rectangular box is the diagonal of that box, that is, the distance from a bottom corner to the opposite upper corner. The diagonal of the box is the hypotenuse of a right triangle in which one leg is the height of the box and the other leg is the bottom of the box. The height of the box is 10 inches. The diagonal of the box bottom is the hypotenuse of a right triangle with legs of 6 inches and 8 inches. Thus, we have a triangle twice the size of a 3-4-5 right triangle, that is, a 6-8-10 right triangle. So the diagonal of the bottom of the box is 10 inches. Thus, both legs of the right triangle whose hypotenuse we seek are 10 inches; it is an isosceles right triangle. The hypotenuse of an isosceles right triangle is the square root of 2 multiplied by the length of a leg of that triangle. Therefore, the length of the hypotenuse, which is the diagonal of the box, is 10 times the square root of 2.

29. **The correct answer is (E).** An approach that seems useful to many problems of this sort is to select a convenient original price to work with. Suppose the widget was priced at \$100 before 1981. After a 20% increase in 1981, the price rose to 100 + (.2)(100) = \$120. After the 10% increase in 1982, the price rose to 120 + (.1)(120) = \$132. This means that the price would have to be decreased by \$32 to return it to the pre-1981 price of \$100. Now the question becomes: What percentage of \$132 is \$32? This is $\frac{32}{132}$ times 100%, which is a little more than 24%.

30. **The correct answer is (C).** This question can be solved algebraically. We know that the original investment plus interest earned equals \$781.00:

Original Investment + Interest = \$781.00

But how much interest was earned? We know that the money earned 4 years of interest at 10.5%, which is $4 \times 10.5 = 42\%$ total interest. So Interest = .42 × Original Investment. Using this, we rewrite our original equation:

Original Investment + 42% of Original Investment = \$781

Original Investment + .42 × Original Investment = \$781

$$1.42 \text{ OI} = \$781$$

$$\text{OI} = \frac{\$781}{1.42}$$

$$\text{OI} = \$550$$

31. The correct answer is (E). We calculate the charges as follows. The first $\frac{1}{9}$ mile costs x cents. Every additional $\frac{1}{9}$ miles costs $\frac{x}{5}$ cents. In y miles there are $9y$ $\frac{1}{9}$'s of a mile, but we take away the first $\frac{1}{9}$ (which costs x cents) to find how much the additional mileage will cost:

$$9y - 1\left(\frac{x}{5}\right) = \frac{9xy - x}{5}$$

This is the cost of the additional mileage after the first $\frac{1}{9}$ mile. Now we add in the x cents for the first $\frac{1}{9}$ mile:

$$x + \frac{9xy - x}{5}$$

32. The correct answer is (D). Although the subject matter of this question involves physics, no knowledge of physics is needed to answer it. Instead, you need only to substitute the numbers into the formula provided and solve for the missing variable:

$$v^2 = 2ad$$

$$(20)^2 = 2(10)d$$
$$400 = 20d$$
$$d = 20$$

So the object traveled 20 meters.

33. The correct answer is (B). This question asks you to combine two work rates:

Rate 1 + Rate 2 = Combined Rate

Using the rates provided in the question stem:

$\frac{x}{30}$ minutes + $\frac{x}{60}$ minutes = $\frac{x}{k}$ minutes

(where the unknown k is the solution to the problem). Finding a common denominator and adding the fractions on the left:

$$\frac{2x + x}{60} = \frac{x}{k}$$

Cross-multiplying:

$$k = \frac{60x}{3x} = 20$$

So together the two machines will sort x letters in 20 minutes.

34. The correct answer is (B). You don't need any fancy formulas to attack this problem. If we start with 80 liters of a mixture that is 10% X and 90% Y, we have 8 liters of X and 72 liters of Y. If we add 20 liters of X, we end up with 28 liters of X and 72 liters of Y, for a total of 100 liters of the mixture. Since 28 out of the 100 liters of mixture are X, we have a mixture that is $\frac{28}{100}$ or 28% X.

35. The correct answer is (A). The height of the can is asked for and the diameter is given. The likely connection will be the formula for volume of a cylinder or can, V = $(\pi)(\text{radius})^2(\text{height})$. Since the diameter is given, we know the radius. Since that leaves only one variable in the equation, the volume, in addition to the height, we might well find that one proposition is sufficient. (1) allows us to set up the equation Volume = $(\pi)(r)^2(h) = (10)(\pi)(r)$. The radius is 2 inches, so the equation can be solved for h, so (1) is sufficient. (2) is not sufficient, however. Even knowing the *volume* of the can's contents [as opposed to the *weight* as given by (2)] would not give us the volume of the can itself.

36. The correct answer is (C). The best way to attack this question is to see that the shaded area of the figure can be analyzed into two figures—a rectangle and a triangle:

The area of the rectangle is $30 \times 20 = 600$, and the area of the triangle is $\frac{1}{2}$ (30) (50) = 750. So the area of the composite figure is 1350.

37. **The correct answer is (D).** To find the value of a, we need to establish the value of b and c. From (1), by substituting for c in the equation from the original information, we obtain $a + b + 4a - b = 50$, or $5a = 50$ and $a = 10$. (2) means that $\frac{b+c}{2} = 2a$ or $b + c = 4a$. Substituting $4a$ for $b + c$ in the original equation gives us $a + 4a = 5a = 50$ once again.

PART VII

GMAT MATH REVIEW

Arithmetic

chapter 11

OVERVIEW

- **Operations with Integers and Decimals**
- **Operations with Fractions**
- **Verbal Problems Involving Fractions**
- **Variation**
- **Finding Percents**
- **Verbal Problems Involving Percent**
- **Averages**

1. OPERATIONS WITH INTEGERS AND DECIMALS

The four basic arithmetic operations are addition, subtraction, multiplication, and division. The results of these operations are called **sum, difference, product,** and **quotient,** respectively. Because these words are often used in math problems, you should be thoroughly familiar with them.

ADDING. When adding decimals, remember to keep your columns straight and to write all digits in their proper columns according to place value.

Q Add 43.75, .631, and 5

$$\begin{array}{r} 43.75 \\ .631 \\ +\,5. \\ \hline 49.381 \end{array}$$

A 49.381

SUBTRACTING. When subtracting decimals, it is likewise important to put numbers in their proper columns. Be particularly careful in subtracting a number with more place values after the decimal from a number with less place values after the decimal.

Q Subtract .2567 from 3.8

$$\begin{array}{r} 3.8000 \\ -.2567 \\ \hline 3.5433 \end{array}$$

A 3.5433

In order to perform this subtraction, zeros must be attached to the top number to extend it to equal length with the bottom number. The zeros in this case are only place holders and in no way change the value of the number.

MULTIPLYING. When multiplying decimals, pay particular attention to zeros.

Q Find the product of 403 and 30

$$\begin{array}{r} 403 \\ \times\ 30 \\ \hline 12{,}090 \end{array}$$

A 12,090

When multiplying decimals, remember that the number of decimal places in the product must be equal to the sum of the number of decimal places in the numbers being mutiplied.

Q Find the product of 4.03 and .3

$$\begin{array}{r} 4.03 \\ \times\ .3 \\ \hline 1.209 \end{array}$$

A 1.209

DIVIDING. When dividing, it is also important to watch for zeros.

Q Divide 4935 by 7

A
$$7\overline{)4935} = 705$$

Since 49 is divisible by 7, there is no remainder to carry to the next digit. However, 3 is not divisible by 7, so you must put a 0 into the quotient. Carrying the 3, you can then divide 35 by 7.

When dividing by a decimal, always rename the decimal to a whole number by moving the decimal point to the end of the divisor. To do this, multiply the divisor by a power of 10. (Multiplying by 10 moves a decimal point one place to the right. Multiplying by 100 moves it two places to the right, and so forth.) Then multiply the number being divided by the same power of 10. Since division can always be written as a fraction in which the divisor is the denominator and the number being divided is the numerator, when you remove a decimal point from the divisor, you are really multiplying both parts of the fraction by the same number, which changes its form, but not its value.

Q Divide 4.935 by .07

$$.07\overline{)4.935}$$

(Multiply by 100 to move the decimal point two places to the right.)

A
$$7\overline{)493.5} = 70.5$$

Exercise: Operations with Integers and Decimals

Work out each problem on scratch paper.

Add:

1. 6 + 37 + 42,083 + 125

2. .007 + 32.4 + 1.234 + 7.3

3. .37 + .037 + .0037 + 37

Subtract:

4. 3701 – 371

5. 1000 – 112

6. 40.37 – 6.983

Multiply:

7. 3147 by 206

8. 2.137 by .11

9. .45 by .06

Divide:

10. 12,894 by 42

11. 34.68 by 3.4

12. .175 by 25

Solutions

1.
```
          6
         37
      42083
+       125
-----------
      42251
```

2.
```
       .007
     32.4
      1.234
+     7.3
-----------
     40.941
```

3.
```
       .37
       .037
       .0037
+    37.
-----------
     37.4107
```

4.
```
       3701
–       371
-----------
       3330
```

5.
```
       1000
–       112
-----------
        888
```

6.
```
     40.370
–     6.983
-----------
     33.387
```

7.
```
      3147
×      206
----------
     18882
    629400
----------
    648282
```

8.
```
     2.137
×      .11
----------
      2137
     2137
----------
    .23507
```

9.
```
       .45
×      .06
----------
     .0270
```

10.
```
      307
  42)12894
     126
     ---
      294
      294
      ---
```

11.
```
       10.2
  3.4)34.68
      34
      --
        68
        68
        --
```

12.
```
       .007
   25).175
        175
        ---
```

2. OPERATIONS WITH FRACTIONS

ADDING AND SUBTRACTING. In adding or subtracting fractions, you must remember that the numbers must have the same (common) denominator.

Q Add $\frac{1}{3}+\frac{2}{5}+\frac{3}{4}$

A The smallest number divisible by 3, 5, and 4 is 60. Therefore, use 60 as the common denominator. To add the fractions, divide each denominator into 60 and multiply the result by the given numerator.

$$\frac{20+24+45}{60}=\frac{89}{60}, \text{ or } 1\frac{29}{60}$$

▼ **HINT:** To add or subtract two fractions quickly, remember that a sum can be found by adding the two cross-products and putting this answer over the denominator product.

$$\frac{a}{b}\times\frac{c}{d}=\frac{ad+bc}{bd}$$

A similar shortcut applies to subtraction.

$$\frac{a}{b}\times\frac{c}{d}=\frac{ad-bc}{bd}$$

$$\frac{3}{4}\times\frac{5}{7}=\frac{21-20}{28}=\frac{1}{28}$$

All fractions should be left in their simplest form. That is, there should be no factor common to both numerator and denominator. Often in multiple-choice questions you may find that the answer you have correctly computed is not among the choices but an equivalent fraction is. Be careful!

In simplifying fractions involving large numbers, it is helpful to be able to tell whether a factor is common to both numerator and denominator before a lengthy trial division. Certain tests for divisibility help with this.

Tests for Divisibility

To test if a number is divisible by:	Check to see:
2	if it is even
3	if the sum of the digits is divisible by 3
4	if the number formed by the last two digits is divisible by 4
5	if its last digit is a 5 or 0
6	if it is even *and* the sum of the digits is divisible by 3
8	if the number formed by the last three digits is divisible by 8
9	if the sum of the digits is divisible by 9
10	if its last digit is 0

Q Simplify $\frac{3525}{4341}$

A This fraction is simplifiable by 3, since the sum of the digits of the numerator is 15 and those of the denominator add up to 12, both divisible by 3.

$$\frac{3525}{4341} = \frac{1175}{1447}$$

The resulting fraction meets no further divisibility tests and therefore has no common factor listed above. Larger divisors would be unlikely on a GMAT test.

To add or subtract mixed numbers, it is again important to remember common denominators. In subtraction, you must borrow in terms of the common denominator.

Addition:

$$\begin{array}{r} 43\frac{2}{5} \\ +\ 8\frac{1}{3} \\ \hline \end{array} \qquad \begin{array}{r} 43\frac{6}{15} \\ +\ 8\frac{5}{15} \\ \hline 51\frac{11}{15} \end{array}$$

Subtraction:

$$\begin{array}{r} 43\frac{2}{5} \\ -\ 6\frac{2}{3} \\ \hline \end{array} \qquad \begin{array}{r} 43\frac{6}{15} \\ -\ 6\frac{10}{15} \\ \hline \end{array} \qquad \begin{array}{r} 42\frac{21}{15} \\ -\ 6\frac{10}{15} \\ \hline 36\frac{11}{15} \end{array}$$

MULTIPLYING: To multiply fractions, always try to divide common factors from any numerator and any denominator where possible before actually multiplying. In multiplying mixed numbers, always rename them as improper fractions first.

Multiply: $\frac{2}{\cancel{5}} \cdot \frac{\overset{2}{\cancel{10}}}{11} \cdot \frac{\overset{9}{\cancel{99}}}{\underset{55}{\cancel{110}}} = \frac{18}{55}$

Multiply: $4\frac{1}{2} \cdot 1\frac{2}{3} \cdot 5\frac{1}{5}$

$$\frac{\overset{3}{\cancel{9}}}{\cancel{2}} \cdot \frac{\cancel{5}}{\cancel{3}} \cdot \frac{\overset{13}{\cancel{26}}}{\cancel{5}} = 39$$

DIVIDING: To divide fractions or mixed numbers, remember to multiply by the reciprocal of the divisor (the number after the division sign).

Divide: $4\frac{1}{2} \div \frac{3}{4} = \frac{\overset{3}{\cancel{9}}}{\cancel{2}} \cdot \frac{\overset{2}{\cancel{4}}}{\cancel{3}} = 6$

Divide: $62\frac{1}{2} \div 5 = \frac{\overset{25}{\cancel{125}}}{2} \cdot \frac{1}{\cancel{5}} = 12\frac{1}{2}$

To simplify complex fractions (fractions within fractions), multiply every term by the least common denominator of all fractions.

Q $\dfrac{\frac{1}{2}+\frac{1}{3}}{\frac{1}{4}+\frac{1}{6}}$

A The least number that can be used to clear all fractions is 12. Multiplying each term by 12 yields:

$\dfrac{6+4}{3+2}=\dfrac{10}{5}=2$

Q $\dfrac{\frac{3}{4}+\frac{2}{3}}{1-\frac{1}{2}}$

A Again, multiply by 12. $\dfrac{9+8}{12-6} = \dfrac{17}{6} = 2\dfrac{5}{6}$

Exercise: Operations with Fractions

Work out each problem in the space provided.

Add:

1. $12\frac{5}{6}+2\frac{3}{8}+21\frac{1}{4}$

2. $\frac{1}{2}+\frac{1}{3}+\frac{1}{4}+\frac{1}{5}+\frac{1}{6}$

Subtract:

3. $5\frac{3}{4}$ from $10\frac{1}{2}$

4. $17\frac{2}{3}$ from 50

5. $25\frac{3}{5}$ from $30\frac{9}{10}$

Multiply:

6. $5\frac{1}{4}\bullet 1\frac{5}{7}$

7. $\frac{3}{4}\bullet\frac{3}{4}\bullet\frac{3}{4}$

8. $12\frac{1}{2}\bullet 16$

Divide:

9. $\frac{1}{5}\div 5$

10. $5\div\frac{1}{5}$

11. $3\frac{2}{3}\div 1\frac{5}{6}$

Simplify:

12. $\dfrac{\frac{5}{6}-\frac{1}{3}}{2+\frac{1}{5}}$

13. $\dfrac{3+\frac{1}{4}}{5-\frac{1}{2}}$

Solutions

1.
$$\begin{array}{r} 12\frac{5}{6} = \frac{20}{24} \\ 2\frac{3}{8} = \frac{9}{24} \\ +\ 21\frac{1}{4} = \frac{6}{24} \\ \hline 35\ +\ \frac{35}{24} = 36\frac{11}{24} \end{array}$$

2.
$$\begin{array}{r} \frac{1}{2} = \frac{30}{60} \\ \frac{1}{3} = \frac{20}{60} \\ \frac{1}{4} = \frac{15}{60} \\ \frac{1}{5} = \frac{12}{60} \\ +\ \frac{1}{6} = \frac{10}{60} \\ \hline \frac{87}{60} = 1\frac{27}{60} = 1\frac{9}{20} \end{array}$$

3.
$$\begin{array}{r} 10\frac{1}{2} = 9\frac{3}{2} = 9\frac{6}{4} \\ -5\frac{3}{4} \\ \hline 4\frac{3}{4} \end{array}$$

4.
$$\begin{array}{r} \overset{49}{\cancel{50}}\frac{3}{3} \\ -17\frac{2}{3} \\ \hline 32\frac{1}{3} \end{array}$$

5.
$$\begin{array}{r} 30\frac{9}{10} \\ -\ 25\frac{3}{5} = \left(\frac{6}{10}\right) \\ \hline 5\frac{3}{10} \end{array}$$

6. $\frac{\overset{3}{\cancel{21}}}{\cancel{4}} \bullet \frac{\overset{3}{\cancel{12}}}{\cancel{7}} = 9$

7. $\frac{3}{4} \bullet \frac{3}{4} \bullet \frac{3}{4} = \frac{27}{64}$

8. $\frac{25}{\cancel{2}} \bullet \overset{8}{\cancel{16}} = 200$

9. $\frac{1}{5} \bullet \frac{1}{5} = \frac{1}{25}$

10. $5 \bullet 5 = 25$

11. $\frac{\cancel{11}}{\cancel{3}} \bullet \frac{\overset{2}{\cancel{6}}}{\cancel{11}} = 2$

12. $\frac{25-10}{60+6} = \frac{15}{66} = \frac{5}{22}$

Each term was multiplied by 30.

13. $\frac{12+1}{20-2} = \frac{13}{18}$

Each term was multiplied by 4.

3. VERBAL PROBLEMS INVOLVING FRACTIONS

Fraction problems deal with parts of a whole.

Q If a class consists of 12 boys and 18 girls, what part of the class is boys?

A 12 out of 30 students, or $\frac{12}{30} = \frac{2}{5}$

Read all the questions carefully. Often a problem may require more than one calculation.

Q $\frac{1}{4}$ of this year's seniors have averages above 90. $\frac{1}{2}$ of the remainder have averages between 80 and 90. What part of the senior class have averages below 80?

A $\frac{1}{4}$ have averages above 90.

$\frac{1}{2}$ of $\frac{3}{4}$ or $\frac{3}{8}$ have averages between 80 and 90.

$\frac{1}{4} + \frac{3}{8} = \frac{2}{8} + \frac{3}{8} = \frac{5}{8}$ have averages above 80.

Therefore, $\frac{3}{8}$ of the class have averages below 80.

▼ **HINT:** *Use Algebra.* When a problem can easily be translated into an algebraic equation, remember that algebra is a very useful tool.

Q 14 is $\frac{2}{3}$ of what number?

A $14 = \frac{2}{3}x$

Multiply each side by $\frac{3}{2}$:

$21 = x$

▼ **HINT:** *Substitute numbers.* If a problem is given with letters in place of numbers, the same reasoning must be used as if numbers were given. If you are not sure how to proceed, replace the letters with numbers to determine the steps that must be taken.

Q If John has p hours of homework and has worked for r hours, what part of his homework is yet to be done?

A If John had 5 hours of homework and had worked for 3 hours, you would first find he had 5 – 3 hours, or 2 hours, yet to do. This represents $\frac{2}{5}$ of his work. Using letters, his remaining work is represented by $\frac{p-r}{p}$.

Exercise: Verbal Problems Involving Fractions

Work out each problem.

1. A team played 30 games of which it won 24. What part of the games played did it lose?

   (A) $\frac{4}{5}$

   (B) $\frac{1}{4}$

   (C) $\frac{1}{5}$

   (D) $\frac{3}{4}$

   (E) $\frac{2}{3}$

2. If a man's weekly salary is $\$X$ and he saves $\$Y$, what part of his weekly salary does he spend?

   (A) $\frac{X}{Y}$

   (B) $\frac{X-Y}{X}$

   (C) $\frac{X-Y}{Y}$

   (D) $\frac{Y-X}{X}$

   (E) $\frac{Y-X}{Y}$

3. What part of an hour elapses between 11:50 A.M. and 12:14 P.M.?

   (A) $\frac{2}{5}$

   (B) $\frac{7}{30}$

   (C) $\frac{17}{30}$

   (D) $\frac{1}{6}$

   (E) $\frac{1}{4}$

4. One-half of the employees of Acme Co. earn salaries above \$18,000 annually. One-third of the remainder earn salaries between \$15,000 and \$18,000. What part of the staff earns below \$15,000?

   (A) $\frac{1}{6}$

   (B) $\frac{2}{3}$

   (C) $\frac{1}{2}$

   (D) $\frac{1}{10}$

   (E) $\frac{1}{3}$

5. David received his allowance on Sunday. He spends $\frac{1}{4}$ of his allowance on Monday and $\frac{2}{3}$ of the remainder on Tuesday. What part of his allowance is left for the rest of the week?

   (A) $\frac{1}{3}$

   (B) $\frac{1}{12}$

   (C) $\frac{1}{4}$

   (D) $\frac{1}{2}$

   (E) $\frac{4}{7}$

6. 12 is $\frac{3}{4}$ of what number?

   (A) 16

   (B) 9

   (C) 36

   (D) 20

   (E) 15

7. A piece of fabric is cut into three sections so that the first is three times as long as the second and the second section is three times as long as the third. What part of the entire piece is the smallest section?

(A) $\frac{1}{12}$

(B) $\frac{1}{9}$

(C) $\frac{1}{3}$

(D) $\frac{1}{7}$

(E) $\frac{1}{13}$

8. What part of a gallon is one quart?

(A) $\frac{1}{2}$

(B) $\frac{1}{4}$

(C) $\frac{2}{3}$

(D) $\frac{1}{3}$

(E) $\frac{1}{5}$

9. A factory employs M men and W women. What part of its employees are women?

(A) $\frac{W}{M}$

(B) $\frac{M+W}{W}$

(C) $\frac{W}{M-W}$

(D) $\frac{W}{M+W}$

(E) W

10. A motion was passed by a vote of 5:3. What part of the votes cast were in favor of the motion?

(A) $\frac{5}{8}$

(B) $\frac{5}{3}$

(C) $\frac{3}{5}$

(D) $\frac{2}{5}$

(E) $\frac{3}{8}$

11. If the ratio of x:y is 9:7, what is the value of $x + y$?

(A) 2

(B) 14

(C) 16

(D) 63

(E) It cannot be determined from the information.

12. In a certain class the ratio of men to women is 3:5. If the class has 24 people in it, how many are women?

(A) 9

(B) 12

(C) 15

(D) 18

(E) 21

13. If the ratio of men to women in a class is 3:5 and the class contains 24 people, how many additional men would have to enroll to make the ratio of men to women 1:1?

(A) 3

(B) 6

(C) 9

(D) 12

(E) 15

14. If x is $\frac{2}{3}$ of y and y is $\frac{3}{4}$ of z, what is the ratio of $z : x$?

(A) 1:2

(B) 1:1

(C) 2:1

(D) 3:2

(E) 4:3

15. What fraction of 8 tons is 1,000 lbs.?

(A) $\frac{1}{32}$

(B) $\frac{1}{16}$

(C) $\frac{1}{8}$

(D) $\frac{8}{1}$

(E) $\frac{16}{1}$

Solutions

1. **The correct answer is (C).** The team lost 6 games out of 30. $\frac{6}{30} = \frac{1}{5}$
2. **The correct answer is (B).** The man spends $X - Y$ out of X. $\frac{X-Y}{X}$
3. **The correct answer is (A).** 10 minutes elapse by noon, and another 14 after noon, making a total of 24 minutes. There are 60 minutes in an hour. $\frac{24}{60} = \frac{2}{5}$
4. **The correct answer is (E).** One-half earn over \$18,000. One-third of the other $\frac{1}{2}$, or $\frac{1}{6}$, earn between \$15,000 and \$18,000. This accounts for $\frac{1}{2} + \frac{1}{6}$, or $\frac{3}{6} + \frac{1}{6} = \frac{4}{6} = \frac{2}{3}$ of the staff, leaving $\frac{1}{3}$ to earn below \$15,000.
5. **The correct answer is (C).** David spends $\frac{1}{4}$ on Monday and $\frac{2}{3}$ of the other $\frac{3}{4}$, or $\frac{1}{2}$, on Tuesday, leaving only $\frac{1}{4}$ for the rest of the week.
6. **The correct answer is (A).** $12 = \frac{3}{4}x$. Multiply each side by $\frac{4}{3}$. $16 = x$
7. **The correct answer is (E).** Let the third or shortest section $= x$. Then the second section $= 3x$, and the first section $= 9x$. The entire piece of fabric is then $13x$, and the shortest piece represents $\frac{x}{13x}$ or $\frac{1}{13}$ of the entire piece.
8. **The correct answer is (B).** There are four quarts in one gallon.
9. **The correct answer is (D).** The factory employs $M + W$ people, out of which W are women.
10. **The correct answer is (A).** For every 5 votes in favor, 3 were cast against. 5 out of every 8 votes cast were in favor of the motion.
11. **The correct answer is (E).** Remember, a ratio is a fraction. If x is 18 and y is 14, the ratio $x : y$ is 9:7, but $x + y$ is 32. The point of this problem is that x and y can take on *many* possible values, just as long as the ratio 9:7 is preserved. Given the multiplicity of possible values, it is not possible here to establish *one* definite value for the sum of x and y.
12. **The correct answer is (C).** The ratio of women to the total number of people is 5:8. We can set up a proportion. If $\frac{5}{8} = \frac{x}{24}$, then $x = 15$.
13. **The correct answer is (B).** From the previous problem we know that the class contains 15 women and 9 men. In order to have the same number of men and women, 6 additional men would have to enroll.
14. **The correct answer is (C).** There are several ways to attack this problem. If x is $\frac{2}{3}$ of y then y is $\frac{3}{2}$ of x. If y is $\frac{3}{4}$ of z then z is $\frac{4}{3}$ of y. Therefore, y is $\frac{3}{2}x$ and $z = 2x$. The ratio of z:x is 2 : 1. You could also plug in a real number and solve. If x is 2, figure out what y and z would be. y would be 3 and z would be 4, so the ratio of z to x is 2 : 1.
15. **The correct answer is (B).** A ton contains 2,000 pounds. So the fraction would be $\frac{1,000}{16,000}$, which is $\frac{1}{16}$.

4. VARIATION

DIRECT VARIATION. Two quantities are said to vary directly if they change in the same direction. As one increases, the other increases.

For example, the amount owed to the milkman varies directly with the number of quarts of milk purchased. The amount of sugar needed in a recipe varies directly with the amount of butter used. The number of inches between two cities on a map varies directly with the number of miles between the cities.

▼ **HINT:** Whenever two quantities vary directly, you can find a missing term by setting up a proportion. However, be very careful to compare the same units, in the same order, on each side of the equal sign.

Q If a two-ounce package of peanuts costs 20¢, what is the cost of a pound of peanuts?

A Here you are comparing cents with ounces, so $\frac{20}{2} = \frac{x}{16}$

In solving a proportion, it is easiest to cross-multiply, remembering that the product of the means (the second and third terms of a proportion) is equal to the product of the extremes (the first and last terms of a proportion).

$$2x = 320$$
$$x = 160$$

Remember that the original units were cents, so the cost is $1.60.

When two fractions are equal, as in a proportion, it is sometimes easier to see what change has taken place in the given numerator or denominator and then to apply the same change to the missing term. In keeping fractions equal, the change will always involve multiplying or dividing by a constant. In the previous example, the denominator was changed from 2 to 16. This involved multiplication by 8; therefore, the numerator (20) must also be multiplied by 8, giving 160 as an answer without any written work necessary. Since time is a very important factor in this type of examination, shortcuts such as this could be critical.

Q If a truck can carry m pounds of coal, how many trucks are needed to carry p pounds of coal?

A You are comparing trucks with pounds. This again is a direct variation, because the number of trucks increases as the number of pounds increases.

$$\frac{1}{m} = \frac{x}{p}$$
$$mx = p$$
$$x = \frac{p}{m}$$

INVERSE VARIATION. Two quantities are said to vary inversely if they change in opposite directions. As one increases, the other decreases.

For example, the number of workers hired to paint a house varies inversely with the number of days the job will take. A doctor's stock of flu vaccine varies inversely with the number of patients injected. The number of days a given supply of cat food lasts varies inversely with the number of cats being fed.

▼ **HINT:** Whenever two quantities vary inversely, you can find a missing term by using multiplication. Multiply the first quantity by the second and set the products equal.

Q If a case of cat food can feed 5 cats for 4 days, how long would it feed 8 cats?

A Since this is a case of inverse variation (the more cats, the fewer days), multiply the number of cats by the number of days in each instance and set them equal.

$$5 \times 4 = 8 \times x$$
$$20 = 8x$$
$$2\frac{1}{2} = x$$

Exercise: Variation

Work out each problem.

1. If 60 feet of uniform wire weighs 80 pounds, what is the weight of 2 yards of the same wire?

(A) $2\frac{2}{3}$
(B) 6
(C) 8
(D) 120
(E) 2400

2. A gear 50 inches in diameter turns a smaller gear 30 inches in diameter. If the larger gear makes 15 revolutions, how many revolutions does the smaller gear make in that time?

(A) 9
(B) 12
(C) 20
(D) 25
(E) 30

3. If x men can do a job in h days, how long would y men take to do the same job?

(A) $\frac{x}{h}$
(B) $\frac{xh}{y}$
(C) $\frac{hy}{x}$
(D) $\frac{xy}{h}$
(E) $\frac{x}{y}$

4. If a furnace uses 40 gallons of oil in a week, how many gallons, to the nearest gallon, does it use in 10 days?

(A) 4
(B) 28
(C) 57
(D) 58
(E) 400

5. A recipe requires 13 ounces of sugar and 18 ounces of flour. If only 10 ounces of sugar are used, how much flour, to the nearest ounce, should be used?

(A) 13

(B) 14

(C) 15

(D) 23

(E) 24

6. If a car can drive 25 miles on two gallons of gasoline, how many gallons will be needed for a trip of 150 miles?

(A) 3

(B) 6

(C) 7

(D) 10

(E) 12

7. A school has enough bread to feed 30 children for 4 days. If 10 more children are added, how many days will the bread last?

(A) $1\frac{1}{3}$

(B) $2\frac{2}{3}$

(C) 3

(D) $5\frac{1}{3}$

(E) 12

8. At c cents per pound, what is the cost of a ounces of salami?

(A) $\frac{c}{a}$

(B) $\frac{a}{c}$

(C) ac

(D) $\frac{ac}{16}$

(E) $\frac{16c}{a}$

9. If 3 miles are equivalent to 4.83 kilometers, then 11.27 kilometers are equivalent to how many miles?

(A) 2

(B) 5

(C) 7

(D) $6\frac{1}{2}$

(E) $7\frac{1}{3}$

10. If p pencils cost d dollars, how many pencils can be bought for c cents?

(A) $\frac{100pc}{d}$

(B) $\frac{pc}{100d}$

(C) $\frac{pd}{c}$

(D) $\frac{pc}{d}$

(E) $\frac{cd}{p}$

Solutions

1. **The correct answer is (C).** You are comparing *feet* with pounds. The more feet the more pounds. This is DIRECT. Remember to rename yards as feet:

$$\frac{60}{80}=\frac{6}{x}$$
$$60x=480$$
$$x=8$$

2. **The correct answer is (D).** The larger a gear, the fewer times it revolves in a given period of time. This is INVERSE.

$$50 \cdot 15 = 30 \cdot x$$
$$750 = 30x$$
$$25 = x$$

3. **The correct answer is (B).** The more men, the fewer days. This is INVERSE.

$$x \cdot h = y \cdot ?$$
$$\frac{xh}{y} = ?$$

4. **The correct answer is (C).** The more days, the more oil. This is DIRECT. Remember to rename the week as 7 days.

$$\frac{40}{7}=\frac{x}{10}$$
$$7x=400$$
$$x=57\frac{1}{7}$$

5. **The correct answer is (B).** The more sugar, the more flour. This is DIRECT.

$$\frac{13}{18}=\frac{10}{x}$$
$$13x=180$$
$$x=13\frac{11}{13}$$

6. **The correct answer is (A).** The more miles, the more gasoline. This is DIRECT.

$$\frac{25}{2}=\frac{150}{x}$$
$$25x=300$$
$$x=12$$

7. **The correct answer is (C).** The more children, the fewer days. This is INVERSE.

$$30 \cdot 4 = 40 \cdot x$$
$$120 = 40x$$
$$3 = x$$

8. **The correct answer is (D).** The more salami, the more it will cost. This is DIRECT. Remember to rename the pound as 16 ounces.

$$\frac{c}{16}=\frac{x}{a}$$
$$x=\frac{ac}{16}$$

9. **The correct answer is (C).** The more miles, the more kilometers. This is DIRECT.

$$\frac{3}{4.83}=\frac{x}{11.27}$$
$$4.83x=33.81$$
$$x=7$$

10. **The correct answer is (B).** The more pencils, the more cost. This is DIRECT. Remember to rename dollars as cents.

$$\frac{p}{100d}=\frac{x}{c}$$
$$x=\frac{pc}{100d}$$

5. FINDING PERCENTS

PERCENT EQUIVALENTS. "Percent" means "out of 100." If you understand this concept, it becomes very easy to rename a percent as an equivalent decimal or fraction.

$$5\% = \frac{5}{100} = .05$$

$$2.6\% = \frac{2.6}{100} = .026$$

$$c\% = \frac{c}{100} = \frac{1}{100} \bullet c = .01c$$

$$\frac{1}{2}\% = \frac{\frac{1}{2}}{100} = \frac{1}{100} \bullet \frac{1}{2} = \frac{1}{100} \bullet .5 = .005$$

▼ **HINT:** To rename a % as a decimal, remove the % sign and divide by 100. This has the effect of moving the decimal point two places to the LEFT.

$$37\% = .37$$

▼ **HINT:** To rename a decimal as a %, add the % sign and multiply by 100. This has the effect of moving the decimal point two places to the RIGHT.

$$.043 = 4.3\%$$

▼ **HINT:** To rename a % as a fraction, remove the % sign and divide by 100. This has the effect of putting the % over 100 and simplifying the resulting fraction.

$$75\% = \frac{75}{100} = \frac{3}{4}$$

▼ **HINT:** To rename a fraction as a %, add the % sign and multiply by 100.

$$\frac{1}{8} = \frac{1}{8} \bullet 100\% = \frac{100}{8}\% = 12\frac{1}{2}\%$$

Certain fractional equivalents of common percents occur frequently enough that they should be memorized. Learning the values in the following table will make your work with percent problems much easier.

PERCENT–FRACTION EQUIVALENT TABLE

$50\% = \frac{1}{2}$		
$25\% = \frac{1}{4}$	$33\frac{1}{3}\% = \frac{1}{3}$	$12\frac{1}{2}\% = \frac{1}{8}$
$75\% = \frac{3}{4}$	$66\frac{2}{3}\% = \frac{2}{3}$	$37\frac{1}{2}\% = \frac{3}{8}$
$10\% = \frac{1}{10}$	$20\% = \frac{1}{5}$	$62\frac{1}{2}\% = \frac{5}{8}$
$30\% = \frac{3}{10}$	$40\% = \frac{2}{5}$	$87\frac{1}{2}\% = \frac{7}{8}$
$70\% = \frac{7}{10}$	$60\% = \frac{3}{5}$	$16\frac{2}{3}\% = \frac{1}{6}$
$90\% = \frac{9}{10}$	$80\% = \frac{4}{5}$	$83\frac{1}{3}\% = \frac{5}{6}$

Most percentage problems can be solved by using the following proportion:

$$\frac{\%}{100} = \frac{\text{part}}{\text{whole}}$$

Although this method works, it often yields unnecessarily large numbers that are difficult to compute. Following are examples of the four basic types of percent problems and different methods for solving them.

To Find a % of a Number

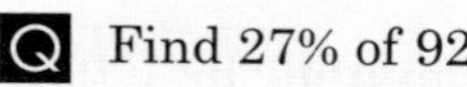

Q Find 27% of 92.

A

PROPORTION METHOD

$$\frac{27}{100} = \frac{x}{92}$$

$$100x = 2484$$

$$x = 24.84$$

SHORTER METHOD

Rename the % as its decimal or fraction equivalent and multiply. Use fractions only when they are among the familiar ones given in the previous table.

Q Find $12\frac{1}{2}\%$ of 96.

A

PROPORTION METHOD	DECIMAL METHOD	FRACTION METHOD
$\frac{12\frac{1}{2}}{100} = \frac{x}{96}$ $100x = 1200$ $x = 12$	96 $\times .125$ 480 192 96 12.000	$\frac{1}{8} \cdot 96 = 12$

Which method is easiest? It really pays to memorize those fractional equivalents.

To Find a Number When a % of It Is Given

Q 7 is 5% of what number?

A

PROPORTION METHOD	SHORTER METHOD
$\frac{5}{100} = \frac{7}{x}$ $5x = 700$ $x = 140$	Translate the problem into an algebraic equation In doing this, the % must be written as a fraction or decimal. $7 = .05x$ $700 = 5x$ $140 = x$

Q 20 is $33\frac{1}{3}\%$ of what number?

A

PROPORTION METHOD	SHORTER METHOD
$\frac{33\frac{1}{3}}{100} = \frac{20}{x}$ $33\frac{1}{3}x = 2000$ $\frac{100}{3}x = 2000$ $100x = 6000$ $x = 60$	$20 = \frac{1}{3}x$ $60 = x$

Just think of the time you save and the number of extra problems you will get to solve if you know that $33\frac{1}{3}\% = \frac{1}{3}$.

To Find What % One Number Is of Another

Q 90 is what % of 1500?

A

PROPORTION METHOD	SHORTER METHOD
$\frac{x}{100}=\frac{90}{1500}$ $1500x=9000$ $15x=90$ $x=6$	Put the part over the whole. Simplify the fraction and multiply by 100. $\frac{90}{1500}=\frac{9}{150}=\frac{3}{50}\bullet 100=6$

Q 7 is what % of 35?

A

PROPORTION METHOD	SHORTER METHOD
$\frac{x}{100}=\frac{7}{35}$ $35x=700$ $x=20$	$\frac{7}{35}=\frac{1}{5}=20\%$

Q 18 is what % of 108?

A

PROPORTION METHOD	SHORTER METHOD
$\frac{x}{100}=\frac{18}{108}$ $108x=1800$ Time-consuming long division is necessary to get: $x=16\frac{2}{3}$	$\frac{18}{108}=\frac{9}{54}=\frac{1}{6}=16\frac{2}{3}\%$ Once again, if you know the fraction equivalents of common percents, computation can be done in a few seconds.

To Find a % Over 100

Q Find 125% of 64.

A

PROPORTION METHOD	DECIMAL METHOD	FRACTION METHOD
$\frac{125}{100}=\frac{x}{64}$ $100x=8,000$ $x=80$	64 × 1.25 320 128 64 80.00	$1\frac{1}{4}\bullet 64$ $\frac{5}{\not 4}\bullet \overset{16}{\not 64}=80$

Q 36 is 150% of what number?

A

PROPORTION METHOD

$$\frac{150}{100}=\frac{36}{x}$$
$$150x = 3600$$
$$15x = 360$$
$$x = 24$$

DECIMAL METHOD

$$36 = 1.50x$$
$$360 = 15x$$
$$24 = x$$

FRACTION METHOD

$$36 = 1\frac{1}{2}x$$
$$36 = \frac{3}{2}x$$
$$72 = 3x$$
$$24 = x$$

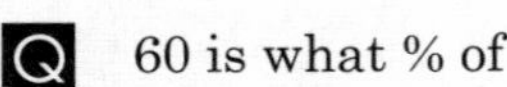

Q 60 is what % of 50?

A

PROPORTION METHOD

$$\frac{x}{100}=\frac{60}{50}$$
$$50x = 6000$$
$$5x = 600$$
$$x = 120$$

FRACTION METHOD

$$\frac{60}{50}=\frac{6}{5}=1\frac{1}{5}=120\%$$

Exercise: Finding Percents

Work out each problem.

1. Write .2% as a decimal.

(A) .2

(B) .02

(C) .002

(D) 2

(E) 20

2. Write 3.4% as a fraction.

(A) $\frac{34}{1000}$

(B) $\frac{34}{10}$

(C) $\frac{34}{100}$

(D) $\frac{340}{100}$

(E) $\frac{34}{10,000}$

3. Write $\frac{3}{4}$% as a decimal.

(A) .75

(B) .075

(C) .0075

(D) .00075

(E) 7.5

4. Find 60% of 70.

(A) 420

(B) 4.2

(C) $116\frac{2}{3}$

(D) 4200

(E) 42

5. What is 175% of 16?

(A) $9\frac{1}{7}$

(B) 28

(C) 24

(D) 12

(E) 22

6. What percent of 40 is 16?

(A) 20

(B) $2\frac{1}{2}$

(C) $33\frac{1}{3}$

(D) 250

(E) 40

7. What percent of 16 is 40?

(A) 20

(B) $2\frac{1}{2}$

(C) 200

(D) 250

(E) 40

8. $4 is 20% of what?

(A) $5

(B) $20

(C) $200

(D) $5

(E) $10

9. 12 is 150% of what number?

(A) 18

(B) 15

(C) 6

(D) 9

(E) 8

10. How many sixteenths are there in $87\frac{1}{2}$%?

(A) 7

(B) 14

(C) 3.5

(D) 13

(E) 15

Solutions

1. **The correct answer is (C).**

   .2% = .002 The decimal point moves to the LEFT two places.

2. **The correct answer is (A).**

   $3.4\% = \frac{3.4}{100} = \frac{34}{1000}$

3. **The correct answer is (C).**

   $\frac{3}{4}\% = .75\% = .0075$

4. **The correct answer is (E).**

   $60\% = \frac{3}{5} \quad \frac{3}{5} \bullet 70 = 42$

5. **The correct answer is (B).**

   $175\% = 1\frac{3}{4} \quad \frac{7}{4} \bullet 16 = 28$

6. **The correct answer is (E).**

   $\frac{16}{40} = \frac{2}{5} = 40\%$

7. **The correct answer is (D).**

   $\frac{40}{16} = \frac{5}{2} = 2\frac{1}{2} = 250\%$

8. **The correct answer is (B).**

   $20\% = \frac{1}{5}$, so $4 = \frac{1}{5}x \quad 20 = x$

9. **The correct answer is (E).**

   $150\% = 1\frac{1}{2} \quad \frac{3}{2}x = 12 \quad 3x = 24 \quad x = 8$

10. **The correct answer is (B).**

    $87\frac{1}{2}\% = \frac{7}{8} = \frac{14}{16}$

6. VERBAL PROBLEMS INVOLVING PERCENT

Certain types of business situations are excellent applications of percent.

Percent of Increase or Decrease

The percent of increase or decrease is found by putting the amount of increase or decrease over the original amount and renaming this fraction as a percent, as explained in a previous section.

Q Over a five-year period, the enrollment at South High dropped from 1,000 students to 800. Find the percent of decrease.

A $\frac{200}{1000} = \frac{20}{100} = 20\%$

Q A company normally employs 100 people. During a slow spell, it fired 20% of its employees. By what percent must it now increase its staff to return to full capacity?

A $20\% = \frac{1}{5} \quad \frac{1}{5} \bullet 100 = 20$

The company now has 100 – 20 = 80 employees. If it then increases by 20, the percent of increase is $\frac{20}{80} = \frac{1}{4}$, or 25%.

Discount

A discount is usually expressed as a percent of the marked price that will be deducted from the marked price to determine the sale price.

Q Bill's Hardware offers a 20% discount on all appliances during a sale week. If they take advantage of the sale, how much must the Russells pay for a washing machine marked at $280?

A

LONG METHOD

$$20\% = \frac{1}{5}$$

$$\frac{1}{5} \bullet 280 = \$56 \text{ discount}$$

$$\$280 - \$56 = \$224 \text{ sale price}$$

The danger inherent in this method is that $56 is sure to be among the multiple-choice answers.

SHORTCUT METHOD

If there is a 20% discount, the Russells will pay 80% of the marked price.

$$80\% = \frac{4}{5}$$

$$\frac{4}{5} \bullet 280 = \$224 \text{ sale price}$$

Q A store offers a television set marked at $340 less discounts of 10% and 5%. Another store offers the same set with a single discount of 15%. How much does the buyer save by buying at the better price?

A In the first store, the initial discount means the buyer pays 90% or $\frac{9}{10}$ of 340, which is $306. The additional 5% discount means the buyer pays 95% of $306, or $290.70. Note that the second discount must be figured on the first sale price. Taking 5% off $306 is a smaller amount than taking the additional 5% off $340. The second store will therefore have a lower sale price. In the second store, the buyer will pay 85% of $340, or $289, making the price $1.70 less than in the first store.

Commission

Many salespeople earn money on a commission basis. In order to encourage sales, they are paid a percentage of the value of goods sold. This amount is called a commission.

Q A salesperson at Brown's Department Store is paid $80 per week in salary plus a 4% commission on all her sales. How much will that salesperson earn in a week in which she sells $4,032 worth of merchandise?

A Find 4% of $4,032 and add this amount to $80.

$$\begin{array}{r} 4032 \\ .04 \\ \hline \end{array}$$

$$\$161.28 + \$80 = \$241.28$$

Q Bill Olson delivers newspapers for a dealer and keeps 8% of all money collected. One month he was able to keep $16. How much did he forward to the newspaper?

A First, determine how much he collected by finding the number that 16 is 8% of.

$$\begin{aligned} 16 &= .08x \\ 1600 &= 8x \\ 200 &= x \end{aligned}$$

If Bill collected $200 and kept $16, he gave the dealer $200 – $16, or $184.

Taxes

Taxes are a percent of money spent or money earned.

Q Noname County collects a 7% sales tax on automobiles. If the price of a car is $8,532 before taxes, what will this car cost once sales tax is added in?

A Find 7% of $8,532 to determine tax and then add it to $8,532. This can be done in one step by finding 107% of $8,532.

$$\begin{array}{r} 8532 \\ \times\ 1.07 \\ \hline 59724 \\ 85320 \\ \hline \$9129.24 \end{array}$$

Q If the tax rate in Anytown is $3.10 per $100, what is the annual real estate tax on a house assessed at $47,200?

A Annual tax = Tax rate × Assessed value

$$\begin{aligned} &= (\$3.10/\$100)\ (\$47,200) \\ &= (.031)\ (47,200) \\ &= \$1463.20 \end{aligned}$$

Exercise: Verbal Problems Involving Percent

Work out each problem.

1. A suit marked at $80 is sold for $68. What is the rate of discount?

   (A) 15%

   (B) 12%

   (C) $17\frac{11}{17}\%$

   (D) 20%

   (E) 24%

2. What was the original price of a radio that sold for $70 during a 20%-off sale?

   (A) $84

   (B) $56

   (C) $87.50

   (D) $92

   (E) $90

3. How many dollars does a salesperson earn on a sale of s dollars at a commission of r%?

   (A) rs

   (B) $\frac{r}{s}$

   (C) $100rs$

   (D) $\frac{r}{100s}$

   (E) $\frac{rs}{100}$

4. At a selling price of $273, a refrigerator yields a 30% profit on the cost. What selling price will yield a 10% profit on the cost?

   (A) $210

   (B) $231

   (C) $221

   (D) $235

   (E) $240

5. What single discount is equivalent to two successive discounts of 10% and 15%?

   (A) 25%

   (B) 24%

   (C) 24.5%

   (D) 23.5%

   (E) 22%

6. The net price of a certain article is $306 after successive discounts of 15% and 10% off the marked price. What is the marked price?

   (A) $234.09

   (B) $400

   (C) $382.50

   (D) $408

   (E) None of these

7. If a merchant makes a profit of 20% based on the selling price of an article, what percent does the merchant make on the cost?

   (A) 20

   (B) 40

   (C) 25

   (D) 80

   (E) None of these

8. A certain radio costs a merchant $72. At what price must the merchant sell this radio in order to make a profit of 20% of the selling price?

   (A) $86.40

   (B) $92

   (C) $90

   (D) $144

   (E) $148

9. A baseball team has won 40 games out of 60 played. It has 32 more games to play. How many of these must the team win to make its record 75% for the season?

   (A) 26
   (B) 29
   (C) 28
   (D) 30
   (E) 32

10. If prices are reduced 25% and sales increase 20%, what is the net effect on gross receipts?

   (A) They increase by 5%.
   (B) They decrease by 5%.
   (C) They remain the same.
   (D) They increase by 10%.
   (E) They decrease by 10%.

11. A salesperson earns 5% on all sales between \$200 and \$600, and 8% on all sales over \$600. What is her commission in a week in which her sales total \$800?

   (A) \$20
   (B) \$46
   (C) \$88
   (D) \$36
   (E) \$78

12. If the enrollment at State U. was 3,000 in 1965 and 12,000 in 1990, what was the percent of increase in enrollment?

   (A) 125%
   (B) 25%
   (C) 300%
   (D) 400%
   (E) 3%

13. If 6 students, representing $16\frac{2}{3}\%$ of the class, failed algebra, how many students passed the course?

   (A) 48
   (B) 36
   (C) 42
   (D) 30
   (E) 32

14. If 95% of the residents of Coral Estates live in private homes and 40% of these live in air-conditioned homes, what percent of the residents of Coral Estates live in air-conditioned homes?

   (A) 3%
   (B) 30%
   (C) 3.8%
   (D) 40%
   (E) 38%

15. A salesperson receives a salary of \$100 a week and a commission of 5% on all sales. What must be the amount of sales for a week in which the salesperson's total weekly income is \$360?

   (A) \$6,200
   (B) \$5,200
   (C) \$2,600
   (D) \$720
   (E) \$560

Solutions

1. **The correct answer is (A).** The amount of discount is \$12. Rate of discount is figured on the original price.

$\frac{12}{80} = \frac{3}{20} \quad \frac{3}{20} \bullet 100 = 15\%$

2. **The correct answer is (C).** \$70 represents 80% of the original price.

$$70 = .80x$$
$$700 = 8x$$
$$\$87.50 = x$$

3. **The correct answer is (E).**

$r\% = \frac{r}{100}$

The commission is $\frac{r}{100} \bullet s = \frac{rs}{100}$

4. **The correct answer is (B).** \$273 represents 130% of the cost.

$$1.30x = 273$$
$$13x = 2730$$
$$x = \$210 = \text{ cost}$$

The new price will add 10% of cost, or \$21, for profit.

New price = \$231

5. **The correct answer is (D).** Work with a simple figure, such as 100.

First sale price is 90% of \$100, or \$90.

Final sale price is 85% of \$90, or \$76.50

Total discount is \$100 – \$76.50 = \$23.50

% of discount = $\frac{23.50}{100}$ or 23.5%

6. **The correct answer is (B).** If marked price = m, first sale price = $.85m$ and net price = $.90(.85m) = .765m$

$.765m = 306$

$m = 400$

In this case, it would be easy to work from the answer choices.

15% of \$400 is \$60, making a first sale price of \$340.

10% of this price is \$34, making the net price \$306.

Choices (A), (C), and (D) would not give a final answer in whole dollars.

7. **The correct answer is (C).** Use an easy amount of \$100 for the selling price. If the profit is 20% of the selling price, or \$20, the cost is \$80. Profit based on cost is

$\frac{20}{80} = \frac{1}{4} = 25\%$

8. **The correct answer is (C).** If the profit is to be 20% of the selling price, the cost must be 80% of the selling price.

$$72 = .80x$$
$$720 = 8x$$
$$90 = x$$

9. **The correct answer is (B).** The team must win 75%, or $\frac{3}{4}$, of the games played during the entire season. With 60 games played and 32 more to play, the team must win $\frac{3}{4}$ of 92 games in all. $\frac{3}{4} \bullet 92 = 69$. Since 40 games have already been won, the team must win 29 additional games.

10. **The correct answer is (E).** Let original price = p, and original sales = s. Therefore, original gross receipts = ps. Let new price = $.75p$, and new sales = $1.20s$. Therefore, new gross receipts = $.90ps$. Gross receipts are only 90% of what they were.

11. **The correct answer is (D).** 5% of sales between \$200 and \$600 is .05(600) = \$20. 8% of sales over \$600 is .08(200) = \$16. Total commission = \$20 + \$16 = \$36.

12. **The correct answer is (C).** Increase is 9,000. Percent of increase is figured on original.

$\frac{9000}{3000} = 3 = 300\%$

13. The correct answer is (D).

$16\frac{2}{3}\% = \frac{1}{6}$

$6 = \frac{1}{6}x$

$36 = x$

36 students in class. 6 failed. 30 passed.

14. The correct answer is (E).

$40\% = \frac{2}{5}$

$\frac{2}{5}$ of 95% = 38%

15. The correct answer is (B). Let s = sales:

$\$100 + .05s = 360$

$.05s = 260$

$5s = 26{,}000$

$s = \$5{,}200$

7. AVERAGES

ADD, THEN DIVIDE. The concept of average is familiar to most students. To find the average of n numbers, simply add the numbers and divide by n.

Q Find the average of 32, 50, and 47.

A

$$\begin{array}{r} 32 \\ 50 \\ +47 \\ \hline 129 \end{array} \qquad 3\overline{)129} = 43$$

A more frequently encountered type of average problem will give the average and ask you to find a missing term.

Q The average of three numbers is 43. If two of the numbers are 32 and 50, find the third number.

A Using the definition of average, write the equation:

$$\frac{32 + 50 + x}{3} = 43$$

$$32 + 50 + x = 129$$

$$82 + x = 129$$

$$x = 47$$

WEIGHTED AVERAGE. Another concept to understand is the weighted average.

Q Andrea has four grades of 90 and two grades of 80 during the spring semester of calculus. What is her average in the course for this semester?

A

$$\begin{array}{r} 90 \\ 90 \\ 90 \\ 90 \\ 80 \\ +\ \underline{80} \\ 6\overline{)\,520} \\ 86\frac{2}{3} \end{array} \qquad \text{or} \qquad \begin{array}{r} 90 \cdot 4 = 360 \\ 80 \cdot 2 = \underline{160} \\ 6\overline{)520} \\ 86\frac{2}{3} \end{array}$$

Be sure to understand that you cannot simply average 90 and 80, since there are more grades of 90 than 80.

AVERAGE RATE. The final concept of average that you should master is average rate. The average rate for a trip is the total distance covered, divided by the total time spent.

Q In driving from New York to Boston, Mr. Portney drove for 3 hours at 40 miles per hour and 1 hour at 48 miles per hour. What was his average rate for this portion of the trip?

A $\text{Average rate} = \dfrac{\text{Total distance}}{\text{Total time}}$

$$\text{Average rate} = \frac{3(40)+1(48)}{3+1}$$

$$\text{Average rate} = \frac{168}{4} = 42 \text{ miles per hour}$$

Since more of the trip was driven at 40 mph than at 48 mph, the average should be closer to 40 than to 48, which it is. This will help you to check your answer, or to pick out the correct choice in a multiple-choice question.

Exercise: Averages

Work out each problem.

1. Dan had an average of 72 on his first four math tests. After taking the next test, his average dropped to 70. Which of the following is his most recent test grade?

   (A) 60
   (B) 62
   (C) 64
   (D) 66
   (E) 68

2. What is the average of $\sqrt{.64}$, .85, and $\frac{9}{10}$?

   (A) $\frac{21}{25}$
   (B) 3.25
   (C) 2.55
   (D) 85%
   (E) $\frac{4}{5}$

3. The average of two numbers is XY. If the first number is Y, what is the other number?

   (A) $2XY - Y$
   (B) $XY - 2Y$
   (C) $2XY - X$
   (D) X
   (E) $XY - Y$

4. 30 students had an average of X, while 20 students had an average of 80. What is the average for the entire group?

   (A) $\frac{X+80}{50}$
   (B) $\frac{X+80}{2}$
   (C) $\frac{50}{X+80}$
   (D) $\frac{3}{5}X+32$
   (E) $\frac{30X+80}{50}$

5. What is the average of the first 15 positive integers?

   (A) 7
   (B) 7.5
   (C) 8
   (D) 8.5
   (E) 9

6. A man travels a distance of 20 miles at 60 miles per hour and then returns over the same route at 40 miles per hour. What is his average rate for the round trip in miles per hour?

   (A) 50
   (B) 48
   (C) 47
   (D) 46
   (E) 45

7. A number p equals $\frac{3}{2}$ the average of 10, 12, and q. What is q in terms of p?

   (A) $\frac{2}{3}p-22$
   (B) $\frac{4}{3}p-22$
   (C) $2p-22$
   (D) $\frac{1}{2}p+11$
   (E) $\frac{9}{2}p-22$

8. Susan has an average of 86 in three examinations. What grade must she receive on her next test to raise her average to 88?

   (A) 94
   (B) 90
   (C) 92
   (D) 100
   (E) 96

9. The heights of the five starters on Redwood High's basketball team are 5′11″, 6′3″, 6′, 6′6″, and 6′2″. The average height of these players is

(A) 6′1″

(B) 6′2″

(C) 6′3″

(D) 6′4″

(E) 6′5″

10. What is the average of all numbers from 1 to 100 that end in 2?

(A) 46

(B) 47

(C) 48

(D) 50

(E) None of these

Solutions

1. **The correct answer is (B).**

$$\frac{4(72)+x}{5}=70$$
$$288+x=350$$
$$x=62$$

2. **The correct answer is (D).** In order to average these three numbers, they should all be expressed as decimals.

$$\sqrt{.64}=.8$$
$$.85=.85$$
$$\frac{9}{10}=.9$$
$$\text{Average}=\frac{.8+.85+.9}{3}=\frac{2.55}{3}=.85$$

This is equal to 85%.

3. **The correct answer is (A).**

$$\frac{Y+x}{2}=XY$$
$$Y+x=2XY$$
$$x=2XY-Y$$

4. **The correct answer is (D).**

$$\frac{30(X)+20(80)}{50}=\text{Average}$$
$$\frac{30(X)+1600}{50}=\frac{3X+160}{5}=\frac{3}{5}X+32$$

5. **The correct answer is (C).** Positive integers begin with 1.

$$\frac{1+2+3+4+5+6+7+8+9+10+11+12+13+14+15}{15}$$

Since these numbers are evenly spaced, the average will be the middle number, 8.

6. **The correct answer is (B).**

Average rate = $\frac{\text{Total distance}}{\text{Total time}}$

Total distance = 20 + 20 = 40

Since time = $\frac{\text{distance}}{\text{time}}$, time for first part of trip is $\frac{20}{60}$, or $\frac{1}{3}$ hour, while time for the second part of trip is $\frac{20}{40}$, or $\frac{1}{2}$ hour.

Total time = $\frac{1}{3}+\frac{1}{2}$, or $\frac{5}{6}$ hour.

Average rate $\frac{40}{\frac{5}{6}}=40\bullet\frac{6}{5}=48$ mph

7. **The correct answer is (C).**

$$p=\frac{3}{2}\left(\frac{10+12+q}{3}\right)$$
$$p=\frac{10+12+q}{2}$$
$$2p=22+q$$
$$2p-22=q$$

8. **The correct answer is (A).**

$$\frac{3(86)+x}{4}=88$$
$$258+x=352$$
$$x=94$$

9. **The correct answer is (B).**

$$\begin{array}{r} 5'11'' \\ 6'\,3'' \\ 6' \\ 6'\,6'' \\ \underline{6'\,2''} \end{array}$$

$$29'22'' = 5\overline{)\,30'\,10''}\quad 6'2''$$

10. **The correct answer is (B).**

$$\frac{2+12+22+32+42+52+62+72+82+92}{10}$$

Since these numbers are equally spaced, the average is the middle number. However, since there is an even number of addends, the average will be halfway between the middle two. Halfway between 42 and 52 is 47.

chapter 12

Algebra

OVERVIEW

- **Signed Numbers**
- **Linear Equations**
- **Exponents**
- **Quadratic Equations**
- **Literal Expressions**
- **Roots and Radicals**
- **Factoring and Algebraic Fractions**
- **Problem Solving in Algebra**
- **Inequalities**
- **Defined Operation Problems**

1. SIGNED NUMBERS

To solve algebra problems, you must be able to compute accurately with signed numbers.

Addition: To add signed numbers with the same sign, add the magnitudes of the numbers and keep the same sign. To add signed numbers with different signs, subtract the magnitudes of the numbers and use the sign of the number with the greater magnitude.

Subtraction: Change the sign of the number being subtracted and follow the rules for addition.

Multiplication: If there are an odd number of negative signs, the product is negative. An even number of negative signs gives a positive product.

Division: If the signs are the same, the quotient is positive. If the signs are different, the quotient is negative.

Exercise: Signed Numbers

Work out each problem.

1. When +3 is added to –5, the sum is
   (A) –8
   (B) +8
   (C) –2
   (D) +2
   (E) –15

2. When –4 and –5 are added, the sum is
   (A) –9
   (B) +9
   (C) –1
   (D) +1
   (E) +20

3. When –6 is subtracted from +3, the result is
   (A) –3
   (B) +3
   (C) +18
   (D) –9
   (E) +9

4. When –5 is subtracted from +10, the result is
   (A) +5
   (B) +15
   (C) –5
   (D) –15
   (E) –50

5. (–6)(–3) equals
   (A) –18
   (B) +18
   (C) +2
   (D) –9
   (E) +9

6. The product of $(-6)(+\frac{1}{2})(-10)$ is
   (A) $-15\frac{1}{2}$
   (B) $+15\frac{1}{2}$
   (C) –30
   (D) +30
   (E) +120

7. When the product of (–4) and (+3) is divided by (–2), the quotient is
   (A) $\frac{1}{2}$
   (B) $3\frac{1}{2}$
   (C) 6
   (D) $-\frac{1}{2}$
   (E) – 6

Solutions

1. **The correct answer is (C).** In adding numbers with opposite signs, subtract their magnitudes (5 – 3 = 2) and use the sign of the number with the greater magnitude (negative).

2. **The correct answer is (A).** In adding numbers with the same sign, add their magnitudes (4 + 5 = 9) and keep the same sign.

3. **The correct answer is (E).** Change the sign of the bottom number and follow the rules for addition.

$$\begin{array}{rr} + & 3 \\ +\ \ominus & 6 \\ + & 9 \end{array}$$

4. **The correct answer is (B).** Change the sign of the bottom number and follow the rules for addition.

$$\begin{array}{rr} + & 10 \\ +\ \ominus & 5 \\ + & 15 \end{array}$$

5. **The correct answer is (B).** The product of two negative numbers is a positive number.

6. **The correct answer is (D).** The product of an even number of negative numbers is positive.

$$(\overset{3}{\cancel{6}})\left(\frac{1}{\cancel{2}}\right)(10) = 30$$

7. **The correct answer is (C).**

$(-4)(+3) = -12$

Dividing a negative number by a negative number gives a positive quotient.

$$\frac{-12}{-2} = +6$$

2. LINEAR EQUATIONS

The next step in solving algebra problems is mastering linear equations. Whether an equation involves numbers or only variables, the basic steps are the same.

Strategy:

❶ If there are fractions or decimals, remove them by multiplication.

❷ Collect all terms containing the unknown for which you are solving on the same side of the equation. Remember that whenever a term crosses the equal sign from one side of the equation to the other, it must pay a toll. That is, it must change its sign.

❸ Determine the coefficient of the unknown by combining similar terms or factoring when terms cannot be combined.

❹ Divide both sides of the equation by this coefficient.

Q Solve for x: $5x - 3 = 3x + 5$

A $2x = 8$
$x = 4$

Q Solve for x: $ax - b = cx + d$

A
$$ax - cx = b + d$$
$$x(a - c) = b + d$$
$$x = \frac{b + d}{a - c}$$

Q Solve for x: $\frac{3}{4}x + 2 = \frac{2}{3}x + 3$

A Multiply by 12: $9x + 24 = 8x + 36$

$$x = 12$$

Q Solve for x: $.7x + .04 = 2.49$

A Multiply by 100: $70x + 4 = 249$

$$70x = 245$$
$$x = 3.5$$

SIMULTANEOUS EQUATIONS. In solving equations with two unknowns, you must work with two equations simultaneously. The object is to eliminate one of the two unknowns, and solve for the resulting single unknown.

Q Solve for x: $2x - 4y = 2$
$3x + 5y = 14$

A Multiply the first equation by 5: $10x - 20y = 10$

Multiply the second equation by 4: $12x + 20y = 56$

Since the y terms now have the same numerical coefficients, but with opposite signs, you can eliminate them by adding the two equations. If they had the same signs, you would eliminate them by subtracting the equations.

Add the equations:

$$10x - 20y = 10$$
$$12x + 20y = 56$$
$$22x = 66$$
$$x = 3$$

Since you were only asked to solve for x, stop here. If you were asked to solve for both x and y, you would now substitute 3 for x in either equation and solve the resulting equation for y.

$$3(3) + 5y = 14$$
$$9 + 5y = 14$$
$$5y = 5$$
$$y = 1$$

Q Solve for x:

$ax + by = c$
$dx + ey = f$

A Multiply the first equation by e: $aex + bey = ce$

Multiply the second equation by b: $bdx + bey = bf$

Since the y terms now have the same coefficient, with the same sign, eliminate these terms by subtracting the two equations.

$$\begin{array}{l} aex + bey = ce \\ \underline{-(bdx + bey = bf)} \\ aex - bdx = ce - bf \end{array}$$

Factor to determine the coefficient of x: $x(ae - bd) = ce - bf$

Divide by the coefficient of x: $x = \dfrac{ce - bf}{ae - bd}$

Exercise: Linear Equations

Work out each problem.

1. If $5x + 6 = 10$, then x equals

(A) $\frac{16}{5}$

(B) $\frac{5}{16}$

(C) $-\frac{5}{4}$

(D) $\frac{4}{5}$

(E) $\frac{5}{4}$

2. Solve for x: $ax = bx + c, a \neq b$

(A) $\frac{b+c}{a}$

(B) $\frac{c}{a-b}$

(C) $\frac{c}{b-a}$

(D) $\frac{a-b}{c}$

(E) $\frac{c}{a+b}$

3. Solve for k: $\frac{k}{3} + \frac{k}{4} = 1$

(A) $\frac{11}{8}$

(B) $\frac{8}{11}$

(C) $\frac{7}{12}$

(D) $\frac{12}{7}$

(E) $\frac{1}{7}$

4. If $x + y = 8p$ and $x - y = 6q$, then x is

(A) $7pq$

(B) $4p + 3q$

(C) pq

(D) $4p - 3q$

(E) $8p + 6q$

5. If $7x = 3x + 12$, then $2x + 5 =$

(A) 10

(B) 11

(C) 12

(D) 13

(E) 14

6. In the equation $y = x^2 + rx - 3$, for what value of r will $y = 11$ when $x = 2$?

(A) 6

(B) 5

(C) 4

(D) $3\frac{1}{2}$

(E) 0

7. If $1 + \frac{1}{t} = \frac{t+1}{t}$, what does t equal?

(A) +1 only

(B) +1 or –1 only

(C) +1 or +2 only

(D) No values

(E) All values except 0

8. If $.23m = .069$, then $m =$

(A) .003

(B) .03

(C) .3

(D) 3

(E) 30

9. If $35rt + 8 = 42rt$, then $rt =$

(A) $\frac{8}{7}$

(B) $\frac{8}{87}$

(C) $\frac{7}{8}$

(D) $\frac{87}{8}$

(E) $-\frac{8}{7}$

10. For what values of n is $n + 5$ equal to $n - 5$?

(A) No value

(B) 0

(C) All negative values

(D) All positive values

(E) All values

Solutions

1. **The correct answer is (D).**

$5x = 4$

$x = \frac{4}{5}$

2. **The correct answer is (B).**

$ax - bx = c \quad x(a - b) = c \quad x = \frac{c}{a - b}$

3. **The correct answer is (D).** Multiply by 12: $4k + 3k = 12$

$7k = 12$

$k = \frac{12}{7}$

4. **The correct answer is (B).** Add equations to eliminate y:

$x + y = 8p$

$x - y = 6q$

$2x = 8p + 6q$

Divide by 2: $x = 4p + 3q$

5. **The correct answer is (B).** Solve for x:

$4x = 12$

$x = 3$

$2x + 5 = 2(3) + 5 = 11$

6. **The correct answer is (B).** Substitute given values:

$11 = 4 + 2r - 3$

$10 = 2r$

$r = 5$

7. **The correct answer is (E).** Multiply by t: $t + 1 = t + 1$

This is an identity and is therefore true for all values. However, since t was a denominator in the given equation, t may not equal 0, because you can never divide by 0.

8. **The correct answer is (C).** Multiply by 100 to make coefficient an integer.

$23x = 6.9$

$x = .3$

9. The correct answer is (A). Even though this equation has two unknowns, you are asked to solve for *rt*, which may be treated as a single unknown.

$8 = 7rt$

$\frac{8}{7} = rt$

10. The correct answer is (A). There is no number such that when 5 is added, you get the same result as when 5 is subtracted. Do not confuse choices (A) and (B). Choice (B) would mean that the number 0 satisfies the equation, which it does not.

3. EXPONENTS

DEFINITIONS. An **exponent** is a mathematical notation indicating that a number, called the **base**, has been multiplied one or more times by itself. For example, in the term 2^3, the 2 is the base and the ^{3} is the exponent. This term means "2 times 2 times 2" and is read "two to the third power." The word **power** tells how many times the base number appears in the multiplication.

$x^3 = x$ times x times x
$x^2 = x$ times x
$x^1 = x$
$x^0 = 1$

THE RULES OF EXPONENTS

1. To multiply powers of the same base, add the exponents.
   x^2 times $x^3 = x^{2+3} = x^5$
   x^5 times $x^4 = x^{5+4} = x^9$

2. To divide powers of the same base, subtract the exponent of the divisor from the exponent of the dividend.

   $\frac{x^6}{x^2} = x^{6-2} = x^4$

   $\frac{x^{10}}{x^3} = x^{10-3} = x^7$

3. To find the power of a power, multiply the exponents.
   $(x^2)^3 = x^{(2)(3)} = x^6$
   $(x^3y^5)^2 = x^{(3)(2)}y^{(5)(2)} = x^6y^{10}$

A variable base with an even exponent has two values, one positive and one negative.

$x^2 = 25$ x could be positive 5 or negative 5.

A variable base can be zero (unless otherwise stated in the problem). In that case, no matter what the exponent, the value of the term is zero.

Is x^4 always greater than x^2? No; if x is zero, then x^4 and x^2 are equal.

When the base is a fraction between 0 and 1, the larger the exponent, the smaller the value of the term.

Which is greater, $\left(\frac{37}{73}\right)$ or $\left(\frac{37}{73}\right)^2$? The correct answer is $\left(\frac{37}{73}\right)$. $\left(\frac{37}{73}\right)$ is almost $\frac{1}{2}$, while $\left(\frac{37}{73}\right)^2$ is about $\frac{1}{4}$.

Exercise: Exponents

Work out each problem.

1. If x and y are not equal to 0, then $x^{12}y^6$ must be
   I. Positive
   II. Negative
   III. An integer
   IV. A mixed fraction
   (A) I only
   (B) II only
   (C) III only
   (D) IV only
   (E) I and III

2. $(x^2y^3)^4 =$
   (A) x^6y^7
   (B) x^8y^{12}
   (C) $x^{12}y^8$
   (D) x^2y
   (E) x^6y^9

3. $\frac{x^{16}y^6}{x^4y^2} =$
   (A) $x^{20}y^8$
   (B) x^4y^3
   (C) x^5y^6
   (D) $x^{12}y^3$
   (E) $x^{12}y^4$

4. If $x^4 = 16$ and $y^2 = 36$, then the *maximum* possible value for $x - y$ is
   (A) –20
   (B) 20
   (C) –4
   (D) 6
   (E) 8

5. $p^8 \times q^4 \times p^4 \times q^8 =$
   (A) $p^{12}q^{12}$
   (B) p^4q^4
   (C) $p^{32}q^{32}$
   (D) $p^{64}q^{64}$
   (E) $p^{16}q^{16}$

Solutions

1. **The correct answer is (A).** If x and y are not 0, then the even exponents would force x^{12} and y^6 to be positive.

2. **The correct answer is (B).** To raise a power to a power, multiply the exponents. $x^{(2)(4)}y^{(3)(4)} = x^8y^{12}$

3. **The correct answer is (E).** All fractions are implied division. When dividing terms with a common base and different exponents, subtract the exponents. 16 – 4 = 12 and 6 – 2 = 4.

4. **The correct answer is (E).** x could be positive 2 or negative 2. y could be positive 6 or negative 6. The four possible values for $x - y$ are as follows:

$2 - 6 = -4$
$2 - (-6) = 8$
$-2 - 6 = -8$
$-2 - (-6) = 4$

The maximum value would be 8.

5. **The correct answer is (A).** The multiplication signs do not change the fact that this is the multiplication of terms with a common base and different exponents. Solve this kind of problem by adding the exponents.

$p^{8+4} \times q^{4+8} = p^{12}q^{12}$

4. QUADRATIC EQUATIONS

ROOTS AND FACTORING. In solving quadratic equations, remember that there will always be two roots, even though these roots may be equal. A complete quadratic equation is of the form $ax^2 + bx + c = 0$ and, in the GMAT, can always be solved by factoring.

Q Factor: $x^2 + 7x + 12 = 0$

A $(x \quad)(x \quad) = 0$

The last term of the equation is positive; therefore, both factors must have the same sign, since the last two terms multiply to a positive product. The middle term is also positive; therefore, both factors must be positive, since they also add to a positive sum.

$(x + 4)\ (x + 3) = 0$

If the product of two factors is 0, each factor may be set equal to 0, yielding the values for x of -4 or -3

Q Factor: $x^2 + 7x - 18 = 0$

A $(x \quad)(x \quad) = 0$

Now you are looking for two numbers with a product of -18; therefore, they must have opposite signs. To yield +7 as a middle coefficient, the numbers must be +9 and −2.

$(x + 9)\ (x - 2) = 0$

This equation gives the roots −9 and +2.

Incomplete quadratic equations are those in which b or c is equal to 0.

Q Solve for x: $x^2 - 16 = 0$

A $x^2 = 16$
$x = \pm 4$ Remember, there must be 2 roots.

Q Solve for x: $4x^2 - 9 = 0$

A $4x^2 = 9$

$x^2 = \frac{9}{4}$

$x = \pm\frac{3}{2}$

Q Solve for x: $x^2 + 4x = 0$

A Never divide through an equation by the unknown, as this would yield an equation of lower degree having fewer roots than the original equation. Always factor this type of equation.

$x(x + 4) = 0$

The roots are 0 and –4.

Q Solve for x: $4x^2 - 9x = 0$

A $x(4x - 9) = 0$

The roots are 0 and $\frac{9}{4}$.

RADICALS. In solving equations containing radicals, always get the radical alone on one side of the equation; then square both sides to remove the radical and solve. Remember that all solutions to radical equations must be checked, as squaring both sides may sometimes result in extraneous roots.

Q Solve for x: $\sqrt{x+5} = 7$

A $x + 5 = 49$

$x = 44$

Checking, we have $\sqrt{49} = 7$, which is true.

Q Solve for x: $\sqrt{x} = -6$

A $x = 36$

Checking, we have $\sqrt{36} = -6$, which is not true, as the radical sign means the positive, or principal, square root only. $\sqrt{36} = 6$, not –6, and therefore this equation has no solution.

Q Solve for x: $\sqrt{x^2+6}-3=x$

$$\sqrt{x^2+6}=x+3$$
$$x^2+6=x^2+6x+9$$
$$6=6x+9$$
$$-3=6x$$
$$-\frac{1}{2}=x$$

A Checking, we have $\sqrt{6\frac{1}{4}}-3=-\frac{1}{2}$

$$\sqrt{\frac{25}{4}}-3=-\frac{1}{2}$$
$$\frac{5}{2}-3=-\frac{1}{2}$$
$$2\frac{1}{2}-3=-\frac{1}{2}$$
$$-\frac{1}{2}=-\frac{1}{2}$$

This is a true statement. Therefore, $-\frac{1}{2}$ is a true root.

Exercise: Quadratic Equations

Work out each problem.

1. Solve for x: $x^2 - 2x - 15 = 0$
   (A) + 5 or – 3
   (B) – 5 or + 3
   (C) – 5 or – 3
   (D) + 5 or + 3
   (E) None of these

2. Solve for x: $x^2 + 12 = 8x$
   (A) + 6 or –2
   (B) –6 or + 2
   (C) –6 or –2
   (D) + 6 or + 2
   (E) None of these

3. Solve for x: $4x^2 = 12$
   (A) $\sqrt{3}$
   (B) 3 or –3
   (C) $\sqrt{3}$ or $-\sqrt{3}$
   (D) $\sqrt{3}$ or $\sqrt{-3}$
   (E) 9 or –9

4. Solve for x: $3x^2 = 4x$
   (A) $\frac{4}{3}$
   (B) $\frac{4}{3}$ or 0
   (C) $-\frac{4}{3}$ or 0
   (D) $\frac{4}{3}$ or $-\frac{4}{3}$
   (E) None of these

5. Solve for x: $\sqrt{x^2+7}-2=x-1$

(A) No values

(B) $\frac{1}{3}$

(C) $-\frac{1}{3}$

(D) –3

(E) 3

Solutions

1. **The correct answer is (A).**

$$(x-5)(x+3) = 0$$
$$x = 5 \text{ or } -3$$

2. **The correct answer is (D).**

$$x^2-8x+12=0$$
$$(x-6)(x-2)=0$$
$$x=6 \text{ or } 2$$

3. **The correct answer is (C).**

$$x^2=3$$
$$x=\pm\sqrt{3}$$

4. **The correct answer is (B).**

$$3x^2-4x=0$$
$$x(3x-4)=0$$
$$x=0 \text{ or } \frac{4}{3}$$

5. **The correct answer is (E).**

$$\sqrt{x^2+7}=x+1$$
$$x^2+7=x^2+2x+1$$
$$6=2x$$
$$x=3$$

Checking: $\sqrt{16}-2=3-1$
$$4-2=3-1$$
$$2=2$$

5. LITERAL EXPRESSIONS

If you can compute with numbers, working with variables should be easy. The computational processes are exactly the same. Just think of how you would do the problem with numbers and do exactly the same thing with variables.

Q Find the number of inches in 2 feet 5 inches.

A Since there are 12 inches in a foot, multiply 2 feet by 12 to change it to 24 inches and then add 5 more inches, giving an answer of 29 inches.

Q Find the number of inches in f feet and i inches.

A Doing exactly as you did above, multiply f by 12, giving $12f$ inches, and add i more inches, giving an answer of $12f + i$ inches.

Q A telephone call from New York to Chicago costs 85 cents for the first 3 minutes and 21 cents for each additional minute. Find the cost of an 8-minute call at this rate.

A The first 3 minutes cost 85 cents. There are 5 additional minutes above the first 3. These 5 are billed at 21 cents each, for a cost of \$1.05. The total cost is \$1.90.

Q A telephone call costs c cents for the first 3 minutes and d cents for each additional minute. Find the cost of a call that lasts m minutes if $m > 3$.

A The first three minutes cost c cents. The number of *additional* minutes is $(m - 3)$. These are billed at d cents each, for a cost of $d(m - 3)$ or $dm - 3d$. Thus, the total cost is $c + dm - 3d$. Remember that the first three minutes have been paid for in the basic charge; therefore, you must subtract from the total number of minutes to find the *additional* minutes.

Exercise: Literal Expressions

Work out each problem.

1. David had d dollars. After a shopping trip, he returned with c cents. How many cents did he spend?

(A) $d - c$

(B) $c - d$

(C) $100d - c$

(D) $100c - d$

(E) $d - 100c$

2. How many ounces are there in p pounds and q ounces?

(A) $\frac{p}{16} + q$

(B) pq

(C) $p + 16q$

(D) $p + q$

(E) $16p + q$

3. How many passengers can be seated on a plane with r rows, if each row consists of d double seats and t triple seats?

(A) rdt

(B) $rd + rt$

(C) $2dr + 3tr$

(D) $3dr + 2tr$

(E) $rd + t$

4. How many dimes are there in $4x - 1$ cents?

(A) $40x - 10$

(B) $\frac{2}{5}x - \frac{1}{10}$

(C) $40x - 1$

(D) $4x - 1$

(E) $20x - 5$

5. If u represents the tens' digit of a certain number and t represents the units' digit, then the number with the digits reversed can be represented by

(A) $10t + u$

(B) $10u + t$

(C) tu

(D) ut

(E) $t + u$

6. Joe spent k cents of his allowance and has r cents left. What was his allowance in dollars?

(A) $k + r$

(B) $k - r$

(C) $100(k + r)$

(D) $\frac{k + r}{100}$

(E) $100kr$

7. If p pounds of potatoes cost \$$k$, find the cost (in cents) of one pound of potatoes.

(A) $\frac{k}{p}$

(B) $\frac{k}{100p}$

(C) $\frac{p}{k}$

(D) $\frac{100k}{p}$

(E) $\frac{100p}{k}$

8. Mr. Rabner rents a car for d days. He pays m dollars per day for each of the first 7 days, and half that rate for each additional day. Find the total charge if $d > 7$.

(A) $m + 2m(d-7)$

(B) $m + \frac{m}{2}(d-7)$

(C) $7m + \frac{m}{2}(d-7)$

(D) $7m + \frac{md}{2}$

(E) $7m + 2md$

9. A salesperson earns 900 dollars per month plus a 10% commission on all sales over 1,000 dollars. One month she sells r dollars' worth of merchandise where $r > \$1000$. How many dollars does she earn that month?

(A) $800 + .1r$

(B) $800 - .1r$

(C) $900 + 1r$

(D) $900 - .1r$

(E) $810 + .1r$

10. Elliot's allowance was just raised to k dollars per week. He gets a raise of c dollars per week every 2 years. How much will his allowance be per week y years from now?

(A) $k + cy$

(B) $k + 2cy$

(C) $k + \frac{1}{2}cy$

(D) $k + 2c$

(E) $ky + 2c$

Solutions

1. **The correct answer is (C).** Since the answer is to be in cents, change d dollars to cents by multiplying it by 100 and subtract from that the c cents he spent.

2. **The correct answer is (E).** There are 16 ounces in a pound. Therefore, you must multiply p pounds by 16 to change it to ounces and then add q more ounces.

3. **The correct answer is (C).** Each double seat holds 2 people, so d double seats hold $2d$ people. Each triple seat holds 3 people, so t triple seats hold $3t$ people. Therefore, each row holds $2d + 3t$ people. There are r rows, so multiply the number of people in each row by r.

4. **The correct answer is (B).** To change cents to dimes, divide by 10.

$$\frac{4x-1}{10} = \frac{4}{10}x - \frac{1}{10} = \frac{2}{5}x - \frac{1}{10}$$

5. **The correct answer is (A).** The original number would be $10u + t$. The number with the digits reversed would be $10t + u$.

6. **The correct answer is (D).** Joe's allowance was $k + r$ cents. To change this to dollars, divide by 100.

7. **The correct answer is (D).** This can be solved by using a proportion. Remember to change $\$k$ to $100k$ cents.

$$\frac{p}{100k}=\frac{1}{x}$$
$$px=100k$$
$$x=\frac{100k}{p}$$

8. **The correct answer is (C).** He pays m dollars for each of 7 days, for a total of $7m$ dollars. Then he pays $\frac{1}{2}m$ dollars for $(d-7)$ days, for a cost of $\frac{m}{2}(d-7)$.

   The total charge is $7m+\frac{m}{2}(d-7)$.

9. **The correct answer is (A).** She gets a commission of 10% of $(r-1000)$, or $.1(r-1000)$, which is $.1r-100$. Adding this to 900 yields $800+.1r$.

10. **The correct answer is (C).** Since he gets a raise only every 2 years, in y years, he will get $\frac{1}{2}y$ raises. Each raise is c dollars, so with $\frac{1}{2}y$ raises his present allowance will be increased by $c(\frac{1}{2}y)$.

6. ROOTS AND RADICALS

ADDING AND SUBTRACTING. Rules for adding and subtracting radicals are much the same as for adding and subtracting variables. Radicals must be exactly the same if they are to be added or subtracted, and they merely serve as a label that does not change.

$$4\sqrt{2}+3\sqrt{2}=7\sqrt{2}$$

$\sqrt{2}+2\sqrt{3}$ cannot be added.

$\sqrt{2}+\sqrt{3}$ cannot be added.

Sometimes, when radicals are not the same, simplification of one or more radicals will make them the same. Remember that radicals are simplified by factoring out any perfect square factors.

$$\sqrt{27}+\sqrt{75}\quad\sqrt{9\bullet 3}+\sqrt{25\bullet 3}\quad 3\sqrt{3}+5\sqrt{3}=8\sqrt{3}$$

MULTIPLYING AND DIVIDING. In multiplying and dividing, treat radicals in the same way as you treat variables. They are factors and must be handled as such.

$$\sqrt{2}\bullet\sqrt{3}=\sqrt{6}$$
$$2\sqrt{5}\bullet 3\sqrt{7}=6\sqrt{35}$$
$$(2\sqrt{3})^2=2\sqrt{3}\bullet 2\sqrt{3}=4\bullet 3=12$$

$$\frac{\sqrt{75}}{\sqrt{3}}=\sqrt{25}=5$$
$$\frac{10\sqrt{3}}{5\sqrt{3}}=2$$

SIMPLIFYING. To simplify radicals that contain a sum or difference under the radical sign, add or subtract first, then take the square root.

$$\sqrt{\frac{x^2}{9}+\frac{x^2}{16}}$$

$$\sqrt{\frac{16x^2+9x^2}{144}}=\sqrt{\frac{25x^2}{144}}=\frac{5|x|}{12}$$

If you take the square root of each term before combining, you would have $\frac{x}{3}+\frac{x}{4}$, or $\frac{7x}{12}$, which is clearly not the same answer. Remember that $\sqrt{25}$ is 5. However, if you write that $\sqrt{25}$ as $\sqrt{16+9}$, you cannot say it is 4 + 3 or 7. *Always* combine the quantities within a radical sign into a single term before taking the square root.

FINDING SQUARE ROOTS. To find the number of digits in the square root of a number, remember that the first step in the procedure for finding a square root is to pair off the numbers in the radical sign on either side of the decimal point. Every pair of numbers under the radical gives one number in the answer.

$\sqrt{32\ 14\ 89}$ will have 3 digits.

▼ **HINT:** If you are given several choices for $\sqrt{321489}$, look first for a three-digit number. If there is only one among the answers, that is the one you should select. If there is more than one, you will have to reason further. If a number ends in 9, such as in the example, its square root would have to end in a digit that would end in 9 when multiplied by itself. This might be either 3 or 7. Only one of these would probably be among the choices, as very few GMAT problems call for much computation.

Q The square root of 61504 is exactly

(A) 245

(B) 246

(C) 247

(D) 248

(E) 249

A The only answer among the choices that will end in 4 when squared is (D).

Exercise: Roots and Radicals

Work out each problem.

1. What is the sum of $\sqrt{12}+\sqrt{27}$?

(A) $\sqrt{29}$
(B) $3\sqrt{5}$
(C) $13\sqrt{3}$
(D) $5\sqrt{3}$
(E) $7\sqrt{3}$

2. What is the difference between $\sqrt{150}$ and $\sqrt{54}$?

(A) $2\sqrt{6}$
(B) $16\sqrt{6}$
(C) $\sqrt{96}$
(D) $6\sqrt{2}$
(E) $8\sqrt{6}$

3. What is the product of $\sqrt{18x}$ and $\sqrt{2x}$?

(A) $6x^2$
(B) $6x$
(C) $36x$
(D) $36x^2$
(E) $6\sqrt{x}$

4. If $\frac{1}{x} = \sqrt{.25}$, what does x equal?

(A) 2
(B) .5
(C) .2
(D) 20
(E) 5

5. If n = 3.14, find n^3 to the nearest hundredth.

(A) 3.10
(B) 30.96
(C) 309.59
(D) 3095.91
(E) 30959.14

6. The square root of 24336 is exactly

(A) 152
(B) 153
(C) 155
(D) 156
(E) 158

7. The square root of 306.25 is exactly

(A) .175
(B) 1.75
(C) 17.5
(D) 175
(E) 1750

8. Divide $6\sqrt{45}$ by $3\sqrt{5}$.

(A) 9
(B) 4
(C) 54
(D) 15
(E) 6

9. $\sqrt{\frac{y^2}{25}+\frac{y^2}{16}} =$

(A) $\frac{2|y|}{9}$
(B) $\frac{9|y|}{20}$
(C) $\frac{|y|}{9}$
(D) $\frac{|y|\sqrt{41}}{20}$
(E) $\frac{41|y|}{20}$

10. $\sqrt{a^2+b^2}$ is equal to

(A) $a+b$
(B) $a-b$
(C) $(a+b)(a-b)$
(D) $\sqrt{a^2}+\sqrt{b^2}$
(E) None of these

Solutions

1. **The correct answer is (D).**

$$\sqrt{12} = \sqrt{4}\sqrt{3} = 2\sqrt{3}$$
$$\sqrt{27} = \sqrt{9}\sqrt{3} = 3\sqrt{3}$$
$$2\sqrt{3} + 3\sqrt{3} = 5\sqrt{3}$$

2. **The correct answer is (A).**

$$\sqrt{150} = \sqrt{25}\sqrt{6} = 5\sqrt{6}$$
$$\sqrt{54} = \sqrt{9}\sqrt{6} = 3\sqrt{6}$$
$$5\sqrt{6} - 3\sqrt{6} = 2\sqrt{6}$$

3. **The correct answer is (B).**

$$\sqrt{18x} \bullet \sqrt{2x} = \sqrt{36x^2} = 6x$$

4. **The correct answer is (A).**

$$\sqrt{.25} = .5$$
$$\frac{1}{x} = .5$$
$$1 = .5x$$
$$10 = 5x$$
$$2 = x$$

5. **The correct answer is (B).** $(3)^3$ would be 27, so the answer should be a little larger than 27.

6. **The correct answer is (D).** The only answer that will end in 6 when squared is (D).

7. **The correct answer is (C).** The square root of this number must have two digits before the decimal point.

8. **The correct answer is (E).**

$$\frac{6\sqrt{45}}{3\sqrt{5}} = 2\sqrt{9} = 2 \bullet 3 = 6$$

9. **The correct answer is (D).**

$$\sqrt{\frac{y^2}{25} + \frac{y^2}{16}} = \sqrt{\frac{16y^2 + 25y^2}{400}}$$
$$= \sqrt{\frac{41y^2}{400}} = \frac{y\sqrt{41}}{20}$$

10. **The correct answer is (E).** Never take the square root of a sum separately. There is no way to simplify $\sqrt{a^2 + b^2}$.

7. FACTORING AND ALGEBRAIC FRACTIONS

SIMPLIFYING. To simplify algebraic fractions, you must divide the numerator and denominator by the same factor, just as you do in arithmetic. You can never cancel terms, as this would be adding or subtracting the same number from the numerator and denominator, which changes the value of the fraction. When you simplify $\frac{6}{8}$ to $\frac{3}{4}$, you are really saying that $\frac{6}{8} = \frac{2 \cdot 3}{2 \cdot 4}$ and then dividing numerator and denominator by 2. You do not say $\frac{6}{8} = \frac{3+3}{3+5}$ and then say $\frac{6}{8} = \frac{3}{5}$. This is faulty reasoning in algebra as well. If you have $\frac{6t}{8t}$, you can divide numerator and denominator by 2t, giving $\frac{3}{4}$ as an answer. However, if you have $\frac{6+t}{8+t}$, you can do no more, as there is no factor that divides into the entire numerator as well as the entire denominator. Canceling terms is one of the most frequent student errors. Don't get caught! Be careful!

Q Simplify $\frac{3x^2+6x}{4x^3+8x^2}$ to its simplest form.

A Factor the numerator and denominator to get $\frac{3x(x+2)}{4x^2(x+2)}$. The factors common to both numerator and denominator are x and $(x + 2)$. Divide these out to arrive at the correct answer of $\frac{3}{4x}$.

ADDING AND SUBTRACTING. To add or subtract fractions, work with a common denominator and the same shortcuts used in arithmetic.

Q Find the sum of $\frac{1}{a}$ and $\frac{1}{b}$.

A Remember to add the two cross products and put the sum over the denominator product. $\frac{b+a}{ab}$

Add: $\frac{2n}{3} + \frac{3n}{2}$

$\frac{4n+9n}{6} = \frac{13n}{6}$

MULTIPLYING AND DIVIDING. To multiply or divide fractions, divide a factor common to any numerator and any denominator. Always remember in division to multiply by the reciprocal of the fraction following the division sign. Where exponents are involved, they are added in multiplication and subtracted in division.

Q Find the product of $\frac{a^3}{b^2}$ and $\frac{b^3}{a^2}$.

A Divide a^2 into the first numerator and second denominator, giving $\frac{a}{b^2} \bullet \frac{b^3}{1}$. Then divide b^2 into the first denominator and second numerator, giving $\frac{a}{1} \bullet \frac{b}{1}$. Finally, multiply the resulting fractions, giving an answer of *ab*.

Q Divide $\frac{6x^2y}{5}$ by $2x^3$.

A $\frac{6x^2y}{5} \bullet \frac{1}{2x^3}$. Divide the first numerator and second denominator by $2x^2$, giving $\frac{3y}{5} \bullet \frac{1}{x}$. Multiply the resulting fractions to get $\frac{3y}{5x}$.

COMPLEX FRACTIONS. Complex algebraic fractions are simplified by the same methods used in arithmetic. Multiply each term of the complex fraction by the least common denominator of all fractions within the fraction.

Q Simplify: $\dfrac{\frac{1}{a}+\frac{1}{b}}{ab}$

A Multiply *each term* by *ab*, giving $\frac{b+a}{a^2b^2}$. Since no simplification beyond this is possible, $\frac{b+a}{a^2b^2}$ is the final answer.

DIFFERENCE OF TWO SQUARES. Certain types of problems may involve factoring the difference of two squares. If an expression consists of two terms that are perfect squares separated by a minus sign, the expression can always be factored into two binomials, with one containing the sum of the square roots and the other the difference of the square roots.

Q If $x^2 - y^2 = 100$ and $x + y = 2$, find $x - y$.

A Since $x^2 - y^2$ can be written as $(x + y)(x - y)$, these two factors must multiply to 100. If one is 2, the other must be 50.

Q If $a + b = \frac{1}{2}$ and $a - b = \frac{1}{4}$, find $a^2 - b^2$.

A $a^2 - b^2$ is the product of $(a + b)$ and $(a - b)$. Therefore, $a^2 - b^2$ must be equal to $\frac{1}{8}$.

Exercise: Factoring and Algebraic Fractions

Work out each problem.

1. Find the sum of $\frac{n}{6}+\frac{2n}{5}$.
   (A) $\frac{13n}{30}$
   (B) $17n$
   (C) $\frac{3n}{30}$
   (D) $\frac{17n}{30}$
   (E) $\frac{3n}{11}$

2. Combine into a single fraction: $1-\frac{x}{y}$
   (A) $\frac{1-x}{y}$
   (B) $\frac{y-x}{y}$
   (C) $\frac{x-y}{y}$
   (D) $\frac{1-x}{1-y}$
   (E) $\frac{y-x}{xy}$

3. Divide $\frac{x-y}{x+y}$ by $\frac{y-x}{y+x}$
   (A) 1
   (B) –1
   (C) $\frac{(x-y)^2}{(x+y)^2}$
   (D) $-\frac{(x-y)^2}{(x+y)^2}$
   (E) 0

4. Simplify: $\dfrac{1+\frac{1}{x}}{\frac{y}{x}}$
   (A) $\frac{x+1}{y}$
   (B) $\frac{x+1}{x}$
   (C) $\frac{x+1}{xy}$
   (D) $\frac{x^2+1}{xy}$
   (E) $\frac{y+1}{y}$

5. Find an expression equivalent to $\left(\frac{2x^2}{y}\right)^3$.

(A) $\frac{8x^5}{3y}$

(B) $\frac{6x^6}{y^3}$

(C) $\frac{6x^5}{y^3}$

(D) $\frac{8x^5}{y^3}$

(E) $\frac{8x^6}{y^3}$

6. Simplify: $\frac{\frac{1}{x}+\frac{1}{y}}{3}$

(A) $\frac{3x+3y}{xy}$

(B) $\frac{3xy}{x+y}$

(C) $\frac{xy}{3}$

(D) $\frac{x+y}{3xy}$

(E) $\frac{x+y}{3}$

7. $\frac{1}{a}+\frac{1}{b}=7$ and $\frac{1}{a}-\frac{1}{b}=3$. Find $\frac{1}{a^2}-\frac{1}{b^2}$.

(A) 10

(B) 7

(C) 3

(D) 21

(E) 4

8. If $(a-b)^2=64$ and $ab=3$, find a^2+b^2.

(A) 61

(B) 67

(C) 70

(D) 58

(E) 69

9. If $c+d=12$ and $c^2-d^2=48$, then $c-d=$

(A) 4

(B) 36

(C) 60

(D) 5

(E) 3

10. The trinomial x^2+x-20 is exactly divisible by

(A) $x-5$

(B) $x+4$

(C) $x-10$

(D) $x-4$

(E) $x-2$

Solutions

1. **The correct answer is (D).**

$$\frac{n}{6}+\frac{2n}{5}=\frac{5n+12n}{30}=\frac{17n}{30}$$

2. **The correct answer is (B).**

$$\frac{1}{1}-\frac{x}{y}=\frac{y-x}{y}$$

3. **The correct answer is (B).**

$$\frac{x-y}{x+y}\bullet\frac{y+x}{y-x}$$

Since addition is commutative, you can divide $x+y$ with $y+x$, as they are the same quantity. However, subtraction is not commutative, so you cannot divide $x-y$ with $y-x$, as they are *not* the same quantity. Change the form of $y-x$ by factoring out a -1. Thus, $y-x=(-1)(x-y)$. In this form, you can divide $x-y$, leaving an answer of $\frac{1}{-1}$, or -1.

4. **The correct answer is (A).** Multiply every term of the fraction by x, giving $\frac{x+1}{y}$.

5. **The correct answer is (E).**

$$\frac{2x^2}{y} \bullet \frac{2x^2}{y} \bullet \frac{2x^2}{y} = \frac{8x^6}{y^3}$$

6. **The correct answer is (D).** Multiply every term of the fraction by xy, giving $\frac{y+x}{3xy}$.

7. **The correct answer is (D).**

$\frac{1}{a^2} - \frac{1}{b^2}$ is equivalent to $\left(\frac{1}{a}+\frac{1}{b}\right)\left(\frac{1}{a}-\frac{1}{b}\right)$.

Therefore, multiply 7 by 3 for an answer of 21.

8. **The correct answer is (C).**

$(a-b)^2$ is $(a-b)(a-b)$, or $a^2 - 2ab + b^2$, which is equal to 64.

$$a^2 - 2ab + b^2 = 64$$
$$a^2 + b^2 = 64 + 2ab$$

Since $ab = 3$, $2ab = 6$, and $a^2 + b^2 = 64 + 6$, or 70.

9. **The correct answer is (A).**

$$\begin{aligned} c^2 - d^2 &= (c+d)(c-d) \\ 48 &= 12(c-d) \\ 4 &= (c-d) \end{aligned}$$

10. **The correct answer is (D).** The factors of $x^2 + x - 20$ are $(x+5)$ and $(x-4)$.

8. PROBLEM SOLVING IN ALGEBRA

In solving verbal problems, the most important technique is to read accurately. Be sure you understand exactly what you are asked to find. Once this is done, represent what you are looking for algebraically. Write an equation that translates the words of the problem to the symbols of mathematics. Then solve that equation by the techniques reviewed previously.

This section reviews the types of algebra problems most frequently encountered on the GMAT. Thoroughly familiarizing yourself with the problems that follow will help you to translate and solve all kinds of verbal problems.

Coin Problems

In solving coin problems, it is best to change the value of all monies involved to cents before writing an equation. Thus, the number of nickels must be multiplied by 5 to give their value in cents; dimes must be multiplied by 10; quarters by 25; half dollars by 50; and dollars by 100.

Q Richard has $3.50 consisting of nickels and dimes. If he has 5 more dimes than nickels, how many dimes does he have?

A

$$\begin{aligned} \text{Let } x &= \text{the number of nickels} \\ x+5 &= \text{the number of dimes} \\ 5x &= \text{the value of the nickels in cents} \\ 10x+50 &= \text{the value of the dimes in cents} \\ 350 &= \text{the value of the money he has in cents} \\ 5x+10x+50 &= 350 \\ 15x &= 300 \\ x &= 20 \end{aligned}$$

He has 20 nickels and 25 dimes.

▼ **HINT:** In a problem such as this, you can be sure that 20 would be among the multiple-choice answers. You must be sure to read carefully what you are asked to find and then continue until you have found the quantity sought.

Consecutive Integer Problems

Consecutive integers are one apart and can be represented by x, $x + 1$, $x + 2$, etc. Consecutive even or odd integers are two apart and can be represented by x, $x + 2$, $x + 4$, etc.

Q Three consecutive odd integers have a sum of 33. Find the average of these integers.

A Represent the integers as x, $x + 2$, and $x + 4$. Write an equation indicating the sum is 33.

$$\begin{aligned} 3x + 6 &= 33 \\ 3x &= 27 \\ x &= 9 \end{aligned}$$

The integers are 9, 11, and 13. In the case of evenly spaced numbers such as these, the average is the middle number, 11. Since the sum of the three numbers was given originally, all you really had to do was divide this sum by 3 to find the average, without ever knowing what the numbers were.

Age Problems

Problems of this type usually involve a comparison of ages at the present time, several years from now, or several years ago. A person's age x years from now is found by adding x to his present age. A person's age x years ago is found by subtracting x from his present age.

Q Michelle was 12 years old y years ago. Represent her age b years from now.

A Her present age is $12 + y$. In b years, her age will be $12 + y + b$.

Interest Problems

The annual amount of interest paid on an investment is found by multiplying the amount of principal invested by the rate (percent) of interest paid.

Principal • Rate = Interest income

Q A student invests \$4,000, part at 6% and part at 7%. The income from these investments in one year is \$250. Find the amount invested at 7%.

A Represent each investment.

Let x = the amount invested at 7%. Always try to let x represent what you are looking for.

$$\begin{aligned} 4000 - x &= \text{the amount invested at 6\%} \\ .07x &= \text{the income from the 7\% investment} \\ .06(4000 - x) &= \text{the income from the 6\% investment} \\ .07x + .06(4000 - x) &= 250 \\ 7x + 6(4000 - x) &= 25000 \\ 7x + 24000 - 6x &= 25000 \\ x &= 1000 \end{aligned}$$

The student invested \$1,000 at 7%.

Fraction Problems

A fraction is a ratio between two numbers. If the value of a fraction is $\frac{2}{3}$, it does not mean the numerator must be 2 and the denominator 3. The numerator and denominator could be 4 and 6, respectively, or 1 and 1.5, or 30 and 45, or any of infinitely many other combinations. All you know is that the ratio of numerator to denominator will be 2:3. Therefore, the numerator may be represented by $2x$, the denominator by $3x$, and the fraction by $\frac{2x}{3x}$.

Q The value of a fraction is $\frac{3}{4}$. If 3 is subtracted from the numerator and added to the denominator, the value of the fraction is $\frac{2}{5}$. Find the original fraction.

A Let the original fraction be represented by $\frac{3x}{4x}$. If 3 is subtracted from the numerator and added to the denominator, the new fraction becomes $\frac{3x-3}{4x+3}$.

The value of the new fraction is $\frac{2}{5}$. $\frac{3x-3}{4x+3} = \frac{2}{5}$

Cross-multiply to eliminate fractions.

$$\begin{aligned} 15x - 15 &= 8x + 6 \\ 7x &= 21 \\ x &= 3 \end{aligned}$$

Therefore, the original fraction is: $\frac{3x}{4x} = \frac{9}{12}$

Mixture Problems

DRY MIXTURES. There are two kinds of mixture problems with which you should be familiar. The first is sometimes referred to as dry mixture, in which dry ingredients of different values are mixed. Also solved by the same method are problems such as those dealing with tickets at different prices. In solving this type of problem, it is best to organize the data in a chart of three rows and three columns, labeled as illustrated in the following example.

Q A dealer wishes to mix 20 pounds of nuts selling for 45 cents per pound with some more expensive nuts selling for 60 cents per pound to make a mixture that will sell for 50 cents per pound. How many pounds of the more expensive nuts should be used?

	No. of lbs. •	Price/lb. =	Total Value
Original	20	.45	.45(20)
Added	x	.60	.60(x)
Mixture	20 + x	.50	.50(20 + x)

A The value of the original nuts plus the value of the added nuts must equal the value of the mixture. Almost all mixture problems require an equation that comes from adding the final column:

$$.45(20) + .60(x) = .50(20 + x)$$

Multiply by 100 to remove the decimals.

$$\begin{aligned} 45(20) + 60(x) &= 50(20 + x) \\ 900 + 60(x) &= 1000 + 50x \\ 10x &= 100 \\ x &= 10 \end{aligned}$$

The dealer should use 10 lbs. of 60-cent nuts.

CHEMICAL MIXTURES. The second type of mixture problem concerns chemical mixtures. These problems deal with percents rather than prices and with amounts instead of values.

Q How much water must be added to 20 gallons of a solution that is 30% alcohol to dilute it to a solution that is only 25% alcohol?

	No. of gals. •	% alcohol =	Amt. alcohol
Original	20	.30	.30(20)
Added	x	0	0
Mixture	20 + x	.25	.25(20 + x)

A Note that the percent of alcohol in water is 0. Had you added pure alcohol to strengthen the solution, the percent would have to be 100. The equation again comes from the last column. The amount of alcohol added (none in this case) plus the amount you had to start with must equal the amount of alcohol in the new solution.

$$\begin{aligned} .30(20) &= .25(20 + x) \\ 30(20) &= 25(20 + x) \\ 600 &= 500 + 25x \\ 100 &= 25x \\ x &= 4 \end{aligned}$$

Motion Problems

The fundamental relationship in all motion problems is that of Rate • Time = Distance. The problems at the level of this examination usually derive their equations from relationships concerning distance. Most problems fall into one of three types:

1. *Motion in opposite directions.* When two objects start at the same time and move in opposite directions, or when two objects start at points at a given distance apart and move toward each other until they meet, the total distance traveled equals the sum of the distances traveled by each object.

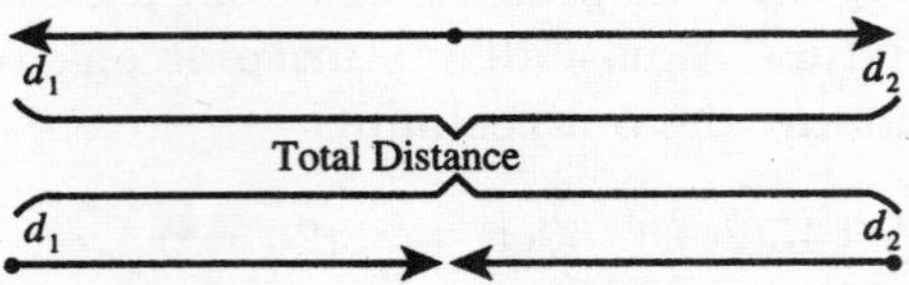

   In either of the above cases, $d_1 + d_2$ = total distance.

2. *Motion in the same direction.* This type of problem is sometimes called the "catch-up" problem. Two objects leave the same place at different times and different rates, but one "catches up" to the other. In such a case, the two distances must be equal.
3. *Round trip.* In this type of problem, the rate going is usually different from the rate returning. The times are also different. But if you go somewhere and then return to the starting point, the distances must be the same.

To solve any motion problem, it is helpful to organize the data in a box with columns for rate, time, and distance. Use a separate line for each moving object. Remember that if the rate is given in *miles per hour*, the time must be in *hours* and the distance in *miles*.

Q Two cars leave a restaurant at 1 P.M., with one car traveling east at 60 miles per hour and the other west at 40 miles per hour along a straight highway. At what time will they be 350 miles apart?

	Rate •	Time =	Distance
Eastbound	60	x	$60x$
Westbound	40	x	$40x$

A Notice that the time is unknown, since it is necessary to find the number of hours traveled. However, since the cars start at the same time and stop when they are 350 miles apart, their times are the same.

$$\begin{aligned} 60x + 40x &= 350 \\ 100x &= 350 \\ x &= 3\frac{1}{2} \end{aligned}$$

In $3\frac{1}{2}$ hours, it will be 4:30 P.M.

Q Gloria leaves home for school, riding her bicycle at a rate of 12 mph. Twenty minutes after she leaves, her mother sees Gloria's English paper on her bed and leaves to bring it to her. If her mother drives at 36 mph, how far must she drive before she reaches Gloria?

	Rate	• Time	= Distance
Gloria	12	x	$12x$
Mother	36	$x-\frac{1}{3}$	$36\left(x-\frac{1}{3}\right)$

A Notice that 20 minutes has been changed to $\frac{1}{3}$ of an hour. In this problem the times are not equal, but the distances are.

$$\begin{aligned} 12x &= 36\left(x-\frac{1}{3}\right) \\ 12x &= 36x-12 \\ 12 &= 24x \\ x &= \frac{1}{2} \end{aligned}$$

If Gloria rode for $\frac{1}{2}$ hour at 12 mph, the distance covered was 6 miles.

Q Judy leaves home at 11 A.M. and rides to Mary's house to return Mary's bicycle. She travels at 12 miles per hour and arrives at 11:30 A.M. She turns right around and walks home. How fast does she walk if she returns home at 1 P.M.?

	Rate	• Time	= Distance
Going	12	$\frac{1}{2}$	6
Return	x	$1\frac{1}{2}$	$\frac{3}{2}x$

A The distances are equal.

$$\begin{aligned} 6 &= \frac{3}{2}x \\ 12 &= 3x \\ x &= 4 \end{aligned}$$

She walked at 4 mph.

Work Problems

In most work problems, a complete job is broken into several parts, each representing a fractional part of the entire job. For each fractional part, which represents the portion completed by one person, one machine, one pipe, etc., the numerator should represent the time actually spent working, while the denominator should represent the total time needed to do the entire job alone. The sum of all the individual fractions should be 1.

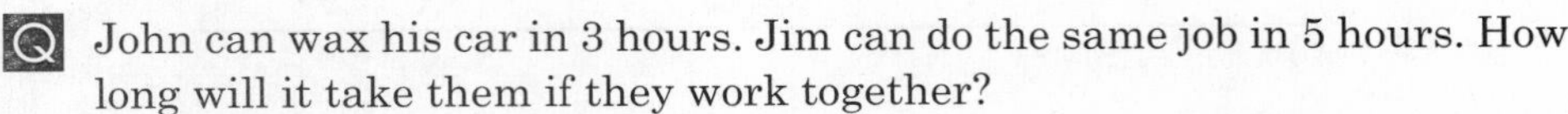

Q John can wax his car in 3 hours. Jim can do the same job in 5 hours. How long will it take them if they work together?

A If multiple-choice answers are given, you should realize that the correct answer must be smaller than the shortest time given, for no matter how slow a helper may be, he will do some of the work. Therefore, the job will be completed in less time than it would take for one person working alone.

$$\frac{\text{Time spent}}{\text{Total time needed to do job alone}}: \quad \overset{\text{John}}{\frac{x}{3}} + \overset{\text{Jim}}{\frac{x}{5}} = 1$$

Multiply by 15 to eliminate fractions.

$$\begin{aligned} 5x + 3x &= 15 \\ 8x &= 15 \\ x &= 1\frac{7}{8} \text{ hours} \end{aligned}$$

Exercise: Problem Solving in Algebra

Work out each problem.

1. Sue and Nancy wish to buy a snack. They combine their money and find they have \$4.00, consisting of quarters, dimes, and nickels. If they have 35 coins and the number of quarters is half the number of nickels, how many quarters do they have?

   (A) 5
   (B) 10
   (C) 20
   (D) 3
   (E) 6

2. Three times the first of three consecutive odd integers is 3 more than twice the third. Find the third integer.

   (A) 9
   (B) 11
   (C) 13
   (D) 15
   (E) 7

3. Robert is 15 years older than his brother Stan. However, y years ago Robert was twice as old as Stan. If Stan is now b years old and $b > y$, find the value of $b - y$.

   (A) 13
   (B) 14
   (C) 15
   (D) 16
   (E) 17

4. How many ounces of pure acid must be added to 20 ounces of a solution that is 5% acid to strengthen it to a solution that is 24% acid?

   (A) $2\frac{1}{2}$
   (B) 5
   (C) 6
   (D) $7\frac{1}{2}$
   (E) 10

5. A dealer mixes a pounds of nuts worth b cents per pound with c pounds of nuts worth d cents per pound. At what price should he sell a pound of the mixture if he wishes to make a profit of 10 cents per pound?

   (A) $\frac{ab+cd}{a+c}+10$
   (B) $\frac{ab+cd}{a+c}+.10$
   (C) $\frac{b+d}{a+c}+10$
   (D) $\frac{b+d}{a+c}+.10$
   (E) $\frac{b+d+10}{a+c}$

6. Barbara invests \$2,400 in the National Bank at 5%. How much additional money must she invest at 8% so that the total annual income will be equal to 6% of her entire investment?

   (A) \$2,400
   (B) \$3,600
   (C) \$1,000
   (D) \$3,000
   (E) \$1,200

7. Frank left Austin to drive to Boxville at 6:15 P.M. and arrived at 11:45 P.M. If he averaged 30 miles per hour and stopped one hour for dinner, how far is Boxville from Austin?

(A) 120
(B) 135
(C) 180
(D) 165
(E) 150

8. A plane traveling 600 miles per hour is 30 miles from Kennedy Airport at 4:58 P.M. At what time will it arrive at the airport?

(A) 5:00 P.M.
(B) 5:01 P.M.
(C) 5:02 P.M.
(D) 5:20 P.M.
(E) 5:03 P.M.

9. Mr. Bridges can wash his car in 15 minutes, while his son Dave takes twice as long to do the same job. If they work together, how many minutes will the job take them?

(A) 5
(B) $7\frac{1}{2}$
(C) 10
(D) $22\frac{1}{2}$
(E) 30

10. The value of a fraction is $\frac{2}{5}$. If the numerator is decreased by 2 and the denominator increased by 1, the resulting fraction is equivalent to $\frac{1}{4}$. Find the numerator of the original fraction.

(A) 3
(B) 4
(C) 6
(D) 10
(E) 15

Solutions

1. **The correct answer is (B).**

Let x= number of quarters
$2x$= number of nickels
$35 - 3x$= number of dimes

Write all money values in cents.

$$25(x) + 5(2x) + 10(35 - 3x) = 400$$
$$25x + 10x + 350 - 30x = 400$$
$$5x = 50$$
$$x = 10$$

2. **The correct answer is (D).**
Let x= first integer
$x + 2$ = second integer
$x + 4$ = third integer

$$3(x) = 3 + 2(x + 4)$$
$$3x = 3 + 2x + 8$$
$$x = 11$$

The third integer is 15.

3. **The correct answer is (C).**

b = Stan's age now
$b + 15$ = Robert's age now
$b - y$ = Stan's age y years ago
$b + 15 - y$ = Robert's age y years ago

$$b + 15 - y = 2(b - y)$$
$$b + 15 - y = 2b - 2y$$
$$15 = b - y$$

4. **The correct answer is (B).**

	No. of oz.	• % acid	= Amt. acid
Original	20	.05	1
Added	x	1.00	x
Mixture	$20 + x$	.24	$.24(20 + x)$

$1 + x = .24(20 + x)$.

Multiply by 100 to eliminate decimal.

$$100 + 100x = 480 + 24x$$
$$76x = 380$$
$$x = 5$$

5. **The correct answer is (A).** The a pounds of nuts are worth a total of ab cents. The c pounds of nuts are worth a total of cd cents. The value of the mixture is $ab + cd$ cents. Since there are $a + c$ pounds, each pound is worth $\frac{ab+cd}{a+c}$ cents.

Since the dealer wants to add 10 cents to each pound for profit, and the value of each pound is in cents, add 10 to the value of each pound.

6. **The correct answer is (E).** If Barbara invests x additional dollars at 8%, her total investment will amount to $2400 + x$ dollars.

$$.05(2400) + .08(x) = .06(2400 + x)$$
$$5(2400) + 8(x) = 6(2400 + x)$$
$$12000 + 8x = 14400 + 6x$$
$$2x = 2400$$
$$x = 1200$$

7. **The correct answer is (B).** Total time elapsed is $5\frac{1}{2}$ hours. However, one hour was used for dinner. Therefore, Frank drove at 30 mph for $4\frac{1}{2}$ hours, covering 135 miles.

8. **The correct answer is (B).**

$$\text{Time} = \frac{\text{Distance}}{\text{Rate}} = \frac{30}{600} = \frac{1}{20} \text{ hour,}$$

or 3 minutes

9. **The correct answer is (C).** Dave takes 30 minutes to wash the car alone.

$$\frac{x}{15} + \frac{x}{30} = 1$$
$$2x + x = 30$$
$$3x = 30$$
$$x = 10$$

10. **The correct answer is (C).**
Let $2x$ = original numerator
$5x$ = original denominator

$$\frac{2x-2}{5x+1} = \frac{1}{4}$$

Cross-multiply:

$$8x - 8 = 5x + 1$$
$$3x = 9$$
$$x = 3$$

Original numerator is 2(3), or 6.

9. INEQUALITIES

Algebraic inequality statements are solved just as equations are solved. However, you must remember that whenever you multiply or divide by a negative number, the order of the inequality, that is, the inequality symbol, must be reversed.

Q Solve for x: $3 - 5x > 18$

A Add –3 to both sides:
$-5x > 15$
Divide by –5, remembering to reverse the inequality:
$x < -3$

Q $5x - 4 > 6x - 6$

A Collect all x terms on the left and numerical terms on the right. As with equations, remember that if a term crosses the inequality symbol, the term changes sign.
$-x > -2$
Divide (or multiply) by –1:
$x < 2$

In working with geometric inequalities, certain postulates and theorems should be reviewed. The list follows:

POSTULATES AND THEOREMS

1. If unequal quantities are added to unequal quantities of the same order, the result is unequal quantities in the same order.
2. If equal quantities are added to, or subtracted from, unequal quantities, the results are unequal in the same order.
3. If unequal quantities are subtracted from equal quantities, the results are unequal in the opposite order.
4. Doubles or halves of unequals are unequal in the same order.
5. If the first of three quantities is greater than the second, and the second is greater than the third, then the first is greater than the third.
6. The sum of two sides of a triangle must be greater than the third side.
7. If two sides of a triangle are unequal, the angles opposite these sides are unequal, with the greater angle opposite the greater side.
8. If two angles of a triangle are unequal, the sides opposite these angles are unequal, with the greater side opposite the greater angle.
9. An exterior angle of a triangle is greater than either remote interior angle.

Q If BCD is a straight line and $m\angle A = 40°$, then angle ACD contains

(A) 40°

(B) 140°

(C) less than 40°

(D) more than 40°

(E) 100°

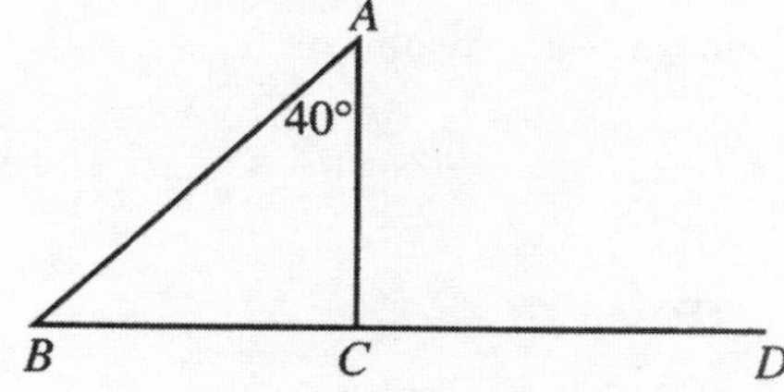

A **The correct answer is (D),** since an exterior angle of a triangle is always greater than either of the remote interior angles.

Q Which of the following statements is true regarding the triangle?

(A) $AB > AC$

(B) $AC > BC$

(C) $AB > BC$

(D) $AC > AB$

(E) $BC > AB + AC$

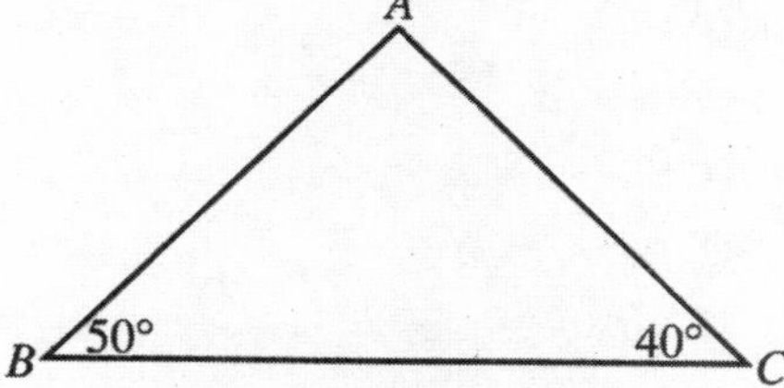

A **The correct answer is (D),** since a comparison between two sides of a triangle depends upon the angles opposite these sides. The greater side is always opposite the greater angle. Since angle A contains 90°, the greatest side of this triangle is BC, followed by AB and then AC.

Exercise: Inequalities

Work out each problem.

1. If $x < y$, $2x = A$, and $2y = B$, then
   (A) $A = B$
   (B) $A < B$
   (C) $A > B$
   (D) $A < x$
   (E) $B < y$

2. If $a > b$ and $c > d$, then
   (A) $a = c$
   (B) $a < d$
   (C) $a + d = b + c$
   (D) $a + c < b + d$
   (E) $a + c > b + d$

3. If $ab > 0$ and $a < 0$, which of the following is negative?
   (A) b
   (B) $-b$
   (C) $-a$
   (D) $(a - b)$
   (E) $-(a + b)$

4. If $4 - x > 5$, then
   (A) $x > 1$
   (B) $x > -1$
   (C) $x < 1$
   (D) $x < -1$
   (E) $x = -1$

5. Point X is located on line segment AB and point Y is located on line segment CD. If $AB = CD$ and $AX > CY$, then
   (A) $XB > YD$
   (B) $XB < YD$
   (C) $AX > XB$
   (D) $AX < XB$
   (E) $AX > AB$

6. If $w > x$, $y < z$, and $x > z$, then which of the following must be true?
   (A) $w > x > y > z$
   (B) $w > x > z > y$
   (C) $x > z > y > w$
   (D) $z < y < x < w$
   (E) $z < x < y < w$

7. If x and y are positive integers such that $0 < (x + y) < 10$, then which of the following must be true?
   (A) $x < 8$
   (B) $x > 3$
   (C) $x > y$
   (D) $x + y = 5$
   (E) $x - y \leq 7$

8. In the diagram below, which of the following is always true?

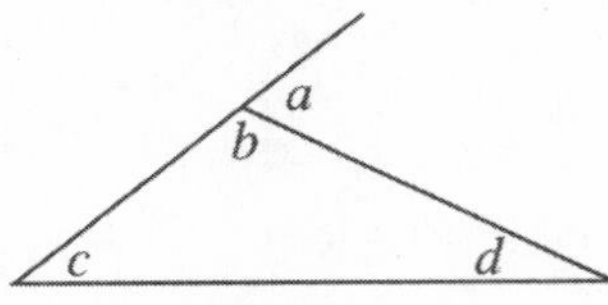

   I. $a > b$
   II. $c > a$
   III. $d > a$
   (A) I only
   (B) II and III only
   (C) I, II, and III
   (D) II only
   (E) None of these

9. If point X is on line segment AB, all of the following may be true except
(A) $AX = XB$
(B) $AX > XB$
(C) $AX < XB$
(D) $AB > XB$
(E) $AX + XB < AB$

10. If $x > 0$, $y > 0$, and $x - y < 0$, then
(A) $x > y$
(B) $x < y$
(C) $x + y < 0$
(D) $y - x < 0$
(E) $x = -y$

Solutions

1. **The correct answer is (B).** Doubles of unequals are unequal in the same order.

2. **The correct answer is (E).** If unequal quantities are added to unequal quantities of the same order, the results are unequal in the same order.

3. **The correct answer is (A).** If the product of two numbers is > 0 (positive), then either both numbers are positive or both are negative. Since $a < 0$ (negative), b must also be negative.

4. **The correct answer is (D).**

$$4 - x > 5$$
$$-x > 1$$

Divide by –1 and change the inequality sign.

$$x < -1$$

5. **The correct answer is (B).**

If unequal quantities are subtracted from equal quantities, the results are unequal in the same order.

6. **The correct answer is (B).** The first and third statements assert:

$w > x$ and $x > z$, therefore $w > x > z$

The second statement says that y is less than z. Therefore:

$w > x > z > y$

7. **The correct answer is (E).** Perhaps using numbers is the easiest way to explain this item:

(A) x could be 8 and y could be 1: $0 < (8 + 1) < 10$

(B) x could be 3 and y could be 6: $0 < (3 + 6) < 10$

(C) This is wrong as just shown above.

(D) This too is wrong as shown above.

(E) The largest possible value for x is 8, and the smallest possible value for y is 1. So the greatest possible value for $x - y$ is 7.

8. **The correct answer is (E).** An exterior angle of a triangle must be greater than either remote interior angle. There is no fixed relationship between an exterior angle and its adjacent interior angle.

9. **The correct answer is (E).** Point X could be so located to make each of the other choices true, but the whole segment AB will always be equal to the sum of its parts AX and XB.

10. **The correct answer is (B).** If x and y are both positive, but $x - y$ is negative, then y must be a greater number than x.

10. DEFINED OPERATION PROBLEMS

"Defined operation" is another name for "function." A function problem might look like this: The function of x is obtained by squaring x and then multiplying the result by 3. If you wanted to know $f(4)$, you would square 4 and multiply that product by 3; the answer would be 48. On the GMAT the $f(x)$ symbol is not normally used. Instead the test-makers use arbitrary symbols and define what function they represent. You approach these symbols as you would a function: Talk to yourself about what the function does. In math you usually change words into mathematical notation, but with functions you change mathematical notation into words.

$!x = 2x + 4$

What does the "!" do in this problem? It takes x and doubles it and then adds four.

Q What is the value of !6?

A $!6 = 2(6) + 4 = 16$

Exercise: Defined Operation Problems

Work out each problem.

1. &x is such that &$x = \frac{x^3}{2}$. What is the value of &4?

   (A) 8
   (B) 16
   (C) 32
   (D) 40
   (E) 64

2. \$$x$ is such that \$$x$ is equal to the nearest integer less than x. What is the value of \$6.99 times \$ –2.01?

   (A) 18
   (B) 12
   (C) –12
   (D) –18
   (E) –21

3. The operation # is defined in the following way for any two numbers:

   $p \# q = (p - q)$ times $(q - p)$

   If $p \# q = -1$, then which of the following are true?

   I. p could equal 5 and q could equal 4
   II. p could equal 4 and q could equal 5
   III. p could equal 1 and q could equal –1
   IV. p could equal –1 and q could equal 1

   (A) I and II only
   (B) I and III only
   (C) II and IV only
   (D) III and IV only
   (E) I, II, III, IV

4. Every letter in the alphabet has a number value that is equal to its place in the alphabet; thus, the letter A has a value of 1 and C a value of 3. The number value of a word is obtained by adding up the value of the letters in the word and then multiplying that sum by the length of the word. The word "DFGH" would have a number value of

   (A) 22
   (B) 44
   (C) 66
   (D) 100
   (E) 108

5. Let &x be defined such that &$x = x + \frac{1}{x}$. The value of &6 + &4 + &2 is

   (A) 12
   (B) $12\frac{7}{12}$
   (C) $12\frac{11}{12}$
   (D) $13\frac{1}{12}$
   (E) $13\frac{5}{12}$

Solutions

1. **The correct answer is (C).** $4^3 = 64$ and 64 divided by 2 is 32.

2. **The correct answer is (D).** The key phrase in the problem is "the nearest less integer." The nearest least integer to 6.99 is 6 (not 7, this problem does not say to round the numbers) and the nearest least integer to –2.01 is –3 (not –2 as –2 is greater than –2.01).

3. **The correct answer is (A).** The best way to solve this is to plug the values into the equation:

$$(5 - 4) \times (4 - 5) = -1$$

$$(4 - 5) \times (5 - 4) = -1$$

$$(1 - {}^{-}1) \times (-1 - 1) = -4$$

$$(-1 - 1) \times (1 - {}^{-}1) = -4$$

Statements I and II give the stated value, –1.

4. **The correct answer is (D).** D = 4, F = 6, G = 7, and H = 8 so the sum of the letters would be 25. 25 multiplied by 4 (the length of the word) is 100.

5. **The correct answer is (C).** The work of this problem is adding up the reciprocals of the numbers.

6 + 4 + 2 is clearly 12.

$$\frac{1}{6} + \frac{1}{4} + \frac{1}{2} = \frac{2}{12} + \frac{3}{12} + \frac{6}{12} = \frac{11}{12}$$

chapter 13

Geometry

OVERVIEW

- **Areas**
- **Perimeters**
- **Circles**
- **Volumes**
- **Triangles**
- **Right Triangles**
- **Parallel Lines**
- **Polygons**
- **Similar Polygons**
- **Coordinate Geometry**

Here are some of the most important geometry formulas that you should know for the GMAT.

1. AREAS

1. Rectangle = bh

   Area = $6 \cdot 3 = 18$

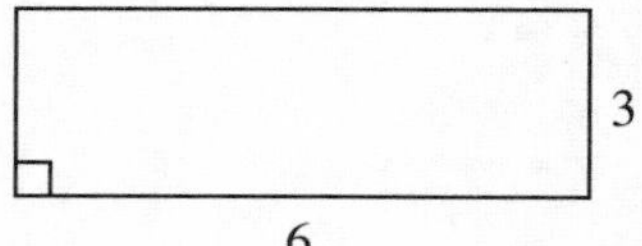

2. Parallelogram = bh

   Area = $8 \cdot 4 = 32$

3. Rhombus = $\frac{1}{2}d_1d_2$

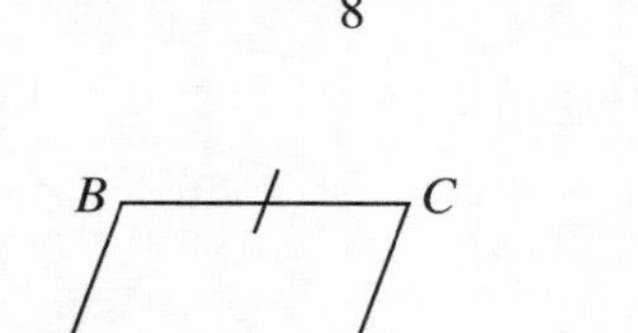

If $AC = 10$ and $BD = 8$, then area is $\frac{1}{2}(10)(8) = 40$.

4. Square = s^2 or $\frac{1}{2}d^2$
Area = $6^2 = 36$

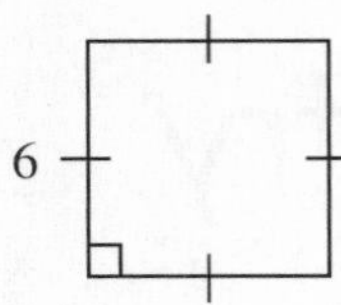

Area = $\frac{1}{2}(10)(10) = 50$

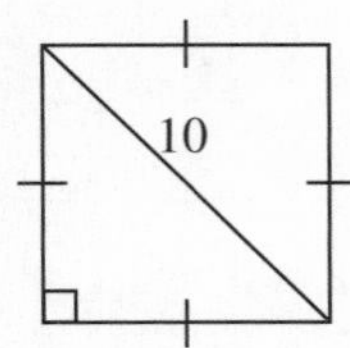

5. Triangle = $\frac{1}{2}bh$
Area = $\frac{1}{2}(12)(4) = 24$

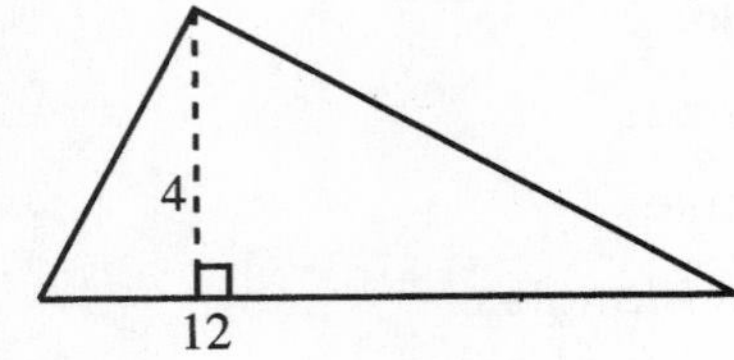

6. Equilateral triangle = $\frac{s^2}{4}\sqrt{3}$
Area = $\frac{36}{4}\sqrt{3} = 9\sqrt{3}$

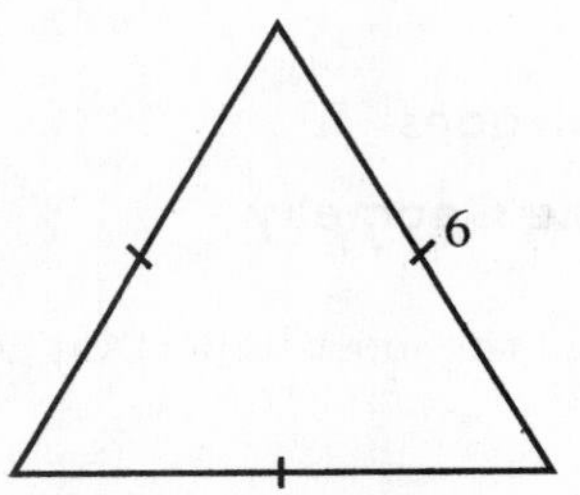

7. Trapezoid = $\frac{1}{2}h(b_1 + b_2)$

Area = $\frac{1}{2}(5)(16) = 40$

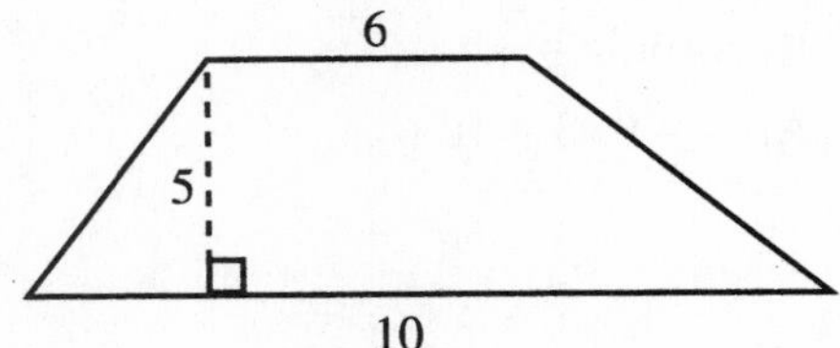

8. Circle = πr^2
Area = $\pi(6)^2 = 36\pi$

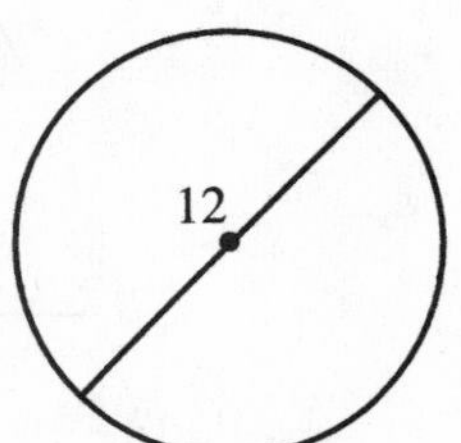

2. PERIMETERS

1. Any polygon = sum of all sides

   P = 5 + 8 + 11 = 24

   5 8 11

2. Circle = $2\pi r$

   (called circumference)

   Circle = $\pi(12) = 12$

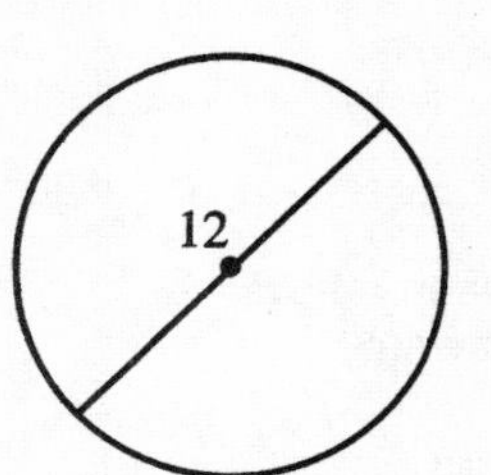

3. The distance covered by a wheel in one revolution is equal to the circumference of the wheel.

   In one revolution, this wheel covers $\pi \cdot \frac{14}{\pi}$, or 14 feet.

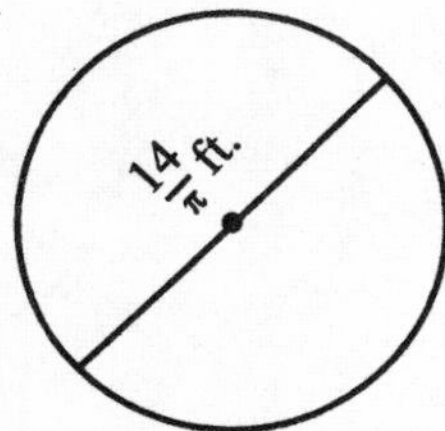

3. CIRCLES

1. A central angle is equal in degrees to its intercepted arc.

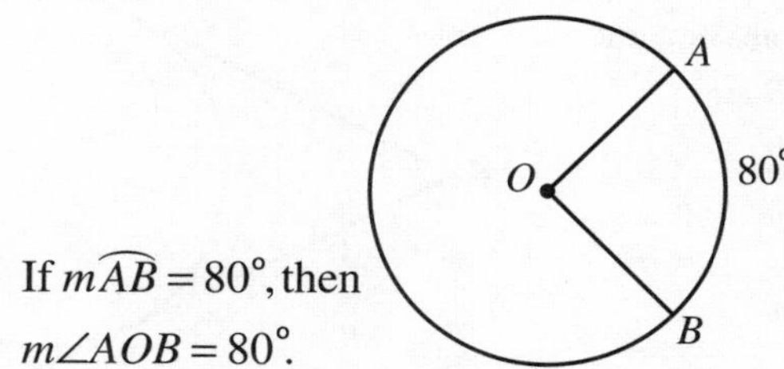

2. An inscribed angle is equal in degrees to one-half its intercepted arc.

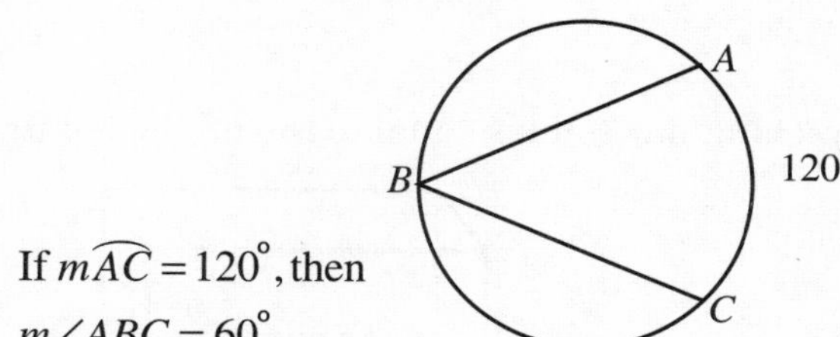

3. An angle formed by two chords intersecting in a circle is equal in degrees to one-half the sum of its intercepted arcs.

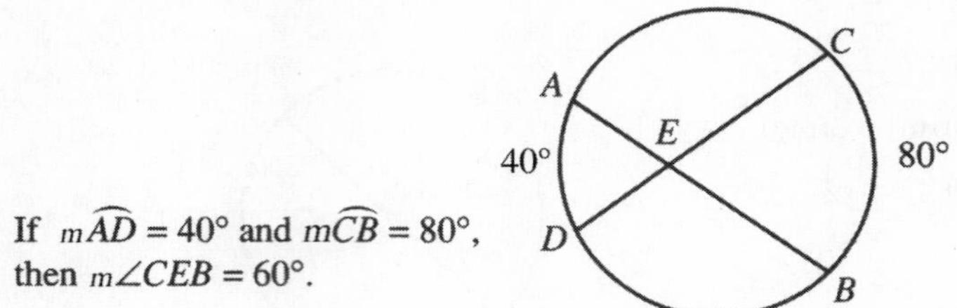

If $m\widehat{AD} = 40°$ and $m\widehat{CB} = 80°$, then $m\angle CEB = 60°$.

4. An angle formed outside a circle by two secants, a secant and a tangent, or two tangents is equal in degrees to one-half the difference of its intercepted arcs.

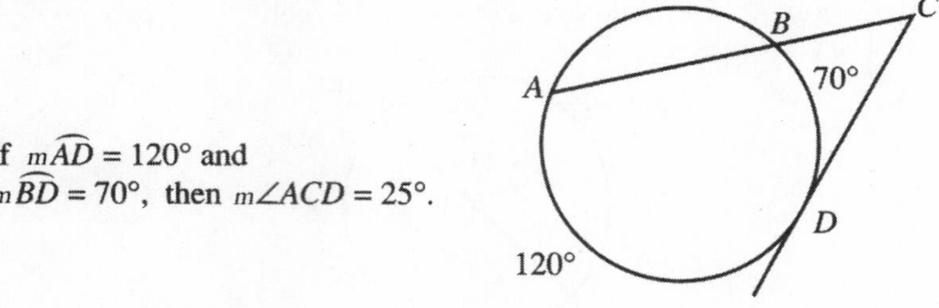

If $m\widehat{AD} = 120°$ and $m\widehat{BD} = 70°$, then $m\angle ACD = 25°$.

5. Two tangent segments drawn to a circle from the same external point are congruent.

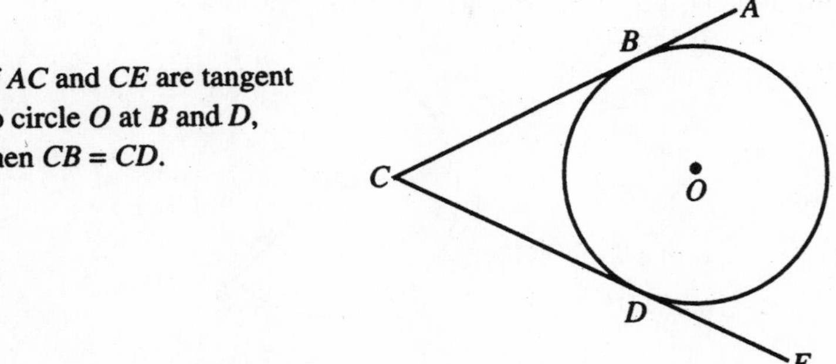

If AC and CE are tangent to circle O at B and D, then $CB = CD$.

4. VOLUMES

1. The volume of a rectangular solid is equal to the product of its length, width, and height.

   $V = lwh$

   $V = (6)(2)(4) = 48$

2. The volume of a cube is equal to the cube of an edge.

$V = e^3$

$V = (5)^3 = 125$

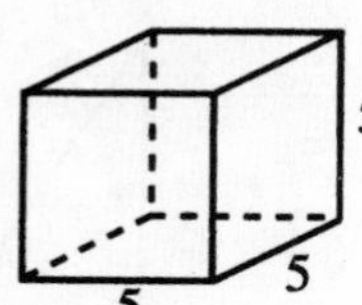

3. The volume of a cylinder is equal to π times the square of the radius of the base times the height.

$V = \pi r^2 h$

$V = \pi(5)^2(3) = 75\pi$

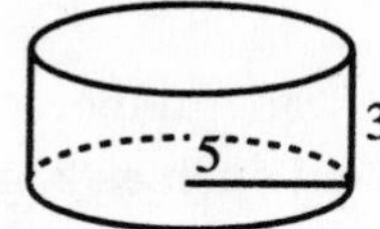

5. TRIANGLES

1. If two sides of a triangle are congruent, the angles opposite these sides are congruent.

If $AB \cong AC$, then

$\angle B \cong \angle C$.

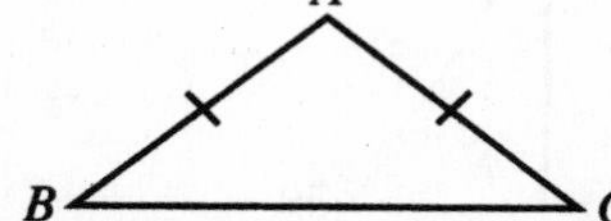

2. If two angles of a triangle are congruent, the sides opposite these angles are congruent.

If $\angle B \cong \angle C$, then

$AB \cong AC$.

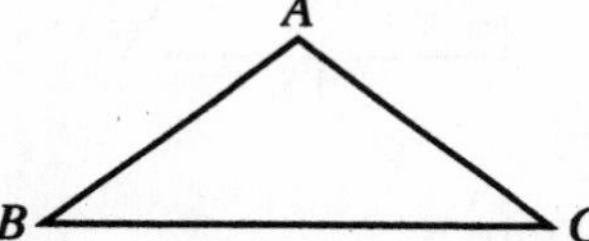

3. The sum of the measures of the angles of a triangle is 180°.

4. The measure of an exterior angle of a triangle is equal to the sum of the measures of the two remote interior angles.

$m\angle 1 = 130°$

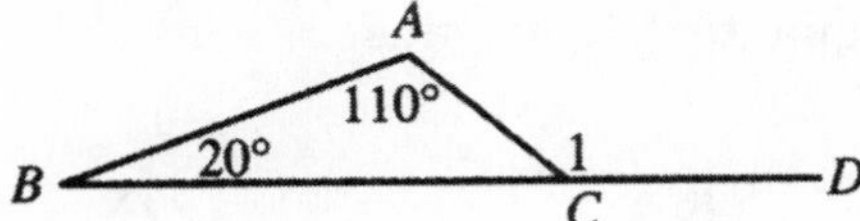

5. If two angles of one triangle are congruent to two angles of a second triangle, the third angles are congruent.

$\angle D \cong \angle A$

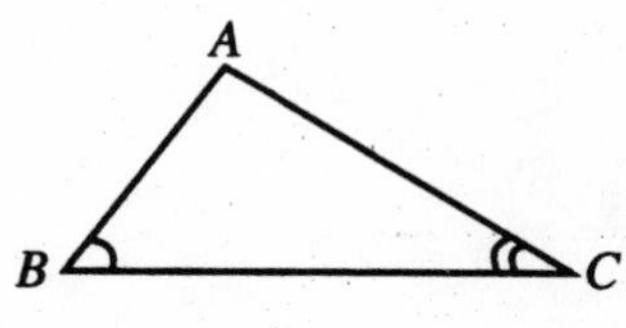

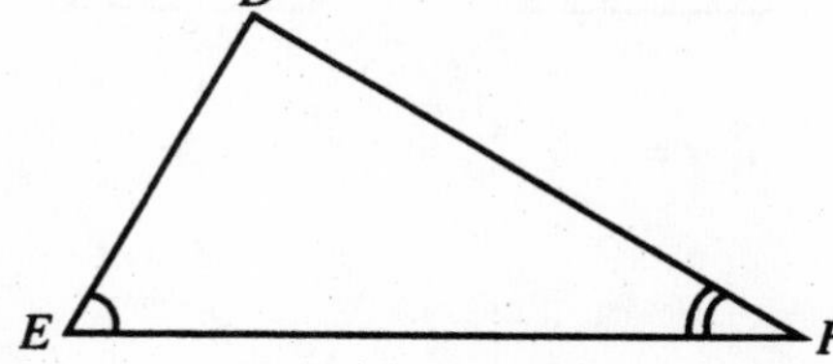

6. RIGHT TRIANGLES

1. Pythagorean Theorem

$$(\text{leg})^2 + (\text{leg})^2 = (\text{hypotenuse})^2$$
$$4^2 + 5^2 = x^2$$
$$16 + 25 = x^2$$
$$41 = x^2$$
$$\sqrt{41} = x$$

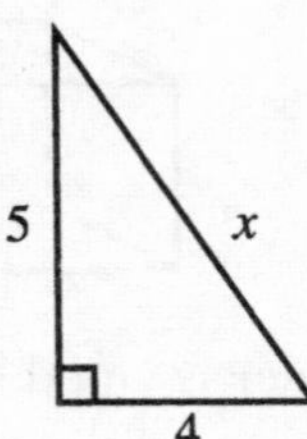

2. Pythagorean triples: These are sets of numbers that satisfy the Pythagorean Theorem. When a given set of numbers such as 3, 4, 5 forms a Pythagorean triple ($3^2 + 4^2 = 5^2$), any multiples of this set such as 6, 8, 10 or 15, 20, 25 also form a Pythagorean triple. The most common Pythagorean triples, which should be memorized, are:

3, 4, 5
5, 12, 13
8, 15, 17
7, 24, 25

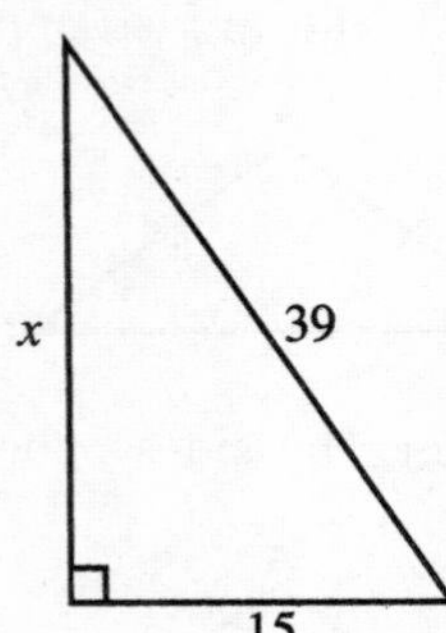

Squaring these numbers in order to apply the Pythagorean Theorem would take too much time. Instead, recognize the hypotenuse as 3(13). Suspect a 5, 12, 13 triangle. Since the given leg is 3(5), the missing leg must be 3(12), or 36, with no computation and a great saving of time.

3. The 30°-60°-90° triangle:
   a) The leg opposite the 30° angle is $\frac{1}{2}$ hypotenuse.
   b) The leg opposite the 60° angle is $\frac{1}{2}$ hypotenuse $\cdot \sqrt{3}$.
   c) An altitude in an equilateral triangle forms a 30°-60°-90° triangle and is therefore equal to $\frac{1}{2}$ hypotenuse $\cdot \sqrt{3}$.

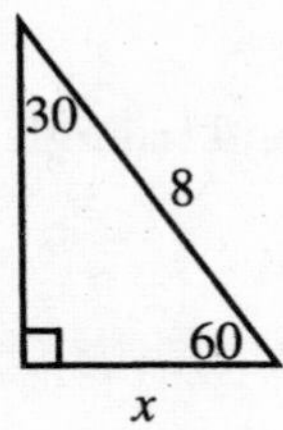

$x = 4$

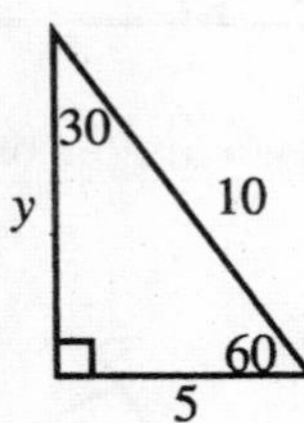

$y = 5\sqrt{3}$

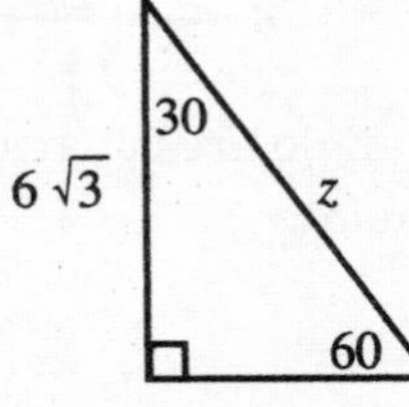

$z = 12$

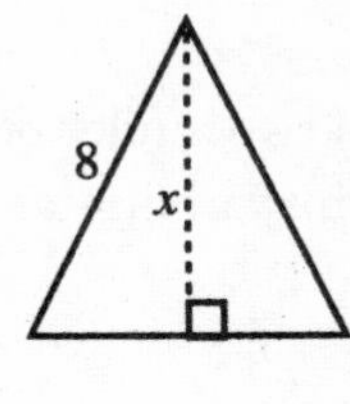

$x = 4\sqrt{3}$

4. The 45°-45°-90° triangle (isosceles right triangle):
   a) Each leg is $\frac{1}{2}$ hypotenuse · $\sqrt{2}$.
   b) Hypotenuse is leg · $\sqrt{2}$.
   c) The diagonal in a square forms a 45°-45°-90° triangle and is therefore equal to a side · $\sqrt{2}$.

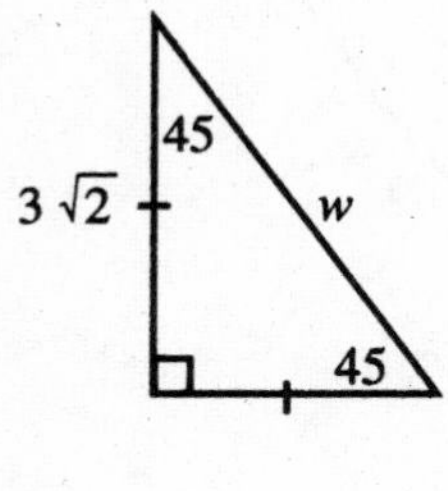

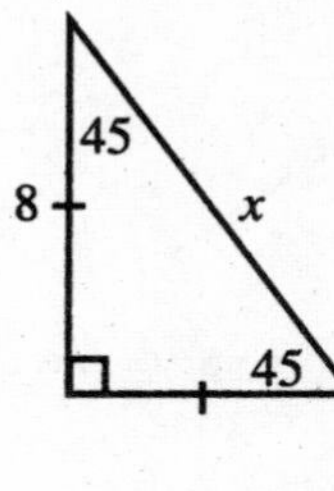

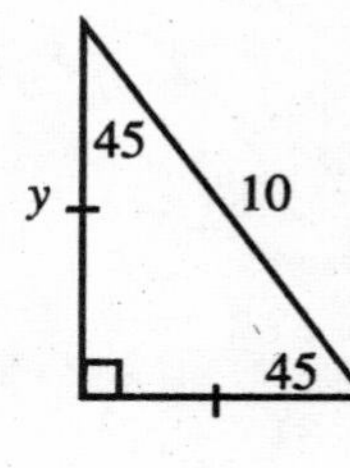

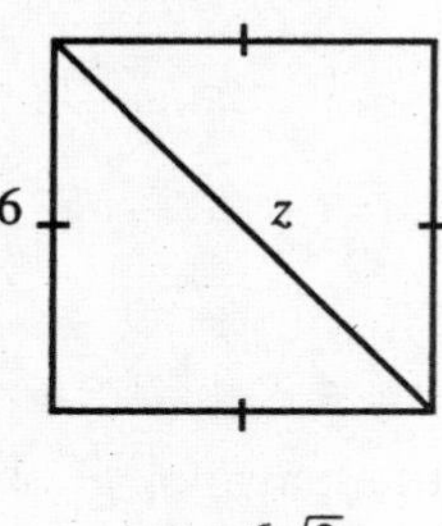

$w = 6$ $x = 8\sqrt{2}$ $y = 5\sqrt{2}$ $z = 6\sqrt{2}$

7. PARALLEL LINES

1. If two parallel lines are cut by a transversal, the alternate interior angles are congruent.

If $AB \parallel CD$, then
$\angle 1 \cong \angle 3$ and
$\angle 2 \cong \angle 4$.

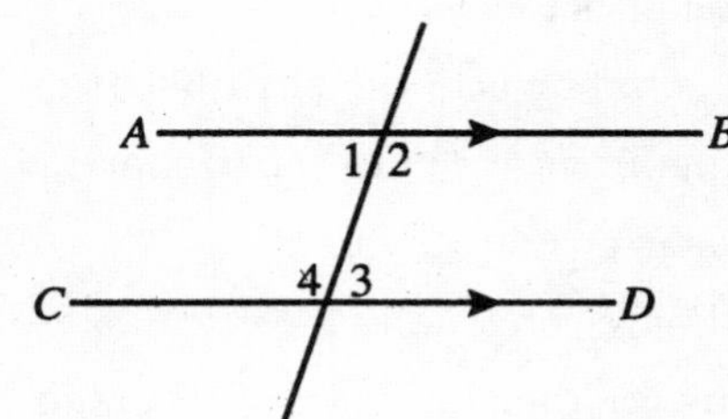

2. If two parallel lines are cut by a transversal, the corresponding angles are congruent.

If $AB \parallel CD$, then
$\angle 1 \cong \angle 5$,
$\angle 2 \cong \angle 6$,
$\angle 3 \cong \angle 7$, and
$\angle 4 \cong \angle 8$.

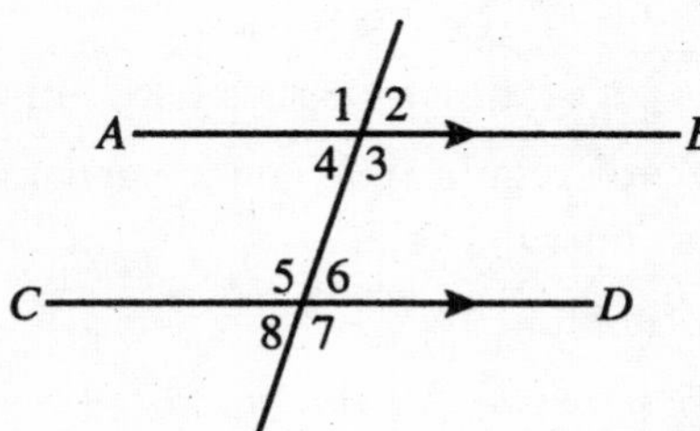

3. If two parallel lines are cut by a transversal, interior angles on the same side of the transversal are supplementary.

If $AB \parallel CD$, then
$\angle 1$ is supplementary to $\angle 4$ and
$\angle 2$ is supplementary to $\angle 3$.

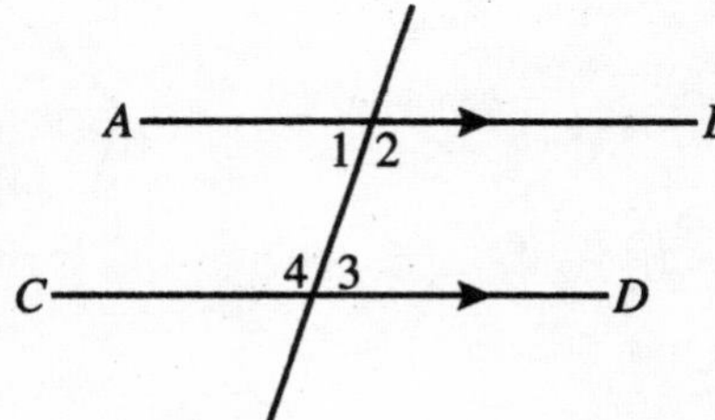

8. POLYGONS

1. The sum of the measures of the angles of a polygon of n sides is $(n - 2)180°$.

   Since $ABCDE$ has 5 sides,

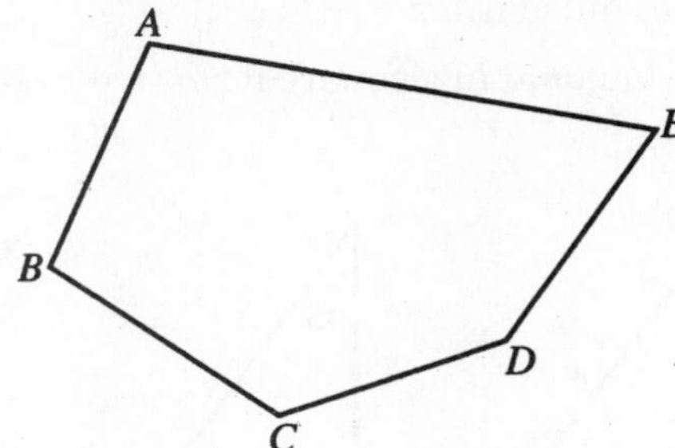

   $m\angle A + m\angle B + m\angle C + m\angle D + m\angle E = (5 - 2)180 = 3(180) = 540°$

2. In a parallelogram:
   a) Opposite sides are parallel.
   b) Opposite sides are congruent.
   c) Opposite angles are congruent.
   d) Consecutive angles are supplementary.
   e) Diagonals bisect each other.
   f) Each diagonal bisects the parallelogram into two congruent triangles.

3. In a rectangle, in addition to the properties listed in (2), above:
   a) All angles are right angles.
   b) Diagonals are congruent.

4. In a rhombus, in addition to the properties listed in (2), above:
   a) All sides are congruent.
   b) Diagonals are perpendicular.
   c) Diagonals bisect the angles.

5. A square has *all* of the properties listed in (2), (3), and (4), above.

6. The apothem of a regular polygon is perpendicular to a side, bisects that side, and also bisects a central angle.

   OX is an apothem.

   It bisects AB, is perpendicular to AB,

   and bisects $\angle AOB$.

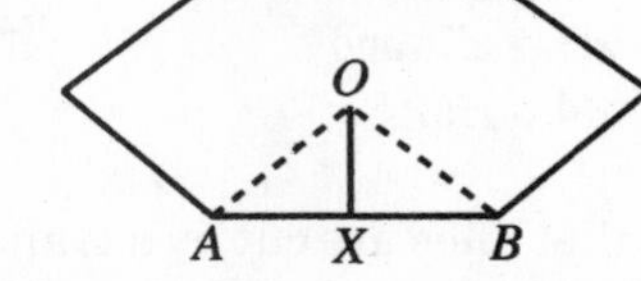

7. The area of a regular polygon is equal to one-half the product of its apothem and perimeter.

   $A = \frac{1}{2}(3)(30) = 45$

9. SIMILAR POLYGONS

1. Corresponding angles of similar polygons are congruent.
2. Corresponding sides of similar polygons are in proportion.

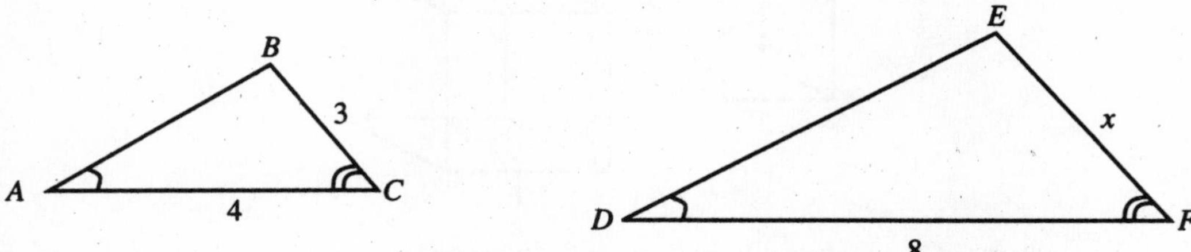

If triangle *ABC* is similar to triangle *DEF,* and the sides are given as marked, then *EF* must be equal to 6, as the ratio between corresponding sides is 4:8 or 1:2.

3. When figures are similar, all corresponding linear ratios are equal. The ratio of one side to its corresponding side is the same as perimeter to perimeter, apothem to apothem, altitude to altitude, etc.
4. When figures are similar, the ratio of their areas is equal to the square of the ratio between two corresponding linear quantities.

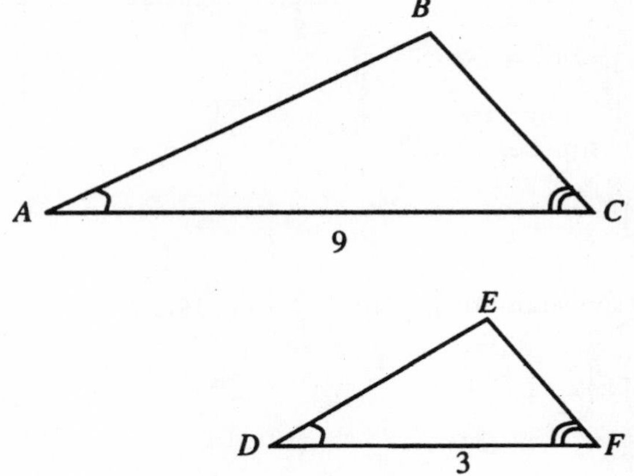

If triangle *ABC* is similar to triangle *DEF,* the area of triangle *ABC* will be 9 times as great as that of triangle *DEF.* The ratio of sides is 9:3, or 3:1. The ratio of areas will be the square of 3:1, or 9:1.

5. When figures are similar, the ratio of their volumes is equal to the cube of the ratio between two corresponding linear quantities.

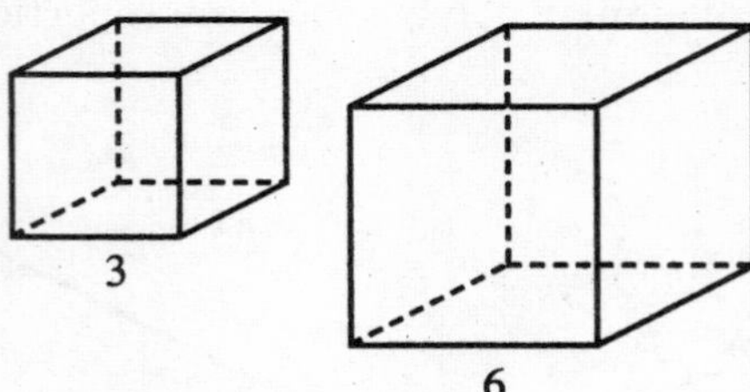

The volume of the larger cube is 8 times as large as the volume of the smaller cube. If the ratio of sides is 3:6, or 1:2, the ratio of volumes is the cube of this, or 1:8.

10. COORDINATE GEOMETRY

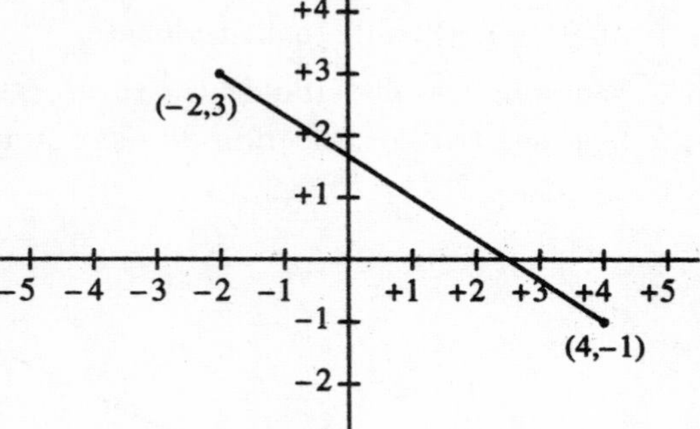

1. Distance between two points:

$$\sqrt{(x_2 - x_1)^2 + (y_2 - y_1)^2}$$

The distance from (–2, 3) to (4, –1) is:

$$\sqrt{[4-(-2)]^2 + [-1-(3)]^2}$$

$$\sqrt{(6)^2 + (-4)^2} = \sqrt{36+16} = \sqrt{52}$$

2. The midpoint of a line segment:

$$\left(\frac{x_1 + x_2}{2}, \frac{y_1 + y_2}{2}\right)$$

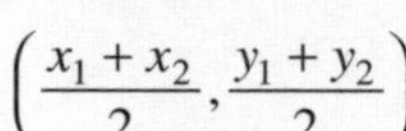

The midpoint of the segment joining (–2, 3) to (4, –1) is:

$$\left(\frac{-2+4}{2}, \frac{3+(-1)}{2}\right) = \left(\frac{2}{2}, \frac{2}{2}\right) = (1,1)$$

Exercise: Geometry

Work out each problem.

1. If the angles of a triangle are in the ratio 2:3:7, the triangle is
   (A) acute
   (B) isosceles
   (C) obtuse
   (D) right
   (E) equilateral

2. If the area of a square of side x is 5, what is the area of a square of side $3x$?
   (A) 15
   (B) 45
   (C) 95
   (D) 75
   (E) 225

3. If the radius of a circle is decreased by 10%, by what percent is its area decreased?
   (A) 10
   (B) 19
   (C) 21
   (D) 79
   (E) 81

4. A spotlight on the ceiling is 5 feet from one wall of a room and 10 feet from the wall at right angles to it. How many feet is it from the intersection of the two walls?
   (A) 15
   (B) $5\sqrt{2}$
   (C) $5\sqrt{5}$
   (D) $10\sqrt{2}$
   (E) $10\sqrt{5}$

5. A dam has the dimensions indicated in the figure. Find the area of this isosceles trapezoid.

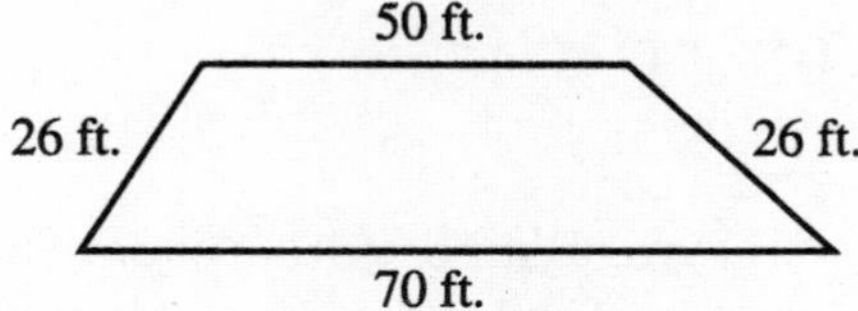

   (A) 1300
   (B) 1560
   (C) 1400
   (D) 1440
   (E) It cannot be determined from the information given.

6. In parallelogram $PQRS$, angle P is four times angle Q. What is the measure in degrees of angle P?
   (A) 36
   (B) 72
   (C) 125
   (D) 144
   (E) 150

7. If $PQ \cong QS$, $QR \cong RS$ and the measure of angle $PRS = 100°$, what is the measure, in degrees, of angle QPS?

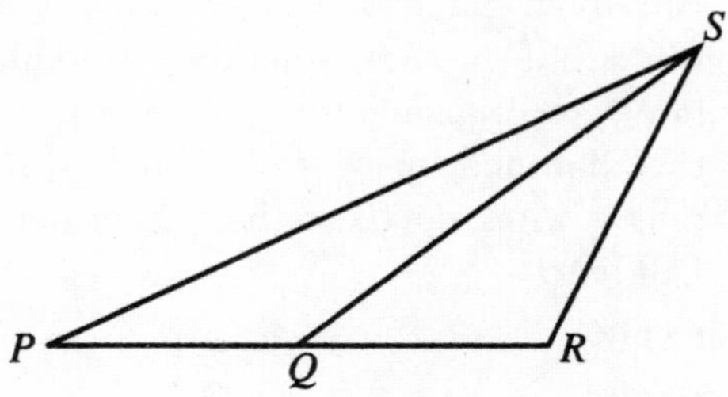

   (A) 10
   (B) 15
   (C) 20
   (D) 25
   (E) 30

8. A line segment is drawn from the point (3, 5) to the point (9, 13). What are the coordinates of the midpoint of this line segment?

(A) (3, 4)

(B) (12, 18)

(C) (6, 8)

(D) (9, 6)

(E) (6, 9)

9. A rectangular box with a square base contains 6 cubic feet. If the height of the box is 18 inches, how many feet are there in each side of the base?

(A) 1

(B) 2

(C) $\sqrt{3}$

(D) $\frac{\sqrt{3}}{3}$

(E) 4

10. The surface area of a cube is 150 square feet. How many cubic feet are there in the volume of the cube?

(A) 30

(B) 50

(C) 100

(D) 125

(E) 150

11. Peter lives 12 miles west of school and Bill lives north of the school. Peter finds that the direct distance from his house to Bill's is 6 miles shorter than the distance by way of school. How many miles north of the school does Bill live?

(A) 6

(B) 9

(C) 10

(D) $6\sqrt{2}$

(E) None of these

12. A square is inscribed in a circle of area 18π. Find a side of the square.

(A) 3

(B) 6

(C) $3\sqrt{2}$

(D) $6\sqrt{2}$

(E) It cannot be determined from the information given.

13. A carpet is y yards long and f feet wide. How many dollars will it cost if the carpet sells for x cents per square foot?

(A) xyf

(B) $3xyf$

(C) $\frac{xyf}{3}$

(D) $\frac{.03yf}{x}$

(E) $.03xyf$

14. If a triangle of base 6 has the same area as a circle of radius 6, what is the altitude of the triangle?

(A) 6π

(B) 8π

(C) 10π

(D) 12π

(E) 14π

15. The vertex angle of an isosceles triangle is p degrees. How many degrees are there in one of the base angles?

(A) $180 - p$

(B) $90 - p$

(C) $180 - 2p$

(D) $180 - \frac{p}{2}$

(E) $90 - \frac{p}{2}$

16. In a circle with center O, the measure of arc $RS = 132$ degrees. How many degrees are there in angle RSO?

(A) 66°

(B) 20°

(C) 22°

(D) 24°

(E) 48°

17. The ice compartment of a refrigerator is 8 inches long, 4 inches wide, and 5 inches high. How many ice cubes will it hold if each cube is 2 inches on an edge?

(A) 8

(B) 10

(C) 12

(D) 16

(E) 20

18. In the figure, PSQ is a straight line and RS is perpendicular to ST. If the measure of angle $RSQ = 48°$, how many degrees are there in angle PST?

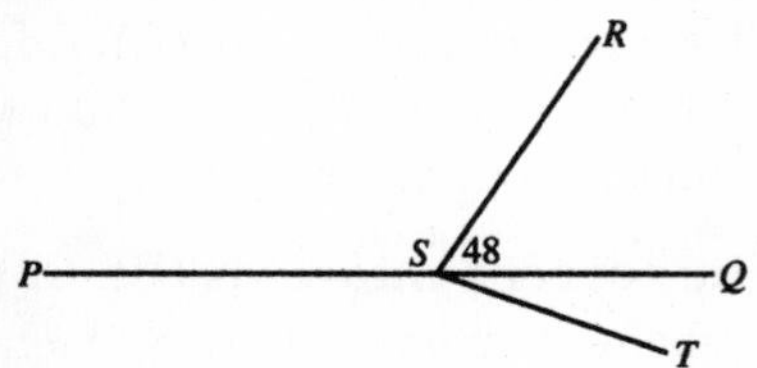

(A) 48°

(B) 132°

(C) 90°

(D) 136°

(E) 138°

19. A cylindrical pail has a radius of 7 inches and a height of 9 inches. If there are 231 cubic inches to a gallon, approximately how many gallons will this pail hold?

(A) 6

(B) $\frac{12}{7}$

(C) 7.5

(D) 8.2

(E) 9

20. In triangle PQR, QS and SR are angle bisectors and the measure of angle $P = 80°$. How many degrees are there in angle QSR?

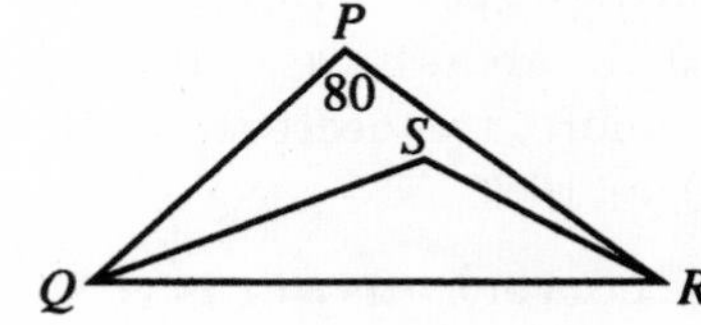

(A) 115°

(B) 120°

(C) 125°

(D) 130°

(E) 135°

Solutions

1. **The correct answer is (C).** Represent the angles as $2x$, $3x$, and $7x$.

$$2x + 3x + 7x = 180^\circ$$
$$12x = 180^\circ$$
$$x = 15^\circ$$

The angles are 30°, 45°, and 105°. Since one angle is between 90° and 180°, the triangle is called an obtuse triangle.

2. **The correct answer is (B).** If the sides have a ratio 1:3, the areas have a ratio 1:9. Therefore, the area of the large square is 9(5), or 45.

3. **The correct answer is (B).** If the radii of the two circles have a ratio of 10:9, the areas have a ratio of 100:81. Therefore, the decrease is 19 out of 100, or 19%.

4. **The correct answer is (C).**

$$5^2 + 10^2 = x^2$$
$$25 + 100 = x^2$$
$$x^2 = 125$$
$$x = \sqrt{125} = \sqrt{25}\sqrt{5} = 5\sqrt{5}$$

5. **The correct answer is (D).**

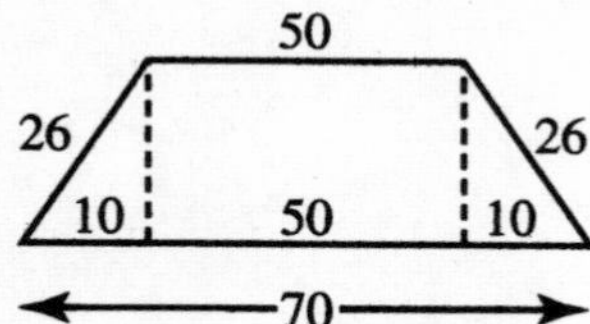

When altitudes are drawn from both ends of the upper base in an isosceles trapezoid, the figure is divided into a rectangle and two congruent right triangles. The center section of the lower base is equal to the upper base, and the remainder of the lower base is divided equally between both ends. The altitude can then be found using the Pythagorean Theorem. In this case, we have a 5, 12, 13 triangle with all measures doubled, so the altitude is 24.

The area is $\frac{1}{2}(24)(120)$, or 1440.

6. **The correct answer is (D).** The consecutive angles of a parallelogram are supplementary, so

$$x + 4x = 180^\circ$$
$$5x = 180^\circ$$
$$x = 36^\circ$$

Angle P is 4(36), or 144°.

7. **The correct answer is (C).**

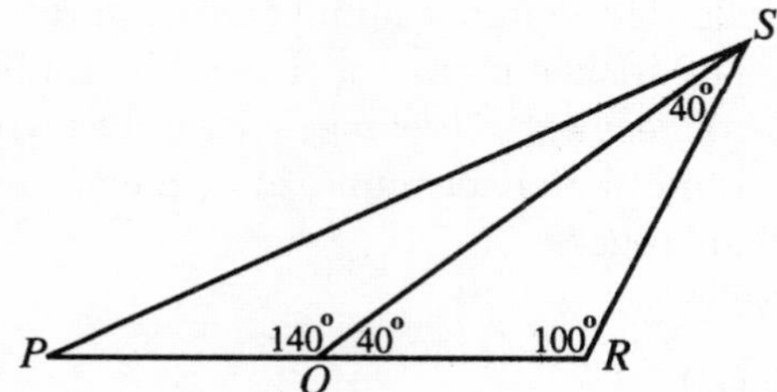

Since $QR \cong RS$, $\angle RQS \cong \angle RSQ$. There are 80° left in the triangle, so each of these angles is 40°. $\angle SQP$ is supplementary to $\angle SQR$, making it 140°. Since $QP \cong QS$, $\angle QPS \cong \angle QSP$. There are 40° left in the triangle, so each of these angles is 20°.

8. **The correct answer is (E).** Add the x values and divide by 2. Add the y values and divide by 2.

9. **The correct answer is (B).** Change 18 inches to 1.5 feet. Letting each side of the base be x, the volume is $1.5x^2$.

$$1.5x^2 = 6$$
$$15x^2 = 60$$
$$x^2 = 4$$
$$x = 2$$

10. **The correct answer is (D).** The surface area of a cube is made up of 6 equal squares. If each edge of the cube is x, then

$$6x^2 = 150$$
$$x^2 = 25$$
$$x = 5$$

Volume = $(\text{edge})^3 = 5^3 = 125$

11. **The correct answer is (B).**

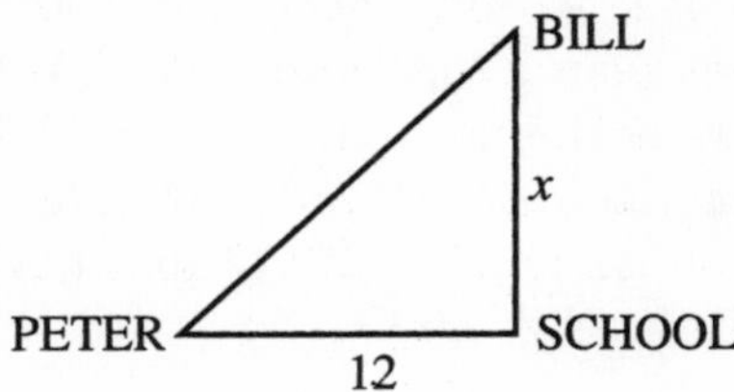

The direct distance from Peter's house to Bill's can be represented by means of the Pythagorean Theorem as $\sqrt{144+x^2}$. Then

$\sqrt{144+x^2} = (12 + x) - 6$

$\sqrt{144+x^2} = x + 6$

Square both sides.

$$144 + x^2 = x^2 + 12x + 36$$
$$144 = 12x + 36$$
$$108 = 12x$$
$$9 = x$$

12. **The correct answer is (B).**

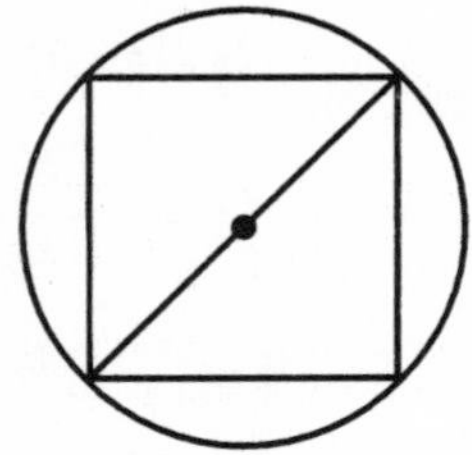

The diagonal of the square will be a diameter of the circle.

$$\pi r^2 = 18\pi$$
$$r^2 = 18$$
$$r = \sqrt{18} = \sqrt{9}\sqrt{2} = 3\sqrt{2}$$

The diameter is $6\sqrt{2}$ and, since the triangles are 45°-45°-90°, a side of the square is 6.

13. **The correct answer is (E).** To find the area in square feet, change y yards to $3y$ feet. The area is then $(3y)(f)$, or $3yf$ square feet. If each square foot costs x cents, change this to dollars by dividing x by 100. Thus, each square foot costs $\frac{x}{100}$ dollars.

The cost of $3yf$ square feet will be $(3yf)\left(\frac{x}{100}\right)$, or $\frac{3xyf}{100}$.

Since $\frac{3}{100} = .03$, the correct answer is (E).

14. **The correct answer is (D).** The area of the circle is $(6)^2\pi$, or 36π.

In the triangle $\frac{1}{2}(6)(h) = 36\pi$

$$3h = 36\pi$$
$$h = 12\pi$$

15. **The correct answer is (E).** There are $(180 - p)$ degrees left, which must be divided between 2 congruent angles. Each angle will contain $\frac{(180-p)}{2}$, or $90 - \frac{p}{2}$ degrees.

16. **The correct answer is (D).**

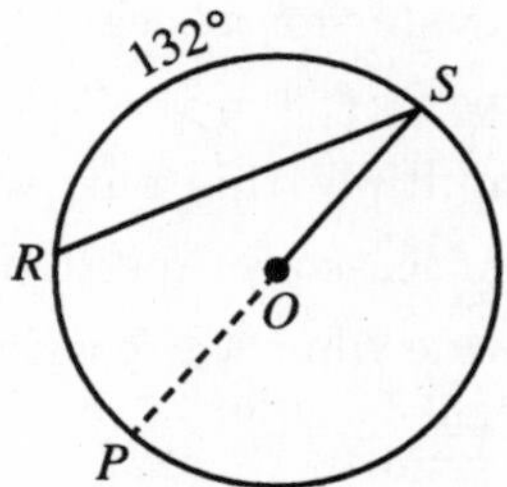

By extending SO until it hits the circle at P, arc PRS is a semicircle. Therefore, the measure of arc PR = 48°, and the measure of the inscribed angle RSO = 24°.

17. **The correct answer is (D).**

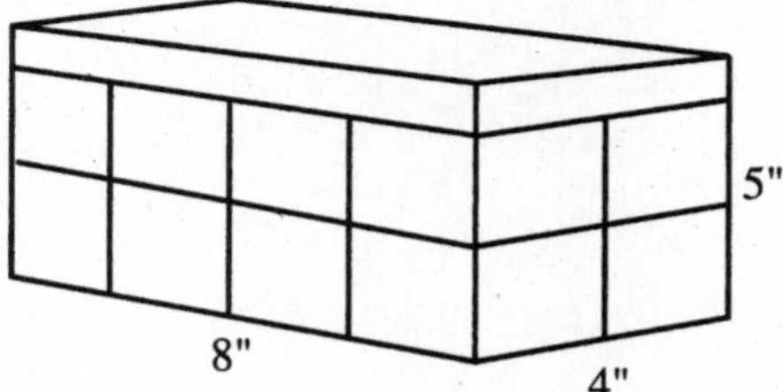

The compartment will hold 2 layers, each of which contains 2 rows of 4 cubes each. This leaves a height of 1 inch on top empty. Therefore, the compartment can hold 16 cubes.

18. **The correct answer is (E).**

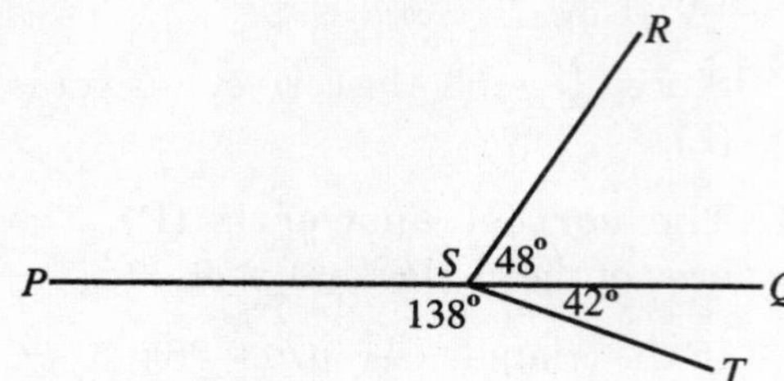

Since $\angle RST$ is a right angle, 42° are left for $\angle QST$. Since PSQ is a straight angle of 180°, $\angle PST$ contains 138°.

19. **The correct answer is (A).** The volume of the pail is found using the formula $V = \pi r^2 h$. Since the answers are not in terms of π, it is best to use $\frac{22}{7}$ as a value for π because the 7 will divide with r^2: $V = \frac{22}{\cancel{7}} \cdot \cancel{49}^7 \cdot 9$. Rather than multiply this out, which will take unnecessary time, divide by 231 and divide wherever possible.

$$\frac{\cancel{22}^2 \cdot \cancel{7} \cdot \cancel{9}^3}{\cancel{231}\,1} = 6$$

$\cancel{33}$

$\cancel{3}$

20. **The correct answer is (D).** If $m\angle P = 80°$, there are 100° left between $\angle PQR$ and $\angle PRQ$. If they are both bisected, there will be 50° between $\angle SQR$ and $\angle SRQ$, leaving 130° in triangle SRQ for $\angle QSR$.

PART VIII

APPENDICES

Creating Your B-School Application

appendix A

In order to create the most effective application you can, you must understand and appreciate the goals of the process by which some applicants are selected (and others not) as a social and economic process. With this knowledge, you can intelligently craft an application that is consistent with the workings of these processes—one that has the maximum chance of success.

Application success is no accident. You must have a plan that incorporates these goals:

- Your completed application must hang together as a coherent whole.Your GPA, your GMAT score, and your application form the core of this whole.
- Your personal statement should incorporate some of the most important themes from the application itself and weave them into a story or an argument for why you should be accepted.
- Your letters of recommendation should come from people who know you well enough to echo some of the points contained in both the core and your personal statement.

UNDERSTANDING THE APPLICATION PROCESS

If you're like most candidates, at the outset you think of the application process as taking a test, answering a few questions about your educational background and employment history, writing a personal statement, and arranging for a couple of recommendations. After which, you put everything into an envelope (with a check) and then wait for an answer.

The application process is much, much more than this. The cost of the application process routinely exceeds $1,000. The fees that you pay to take the Graduate Management Admission Test and for score and grade reports could be more than $200. Further, the application fees charged by schools run between $50 and $75. Assuming that you apply to ten schools, you could easily spend $750 on application fees. In addition, you will probably spend at least $100 on administrative details such as document preparation, copying, postage, and long-distance telephone calls. Add another $300 or so for test preparation for the GMAT, and you have already committed well over $1,000.

The total cost of a B-school education can be more than $100,000, and many applicants try to analyze it as an investment. You might want to run your own spread sheet. Use those factors that you think are relevant (e.g., tuition and fees on one side and prospective earnings on the other), but some words of advice about constructing your model: First, be careful how you factor in living expenses. You have to eat and have a place to live no matter what you're doing; therefore, only *increases* in the cost of living associated with obtaining the degree are relevant. Second, assuming foregone opportunity cost as measured by two years' annual salary is a gross oversimplification. You will be able to work in the summer between your first and second years (perhaps in a very good position as part of a firm's recruiting policy); and, in any event, you graduate in June. So, at the most, lost income is really only six quarters and not eight. And there is the greater return that you expect after graduation. And all of this pales in comparison to the fun you'll have in school (even though it is hard work) and the increase in job satisfaction—factors that are impossible to value in economic terms.

Don't let those numbers frighten you. They are not intended to dissuade you from pursuing your education, but rather to dramatize a point. The decision to apply to a B-school has significant financial implications for you as an individual (and probably for your family). To create the most powerful application possible given your GPA, test score, and background, you need to be aware of the criteria the business school will use when it reviews your application. That way, you can craft an application that, in its every detail, answers the concerns of the admission committee.

THE BUSINESS OF BUSINESS EDUCATION

From the perspective of the school, there are financial as well as social implications. A B-school, like any educational institution, is a corporate individual, and its admissions decisions reflect financial and social policies adopted by the corporation. Consider first some of the financial implications that influence a B-school to accept or reject an applicant.

The school has to be run as a business. It has employees; it owns or rents property; it operates a library; it buys furniture and office equipment; it pays utility bills; and so on. A large part of those expenses is paid using student tuition. A school, therefore, is dependent on a steady flow of tuition money. So admissions decisions must be made in the context of budgetary constraints. A school simply cannot afford to have large numbers of students dropping out of school.

One concern of an admissions officer is to ensure that those applicants who are accepted are committed to completing the course of study. Additionally—though this may not be an explicit concern—schools rely heavily on alumni donations. So it should not be surprising to learn that an applicant who shows considerable professional promise would be considered favorably. And a school that graduates successful professionals gets a reputation for being a good school and such a reputation in turn tends to attract highly qualified applicants.

Financial considerations are only one aspect of the admissions decision. Schools also have a sense of the social responsibility they bear as educators. They meet this responsibility in some fairly obvious ways such as actively seeking applications from groups who have traditionally been under-represented.

The Competition

The admissions process, then, is the interface between two perspectives. The process is designed to match individuals and institutions who can mutually satisfy each other's needs. This matching function, however, is somewhat skewed. There are more people interested in graduate study in business (at least at the competitive schools) than there are seats available. As a consequence, applicants are competing for seats. Given the mismatch between the number of seats and the number of applicants, the application process is turned into a competition. You will have to compete against others for a place (or at least for a place at the business school of your choice). To do this, you must make yourself attractive to a school. You must persuade the admissions committee that you will help them satisfy their economic and social needs,and that thought must guide you as you create your application.

You can learn a lot about your chances of acceptance at particular schools by visiting their web sites and by reading their admissions literature.

And don't forget to tell them what they want to hear. Business schools want to hear that you have both the ability to handle the curriculum and the motivation to study hard plus that you'll be an interesting addition to the business school. Everything that goes into the application should bear on one of these points.

BEHIND CLOSED DOORS: AN INSIDE LOOK AT THE ADMISSIONS PROCESS

What goes on behind the closed doors of the admissions office? Well, the first thing that you should know about the admissions process is that there is no one admissions process. Rather, each school has its own individual admissions process that differs somewhat from that of every other school in the country.

At some schools, the decisions are made by faculty committees. At such schools, decisions may be made by majority vote, or unanimous agreement may be required before an acceptance is extended to an applicant. At other schools, the decisions may be made by a single professional admissions officer or by a dean of admissions who is not a faculty member. At other schools, decisions may be made by a committee with members drawn from both administration and faculty. And at some schools, students themselves may have some input into admissions decisions.

The GMAT/GPA Factors and the "Admissions Index"

Despite the variety of formal structures, one generalization is possible: Every school relies to some extent on the applicant's Grade Point Average (GPA) and GMAT score, but there are few (if any) schools that rely only on these quantitative factors. What does this statement mean for you? First, it says that every school uses the GPA and the

GMAT score. The exact use of these numbers varies from school to school, but many use a formula that combines the two together into an index. The formula is designed to weight the two numbers approximately equally to give admissions officers some idea of how one applicant stacks up against other applicants.

Note that, for many years, Harvard Business School was an exception to the rule and not only did not use but didn't even accept GMAT scores. More recently, however, even Harvard climbed aboard the GMAT bandwagon.

The GMAT is scored on a scale from 200 (the minimum) to 800 (the maximum). (You may notice that this is the same scale that is used by the SAT.) The 200-to-800 point scale has a special relation to the 0-to-4 grading system used by most colleges: 800 is 200 times 4. This permits the use of a formula to combine the two measures. For example:

$$\text{Index} = (\text{GMAT}) + (200 \times \text{GPA})$$

This formula combines the two numbers to create an index. Let's use some numbers, say a GPA of 3.5 and a GMAT score of 700:

$$I = (\text{GMAT}) + (200 \times \text{GPA})$$

$$I = (700) + (200 \times 3.5) = 1400$$

Thus, the index for this particular applicant is a 1400—an artificial number, but one that will make sense to the admissions committee because all other applications at their school are classified in the same manner.

Another index formula might generate a number with a more familiar look:

$$\text{Index} = \frac{\frac{\text{GMAT}}{200} + \text{GPA}}{2}$$

A GMAT score of 600 and a GPA of 3.5 would generate the value 3.25 using this formula, and the 3.25 is a fairly inuitive number: this applicant is a B+ student.

What does the index do? That varies from school to school. Some schools have a fairly mechanical admissions process that emphasizes the index. The school may set a minimum index below which applications receive little or no attention because they are probably going to be rejected anyway. Such schools may also have a second, higher minimum that triggers an automatic acceptance (unless the application shows some glaring weakness—say a letter of recommendation that torpedoes the application). At the opposite extreme are schools that minimize the importance of the "numbers." These schools may not even calculate an index. Such schools have a very flexible admissions process.

Most schools fall somewhere in between these extremes. Many schools use the index as a screening device to determine how much attention will be given to an application. Applications with very low indexes will receive little attention. The schools reason that unless there is something obvious and compelling in the application to offset the low numbers, then the applicant will be rejected. Applications with very high indexes will also receive little attention. The reasoning is that unless there is something obvious and compelling in the application to reject it, it should be accepted. On this theory, the applications with indexes in the middle receive the greatest attention. These are applications from candidates who are at least competitive for the school but who do not command an automatic acceptance. It is in this pool that competition is the most severe.

Here is a table that illustrates what happens at most B-schools (business schools are somewhat edgy about releasing this kind information, so the table is a composite based on data from several schools):

ADMISSIONS CHANCES

		GMAT (Percentile Rankings)			
		61–70	**71–80**	**81–90**	**90+**
G	**3.75+**	2/19	40/101	102/116	72/79
P	**3.50–3.74**	6/112	75/275	301/361	120/129
A	**Below 3.50**	10/160	90/601	375/666	201/250

(The number to the right of the slash shows the number of applicants; the number to the left of the slash shows the number of applicants accepted.)

In the category in the upper-right-hand corner are candidates with scores above the 90th percentile and GPAs above 3.75. The table shows that 72 of the 79 were accepted and seven rejected.

Interestingly, the table also shows that some candidates with higher indexes were rejected in favor of candidates with lower numbers. For example, of those candidates with scores between the 81st and 90th percentiles, 74 more candidates were accepted with a GPA below 3.50 than the higher GPA between 3.5 and 3.74. Why would a business school reject an applicant with higher numbers for one with lower numbers? Because of the unquantifiable factors such as motivation, commitment, leadership, experience, and so on. (More information on the role of these characteristics and how you can demonstrate that you have them is given later in this appendix.)

As you prepare your applications, you are, of course, saddled with your GPA and your GMAT score. There is nothing you can do to change those factors. This means that you have to work hard to craft an application that presents your credentials in the best light.

Want to know more about your chances for success at a particular school? Look at the admission literature for information about average or median GMAT and GPA of entering students.

ROLLING ADMISSIONS

Rolling admissions is a device used by schools that regulates the release of acceptances. A typical application season opens in October and closes in February or perhaps March. Applications will be received throughout the application season, and decisions are made on an ongoing basis. Rather than saving all applications until the deadline for applications has passed and then making decisions, rolling admissions allows schools to notify applicants on an ongoing basis.

To make the rolling admission plan work, the school begins by "targeting" an entering class: Based on its admissions history, a school will estimate what it thinks will be the range of GMAT scores and the range of GPAs of the students it will accept for the upcoming year. Then, as it receives applications (say, month by month), the school will act on them. Students with very strong applications compared with the target group will receive acceptances, and students with weak ones, rejections. Applications that are neither weak nor strong (but rather in the middle) will be carried over—these applicants receive no notification that the application is still pending. The rolling admissions process has advantages for both the school and the applicant. From the applicant's point of view, the earlier the notification of the disposition of an application the better. That is, you know whether you were accepted or rejected and can go on from there. From the school's viewpoint, the entering class (and the stability of the budget) begins to take shape as early as possible.

The rolling admissions process is also a tool you can use to your advantage: Apply early. Obviously, schools have greater flexibility earlier in the admission season than later—there are more seats available earlier in the year. That is not to say that if you apply late in the season you will be rejected. In fact, it is impossible to quantify exactly the advantage that applications received earlier rather than later enjoy. Still, if you want to maximize your chances of acceptance, apply early!

And don't downplay the advantages of early admissions applications; they can benefit you in ways that extend beyond admissions. The early bird gets the worm, and you may have advantages in terms of financial aid and other university services such as a housing lottery that are administered on a "first come, first served" basis. Also, the earlier you receive a notification, the sooner you can start making plans for a major transition in your life.

DECIDING WHERE TO APPLY

Given the financial commitment that you will be making, one of the obvious questions on your mind will be "Where should I apply?"

Let's assume that you have the resources to apply to ten schools and that you have an above-average GPA and GMAT score. Depending on the exact numbers, you may very well have a chance at one of the top business schools. But those are your long-shot schools. You are almost a sure thing at many schools. And there is a long list of schools in the middle at which your application will almost surely receive serious consideration but is not guaranteed for acceptance. Given these considerations, you should select two or perhaps three long-shot schools. As the term "long shot" implies, the odds of your being accepted at these schools are not very good, but the potential pay-off justifies the gamble.

On the other hand, you should also select one or two sure-thing schools. To do this, you may have to apply to a school in your geographical area that doesn't enjoy a particularly good reputation or to a school that is located in another part of the country. The rest of your applications should go to your good-bet schools—schools for which the chances for acceptance are 40% to 75%.

Hedge your application bets. Given your GMAT score and GPA, classify schools on your list as "sure things" (odds of acceptance are better than 4 out of 5), "long shots" (odds are worse than 1 out of 5), and "solid favorites" (odds are 2 out of 5 to 4 out of 5). Put most of your "money" on the solid favorites with lesser amounts on sure things and long shots. (The exact proportions will depend on your personal risk-taking preferences.)

This strategy of "stacking" your applications will maximize your chances of acceptance at a school you want while minimizing the chance that you won't get in to any school. Of course, the way the strategy gets implemented will vary from person to person. For people who are lucky enough to have a high GPA and a top GMAT score, the middle and bottom tier schools collapse into a single tier. And at the other extreme, those who are unlucky enough to have a GPA and GMAT score that are below what most schools accept will have to work with the second and third tiers.

As you prepare to implement your strategy, make a realistic assessment of your chances. Candidates unfortunately tend to overestimate the importance of what they believe to be their own interesting or unique factors. It is not unusual to hear candidates make statements such as "Well sure my GPA is a little low, but I had to work part-time while I was in school" and "I know my GMAT score is not that good, but I was a member of the University Senate." These are valid points and are usually taken into consideration by admissions officers. But the question is how much weight they will be given since they (or some similar point) are true of most of the people who are applying to business school.

And finally, be realistic. If you are thinking of applying to a school like Wharton, Sloan, Tuck, or Kellogg, and you have a 3.25 GPA and a GMAT score of 75th percentile, then there had better be something really special in your background—like a stint as CEO of General Electric. These schools turn down a lot of applications with "supernumbers" and even more with good-to-excellent numbers.

WHICH B-SCHOOL IS THE BEST?

A question related to the "Where should I apply?" question is "What are the top schools in the country?" Since there is no single criterion for "best school" that would be accepted by everyone, it is arguable that this question simply cannot be given a meaningful answer. But even though no unequivocal answer can be given, it is possible to get an approximate answer.

One way of evaluating B-schools is to think of them as falling into one of three groups: national schools, regional schools, and local schools. National schools are those with substantial academic reputations, such as Chicago, Columbia, Harvard, Kellogg, Michigan, Sloan, Stanford, Tuck, Wharton, and Yale. This group could also include Carnegie Mellon, Cornell (Johnson), Berkeley (Haas), Hastings, UCLA (Anderson), Duke (Fuqua), Georgetown, NYU (Stern), University of Texas (Austin), and the University of Virginia (Darden). Regional schools have a substantial regional reputation but are not known nationally as "top" schools. Local schools are those whose educational mission is providing theoretical instruction to supplement students' practical experience and often offer part-time, evening programs. If your goal is a partnership track position with a top consulting firm in a big city, then you should aim for a "national" school. On the other hand, if you want the MBA for advancement on the career track you're already on, then it probably won't make a lot of difference where you go to school.

Do your research and keep an open mind when you're deciding which school is "the best." Admissions officers often say that there are 20 B-schools in the top ten.

CRAFTING YOUR APPLICATION

To maximize your chances of success, you must create an application that satisfies the needs of the school to which you are applying. This does not mean that you create an application out of whole cloth, but it does mean that you organize and present your experiences in a way that depicts you in the most favorable light.

Answering the "Short Answer" Application Questions

Most of the questions you will be asked need only short answers, for example, "Did you work while you were in school?," "What clubs did you join?," and "What honors or awards did you receive?" You don't have much room to maneuver here. But you should try to communicate as much information as possible in your short answers. Compare the following pairs of descriptions:

Good	Member of the College Orchestra
Better	Second Violinist of the College Orchestra
Good	Played Intra-Mural Volleyball
Better	Co-captain of the Phi Kappa Volleyball Team
Good	Member of the AD's CSL
Better	One of three members on the Associate Dean's Committee on Student Life
Good	Worked at Billy's Burger Barn
Better	Assistant Manager at Billy's Burger Barn (25 hours/week)

In addition to the short-answer questions, most applications require one or more personal statements. Some of these are very narrow and to the point, e.g., "What has been your biggest failure and why did it happen?" An application may also include a general invitation to make a non-specific personal statement. Some applications ask for very little, for example, "In a paragraph explain to us why you want to go to business school." Other applications are open-ended: "On a separate sheet of paper, tell us anything else you think we ought to know about you." The point of the question is to give you the opportunity to give the admissions committee any information that might not be available from the GMAT score, GPA, and short-answer questions.

Before filling out any applications, sit down and make a list of all of your accomplishments. Include everything, then prioritize the list. Keep only the ones that are likely to be meaningful to an admissions committee.

Writing an Effective Personal Statement

For two reasons, you should consider the personal statements to be the most important part of your application. First, the personal statements should give an admissions committee a reason or reasons to accept you. Second, the personal statements are the one aspect of the application over which you can exercise any real control. Your GPA is already settled; your work experience was accumulated over years; your GMAT has been scored. Those are aspects of the application that cannot easily be manipulated. The personal statements, however, are under your control.

For an in-depth look at crafting this critical component of your application, see Appendix B, "Workshop: The Personal Statement," later in this book.

Choosing Your Statement's Content

What should go into a non-specific personal statement? Arguments that interpret your academic, employment, and personal history in such a way as to indicate that you have the ability to do business school studies and that you are committed to studying and later to applying what you've learned. Importantly, the personal statements must not be a simple restatement of facts already in the application.

Imagine, for example, a personal statement that reads as follows:

> I went to State University where I got a 3.5 GPA. I was a member of the Associate Dean's Committee on Student Life, and I worked as the assistant manager on the night shift at Billy's Burger Barn. Then I took the GMAT and got a 600. I know I will make a really good business-school student and later a fine professional manager.

Not very interesting. Furthermore, all of that information is already included in the answers to the standard questions on the application. There is no point in simply repeating it.

Instead, your personal statement should interpret the facts of your life to make them reasons why you should be accepted into business school. Let's start with the GPA. Try to bring out facts that suggest that the GPA is really better than it looks:

- Did you have one particularly bad semester during which you took Physics, Calculus, and Latin that pulled your average down?
- Was there a death in the family or some other difficult time that interfered with your studies?
- How many hours did you work in an average week?
- What extracurricular or family commitments took time away from your studies?
- Did you follow an unusual course of study such as an honors program or a double major?
- Was your major a particularly challenging one?
- Did you participate in any unusual courses such as field research?

These are the points that the admissions committee wants to hear. For example:

> The committee will see that my final GPA is 3.5. I should point out that the average would have been higher had I not had to work 20 hours each week to finance my education. Additionally, my grades in the first semester of my junior year were disappointing because my grandmother, who lived with my family and with whom I was very close, died. Finally, in order to fulfill the requirements for the honors program, I wrote a 50-page honors thesis on the economics of the Dutch fishing industry of the 18th century. I have included with this application a copy of the introduction to this paper.

You should take the same approach to your work experience. For example:

> During my junior and senior years in college, I worked an average of 20 hours per week at Billy's Burger Barn as the manager on the night shift. I reported to work at midnight and got off at four a.m. As night manager, I supervised eight other employees and was responsible for making emergency repairs on kitchen equipment. For example, once I was able to keep the deep fryer in operation by using a length of telephone cable to repair a faulty thermostat. The night manager was also responsible for maintaining order. It's no easy job to convince intoxicated students who become too rowdy to leave without calling the police. And we were robbed at gunpoint not once but twice.

Of course, if you have considerable work experience, e.g., if you graduated from college several years ago, you will want to go into your experience in more detail than student work-experience merits.

Can you say anything about the GMAT? Probably not much. The GMAT score is not usually open to interpretation, but there are some exceptions. One such exception is a history of poor scores on standardized exams. Consider the following:

> I believe that my GMAT score of 600 understates my real ability for I have never had much success on aptitude tests. My SAT score was only 925. Yet, I finished college with a 3.6 GPA.

Or:

> The committee will see that I have two GMAT scores, 300 and 600. During the first test, I had the flu and a fever and simply could not concentrate.

These are the two most common excuses for a disappointing GMAT score.

Finally, you must also persuade the admissions committee that you are serious about studying business. It won't do to write "I really admire Lee Iaccoca." You must be able to show the committee something in your background that explains why you want to go to business school. Also, it will help your case if you can suggest what you might do with an MBA. For example:

> As a chemistry major, I joined the Student Environmental Association. Working with professors, we helped the local paper mill develop a plan to stop polluting Three-Mile Run Creek. I hope to help a large business manage its operations in an environmentally acceptable manner.

Your career objectives have to be believable. It won't do to write "I plan to be a captain of industry." That's much too abstract. You need to be much more specific. Even if you can't identify a particular position that you would like to have, you need to think about the conditions that would give you the job satisfaction you're looking for and then describe those conditions.

Finally, you may also wish to include in your personal statement information that shows that you have something that will help the school create a diverse student body. This additional information can be something dramatic:

> One morning, a patron choked on a burger and lost consciousness. I used the Heimlich maneuver to dislodge the food and performed CPR until a team of paramedics arrived. The patron recovered fully in large part, according to her doctors, because of my first aid.

Or the information may not be dramatic:

> My parents are Armenian immigrants, so I am fluent in Armenian as well as English. I would enjoy meeting others who share an interest in the politics, business, and culture of that part of the world.

Don't overestimate the value of this kind of information. It is, so to speak, the icing on the cake. It makes you a more interesting individual and might tip the scale in your favor when all other things are equal. It will not, however, get you an acceptance at a school for which you are not otherwise competitive in terms of GMAT and GPA.

Diversity is important. Take Wharton, for example. It says that about 30 percent of its students are women, 18 percent are members of minority groups, and 32 percent are foreign nationals. At its web site, Harvard Business School features a half dozen students who have strikingly unusual experiences.

Organizing Your Argument

Your personal statement presents your "arguments" for acceptance into the school to which you're applying. When you marshal your arguments for acceptance, you need to present them in an organized fashion. There is no single preferred format, but you might start with the following outline:

I. I have the ability.
   A. My college studies were good.
      i. I had one bad semester.
      ii. I was in the honors program.
      iii. I wrote a thesis.
   B. My work experience is good.
      i. I was promoted to VP of my firm.
      ii. I worked while in college.

II. I want to become a business executive.
   A. I worked with executives on the financial problems of Company X.
   B. I would become a specialist in mergers.

III. There is something interesting about me.

You should create your outline, using all the arguments you can think of. Then you must begin to edit. For most people, the final document should not be more than a page to a page and a half—typed of course! (Particular schools may have even more stringent limitations; abide by them.) During the editing process, you should strive for an economy of language so that you can convey as much information as possible. Additionally, you will be forced to make considered judgments about the relative importance of various points. You will be forced to delete those ideas that aren't really that compelling. To obtain a really good personal statement, it may be necessary to reduce five or six pages to a single page, and the process may require more than 20 drafts.

If your numbers (GMAT and GPA) are in the ballpark, then your personal statement is likely to be the most important part of the application. It will never be perfect, but make it as much so as possible. Ask professors, friends, and co-workers to read it and to comment on it. You might even want to consult a professional advisor to help to construct the application.

Regardless of where you intend to apply, you should take time to look at some applications from top business schools. The wording of their essay prompts can give you some good ideas of what you might want to write for any application. One school, for example, asks "What are your three most important strengths and your three most serious weaknesses and how do you think an MBA education will affect them?" It's excellent food for thought.

LETTERS OF RECOMMENDATION

Perhaps the best advice about so-called letters of recommendation is to think of them as evaluations rather than recommendations. Indeed, many admissions officers refer to letter-writers as evaluators. These letters can be very important factors in an application, so you need to choose their authors carefully.

First, let's dispose of a common misunderstanding. A letter of evaluation does not have to come from a famous person. How effective is the following letter?:

> William Hardy, CEO
> MegaBucks Holding Company
>
> To the Admissions Committee:
>
> I am recommending Paul Roberts for your business school. My Head of Financial Operations knows his father, Mark, who works in our Bonds Division and says that Mark is a very hard worker. If Paul is anything like his father, he too will be a good employee.
>
> Sincerely,
>
> William Hardy

The letterhead holds out great promise, but then the letter itself is worthless. It is obvious that the letter-writer doesn't really have any basis for the conclusion that the candidate will be a good MBA student.

Too many applicants choose evaluators because they think they need character witnesses (the applicant is honest and trustworthy) or endorsements from powerful people (So-and-So, CEO of MegaWorks, Inc.). But admissions officers are not really interested in either of those. Instead, they want to hear from someone who knows you well, in detail, about the characteristics that you have that would make you a good business student, to wit, the ability to do the curriculum and the motivation to work hard.

The best letters of evaluation will come from people who know you very well, e.g., a professor with whom you took several courses, your immediate supervisor at work, or a business associate with whom you have worked closely. A good evaluation will incorporate the personal knowledge into the letter and will make references to specific events and activities. For example:

Mary P. Weiss
White, Weiss, and Blanche

To the Admissions Committee:

White, Weiss, and Blanche is a consulting firm that advises businesses on environmental matters. Paul Roberts has worked for us for the past two summers. His work is outstanding, and he is an intelligent and genial person.

Last summer, as my assistant, Paul wrote a 25-page report that outlined a way of altering a client's exhaust stack to reduce sulfur emissions. The report was organized so that it was easy to follow and written in a style that was clear and easy to understand. Additionally, Paul made the live presentation during a meeting with the client's board of directors, engineers, and lawyers. He was confident and handled some very difficult questions in an easy manner. I should note that we have used Paul's innovation in several other plants.

Finally, I would note that Paul made an important contribution to our company softball team. The team finished in last place, but Paul played in every game. His batting average wasn't anything to brag about, but his enthusiasm more than made up for it.

Sincerely,

Mary Weiss

To get a letter such as this, you will have to ask someone who knows you well. It may also help to provide them with some "suggestions" about what should go into the letter. So if you have not been in recent contact, send a resume with a cover letter reminding them of some of the important points that you might want them to mention.

A POST SCRIPT

You are about to make a huge investment in your future. The cost of applying to B-school is virtually nothing when compared to the cost of an MBA education. And the cost of the education minuscule when compared with your earnings potential over a lifetime—depending on where you get in. More importantly, it is your life—your time needed to complete applications, two years in school, and a career. So explore all options and maximize your opportunities.

Workshop: The Personal Statement

appendix B

This part gives you a look at the "before" and "after" of two personal statements. The case studies used are composites, suitably sanitized, that have been created from two or more actual files in order to illustrate a wider range of points. For each case study, there is a summary of the candidate's credentials, a first version of the personal statement, a critique of the first version, and an "improved version" of the personal statement. The "improved version" should not be taken as a final version. Even the "improved version" needs further work, but the work becomes a matter of careful attention to detail rather than a major reorganization.

CASE STUDY 1: J.V.

J.V. was 27 when she decided to apply to business school. At the time, she was a civil service worker for a government agency. She realized that while she enjoyed considerable job security, that job security also meant a fairly tedious day-to-day routine and a plodding career track. She took the LSAT and got a 154 and the GMAT and got a 610. She decided to apply to business school. Her undergraduate grade point average was 3.7. After considering her options, she selected six schools—three Ivy League schools, two "second tier" schools, and one local school at which admission was all but assured. See the resume of J.V. on the next page.

One of the most common mistakes made by applicants is to write a personal statement that "moves across the surface" and that is the main weakness of this statement. For example, paragraph one simply repeats a chronology that will be available to the reader elsewhere in the application. (Just as it is available in the resume.) It simply reiterates "what" happened without addressing the "why" of the events. What is the significance of the transfer from the School of Education to the College of Arts and Sciences? And if it doesn't have any significance (from the perspective of an admissions officer), then it doesn't belong in the personal statement.

RESUME OF J.V.

Personal Information

Address: 355 West Oak Street
Anywhere, USA 12345
Telephone: 555-1212 (Day); 555-2323 (Evening)

Educational Background

M.A. STATE UNIVERSITY, FRENCH LITERATURE, 1994

Thesis: Deconstructing the Sartre-de Beauvoir Correspondence
Activities: University Graduate Student Council
French Literature & Philosophy Forum

B.A. STATE COLLEGE, 1993 (HONORS) ROMANCE LANGUAGES

Activities: Junior Year Abroad, Paris
University Choral Society
Italian-American Caucus

Employment History

1994-Present: **Social Security Administration**
Supervise 25 claims agents; responsibility for reviewing claimant appeals for benefits.
1987-1988: **State University, French Dept.**
Adjunct Professor

Other Interests

Music (Opera and Piano)
Travel

(Here's the first version of J.V.'s PERSONAL STATEMENT)

WHY I WANT TO GO TO BUSINESS SCHOOL

The decision to apply to business school represents the third and final important reorientation in my life. I came to college certain that I would want to pursue a teaching career and entered the School of Education. After a semester, I realized that I did not want to teach on the elementary or even secondary level, so I transferred to the College of Arts and Sciences to study languages and become a college teacher. After graduation, I took a Master's in French while I taught on the college level. During that year, I realized that even college teaching was not for me. At the end of that time, I took a job with the Federal Government.

While with the Federal Government, I have received several promotions. In my present capacity, I am a Supervisor for the Social Security Administration. I have the responsibility for supervising 25 Claims Agents. This means that I supervise their day-to-day activities (assigning cases and monitoring progress) and handle crisis situations (such as labor union grievances). One of my most important duties is to review the appeals of people whose claims for benefits have been denied. In order to do this, I have to have a detailed knowledge of the regulations governing the eligibility of claimants. I believe that my experience managing this office has been good training for a career in private business.

Finally, I would add that my outside interests include both travel and music. Over the past five years, I have visited Mexico, Peru, Spain, and Israel. I have studied piano since I was a small child, and I have been involved with several opera workshops.

Next, why explain the move from academia to government service? On its face, the move looks like the applicant taught for a year while doing an MA and then moved on to the "real world." Unless there is something more to the event than that, it speaks for itself and doesn't need to be addressed in the personal statement—particularly since it happened so long ago.

The second paragraph likewise "moves across the surface." Much of the information provided there will already have been included in the "Q and A" part of the application. As you can see, the second paragraph really does not add anything to this. The last part of the second paragraph attempts to explain the significance that the employment experience has in terms of a B-school application. This part should be expanded, and more detail should be included.

The third paragraph is a good idea, but its treatment is too cursory. How much time did the applicant spend in the places mentioned? If just a week or two, then this travel probably won't mean much to an admissions officer. Additionally, the effectiveness of the discussion about musical talent would be considerably enhanced with some more detail.

As it turns out, further discussion with this applicant revealed some important information that was not apparent from the resume (and likely would not have shown up in the "Q and A" part of the application). After reworking, the applicant's statement has much greater impact.

With these points in mind, here you see the revised version of J.V.'s PERSONAL STATEMENT:

WHY I WANT TO GO TO BUSINESS SCHOOL

My decision to apply to business school was made after careful reflection. My present employment affords me a comfortable standard of living and considerable job security, but the position no longer offers the challenges and variety that it once did. To be sure, there are occasional surprises. A few months ago, for example, a male employee filed a grievance claiming that he was the victim of sexual harassment in the workplace. (He alleged that two female co-workers had made suggestive remarks about parts of his anatomy.) As it turns out, what really happened was that a male co-worker reported to the complainant that such remarks had been made. Since they were not made directly to the complainant, there was no ground under our rules for any action. (And the comments of the male co-worker were not, in and of themselves, sexual harassment.) By and large, however, the supervisory duties are fairly routine.

Sometimes appeals claims offer a surprise. Last year, for example, a claimant appeared at a hearing accompanied by an advisor/translator. The advisor/translator would translate my questions (stated in English) into Spanish. What the advisor/translator did not realize is that I am fluent in Spanish, and I knew that throughout the hearing that the advisor/translator was instructing the claimant on how to fabricate a claim. At the end of the hearing, both claimant and advisor/translator were flabbergasted when I told them in Spanish that they were both being charged with attempted fraud. By and large, however, even the appeals on denied claims are usually fairly routine.

What I would hope to find in school and later in business is more of the very best moments of the position I currently have. Even though I know that every occupation has its tedium, I expect that business would offer greater variety and challenge. Most of the managerial situations I confront are similar in their details. Even those that present unusual facts are resolved by reference to a fairly compact body of internal regulations. I look forward with anticipation to the opportunity to handle new situations with variety and surprises and to the need to address a much wider range of managerial concepts.

I am confident in my ability to handle the business school curriculum. My college transcript shows that I graduated with "General Honors" (top 15 percent), but it does not show that my studies made me fluent in French and Italian (as well as Spanish). I anticipate that this facility with languages will be useful as businesses become more global. While a graduate student, I was a member of the French Literature & Philosophy Forum. I presented a paper to the Forum entitled "Contextualizing Correspondence." (I have enclosed a copy for the Committee's review.)

Finally, in addition to my experience in a government agency and my academic perspective, I think that I can add something to school life on a personal level. I have studied voice for nearly ten years. I am a Mezzo-Soprano, and I have participated in several opera workshops. Most recently, I sang the role of Dorabella in Mozart's *Cosi Fan Tutte* with the Northern State Regional Opera Company. This was a particularly satisfying experience because, unlike most workshop productions, this one was done with an orchestra instead of just piano, and the orchestra included several well-known members of the City Orchestra.

In addition to eliminating the weaknesses mentioned, the revised version contains a couple of very nice features. The additional detail—the name of the paper, the role of Dorabella, the importance of the orchestra—all make the revised version more readable as well as more credible. Also, the anecdote that illustrates the use of Spanish is a nice touch. It's interesting, in and of itself, as a story. In fact, don't underestimate the importance of holding the reader's attention. Admissions officers may be reading a dozen or more personal statements an hour and hundreds in just a few weeks. You need something that will make yours stand out.

CASE STUDY 2: P.D.

P.D. was 20 and a junior in college when he decided on a career in business. He took the GMAT in the spring of his junior year and scored 480. He took the exam a second time in the fall of his senior year and scored 620. His GPA through the first six semesters was 3.4. In order to maximize his options, P.D. decided to apply to ten schools—only one top-tier school, two second-tier schools, and seven schools with various distinguishing features. (The following application document was completed in the fall of P.D.'s senior year, so some information was not yet available.)

Application for Admission

Educational Background

List the official names of all colleges, universities, and other postsecondary institutions attended, including those for summer session or evening class.

Institution	Dates	Major	Degree	Date
Loyola U.	94–	History	A.B.	NA
Kramer CC	Sum '93	NA	NA	NA

LIST ACADEMIC HONORS AND OTHER AWARDS RECEIVED

Dean's List (2 Semesters)
Honorable Mention, Robertson Prize in History

Employment History

Loyola U., Public Relations, Summer '96, 40 hours per week
City News, Account Rep., Summer '95, 40 hours per week
TV Cable Co., Installer, Summer '94, 40 hours per week
City News, Carrier, Spring '96, 15 hours per week
City News, Carrier, Spring '95, 10 hours per week

Personal Statement

Staple to this page a typed, signed personal statement that tells us why you want to pursue an MBA. Please discuss personal and professional goals that are important to you. You should consider this an opportunity to introduce yourself to us.

PERSONAL STATEMENT OF P.D. (First Version)

I want to take this opportunity to introduce myself to the Admissions Committee. I will graduate from Loyola University next spring with a major in history. I want to get an MBA because I am vitally concerned with the important economic problems that face us as a society. These include issues such as globalization, inefficiency, and economic injustice. As a high-level manager, I know that I will be in a position to address these important matters.

If the Committee reviews my record, they will see that I have a strong academic background. Through my first six semesters, I have a 3.4 GPA, and I expect to do better during the next two semesters. I have taken the GMAT twice because I did not do very well the first time (scoring only 480), but the second time I got a 620. I have been on the Dean's List twice, and my paper on the Federalist Papers received "Honorable Mention" in the History Department's Robertson Competition. I would point out that I achieved these accomplishments while working part-time. I even took courses at the community college during the summer.

My employment also demonstrates that I have the ability to do well in business. While it is true that my first summer in college I worked as a laborer for TV Cable installing cable, my second summer I was an Account Representative for the City News. In that capacity, I dealt with people on a daily basis and had to think on my feet. After that I worked for the University in its Public Relations Office.

As a member of the Student Government, I had to deal with a lot of different people on a variety of issues. I was able to observe first hand the give and take that goes into the making of policy. Plus I was a member of the Demosthenes Club and a member of an intramural basketball team.

The problem that P.D. faces—and it is one faced by thousands of candidates who are applying for admission directly out of college—is that it may be difficult to articulate specific reasons why one wants an MBA. To be sure, many undergraduates may have fairly settled career goals; and if you are one of them, you should not hesitate to state your goals. Other students, however, may have only the vaguest idea of what they want to do "when they grow up"; and if you are one of them, you should not overstate your case. Instead, you should address the issue in general terms and let your record speak for you. Let's look at P.D.'s personal statement a bit more closely. There is nothing particularly wrong with the first paragraph. There may be better ways of beginning this type of essay, but certainly it cannot be said that this style is completely inappropriate.

The beginning of the next paragraph is pretty much useless. The explanation regarding the GMAT score is typical of many personal statements: I didn't do well the first time I took the test, so I took it again. That fact is apparent. If you are going to address the fact that you have taken the GMAT more than once, then you must be prepared with an explanation: The first time I took the GMAT I got a 480, but I was very ill with the flu that day. My second test, taken when I felt well, is a better indicator of my ability.

The last part of that paragraph has the merit of mentioning the title of the paper that earned P.D. the "Honorable Mention." This is something that is probably not covered elsewhere in the application and so should be expanded. It might even be a good idea to include a copy of the paper or at least the introduction. One would not expect that an Admissions Committee would read it as thoroughly as a professor would, but one might hope that an admissions officer might say "Mmmmm, I don't have time to read all of this, but it does look like a good piece of work." The third and fourth paragraphs don't say very much beyond what is already evident in the rest of the application. It is important to explain to an admissions officer the significance of events and accomplishments.

As for the entry about intramural basketball, P.D. was twice a member of the Intramural Allstars; and at this college, each spring the Intramural Allstars play an exhibition game in the arena against members of the college's varsity basketball team. This experience alone obviously does not qualify P.D. to study business at Yale, but it is an experience that few other applicants at any school will have had—and it may count for something.

With these points in mind, P.D. can revise his personal statement to carry much more impact, as shown on the next page.

P.D.'S PERSONAL STATEMENT (Revised Version)

I want to take this opportunity to introduce myself to the Admissions Committee and to provide you with some information that is not included in other parts of my application. I want to discuss further both the issue of my ability to succeed in business school and my reasons for wanting to earn an MBA.

First, my GPA alone does not describe the full extent of my academic ability. It is lower than it otherwise would have been because my performance in my freshman year was not particularly good. Additionally, it was financially necessary for me to work the past two spring semesters, and you will observe that my grades during the spring semesters are lower than those of the fall semesters. Finally, I devoted considerable time to extracurricular activities.

As for the GMAT, the first time I took the exam I was sick with the flu and obviously did not do as well as I could. My second score is a better measure of my real ability.

Setting aside the considerations above, if the Admissions Committee is looking for a good example of my ability, you should look at my paper "Implicit Religious Convictions in the Federalist Papers." I wrote this paper for Professor M.V., a notoriously hard grader, who not only gave it an "A" but encouraged me to enter it in the Robertson Competition. The Robertson Competition is sponsored by the History Department each year as part of its Colloquium on American History and is open to both graduate and undergraduate students. Twelve students read papers to a panel of distinguished historians from universities across the nation. One paper receives the "Robertson Award" and two others receive "Honorable Mention." I have enclosed a copy of this paper.

I have decided on a career in business because I enjoy doing those things that I know will be required of me. The Demosthenes Club is a debating society with 35 active members. We meet for three hours every other week to debate a topic such as "Capital Punishment" or "U.S. Military Commitments." The schedule allows members time to do some additional background research on announced topics. I particularly enjoy debating various policy options in terms of their costs and expected outcomes. Additionally, I enjoy writing, and my work in the University's Public Relations Office has been particularly helpful in this regard. A press release has to be carefully crafted because it usually deals with a complex situation that must be described in terms that those not familiar with its details can grasp.

Finally, I noted in your Bulletin that you sponsor an intramural basketball league. In high school, I dreamed of playing college basketball; and, in a way, I fulfilled this dream. Each year, the Intramural Allstars play members of the Varsity in an exhibition game in the Arena, and I was selected to play for the Allstars twice. Thus, I have had the privilege of being soundly defeated by some of the best in college basketball.

You'll notice that the revised statement answers all of the objections that were raised in response to the first version. Beyond that, the revised version is an improvement in a couple of other ways. First, the mention of the paper (as recommended) drives the point home: it's an impresssive title suggesting critical analysis and research. The further detail about the debating society is also useful since it hints at skills a lawyer ought to have. Finally, the mention of the basketball game is good fun. And the self-deprecating tone of that paragraph, because it is in good humor, avoids the danger of sounding like a boast.

Ask the Experts

appendix C

The following questions and answers explore a number of issues that surround choosing the right business school, writing successful applications, timing your application process, assessing your chances for acceptance, and more.

1. The term "MBA" seems to mean different things to different people. What *exactly* is an MBA?

The Master of Business Administration is the degree granted after a general course of graduate study in management. The term MBA is also used loosely to refer to a number of other higher education degrees that are awarded for study in particular areas, degrees such as the Master of Accounting, Master of Health Administration, Master of Public Health, and Master of Taxation. The terms "business school" and the even shorter "B-school" are used to refer to all such programs of graduate study in management in lieu of the phrase "graduate school of management." Earning an MBA usually requires two years of full-time study or three to four years of partime study beyond the bachelor's degree.

2. What are the advantages of getting an MBA?

An MBA is the business manager's analog of the lawyer's JD or the doctor's MD. The MBA program focuses on administration: the curriculum aims to train professional managers rather than researchers or academics. Although an MBA is not a licensing requirement for business in general, employers in certain areas, such as investment banking, informally make the MBA a requirement by giving preferential hiring treatment to MBAs over JDs or MAs and over those who have no graduate degree at all. Furthermore, MBAs generally receive higher starting salaries than those who have only a bachelor's degree. Finally, as a rule MBAs are promoted faster and farther than people who have only a bachelor's degree.

3. Is the MBA losing its value?

That depends. An MBA degree can still be an important asset, but the picture is a bit more complicated than it was 30 years ago. In the late 1970s, the MBA became a hot ticket. The degree came to be regarded as a pass key that could open any door, and so quite naturally more and more people wanted to go to business school. And also quite naturally, more and more universities either added a new MBA program or expanded an existing one in order to capture a share of the tuition dollars generated by the increase in demand for the degree. Economic theory predicts that the value of the degree would be lowered by this rapid growth simply because the degree is no longer as scarce as it would otherwise have been. Beyond that, however, not all MBA programs were created equal. And the degrees awarded by business schools with marginal programs are really much less valuable in objective terms than those offered by top business schools.

4. Is it difficult to get into an MBA program?

It's difficult to gain admission to *some* schools, easy to get into others. In a typical year, about 200,000 people start the business school application process by taking the Graduate Management Admission Test (GMAT), which most business schools require. At top schools, the ratio of admission offers to total applications may be as low as one to five or even one to six. On the other hand, there are several hundred business schools to choose from (about 900 worldwide use the GMAT), and some accept virtually everyone who applies. Thus, it is in a sense easy to get into business school, if an applicant is willing to enter any MBA program.

Of course, business school seats are not assigned by lottery, so the chance of a particular person's getting into a certain school depends very much on that person's qualifications, undergraduate grade point average, or GPA, work experience, extracurricular activities, and score on the Graduate Management Admission Test. Admissions officers take all of those things into account.

5. Which U.S. business schools are considered the best?

School rankings depend on which factors are considered and how these factors are weighted. However, any list of top business schools would have to include Chicago, Columbia, Dartmouth, Harvard, Michigan, Northwestern, Pennsylvania, and Stanford—not necessarily in that order.

6. How reliable are published rankings?

Each year *U.S. News & World Report* magazine publishes a ranking of top business schools based upon a survey that it conducts. And *Business Week* has created a book entitled *The Best Business Schools*. Those are useful guides so long as you don't put too much emphasis on small differences in rankings. That is, if a ranking puts Northwestern first, Harvard second, Chicago third, Pennsylvania fourth, and Dartmouth fifth, there is good reason to believe that those are top business schools, but not that they necessarily stack up against each other in exactly that order. A better use of a ranking is to think in terms of clusters of schools. The top eight or nine schools are the super-elite; the next eight or nine are the elite; and so on.

7. When should applications be submitted?

Applications should be submitted well in advance of the deadline for two reasons. First, Murphy's Law operates with full force in the area of business school admissions: if something can go wrong, it will. Make sure that you leave yourself plenty of time to correct any errors or omissions. If you learn in November that one of your recommenders has not yet submitted a recommendation to a school with a March 1 deadline, then you have plenty of time to correct the omission, but if you don't learn of the problem until March 15, then it is too late. Second, some business schools use a rolling admissions process under which applications are processed throughout the application season. As the season progresses and offers of admissions are made to successful applicants, fewer and fewer seats remain for those who apply later in the year. You will maximize your chances if you apply early.

8. How many schools should a person apply to?

In terms of targeting schools for applications, "the more the merrier." But, of course, most people do not have unlimited funds and must therefore choose a small number of schools. People may want to arrange their applications according to a pyramid that represents their competitiveness in the overall applicant pool. For example, if someone has above-average but not superior credentials and plans to apply to a total of ten business schools, this person can target one or perhaps two of the top ten schools. The chance of acceptance at those schools may be only one out of ten, but the potential gain justifies the risk. Then, the person should select five or six "bread and butter" schools, schools for which the person fits the profile of a typical student. Finally, in order to guard against the unexpected, the person should add one or two "safeties," schools for which he or she seems to be overqualified.

Of course, this strategy has to be adjusted to one's own qualifications. Someone with an outstanding academic background, a very high GMAT score, and considerable work experience can feel confident of being accepted at a top school but should still include one or two "safeties." For someone with relatively weak credentials, it may not make any sense to apply to a top school. That person should concentrate all resources on schools that seem to provide the best opportunity for acceptance.

9. How can a person know in advance whether an application is likely to be successful at a particular school?

One cannot really know in advance. The admissions process is just too complex to permit that kind of certainty. But applicants will surely want to consult the descriptive bulletins distributed by the school. Most contain information about median or average GMAT score and GPA of students enrolled. That way, people can then compare their own quantitative factors with the numerical profiles provided by the schools themselves.

10. If a person has a GPA or a GMAT score that is below that typically accepted by a school, is it a waste of time and money to apply there?

Not necessarily. Remember that the GPA and the GMAT are simply evidence of the characteristics sought by admissions officers. A somewhat low GPA might be offset by a dazzling GMAT score, or a somewhat disappointing GMAT score might be balanced out by an excellent academic record. But if both numerical measures are below those typically accepted by the school, it will take some extraordinary employment experience or personal achievement to make the application competitive. And in the absence of some additional asset, it might be better to pass up the school.

11. Who makes the admissions decisions?

The title "admissions officer" designates different people at different schools. Each business school has an admissions office that is responsible for reviewing and acting on applications for admissions to that school, and that admissions office designs its own procedures. The decision-making authority may be given to a committee of faculty members, or it may be given to a dean or to a professional admissions officer; it may be shared by faculty members and professional admissions officers; and some authority may even be given to selected students. "Admissions officer" can mean anyone who has the decision-making authority regarding applications for admission to an MBA program.

12. What is the practice of "indexing" applications?

Some business schools use a mathematical formula to combine an applicant's GPA and score on the GMAT in approximately equal weights to generate a single numerical value for the application. In fact, the scoring system of the GMAT was designed to make quantitative evaluations of candidates easy. Here is an example of a mathematical formula that produces an index that gives approximately equal weight to the GPA and the GMAT score:

$$\text{Index} = \frac{\frac{\text{GMAT}}{200} + \text{GPA}}{2}$$

Since the GMAT is scored on a scale of 200 (the minimum) to 800 (the maximum), a division by 200 generates a number on a scale from 1 to 4, a 4-point scale that is similar to the grading system used by most U.S. colleges and universities. And the reduced GMAT score and the GPA are simply averaged.

Thus, if a candidate has a GPA of 3.5 and a GMAT score of 500, the application is assigned an index of 3.0:

$$\text{Index} = \frac{\frac{500}{200} + 3.5}{2} = 3.0$$

A similar result can be achieved by using a formula that converts the GPA to the GMAT scoring scale by multiplying the GPA by 200:

$$\text{Index} = \text{GMAT} + (200 \times \text{GPA})$$

Using this system, our hypothetical application would be assigned an index of 1200:

$$\text{Index} = 500 + (200 \times 3.5) = 1200$$

The 1200 is a number on an artificial scale, but it will have meaning for admissions officers.

13. Do admissions officers at the various business schools assign each application an index and just take the ones with the highest index?

Not at all. In the first place, not every business school uses an indexing system. In the second place, even among those that do, no school makes its decisions solely on the basis of an indexing formula.

14. Do business schools have numerical cutoffs and reject applications that fall below those cutoffs?

Some do; some don't. No business school uses only the GMAT score and the GPA to make its decisions. Some set minimum numbers below which applications are not accepted. The minimum may be a minimum GPA, or a minimum GMAT, or a minimum index combining both GPA and GMAT. Business schools that have set such minimums usually announce the fact in their catalogs and application forms.

15. How important are the GPA/GMAT "numbers" in the admissions process?

The GPA and GMAT scores are extremely important. If you look at the statistics that are released by the admissions offices of the various business schools, you will see clearly that applicants with higher GPAs and GMAT scores are more likely to be accepted than those with lower GPAs and GMAT scores.

16. What other than the GPA and GMAT score goes into the admissions process?

Most business school admissions processes are designed to select for both ability and motivation. Business schools want students who will graduate with a strong academic record and who will then go on to successful careers. Such students and graduates are great salespeople for the school's MBA program. No matter how intellectually gifted an applicant may be, many schools will reject an applicant who cannot demonstrate the motivation necessary to apply those gifts to academic and career success.

17. Why is the GPA not a complete measure of ability?

First, a grade point average is just that, an average. And averages, while convenient, tend to obscure important details. A simple GPA number will not tell, for example, about the difficulty of a candidate's curriculum, and there is a big difference between a 3.5 earned in "ballroom dancing" and a 3.5 earned in history or biology. Second, an average tells nothing about the individual circumstances of the candidate. A candidate who worked full-time while in school who earns a 3.5 has achieved something considerably more remarkable than a candidate who earned the same 3.5 but had the luxury of studying at leisure. Third, an average conceals any trends in a candidate's academic performance. Some candidates may have a relatively low GPA but show improved performance later in their undergraduate careers. And this later, better performance may very well be a truer indicator of ability and motivation than the earlier disappointing performance. Finally, all schools are not equal: some consideration may be given to the academic reputation of an undergraduate institution—even if it isn't possible to quantify the adjustment very precisely.

18. Ok, so how do admissions officers obtain this additional information?

From the applicants. Applicants are required to submit transcripts or to arrange for them to be sent by the various schools that they have attended. The transcripts demonstrate a thorough record of what courses the student embarked upon, how well the student performed within those courses, as well as how the student's overall performance ranks. Further, the application includes questions such as "What jobs did you hold as a student?," "How many hours a week did you work?," and "What extracurricular activities did you participate in while in college?"

19. What "other factors" should I mention on my application to best demonstrate ability and motivation?

Active participation in extracurricular activities, or civic activities, or professional organizations could be evidence of both characteristics. So could individual accomplishments such as mastery of a second or third language, proficiency with a musical instrument, and participation in a group activity, whether competitive such as individual sports like golf and tennis or cooperative such as team sports like soccer and basketball.

Admissions officers are looking for students who work and play well with one another, so "interesting accomplishments" would make a candidate more attractive. Such accomplishments by themselves are not likely to be sufficient reason to accept an applicant. Almost any significant experience or accomplishment can provide evidence of one of the three characteristics: ability, motivation, or interesting personality. It is very important to remember that, from the perspective of an admissions officer, it is not the fact of the experience or accomplishment that is important but the significance of that experience or accomplishment, that is, what it means in terms of ability and motivation, and perhaps what it can add to the diversity of the school's student body.

20. How does participation in a sport like basketball prove that a person will succeed in business school?

It doesn't prove that a person will succeed, but it does provide evidence of several characteristics. First, it demonstrates that the applicant is a team player, and that may be important for projects both in business school and later in the business world. Second, it is evidence that the applicant has drive and ambition—aspects of motivation that, when properly harnessed, help to put intellectual energy to productive use. Third, people who have personal accomplishments are in general more interesting than those who have none.

21. Where in the application form can one mention these additional experiences and accomplishments?

Application forms include lines for applicants to list their activities and accomplishments. Many applications also require essay responses to questions such as "Identify your three most important accomplishments and explain why you consider them to be important" or "What is your biggest professional weakness and how do you think that a business school education will correct it?" The short-answer questions help admissions officers learn what applicants have done and the essay questions help them learn why those accomplishments are significant.

22. Do admissions officers also consider post-college employment?

Because the objective of the admissions process is to identify those candidates who have ability and motivation, admissions officers are indeed interested in a candidate's professional background, including promotions, responsibilities, and so on.

23. How much weight is given to employment experience when compared to academic record?

The answer to that question will depend on the educational philosophy of each business school. Some business schools actually require that applicants have one or two years of work experience and simply will not consider candidates who do not. This requirement reflects a determination by the faculty that what it has to teach cannot be learned effectively until one has a certain amount of real-world experience. Other business schools have adopted such a requirement as a general rule but allow certain exceptions because they feel that some people can acquire the requisite experience in an academic setting or while working in college. Other schools do not have such a requirement; but even there, employment experience may be considered a valuable asset that adds weight to an application that shows good academic performance.

24. How important are personal interviews?

Personal interviews add another dimension to the evaluation process, but business schools have different policies on interviewing. Some business schools do not have sufficient administrative resources to conduct any interviews at all. Others do not make an interview part of the evaluation process but do encourage applicants to visit for informational purposes. Still others grant interviews when applicants request them. At other business schools, interviews are not required but are strongly encouraged. Finally, some schools require interviews whether in person or by telephone.

25. What guidelines should one follow when answering essay or interview questions?

Your basic goal should be to create answers that are well-considered and thoughtful. Most essay or interview questions do not have right and wrong answers in the sense that they must have a certain content in order to please an admissions officer. But answers should have a certain style. A well-considered and thoughtful response will express the applicant's general philosophy on some issue as illustrated by concrete examples; it will sound honest and sincere because it is a reflection of the applicant's true feelings; and it will be well presented, which means that written responses will be carefully edited and typed and oral responses given in an interview will be spontaneous, not rehearsed, because they articulate conclusions that the applicant has arrived at through serious consideration.

26. How important are recommendations?

Recommendations can be extremely important. Many applicants mistakenly believe that a recommendation will be effective only if it comes from an important person whose name is likely to be familiar to an admissions officer, so they launch a "star search" for the biggest "name" that they can find who will submit a recommendation. The result, however, may be a recommendation without very much content. The most important criteria for choosing a recommender are: (1) the recommender must know the purpose of an MBA program, (2) the recommender should know the applicant well, and (3) the recommender should specifically describe the connection between (1) and (2). If it happens that the recommender is also a prominent person, so much the better; but prominence alone does not qualify a person as a recommender.

27. What can one do in order to obtain the maximum GMAT score possible?

Make sure that you are prepared for the exam. A good preparation program has three components:

- a review of the substantive skills tested
- strategies and techniques useful for the particular test in question
- practice, practice, practice

28. Should applicants take the GMAT for practice?

No! You can take the GMAT as many times as you care to, but multiple scores are reported to the business schools that you designate to receive your scores whether you want them reported or not. Obviously, you don't want a "practice" score reported along with a "real" score. Instead, people can find plenty of material for practice in this book.

About the Author

Professor Thomas H. Martinson is widely acknowledged to be America's leading authority on test preparation. Educated at Harvard University with an advanced degree and twelve years of postgraduate research, Professor Martinson has published over three dozen books on test preparation. He is routinely invited to lecture on test preparation and related topics at top colleges and universities throughout the United States and abroad.

The *Master the GMAT CAT* is published with and without CD. If you have purchased the CD version of our book, you will be able to practice what you have learned using state-of-the-art computer adaptive software. The software was created by Cambridge Educational Services, 2720 River Road, Ste. 36, Des Plaines, IL 60018.

NOTES

NOTES

NOTES

NOTES

NOTES